Collaboration, Consultation, and Teamwork for Students with Special Needs

Peggy Dettmer

Kansas State University

Ann Knackendoffel

Kansas State University

Linda P. Thurston

Kansas State University

Boston Columbus Indianapolis New York San Francisco Upper Saddle River
Amsterdam Cape Town Dubai London Madrid Milan Munich Paris Montreal Toronto
Delhi Mexico City São Paulo Sydney Hong Kong Seoul Singapore Taipei Tokyo

Executive Editor and Publisher: *Stephen D. Dragin*
Editorial Assistant: *Katherine Wiley*
Marketing Manager: *Joanna Sabella*
Production Project Manager: *Maggie Brobeck*
Manager, Central Design: *Jayne Conte*
Cover Designer: *Bruce Kenselaar*
Cover Image: *ImageZoo/Alamy*
Full Service Project Management and Composition Service: *Vivek Khandelwal/Element LLC*
Text Printer/Binder: *Courier Companies, Inc.*
Cover Printer: *Courier Companies, Inc.*
Text Font: *Times LT Std 10/12*

Credits and acknowledgments borrowed from other sources and reproduced, with permission, in this textbook appear below and on the appropriate page within text.

Cartoons: Jane More Loeb

Many of the designations by manufacturers and sellers to distinguish their products are claimed as trademarks. Where those designations appear in this book, and the publisher was aware of a trademark claim, the designations have been printed in initial caps or all caps.

Library of Congress Cataloging-in-Publication Data
   Dettmer, Peggy.
   Collaboration, consultation, and teamwork for students with special needs/Peggy Dettmer,
Ann Knackendoffel, Linda P. Thurston.—7th ed.
        p. cm.
   Prev. edition entered under title.
   ISBN 978-0-13-265967-3 (alk. paper)
 1. Children with disabilities—Education—United States.   2. Special
education—United States.   3. Educational consultants—United States.   4. Teaching
teams—United States.   I. Knackendoffel, Ann.   II. Thurston, Linda P.
III. Title.
   LC4031.D47 2013
   371.90973--dc23

                                                    2012011179

10 9 8 7 V092 15

ISBN 13: 978-0-13-265967-3
ISBN 10: 0-13-265967-0

About the Authors

Peggy Dettmer is professor emeritus of Education at Kansas State University, where she earned an M.S. in Special Education and a Ph.D. in Educational Psychology. She chaired the Educational Psychology and Counseling Department and directed the College of Education honors program for several years. Her 42 years of teaching experience was divided somewhat evenly between K–8 public schools and the teacher education program at Kansas State University, where her areas of emphasis were educational psychology, assessment for effective teaching, education of gifted and talented students, collaborative school consultation, creativity, and professional development. She has written a number of books and articles for refereed journals and conducted many professional development activities on these topics.

Dr. Dettmer chaired the Professional Development Division for the National Association of Gifted Children (NAGC) and participated in construction of the NAGC gifted program standards. Her main areas of professional interest include the constructive use of adult differences and providing responsive environments to nurture creativity in children and youth.

Ann Knackendoffel, assistant professor in Special Education at Kansas State University, earned a Ph.D. in Special Education from the University of Kansas. Her interest in collaboration and consulting began with her dissertation research on collaboration between general educators and special educators, and it continued with co-authoring a book on collaborative problem solving.

Dr. Knackendoffel has been a teacher at both elementary and secondary levels and a special educator for students with intellectual and learning disabilities as well as students with emotional and behavior disorders. She currently teaches a graduate-level course in consultation and collaboration for special educators at Kansas State University and has conducted numerous workshops and conference presentations on collaborative school consultation. She also teaches courses for general education majors focusing on students with special needs, academic intervention techniques for them, and assistive technology. Her particular interests are in collaborative problem solving, and the utilization and supervision of paraeducators.

Linda P. Thurston, professor and assistant dean at Kansas State University, earned an M.A. in Experimental Psychology at the University of Texas–El Paso and a Ph.D. in Behavioral Science from the University of Kansas.

In addition to teaching graduate courses in program evaluation, women and leadership, and special education, she is the founding director of the Office of Educational Innovation and Evaluation and the first coordinator of the new faculty mentoring program in Kansas State University's College of Education. Thurston has published and taught in the areas of disabilities, gender, family, and poverty issues, as well as evaluation. She has been principal investigator on more than $10 million in external funding related to those areas. Thurston served as a program officer in the Education and Human Resources Directorate at the National Science Foundation for several years.

Contents

5 *Problem-Solving Strategies for Collaborative School Consultation and Teamwork* **117**

6   *Organization and Management of Collaborative School Consultation*   *150*

PART III   Processes for Working Together as Co-Educators   183

7   *Communicating as Collaborators, Consultants, and Team Members*   *185*

15 *Synthesis and Support for Working Together as Co-Educators*   425

Preface

Revisions of textbooks are needed from time to time. This is particularly germane in the field of special education, where school reforms and program changes occur regularly. Reasons for updates typically include legislative actions, new research findings, outcomes of new professional development programs, expanded roles of school personnel, outcomes from action research by educators, heightened involvement of families and communities in educational matters, altered goals of funding agencies, and increased public attention to education.

NEW TO THIS EDITION

New and updated material in this seventh edition of the book, as guided by feedback from our students, input from our colleagues in education, suggestions from reviewers and other users of the book, and our own teaching and studies, include:

- *Reorganization of chapters and content* within chapters to reflect the changing needs of school educators and home educators for methods and models to help students with very special needs become successful in school and fulfill their potential
- *New and updated coverage of educational designs and reforms*, including Response to Intervention, Universal Design for Learning, professional learning communities, communities of practice, and Common Core Standards
- *Attention in each chapter to tools of technology* for collaboration and communication, including social media tools for communication and meetings, resource-sharing tools, planning and management tools, evaluation tools, and more
- *A new chapter on paraeducators* featuring discussion of how general educators and special educators coordinate and supervise paraeducators (paras), how to decide when a para is really needed, ways to use paras effectively, supervision and evaluation of paras, and how to get going on the right foot and stay connected with paraeducators
- A chapter that was new in the previous edition and has now been expanded into *two chapters*, one that focuses on *differences in professional perspectives* of educators and the other on *differences in personal preferences of educators* that influence their aims to collaborate and co-teach. Factors of tradition, territory, time, talents, and trust must be managed to build strong collaborative relationships, and diversity in educational partnerships can strengthen team efforts
- *A new chapter on evaluation of collaborative school consultation* that includes purposes and types of evaluation for collaborative school consultation; steps in designing an evaluation plan; determining the measures; collecting, analyzing, and reporting data; self-evaluation of collaborative consultation skills; and large-program evaluations
- *Inclusion of attention to the exceptional learning needs of students with high ability and talent* for whom collaborative school consultation programs can be so beneficial and yet are too often overlooked in special education–focused textbooks.

- *Additional material on working smarter rather than harder* in managing meetings, interruptions, technology, and stress, as well as in making connections with students' families
- *Helps for novice and early-career teachers* to enter into collaborative school consultation and co-teaching comfortably and enthusiastically
- *Vignettes* and *case studies*, as well as *Reflections* (for pondering) and *Actions* (for doing) in all chapters
- *An updated Instructor's Resource Guide with objective-/subjective-item test bank, additional scenarios, and activities for use in class or as assignments for further study, as well as class-ready PowerPoints* prepared by the book's authors, all available online

As educators, we aspire to have our students become knowledgeable, caring, and self-fulfilling individuals in this increasingly complex and interconnected world. Their educational roles will demand much more of them than basic knowledge and its application in the classroom. They will need skills in problem identification and problem solving, communicating and collaborating with others, thinking critically and creatively, recognizing and caring about the needs of others, speaking and listening and writing effectively, knowing how to learn new things, using technology effectively, and evaluating their own work for accountability purposes.

To help our students achieve these lofty aims, it is vital that we prepare them to connect and interact through solid relationships with co-educators. This includes general education teachers, special education teachers, families of students, general education and special education administrators, early childhood education teachers, school psychologists, school counselors, related services and support personnel, professional development and curriculum personnel, and community leaders. To draw a line of demarcation between general education and special education would be the ultimate labeling and exclusion. Special education teachers and general education teachers must engage in a continuous flow of collaborative teaching and learning to serve special needs in an inclusive educational environment.

Not all educators are comfortable working with other educators in collaborative environments. Teacher education programs in the past did not stress the development of interpersonal skills among colleagues. This book is a vehicle for developing such skills. It is designed to be a bridge between *theories* of interrelationships in the school context and *practices* of the processes and content that can facilitate working together for students' needs. Teachers also learn from their students. When they pay attention to students and colleagues, updating and refining their curriculum as guided by learner input, they become wiser educators, more insightful consultants, and more effective as collaborative instructional partners. Teachers who observe and listen to learners show that they are receptive to others' ideas and know that they never will lack for new, relevant material.

The book's fifteen chapters are organized into five parts on contexts, content, processes, practices, and support. Each chapter begins with focusing questions and a list of key terms. Vignettes set the stage for chapter content. Activities within the chapter text are called Reflections (for thinking about) and Actions (for doing). Figures provide additional examples to embellish the content, visual representations, and practical checklists. A list of tips at the end of each chapter offers succinct, practical suggestions for putting the concepts to use. The brief Additional Resources section at the end of each chapter suggests a few other sources for expanding on the chapter's topics.

Our aim for this book from its inception has been to promote school collaboration, consultation, and teamwork as a means of transforming school learning environments into settings where education is special for *every* student and where *all* educators are successful in their complex, demanding roles.

NEW! COURSESMART eTEXTBOOK AVAILABLE

CourseSmart is an exciting new choice for students looking to save money. As an alternative to purchasing the printed textbook, students can purchase an electronic version of the same content. With a CourseSmart eTextbook, students can search the text, make notes online, print out reading assignments that incorporate lecture notes, and bookmark important passages for later review. For more information, or to purchase access to the CourseSmart eTextbook, visit www.coursesmart.com.

Acknowledgments

The six previous editions of this book were dedicated to various groups of educators and students for whom the book has been developed and has evolved over the years. Now we dedicate this seventh edition to our co-author for the first five editions, Norma Dyck Sellberg, who passed away in the fall of 2009, after a long, courageous battle with cancer.

Dr. Dyck, professor emeritus in Special Education at Kansas State University, developed an original proposal in the 1980s that resulted in a federally funded special education consulting project to prepare teachers for collaborative school consultation. That program was the catalyst for the first edition of this book.

Dr. Dyck's daughter, Kari Woods, now a program associate at the University of Kansas, and at one time a partner with her mother in developing curriculum materials for teachers of students with special needs, wrote this about her mother's work:

> She did not write about consultation, collaboration, and teamwork as just a theory, but valued the processes highly and practiced them regularly. She often spoke of her joy as a faculty member at Kansas State University where she collaborated with the co-authors of this book to advance the mission of teacher preparation and professional development. She maintained contact with former students who entered the teaching profession and provided consultation when asked to do so. After her retirement from the University, she and I led a team that provided teacher training materials, professional development workshops, and consultation with schools on ways to include students with disabilities in general education.
>
> Whatever the context, her foremost concern was for children who struggled to learn. Her desire to help these students overcome their difficulties in learning was the driving force behind all of her work. In doing so, she demonstrated that this work could not be an independent undertaking. Collaboration, consultation, and working in teams were the best means to that end.

We are pleased to recognize other individuals who also have contributed to the thinking and writing that molded these pages. In a collaborative process, it is not easy to tell where the contribution of one appears, another interfaces, and yet another goes on from there. This demonstrates once again the complexity and the beauty of working together toward lofty aims.

We thank our editors and assistants for their guidance and oversight to the project: Steve Dragin, Jamie Bushell, and Annette Joseph.

We also extend our appreciation to the reviewers: Sungho Park, California State University, Los Angeles, and Denise M. Skarbek, Indiana University–South Bend. Once again, we give posthumous recognition to Jane More Loeb for her pen-and-ink drawings. Jane, as teacher, mentor, curriculum specialist for children with learning and behavioral disorders, devoted wife, and dedicated mother, influenced so many with her teaching and mentorship programs, photography, and artwork.

We trust that the material presented here and in the *Instructor's Resource Guide with Test Bank* and PowerPoint package, both available online, will be helpful and inspirational to those who use them. The suggestions and contributions of students, families, teaching colleagues, reviewers, and editorial staff have been an important part of the process and the product. That is what collaborative school consultation and teamwork are all about.

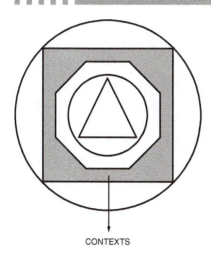

CONTEXTS

Contexts for Working Together as Co-Educators

PART I, INDICATED BY THE SHADED SQUARE, frames contexts for collaboration, consultation, and teamwork in inclusive schools. Chapter 1 places co-educators in collaborative school consultation situations where teamwork is, or can become, a natural and welcomed part of an ethical school climate. Chapter 2 addresses differences in professional perspectives among co-educators. Chapter 3 continues the discussion of differences by focusing on the diversity in personal preferences among co-educators.

Working Together in Collaboration, Consultation, and Teams

COLLABORATION, CONSULTATION, AND TEAMWORK PROBABLY began around cave fires ages ago, as humans discovered it was good to talk things over. It is likely that as they learned to explore wider territories, construct things, and use and trade things, they found it helpful to communicate by smoke signal and drumbeat. They formed connections and networks and began to consult and collaborate with those they trusted. Through social interaction, they learned helpful things from others and enjoyed expressing their own views to others as well. When they planned hunting and food-gathering forays and eventually began to plant and harvest, they developed methods for teamwork that earned them even more success as hunters, gatherers, and growers.

So it has been that throughout the ages, people most likely improved their quality of life by working together. Now, as our global world "shrinks," interpersonal skills are even more essential for progress and well-being in this increasingly complex, interconnected world. Individuals will continue to have their own perspectives and preferences in their own contexts (see shaded square in Figure 1.1) about many things, but those who can and do interact and work together successfully will fare best.

Relating to others, communicating, and respecting the viewpoints of others should begin at an early age. Toddlers at home, in their neighborhoods, and especially in day care centers, are expected to outgrow egocentrism and learn how to interact with others. Pre-school children are encouraged to work cooperatively with others. School becomes their next learning field for interrelating. Educators who introduce and model collaboration and productive teamwork are teaching students how to succeed in the world they will inherit and the places they will have in it.

FOCUSING QUESTIONS

1. What factors influence educators to become collaborative, collegial co-educators rather than teachers in more traditionally isolated roles?

2. How are collaboration, consultation, and team methods such as co-teaching defined and delineated?

3. What is collaborative school consultation in practice, and what is it *not*?

4. What educational reform movements and legislation propelled schools toward practices such as collaborative school consultation, co-teaching, partnerships with support agencies, and interrelationships with families of students?

5. How can technological advances in education benefit co-educators and their students?

6. What is an ethical climate for collaborative teaching and learning?

KEY TERMS

case study
client
co-educator
collaboration
collaborative ethic
collaborative school
consultation
Common Core Standards
consultant

consultation
consultative service
consultee
co-teaching
exceptional learning need
(ELN)
free appropriate public
education (FAPE)
network

No Child *Held* Behind
(NC*H*B)
No Child Left Behind
(NCLB)
professional learning
community (PLC)
synchronous/asynchronous
team
teamwork

VIGNETTE 1*

The setting is the faculty room of a typical high school, where four faculty members are sharing school news and airing their concerns during lunch break.

English Teacher: I'm getting another special education student next week—with rather severe learning disabilities this time, I'm told. I'll have this student in my composition and literature classes, along with a student with behavior disorders I've been coping with already. On top of that, as you all know, state assessments are coming up and our district curriculum standards committee is in the midst of who-knows-how-many meetings that seem to never end, and on it goes.

Geometry Teacher: I hear you. What's more, our special ed teachers don't seem to be working with these kids separately like they did when I first started teaching. But that was before inclusion, collaboration, and co-teaching became part of our teaching vocabulary.

Music Teacher: And before national "experts" had come up with things like No Child Left Behind and Common Core Standards.

English Teacher: Well, anyway, I was told that one of the special ed teachers is coming to our next departmental meeting to consult with us and talk about our roles in helping these students with their special needs. I understand we're going to be asked to set aside time to collaborate with the special ed teachers. That's along with all the other things we do, of course. We may even be encouraged to do some co-teaching with other teachers.

Physical Education Teacher/Coach: Hmmm, don't those two words cancel each other out? "Consult" and "collaborate," I mean. I believe you English teachers call that an oxymoron.

Music Teacher: I guess I'd be inclined to consult a tax accountant for some expert advice, but I think of collaboration as where everyone works together—you know, collaboration as in laboring together—to accomplish some common goals they've agreed on. As for co-teaching, I can tell you what a difficult process that is when you have a group of independent thinkers and free spirits who like to do things their own way and want to be the star of the show!

English Teacher: Well, frankly, I'm not interested in word games right now. I'm more concerned about finding out where that time is going to come from to do one more thing. I feel like the clock is my enemy. My schedule is packed, and my few minutes of free time don't jibe with anyone else's except for this brief lunch period. Most of all, I want to know who will have bottom-line responsibility for which students, and when, and where—and how!

Geometry Teacher: Right. I've had some questions about how to include all students in my instruction and testing. I think we need more help to do all of this and do it right. I hope we get it.

*We recommend that persons using this book in a group setting read each vignette aloud in conversational tone and style. In this way, the situations will seem relevant and facilitative rather than artificial and contrived. If the vignettes are not used by a group, they should be regarded as part of a chapter's content and read by the individual reader.

TEACHER ISOLATION IN THE PAST

In the past, teachers worked alone in their classrooms for the most part. They marked attendance forms, took lunch counts, completed other daily procedures, and then closed their classroom doors to begin instruction of the required content. They tried to handle each learning situation with minimal outside help. Asking for assistance would have been tantamount to showing insecurity or demonstrating incompetence. After all, hardy and capable teachers in the past had managed eight grades in one-room schoolhouses without help, hadn't they?

In more recent times, schools have become multidimensional centers of activity and much more social places. But an individual educator with myriad responsibilities and goals not only for student success but personal success can still feel stranded in a crowded setting devoid of adult interactions and professional stimulation. Teachers may be just next door or down the hall from other adults, yet paradoxically they are somewhat insulated from each other during the school day. Most tend to go about their responsibilities alone, without much meaningful adult interaction. This can make teaching a lonely occupation in a very public place. (See Figure 1.2.)

The insularities of some subjects and departmental boundaries are barriers to meaningful collaboration where, even if teachers would want to collaborate and co-teach, lack of time and a place limit the opportunity.

FIGURE 1.2   "I feel so alone!"

REFLECTION 1.1

Interaction to Save the Day

Using Figure 1.2 to stir your memory, put yourself in that chair and recall one or more times when your feeling of isolation on the job seemed almost overwhelming and interaction with a colleague or a friend who understood that feeling of professional loneliness would have "saved the day." Could meaningful interaction with an understanding, caring educator have helped? Who could have provided it? How, when, and where might it have taken place?

Many teachers, particularly those who are just beginning their careers, have been reluctant to discuss their concerns or ask for assistance from support personnel, lest their confidence and competency be called into question. In the meantime, others who are resource teachers, related services personnel, and support personnel have waited in the wings until called on for assistance. Too often the teachers desiring help and their potential helpmates are brought together only when situations reach a crisis level, if at all. How much better for all concerned if they could have had more immediate and directed interaction to identify needs and plan early interventions for students with special needs. As a teacher's array of responsibilities grows, and time allocated for instructing and managing classes as an intact group becomes shorter, the burden of trying to meet the needs of every student grows heavier and more complex.

In many situations, chunking of the typical school day further insulates teachers from sources of ideas beyond their own background of experiences. This is particularly evident at the high school level, where teachers might have five classes and several different preparations daily, along with building duties and extracurricular activities, while interacting with more than 100 students during the course of the day and sometimes into the evening.

Adding to the complexity of the school day with its myriad curricular and extracurricular activities is the growing awareness by perceptive teachers that *every* student has special needs that require special attention. Furthermore, every student has unique abilities and talents to be nurtured. The task of developing the potential of all students and preparing them for future careers, further education, and eventual participation as citizens can be overwhelming. That "little red schoolhouse" with one teacher serving a wide range of student ages and needs in an isolated setting just will not do.

REFLECTION 1.2

From Responsibilities to Opportunities

Review Vignette l, the scene in the high school faculty room. Give some thought to the frustrations of the English teacher who feels overworked and ill prepared for addressing more special needs in her classroom, along with finding time to meet with special education teachers and perhaps even plan for co-teaching with them. If you were the *concerned English teacher*, what might you be overlooking that could be potentially helpful for both of you and the new student?

If you were the *special education consulting teacher* assigned to work with that English teacher and you overheard or found out about that brief four-teacher conversation in the faculty room, how would you get ready for your first interaction with her? Later in the chapter, Vignette 1 and this Reflection 1.2 will become a case study for exploring ways to prepare for and engage in that first meeting.

WHY WORK TOGETHER AS EDUCATORS?

In our increasingly interdependent and specialized world, it is unlikely that any one person has enough knowledge and ability in any field of endeavor to handle every circumstance. So it is reasonable and prudent to consult, collaborate, and team up in partnerships with others to achieve common goals. Consultation and collaboration are routine in fields as varied as medicine, law, industry, fashion, sports, film making, construction, scientific research, journalism, decorating, finance—the list is endless. Some consultants even have their own consultants!

Teamwork is emphasized frequently in these times across a diverse range of work settings. In fields that encourage networking with others who have similar yet helpfully different perspectives, results have been dramatic. Processes of sharing expertise and challenging basic assumptions can stimulate growth in exciting ways when colleagues team up as productive partners.

So what about education? Does teaching lend itself to working together? It is definitely a multidimensional activity. The educator role has never been easy, and it becomes more challenging each year. School personnel are bombarded with more and more responsibilities, even as legislatures and the general public raise expectations for student achievement and hold educators accountable for measurable yearly progress of their students. Teacher burnout and attrition (to be discussed in Chapter 6) are major concerns in special education, an area of teaching that has experienced major shortages for some time. Cosmetic alteration of existing programs and practices will not be enough to address such complex issues and multiple concerns. Responsibilities have escalated and expanded for instruction, management of the learning environment, assessment of student achievement, professional development activity, and networking with a broad range of school personnel and families.

ACTION 1.1
Identifying Teacher Responsibilities

What does a teacher do in the course of a day, week, and school year? With short phrases, describe all the responsibilities you can think of that teachers typically perform. Draw upon your recollections of what teachers did in your student days, what professors did in your teacher preparation and student teaching programs, and any teaching experiences during or beyond your school days that you have had. Remember to include not only instruction and curriculum preparation but also things such as assessment, classroom management, extracurricular and supervisory duties, classroom maintenance responsibilities, conferences with families of students, professional development, and much more. Expect to come up with dozens and dozens of areas that reflect the teacher's professional day, week, and year. Include professionally focused summer duties to offset the mistaken idea that "teachers don't have to work in the summertime."

If you collaborate with other teachers in various grade levels, content areas, and specialized roles to do this activity, your combined lists will become a colorful and impressive collection of teaching responsibilities. The discussion itself will be an example of collaborative consultation, where each person is consulting with others and contributing information from his or her own perspectives and experiences. Save these lists for the Action 1.3 activity later on.

DESCRIBING CONSULTATION, COLLABORATION, AND TEAMWORK

Practical definitions of collaboration, consultation, and teamwork for school settings must be general enough to apply to a wide range of school structures and circumstances yet flexible enough for adapting to many types of schools and communities. Defining is difficult due to the challenges of drawing meaningful boundaries and the risks of being too limiting or too broad (John-Steiner, Weber, & Minnis, 1998).

Issues of definition or descriptions require careful attention to semantics because meanings can vary from user to user and from context to context. People who say, "Oh, that's just semantics; don't bother about it" fail to recognize the importance of appropriate word selection for verbal or written communication (or signs in signed communication). Consider the foreign diplomat in a press conference who is striving to communicate complex ideas and present delicate nuances of meanings that are critical to matters on the world stage. Flawed interpretations and inaccurate translations can produce serious misunderstandings on an international level. In similar fashion, teachers who communicate poorly about abstract concepts such as achievement, effort, behavior, and expectations can erect barriers to important interactions that need to take place.

Webster's Third New International Dictionary (1976), *Webster's New Collegiate Dictionary* (1996), and *World Book Dictionary* (2003) provide several shades of meaning and a number of synonyms relevant for schools and education. The words and synonyms complement each other to form a conceptual foundation for collaboration, consultation, and teamwork in educational environments.

By analyzing synonyms from these sources for a particular word, we can find meanings that are useful in complex situations and construct definitions that will be helpful to our purposes here:

- *collaborate:* To labor together or work jointly in cooperative interaction to attain a shared goal
- *collaborative ethic:* A philosophy of shared spirit and interdependence among those who are working together for common causes

- *teamwork, teaming:* Joint action in which persons work cooperatively to achieve shared goals; also, joining forces or efforts so that each individual contributes a clearly defined portion of the effort and subordinates personal prominence to the effectiveness of the whole (Recall the popular saying, "There's no 'I' in the word 'team.'")
- *consult:* To advise or seek advice, confer, confab, huddle, parley, counsel, discuss, deliberate, consider, examine, refer to, or communicate in order to decide or plan something, seek an opinion as a guide to one's own judgment, request information or facts, or talk over a situation or subject with someone
- *consultation:* Advisement, counsel, conference, or formal deliberation to provide direct services focused on needs and concerns
- *consultant:* One who gives professional advice or renders professional services in a field of special knowledge and training, or more simply, one who consults with another
- *client:* Individual, group, agency, or other entity receiving services to enhance abilities for learning and for doing (In some instances, *target* is a synonym for client, but the word is best avoided when referring to people.)
- *consultee:* One who confers with the consultant to gather and exchange information, generate ideas, and apply them to a client's needs (The consultee in school settings is often, but by no means always, the general education or classroom teacher.)
- *co-educator:* An educator who collaborates, consults, teams with, co-teaches, or networks with the other educator(s) to address students' needs for learning and doing (This may be school educator, home educator—parent or other family member or caregiver—or community resource person.)
- *co-teaching:* Two or more teachers planning and implementing instruction and monitoring and assessing student achievement, often in an inclusive classroom setting
- *network:* A system of connections among individuals or groups who have similar interests and interact to accomplish shared goals

Drawing from the words just described, the following definitions frame major concepts presented in this book:

- Collaborative school consultation with teamwork is an interactive process in which school personnel in general education and special education, related services and support personnel, families of students, and the students themselves are working together and sharing their diversity of knowledge and expertise in order to define needs and then plan, implement, assess, follow through, and follow up on ways of helping learners develop to their fullest.
- Co-educators are persons who collaborate, consult, and work as a team to provide appropriate learning experiences for learners' diverse needs. Co-educators can be school based, such as teachers and related services or support personnel; home based, such as family members or caregivers for students; and community based in support roles.
- Teamwork in the collaborative school environment is the process by which a group of co-educators work to address common purposes and strive to achieve shared goals for the benefit and ultimate successes of children and youth.

The word *collaborate* has come a long way from days when it often was construed to mean working in collusion with an enemy. A collaborative school consultation relationship is characterized by mutual trust and behaviors that facilitate joint exploration of ways to help students. The consultant and consultee join as a team to plan and solve problems for the needs of the client. They may draw others into the team, such as family members, related services, or support personnel who could be of help.

How do collaboration and consultation differ in purpose? Sheridan (1992) has characterized consultation as a form of collaboration. Consultation helps consultees develop skills to solve current problems and generalize those skills to other problems. In its most effective form, it is interactive and requires active participation, or collaborative effort, by the consultee. Sheridan calls for consultants to engage in self-reflection and self-evaluation about the impact they will have on the interactive process of consultation.

The Reflection and Action features in this book present opportunities to think about the issues brought forth and then interact with others to share reflections and act on ways of serving exceptional learning needs. Through collaborative school consultation and teamwork, co-educators become more capable and have more confidence in their abilities than when teaching in isolated contexts. Co-educators put student needs first, with collaborative efforts helping educators guide and instruct in ways that promote student learning (Brownell, Adams, Sindelar, Waldron, & Vanhover 2006).

Much of the collaboration in school settings has been more occasional and happenstance than frequent and planned. Available and congruent time blocks are necessary for productive interaction with colleagues, and these opportunities are few in the course of a busy school day. Planning and preparation for working together in new, less familiar roles have been minimal. Then, too, careful assessment of collaborative outcomes has been the exception, not the rule. (This neglected area will be addressed in Chapter 12.) Nevertheless, the growing complexities of teaching and escalating demands for student achievement and school accountability point to a strong need for working together in many dimensions. Collaborative school consultation and team interactions by educators are receiving increased attention among school professionals.

ACTION 1.2
Collaboration Throughout the Global Community

The word *collaboration* is appearing more and more in all sorts of venues—news periodicals, newscasts, speeches, documentaries, medical and science reports, sports reviews, entertainment and media discussions, political panels, industrial plans, organizational reports, weblogs, music production, community meetings, casual conversations—the list of examples could go on and on. If you make it a point to listen and look for the word or its derivatives, such as *collaborate* and *collaborative*, for a week, you may be surprised at the result. Just tally on a card each time you see or hear it and note in what context it appeared. If marking a tally is not convenient at the time, then make a mental note: "There it is. I did hear the word *collaboration* in today's newscast describing collaborative activities among journalists and humanitarian groups." Or, "I did see *collaborate* in a magazine article featuring collaborative consumption—an amazing concept in economics." If you read a morning newspaper, you may come across the word right there. After a week, consolidate your findings with those of others who are watching for it and discuss when, where, and how the word was used.

WHY WORK TOGETHER FOR SPECIAL NEEDS?

Terms for describing exceptionality can vary among federal, state, and local agencies, but typical ones include autism, behavioral disorder, communicative disability, cultural and linguistic diversity, deafness or being hard of hearing, developmental disability or mental retardation, dual sensory impairment, emotional disturbance, learning disability, multiple disabilities, physical disability, traumatic brain injury, and visual impairment or blindness. More than half of the states in the United States also include gifted and talented students as a part of special education because of their exceptional learning needs.

In Vignette 1 earlier in this chapter, the client was the new student with severe learning disabilities. To address the student's exceptional learning needs, the learning disabilities consultant would serve the student indirectly for the most part by collaborating with the classroom English teacher, who would be consultee and provider of direct services to the student. Some direct service could be given to the student by the learning disabilities consultant if her co-educators decided on that, but direct service would come to the student primarily from the classroom teacher.

Those in the consultant role do not hold claim to all the expertise. Competent consultants also listen and learn. They help consultees discover what they already know. They help consultees recognize their own talents and trust their own skills. Not only does this benefit the student with exceptional learning needs; it also has the potential benefit of helping the consultee serve other students' special needs when the skills and strategies learned for one student can be put to use successfully with other students.

ACTION 1.3
Categorizing Teacher Responsibilities

Sort the list of teacher responsibilities you compiled in Action 1.1 into categories of tasks with these headings: instructional; curricular, managerial, evaluative, supportive, and professional growth related. Then decide which tasks might be carried out most productively and enjoyably in collaborative contexts. As one example for the category of managerial responsibility for ordering books and supplies, teams of teachers might collaborate to pool their media and library allocations and make decisions about materials that could be shared or used for team teaching. Are you already doing that? Then teams could explore their basal series texts together to find areas of overlap and identify potential topics for unifying curriculum content across several subject areas.

Mark with an asterisk (*) other tasks that have collaborative potential and add more that may have been overlooked in the Action 1.1 list, such as "organizing cross-grade tutors and study-buddies," or "involving families in preparing a notebook of potential community resources." Discuss how collaborative discussion groups and teamwork activities could use those ideas.

WHAT COLLABORATIVE SCHOOL CONSULTATION IS AND WHAT IT IS *NOT*

Collaborators work for the good of the whole, where individual preferences are set aside to address a greater purpose. The concept is based on the adage that many heads and hearts are better than one, and the pooled experiences, talents, knowledge, and ideas of a group are even better than the sum of the individual parts. Various forms for collaboration, consultation, and teaming exist, and many different terms can be used to describe those processes— for example, consulting teacher, collaborative consultation, team teaching, co-teaching, cooperative teaching, and collaborative teaching.

All three processes—collaboration, consultation, and teamwork—as they occur in the school context involve interaction among school personnel, families and students, and the community in working together to achieve common goals. However, there are subtle distinctions. In school consultation, a consultant contributes specialized expertise toward an educational problem, and the consultee then delivers the direct service utilizing that expertise. Consultants and consultees are collaborators when they assume equal ownership in identifying a problem and finding solutions. Collaboration is a way of working in which power struggles and feigned politeness are counterproductive to team goals. Researchers and practitioners stress that collaboration must be voluntary, not required or coerced. An educator *willingly* assists another to address needs of a third party. Successful collaborative consultants use different styles of interaction under different circumstances in different situations.

Collaborating as a teaching team is catalytic in generating group spirit. One of the best examples of collaboration is a musical ensemble. Whether one is accompanying a soloist; performing with a small group; or playing with an orchestra, it is the united effort that creates the musical experience. Musicians of many instruments typically are not brought together to play the same note with instruments that make the same sound. Doing so would make the music only louder, not richer and more harmonious. In similar fashion, co-teachers work in harmonious concert, rarely in unison, to provide rich learning experiences. Teaming up to co-teach or partner in learning activities will generate many opportunities for interaction in which each person is learning from and building on the strengths and expertise of the others.

Welch (1998) deconstructs the term *collaboration* and comes up with a unique concept of working together for mutual benefit. It is different from cooperation, in which all come to agreement but perhaps not all are benefiting. Welch says that schools have tended to be more cooperative than collaborative and gives as an example the parallel but sometimes uneasy coexistence of general and special education. Welch faults the Individual Education Plan (IEP) process as often involving little or no collaboration during development and implementation; the plan may be drafted before a meeting using a generalized template and then quickly reviewed and hastily approved by those present, thus "essentially disempowering the 'I' in the IEP process" (Welch, 1998, p. 128.). One way to improve the process would be for the classroom teacher, who is required by the Individuals with Disabilities Education Act (IDEA) to be involved, to participate as a very active member rather than a relatively passive observer.

Another is to use family wisdom as well as professional wisdom, drawing on both family values and professional values. The collaborating consultant must *first do no harm* and then deliver services that are academically and ethically sound (Wesley & Buysse, 2006).

When educators—special education teachers, classroom teachers, school administrators, related services and support personnel—and families and community agencies are consulting and collaborating as members of an educational team, what specifically are the kinds of things they can be observed doing? A comprehensive list would include several or all of the following:

- Discussing students' needs with co-educators and planning ways of addressing those needs
- Listening to colleagues' concerns about a particular teaching situation
- Assisting families with their students who are in a transition period—from early childhood education programs to kindergarten, from elementary to middle school, from middle school to high school, or from high school to work or postsecondary education
- Recommending classroom alternatives as first-to-be-tried interventions for students with special learning and behavior needs
- Providing direct assistance to colleagues, as in co-teaching or demonstration teaching for special needs
- Leading or participating in professional development activities that focus on special needs
- Locating and sharing resources, instructional materials, and teaching strategies
- Using technology for efficient, productive interactions among colleagues, students, and their families
- Engaging in classroom observations, assessment of students, and evaluation of services
- Serving on curriculum committees, textbook committees, extracurricular activities committees, and school advisory councils
- Following through and following up on educational issues and concerns with co-educators, students and their families, and community members
- Networking with other educational professionals and agencies who can be resources for students' needs and school improvements in general

These are just some of the activities that educators engage in when they are collaborating.

So what kinds of activity are *not* considered collaborative school consultation? Collaborative school consultation is not counseling; neither is it therapy or supervision. The focus instead must be on issues and educational concerns relevant to the welfare of the client rather than on problems of consultees. Conoley and Conoley (1982) caution that the consultant must collaborate for issues and needs of the client, typically the student, and not the consultee, who typically is the teacher.

It is important that consulting teachers shed the "expert" image, but also be recognized as having expertise and resourcefulness to contribute. Collaborative consultation can emanate from any role pertinent to the case if the participants are well informed. As a professional in the medical field commented, patients collaborate effectively with their doctors precisely because they are so well informed about their own conditions. No consultant is the be-all, end-all expert, and any co-educator can serve in the consulting role when circumstances dictate.

Collaboration among professional colleagues is not talk or discussion for its own sake. Furthermore, collaboration during co-teaching must not be hierarchical or judgmental but voluntary and entered into with parity among the teaching partners. Collaborative services should not be used as a money-saving strategy in inclusive settings to eliminate or reduce the number of school personnel. Importantly, consultative and collaborative structures that provide indirect service must not be substituted in cases for which there is a strong need for direct services.

As cautioned earlier and as will be emphasized repeatedly throughout this book, collaborative school consultation and co-teaching cannot be forced on educators; these processes must be entered into by choice. There will be times when teachers relish having autonomy in their work. Busy, multitasking educators need private, personal think-and-do time. It is important for teachers to develop some instructional ideas that are theirs alone, for in many cases, this was a compelling reason that they chose the profession. Most teachers are willing to share ideas and lend help to colleagues; however, they should not be asked to give up their specialties any more than chefs would be expected to relinquish their most prized recipes. Such unnecessary behavior would mean giving up practices that are personally satisfying. That is not the purpose of collaboration, nor should it be a presumed condition of co-teaching. Instead, collaborators should help colleagues develop their own skills and talents and instructional specialties.

MOTIVATION FOR WORKING COLLABORATIVELY

Reports from school districts throughout the United States identify collaboration as a key variable in the successful implementation of inclusive education (Villa & Thousand, 2003). In a collaborative climate, differentiated tasks can be allocated to individuals with a variety of skills to contribute. This means recognizing differences and finding ways to capitalize on those differences. The collaborative process is enriched by diversity among collaborators—diversity of backgrounds, experiences, perspectives, values, skills, talents, and interests. Individual differences of adults who consult and collaborate are rich ingredients for successful collaborations. This concept will be developed further in Chapters 2 and 3.

Collaborators do not compromise and cooperate so much as they confer and concur. Compromise seems to suggest giving up or conceding a point; cooperation may dilute interaction so that it misses the mark for everyone. This would be particularly problematic for students with exceptional learning needs. Making an unwanted compromise or giving way to pressure in order to "just cooperate so we can get on with it" can result in an inferior plan developed out of frustration and expediency, not satisfaction with the proposal. Collaboration, on the other hand, involves ongoing talking and planning, disagreeing, contributing, amending, adding to, and coming to consensual agreement so *all* can benefit.

Collaborators need models that provide structure, practice, encouragement, and positive feedback in order to perform the sophisticated and demanding functions called for in collaborative school consultation. Many school systems have adopted a professional learning community (PLC) approach for using assessment data and student work as tools to select instructional strategies for students' learning needs (Thessin & Starr, 2011). DuFour (2004) suggests that educators in the PLC may equate collaboration with congeniality and camaraderie; nevertheless, they must have the right structures to work in if they are to build a culture of collaboration. Thessin and Starr (2011, p. 49) assert that "Teachers do not magically know how to work with colleagues; districts must support and lead that work if PLCs are to live up to their potential." In their analysis, they found that previously, when common planning periods had been scheduled, the focus tended to be on planning events and field trips. Then, when the focus was turned toward supporting and improving student achievement, the immediate result was confusion and frustration. So educators found that districts needed to provide guidance for administrators and teachers on how to work together in PLCs effectively. (See the Additional Resources section for a description of one school district's PLC plan.)

CO-EDUCATOR RESPONSIBILITIES IN COLLABORATIVE ENDEAVORS

When collaborators-to-be first contemplate the role, they often voice their initial concerns with questions such as these:

- Who am I in the collaborative role?
- How do I carry out the responsibilities of this role?
- How will I know whether I am succeeding?
- How can I prepare for the collaborative role?
- Will I have my own place and space in the school(s)?
- Will I be able to work with children—my main love in teaching—or only with adults?

To address these questions, it is essential that central administrators and policymakers such as school board members sell the importance and benefits of consultative, collaborative, and co-teaching roles to their school personnel and community members. Then building-level administrators must sell the ideas to faculty and staff in their own attendance centers, and to students' families. A key factor of collaborative school consultation for the selling and the ultimate success of the concept is allocation of real and sufficient time for the interactions that are expected to occur. This will be addressed in much more detail in later chapters.

Teachers need encouragement to share the responsibilities enthusiastically for all students. Related services personnel and support personnel should be integrated into a collaborative context. Families must receive convincing information that assures them such services are right for their children and do not take away attention from their needs. Students should be an integral part of the planning process by participating as young collaborators who are intensely involved in their own educational programs. Ultimately, the community must support establishment of a collaborative climate and anticipate its potential benefits for all.

INTERCHANGEABLE ROLES AND RESPONSIBILITIES

Role delineation will be a major topic in Chapter 4. For now, let it be said that anyone who consults in one situation might be a consultee or even a client in another. In each of these instances, both consultant and consultee share responsibility for working out a plan to help the client. A special education teacher might be a consultant in one situation or a consultee in another situation for which the general education teacher is the consultant. The student typically is the client but in some cases could be a consultee or even a consultant. A social worker, special reading teacher, or general classroom teacher might initiate consultative service. A school counselor or a student's family member might request collaborative consultation. The combinations of "people roles" that may participate in school collaboration and consultation needed to help students and teachers are virtually limitless. In Figure 1.3,

FIGURE 1.3   Collaborators in the Consultant, Consultee, or Client Role

Special education teacher	Student with learning disability
General classroom teacher	Student with behavioral disorder
School psychologist	Preschool student
School counselor	Student with mental retardation
Reading specialist	Student with high aptitude/talent
Building administrator	Student with attention deficit disorder
Gifted program facilitator	Student with physical disability
School nurse	Parent of student with disability
Media specialist	Parent of student with high aptitude/talent
Technology specialist	Community-based mentor
Resource room teacher	Student with autism or Asperger's syndrome
School cafeteria personnel	Medical doctor/dentist
School bus driver	University professor in special education
School custodian	Speech and language pathologist
Special education director	University professor in general education
Early childhood teacher	Probation officer
Curriculum specialist	Head Start personnel
Professional development personnel	State Department of Education personnel
Student (preservice) teacher	Paraeducator
Social worker	Minister/priest/rabbi/imam
School advisory council member	School board member
School district administrator	Other?

each collaborator, depending on the situation, could be a consultant, a consultee, or a client. Although roles and responsibilities may vary among individuals and across situations, when there is understanding about the nature of the role and appreciation for its possibilities, a collaborative and facilitative spirit will prevail.

REFLECTION 1.3

Showing Role Interchangeability

Select any three roles from Figure 1.3. Label one as consultant, another as consultee, and a third as client with special needs. Think about a scenario in which this configuration might be formed to help the client (having special needs that you determine). Without delving into what could or should happen, select another group of three and envision a different scenario where collaborative school consultation could be activated. Select more groups of three roles or sometimes four or five and pose situations in which they could be involved. (On occasion, IEP teams have included a dozen or so participants!) In a later chapter, these configurations can be put into practice using problems that will be introduced there.

THE CASE STUDY AS A WAY TO EXPLORE EDUCATIONAL ISSUES

A case study is a short, focused vignette that offers a situation in which participants are to make decisions about a simulated problem. They do so by first studying the dynamics of the situation and then analyzing the known facts, identifying the initiator of service, defining the problem, generating possible action(s), evaluating the proposed plan for action, making a decision about it, and following up and following through on the outcomes.

Originally developed at Harvard Law School (Hawthorne, 1991), the case study is a helpful instructional technique for a number of disciplines including education. Some guidelines for using case studies to practice content-area problem solving are:

- Every participant should have studied the case and come prepared to participate in the discussion.
- No new facts should be added to the case during the discussion.
- Participating groups should be small enough (fewer than twelve, with six or eight being better) so that all participate.
- Participants could role play from different perspectives to explore alternative solutions.

Case studies are effective because they tell appealing stories about things most participants have experienced (Hutchings, 1993). They also bring to light issues that may not have been seen or considered previously or may have been slipped under the proverbial rug.

The situation described in Vignette 1 is useful here for illustrating a case study approach and providing an organizational template to outline components of a typical

FIGURE 1.4   Template for a Case Study

A. Description of the Scene or Situation

B. Initiator/Convener of the Collaborative Consultation Activity

C. Processes for:

    1. Defining of Problem(s) and Need(s)

    2. Developing Possible Collaborative Action(s), with Critique of Them

    3. Determining Plan for Collaborative Action(s)

    4. Making Collaborative Decision about Activating Proposed Plan

    5. Follow-Through Action and By Whom

    6. Follow-Up Action by When and by Whom

    7. Evaluation of the Collaborative Consultation Process

collaborative school consultation process. A variety of other case study methods and examples will appear in later chapters. (See Figure 1.4 for one form of a case study template, keeping in mind that it can be altered to fit other contexts.)

Practical application of the template might go like this: The Vignette 1 *situation* involves the English teacher (let's call her Meg) and the special education consulting teacher for learning disabilities (let's refer to her as Rachel) who are entering the first stage of collaborative instructional teaming to assist a high-school student who has severe learning disabilities. (Keep in mind that the focus here is not on problem solving for the student's needs, but on examining how the collaborative consultation process is developing.) From earlier comments made by English teacher Meg to some of her high school colleagues in the faculty room, we assume that the *initiator/convener* of their first interaction will be special educator Rachel. When they do meet, the information that they have to share comprises the *known facts*. They will use this information and more, if they can obtain more, to think up *a course of action* that will help this student (let's call him Steve) in Meg's classes. As they pool their knowledge about Steve and his school and family backgrounds, each will aim to become familiar with the other's curriculum and instructional strategies that could be used to address his needs. Rachel will learn about Meg's conventional English curriculum for the class Steve is entering, while Meg will learn about Rachel's special education curriculum that can provide opportunities for Steve to succeed in the English classes. Each needs to know what the other can do for him. This is a very important part of determining *possible actions* that consultee Meg and consultant Rachel can take to assist each other for client Steve's benefit.

The two teachers will want to discuss instructional practices that could be used to formulate *a plan of action* for Steve, such as accommodations and modifications in grading policies, homework requirements, incentives, the structure of the classroom environment, home support, and much more. After critique of the possibilities, they make a *collaborative decision to activate the plan*, set dates for future meetings (including IEP conferencing, if required), and discuss other resources for helping this student. It is not unreasonable to assume that each might pick up ideas from this collaboration for working with other students they have who need some assistance.

As a team, they would continue with the important step of scheduling *follow through* that involves consultee, consultant, and client in monitoring progress toward the team-crafted goals. They also would specify a later time to *follow up* on progress to date. Last but by no means least, before and after the follow-up date, they would *evaluate* the collaborative consultation *process* as it was carried out in this situation. They would like for it to have the positive ripple effect of serving other students beyond this one client and situation.

A LITTLE HISTORY OF EDUCATIONAL REFORM MOVEMENTS

Now that the case is made and the stage is set for working together as co-educators, a very brief review of special education history can be illuminative. Most readers will have studied these historical accounts previously; nonetheless, a look back at schools, from the days of teaching in isolation to the present where educators are encouraged to work in teams and groups, will promote better understanding of the rationale and recommendations for topics to come.

In the 1960s, professional and lay advocates representing special needs pressed for the right of those with mental retardation to have opportunities as similar as possible to those in mainstream society. Public attention to needs of preschoolers from disadvantaged environments was gaining momentum. In 1965, passage of the Elementary and Secondary Education Act (ESEA) authorized funding and made specific provisions for students with disabilities (Talley & Schrag, 1999). Reauthorizations of that legislation in 1988 and 1994 mandated parent involvement in early childhood programs such as Head Start, encouraging school- and community-linked services through the Community Schools Partnership Act. *Consultation* and *collaboration* became essential elements in coordinating the array of services provided for students with special needs.

During the 1970s through the early 2000s, educators witnessed an explosion of reports, proposals, and legislative mandates calling for educational reform and fueling the mainstreaming movement with its concept of least restrictive environment (LRE). In 1975 Public Law 94-142 (a law put forth by the 94th Congress as its 142nd piece of legislation) was passed. After that, educators could no longer place individuals with disabilities arbitrarily in a special school or self-contained classroom. A continuum of service options was to be available, and the type of service or placement was to be as close to the normal environment as possible, with general education teachers responsible for the success of those students. In order to meet this new responsibility, *general education teachers were to receive help from special education personnel*. This was an important provision, and it opened eyes to the need for general education and special education to work together.

The 1980s brought about the development of collegial, participatory environments among students and staff, with particular emphasis on personalizing school environments and designing curriculum for deeper understanding (Michaels, 1988). A position paper issued by Madeline Will (1986), former director of the U.S. Office of Special Education and Rehabilitative Services, stated that too many children were being inappropriately identified and placed in learning disabilities programs. In that paper, Will called for *collaboration* between special education personnel and general education personnel to provide special services within the general classroom. This generated the Regular Education Initiative (REI), referred to by some educators as the General Education Initiative (GEI), which caused major changes in the way education is delivered. All students, with the exception of those with severe disabilities, were from that time to be served primarily in a regular education setting. Furthermore, cooperative school–parent relationships would be enhanced (Will, 1986).

In 1986, P.L. 94-142 was amended by P.L. 99-457 to mandate free appropriate public education (FAPE) for preschool children ages three to five having disabilities. An Individualized Family Service Plan (IFSP) was required for each child served, thus extending the concept of the IEP to provide support for child *and* family (Smith, 1998). Because most disabilities of children in early intervention programs are severe, services of specialists from several disciplines were deemed essential for children in the programs. Families were to have an integral part in the therapy through home-based programs. Families were described in a broad sense, not necessarily as a father-and-mother unit, so as to include parents, grandparents, older siblings, aunts and uncles, or others who are functioning in the caregiver role. The IFSP was to be developed by a multidisciplinary team, with family members as active participants.

In 1990, early into a third wave of reform, P.L. 94-142 was amended with the passage of P.L. 101-476, the Individuals with Disabilities Education Act (IDEA). This was when references to *handicapped children* were changed to *children with disabilities*. In addition, more emphasis was placed on requirements to provide transition services for students 16 years of age and older. Goals of special education advocates included merging special and general education into one inclusive system, increasing dramatically the number of children with disabilities who would be in mainstream classrooms, and aiming to strengthen academic achievement of students with mild and moderate disabilities, as well as that of underachievers without disabilities.

In 1997, after much study and discussion nationwide, reauthorization and amendments for IDEA were approved by Congress and signed into law by U.S. President Bill Clinton. A focus of IDEA 1997 was *collaboration* among general educators and special educators, parents, related services personnel, and other service providers; this inclusion meant that general educators in particular must be actively engaged in selecting program modifications and supports, alternative-grading procedures, and assistive technology devices (Williams & Martin, 2001). Transition services and interagency linkages were noted as vital areas of assistance.

The concept of inclusion that swept the nation did not suddenly emerge out of a vacuum. It emanated from the long line of special education movements and mandates briefly described above and charted in Figure 1.5. Inclusive schools *include* students with special needs in the total school experience, rather than "exclude" them by placement in special schools or classrooms.

Collaboration is essential to inclusion because successful inclusion presumes that "no one teacher can or ought to be expected to have all the expertise required to meet

FIGURE 1.5 **Historic Path of Important Educational Movements**

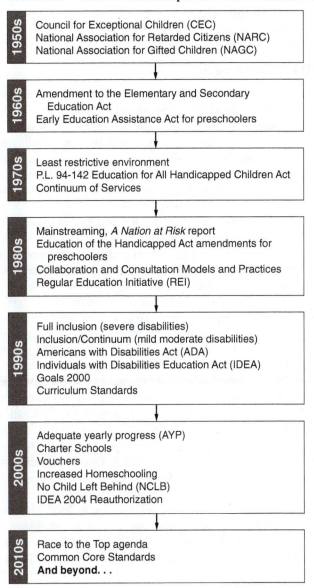

the educational needs of all students in the classroom" (Lipsky, 1994, p. 5). All educators share responsibility for student achievement and behavior. There must be total commitment from principal to school custodian (Federico, Herrold, & Venn, 1999). Every inclusive school looks different, but all inclusive schools are characterized by a sense of community, high standards, collaboration and cooperation, changing roles and an array of services, partnership with families, flexible learning environments, strategies based on research, new forms of accountability, and ongoing professional development (Federico, Herrold, & Venn, 1999; Working Forum on Inclusive Schools, 1994).

The No Child Left Behind Legislation

The No Child Left Behind Act (NCLB) of 2001 mandated requirements and added specificity to elements of the 1965 Elementary and Secondary Education Act. Purposes of this legislation were summarized as accountability, assessment, and high standards. NCLB unleashed a flurry of high-stakes testing in specific curricular areas (reading and math as the first subjects to be tested), inclusion of children with disabilities in the testing scheme, intensive preparations for the tests, high-profile reports of schools that made or failed to make adequate yearly progress (AYP), higher standards for teacher certification, and more accountability of schools for student achievement.

The NCLB legislation was not adequately funded, and its enactment received much additional criticism from the educational community. Many have stressed that education is not conducive to high-stakes testing. Children do not learn the same amount at the same rate and at the same ages. Furthermore, success of schools cannot be measured by tests. Test results should be used to guide instruction, not to signify school success or failure.

The focus of NCLB on high-stakes testing has narrowed the school curriculum considerably for all students. Heavy emphasis on students who are below proficiency levels shifts attention and resources from very able learners who need challenge and advancement; consequently, they are being *held* behind—invoking the need for a new term, No Child *Held* Behind (NC*H*B). Still another concern is that standardized tests and assessment of adequate yearly progress in cognitive areas do not assess student growth in the emotional, physical, self-expressive, and social areas that also are vital for student development (Dettmer, 2006). All children need development in fine arts, physical education, practical arts, problem solving, and working together collaboratively, to mention only some of the elements that should be present in a rich curriculum structure but have been curtailed or eliminated altogether by demands and burdens of NCLB. One of the harshest criticisms of NCLB has been that it ties teacher accountability to test scores when so many other elements should be examined as major factors in student success or failure.

The NCLB legislation was overdue for reauthorization in 2007, after the rewriting of the ESEA, as amended in 2002 by NCLB. The reauthorization that did not happen was replaced by U.S. President Barack Obama's 2010 Race to the Top agenda. It focuses even more on test scores as ultimate measures of educational quality (Ravitch, 2011). Its agenda of testing, accountability, school choice, and more federal control include use of test scores to evaluate teaching, a policy that many in the professional community believe does not bode well for students or their teachers. Proposals for improvement to public education that have been catalyzed by disillusionment over NCLB and the Race to the Top agenda include:

- Expanding the curriculum
- Discouraging the practice of teaching to the test
- Improving high school graduation rates

- Providing better tests for measuring accountability
- Putting stronger emphasis on preparing students for work and college
- Implementing assessments that reflect critical thinking and problem solving
- Retaining excellent teachers by means of career ladders and mentors

Each of these proposals could benefit from strong collaborations among professional educators, in partnership with families and communities.

Collaborative School Consultation as Change Agent in Special Education

The need for special education in public schools probably dates back to the mid-nineteenth century, when state after state (Rhode Island in 1840, then Massachusetts in 1852, followed in time by all the other states) passed compulsory school attendance laws mandating formal education for every school-age child, regardless of disability, giftedness, or other special need. Now, in the twenty-first century, up to one-third of all school-age children in the United States are designated as experiencing difficulties in school because of special needs, and if the significant needs of gifted students for acceleration and enrichment were included, this figure would be substantially higher. These realities, along with various social issues and pressures of the times, have spurred interest in a variety of ideas to "fix" schools and the students in them.

Charter schools, voucher systems, dual-language classrooms, professional learning communities, multi-grade classrooms, and block scheduling are just the tip of the panoply of ideas that make up the school-reform iceberg. However, interest has been escalating for more than a half-century in the relatively unheralded and uncomplicated process of collaborative school consultation and its related forms of teamwork such as co-teaching, mentoring, cooperative learning, and various tutoring structures. This informal movement has fueled an escalating number of conferences, publications, research studies, pilot programs, federal and state grants, and training projects, as well as several teacher preparation courses and programs, for increasing the understanding of collaborative school consultation and applying collaborative practices in schools. Meanwhile, collaboration has become the go-to word in dozens of social and career fields for describing how people should be working together and helping each other across all societal venues.

ACTION 1.4
Collaboration Is in Style!

In Action 1.2 you were asked to watch for the word *collaboration* in your everyday coming and going. How is that going? What are the most unexpected areas in which you have noticed the word being used? Entertainment? Politics? Religion? Industry? Science? Sports? Pool your findings with those of others to expand your outlook on collaborative potential.

Where did the idea for consultation and collaboration in schools come from? School consultation probably originated in the mental health and management fields (Reynolds & Birch, 1988). Gerald Caplan (1970) developed consultation programs to train staff members for working with troubled adolescents in Israel after World War II. Building upon this Caplanian mental health consultation concept (Caplan, Caplan, & Erchul, 1995), mental health services escalated and moved into school settings, where consultation services provided by school psychologists produced promising results. The role of consultation in school psychology was broadened to encourage collaborative relationships (Gallessich, 1974; Pryzwansky, 1974). Such relationships helped teachers, administrators, and students' families deal with future problems as well as immediate concerns.

Examples of consulting in the areas of speech and language therapy, and in programs for hearing-impaired and visually impaired students, date from the late 1950s. Examples of teacher consultation for students with learning disabilities and behavioral disorders appeared in the literature as early as the mid-1960s. At that time, consultants for the most part were not special educators but clinical psychologists and psychiatric social workers.

By the mid-1960s the term *school consultation* was listed in *Psychological Abstracts* (Friend, 1988). School counselors began to promote the concept of proactive service, so that by the early 1970s, consultation was being recommended as an integral part of contemporary counseling service. Interest in collaborative relationships on the part of counselors and psychologists signaled a desire to influence the systems that most profoundly affect students (Brown, Wyne, Blackburn, & Powell, 1979).

The behavioral movement had been gaining momentum in the late 1960s, and it fueled interest in alternative models for intervention and the efficient use of time and other resources. This interest sparked development of a text by Tharp and Wetzel (1969), in which they presented a triadic consultation model using behavioral principles in school settings. The triadic model is the basic pattern upon which many subsequent models and methods for consultation have been structured. This will be reiterated and emphasized with methods and models in Chapter 4.

The 1970s decade was a very busy time in the field of special education. By the mid-1970s, consultation was regarded as a significant factor in serving students with special needs. Special education became a major catalyst for promoting consultation and collaboration in schools (Friend, 1988). By the mid-1980s, consultation was one of the most significant educational trends for serving students with special needs.

In the 1990s, leaders in school consultation reconceptualized existing models to fimore appropriately with inclusive schools and expanded roles of school personnel. Bergan (1995) describes an evolution from the school psychologist's behavioral consultation focus on assessment, labeling, and placement activities to an expanded role of consultative and collaborative problem solving for students' needs. The framework for behavioral consultation was revised to become a case-centered, problem-solving approach that could be teacher-based, parent-based, or conjoint-based (parent–teacher) consultation in which the consultee's involvement is critical to success of positive client outcomes (Kratochwill & Pittman, 2002).

Gifted education programs became one of the most promising fields for extensive use of collaborative consultation (Dettmer, 1989). Dettmer and Lane (1989) and Idol-Maestas and Celentano (1986) stressed the need for collaborative consultation practices to assist with learning needs of gifted and talented students who spend most of their school day in regular classrooms. Dyck and Dettmer (1989) promoted methods for facilitating learning programs of twice exceptional, gifted learning-disabled students within a consulting teacher plan.

The public in the new millennium is becoming more and more aware that teaching is not just the responsibility of professional educators within a school's walls. Community members and resource personnel beyond school campuses are acknowledged as important collaborators and team members in providing students with rich, authentic learning experiences.

Team teaching by co-educators across their classrooms is regarded by many dedicated teachers as a promising way of bringing students closer to achievement of standards (Kluth & Straut, 2001).

The next several years will be critical for professional educators as they choose to work together, learn best methods of working together, and find that they *enjoy* doing it. It will be important for them to model such activity because their students will be expected to work collaboratively as adults in their own careers and community roles of the future. Strong partnerships between home and school educators will be an increasingly essential part of helping students become competent, ethical leaders for the future. That said, participants in collaborative school consultation must work through their feelings of doubt, insecurity, and other concerns as they sort out the dynamics of partnering roles. School administrators have a responsibility to invite open, candid interaction about the insecurities and other concerns of co-educators related to educational issues, and provide opportunities for talking them over in transparent, constructive discussions.

COMMON CORE STANDARDS

The Common Core Standards document,[1] sponsored by the National Governors Association and the Council of Chief State School Officers, was presented in June 2010 (Conley, 2011). These standards outline real-life knowledge and skills students should learn in order to be "college ready," so that educators will know how to provide the appropriate instruction for them. State entities controlled the development process and content of the standards. It is not surprising, then, that most states quickly adopted the standards as replacement for their own state content standards. Common Core Standards (2010) are intended to:

- Point out key knowledge and skills that teachers need to focus on
- Raise expectations for achievement levels to those of the best education systems in the world
- Bring national consistency to expectations for high quality of curriculum materials
- Align teacher education programs with the standards
- Make available student achievement data and research findings to determine what works in education

The U.S. Department of Education is funding development of assessments to measure student learning of the standards in wider, more multidimensional ways (Conley, 2011). This will include using formative measures at more frequent intervals to provide feedback on student progress through the school year.

The standards include several measures that are particularly relevant to special education, such as:

- Skill to articulate a personal philosophy of special education
- Roles of individuals with exceptional learning needs, families, and school and community personnel in planning individualized programs
- *Models and strategies for consultation and collaboration*
- Several other measures focusing on assessment, communication, paraeducators, and families.

The Common Core Standards stipulate that students supported by the Individuals with Disabilities Act (IDEA) are to have the same rigorous coursework general education students receive. No provisions are given for ways of accomplishing this; however, concessions are made in the area of reading to allow the use of Braille, screen-reader technology, and other assistive devices, and the area of writing to include the use of a scribe, computer, or speech-to-text technology.

The overarching goal is achievement of world-class learning outcomes for all students. Nevertheless, just as with the NCLB legislation, there has been some skepticism toward whether the Common Core Standards will make a difference in student learning nationwide (Lee, 2011). Debate also has focused on whether the federal government should make receipt of federal funds contingent on states' adoptions of common academic standards such as in language arts and mathematics (Jennings, 2011). Therefore, it is especially important that teachers, family members, and students be "on the same page" in working toward common goals. This will require dedicated efforts in working collaboratively and in partnerships as co-educators. It is a positive sign that one of the Common Core Standards identifies Collaboration Knowledge as an area where numerous skills are to be developed including communication, teamwork, respectful and beneficial relationships, and group problem solving.

TECHNOLOGY FOR WORKING TOGETHER EFFECTIVELY

Modern technology has revolutionized many areas of work, study, and play in the past several decades, with the promise of many more exciting advances in the years to come. Although education has not been in the forefront of most technological breakthroughs, educators have found countless ways to use the breakthroughs in ways that help them connect with colleagues resourcefully and engage students successfully. Throughout this book the topic of technology will appear frequently, but not as an element to be taught. Rather, it will be treated as a useful *tool* for instruction and collaboration in inclusive learning environments.

Five categories of application for putting technology tools to work appear to be particularly helpful for collaborating teachers and support personnel:

1. Gathering and sharing information
2. Communicating with co-educators in schools, homes, and communities
3. Developing resources for curriculum and instruction
4. Organizing and managing data
5. Networking with co-educators and support services

It is illuminating to explore the various technologies put into play in the education arena. It will be important to reflect in later chapters on both contributions *and* cautions that are integral to the use of these technological tools for teaching and learning. For now, we will examine briefly their potential in the first two areas—information and communication—for assisting with student growth and achievement.

Information Gathering and Sharing

Information is "out there" to be retrieved any time on just about any topic that teachers or students are seeking. Technology tools provide pathways for co-educators and students to be informed and engaged. Consultants, teachers, and students are connected to large information systems that offer a variety of options, ranging from electronic listservs to conferencing capabilities. Potential uses for consultants and teachers include library searches and information bulletins relating to special needs of students with disabilities.

At the local level, list servers can be created using the Internet to manage mailing lists for groups of users. A list server system can send messages automatically to multiple e-mail addresses on the mailing lists used by teachers in a building or a school district. Collaborating educators could use systems such as Listserv or Majordomo to share ideas with co-educators that have worked well with other educators and schools.

Most preservice students today, as well as younger students still in school, grew up with technology and can grasp it with keen understanding from the moment it is available. They communicate with each other and absorb much of their information by using asynchronous communication that they can access any time they wish, not just at set intervals. As one university professor put it, "My students are always connected and always on, 24-7." Differences in professional perspectives stemming from generational gaps fade away or, more often, are turned upside down as novice and preservice teachers come to their first classrooms more prepared technologically than veteran teachers. The mentor–mentee relationship in such instances often is reversed, enhancing the beginning teacher's feelings of confidence in belonging to the group as a useful co-educator.

Some veteran teachers who completed their teacher preparation programs years ago are not adequately schooled in the use of technology. But they are learning to learn and to incorporate students' high-level skills into the lessons and their instruction. They do so through several avenues, including self-study, tutorials, professional development activities, and networking via electronic communication. Sometimes they are disposed to become the mentees in technology and welcome having students as their mentors. The entire process of using technology in teaching and learning extends across all disciplines and generations, with many opportunities yet to come for professional collaboration and teamwork.

Communicating with Co-Educators

School personnel who collaborate and co-teach obviously must communicate often to coordinate their efforts. Time is always at a premium for busy educators, but new computer technology and other electronic social media are improving the situation. Now communication can take place asynchronously, that is, intermittently without the need of a "common clock" for transmitting communications between sender and receiver. Collaborators need not wait for congruent schedules and compatible locations, as they had to do when connecting in a synchronous mode. This is a big help in dealing with the scarcity of time—a nonrenewable resource that has such an important impact on co-educator interactions. The topics of time and communication will continue to be addressed throughout the book.

ETHICS FOR WORKING TOGETHER AS CO-EDUCATORS

An ethical climate for collaborative school consultation and teamwork calls for a system of values and principles in which beliefs and actions about working together will guide practices and inspire excellence. Some educators may ask why there is need for studying ethical principles and practices when their professional aims are lofty and their principles already reflect high ideals. A better question for teachers to ask is how they, as models for future leaders, can create an ethical climate to convey those principles and values to their students because young people of the future will need to practice ethics in any field of endeavor they eventually choose. Educators can begin by demonstrating ethical principles in all facets of their roles, including the interrelationships among professional colleagues.

Collaborators must create environments in which respect and caring characterize their professional interactions as they engage in the education of children and youth. They must strive to maintain personal integrity, even when under pressure from others, by standing firm as a model and monitoring potential violations of ethical principles or bending of important rules by others.

Ethical collaborators respect the worth and potential of every individual. General educators and special educators acknowledge that *every* child is a minority of one with unique backgrounds, situations, abilities, and needs. They strive to serve special needs with diligence and perseverance, not because it is legislated but because it is the right thing to do. They acknowledge without rancor that some educators may not be keen on collaborating or co-teaching, but they continue to encourage participation by colleagues because they believe it will benefit students.

Special needs of students are the focus of many collaborative interactions. In the course of addressing those special needs, it is important to keep in mind that collaborative school consultants have complex roles laced with heavy responsibilities that include protection of privacy and caretaking of confidential material. Each chapter to come will conclude with a look at ethical considerations pertaining to the chapter's content. Conclusions will be drawn about the ways in which collaborative school consultants should conduct their responsibilities ethically within an ethical climate that they help create.

TIPS FOR WORKING TOGETHER IN SCHOOLS

1. Value and find ways to demonstrate beyond token lip service the value of consultation, collaboration, and teamwork as tools for planning and coordinating instruction.
2. Survey the school context for ways to collaborate, consult, and team teach.
3. Encourage each member of a collaborative group to share knowledge and perceptions about an issue in order to establish a solid framework in which to discuss the issue.
4. Try not to press for personally favored solutions to school needs, co-educator needs, or student needs but instead strive instead for collaborative efforts to solve problems together even if it means setting aside some of your own agenda.
5. Explore possibilities that technological tools have for making interactions with co-educators and students' families efficient, effective, and enjoyable.
6. Ask for help when *you* come up against a problem; doing so has a humanizing, rapport-building effect.
7. Interact in positive fashion with every co-educator in the building(s) regularly.
8. Learn all you can about methods of consulting, collaborating, co-teaching, and engaging in other kinds of collegial teamwork, analyzing what seems to work and not work, as it would be applicable to your environment.
9. Do not wait to be approached for opportunities to consult, collaborate, and co-teach.
10. Leave the door open, both figuratively and literally, for future partnerships and collaborations.

ADDITIONAL RESOURCES

Journal for Educational and Psychological Consultation. All issues. This journal offers theory-based and research-based articles on the use of collaboration and consultation in teaching, psychology, counseling, and other education-relevant professions.

Correa, V. I., Jones, H. A., Thomas, C. C., & Morsink, C. V. (2004). *Interactive teaming: Enhancing programs for students with special needs* (4th ed.). Upper Saddle River, NJ: Prentice Hall.

Thessin, R. A., & Starr, J. P. (2011). Supporting the growth of professional learning communities. *Phi Delta Kappan, 92*(6), 48–54.

Williams, J. M., & Martin, S. M. (2001). Implementing the Individuals with Disabilities Education Act of 1997: The consultant's role. *Journal of Educational and Psychological Consultation, 12*(1), 59–81.

2

Working Together with Professional Perspectives That Differ

A PATCHWORK QUILT IS MADE UP OF MANY COLORS, textures, shapes, and sizes. In your mind's eye, see a beautiful patchwork quilt, carefully planned and skillfully put together. Each piece contributes something unique to the whole. Some of the pieces may seem to clash a bit, but if every piece in the quilt were the same, it would be drab and dull. When put together, all of the pieces form a collage in which each one contributes to the beauty of the whole.

In much the same way, a school is a patchwork of background, education, experiences, attitudes, personalities, values, interests, talents, and skills, all blending into a human collage. Each person within the school environment is different from the others and contributes special qualities to enrich the whole. People may differ markedly and even take serious issue with one another on occasion because of their differences. But the wonderful array of individuals who come together in schools each day creates a montage of unlimited opportunity for working collaboratively in that context (shaded square in Figure 2.1).

Educators are attuned to individual differences of *students* as they plan for learning needs, but too often they overlook the individual differences among *adults* with whom they work. Why is this so important? It is important because the synergy created by adult differences, if recognized, respected, and used in constructive ways, will help educators to be better instructors and allow their students to be better learners.

FOCUSING QUESTIONS

1. How do professional differences affect collaborative relationships among co-educators, and how can those differences be addressed for positive outcomes?

2. In what ways do factors of tradition, time, territory, talent, and trust influence school environments?

3. How do educational taxonomies for cognitive, affective, sensorimotor, and social domains guide the teaching and learning of students with special needs?

4. How can collaborative school consultation address students' needs effectively when co-educators have such wide variations in their professional perspectives?

5. What important technological advances can help co-educators strengthen collaborative connections and develop networks for the benefit of students with exceptional learning needs?

6. What ethical considerations are most relevant to co-educators in making constructive use of their inevitable professional differences?

KEY TERMS

instructional objectives	onedownsmanship	thinking-and-doing processes
learning theory (cognitive, behavioral, social)	sensorimotor	transfer (low-road, high-road)
	taxonomies	

VIGNETTE 2

On the morning after a professional development (PD) day for the faculty of a midsize middle school, comments could be heard in the central hallway as teachers checked in for the day and gathered materials to take up instruction where they had left off two days before. The theme for yesterday's professional development activity had been introduction and exploration of implementing a community-member and young-teen student mentoring program that the school administrators had learned about at their last statewide school administrators' convention. Several teachers could be overheard sharing their views about the professional development experience.

"I'm eager to try that new teaching strategy in our school. It's been working well in other schools I've read about."

"Here we go again. Another iffy program to spin us around for another dizzy ride on the school reform merry-go-round."

"In our department we seem to see eye to eye on everything that's important. We'll want to try out this program. What a great group of colleagues I work with."

"Why are some people so negative toward new ideas before they even try them out? They could at least wait and see what happens after other people have the gumption to try them."

"I say let's take some risks and do something innovative for a change, like this program."

"Seems like we do the same old thing, or we get all enthused over dubious ideas like this program. Then people fall into line like sheep.

I'm skeptical about this program and I'll speak up to that effect."

"Yep, a wasted day. It dragged on and on, and we have nothing to show for it except a stack of yesterday's papers to grade and some notes about bad behavior yesterday that I will have to deal with today."

"I like the direction our school is heading as we try out these new ideas with people in our community."

"It was my first inservice and I picked up every handout, but I don't know when I'll have time to read them."

"I just can't figure out where our principal and professional development coordinator came up with this one. We wouldn't have given it the time of day in the school where I was last year."

"What a fiasco that professional day was! I don't plan to be part of that program and I didn't bring back a single thing I could use in my classroom. Besides that, the lunch was terrible."

"Wasn't that a great workshop? With what I came away learning about young-teen students, I have some new ideas on how to plan lessons."

PROFESSIONAL DIFFERENCES AMONG CO-EDUCATORS IN EDUCATIONAL ENVIRONMENTS

People in all walks of life bring their own perspectives to their work. The focus of this chapter is on differences in *professional perspectives* of educators who work together for a common purpose. Then Chapter 3 will address *personal preferences* that affect interpersonal relationships among educators when they consult and collaborate and co-teach.

Individuals sometimes set aside their own perspectives and preferences for the good of a group. Teachers may do so to foster unanimity, or perhaps so they will not call attention to themselves. Deference to other teachers' perspectives can occur when groups try to reach agreement on potentially divisive matters such as grading systems, or class rules, or amount and time of homework assigned, or modification of tests for students with learning disabilities. Teachers generally are not hesitant about using their own preferred ways of setting up their classroom, teaching a favorite unit, deciding whether to use portfolios, and providing feedback on student work, because those areas have fewer ripple effects through the system.

To bring semantics into the picture again briefly, we can look upon *perspective* as a mental view of facts and ideas and a style of seeing relevant data in meaningful relationships. Perspectives are philosophical in nature—such as arriving at reasons for choosing one's profession, developing individual work ethics, having views on what one's role is and what it should be, forming opinions about how the work should be done, and implementing instructional strategies with appropriate measures for assessing outcomes.

FACTORS OF TRADITION, TIME, TERRITORY, TALENT, AND TRUST IN SCHOOLS

Co-educators differ in opinions and practices on a number of factors that are integral parts of the school environment. Some are minor differences and some are major enough to be potential impediments to constructive interaction. Examples of particular relevance are tradition, time, and territoriality. Other examples of interest are talent and trust.

Tradition in Schools

Customs and conventions that are carried out in schools through habit and/or convenience, or that sometimes just drag on through benign neglect, can solidify into traditions that are hard to set aside even when they no longer serve educators and learners well and may even be harmful. Examples of traditions are:

- Treating special education as a *place* where students who need special help are to *go*
- Labeling children for placement in special services for an unspecified length of time
- Referring to students in special education classes as "your" kids, not *our* kids
- Viewing children as needing special education services when there might really be a misfit between their abilities and the demands made on them by an inflexible school situation

- Looking on families as part of the problem rather than as part of the solution when students are at risk of failure
- Regarding support services from agencies as if they and school personnel were boats passing in the stream rather than as integral components in programs for students with major needs
- Thinking of consultants as experts with all the answers instead of as collaborative colleagues working with teachers who are experts in their own right

One more tradition deserves mention because it has the potential to cast a pall over the school atmosphere. It is the inclination to envision and describe schools and the educational process with vocabulary that is negatively nuanced. Examples are *target* (a word used sparingly here and replaced with others such as *focus*), *training* (also to be avoided and replaced with *preparation*), *intervention*, *remediation*, and others that connote sickness, such as *diagnostic*, *prescriptive*, *treatment*, *impaired*, *monitor*, *referral*, *disability*, *adaptive*, and *label*. When words with more positive tones can be used, they should be used. Once again, it is important to discard the false notion that semantics are unimportant. Inappropriate words and terms become a thick barrier to understanding that collaborative educators must reckon with.

On a more positive note, traditions *can* be altered or overturned and customs and beliefs *can* be changed with sensitivity and clear reasoning. One example of successful tradition breaking in semantics is the now-frowned-on use of the term *handicapped* to reference children and adults who have special needs.

Time in Schools

"Where will I find the time to get together with my colleagues?" says an overscheduled teacher with an overextended caseload. But the reality is that time has not gone missing; it has just been used for other things.

Time is an unredeemable resource with an ultimately fair distribution—everyone gets the same amount. As for *how* it is used—that's the challenge. Use of time is a combination of choice, necessity, fate, and a little luck, and that is where the unfairness begins. Few teachers would question that time is the single most problematic aspect of trying to collaborate and work in teams within a traditional school setting. They have to choose to "spend" some of their time in this different way while attending to whatever their designated responsibilities are, knowing that fate may deal them less time by needing to do double bus duty for a sick colleague or deal them more time with a little luck from a canceled meeting—all beyond their control in managing the precious resource of time.

Teachers never have enough time, and if they do manage to carve out a bit here and there, they are lucky if those minutes match with prospective collaborators' free minutes. Refer again to your collection of teacher responsibilities from Action 1.1 and recall the suggestion that it should include summer-school teaching, advanced coursework in the summer, professional development and workshops, tutoring, gathering and constructing materials for the next school year, and the like. (Often there is an insensitive, unknowledgeable person or two around who can push a teacher's hot button by expressing envy—usually loudly, about teachers' "easy work schedules and long summer vacations.")

Does your list show the time consumed in just *thinking* about planning the curriculum, instruction, and assessments? A teacher may spend hours and hours conceptualizing a unit, backtracking and altering until the perfect plan finally pops into clear perspective. Then there are resource gathering and lesson preparation, just for starters. Much of this effort, contrary to effort demanded in many other work roles, is carried out on the teacher's *own time*. Furthermore, planning and preparing ways to differentiate a unit for students with special needs typically requires even more time and effort beyond conventional preparations.

Some time and opportunity for gathering new ideas from colleagues and revitalizing professional enthusiasm through interaction with co-educators might occur during professional development sessions, but these activities are often too ill timed, highly structured and short-lived to allow for productive interaction. Some sessions are scheduled unwisely to take place at the end of a hectic day, when teachers are tired and want to reflect a bit on their teaching day, set things up for the next day, and then turn their attention toward home or community activities.

Educators may wish for more small-group meetings to address mutual professional concerns and talk about common curricular interests, but that does not necessarily signal a desire to collaborate or co-teach. They may appreciate the value of conferring with students' families beyond the expected parent-teacher conference, but feel apprehensive about making a home- or neutral-site visit or asking a parent to come to school for a daytime or evening visit. Opportunities to observe other teachers and visit other schools may have appeal, but teachers are torn between the anxiety of leaving their classrooms in the care of others and the prospect of learning something new when observing in other classrooms. Indeed, opportunities may be rare and hard to arrange for well-timed and properly focused observations of other educators in other school settings.

Some school systems encourage co-teaching as a way of allowing teachers to interact with and observe other teachers in a collegial way. But well-intentioned efforts to set up co-teaching environments can be less than collaborative if not planned carefully. Unfortunately, the outcome of poor planning could be simply turn-teaching—"You teach this part of the lesson and then take a break or make the copies we need for next hour, while I handle the part coming up." Co-teaching is based on much planning and organization, and that takes *time*. Nevertheless, hard-working, time-challenged educators may relish the thought of team teaching, or engaging in pleasant interaction with other adults during the school day, or venting frustrations to a sympathetic ear, or bouncing new teaching ideas off interested colleagues for their reactions.

Although many educators appreciate the interaction and camaraderie that co-teaching and collaborative consultation offer, some say candidly that they did not choose teaching as a career to work all that much with adults. Others feel that teaming up with co-teachers or consulting teachers will be perceived as a red flag to mark their weaker areas or a no-confidence vote in their abilities. Yet another aspect that troubles special education teachers is the possibility that collaboration may siphon off precious minutes needed for direct services to students. Teachers could argue convincingly there is just too little time for the careful planning and concentrated effort that productive collaboration requires, picking up on the familiar complaint that "It will just be a waste of time."

So where is time to be begged, borrowed, or found for collaborating, teaming, and networking? For starters, a very simple tactic is to steal back some time from one of its greediest thieves—*the meeting*. Recall English teacher Meg's concern in Chapter 1 about meetings. Rachel, the convener of their collaboration, learned of her concern and determined that she would distribute a concise agenda before the meeting, listing items to be addressed and designating a five-minute wrap-up period with a definite stop time imposed and unfinished business tabled for another time. Thus, a planned thirty-minute meeting would not become a frustrating, loosely organized activity dragging on for fifty minutes or more and leaving participants exhausted with little or no closure. They would know what to expect and collaboratively use the valuable minutes to work and then to conclude on time. It's a simple idea, but how many meetings truly do not work this well and thus become time thieves?

Another way to carve out more time is to restructure professional development days. Some of the time for attending presentations or for doing individual work in classrooms might be set aside for periods of *well-organized* collaborative interaction as grade-level teams, or curriculum departments, or fine arts and humanities faculty, or even more interestingly, a purposeful mix of various areas and grade levels. Having a coordinated, collaborative meeting to discuss this possibility could be a valuable team activity on its own. Such a practice is beginning to take hold in school districts around the country. For every element of the school day and every structure for the school year, time is a defining feature with the potential for posing problems or creating benefits for school personnel.

Territory in Schools

Issues of territory, or "turf," arise in areas of school life as varied as curriculum development, selection of materials, allocation of academic time, scheduling, shared classrooms and equipment, shared paraeducators, noise levels, discipline procedures, grading policies, homework policies, incentives to encourage student effort, and much, much more. These kinds of concerns stem from a number of realities and practicalities that emanate from differences among educators in their professional perspectives.

Educators cannot be coerced into being collegial and working together closely. Teachers who are accustomed to being in charge and making virtually all the day-to-day decisions in their classrooms cannot be ordered to just go out and collaborate with each other or co-teach to any great degree. Likewise, teachers who have favorite subjects, preferred ways of planning and instructing, and definite ideas about teaching and assessment will not give them up lightly. Some are displeased when teaching partners are selected *for* them. They would prefer to choose their own collaborator or to continue in partnerships that are established. However, this may not be an option if it is a case of general education and special education personnel. Special educator services in many districts are stretched thin and must be shared among several buildings and classrooms.

Some teachers speak out to say that they just need their "space." They acknowledge that they don't like others looking over their shoulder while they teach or breathing down their neck when they sort through materials or critique student work. Dealing with differences in professional perspectives is a challenging task because even in a collaborative, sharing environment, having one's place and routines—one's turf—continues to be important to the educator. Turf and ownership issues can be problematic for novice teachers who are settling into their first teaching positions. They want to get off to a good start with colleagues, but they also have ideas for setting up a dream classroom that they have preparing for and designing in their mind for years. Striking out to do things one's own way as a novice teacher is a bit scary but also invigorating; this is what teacher education students work hard for in their classes and student teaching experiences. Collaboration for them must be an opportunity to learn but also a chance to share *their* often new and bold ideas, and veteran teachers must make sure they can do so.

An insightful building administrator will recognize that the issue of territory is a potential threat to successful interactions, so they will watch for signs of discord. If there is evidence that tension is brewing, several possibilities can be explored to alleviate the pressures: individual conferences, printed material from the administrators to promote collaborative enterprises, a focused inservice session, bulletin boards featuring staff working together as a team, an agenda-specific departmental meeting, or, in extreme cases, rearrangement of teaching assignments with agreement by the individuals involved.

Before leaving the issue of territoriality, one other aspect bears mentioning—territoriality within a classroom. Sometimes teachers carve out a space and stay there until they are reminded, or come to realize it themselves, that they are slighting certain areas of the room and perhaps the students or resource personnel who choose to be located there or are assigned to be there. It is to collaborative teachers' advantage to move about, sharing enthusiasm and encouraging participation, yet taking care not to intimidate or close in on students in a domineering manner. If two or more teachers are teaming, the "teacher wealth" can be spread around to cover all "turf" and have more engagement with students.

Talent in Schools

Much talent resides within a pool of educators. This deep and wide pool, one of the best resources that schools can offer to students, is an important component of the educational environment. Talent even has the potential for defusing turf tension because when every individual's talents are recognized and encouraged to shine, protecting one's place becomes less important, perhaps even inconsequential.

Some talent is group talent—as in the cases of a Final Four basketball team, a renowned acting troupe, and a team of widely acclaimed surgeons. Other talent is individual—such as that of a stand-up comedian, an award-winning chef, and a master teacher—that could become an aspect of team talent if shared in partnerships and mentorships.

Schools are filled with budding talents of students at all grade levels. However, teacher talent may stay hidden under heavy caseloads and unforgiving time clocks. But in these adult talents are opportunities for constructing teams of talented individuals. Once formed, they can work together for student growth, faculty development, and school improvement. A parent–teacher organization might channel talents into teams for a major fund-raising effort to supply resources needed after budget cuts. Teachers from the language arts, drama, art, music, vocational arts, and journalism classes might collaborate to offer a class in filmmaking or to put on a demonstration play that includes writing, acting, directing, construction, costuming, photography, music, and art.

Talent is a fine vehicle through which to diversify instruction for students with developmental disabilities and showcase the results. One classroom for teen-age students with developmental delays discovered cooking talent in their midst. They began to make healthy snacks and treats, first for themselves and then for students and teachers in their building. With the money left over after buying ingredients, they expanded their operation to include other attendance centers. After several months of success, and a few trials and setbacks from which they learned much, they developed a catering service that reached beyond school walls into the community with its excellent reputation and products. A number of consultants and collaborators, including district and building administrators, were involved in this exceedingly successful venture, but the kudos and recognitions were theirs to relish. Students in special education classes have much to contribute, and will learn many things as they are doing so, when they and their teachers are given the opportunities to develop and use their talents.

Trust in Schools

Trust is an enigmatic and elusive construct when applied to the work setting. Although daily news reports from national media trumpet instance upon instance of failed trust in areas such as finance, government, business, industry, sports, and the like, educators who have been entrusted with the public's most precious commodity of all—children and youth, are expected to function in trustworthy fashion at all times to prepare their students for an honorable future among others who may be trustworthy or not.

Building trust in young students requires careful instruction and modeling by caring educators. Expecting to find trust in others is in and of itself an act of trust. The example of the successful catering service built and operated by teenage students with developmental delays was a case of talent and expertise built on a mountain of trust.

Numerous national reports have laid out the competencies that young people will need for their future roles, emphasizing the ability to work with others, trust in them, and rely on them during problem-finding and problem-solving activities. Trust emanates from the collaborative ethic that must be present with every interaction in and for schools, whether between classroom teacher and student, administrator and parent, paraeducator and special education teacher, or school board members and community members.

Trust is demonstrated when teachers observe, visit, and look over other teachers' shoulders in their classrooms. It is solidified by courteous exits and respectful post-observation discussions where, just as teachers do in a parent–teacher conference, visitors certainly will want to begin and end with positive things to say about their visits. Trust is needed most when educators are keepers of confidential information about students that must be handled in a discreet but constructive way.

ACTION 2.1
Demonstrating Trust

Identify another teacher with whom you feel comfortable talking about your professional concerns. Invite that teacher to visit your classroom and then exchange roles to visit that person's classroom. Follow the visits with a discussion about what each of you learned and would like to share.

As a deeper demonstration of trust, initiate and follow through in the same fashion with a teacher for whom you have not yet gained that level of trust. Before you make the visit, remember the good things about your visitation with the first person, and put yourself into that frame of mind and trust. In other words, expect to have a good time and profit from the experience.

Finally, suggest to your colleagues that rotating faculty meetings among classrooms would be a productive experience. The aim would be, once again, to have an enjoyable time with this change of perspective, and to profit from it. A sign-up sheet where each one signs for a preferred time might be a good way to initiate this arrangement. This is especially constructive if the group is a mix of general and special education staff. During these times of visitation and follow-up discussions, make a strong effort to listen. Listen long enough to find areas of agreements *and* disagreements, and to feel the pull of others' convictions in each instance.

RECOGNIZING INDIVIDUAL DIFFERENCES IN PROFESSIONAL PERSPECTIVES

In Chapter 1 you were given a challenge to list 100 or more responsibilities that school personnel perform in their roles. What if the challenge were to compile a list of how many *different* ways educators go about *carrying out* these responsibilities? For example, some arrive early in the morning to prepare for classes; others stay late and prepare for the next day. Some plan curriculum by the week and others by the month. Some use cooperative learning techniques; others like to have peer tutors or volunteer aides. Some arrange student seating in rows or groups; a few have removed the seats from their classrooms! Differences in a wide array of teaching practices can set co-educators apart from one another when they set out to collaborate for instruction and classroom management.

ACTION 2.2
Identifying Areas of Difference

What factors could partition educators into categories? Begin with the obvious ones—for example, age or generation, years of teaching experience, curriculum areas taught, age or grade levels taught, geographic location of school (urban, suburban, consolidated, rural), teacher education program attended, and so forth. As suggested in Chapter 1, if this activity is done in collaboration with teachers from other grade levels, content areas, school sizes and locations, the list that is generated will be even richer. Discuss what effects these differences could have on teaching and classroom management. For example, do teachers of the baby-boom generation differ in perspectives on discipline from those of generation X? What about gender of teachers? If that is not considered important as a category of difference, then why do elementary schools often seek out male applicants for lower-grade teaching positions?

In analyzing the problem-solving capacities of groups that are engaged in various team endeavors, Page (2007) determined that those with different types of disciplinary training bring different tools and diverse understandings to the task. Pursuing this analysis further, Conoley (1994) states,

> It requires courage to detail differences from the accepted ways of seeing, knowing, and doing. . . . If I say I am interested in learning about the world, but wish to do so in a way that puts a focus on connections, I hope that can be understood as another way. If you say you are interested in learning about the world, but wish to do so in a way that puts a focus on isolated events, I hope that can be understood as just another way. There are many ways to a truth with many faces. (p. 49)

General Education and Special Education Collaborators

The school days of "us" versus "them" between general educators and special educators are past, just as the phrase "my students" has been replaced in favor of newer language emphasizing *our students* and *in our classrooms.* Nonetheless, the evidence is not so clear that each faction's instructional style and content are well understood by the other. If one teacher does not know the other's curriculum, they will be just helping, not collaborating. Many educators acknowledge that they feel unprepared for collaborative consultation; therefore, they learn little from teachers who have different perspectives. If they do adapt new ideas learned, implementation of those ideas may vary in depth and quality due to variance in their knowledge and beliefs (Brownell, Adams, Sindelar, Waldron, & Vanhover, 2006). (See Figure 2.2.)

Even though collaboration is becoming more widely recognized and promoted as an essential component in improving the ability of general and special educators to work together effectively, teachers whose perspectives differ most significantly are the least likely to collaborate (Brownell et al., 2006). This underscores the importance of having co-educators understand what their colleagues are thinking, feeling, doing, and bringing into the school environment for the instruction of *all* students. As Tiegerman-Farber and Radziewicz (1998) put it, from shared perceptions will come a set of shared expectations for schools and students. Mismatches between teachers, whether between general education and special education, or elementary and secondary, or fine arts and vocational/ technical arts, or teachers from older and younger generations, to cite just a few examples, if not addressed and smoothed, will create discord and stolidly independent thinking rather than shared discourse and solidly productive problem solving.

Every educator needs to have a "big picture" of both general and special education curriculums, along with wide-scope understandings of state and local standards, instructional approaches for diverse learning needs, ways of aligning goals with curriculum, teaching and behavioral management strategies for special needs, and assessment methods for grading and reporting on outcomes (McDonnell, McLaughlin, & Morrison, 1997; Walsh, 2001). During a professional development day, with careful planning and a competent moderator, having a "big-picture discussion" to find commonalities and discover

FIGURE 2.2 Sharing Perspectives and Preferences

interesting differences could make teaching, coaching, and monitoring student development more exciting and rewarding.

It is up to school administrators, counselors, school psychologists, experienced teachers, and parents to increase their understandings of learning goals and assessment processes, and to promote the best practices for the best reasons. These understandings can be built through staff development activities, scheduled collaborative events, conferences with family members, and informal consultative dialogues.

Walsh (2001) asserts that one major decision to be made by both general and special education teachers is to determine what is not absolutely necessary for all students to learn in order to meet content standards. They also must decide how it has been determined that students have learned the content at an acceptable level. The foundation for these understandings should be laid in teacher preparation programs before new teachers enter the hustle and bustle of school life to assume responsibilities immediately for curriculum and assessment decisions. Novice teachers in particular are challenged when planning instruction and conducting assessments of students with special needs. They need to know when they are doing just fine and be helped by co-teachers when things are not going so well.

A positive point to stress here is that novice teachers bring many assets to their first professional assignments. They are enthusiastic and eager to put into practice the new and creative ideas they have been accumulating. They tend to have been exposed to the most recent educational theories, methods, and materials. Many completed their student teaching experience under the supervision of well-informed, experienced university professors and master teachers in excellent schools. Even so, knowledge does not become wisdom without experience. A major difference between the novice and the veteran teacher, whether in general education or special education, is the experience that guides professionals when making important decisions about complex issues such as, "Yes, this is a promising plan," or "No, we don't want to try it with that student." Collaborators and mentors have opportunities to share their own experiences in ways that will contribute to the novice teacher's growth.

Grade-Level and Curriculum-Area Collaborators

Grade-level differences among elementary and secondary teachers may have less effect on collaboration than general and special education differences because the two groups do not interface all that much; however, there are times when district-wide groups come together for the purpose of aligning curriculum to state standards, or designing testing programs to comply with federal and state regulations, or adopting a district-wide textbook series. Professional perspectives among preschool, elementary, middle school, and high school teachers can vary considerably in regard to policies about prevailing or proposed systems for classroom organization and management such as basal series choices, student recognition programs, grade point systems, absentee and truancy procedures, and the like.

One long-standing mantra for education has been that "elementary schools teach children, and secondary schools teach subjects." This is a flawed assumption greatly in need of revision. Young children are curious about the world and not reluctant to show it; they hunger for interesting, advanced subject matter. Teens feign disinterest while pressuring for more interaction with peers, especially with their friends. This is generalizing to some extent, but with more truth than hyperbole. Joint professional development activities involving elementary- and secondary-level personnel can be a vehicle for planning curriculum with richer, more sophisticated content at the elementary level and more socially interactive curriculum for content at the secondary level.

Curriculum-area differences affect schedules and time in ways that can hamper collaboration and professional development experiences. Physical education teachers may request to be excused from professional development activities because of their coaching duties and supervision of sports events. Practical arts classrooms and shops often are housed apart from the other classrooms, so that it is less convenient to join in. Science projects and lab monitoring may spill over into other class periods, causing schedules and patience levels to fray. Music performance, debate, and academic-competition groups require teachers and coaches to be gone several times during the year. Such realities make the scheduling of both collaborative consultation and professional development activity difficult, particularly at the secondary level. This affects the teachers in many of the curricular areas that are especially important to students with exceptional learning needs and the issue must be addressed thoughtfully.

Instructional Differences in Perspectives among Collaborators

Other areas of variability among teachers that may surface when they gather to consult and collaborate, and particularly when they plan co-teaching strategies, include practices involving:

- Homework: how much, how often, and what kind
- Pull-out or pull-in sessions for individual students or small groups that impinge upon normal class procedures
- Whether to make up work missed during pull-out sessions
- Use of test accommodations and modifications for students with disabilities
- Grading policies, for both general education and special education
- Whether to allow do-over work or extra-credit work for full or partial credit
- Time-out, suspension policies, positive and negative reinforcements, and contract contingencies
- Frequency and type of parent involvement in the classroom
- Noise and activity levels within the classroom and elsewhere on school grounds
- Appearance and upkeep of classrooms, especially shared learning areas
- Being the only one on the teaching staff who is a teacher and not a parent, or the only teacher who is a parent
- Styles and frequency of interacting with co-educators and conducting classroom visitations and observations
- Whether to have student-led conferences and if so, how to coach students for them
- Parent-teacher conference schedules, locations, and formats
- Spending personal money for classroom teaching supplies, a practice looked on with disfavor by some teachers who cannot or will not do it, with occasional fall-out of parent pressure to have their child assigned to the teacher-fortified classroom and building principals sometimes caught in the crossfire.
- The unfortunate possibility that inclusion of students with special needs, especially more than one per class, might cause parent or teacher disgruntlement and activate a request for change in class assignment

Principles of Learning and Teaching for Collaborators

What to do, then, to sort out and manage this myriad of differences in professional perspectives when working together? At the outset, there must be understanding among co-educators, in both general education and special education, on two all-encompassing principles of learning, to which most other principles are connected.

The first principle is this: ***Variation*** *in achievement among students **cannot be eliminated***. The only ways it could be done would be to speed up learning of less able students by artificial means and slow down learning of very able students by stunting or withholding opportunities. Both of these options are, of course, unethical and totally unacceptable. The reality is that there are no Lake Wobegons where all students are above average, and no federal mandates, preschool programs, master plans for parent involvement, or rigorous teaching programs, worthy and necessary as they are, can erase the reality of omnipresent differences in achievement.

The second principle is this: *Good teaching will **increase** individual differences in achievement among students.* This is because learners with lower abilities and students with disabilities ***will** learn* with *good instruction*, while those with more abilities will learn even more *if* not held back by teaching practices and school policies that pull expectations and practices to the middle. When educators make peace with this reality, they are empowered to move on in constructive ways that will benefit *all* students tremendously (Hanna & Dettmer, 2004). However, if collaborating educators are not in accord with these two principles, their efforts toward working together will be off balance from the start. Educators must acknowledge these principles, reflect on their broad meaning for teaching and learning, and then instruct accordingly.

Eight areas, and co-educators' levels of commitment to them, contribute strongly to the formation of day-to-day professional perspectives. Any one of the eight could become a stumbling block on the road to successful consultation and collaboration. But when dedicated teachers deliberate together on how they can facilitate student growth, the best approaches will come into focus. The eight areas are:

1. Goals in the four taxonomic domains of learning and doing—cognitive, affective, sensorimotor, and social
2. Learning theory—behavioral, cognitive, or social
3. Kinds of subject matter—essential, developmental, or ideational
4. Instructional objectives—masterable or nonmasterable
5. Orientations in time and achievement levels—with specific time allowed for mastery, or with learning time open-ended for maximum development
6. Assessment and evaluation—domain referenced for mastery, or norm referenced for comparisons with other specific groups
7. Types of scores—raw scores and percentage scores for referencing to specified criteria, or derived scores for referencing normatively (comparatively) to other groups
8. Interpretations of scores—measuring for mastery, or discriminating among specified others

Taxonomies of Learning and Doing

People learn basic facts and comprehend material; then they use that knowing and understanding for applying, analyzing, synthesizing, and evaluating in complex and novel situations.

This learning and doing occurs in four domains—the cognitive domain of thinking, the affective domain of feeling, the physical domain (renamed here as sensorimotor) of absorbing and performing, and the social domain (a new and necessary domain) of relating to others. Activity in each of these domains can range from simple to complex, providing for what is termed by educational psychologists as low-road transfer to similar material and situations, or high-road transfer to new material and novel situations.

The four domains—cognitive (thinking), affective (feeling), sensorimotor (doing), and social (interacting)—lay out a rich, fertile field of possibilities for co-educators to co-plan, co-instruct, and co-evaluate student learning. Understanding the somewhat hierarchical, but not rigidly so, levels of complexity is necessary when designing differentiated curriculum for all students' needs, and particularly those with exceptional learning needs. So they will be revisited here in abbreviated, and in some places adjusted, forms. For example, the well-known cognitive domain and affective domain are extended by two and three levels respectively. The physical domain is revised and renamed the sensorimotor domain. A new taxonomy is introduced—the social domain that is particularly relevant to collaboration, consultation, and teamwork. (See Figure 2.3.)

Cognitive Domain of Thinking   The *Taxonomy of Educational Objectives, Handbook I: Cognitive Domain* (Bloom et al., 1956) is one of the most frequently cited publications in educational literature. It was developed initially with an aim of improving tests, but the developers soon realized that in order to do that they needed first to focus on constructing good instructional objectives. Recall that this was before the legislative and supportive movements of the 1970s produced laws that generated policies for special education.

The six categories in this very familiar cognitive domain are knowledge, comprehension, application, analysis, synthesis, and evaluation (Bloom et al., 1956). Viewing school content through this classification system has made educators uncomfortably aware that too much instruction is being directed toward simple recall of facts and explaining or restating learned material. Surprisingly, this has been more characteristic of secondary schools than

FIGURE 2.3   Four Domains for Thinking and Doing

DOMAIN	Cognitive	Affective	Sensorimotor	Social
PROCESS	Thinking	Feeling	Sensing-moving	**Interacting**
CONTENT	Mental	Emotional	Physical	**Sociocultural**
PURPOSE	Expand thinking	Enhance feeling	Cultivate senses and movement	**Enrich relationships**
BASIC LEARNING	Know Understand	Receive Respond	Observe React	**Relate Communicate**
APPLIED LEARNING	Apply Analyze Evaluate	Value Organize Internalize	Act Adapt Authenticate	**Participate Negotiate Adjudicate**
IDEATIONAL LEARNING	Synthesize Imagine Create	Characterize Wonder Aspire	Harmonize Improvise Innovate	**Collaborate Initiate Convert**

elementary schools. Excessive time spent on low-order, rote-recall learning crowds out the development of complex skills of thinking and doing and reduces opportunities for creative thinking and production. This is especially debilitating for students who need so much time to learn assigned basics that there is little time left for creativity and complex thinking experiences. *All* students, regardless of exceptionality, should be taught to learn and enjoy open-ended, enriching material. Educators must have high expectations for *all* students whether in general education, gifted education programs, or special education for students with disabilities and developmental delays. Group discussions among collaborating teachers can do much to offset objectionable attitudes of lowered expectations and the resultant absences of opportunities for students having special needs.

Affective Domain of Feeling   In 1964, Krathwohl, Bloom, and Masia directed the development of the *Taxonomy of Educational Objectives, Handbook II: Affective Domain*. The original cognitive-domain committee members had recognized the need for addressing affective functions, but they had been discouraged by the difficulty of designing ways to measure them. Categories in this classification system, as ordered from simplest to most complex, are receiving, responding, valuing, organization, and characterization (Krathwohl et al., 1964).

Extending the Cognitive and Affective Taxonomies   Developers of the cognitive and affective domain taxonomies did not promote their work as the be-all and end-all for processes of thinking and doing. They aimed the taxonomy at a level of generality that allowed for flexibility and growth. They hoped not to abort teachers' thinking and development in regard to curriculum, and they did not want the taxonomies to be used as recipes, which nevertheless some teachers since that time have been prone to do. They thought of them as fluid and unfinished, and they encouraged further development of the concepts.

Rereading the original works by the collaborative Bloom and Krathwohl groups and pondering significances of their profoundly important ideas, can be a rewarding professional development exercise or a rich collaborative experience for educators that should lead to new ideas about teaching and learning. Since the original cognitive and affective domains were conceptualized, interest in creativity has burgeoned, generating research on including creative thinking and development of original products, and authentic assessment of those works, as an important part of school curriculum. So it seems appropriate to extend the domains to include such activity.

Including Creativity and Innovation   Imagination is a cognitive and affective tool with which students explore how the world works in wonderful and mysterious ways (Dettmer, 2006). Therefore, stimulating the imagination should not be treated as a recreational activity for that bit of extra time left between bells or as a reward for getting the "real work" done. Neither should it be reserved for the most able, but provided to *all* students as a means of enhancing the educational value of any lesson. With this in mind, the cognitive taxonomy can be expanded reasonably to include categories for *imagination* and *creativity*. Then because cognitive activities of imagination and creativity have affective components, the categories of *wonder* (that catalyzes one's imagination), *aspire* (where risks are accepted in creative production), and *internalize* (owning the created ideas) are relevant. Imagining and wondering are fluid actions occurring at most any point in the taxonomic hierarchies, depending on the situation. They can be important incentives for students who have been disinterested in learning and find it hard to concentrate on learning goals.

All in all, the order of taxonomic levels need not be perceived rigidly so long as a conceptual demarcation is drawn between low-road thinking and feeling (knowledge and comprehension, receiving and responding) for low-road transfer for similar objectives, and high-order thinking and feeling (everything beyond) for high-road transfer to new or novel situations. Key words for action verbs in both domains, as expanded here, are:

- *Cognitive—know and comprehend*; then *apply, analyze, synthesize, evaluate*, then *imagine, create*
- *Affective—receive and respond*; then *value, organize, internalize*, then *characterize, wonder, aspire*

Sensorimotor Domain of Absorbing and Performing   When Bloom et al. (1956) presented the cognitive taxonomy and Krathwohl et al. (1964) developed the affective taxonomy later, there was little mention of a taxonomy for physical development. But in the years since that time there has been increasing attention to motor skills needed for areas such as athletics, the arts, industry, and technology, and to elements of sensing that are critical to the learning process. Several psychomotor taxonomies have been proposed, including those of Simpson (1972) and Harrow (1972). However, they did not emphasize the senses as being integral components of psychomotor skills.

Senses are especially important to teachers of students who are challenged because of disabilities in hearing, seeing, smelling, touching, tasting, speaking, feeling, moving, being still, and staying in balance. So a taxonomy for the physical realm should not be limited to fine and gross motor activity in physical education classes. A physical perspective needs to include sensory input, with attention to sight, sound, touch, taste, and smell and perhaps other elements such as balance and sensitivity to the elements, as factors that have not yet been emphasized in the school curriculum. Many teachers, particularly at the preschool and elementary levels, do this already because they realize the importance of sensory input for learning. Even students at the intermediate and secondary levels indisputably seek sensorimotor stimulation in a variety of ways. They, too, could benefit from activities designed by collaborating teachers to provide activities for developing sensory and motor skills and using those skills judiciously—for example, driver's education, drug-abuse programs, anger management classes, sound level-control studies, and so forth.

A taxonomic structure that moves beyond the psychomotor realm to include sensorimotor functions can be organized into eight levels:

1. *Observe*—Notice with the senses
2. *React*—Show recognition by means of the senses and movement
3. *Act*—Use physical and sensory responses constructively
4. *Adapt*—Adjust motor and sensory activity to fit unfamiliar situations

5. *Authenticate*—Assess validity of specific sensorimotor processes for conditions and purposes
6. *Harmonize*—Integrate sensorimotor activities into situations effectively
7. *Improvise*—Develop aspects of sensorimotor response for problem solving
8. *Innovate*—Construct new, self-expressive sensorimotor-focused actions and solutions

Students who have special needs benefit exponentially from growth and development in these areas. Again, general educators and special educators can blend their curriculums to the benefit of students with and without exceptional learning needs.

Social Domain of Relating to Others   The social realm of functioning is an aspect that has suffered even greater neglect than the sensorimotor domain. Truth be told, teachers and students relate to each other continuously in sociocultural settings of classes, school organizations, sports, and other socially oriented venues. They develop networks of relationships in richly interactive in-school and after-school functions. Some of the most serious learning needs emanate from problems in this domain.

Layers of relationship are somewhat although not inflexibly hierarchical; they can be arranged into an eight-category taxonomy that forms a new social domain. The categories, described in more detail here than the previous three because they *are* new and apply significantly to collaborative consultation and teamwork, are:

1. *Relating*—Acknowledging the presence of others, making eye contact, attending to words or actions of others, showing awareness of the individuality of another as distinct from the group
2. *Communicating*—Sending or receiving messages from others to speak, gesture, call, sign, signal, listen. Messages are sent verbally and nonverbally, with body language often the more powerful of the two types. The most overlooked aspect of the communication process (featured in Chapter 7) is *listening.*
3. *Participating*—Joining in, volunteering for, going along with, actively and willingly taking part in group activities. Much of school life previews later life and future careers where belonging to, taking part in groups, and influencing others in specific directions, are important developments for successful functioning with others.
4. *Negotiating*—Negotiating often takes place informally. Mediation and arbitration are extensions of negotiation and a means of setting aside singularly personal perspectives and preferences to accommodate and assimilate those of others.
5. *Adjudicating*—Conciliating to reach mutually satisfying agreements and settle differences when they arise. Conciliation is an outcome of effective mediation and arbitration. Those who collaborate, communicate, and negotiate effectively in social settings are more able to mediate differences for the benefit of all.
6. *Collaborating*—Working together for success of the group or the project. Teamwork conducted in a collaborative climate is an important function of family, career, and community life.
7. *Initiating*—Creating opportunities and processes for interaction, even if social risks are involved, in order to catalyze action and reform.
8. *Converting*—Creating social transitions and convincing others to join in for the benefit of all.

Importance of the Taxonomies When Working Collaboratively   Taxonomies in education are instructional tools that help educators plan for student learning in stimulating, challenging, future-oriented ways. Taxonomy-driven goals guide the assessment process so it is facilitative, not punitive. When teaching a concept at cognition's knowledge and comprehension levels (for example, the times tables), and expecting students to attend to the lesson affectively by receiving it and responding to it (seeing how many multiplication problems they can complete correctly), instructors allow sufficient time for learning the material at pre-established, announced competency levels. If the material cannot be mastered and learners must move on, re-teaching and correctives are employed. *Extending activities must be made available* for those who do not need to "mark time' or as one student described it, "rev my motor with my brakes on." Collaborative consultation among teachers and resource personnel is vital for structuring the curriculum differentiation that students with special needs should have.

As collaborating teachers plan together, they should discuss how to nurture student growth in critical thinking and creative thinking skills and help students develop tolerance for differing points of view. When lesson objectives are aimed at higher-order thinking, instructors should designate a level of achievement that is reasonable for open-ended, never-ending learning—for example, second-graders keeping logs of interesting words to use in creative writing activities, or high school students evaluating the benefits of various power sources for an energy-hungry nation, or middle school students comparing the need for harvesting raw materials such as tree logs with a contradictory need to protect endangered species such as fish or owls. Then they should determine the point in time at which the class must move on, thereby accepting the reality of varying levels of achievement among the group. Here general educators and special educators sometimes draw lines in the sand as to what they expect students to accomplish; these lines must be smoothed away so that high expectations and differentiated curriculum are in place for *all* students.

If the objectives for learning are to include creative and innovative thinking, emerging through feelings of wonder and risk-taking, then teachers, mentors, and content-area specialists will need to provide flexible time limits and perhaps revise their plans to extend beyond the essential to the developmental and ideational levels.

Three Types of Learning Theory   Learning theory frames teacher expectations, construction of instructional objectives, and methods of assessment. For our purposes here, the focus will be on three predominant types of learning theory—cognitive, behavioral, and social. Each of these types is appropriate in some contexts and not so well suited in others (Hanna & Dettmer, 2004).

Special education teachers have learned and practiced many behavioral principles. So have some general education teachers. However, many of the latter still prefer the cognitive theory or social cognitive theory approach to instruction for most students. Preservice teachers may have been swayed into an either/or situation to the extent that they profess they are a "behaviorist" or a "cognitivist." Then when they collaborate with other educators to identify student needs and plan instruction for the needs, they may find that their "language" is not being used. One co-educator might focus on concepts of observation, reinforcement conditions for modifying behaviors, responses, prerequisite skills, instructional sequencing, and observable criteria for measurement as in behavioral theory. Another may feature concepts of mental constructs, active processing of information, reinforcement as a means of providing information, and construction of knowledge. A third may speak in terms of a co-constructed process in which people interact and negotiate to understand, apply, and problem solve to guide the teaching and learning. The dissonance among these three perspectives (behavioral, cognitive, and social) and others can hamper collaborative thinking among co-educators when planning curriculum and it may be confusing to a novice teacher jumping to a faulty conclusion that the choice must be either/or.

Three Kinds of Subject Matter   Subject matter can be channeled helpfully into one of three kinds—essential, developmental, and ideational. (Refer to Figure 2.3.) Each kind has its place in a well-designed curriculum at all age and ability levels and in all content areas. The distinctions among the three will mold teacher expectations for student achievement, and the goal setting, instructional strategies, and assessment methods guided by those expectations. They also will influence markedly the teacher–student, teacher–teacher, and teacher–family interactions. Here again, differences of perspective are molded to some extent by an educator's affinity toward a general or special education focus, as well as grade levels, curricular areas, preferred school of learning theory, teaching styles, and assessment methods.

Essential subject matter is at a basic and clear-cut level within a closed, fixed sphere for learning. The objectives can be described with specificity and the material is to be mastered by students. This content is the basis for further learning; it is to be used in low-road transfer to similar situations. Teachers instruct for it with well-defined material and students are to learn the material in its entirety. Time is allocated for mastery; if the material is not learned, remedial or compensatory activities are provided. Examples of essential content to be mastered include:

- Toilet training and recognition of colors by preschoolers
- Letters of the alphabet and simple sight words for kindergarten/primary grades
- Times tables and assigned spelling words for intermediate grades
- Traffic signs and symbols
- Standard keyboard position, procedure for setting up a microscope, music symbols and notation, goal of completing a lap in a relay, or rules for baseball, as examples for older students

Teachers of students with learning disabilities or developmental disability formulate many goals using this type of curriculum material. It is taught and learned for mastery.

The second kind of subject matter is *developmental*. It is specifiable but expansive to the extent that it either cannot be fully mastered, or it need not be fully mastered in order to advance. With developmental material, variable levels of achievement among students are to be expected. That said, *all* students must have opportunities to learn many things at the developmental level. Examples of developmental content are:

- Name the capitals of all countries of the world (This is possible but is it essential?)
- List all vice presidents of the United States (Again, this is possible, but would it really need to be transferred to any other situation except in very unusual circumstances?)
- Learn volleyball techniques (When can all possibilities ever be learned?)
- Weld a metal joint (What is a perfect joint weld?)
- Bake a soufflé (Who among the best chefs attains mastery at this?)

This material is taught for only as much achievement as possible or deemed reasonable and necessary.

Finally, *ideational* subject matter can be neither specified nor mastered. This sphere of learning is broad, open-ended, and novel. Novel outcomes and wide ranges of achievement are expected. Transfer of learning is high road, where material can be used in new situations calling for complex problem solving and innovation. Only a representation of the immense range of material is taught, and only some of what was taught is tested. Some instructed content is *not* tested, and some content that was not taught but is related to the topic *is* tested to find out if there is transfer of learning to more complex problems or new situations. And it is here that advocates must make the strongest case for students with exceptional learning needs—those with disorders in learning and behavior that make it hard for them to climb out of the mastery boxes and stretch into open spaces of application, imagination, and creativity. They must have curricular opportunities to explore these spaces, and teachers must expect them to have success in doing so.

Educators with an orientation toward cognitive theory typically are comfortable with ideational subject matter; those who teach students with high aptitude "live here" when planning instruction for students' needs as dictated by their advanced abilities. Their classrooms are likely to provide learning centers and encourage independent studies. Group discussions with no predetermined outcomes are a vehicle for stimulating deeper and wider learning. Examples of ideational content would be to:

- Show in picture format how addition and multiplication are related
- Illustrate protection of human rights provided by a particular amendment to the U.S. Constitution
- Plan a nutritious menu for a month on a given budget
- Apply principles of energy production and conservation to the concept of global warming

Material here is not masterable, and learning is ongoing. The irony is that many students with learning disabilities can thrive in these environments—and they often do after they reach adulthood and can choose their work environments. But they did not have such opportunities in school to develop these qualities because expectations for mastery of lower-level content consumed their learning time and patience. *Collaborative school consultants can be at their most powerfully effective here* in remedying this flawed, myopic thinking about students' exceptional needs and considerable abilities and allow them to "bubble up" in responsive learning environments.

Differences in professional perspective emanating from general education and special education, grade levels, learning theory orientations, and subject-matter realms will have significant effects on collaboration, consultation, and co-teaching teams. With respect, understanding, and accommodation, and demonstrations of good nature mixed in, they will invigorate teaching practices and stimulate student efforts as well.

Annual Goals and Instructional Objectives   Principles related to learning theories and subject-matter contexts frame the kinds of goals and objectives that teachers formulate. They direct teachers in lesson planning, textbook selections, curriculum meetings, and

IEP conferences, creating another distinct difference in professional perspective between special education personnel and general education teachers.

Special education teachers are well schooled in Mager-type (Mager, 1997) behavioral objectives (recall the behavioral theory perspective) that indicate how goals and objectives will be planned and assessed. So they tend to construct annual goals that outline (1) an observable student behavior, (2) conditions for demonstrating the behavior, and (3) the minimal level of attainment expected.

General education teachers may have been exposed to Mager-based principles and they are required under the reauthorized IDEA legislation to attend some IEP conferences where this process for annual goal development frequently is put into practice. But many prefer to use Gronlund-based instructional objectives (Gronlund, 2000) for planning instruction (recall the cognitive theory perspective) in developmental and ideational subject matter—those large, expansive bodies of content with no expected endpoint in achievement levels. Because such goals are not easily measured, several indicants with measurable verbs are needed for each instructional objective to sample behaviors for determining student progress.

Distinction between goal type—Mager-based and Gronlund-based—was sharpened by legislation such as P.L. 94-142 and by methods emphasized in teacher education literature. Much of the special education curriculum calls for mastery-type learning of essential subject matter, if only to ensure measurability of progress on IEP goals. This disadvantages students with disabilities unless they also have opportunities to learn and do with developmental and ideational subject matter as well. Furthermore, ideational goals and most developmental goals are not strictly measurable by objective means such as paper-and-pencil tests. Evidence of achievement must be determined through authentic assessments carefully designed to demonstrate that progress has been made toward meeting the goals.

So what to do? As a start, to buy the needed instructional time for students who must learn apart from the class or leave the classroom periodically for remedial or practice sessions in a resource room, some of their IEP goals should be embedded into instruction for the general education curriculum. Then some broad, high-road transfer goals for students should be incorporated into both the general education and special education curriculum. This requires resourceful collaboration between general and special education teachers. If that does not occur, there will not be enough time in the school day to provide all the opportunities students should have. *Collaboration between special education and general education teachers* becomes even more imperative. All students must have opportunities to achieve at complex levels regardless of disability or cultural or linguistic diversity; instructional objectives must be interpreted as *minimal* statements of expectations and not the outer limits of the learning (Hanna & Dettmer, 2004).

Students who learn differently or happen to have learning difficulties must not be *left* behind (NCLB), and students with high aptitude and talent should not be *held* behind (NC*H*B). Consultation and collaboration, linked to other educational resources, can help ensure that all students have opportunities to learn, develop their potential, and explore their unique interests. Discussions among collaborative school consultants about this issue could have profound motivational influences and positive effects on higher-order learning by students with disabilities and behavioral problems. Collaboration becomes more valued and sought after when co-educators see it working to the benefit of *all* students.

Time and Achievement Dimensions   Essential material typically is framed in a time dimension, with correctives provided if and when students cannot master the material in the time allowed. In the past, this has often been the point at which the special education teacher assists collaboratively to provide modifications and accommodations, anticipating that the student can and must learn the material in order to move on with the class.

Conversely, developmental subject matter and most assuredly ideational material should be set in the achievement dimension. Students will *not* need to stay with that material until it is mastered because mastery is not required; variance in student achievement is to be expected. But they must have opportunities to learn as much of it as they truly need. This is the juncture at which co-educators must meet to decide what those necessities are, and adapt the curriculum with accommodations and modifications.

Students with disabilities should *not* be denied access to higher levels of thinking and doing; in fact, a case could be made that they need such instruction *more* than students who can function successfully in a more or less self-directed fashion. Collaborators must take such concerns into account when they remove material and when they add remedial strategies for students who have been achieving slowly or at low levels. They must not attempt to have all students—those who learn less easily and need more time, as well as those who learn easily and quickly, "come together in the middle and all be at the same place by the end of the term so the next teacher can begin them at the same place." Not at all! Rather, they must aim toward high expectations for all students from wherever they are, and going as far, with good teaching, as they are able. These are tall orders for general classroom teachers and special education teachers, but this is where collaborative efforts and teamwork can "pay off big time," as one enthusiastic teacher remarked. Collaborators can raise their expectations, aim for success in learning by all students, and design curriculum that will enable every student to master what is truly essential and move on to higher levels of complexity, to the greatest extent of which each is capable.

REFLECTION 2.1

What Would You Do?

As a consulting teacher, choose a favorite lesson or subject area and imagine that you and a consultee will be team-teaching this material. This is your first co-teaching experience together. How would you go about getting ready to prepare for it? That is, how would you lay the groundwork so that your co-planning and co-teaching are pleasant for you both and motivating for students? Is it important that you and your co-teacher know some things about your professional perspectives so that you can discuss them before you begin planning, and why or why not? Do you prefer objective tests or short-answer and essay tests? Do you prefer tangible incentives for rewarding accomplishments, or generous feedback on papers? Would your co-teacher describe your classroom routine as routine, or flexible? Or does any of this matter?

If these differences matter, how could you share this kind of information pleasantly and agreeably with your colleagues, and then learn comparable information about them in order to co-plan and co-teach more pleasantly and productively? If you believe they do not matter, reflect on how you would explain that belief.

Assessment and Evaluation Processes   The next three types of professional perspectives are interwoven, so they are addressed here together: purposes of tests, types of scores, and interpretations of scores. Professional differences in these components of assessment, along with political pressures inside and outside the schools, are extremely important factors in working together amiably because they can be divisive areas without careful thought and collegial exchange of views.

Tests are administered to students for one of two purposes: either to determine levels of achievement on stated criteria or to determine achievement levels in relation to others. So tests are either mastery tests or differentiating tests and they will yield scores that are criterion referenced or norm referenced. Criterion-referenced scores relate to specifiable levels of content learned, while norm-referenced scores relate to broad spheres of learning where scores are compared with scores obtained by a relevant group of people.

For mastery learning, teachers teach to the test; indeed, they *should* inform students precisely what they will be tested on and then provide appropriate instruction so that every student has every opportunity to master the material and be prepared to "ace" the test. Students need to know what they will be accountable for and then they need to know whether they succeeded.

Conversely, teachers must *not* teach explicit content for a differentiating, or discriminatory, test. They teach instead for learning and doing that extends beyond recall and comprehension so that students can apply broad, open-ended content to new problems and novel situations. The instruction must be excellent, of course, with expectations for student learning held high. But co-educators should acknowledge that the tests are intended to differentiate between students who learned (or in many instances already knew before it was presented) how to transfer knowledge and understanding of the material to more complex tasks and novel situations, and those who did not, comparing their achievement with that of others in an appropriate reference group.

Such comparisons of test scores are done to make useful decisions. Most uses are justifiable—to determine class rankings, or facilitate entry to advanced programs or higher education, or award scholarships. In a more immediate and practical vein, important decisions can be made about planning and pacing instruction, grouping or not grouping students, referring students to testing for special education programs, selecting materials for continued learning, and much more that *could not be obtained* from the limited information provided by mastery tests over *specified material in closed content domains.*

Interpretation of test scores often uncovers some important professional differences among educators. In reality, many educators are not well enough acquainted with methods of score interpretation. Too many have never had formal instruction in measurement and testing; unfortunately this is especially true among preservice teachers who will not even have previous teaching experiences on which to rely for making decisions with their first classes of students.

Score types include raw scores and the closely related percentage scores that are suitable for interpreting scores on criterion/domain-referenced material where content is clearcut and is to be mastered—for example, 8 out of 10 words spelled correctly, or 90 percent of the 20 assigned arithmetic problems worked correctly.

The other type of score is the derived score that compares student achievement with that of others. Derived scores are discriminatory by design, to discriminate between those who have learned the material and those who have not. (Note that *discriminate* is a psychometric term referring to comparisons of *scores* and is not to be confused with an odious use of the word for stereotyping or for prejudice toward *people*.) Scores on discriminatory, norm-referenced tests can be reported by several means, some more satisfactory than others. Options are grade equivalencies (GEs) or age equivalencies (AEs); ranks and percentile ranks; and a variety of standard scores, including deviation IQs, stanines, *z*-scores, *T*-scores, and normal curve equivalencies (NCEs).

Professional differences about scores and their interpretations can cause serious friction among co-educators because, as indicated earlier, scores are used for very important reasons: applications for work positions or higher education institutions, placements, grades, school reports to the public, communications with parents, and even assessments of teaching. Most school administrators would not look favorably on teachers who awarded all A grades for every student, nor would they do so on teachers whose composite of student grades never rose above D. They would begin to look at the teacher's planning and instruction as too limited or too demanding.

Unfortunately, professional perspectives on score interpretations are often formed in a flawed manner and can result in quite misleading information. The following are just a few of the most illogical and sensitivity-laden approaches that should be discussed in collaborative settings so they create as little confusion and stir up as little disagreement as possible among teachers *and* parents:

■ *Using percentages to score nonmasterable material*—The folly of this approach should be challenged by collaborating teachers who ask "Let's see—that score is 70 percent of what?" which is of course unanswerable for any of the open-ended subject matter that students should be studying a good part of the time. A score of 70 percent on the week's spelling list makes sense. However, a score of 70 percent on important, globe-encircling causes and effects of World War II does not make sense unless the student was given a chart to memorize and recall verbatim, which would be misclassification of open-ended content as content for mastery. A rigid system of percentage grading would lock content into the mastery mode, where only simple, essential material is taught. This approach can be especially debilitating to students for whom learning is slow and difficult but who are entitled to study rich, application-focused content of open-ended domains as well as masterable material in closed domains. It is important that general education and special education teachers arrive collaboratively at sensible goal-setting for both mastery and open-ended learning experiences, and agree on the ways in which learning will be assessed, graded, and reported.

■ *Confusing percentile scores with percentages*—Percentiles put scores into rank file for comparison with others in a group that has been selected for the comparison. That could be last year's similar classes, this year's multiple sections of the same class, or district-wide classes of the same subject and grade level. Percentiles are understood by parents; however, they represent ranks and as such cannot be summed and averaged in grade books.

■ *Using grade equivalencies (GEs) and age equivalencies (AEs)*—Most uses of GEs and AEs are ill advised because they lead to serious misinterpretations by parents and sometimes even by teachers and administrators. As one example, a parent might ask, "If my fifth-grader scored at the eighth-grade level in both math and reading, shouldn't she be advanced to the eighth grade, or at least elevated to eighth-grade math and reading curriculum?" Or another, "Why is our fourth-grade child reading like a second-grader?" That requires backpedaling and searching for convincing explanations by the teacher to parents, so this score type is better avoided.

■ *Grading on the curve*—Some teachers cling to this very questionable but frequently employed practice for assigning letter grades, and alas, some school district policies dictate that it be used. School handbooks may promote the practice although it is a misuse of student evaluation and an abuse of the learning process. Why is it harshly inappropriate? Because learning is not a zero-sum game with just so much learning to go around. When teachers announce before testing, and sometimes even before teaching the material, that the grade distribution will contain one or two As, for example, and X number of Bs, Cs, Ds, and perhaps Fs, the effects on student effort and interest in learning will be primarily negative.

Students who are graded on the curve will concentrate on competing and "taking away" from others. This is particularly demoralizing in inclusive classrooms where there is a wide range of student abilities and too often a long history of prior failures. Some will withdraw from even trying to learn. The resultant peer pressure, not to mention the damper on the learning process, will be debilitating to motivation and interpersonal relations. Students who openly care about their success will feel they must compete to "bump" others for the few top grades and avoid the inevitable bottom of the distribution. Also, social ramifications of that success can be high, especially for vulnerable teens and tweens. No clearer message for *not* collaborating and working together could be sent. Collaborating teachers can forget about demonstrating collegiality and shared effort if they use a system that subtly but powerfully undermines the collaborative spirit. Percentage grading with definitive cutoff scores for letter grades are a harmful way of going about the business of teaching when taking into account the tender cognitive, affective, and social needs of young learners.

So again, what to do? This is an area of instruction and evaluation that begs for strong, totally committed collaborative efforts by co-educators to understand both the obvious and the underlying problems in order to arrive at sensible answers and formulate defensible practices that work to the advantage of all. One solution is to use a system of modified percentage grading that does not link grades to the top student, but employs a covert kind of norm-referencing system instead. This process would anchor a class's scores to other reference groups, as was suggested in regard to percentiles, and allow for adjustments to be made by the teacher so grade distributions come out as experienced teachers *sense* that they should. Preservice teachers typically have little assessment experience and no previous reference groups to refer to, but they could learn much about this in *collaboration* with veteran teachers who would guide them through their novitiate grading processes. It could very well be that the entire teaching staff and perhaps even some interested parents would welcome an opportunity to join novice teachers in a professional development experience focusing on assessment and evaluation. It would be appropriate for school psychologists and counselors to provide leadership in this experience, bringing their listening skills to the table along with their expertise, and technology support staff could showcase the latest electronic tools for efficient management of test data and score interpretations.

■ *Assessment adaptations for students with disabilities*—Adaptations can be made through accommodations or modifications of testing procedures. Accommodations for testing are changes in regular test conditions, and modifications are techniques that alter the test itself. These special education practices have important educational, social, and legal ramifications that must be understood by school administrators and general classroom teachers as well as special education and resource personnel. Collaborative consultation within a professional development activity is a fitting process for examining and discussing all aspects of these complex issues.

THINKING AND DOING TOGETHER, BUT OFTEN IN DIFFERENT WAYS

To summarize, educators differ markedly in many ways with regard to their professional perspectives on teaching and student learning. But they do not need to think alike; they just need to think *together*. Thinking together divergently is not an oxymoron. It is a sophisticated process that can be very productive. Understanding the unique orientations of various others toward the world and the work they do in it, and valuing their individual perspectives, are key factors in building collegial relationships. Educators who make conscientious efforts to respect the individualism and independence of their students also must respect and value the same for their colleagues as school-based co-educators, and for students' family members as home-based co-educators.

Occasionally it will be necessary for collaborating colleagues simply to agree to disagree on one or more topics and then move on with confidence in the knowledge that their decisions have been made together after much thought and discussion. This would not mean that collaboration and consultation failed and it should not discourage co-educators from seeking out other ways of coming together in the future to revisit the issues.

ACTION 2.3

Share Your Perspectives

In groups of three to six, or as a whole group if there are no more than a dozen or so, share your perspectives on the following, and then as a whole group discuss some of the interesting and helpful things you gained from the activity. You may even decide to generate more either-or questions in order to learn more about your colleagues and their views.

- Would you rather teach in a general education classroom or a special education resource room? Why?
- In order to improve behavior, do you favor using positive reinforcement techniques with contingencies or talking it out and reasoning with students to improve behavior?
- Do you think students should be allowed to redo work and receive full credit or partial credit for the redo or not be allowed to redo work at all?
- Assuming that both teachers would grade fairly, do you want to be perceived by students as "a tough grader" or as "an easy grader"? Why?
- What is your perspective on teaming up a student with disabilities and a student with advanced aptitude as study-buddies or tutor–tutee or members of a small cooperative learning group?
- Do you think teachers should supplement teaching materials with their own resources? Why or why not?

John-Steiner, Weber, and Minnis (1998) assert that if an episode of collaboration fails to examine differences, especially ones such as those discussed above that can create tension, the process cannot be fully utilized. Thinking back to some of the most potentially conflictive issues within this chapter, educators should make efforts to respect different points of view even when they disagree, and to temper their interactions with tolerance, genuine interest, and appreciation for other ways of doing things.

Case Study for Addressing Differences in Professional Perspectives

Review Vignette 2, which appears early in this chapter. Then put yourself as a special education consulting teacher in that central hallway of the middle school on the morning after the scheduled professional development day. As teachers and other staff make their ways along the busy hallway, some coming and some going, you pick up on some of their comments about yesterday's activity. You have your own perspective on the event as well. But you are especially interested in others' reactions because your friend and respected co-educator, a general education teacher who is the new building coordinator for professional activities, planned this event. The assignment carries a minimal stipend and an excuse from hall duty. She often asks for your input on educational matters and you are virtually certain she will do so today because this was the first professional development event that she has directed. Now that you are catching strands of off-the-record comments about the professional development day, what are you thinking? Work through the following case-study template points as slightly modified from Chapter 1 for this situation. As in that case study, the process is not about fixing the professional development plan but about perfecting the collaborative consultation process that could help do that. (Recall that the professional development coordinator does not have hall duty and has not yet gotten feedback about the event.)

- *Situation*—as described
- *Known facts*—as described
- *Initiator/convener*—the general educator as professional development coordinator and personal friend
- *Problem/needs*—how to answer honestly, bringing up important points while remaining supportive and encouraging, such as "This is a program that could do much for our students and community. Some liked it but it was not 100% approval. Did the teachers know about the day's theme? Did they have a say in choosing it or planning for it, such as responding to well-designed needs assessment? Could some of our community leaders have been involved, since it was about a community-based program? And what about parents and students getting involved? They might get really excited about it if they are in on the planning."
- Examples of questions to be asked: What collaborative actions and skills could be used in this interaction? How can teachers have a stake in planning their professional day? What others should participate in the planning *and* assessment of the event?

Evaluate this brief, informal consultation and discuss why it had value or why it did not.

TECHNOLOGY FOR GENERAL EDUCATION AND SPECIAL EDUCATION IN COLLABORATION

In recent years, many changes have occurred in ways educators can interact with colleagues and students. Various forms of modern technology have revolutionized the already interactive processes of collaboration and consultation among co-educators.

Some of the most tedious, time-consuming tasks, such as developing IEPs, preparing reports, and collecting and recording academic and behavioral information, have been made easier and faster by technological advances. Software templates, e-mail, electronic calendars, and a variety of other organizational tools help teachers manage a blizzard of paperwork and use their precious time more efficiently.

Use of such tools and others to be described in subsequent chapters can free up more time for the direct services that some students with disabilities need.

Technology tools with a goodness of fit for students with disabilities can escalate achievement and enhance feelings of self-esteem. They become powerful motivators for students who have experienced much failure and frustration in school yet often are quite comfortable with the complexities of these devices, sometimes even unraveling the complexities for their teachers! Many electronic communication devices allow students with learning and behavioral disorders to speak up and share their views, adding their voices to those of classmates.

Teachers must be prudent in dealing with issues related to use of technology such as firewalls to protect students, equal access to equipment and programs, and other potential problems. Working collaboratively with their co-educators to access the wealth of resources available through the Internet and various websites, even when their perspectives on learning and teaching differ markedly, will yield collective knowledge that improves decision-making in matters of curriculum, instruction, and resource selection.

ETHICAL ISSUES CONCERNING PROFESSIONAL PERSPECTIVES

Teachers who devote much attention to accommodating student individuality may still find it difficult to appreciate the inevitable array of adult differences and adapt to them. Educators should give consideration to divergent points of view among their colleagues and be ready, willing, and able to change their minds when the evidence warrants it. This is particularly important when they will be co-teaching.

The persuasive and personal aspects of consultative service require a close, careful monitoring of ethical concerns (Ross, 1986). Essential behaviors for ethical collaborators are empathy for all and an interactive manner of *onedownsmanship,* or de-emphasis of prior knowledge in order to maintain collegial relationships (Henning-Stout, 1994), along with communication in a climate of parity as equal partners with agreement of mutual ownership. One principled person can exert considerable influence and good conscience on a group. Confident teachers model a willingness to learn from others. They draw others into potentially productive sharing sessions. They demonstrate strong respect for individual variability and work at deep understanding of human development and learning theory. They strive to nurture the cognitive, affective, sensorimotor, and social growth of co-educators as well as students. Most importantly, they listen not only to colleagues but also to their students who have much to say about their own needs and perspectives, if given the opportunity.

A collaborative school consultant must be open to new perspectives and ideas, giving co-educators opportunities to share their viewpoints and letting them enjoy the pleasures of contributing. Disagreements must not be taken personally. Co-educators must keep their channels of interaction open and friendly.

TIPS FOR USING ADULT DIFFERENCES CONSTRUCTIVELY

1. Learn as much as possible about the work, environments, potential difficulties, and most of all, joys and satisfactions that your co-educators experience in their roles.
2. Find ways to promote the value of collaborative school consultation and teamwork.
3. Have lunch, workroom breaks, and informal visits with other staff members often.
4. No one is talented or expert at everything (or nothing), so endeavor to recognize and use the talents and expertise of others.
5. Develop opportunities for special education teachers and general education teachers to interact often.
6. Try not to press for your own favorite ways of carrying out curriculum goals, school programs, and special arrangements for students with exceptional learning needs if other ways are preferred by your co-educators and will be equal to or almost as effective.
7. Practice the art of onedownsmanship in your interactions with other school personnel to avoid coming across as "the expert" who *talks* but does not *do*.
8. Respect the rights of others to hold different beliefs. Even when people do not agree, they should assume that others are acting in ways they believe are appropriate.
9. Reasons exist for things that people do or say, so try to discover them.
10. Be available, available, available when others would like to share or just talk.

ADDITIONAL RESOURCES

Bloom, B. S., Engelhart, M. D., Furst, E. J., Hill, W. H., & Krathwohl, D. R. (1956). *Taxonomy of educational objectives, Handbook I: Cognitive domain.* New York: McKay.

Brownell, M., Adams, A., Sindelar, P., Waldron, N., & Vanhover, S. (2006). Learning from collaboration: The role of teacher qualities. *Exceptional Children, 72*(2), 169–185. This study examined how teachers who readily use strategies acquired in collaboration differed from those who do not. The researchers contend that there is not much in-depth information on how the nature of teachers'

individual beliefs might interact to facilitate or hinder innovations in teaching.

Hanna, G. S., & Dettmer, P. (2004). *Assessment for effective teaching: Context-adaptive planning.* Boston: Allyn & Bacon. Individual differences and variability among students, subject matter, learning theory, taxonomies, testing and grading, and other factors forming professional perspectives are presented in detail.

Krathwohl, D. R., Bloom, B. S., & Masia, B. B. (1964). *Taxonomy of educational objectives, Handbook II: Affective domain.* New York: McKay.

3

Working Together with Personal Preferences That Differ

IT IS EASY IN THE BUSY AND PUBLIC BUT RELATIVELY AUTONOMOUS school setting to overlook the impact that differing values, styles, and interests of colleagues have on working together. People in all walks of life bring a variety of professional perspectives, as discussed in Chapter 2, and a wide range of personal preferences, the focus of this chapter, into their work settings. Unfortunately, a study of adult differences and attention to constructive use of those differences is, for the most part, neglected in traditional teacher preparation programs.

Much of the seemingly random variation in this patchwork quilt of characteristics is actually quite orderly and consistent because it is based on the way people prefer to use their judgment and their perceptions (Keirsey & Bates, 1978; Lawrence, 1993). A situation that is interpreted a certain way by one person might be perceived in a very different way by another. If a person views the world and reacts to it in ways unlike another person, it is because he or she is processing the information differently. One's personality is the sum total of that person's sensory, mental, emotional, and social characteristics. It is the embodiment of a collection of qualities (*Webster's New Collegiate Dictionary*, 1996). Personality traits distinguish individuals and characterize them *in their relationships with others*.

It would be easy and convenient, but somewhat myopic, to endorse only one way of doing something—one's own—while wondering why everyone else is not clever enough and agreeable enough to concur and fall into step. In the school setting, differences among co-educators will become positive, beneficial factors if they are used to maximize opportunities for students. How can collaborators go about doing that? They must begin with a determination to acknowledge differences that exist in various contexts (Figure 3.1) and accept and *value* the differences. Next comes working as a team of co-educators who respond to the challenges and strive to *make constructive use* of their differences.

FOCUSING QUESTIONS

1. How do major differences in personal preferences affect collaborative school consultation and teamwork?

2. How can a self-study of personality traits enlighten individual educators in ways that will enhance collegiality and build strong interrelationships among co-educators?

3. How is diversity among co-educators an asset for working as a team, and what competencies are important for those who do work collaboratively and in teams?

4. What positive outcomes can result from well-implemented collaborative school consultation?

5. What technological tools are important for communication and social networking among collaborating educators, families of students, and resource personnel?

6. How can a collaborative consultation ethic that recognizes and respects differences in personal perspectives among co-educators benefit both teachers and learners?

KEY TERMS

persona	personality inventory	"psychopest"
personality	preference	self-study

VIGNETTE 3

Educators reveal some of their individual preferences and personality characteristics when they are "letting their hair down" in informal chats with colleagues. Most of the time, such comments are for short-term chatting, venting, gaining sympathy, or getting reassurance from someone with a friendly ear and the time to listen. But occasionally a kernel of discontent is articulated that needs to be noted and addressed with the help of a collaborating teacher to forestall more serious problems and frustrations. Teachers can be heard making remarks such as these:

"I think I do have some good, instinctive teaching skills, but I don't seem to get them put together to do what I want."

"I get so fed up with the reports that have to be done on such short notice. If data are turned in hastily and carelessly, like some people I know do, what is their value?"

"I worked really hard on a particular project and then when it came time to give out the recognition, everybody seemed to forget that the ideas were mine."

"I like to lead and get things organized and finished, so I guess I'm not timid about saying what I think should be done, but sometimes I get criticized for that."

"I'm always wondering if I should say what I think or wait and see what everyone else thinks so I'm not totally out in left field making a fool of myself."

"It seems like what I do mostly in my department is put out fires."

"If I didn't show up tomorrow, I'm not sure any of my colleagues would care or even notice, for that matter, just as long as a substitute is there to keep order."

"Lots of days I really feel like the first-year teacher I am. Having a mentor would be good, but asking for help would increase my feelings of insecurity."

THINKING TOGETHER IN DIFFERENT WAYS

To serve students best, educators do not need to think alike—they need to think *together*. The process of thinking together divergently is not an oxymoron; it is a form of dialectical thinking that can be very productive. Understanding and valuing uniqueness among adults in their orientations toward the world, and their styles and preferences for processing information, are key factors in successful collegial relationships. Educators who make conscientious efforts to respect the individualism of their students must respect and protect the rights for adults—teacher colleagues and also family members of the students.

■ ■ ■ ■ ■ ▬▬▬▬▬▬▬▬▬▬▬▬▬▬▬▬▬▬▬▬▬▬▬▬▬▬▬▬▬▬▬▬▬▬▬▬▬▬▬

ACTION 3.1
Constructing Portraits of Diversity

The organizer provides one sheet of paper (blue and bigger than letter size being best) to each group of five or six participants—along with various colors of precut paper flower petals (the number of participants multiplied by ten or so) and a brown, teacup-size circle for each group, that will be the center of each group's flower on which to attach the petals. The only other necessities are school glue and pens or pencils.

Within the groups, discuss things that *everyone* in that group has in common. A member of each group prints those several things on the brown centerpiece and glues it to the center of the paper. Then the group discusses characteristics on which they differ. When one and only one person has a particular characteristic—for example, being a twin or driving a convertible—that person writes it on a petal. Each petal should contain only one phrase that is a unique characteristic within the group.

When the allotted time has expired, all petals of uniqueness are glued around the center of the group likenesses. The completed flowers represent both diversity and commonality. Here is one group's flower portrait and comments:

> In the centerpiece we wrote that we are all female in this group; we are all elementary teachers, we all *don't* have a cat; we all have on jeans this evening; we all like spinach; we all love the movie "Casablanca." There were so many things mentioned that applied to almost everyone. But then there would be one person it didn't fit. It was interesting. At that point our center was very full anyway, so we went on to individual petals. On those, one of us is not married, one of us hates to shop while the others love to, one of us was born in a taxicab, one of us lives on a farm, one of us is of Chinese ancestry, one forgot to put the casserole in the oven before coming here this evening, and one of us has a tattoo. We would have continued with this activity because finding fascinating differences is so interesting and could go on forever, but the allotted time ran out.

An all-important follow-up discussion by the whole group should initiate a delightful sharing of information learned and could bring out possibilities for practical use of the diversities. Later, the flowers could be arranged into a mural and displayed as a collage of both diversity and similarities.

One of the most overlooked but crucial factors in teacher preparation is the ability to relate constructively to others, including colleagues, by responding to them and their preferences and needs with emotional maturity (Jersild, 1955). Noted educator Madeline Hunter (1985) encouraged teachers to move toward dialectical thinking. This would not mean abandoning one's own position, but building correction into one's own viewpoints by taking the opposing view momentarily. Hunter urged all to "come out of armed camps … where we're not collaborating, so that 'I understand why you think it's right for your students to line up while I think it's better for them to come in casually'" (1985, p. 3). She stressed that when educators show respect for others' points of view, they model the cooperation students will need to demonstrate in their future roles.

Today's students will become leaders in a shrinking global community. It is vital that their educators prepare them to function successfully in diverse, multicultural societies. The most effective way of providing this instruction is to model such skills every day in the school setting. Teachers must *live* the "sermon," not "preach" it! Collaborative consultation and co-teaching roles are realistic, appropriate vehicles for modeling constructive use of individual differences among people of all ages.

CULTIVATING AWARENESS OF INDIVIDUAL PREFERENCES

During the 1970s, 1980s, and 1990s, numerous methodologies and instruments were developed as personality inventories to help people understand human behavior and improve human relationships. A number of these instruments have been used in such diverse social service areas as education, counseling (for marriage, family, personal, and career needs), religion, business, and industry. Illustrative data from a variety of occupational and academic groups have been helpful in drawing conclusions about vocational preferences, aesthetic preferences, aptitudes, work habits, family and marriage relationships, creativity, and values.

Assessment of individual differences in personality and temperament can be done with one or more instruments that are available among a wide range of existing tools and techniques. An online search using key words such as *personality instruments* or *learning styles inventories* will bring up a wealth of resources to investigate. Some of the most well-known instruments are Bernice McCarthy's 4MAT system, Anthony Gregorc's Mind Styles™ Model, Gregorc and Butler's Mediation Abilities Model, the Dunn and Dunn Learning Styles assessment, David Keirsey's Please Understand Me: Temperament Character Intelligence, and the nationally and internationally popular Myers-Briggs Type Indicator (MBTI). Each of these systems and inventories has been used in a variety of contexts to increase awareness and understanding of human preferences that influence behavior. To balance the zeal of those who support each system, there are others who caution against over-generalizing and oversimplifying complex human attributes with instruments calling for self-report assessment and dichotomous interpretation—for example, concrete/abstract, morning/evening, extrovert/introvert, or impulsive/reflective comparisons. Nevertheless, Carl Jung, eminent Swiss psychologist on whose work the MBTI is based, detailed with conviction how people differ in fundamental ways even though all have the same instincts driving them from within (Jung, 1923).

Personality distinguishes an individual and characterizes him or her in relationships with others. For example, a person who looks for action and variety, shares experiences readily, prefers to work with others, and tends to get impatient with slow, tedious jobs, is indicating preferences that are quite different from one who prefers working alone, laboring long and hard on one thing, and seeking abundant quiet time for reflection. As another example, an individual who is interested in facts, works steadily and patiently, and enjoys being realistic and practical, contrasts with one who prefers to generate multiple possibilities, attends to the whole aspect of a situation at one time, and anticipates what will be said or done.

As a third example, an individual who likes to have things decided and settled, functions purposefully, and seeks to make conditions as they "should be" is not operating from the same preferences as one who has a more live-and-let-live attitude, leaving things open and flexible, with attitudes of adaptability and tolerance. Finally, a person who needs logical reasons, holds firmly to convictions, and contributes intellectually while trying to be fair and impartial has preferences that differ from one who relates freely to most people, likes to agree with others, and cultivates enthusiasm within the group.

Every person is equipped with a broad spectrum of attributes and can use them as needed but typically *prefers* to focus intensively upon one or the other at a time. This is a very important point that calls for elaboration. Each individual has all of the contrasting elements at her or his disposal to use, but does not prefer them at the same time. Elizabeth Murphy (1987) explains it by using the example of color. Just as red cannot be blue, one cannot *prefer* both simultaneously. One might prefer having a red car, but could live with a blue one if circumstances or practicality necessitated having it. If a person prefers to apply real-life experiences to problems, that person does not prefer simultaneously to apply fanciful imagination to those problems. However, he can call out his imagination to assist if he wants to or needs to.

Remarkably, one's *less* preferred functions can contribute mightily to self-satisfaction and production because when they surface, they provide balance and completeness. They are the well-springs of enthusiasm and energy. One's least preferred, most child*like* (different from child*ish*) and somewhat primitive functions can unleash a certain awkwardness and feeling of unrest that initiate ideas and cultivate innovative thinking. When adults are being a bit playful, perhaps silly, and seemingly frivolous, they may very well be functioning temporarily in their less-often used but most creative mode. However, people generally call upon their preferred functions when confidence, comfort, and efficiency are most important.

SELF-STUDY OF OWN PREFERRED STYLES AND FUNCTIONS

Collaborative and inclusive schools, in order to be successful, must develop and maintain superior working relationships. However, unless individuals reflect on their personal preferences and understand how those factors guide their own functioning, they are apt to view others narrowly through biased and distorted lenses of their own unrecognized needs, fears, desires, anxieties, and sometimes unreceptive impulses (Jersild, 1955). These distortions can jeopardize well-meaning efforts to build relationships of trust and cohesiveness. Understanding and respect are crucial for nurturing a collaborative climate in which the productivity of the group will be more than the sum of its parts would be.

Lessen and Frankiewicz (1992) believed affective attributes of teachers can and should be developed, and put it this way: "As teaching is inevitably a human enterprise, to

suggest that teachers' personalities have no effect on their teaching is to deny their human-
ity" (p. 130).

Dyck, Dettmer, and Thurston (1985), in the federally funded Special Education
Consulting Project, conducted to prepare special education teachers for consultation and
collaboration, determined in analysis of pre- and post-test data that an area of greatest gain by participants was "Awareness of self as a crucial variable in the consultative
process." Other high gains were revealed in "Ability to monitor and change my own
behavior as needed to increase my effectiveness" and "Skill when communicating for
problem solving."

Educators who collaborate should reflect on their own values and preferences before
working intensively with other people who are likely to have differing values and preferences. This can be done informally if the stakes are not too high and the process is kept at a
voluntary, exploratory level. Self-study analyses and follow-up discussions can be undertaken with a variety of methods and settings, including discussion groups, role playing,
reading, conferences, and workshops. These structures help educators become more aware
of their own personal attributes and weave those qualities into new combinations for teaching students with diverse interests and learning needs (Dettmer, 1981).

Six graduate students in a special education graduate class are sharing voluntarily what they learned from their experience with a personality preference indicator
(the MBTI):

Student A: When we split into groups in class, it was interesting to discuss things
   because the way we were grouped, everybody was on the same wave length. It would
   be nice and comfortable if we could work with people like that; however, it would make
   work and life dull. As I was skimming through descriptions of other types from mine,
   I noticed there are some I would tend to go head-to-head with—ones who have to have
   everything organized or think their opinion is the only opinion.

Student B: In reviewing descriptions in the personality instrument, I could visual-
   ize people I know and work with. The information was valuable to me in planning
   teams. I usually gravitate toward those most like me. I always thought we worked
   more quickly and efficiently together. But I see now the importance of a diverse group
   of teachers in preparing the most suitable guidelines and educational plans for exceptional children.

Student C: Something I found interesting is that the most effective groups are those that
   have a span of differences. A teacher must be a facilitator to all students, so she has an
   obligation to be flexible and ingenious with her teaching methods.

Student D: I'm more aware now of different types, especially at meetings I have
   attended. I like to observe and study human behavior and the information I obtained
   has helped me to have better insight as to why people react the way they do in different
   situations. It also helped me understand that I need to have patience for those who don't
   think the way I do.

Student E, an international student: The most valuable benefit I earned from the self-
   report inventory is that I became more understanding of myself and more aware of the
   differences among people. I've been thinking about what kind of person I really am for

a long time. Now, I've discovered some answers. I understand my work habits, communication types, preferred teaching situation, and interaction styles much better. More important, however, is that I've become more respectful of the differences among other people. Each person's individual preferences and values are indispensable for effective teamwork.

Student F: It was an opening of my mind. Being human I have had a tendency to think my personality type is best for teaching. I've learned there is not a best type for teaching. Rather, opposite types have strengths that need to be recognized. So I've learned to accept and openly work with people who are different from me.

Tools for studying personality, temperament, and learning style such as the MBTI and others named earlier are useful when discussed in professional development sessions or departmental meetings that focus on small-group activities to highlight the rich variety inherent in human nature. Of course, no single journal article, book, conference, or training package will ever provide sufficient material to fully understand the sophistication and complexity of individual differences. But too few teacher preparation programs provide opportunities for reflection and study. Conoley (1987) and Dettmer (1981) were early advocates in promoting awareness of individual differences among collaborating adults as a key to the theory and practice of school consultation.

Isabel Briggs Myers, who developed the MBTI, liked to help married couples reconcile their points of view by pointing out three alternatives:

> You can consider that it is wrong of your partner to be different from you, and you can be indignant. This diminishes your partner and gets you nowhere. Or you can consider that it is wrong of you to be different from your partner and be depressed. That diminishes you and gets you nowhere. The proper solution is to consider that the two of you are justifiably and interestingly different, and be amused. (Myers, 1975)

Safran (1991) criticizes the shortsightedness of researchers who omit important factors in interaction, such as personality, interpersonal affect, and "domineeringness," from their research designs that focus on consultation and collaboration. Salzberg and Morgan (1995) contend that variability in personality is a key issue in human interaction, but in their research on teacher preparation for working with paraeducators, the topic is noticeably missing.

One point must be emphasized: It is not necessary to use a formal personality assessment to explore the constructive use of individual differences. There is inherent value in keeping the process informal and somewhat fuzzy so as to be nonthreatening and nonjudgmental. The goals should be simple: to increase self-understanding, broaden one's ability to respect and truly value differences in others, and use that wide range of differences constructively for the benefit of students and co-educators. The Action and Reflection activities in this chapter are intended to be catalysts for implementing constructive use of adult differences in school settings.

To reiterate, oversimplification and overgeneralization of complex constructs such as personality must be avoided. Conclusions should not become labels. Rigid interpretations must give way to open mindedness and respect. With these cautions firmly in mind and a heightened understanding of individual differences among adults, teachers *can* interact with their colleagues more effectively. As an additional incentive, it is interesting and lots of fun!

Respecting Different Viewpoints and Inclinations

An early study by Lawrence and DeNovellis (1974) revealed that teachers with different preferences tend to behave differently from one another in the classroom. So it was understandable that they would interact differently with their collaborating colleagues. Learning styles of teachers as well as students can contribute to interactive tendencies. Lawrence (1993) designated four areas that cause teachers to behave differently from each other in the classroom: cognitive style; attitudes and interests; preferences for learning environments that fit those cognitive styles and interests; and dispositions to use certain instructional tools and avoid others. It would be interesting to know if tendencies for these behaviors also are dependent on subjects taught; for example, reading as compared with science, an area many teachers avoid because they feel ill prepared, or social studies, disliked by some teachers and treated with benign neglect.

In the early days of research on teachers and the Myers-Briggs Type Indicator, Carlyn (1977) studied the relationship between personality characteristics and teaching preferences of prospective teachers. She found that some were more interested in administrative functions and others had a strong need for independence and creativity. Some preferred planning entire school programs, and others enjoyed working with small groups of students. Some people liked action and variety more than quiet and reflection. Some liked to work with their colleagues in groups, but others preferred to work alone or with one person. Some got impatient with slow jobs and complicated procedures. Others could work on one thing for a long time, resenting any interruptions.

Carlyn concluded in her study that teachers of different personality type preferences also prefer different kinds of teaching situations. These kinds of preferences and values help explain why, for example, some teachers experiment with modifications and materials, while others resist or just never seem to get around to doing it. It is important for consulting teachers and co-teachers to be aware of this.

A person's perception of the environment reflects and is filtered through one's own stage of development (Oja, 1980). Is it any wonder that teacher behaviors in the classroom and around the school differ? In an effort to develop collaborative norms for its school context, one district offered enculturation experiences that included getting-to-know-you activities using an instrument titled the Keirsey Temperament Sorter and a companion book *Please Understand Me* (Keirsey & Bates, 1978). Several years later, the participants still remembered the activity as providing their first glimpses of their co-educators' uniqueness and the group's diversity (Roy & O'Brien, 1991).

As teachers reflect on their own preferences and become more adept at discerning those of their colleagues, they also become more insightful about tuning in to students in ways that help them match differentiated curriculum to learners' needs. They are more ready and willing to relate to colleagues' styles—not to do the same work in the same ways but to respect others' aims and merge their efforts.

■ ■ ■ ■ ■

ACTION 3.2
Sharing a Professional Experience

In a small group of four or five people, describe an experience from your teaching days or your school days as a student in which you put forth significant effort but ended up feeling unappreciated, not affirmed, and perhaps a bit of a failure in that instance. After everyone has shared a personal example (with people having the option of passing if they wish), discuss how members of the group felt about each other's disappointing professional experience. To practice feeling empathy for those whose preferences differ from yours, show a genuinely caring attitude for their disappointment, especially if it was not something that would have bothered you all that much. Then discuss together what this group activity meant to you.

When a group of educators with different preferences collaborate, they have the opportunity to contribute a variety of strengths to the interaction. Those who like to bring up new possibilities and suggest ingenious ways of approaching problems will benefit from having other people supply pertinent facts and keep track of essential details. When some are playing devil's advocate to find flaws and resist change, others can contribute by agreeing, conciliating and generating enthusiasm to sell the idea (Myers, 1980). Opposite types may or may not attract, but they definitely need to be present in order to achieve maximum team productivity. Managing differences elegantly is a challenge for a collaborative consultant or co-teacher. As stressed earlier, the primary goal in consulting, collaborating, and working as a team is not to think alike, but to think together. Each one's personal preferences and professional perspectives are important elements for making interactions productive.

In sum, differences in schools and classrooms are not just role-related disagreements between adult and child, or teacher and student, or administrator and teacher, or paraeducator and supervising teacher. They offer individual orientations to a world that encompasses unique learning styles, variability in personal values, and differentiated work styles. These differences, when understood and appreciated, can be quite helpful in determining ways to help those with exceptional learning needs be successful and productive.

REFLECTION 3.1

Plans for a Collaborative Activity

As you did for Reflection 2.1 in Chapter 2, single out one of your favorite lessons or subject areas and imagine that you and a consultee will be team-teaching this material. Think about who would be consulting teacher and who would be consultee. Or perhaps you both would be classroom teachers, getting ready to co-teach. How would you go about preparing for this? Although it is important to know something about your co-teacher's styles and preferences, are there things you should study about *yourself* first before embarking on this team endeavor?

What if the only plan time you can possibly spare is before school and although you are "a lark," you are fairly sure your co-teacher-to-be is "an owl." Besides that, you bring your lunch, and your colleague eats in the school cafeteria. This is just a start on ways you sense the two of you are different. So how can you share information about possible differences pleasantly and agreeably with your colleague in order to move ahead to effective co-planning that will lead to successful co-teaching?

USING ADULT DIFFERENCES CONSTRUCTIVELY IN SCHOOLS

Mutual outlooks and shared frames of reference are important for building rapport and exploring a classroom problem or student need. However, the greatest team success will come from making sincere efforts to respect members' differences, value the contributions, and communicate in ways that both respect *and* accommodate a variety of verbal and non-verbal styles. Needing to view matters through a shared "lens," yet doing so with different "eyes," may seem to be a conundrum but can be a useful exercise. (See Figure 3.2.) Divergent points of view often predispose people to see problems in ways that cause confusion and mild conflict. However, when managed by skilled collaborators who accept diversity as a strength in teamwork, divergent points of view are definite assets to problem solving.

FIGURE 3.2   Viewing Matters through Different Lenses

REFLECTION 3.2

Compare and Contrast

Compare and contrast the following pairs of characteristics and think about which one in each pair suits you best in most instances when you are "free to be you."

I offer my opinions to others readily.	*or*	I pause before responding.
I am very interested in specific facts.	*or*	I am interested in many possibilities.
I tend to hold firmly to my convictions.	*or*	I tend to compromise for agreement.
I like to have things decided and settled.	*or*	I like things open and flexible.
I like to work with others.	*or*	I like to work alone.
I work steadily.	*or*	I work in bursts, slack off, and return to work.

With another person—perhaps one who seems to differ from you in many ways—talk about your preferences and theirs. Then reflect on how these characteristics might surface and whether they would require attention in a school setting where you are co-teaching or working as a partner on a team.

Differences When Communicating

Isabel Briggs Myers, developer of the Myers-Briggs Type Indicator, which has been one of the most widely used instruments of personality assessment for more than a half century, emphasized that many communication problems among people stem from differing outlooks and values. Myers's work demonstrated that a statement can seem clear and reasonable to one person but sound meaningless or preposterous to another (Myers, 1974). One person may want an explicit statement of a problem before considering possible solutions, and another might want at least the prospect of an interesting possibility before buckling down to facts. Still another may demand a beginning, a logically arranged sequence of points, and an end (*especially* an end, Myers cautions). One might listen only if the discussion starts with a concern for people and any possible effects of the issue on people.

Myers (1974) contended that it "is human nature *not* to listen attentively if one has the impression that what is being said is going to be irrelevant or unimportant" (p. 4). Communication is such a critical process in successful consultation and collaboration that it will be the singular topic of Chapter 7; however, for an advance preview, think *listening*. Educators can learn a great deal from talking with (and listening to!) colleagues with whom they differ both in theory and in practice. If a common vocabulary is used and a framework of respect for individuality is in place, teamwork will be much more productive. When individuality is regarded as pleasant and interesting, teamwork will be much more enjoyable.

Differences When Problem Finding and Problem Solving

Individual differences have impacts on the problem-finding and problem-solving processes. Some individuals proceed slowly and methodically to identify problems and work out possible solutions, while others zero in on potential problems right away and propose actions very quickly. One person may focus more on the problem using the facts, while another focuses on the process and meanings behind the facts. To reiterate, the discrepancies may seem frustrating to those involved, but there is considerable benefit to having many approaches represented. If educators must resolve a situation without input from others, they can role-play different types of approaches by generating multiple perspectives and in this way obtain at least some of those benefits.

No specific preference is predictive of success in communication or problem solving within the group; however, research shows that teams with a complete representation of types *outperform virtually any single-type or similar-type team* (Blaylock, 1983). The likelihood of having such team versatility is better than might be expected, for a single group of several individuals will include many variations. With pooled experiences, interests, and abilities, the problem-solving process is enriched.

Differences When Evaluating and Reporting

As mentioned in Chapter 2, there is perhaps no area of teaching that creates more tension and potential discord than testing and grading, whether it be among teachers, between teachers and students, between teachers and parents, between teachers and administrators, and between teachers and the coaches who want their athletes to be eligible to play. Consensus on evaluation methods probably will never be reached across all factions, but thoughtful and candid discussion sessions are a place to start.

Using collaborative consultation services in the area of evaluation can be particularly productive. For such services to be successful, good questions, open minds, and forthright sharing of opinions are required. The dialectical conversation may heat up when hot-button issues of eligibility, rewards, honors, and competitions are part of the conversation. At such times, all of the skills of awareness, responsiveness, and conciliation will be helpful. But having an opportunity to express one's sincere and honest viewpoints on assessment, grading, and reporting policies may defuse potential flare-ups of disagreement and quell discord within school environments and between school and home educators.

Recall the section on social taxonomy stages in Chapter 2. Collaboration and teamwork to develop acceptable policies on assessment and evaluation for an entire school context can help an individual teacher, especially a preservice teacher, feel less isolated and more involved.

■ ■ ■ ■ ■

ACTION 3.3
Preferred Recognition and Reward

Form groups of four to six and discuss ways in which *you* would like to be recognized, and perhaps rewarded, reinforced, or praised, for something you did that demanded effort and skill. Remember to draw upon what was brought to mind for further consideration in

Reflection 3.2 and earlier in Reflection 2.1. Then talk over with the group the variations in outcomes that different individuals prefer. How might this affect a work context such as the school and the teaching profession? What actions could you take to show respect for professional perspectives and personal preferences of others with whom you will work?

FACILITATING TEAM INTERACTIONS

Good teamwork calls for recognition and use of certain valuable differences among all members of the team (Kummerow & McAllister, 1988; Myers, 1974). The most effective teams do not agree all the time, but they use their differences constructively (Kummerow & McAllister, 1988; Truesdell, 1983). Individuals have far more potential than they use at any one time, and *the power of this potential in team settings is exponential.* Outcomes of successful team building are positive interdependence, individual accountability, effective face-to-face interaction, collaborative skills, and group processing skills. These are especially important to introduce and develop in teacher preparation programs. Preservice teachers will need practice and modeling in interaction before they join experienced teachers for such professional activities as IEP conferences, staff meetings, and co-teaching activities.

When problem-solving, the collaborating team should use the strengths of each person to identify the problem or need, and then generate ideas for addressing that need, organize plans and divide up what should be done, determine evaluation procedures, follow through with plans including the assessment, and finally, follow up with further planning if needed. Some pertinent questions to consider when discussing how each person can contribute best to the group are:

- Does our team have a mix of experiences, talents, and preferences? If we think we don't, is there something practical that can be done about it?
- Does the group appreciate the constructive potential of adult differences?
- Is everyone ready and willing to contribute in her or his own way?
- Is each person looking forward to having a good professional relationship while finding ways to help students learn?

By valuing the contribution of each member on the team, the group can come to more fully formed, student-centered decisions. Valuing individual differences requires more than merely tolerating them. It means accepting the fact that people are different and the world is the better for the diversity (E. Murphy, 1987). See Figure 3.3 for a 10-point interaction process that shows respect for diversity and constructive use of differing personal preferences among co-educators.

Researchers have noted that variability in teaching is underplayed, with little information available about how individual knowledge and beliefs may interact to help or hinder innovation (Brownell et al., 2006). Teacher preparation programs must be enterprising and direct in preparing future teachers to understand individual differences among adults who will be their co-educators some day. Teacher reflection also is underrated as an influence on how innovative and resourceful the teacher can be. The

FIGURE 3.3   Personal Preferences: Demonstrating Respect and Constructive Use

1. Talk and listen, really listen, together.
2. Value individual differences of adults just as you do the individual differences of young students.
3. Express your own preferences regarding the issue(s) if pertinent.
4. Explore resolutions or compromises together.
5. Summarize collective discussion points and any tentative agreements.
6. Seek input from other parties and information from other sources if the process becomes stalled.
7. Agree on a plan or procedure, with give-and-take arbitration if necessary.
8. Note who compromised more and who compromised less, so as to reverse next time if at all feasible.
9. After concluding the planning session, talk for a little while about the collaborative process to reflect on outcomes and pinpoint areas that can improve.
10. Follow up on outcomes resulting from the interaction.

Reflection activities here are intended as nonthreatening and easy-to-use activities for developing the reflective process and recursive thinking about teaching and learning.

When a group of educators with different type preferences collaborate, they have the opportunity to contribute a variety of strengths within the interaction. Those who like to bring up new possibilities and suggest ingenious ways of approaching problems will benefit from having other people supply pertinent facts and keep track of essential details. When some are finding flaws and holding to an existing policy, others contribute by selling the idea, conciliating, and arousing enthusiasm (Myers, 1980).

Educators can learn a great deal from talking to colleagues with whom they differ both theoretically and methodologically (Gallessich, 1974). With a common vocabulary and a framework of respect for individuality, teamwork can be much more productive.

CAUTIONS TO NOTE WHEN ADDRESSING INDIVIDUAL DIFFERENCES

The caution "A little knowledge is a dangerous thing" should be heeded when pondering the issue of individual differences among co-educators. First and foremost, as noted previously, collaborators can work from awareness of personality-assessment or learning-style concepts without having the formal profiles of individuals in that group; in fact, for most circumstances they probably *should* do so. It is not always possible, necessary, or even desirable to attempt to ferret out people's preferences with a formal measure. The most important step is to adopt the attitude that human differences are not behaviors acted out with intentions of irritating and alienating each other. Rather, they are systematic, orderly, consistent, often unavoidable realities of the way people prefer to use their perception and judgment. The wonderful offshoot of this is that *each set of preferences is valuable, and at times indispensable, in every field.*

Well-researched personality or temperament theory does not condone or promulgate labeling of individuals. Teachers are aware that learning styles theory and right-brain/left-brain research have fallen victim at times to unwarranted use of labels: "He's so right-brained, that he can't..." and "She's a concrete sequential, so she won't...." The world probably does not need any more labels for individuals, and this is particularly cogent in the field of special education, where a long-standing mantra resonates that "labels are for jelly jars, not kids."

In the matter of personal preferences, advice about labeling probably would hold true for adults as well. Others tend to be wary of people who claim to know all about them and proceed to give unsolicited interpretations. The term "psychopest" was coined for such individuals (Luft, 1984). Linking personal styles to semantics briefly, teachers also should be cautious in using language tools—as just one example, the idiom, which can be a combination of personal preferences, professional perspectives, and off-the-cuff labels. People often use sayings lightly such as, "She has her head in the clouds" or "He operates in the fast lane." Common expressions that are accepted or ignored by persons accustomed to them are sometimes perceived in a negative way by others, especially those for whom English is a second or third language.

As a final caution, it is inappropriate and unwise to assume too much from analysis of individual differences. Recall that every person has all the characteristics within herself or himself, to bring out and use or not, depending on circumstances. No generalization should be applied to a single case, for any case could be an anomaly. Teachers who assume something like "Her type does not like to act" may not invite that student to audition for a part in the school play. If a teacher believes that a student will not enjoy participating in simulations, he may be denying that student necessary opportunities to explore new curricular territory and develop new skills. These lessons were learned "the hard way" in uses and misuses of learning styles theory by others before us and should not have to be repeated and relearned at the expense of our students and colleagues.

All good teaching methods have value for some students at certain times and in particular places. By the same token, each method will be received differently by each student. Valuing individual differences requires more than mere toleration. It means accepting the fact that people *are* different and the world is the better for the diversity (E. Murphy, 1987). Teacher preparation programs must be more enterprising and effective in preparing graduates to have superlative ability for understanding individual differences among their professional colleagues as well as their students. Much more research is needed on the constructive use of individual differences among adults, especially in the areas of school consultation, collaboration, and co-teaching.

REFLECTION 3.3

What Is Your View?

Mr. Garcia, a general classroom teacher, and Ms. Abernathy, a special education consulting teacher, often disagree with each other in meetings and conferences at school. Ms. Abernathy feels the need to suggest ideas and arrangements for the general classroom to teachers of students assigned to her because of special needs. Mr. Garcia tries not to be openly critical but has trouble concealing his perception that her ideas lack focus, practicality, direction, and long-term benefits. He considers her efforts at remediation and intervention to be somewhat hit-or-miss.

Ms. Abernathy does not want to appear pushy or play the "expert" role, but she thinks their shared student is frustrated and bored with the sameness of assignments and the emphasis on correctives. She had hoped that Mr. Garcia would like her ideas for flexibility and risk-taking to motivate the student, especially in the use of new technology that could complement the classroom material. At times the communication between them seems completely shut down, although an air of professional politeness is maintained. Interestingly, at social functions and in casual encounters, they seem to get along well and enjoy sharing ideas and experiences not related to school activities, especially when they talk about how their ancestors came to this country with nothing and made a good life for their families.

1. Reflect on their differences in general principles of type theory, and how these differences may be a damper on their ability to collaborate for students with special needs.

2. Then further reflect on some ways they could be encouraged to sand the rough edges off their differences and combine their best qualities to develop good instructional materials and strategies. Who might initiate movement toward this resolution, and how could that be accomplished?

A PREVIEW OF COMPETENCIES FOR COLLABORATORS

Guided by principles of caring and sharing, co-educators work together voluntarily with equal ownership as a team. Those who would be collaborative school consultants should ready themselves as students in their teacher education programs and continue to prepare themselves through professional development activities for working together. When they collaborate and co-teach, they are modeling the interactive skills their students will need for their future.

Competencies for collaborative consultation can be grouped helpfully into categories for frequent review of progress in development. (See Reflection 3.4.) It is good to keep close at hand a checklist of competencies needed that rise out of material presented in the chapters. A comprehensive checklist will be provided in the final chapter, to be used as a self-assessment tool and a reminder of one's purposes and goals for consultation, collaboration, co-teaching, and teamwork in a variety of venues.

REFLECTION 3.4

Descriptors for Competencies

It is not too hard to think up and jot down lists of abstract words—adjectives in this case, for checklists and rubrics to evaluate people-specific competencies. But what do the words *really* mean? For instance, courageous—what *is* being courageous? Or zany—what is that like?

When we think about what qualities would define a very competent consulting teacher, or collaborative consultant, or co-teacher, we begin to form a mental picture from their characteristics of what it would be like to work with them. What would it be like to collaborate with one who is open to ideas, flexible, and unbiased? Or a consultant who is nonjudgmental and takes ownership of mistakes when things go wrong? How would it be to co-teach with a colleague who is reliable and goes the extra mile?

Select just a few words from one or more of the categories and put them into composites for these roles: a consulting teacher for special education, a collaborative consultant for related services, a co-teacher in a general classroom, a co-educator parent who is very involved in school programs, or an educational role of your choosing. While doing this, consider carefully what the words mean and how they blend into a profile of an educator with whom you would like to work.

- *Facilitative*—This includes listening, being nonjudgmental, open to ideas, flexible, patient, unbiased, objective, properly persistent, diplomatic, owning mistakes, brief when needed, guiding, dependable, open-minded, and putting forth effort.
- *Caring*—This includes being responsive, considerate, thoughtful, reliable, going the extra mile, perceptive, sensitive, empathic, kind, personable, sincere, approachable, respectful, tactful, and positive.
- *Knowledgeable*—For this, one should be skilled, up-to-date, resourceful, wanting to learn, knowledge-linker, applying research, informed about legislation and policies, current on curriculum and teaching strategies, and capable of leading.
- *Ethical*—This involves prioritizing appropriately, being communicative, sharing, punctual, true to word and commitments, preserving privacy and confidentiality, and courageous in thought, word, and deed.

You can turn this Reflection into an Action by discussing combinations of adjectives with others. The descriptions could become want-ads, or recognition posters, or awards plaques. Do you or your group know people who already fit your profiles?

Collaborative consultants support students, families, their schools, and the community while advocating for schools and students at every opportunity. What role could be better suited to the aspirations of would-be teachers?

CASE STUDY FOR ADDRESSING PERSONAL PREFERENCE DIFFERENCES

This event takes place in the school district's conference room, about the same time that Vignette 1 in Chapter 1 is occurring among a few teachers in the high school faculty room. Three special education teachers are talking before their special education director arrives for a planning meeting.

Secondary-Level Learning Disabilities Teacher: I understand we're here to decide how we're going to inform staff and parents about the collaborative consultation practices we'll be implementing soon. I for one am scheduled to begin working with an English teacher at the high school. But I think we here should be on the same page first with the overall picture of just what it is we'll be doing in these kinds of roles.

Behavioral Disorders Teacher: Definitely. I have a really basic question. What am I going to do the first week—make that the first day, as a consulting teacher? I understand you had some experience with collaboration and team teaching in your former position out-of-state, but this is new to the rest of us.

Gifted Education Teacher: I agree. I've been thinking about all those personalities and teaching styles and subject areas we'll be dealing with, not to mention the uniqueness of each student. Teachers won't all like or want the same things for them, even for the students they share.

Secondary Learning Disabilities Teacher: Well, I doubt this is something we can become experts in very quickly because this district has not had a history of teachers working together very much. From my past experience, now that you have mentioned it, I found that the key to success with collaborative consultation and co-teaching is process skills—communicating, listening, organizing, contributing, forgiving, apologizing, trying again—you, know, "people skills."

Gifted Education Teacher: Good that you mentioned co-teaching; I think I'm going to be asked to team teach in a few classes. So that will require some reflection on my part before sitting down and interacting with those people. But at the same time we have to take into account the materials and the methods that each student needs in order to learn. I'm a bit apprehensive about it all, but I'm willing to try it.

Behavioral Disorders Teacher: I guess I am, too. I've been thinking for some time now that our current methods of dealing with learning and behavior problems are not as effective and efficient as they should be. I suppose we must be optimistic and approach it from the perspective of the possible benefits both students *and* we teachers could have when we all get comfortable doing it.

This scene and the Chapter 1 scene involve teachers, but that group is general education teachers and this group is made up of special education personnel. Each group is expecting to interact with the other soon. The special education director is arriving shortly for a planning meeting with the special education consulting teachers. This is the situation and these are the facts. The assumptions are that both groups seem a bit ill at ease about collaboration and wonder how it will affect *them*. Even so, they are well aware that they must think of students' needs first.

As the general education teachers await more information about the collaborative consulting and anticipate that there will be an orientation meeting where they will receiving more information about the program and have an opportunity to interact with the special education teachers, they may be composing some questions for which they will seek answers. What might some of those questions be?

As for the special education group awaiting the arrival of the director, what questions is the director preparing to address? And does the director anticipate any major problems? It is typical for special educators in collaborative consultant roles and occasional co-teaching roles to be concerned about:

- *Space*—for office work and materials storage, for conferencing, and for working with students

- *Opportunity to teach*—to work with students, not just adults
- *Expected protocol*—for making requests of families, interacting with them, and providing feedback on their student's progress; also for requesting plan time with teachers to become acquainted with their curriculums, their teaching practices, and student needs
- *Procedures*—for doing paperwork, scheduling IEP conferences, preserving confidentiality, making contacts with families of students, and grading and reporting
- *Assistance*—from paraeducators, clerical staff, and others
- *Accountability*—how their work will be evaluated and by whom

Undoubtedly there will be more questions, and it is likely that more than one orientation meeting will be needed, because so far this just addresses the concerns from the group. The special education director will have an agenda, also. It will most likely involve:

- Responding to questions from the group
- Assigning attendance centers, supervising administrators, teachers, and students
- Discussing matters of protocol, legality, courtesy, and common sense, such as always checking in with the secretary who needs to be able to find them or report their location, touching base with the building administrator by leaving a card or a friendly wave in person, not taking student photos without the proper signed permissions, and greeting faculty and support staff (including custodians, bus drivers, and food service staff who are all very important in the school lives of students with special needs) as often as possible.

The special education director will provide the school handbook(s) and any other policy documents and probably will ask the group to tour their buildings and become familiar with the layout—including storm shelters, restroom areas, and playgrounds. Far-fetched as this may seem, others have found that it is wise to note the dress code, formal or informal, in each building. One traveling teacher said that in one of her afternoon schools she was treated with reserve until she gathered the courage to discuss it with a key teacher in the building. "You come all dressed up as if you are a supervisor," was the reply, "and we come dressed to work." So, because her morning staff did dress "up," she developed a system of dressing "down" at lunchtime for the afternoon—off with the heels, earrings and blazers, and on with the sneakers and sweater. Rapport with that school staff improved almost immediately.

ACTION 3.4
What Is Your Preference?

In groups of three or four, spend three minutes discussing each of the following:

Would you rather vacation in the Bahamas or in Alaska? Why?

Would you rather work in elementary school or secondary school? Why?

Would you prefer to explore deep ocean or deep space? Why?

Would you rather win a new car or a new, installed kitchen? Why?

Then, with the whole group, share some interesting and unusual things you learned about each other from this activity.

Co-educators who share their contradictory viewpoints and diverse insights with each other will find that if they are valued by colleagues for their differences, they can search politely and professionally for commonalities that will add harmony and efficiency to their interactions. By pooling the differences and maximizing the skills of all, they can generate learning climates in which students also broaden their understanding of human differences and learn to respect and value diversity. They will be modeling the respectful collaboration and productive teamwork that children and youth will be required to demonstrate in their futures.

TECHNOLOGY TO STRENGTHEN COLLABORATIVE SCHOOL CONSULTATION AND TEAMWORK

New tools of technology have the potential to help or to harm. A case in point is that electronic systems provide communication, organization, and management processes that save time and alleviate frustrations from earlier times such as telephone tag; however, they can create misunderstandings and breaches of confidentiality. So they are not to be treated casually. Careful selection of the tools, clear understanding of their functions, and thoughtful use in the appropriate circumstances are essential for educators.

Rapid growth of e-mailing and text messaging have rendered the telephone-tag nuisance a thing of the past. The synchronous characteristic of telephones and face-to-face exchanges seem antiquated and cumbersome compared with the modern capabilities of e-mail and texting to connect and manage messages asynchronously. But a note of caution is in order. There are potential disadvantages that must be addressed if asynchronous systems are to operate in the best interests of students and teachers. Not least is absence of emotional tone and body-language signals that can deliver an electronic message in a flat or puzzling way. Another is the potential for a confidentiality breach resulting from sending to the wrong person or to multiple (unwanted) receivers in error. This would be unfortunate in many cases, but in matters of special education and students identified for special education services, the ramifications could be severe. Privacy is an issue if others can access electronic files, and to carry that a step further, confidentiality is compromised when files can be retrieved inappropriately. These problems may be just as likely to occur with printed material, but the negative effects may be more broadly distributed and less easily rectified.

Cell phones, and now smartphones, can be nuisances in schools, necessitating enforcement of specific rules for their use. Few people have escaped the annoyance of having to listen to one side of a conversation in stores, on planes, in medical waiting rooms, and even walking down the street. Rules can be made for class time, but what to do when it is a class of adult students who have left their children in child care and may receive an emergency call from a panicked child-care provider? Development of a fair and consistent policy could be the productive outcome of collaboration among instructors and students. Just having the discussion might bring about changed behaviors for use of electronic devices!

It is the purpose, not the novelty, that makes technology important for educators. An astute teacher uses electronic tools to enhance learning by encouraging their students to retrieve information that fits the course content or expands their outlook on the subject. Jukes, McCain, and Crockett (2011) indicate that technology can empower students to deal with course material at their own pace, to learn when and where it is best for the individual student. They can take their learning beyond the school grounds and engage in the discovery learning that educators have promoted for decades. Extending this concept even further is the movement toward virtual education, educational opportunity available through Internet connectivity by means of a distance education model. One very significant benefit to be gained from alternative learning options such as virtual education spurred by technology is the potential for increases in high-school graduation rates (Carpenter, 2012).

Some educators have raised issues of practicality, health, and safety that can result from indiscriminate use of electronic technology. Most readers of news articles are aware that there is an ongoing debate about possible effects of hand-held devices on the brain with heavy usage over long periods of time. This concern and others warrant serious discussion among educators who are responsible for the physical and emotional welfare of minors.

Because many technology tools are new, and more are arriving all the time, some devil's advocates questions pinpointing their use and abuse are in order:

- Do these tools make us more effectively communicative or less so?
- Do they make us feel more accessible or more isolated?
- Do they cause us to be more attentive or less attentive when reading and studying?
- Are we more efficient now with these tools, or more burdened?
- Can heavy use of hand-held electronic devices by young people over time cause physiological damage to developing brains?
- Do we monitor attitudes toward technology to ensure we are making the best use of these tools?

Such questions bear analysis and careful study by educators who are exploring ways technology can help, not hinder, their aims. They can do so through self-study, tutorials, professional development activities, and networking with other educators. Or they might want to become mentees in technology. But they should avoid "technopests" (cousins to the "psychopests," who claim to know all about a topic and proceed to give unsolicited interpretations) as being less help and more nuisance in the long run for a busy educator.

Electronically talented students can be excellent mentors for a technologically challenged teacher, especially if that student has special learning needs. The experience could be uplifting for students *and* their teachers. The entire process of developing skills to use technology in teaching and learning spans all disciplines and generations, with many opportunities yet to come for interesting professional collaboration and teamwork.

ETHICS OF COLLABORATION WHEN PERSONAL PREFERENCES DIFFER

Working together in harmony is a subtle, complex process to be developed over time, with an attitude of respect and caring. Each should strive to think and do, with finesse, to function as a consensus-building member of a collaborative team that models personal integrity and genuine consideration for others on the team.

Self-study of personal preferences and ensuing group discussions can be intriguing. Just about everybody likes to share their own likes and dislikes and react to those of others. But occasionally participants may become so enthused that they:

- Share inappropriately
- Generalize unadvisedly
- Stereotype inadvertently
- Draw others out indiscriminately

It is important that not only the leader but also each participant in a group takes active part in keeping discussions practical, helpful, appropriately personal, and objectively impersonal. This is especially important for consulting teachers, who are often out and about the building and the district more than classroom teachers, interacting with many other people in several attendance centers. They must take utmost care to keep sensitive school news in that school and confidential matters confidential. They must not carry tales or violate confidences. It is wise to make as few remarks about other teachers' instruction and classrooms as possible. Finally, they must know when to keep trying in collaborative relationships *and* when it is time to get out. More will be presented on this delicate issue later.

TIPS FOR USING ADULT DIFFERENCES CONSTRUCTIVELY

1. Take the time and effort to assess perspectives and preferences of colleagues for teaching and collaborating.
2. Remember the maxim that minds, like parachutes, work best when they are open.
3. Encourage each member of a collaborative group to share knowledge and perceptions about self and issues so as to establish a solid framework in which to discuss problems and needs.
4. Read material that helps you become more knowledgeable and understanding about people, families, and communities that are very different from your own.
5. Interact with every other staff member as often as you can, even if only for a minute or two (and bearing in mind that sometimes shorter is better).
6. Listen to the other person's point of view and seek to understand that person's ideas and meaning.
7. Really care about other persons' feelings and ideas and show it through your actions.
8. Appreciate perceptions and preferences that are different from your own by engaging in a dialectical conversation, but do not feel that it is necessary to change your position or to convert the other person to your position.

9. Be flexible and adaptable, for change takes time, and it must be preceded by awareness and acceptance of the need to change.

10. Respect the rights of others to hold different beliefs. Even if people do not agree, they must assume that others are acting in ways they believe are appropriate.

ADDITIONAL RESOURCES

Jung, C. G. (1923). *Psychological types*. New York: Harcourt Brace.

Keirsey, D. (1998). *Please understand me II: Temperament character intelligence*. Del Mar, CA: Prometheus Nemesis.

Lawrence, G. (1993). *People types and tiger stripes: A practical guide to learning styles* (3rd ed.).
Gainesville, FL: Center for Applications of Psychological Type.

Myers, I. B. (1980). *Gifts differing*. Palo Alto, CA: Consulting Psychologists Press.

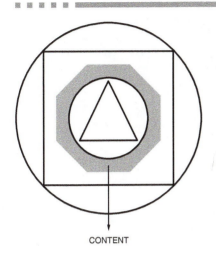

CONTENT

Content for Working Together as Co-Educators

PART II, THE SHADED-OCTAGON CONTENT SECTION, includes three chapters. Chapter 4 introduces facets of frameworks and key components of those frameworks for collaborative school consultation; Chapter 5 focuses on problem finding, problem solving, and planning by co-educators; and Chapter 6 zeros in on skills for managing and organizing consultative and collaborative activities in schools.

4

Components, Structures, and Methods for Collaboration, Consultation, and Teamwork

WHY DO PEOPLE CHOOSE EDUCATION AS A CAREER? Some of us over the course of many years have posed that question to experienced teachers, graduate students in education, and undergraduate students in teacher preparation programs. The aggregate of responses can be summed up in a few sentences:

"I want to make a difference in children's lives."

"I want to do my part to make the world a better place."

"I want to help kids grow and develop their potential."

Some teachers, especially those at the secondary level, also mention having a fondness for their curricular areas and wanting to share that enthusiasm with students. But other factors that educators could have mentioned, such as job opportunity, steady salary, respect from the public, anticipation of several weeks off in the summer, or a desire to follow in the footsteps of an admired teacher, are farther down on their lists.

Goals to mold younger generations and make the world into a better place are lofty ones. In the past such goals were predicated on expectations of being in "my classroom," with "my students," using "the teaching ideas I have been assembling and now can put into practice." But these goals no longer fit neatly into the environment of twenty-first century schools and classrooms. Teachers are being called on to work in more collegial ways by consulting and collaborating and sometimes teaching in partnerships with their colleagues, for *our* students in our *inclusive* classrooms, with our *shared* plans and ideas. Content (see the shaded octagon of Figure 4.1) for addressing collaborative consultation goals in a wide range of educational contexts will be featured in this chapter.

FOCUSING QUESTIONS

1. What four key components are necessary for strong collaborative school consultation programs?
2. What, in brief, are the historical and theoretical bases of collaborative school consultation?
3. What structural facets are inherent in a collaborative school consultation method?
4. What models of collaborative school consultation have been designed and put to use in development of a method for collaborative school consultation?

5. How might educators tailor collaborative school consultation so it is suited to their school contexts, and what tools of technology can facilitate this process?

6. Why is it important to nurture an ethical climate when providing collaborative consultation services for students with exceptional learning needs?

KEY TERMS

collaborative school consultation models

example

Instructional Consultation (IC) model

model

novice teacher

parity

preservice teacher

Professional Development School (PDS)

Resource/Consulting Teacher Program (R/CT) model

Schoolwide Enrichment Model (SEM)

theme interference

triadic model

VIGNETTE 4

The setting is a school administration office where the superintendent, the high school principal, and the special education director are having an early-morning conference.

Special Education Director: I've assigned five people on our special education staff to be collaborative consulting teachers in the schools we targeted at our last meeting.

Principal: I understand the high school is to be one of those schools.

Special Education Director: Yes, several classroom teachers will be involved. I've visited briefly with the English teacher who is getting a new student with learning disabilities and I've also had a special ed staff meeting to discuss collaborative consultation.

Principal: I'm all for trying a new approach, but at this point I'm not sure my staff understands very much about how this way of doing things is going to affect them.

Superintendent: Are you saying we need to spend a little more time at the drawing board to get the kinks out of the plan before handing it to the teachers?

Principal: Yes, and I think the parents also will want to know what will be happening. They'll want us to tell them specifically how this will benefit their child. Any time they think direct services are in jeopardy of being reduced, they get anxious, which is understandable.

Special Education Director: I've been compiling a file of theoretical background, research studies, program descriptions, even some cartoons and funny sayings to add a little levity if there are tense moments—you know the kind, like "a consultant is the one who stops by to borrow your watch and tell you what time it is." The things in the file focus on consultation and collaboration services and may shed light on some of our concerns. I'll get copies of the best of it to you and principals of the other designated schools. Maybe we should plan an inservice for teachers and some awareness sessions for parents, too, before we proceed, especially if we anticipate including some co-teaching.

Superintendent: That sounds good. Draft an outline, and it will be first thing on the agenda at next week's meeting. I'll get the word out to the other principals to be here. And, oh, the way I heard that consultant joke was, "He drives over from the *central office* to borrow your watch and tell you the time!

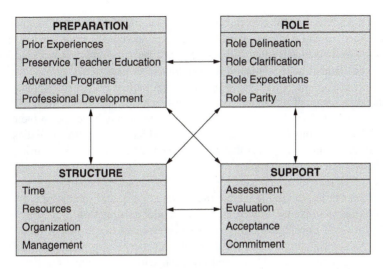

FIGURE 4.2   Key Components in Collaborative School Consultation

Those who will be participating in collaborative consultation services must voice their concerns and work through their feelings of uncertainty about the dynamics of their new roles. School administrators have a responsibility to encourage open, candid expressions of concerns and convene the participants to discuss issues before they escalate into problems.

Four essential components and sixteen subcomponents of consultation, collaboration, and teamwork processes are illustrated in Figure 4.2. The four major components are:

- Preparation
- Role
- Structure
- Support

PREPARATION FOR COLLABORATIVE SCHOOL CONSULTATION

When collaborative school consultation is embraced as a best practice for helping students with exceptional needs, all educators can benefit from preparation activities—administrators, teachers of both general education and special education, and related services and support staff, all of whom are expected to participate in the collaborations and teamwork. Preparation is fundamental for educators in four areas:

- *Prior experiences*—Although not often mentioned as part of formal teacher preparation, preexisting beliefs of would-be teachers that emanate from prior experiences are a core part of successful school-based relationships. Some have children of their own, and others have worked with children and youth in a variety of nonschool venues. Some have fond memories of their school days; others don't. Some may be embarking on teaching as a second career, while others plan to teach for only a few years. All have had life experiences from which they have learned much to form their perspectives and preferences, and to enhance the value of their services in the classroom: An educator is often called on to exercise wisdom when working with young people; the instructive equation is "Knowledge + Experience = Wisdom."

- *Preservice teacher education programs*—Instructors of teacher preparation courses and supervisors of practicum and student-teaching experiences must prepare preservice teachers for roles less autonomous than they may have had in their own teaching days. Students in teacher education should have orientation activities and guided practice in simulated roles that prepare them to become active participants as co-educators in their new teacher roles.
- *Advanced teacher education programs*—Teachers are becoming more supportive of the concept of working in collaborations and teams, and some aspire to have leadership roles in implementing collaborative school consultation.
- *Professional development programs*—Professional development for teachers with experience can strengthen their commitment to working with others as a team and motivate them to collaborate and co-teach with both novice teachers and veteran teacher colleagues.

Preservice Teacher Preparation Programs

Preservice teachers are postsecondary students in their final semesters of undergraduate education, where they are concentrating on many aspects of their chosen profession: curriculum, educational psychology, methods for teaching, development of professional portfolios, field experiences, practicum or student teaching, and involvement in professional organizations. Today's preservice teachers have grown up using the latest technology to connect, interact, and, to some extent, work with colleagues in cooperative groups. But it is not likely that a preservice teacher's interactions and group work have involved being a bona fide advocate for a third party (a client) with exceptional learning and behavioral needs or a consultee responsible for children with such needs. Nevertheless, in only months, if not weeks, preservice teachers will be doing just that—working in parity with experienced co-educators and interacting with families of typical and special needs students.

It is important that programs in teacher education prepare preservice teachers for collaboration with co-educators. College and university instructors need to:

- Assign articles and textbooks for studying the "what for" and "how to" aspects of collaboration, consultation, and co-teaching
- Instruct students in sociological principles that underlie professional interactions
- Model professional interactions in venues such as co-teaching and departmental meetings
- Arrange demonstrations of collaboration in authentic settings, such as observations of practicing teachers' interactions with family members of students, and simulated or actual IEP conferences (with signed permission of students' parents and teachers and coaching by the teachers on preserving confidentiality)
- Present situations and case studies where preservice teachers can respond to new scenarios that call for collaboration

Videotaping or audiotaping sessions with follow-up critique may not be pleasurable, but it certainly can be valuable experience to help novice teachers get ready for their very first professional roles. The more modeling of collaboration that postsecondary personnel can provide for preservice teachers, the better.

An example of collaboration at the institutional level is the Professional Development School (PDS). PDS partnerships around the country are multi-institutional endeavors to review teacher education and K–12 schools simultaneously. One such partnership is the collaborative reconstruction process for PDS involvement at Kansas State University. The College of Arts and Sciences faculty, College of Education faculty, and K–12 public school educators work together in collaboration, inquiry, program assessment, and professional development experiences (Shroyer, Yahnke, Bennett, & Dunn, 2007). This exemplary collaboration on behalf of students has resulted in college course modifications that entail curriculum redesign and development of new teacher education programs. Other universities are working with K–12 schools in PDS activities to improve teaching and learning at all educational levels. Professional development personnel have opportunities for key parts in PDS collaborations.

Although PDS and the professional learning communities noted earlier are two promising trends, some argue that even when university instructors emphasize the importance of collaborative teaching and learning in K–12 schools, not many of them *model* collaboration in their courses (Jones & Morin, 2000). In some districts, mentors and support groups have been established for new teachers to help ensure that they have a good first-year experience and do not fall into the ranks of teachers making early departures from the profession. With dedicated effort on the part of teacher education personnel and school district teachers working as partners, new teachers will be more prepared and comfortable with collaborative consultation and co-teaching formats from their first moments in schools alongside experienced teachers.

Novice Teachers   One new teacher called her first year in the classroom "my first year of learning" (McCaffrey, 2000). Her school setting had class sizes of eight to twelve students, a teacher and three or four paraeducators, and students with needs from physical disability to speech to occupational therapy, moving in and out of the classroom throughout the day. In preparation for each day, she came in early and stayed late, but the result was, nevertheless, frustration on her part and confusion among her students. The situation improved dramatically when she began seeking advice from experienced educators, whom she described as the *most underused and underappreciated resource* for beginning teachers.

New teachers often think that by discussing the problems they are having, they will be committing professional "suicide" (Carver, 2004). But it is not a sign of ineptitude to ask an experienced teacher, "Am I in about the right spot in the text for this time of year?" or "Is my instructional pace in this subject about right?" or "Have I set my expectations for students too high (or too low) or just about right?" In some areas after-school learning communities have been established, with attendance voluntary, as "a lifeline for new teachers in a challenging urban setting" (p. 58). Attendees focus not only on instruction but also on how to "navigate the bureaucracy of a large urban district."

Although first-year teachers have been the focus of numerous studies, few of those studies have focused on first-year *special education* teachers. Whitaker (2000) speaks out on the difficulty of being a beginner in special education and reports on results of focus groups she conducted to explore their concerns. Categories of need that were volunteered by the groups included:

- Mentoring accompanied by emotional support
- Information about special education paperwork
- IEP development and conferencing
- Awareness of school policies and procedures
- Means of locating and accessing materials
- Methods of discipline
- Curriculum building (a standard responsibility and practice for serving special needs)
- Management of routines
- Interaction with co-educators in order to work with them more effectively

To this list it would be realistic and practical to add interaction with families of students. Failure to designate this as a category would indicate a problem in and of itself.

Novice teachers can benefit greatly from observing more experienced colleagues and participating in consultations, by working as part of teaching teams, and by collaborating with a wide range of school personnel. They need knowledge about resources and strategies for sharing them, practice in interactive situations such as IEP conferences and parent conferences, and experience in showing accountability for their expenditures of time and energy in collaboration with co-educators. It bears mentioning again that a particularly important area of preparation for novice teachers while they are still forming their teaching philosophies and strategies is that of relating to families of students and working with them as valued co-educators (Kerns, 1992). A top-twelve list of practical recommendations for first-year teachers is located in the final chapter, Chapter 15, along with a competencies checklist for collaborators.

Two decades ago, Phillips, Allred, Brulle, and Shank (1990) recommended that teacher preparation programs provide introductory education courses in which general and special education preservice teachers participate jointly in practicum experiences that serve a diverse range of children's needs. This insightful plan requires concerted effort by college and university personnel, many of whom are not prepared to engage in collaboration and consultation with their own colleagues, let alone to facilitate development of their students' skills in these areas.

Some veteran educators may be reluctant to have novice teachers engage in consultation practices before they have had teaching experiences in the real world. Nevertheless, the seeds of awareness can and should be planted early to bear fruit later in important ways. After all, for most new teachers there is not much time to acquire experience between the last day of a teacher education program and the first day of stepping into a bustling school environment and their own inclusive classroom.

Mentoring of preservice and novice teachers in a collaborative atmosphere will benefit mentees and help students of those mentees. Mentorships can build confidence in the mentee and contribute professional satisfaction to the mentor as well. This type of professional partnership will be addressed later in more detail.

ACTION 4.1
Practicing Collaboration and Teamwork

This activity has aspects of the jigsaw cooperative learning strategy, but goes beyond a "learning about" action to a *doing for* action.

The whole group divides into three subgroups. One of the three subgroups is given a challenge to design and illustrate a layout for an ideal inclusive classroom. A helpful prelude to this is to find out the dimensions of a typical school room and make the layout somewhat to scale. Plan carefully for two high-traffic areas that can create behavioral and management problems—wastebasket(s) and wall pencil sharpeners—and allocate space for coats and backpacks. Then proceed to the fun part of arranging the room with books, artifacts, charts and boards, plants, and personal touches that reflect one's own teaching personality and style.

The second subgroup is to discuss needs of included students who have conduct and behavior disorders that can disrupt classroom decorum and interfere with other students' learning. After receiving the first subgroup's room plan, they study it and point out any potential problem areas, making suggestions for how the room plan would or might not accommodate the special needs. Does it include space and storage for special-needs equipment? Is the room accessible for all special needs? If the first group has not designated an area for co-teachers to conference, point that out and suggest an appropriate place. Should the room plan be returned for changes?

The third subgroup is charged with examining sets of basal texts and the accompanying instructor's manuals in core subjects to determine what, if any, accommodations and modifications are provided in students' books and instructor manuals. Some will be found sadly lacking but others may be quite good. Then this subgroup will look over the room plan and the special needs adaptations. What resources are available? What more is needed? Which are must-have items, and which are simply nice-to-have? They will want to discuss how faculty could collaborate in curriculum committees to select the best-of-the-best as basal texts and identify other supplementary materials.

Finally, all three subgroups meet to combine their work into a plan that provides a responsive and adaptive physical, academic, and socio-emotional environment for students in an inclusive classroom. With room arrangement, management strategies, and materials carefully planned, participants will be ready for that all-important first day of school.

Advanced Teacher Education Programs

Special education teachers who consult and collaborate with general education colleagues must understand the scope and sequence of grade-level curriculum content, and general education teachers must understand the curriculum and teaching strategies of special education teachers. General education teachers also must be knowledgeable and able to apply instructional and behavioral techniques for students with disabilities or their involvement will have little significant effect. Teacher education programs have far to go to meet these all-encompassing needs.

A source for standards pertaining to collaboration among special educators, families, other educators, related service providers, and community agency personnel is *NCATE/ CEC Program Standards, Programs for the Preparation of Special Education Teachers*, at www.cec.sped.org/Content/NavigationMenu/ProfessionalDevelopment/ProfessionalStandards/.

One of the standards (*Standard 10: Collaboration*) calls for special educators to collaborate with co-educators to ensure that exceptional learning needs (ELNs) of students are addressed in schools. It refers to special educators as resources for their colleagues in understanding the laws and policies of special education and in facilitating transitions of students across many learning settings and contexts.

Some states require preparation in consultation skills for teacher certification. Inclusion of this training in standards for accreditation of teacher education programs is one way to put more emphasis on the presence of collaborative teachers and school environments. Astute school administrators recruit people who welcome opportunities to work collaboratively with their colleagues. Every teacher preparation program and school administration program for collaborative consultation and co-teaching is unique. However, a basic program should include:

- Preparing experienced teachers and preservice teachers, along with school administrators and related services personnel, for working together collegially and productively
- Understanding and delineating co-educator roles
- Developing the frameworks and skills that help educators fulfill those roles
- Evaluating effectiveness of collaborations and co-teaching activities

Graduate and undergraduate degree programs need to provide experiences that extend beyond a "mentioning" mode of superficial exposure to professional interaction. Course syllabi should include not only the conventional learning strategies of lecture, reading, and discussion but also a strong focus on practical experiences and interactions. Small-group activities, simulations and role-plays, interviewing, videotaped and audiotaped consultation practice, reaction and reflection papers, resource gathering, practice with tools and strategies of technology, and assessment of outcomes will help educators to be more comfortable and capable in interactive school roles.

Professional Development Programs

Teachers may enter the profession with credentials that signal competence in content areas and skills in methods, but they are less likely to succeed and more likely to falter if they lack skills in working collaboratively with their colleagues and in partnerships with family members of their students. Consultation and collaboration programs can be planned and implemented through professional development activities that are tailored to each school context. Professional development techniques will be set aside for now but are the focus of Chapter 14.

ROLE RESPONSIBILITIES FOR COLLABORATIVE SCHOOL CONSULTATION

Educators are becoming more aware of the premise that when they collaborate to achieve a common goal, the results are better than when they work in isolation. Recall the well-known phrase "two heads are better than one." Indeed, several heads working together are better yet. Taking that expression even further, the whole of efforts combined is greater than the sum of its parts. A collaborative effort channels each individual educator's strengths and talents into a combined pool of rich resources for serving students' needs.

Role Delineation

A school role such as counselor, general classroom teacher, learning disabilities specialist, speech pathologist, or facilitator for gifted education programs does not automatically determine the situational role for collaborative consultation. Rather, the consultative role emanates from the situation. For example, the consultant might be one who is a parent providing information to the school administrator on the community's views about a school issue, or a learning disabilities teacher helping the coach assess a student athlete's problem in learning the play book, or a mentor giving the gifted program facilitator suggestions for materials to use with a student for enrichment and acceleration.

A consultee, on the other hand, collaborates with a consultant to provide direct service to the client. The client is the one with the identified need or problem. This total concept reflects the contemporary approach to special services where student *needs*, not student labels, determine services and delivery method, and an array of services is targeted and made available to address those needs. As indicated in Chapter 1, these three roles—consultant, consultee, and client—are interchangeable based on need and qualification to serve.

Role Clarification

In the process of collaborative school consultation, the next phase after delineating a role is to clarify how it will be consultative *and* collaborative. Until educators become comfortable with the collaborative concept, ambiguous feelings may persist. Even now teachers and school staff may be unsure of what consulting teachers are supposed to be doing. Classroom teachers may blame their own heavy responsibilities on the seemingly lighter caseloads of consulting teachers. One high school English teacher told a newly appointed consulting teacher, "If you were back in your classroom teaching five hours of English instead of 'facilitating' for a few high-ability students part of the time, my own student numbers wouldn't be so high." Some traveling teachers are envied for having their lunch periods on the road in between schools. Paradoxically, consulting teachers often have excessively demanding workloads due to travel time from school to school, conferences with teachers and students and perhaps parents, preparation of IEPs, and construction or location of special curriculum and materials. During one meeting of a half-dozen or so itinerant special education teachers in a state known for its harsh winters, the group members found that all of them had gone off the road during snow or ice storms at one time or another in their careers. If their workload and hazards of the work are too great, effectiveness of their services will be diminished severely. Time and energy needed for precise coordination and sensitive communication activities will be compromised.

Seamless, well-coordinated instructional plans for students with special needs require keen awareness of role responsibilities and service possibilities among all involved. A classroom teacher and a reading specialist may have information to share in addressing a struggling reader's strengths and deficits, yet know relatively little about each other's curriculum, educational priorities, or expectations for the student. They must coordinate their efforts or those efforts could be counterproductive. Consider this unfortunate situation: A learning disabilities teacher was instructing a student with reading problems to slow down and read more deliberately, while the reading teacher was encouraging him to read much more rapidly and had referred him to the gifted program facilitator. Before the situation came to light in the course of that referral process the student, a pleasant and cooperative child, was trying valiantly to please both teachers simultaneously.

Teachers may have doubts about the ability of a consulting teacher or co-teacher to fit into their classroom structure, especially if that other person is young and inexperienced. As one classroom teacher put it when asked about involving the special education consulting teacher, "I'd never ask *her* for help. What does she know about managing a full classroom of students whose needs are all over the chart? She's never dealt with more than five or six at a time, and she's not been responsible yet for a regular classroom an entire school year." Collaborative school consultation calls for people to relinquish their traditional roles in order to engage in partnerships and sometimes mentorships for sharing their knowledge and expertise and to be ready to learn things from the "new kid on the block." But a few educators are not prepared to trust, abandon lingering school traditions, and respect the budding talent of newer or less experienced colleagues. More than a few simply do not appreciate changes in the usual school structure.

Role Parity

Along with lack of clarification that leads to ambiguity and misunderstanding, special education teachers who travel back and forth among several schools, or who work somewhat apart in the building, may feel an absence of role parity in that they do not belong exclusively to any one school or faculty group. They may feel minimally important to students and the educational system, cut off from general classroom teachers because of differing responsibilities, and even isolated from special education colleagues because of distance and schedules.

As one obvious example of nonparity, when consulting teachers are absent, substitutes often are not provided for them. In fact, on occasion they may even be taken away from their own assignments to be the substitute for absent classroom teachers or to perform other tasks that come up suddenly. Consulting teachers have been asked to guide visitors on a school tour, drive the school bus, and perform secretarial tasks. These feelings are accentuated by the misconception that they have little to no ownership in student welfare and development. Some who travel extensively, usually in their own cars or vans from school to school, have been dubbed "windshield" personnel. As collaborative consultation becomes more widespread, these conditions are improving, but the problems still are far from being overcome.

General education teachers have their own complaints about lack of parity in collaborative enterprises. Oftentimes they are noticeably absent from lists of resources for helping students with needs, so much so that some special education teachers have picked up on the oversight and have asked why no one questions them about what *they* learn from the classroom teachers (Pugach & Johnson, 1989). They feel that not having been trained as specialists suggests that they are less able than the "experts" to consult with and assist. Meanwhile, as classroom teachers they are not going to wait with open arms for the specialists to come and save them. School life will proceed even in the absence of a consulting teacher or co-teacher. School bells will ring, classroom doors will open, and the school day will go on.

Lack of parity could broadcast a message of diminished importance for roles of some educators. Teachers who feel like second-class colleagues, not accepted or appreciated as a vital part of the staff, develop defenses that erode their enthusiasm and effectiveness. Role confusion and inequality also fuel stress that leads to burnout from the profession. Continuous, specific recognition and reinforcement of consulting and collaborating teacher services for student development are important for credibility and professional morale.

Role Expectations

Sometimes co-educators have unreasonable expectations for partnerships or team involvement. They may be anticipating instant success and miraculous student progress in a very short while. Then, if positive results with students are slow to occur, attitudes may range from guarded skepticism to open disapproval of collaborative efforts. But they may simply be expecting too much too soon. A co-teacher or a special services consultant cannot be an instant panacea for every student's difficulties. Furthermore, teachers sometimes neglect to monitor and record results carefully, so day-to-day improvement in work does not stand out and the teacher may think, "I'm not being successful with this child." This is the opposite of not seeing a child for some months and then thinking, "My, how she has grown." Some consultees have been known to pressure consultants unfairly by expecting them to "fix" the student, and then if this does not happen rather soon, or alas, at all, they write off the concept of consultation and collaboration as a waste of precious time.

As noted earlier, some consulting teachers expect to work only with students, not adults, and they prefer it that way. "I was trained to work with kids, and that's what I enjoy," confessed one consulting teacher when assigned to an indirect service role. This situation presents a problem for both consultee and collaborator. A team approach or co-teaching format may be awkward for the staunchly autonomous teacher at first. Unrealistic and unreasonable expectations must be put aside in the early planning stages of school collaboration practices. Co-educators should set reasonable goals for themselves and not expect "the moon." Small, sure steps with a few enthusiastic collaborators will mark the surest path to success with more reluctant colleagues.

Some collaborating consultants may wonder, "If I consult effectively, I may be working myself out of a job." However, that is highly unlikely. The more successful the consultants' services are, the more their fellow teachers and administrators are prone to value them for their contributions in initiating long-range, positive ripple effects. As one example, students who are missed in initial referrals often are noted and subsequently helped as a result of the interactions among classroom teachers and consulting teachers.

Two other points need to be considered. One is that sometimes the most difficult part of a collaborative consultation experience is stepping aside once the consultee experiences some success with students. Another is in those rare situations where the collaboration is not working and after considerable attempts to resolve the difficulties and move on have failed, the collaboration must end for the welfare of all, especially the student who may be caught in the middle. Winding down or ending a collaborative consultation relationship is likely to be a sensitive, stress-inducing process. It is a joint decision in which communication skills are of utmost importance and proper timing is crucial. There is no textbook approach to this (Dougherty, Tack, Fullam, & Hammer, 1996); therefore, it is essential for those involved to prepare themselves for mixed feelings that may include both relief and disappointment when professional and personal relationships must come to an end.

Involvement of as many co-educators as possible through needs assessments, interviews, professional development activities, and both formal and informal communications, will do much to alter inappropriate expectations for consulting and partnership roles. If collaborators can engage in successful teamwork with the more receptive and cooperative colleagues in their schools, it will generate confidence in the approach among others who are not so receptive initially.

STRUCTURES FOR COLLABORATIVE SCHOOL CONSULTATION

School collaboration, consultation, and co-teaching call for structures that provide adequate blocks of time, efficient management of schedules, suitable facilities in which to meet, and careful organization of details so that the interactive processes are carried out as effectively and nonintrusively as possible. These conditions are deceptively simple to describe but much more difficult to put into operation. The first potential barrier to take into consideration is, once again, the unavoidable problem of a lack of time.

Time for Consulting and Collaborating

As discussed in Chapter 2, time is the ultimate nonrenewable resource. One of the most overwhelming and frustrating obstacles to collaborative activity is the lack of time to do it. Sometimes willing teachers use their own planning time for consultation, but that is not an ideal way to instill positive attitudes toward a collaborative approach and it "robs Peter to pay Paul." A typical school day is simply not designed for incorporating collaboration time into the schedule without careful planning, some give and take, and occasionally, personal sacrifice by the collaborating teachers.

Even when a schedule for meeting and following up can be arranged, it may be nearly impossible to find significant blocks of time shared among all potential participants. Working out such a plan is often like working a complex puzzle; it is one of the most formidable tasks of those who want to collaborate, particularly those who have direct teaching responsibilities at specific times in specific buildings. Thus, it is up to administrators to acknowledge the need for this quality time and to exert strong leadership in enabling it to happen. When administrators lend their authority *and* their approval to this endeavor, school personnel are more likely to find ways of getting together and to use that time productively.

Unfortunately, when consulting teachers *first* initiate consultation and collaboration, if it is without formal arrangement, it is very likely that it will come out of their own time—that is, before school, after school, during lunch hours, perhaps even on weekends.

Even so, this *temporary* accommodation should be replaced as soon as possible with a more formal structure for allocation of time and designation of a suitable place during the school day. This is not only for their well-being but to emphasize that consultation and collaboration are not simply add-on services to be carried out by a zealous, dedicated, almost superhuman few.

As time is made available for working together, facilities must be accessible in which to conduct the consultation. The area should be comfortable, quiet, convenient, and relatively private for free exchange of confidences. Such a place is often at a premium in a bustling school community.

Resources for Consulting and Collaborating

It is no secret that districts struggle to find money for their ever-increasing expenses. So there is a risk of letting fiscal issues, rather than factors that focus specifically on student needs, dictate the service delivery method. One such factor is the teacher caseload issue and it must be addressed carefully. Large caseloads may seem to save money in the short run but not in the long run if student performance declines or if there is much attrition from the teaching profession because of heavy assignments. If a collaborating teacher's caseload is too great, direct services will be inadequate, indirect services will be diminished, acceptance of the collaborative approach falters, and the method risks rejection.

Recommended caseload numbers vary depending on school context, travel time required, grade levels, exceptionalities and special needs served, and structure(s) of the interaction method, but the numbers must be kept manageable to fulfill the intent and promise of consultation and collaboration. Part of the solution lies in documenting carefully *all* collaborative consultation and team activities to show the time and personnel required *and* making specific note of what should have been available but was not due to fiscal constraints. Consultants must negotiate with their administrators for reasonable caseload assignments and blocks of time to interact.

Although time is at a premium for busy educators, recent trends in computer technology and other electronic media are improving their situations. Teachers who work in partnerships with colleagues must be very organized and efficient. In recent years tedious, time-consuming tasks such as developing IEPs, preparing reports, collecting academic and behavioral data, and communicating with families and support staff, have become easier with technological advances. Software templates, e-mail, electronic calendars, and a variety of other organizational tools help teachers maximize their time. Tools and vehicles such as these also have allowed teachers to be more connected in networks that enhance collegiality and teamwork. (See the upcoming section on technology.)

Organization for Consulting and Collaborating

It is one thing to design a hypothetical method of consultation but quite another to plan multiple methods for application in different situations, and it is even more challenging to organize and put into motion the right method for each situation. It is easier, of course, if preceded by thoughtful role clarification and genuine role parity, within a climate of appropriate role expectations.

Those who collaborate will want to generate a number of methods for consultation and collaboration in a variety of grade levels, subject areas, and special needs categories, and in suitable contexts for school, community, and families. The consultation structure should fit the context of the system. Some traditional models exist, and newer models for a variety of school contexts have been developed and put into practice. But school personnel should collaborate to design the methods that are custom fit to their schools' needs. Taking a survey of teachers to ask how they would use collaborative activities would be a good way to begin. Studying and observing promising structures in other school systems also can be helpful.

Scientists note that astronomers from all parts of the world collaborate often because there is no one place from which every part of their "work area," the sky, can be observed. This analogy also applies to educators and parents as they address each child's total needs in the cognitive, affective, sensorimotor, and social domains to develop learning and behavior goals. The goals become building blocks for decision making, and without them, the decision making is like a hammer without nails. Educators have long-range and short-term goals. Students have IEPs with annual goals and learning objectives. Schools have mission statements and program goals. Educators' aims, schools' missions, and students' goals should be bases on which to make decisions in educational environments. A goal catalyzes action and provides direction for that action. Reviewing goals will help educators stay focused to sort out and promote the things that are vitally important.

Management for Consulting and Collaborating

Educators with experience as consultants point out several problems that can interfere with the success of consultation, collaboration, or teamwork among educators. By recognizing them and managing them, collaborating teachers will be prepared to sidestep or step over potential hurdles such as:

- Uncertainty about what and how to communicate with those who resist or resent collaboration
- Being regarded as a teacher's aide, "go-fer," or quick-fix expert
- Having consultation regarded as a tutorial for students
- Losing touch with the students when not in direct service with them
- Territoriality of school personnel
- Rigid curriculum and assessment procedures
- Unrealistic expectations (either too high or too low) for the role
- Not having enough information or appropriate materials to share
- Being perceived as a show-off, or an authoritarian expert, or an interloper
- Running into veils of professional politeness that some consultees sometimes use to shield themselves from genuine commitment
- Difficulty managing time and keeping track of resources spread among many schools and classrooms
- Lack of training for the role
- Excessive caseloads that short-circuit effectiveness
- Too many "hats" to wear in the role
- Reluctance of some teachers and school administrators to make changes

Knowing what hurdles may pop up can prevent them from becoming insurmountable barriers. Collaborating teachers can work through role delineation, a consultation framework, adequate evaluation of the process, and careful preparation to develop the necessary skills.

Some of the mystique surrounding special education and support services is reduced when classroom teachers become familiar with the techniques and are led to appreciate and understand special education roles. Jones and Morin (2000) summarize characteristics for successful collaboration as follows:

- Voluntary participation in shared goals
- Mutual respect and parity
- Mutual support with sharing of expertise
- Administrators' support
- Sufficient time

SUPPORT FOR COLLABORATIVE SCHOOL CONSULTATION

The fourth of the key components in collaborative school consultation is support. Support is provided in a number of different ways and at several different levels. Co-educators must document the effectiveness of consultation and collaboration, as described previously in this chapter, to ensure continued support for collaborative consultation service and avoid overlooking small, consistent gains. School personnel are understandably skeptical of indirect services that do not prove their mettle. Co-educators may be involved initially because they are told to be involved or because they have been talked into giving it a try or even because they are intrigued with the possibilities and just want to be collegial. But their interest will wane if the processes become a hassle and a burden, especially if positive results are not forthcoming and convincing.

Assessment for Consulting and Collaborating

Assessment is essential for providing evaluative data to measure outcomes of collaborative school consultation and co-teaching. School personnel will be more accepting if success is demonstrated with carefully collected, valid data. Unfortunately, assessment of collaboration and consultation processes has been minimal and often not well planned and conducted. A few procedures such as rating scales of judgments directed at a variety of skills and activities, and survey estimates of engaged time for the required activities, have been used. Administrators, advisory council members, and policymakers should study carefully the procedures that have been tried and use their authority to insist on development of practical assessment techniques that fit their school contexts. In keeping with the philosophy of collaboration, personnel from diverse roles should design the assessment tools and procedures cooperatively. A needs assessment instrument can be drawn up and field-tested, and co-educators can use it to express their needs and make suggestions for program implementation.

Evaluation for Consulting and Collaborating

Assessment data from self-reports, interviews, and observations are collected for the purpose of evaluation. Formative evaluation provides information for ongoing corrections and improvements. Summative evaluation is used to determine program value and to make decisions about continuation.

Not only should processes and content be evaluated, but the context of the school setting should be evaluated as well. For example, a consultant may have excellent communication skills and a wealth of content with which to consult and collaborate, but if the existing school context provides no time and space for interaction, positive results will be slim to none. Consultants will want to evaluate every stage of the collaborative processes to keep focusing on the right goals.

Assessment and evaluation should include a variety of data-collection methods to provide the kinds of information needed by target groups. Consultation and collaboration practices must not be judged inadequate for the wrong reasons. If time has not been allocated for collaboration, if school personnel have not had preparation and encouragement, and if administrator support is lacking, those components should be targeted for improvement before the collaborative process itself is faulted. Chapter 12 focuses on planning, conducting, and using results of evaluation for collaborative school consultation.

Acceptance for Consulting and Collaborating

Participation in collaborative programs must be a *willing* decision among co-educators who volunteer to adopt this method of serving special needs. There must be parity for all involved, and encouragement by administrators will help to a great extent. By using techniques such as publicizing successes and promoting benefits of consultations and teamwork as they are realized, schools may get the collaboration bandwagon rolling with even the most reluctant persons on board. Most important, however, is involving people right from the start in needs assessments, advisory committees, planning efforts, professional development activities, follow-up activities, and more and more personal contacts.

Commitment to Consulting and Collaborating

Consultation calls for redirection and change in old ways of doing things. The old ways were isolation, "ownership" of students (yours, mine), and sweeping problems under the rug or handing them off to others for direct service "over there in that other area of the school."

True collaboration requires time, energy, and practice. Genuine co-teaching necessitates sharing ownership and territory, and taking risks. These realities make involvement by school personnel more difficult and maintenance of their commitment more challenging. In the minds of many educators, consultation has been associated with exclusionary special education programs and assistance in mainstreamed classes. So, if teachers miss the opportunity for collaborative consultation service and then come to resent having more responsibility for teaching special education students, they may blame the collaborative school consultation approach and those who are collaborative teachers for their situation.

Special education teachers and support personnel need a well-designed plan and a spirited collegial vision that will intrigue and excite them about joining in partnerships. They need to have families of students informed and on board with this approach to helping their children. Most of all, they need strong administrator support or it will be difficult for positive things to happen. (This is addressed further in Chapter 14.) Those who would consult, collaborate, and co-teach must recognize and build on every opportunity to have dedicated, supportive participation by all.

THEORY BASE OF COLLABORATIVE SCHOOL CONSULTATION

School consultation is theory based because it is identified across more than one literature source focusing upon the relationship between consultant and consultee (West & Idol, 1987). At this point, it would be good to bear in mind the adage "There is nothing so practical as a good theory."

West and Idol (1987) identified six prominent models founded on clearly distinguishable theory or theories: mental health, behavioral, process, advocacy, catalyst, and collaborative consultation.

FACETS OF METHODS FOR COLLABORATIVE SCHOOL CONSULTATION

Overlapping philosophies of consultation have evolved from a blending of consultation knowledge and practices in several fields. This overlap creates a tangle of philosophy and terminology that could be problematic for educators. So calling on semantics again, it is helpful to sort out the myriad consultation terms, theories, research findings, and practices, and recast them into useful structures.

When communicating about educational issues, educators will want to avoid using "educationese" (convoluted and redundant phrases), "jargon" (in-house expressions that approximate educational slang), and "alphabet soup" (acronyms that appear to laypeople as a form of code). Communication must be presented in clear language and this requires careful attention to semantics, as noted in Chapter 1. Think about words such as *progress* and its meaning in the context of NCLB; or *misbehavior*, as discussed by parents; or *reinforcers*, when co-teachers plan teaching strategies; or *homework*, as defined by teachers, parents, and some high-profile educational experts. To make the point once again, when some would say, "Never mind, it's just semantics that are causing the problem," educators must keep in mind that it is quite possible semantics *are* the problem, or a big part of it, when analyzing issues.

A practical way of viewing collaborative school consultation and designing a method for implementation in a school context is to describe it semantically as a blend

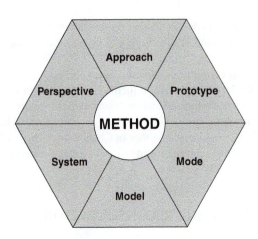

FIGURE 4.3   Structural Facets of Collaborative School Consultation

of facets. Think of the facets as segments of a cut-and-polished gem. These segments (see Figure 4.3) highlight the six elements formulating collaborative consultation method as:

1. *System*—an entity made up of many parts that serve a common purpose
2. *Perspective*—a particular viewpoint or outlook
3. *Approach*—an initial step toward a purpose
4. *Prototype*—a pattern
5. *Mode*—a form or manner of doing
6. *Model*—an example or a replica

For brevity and clarity, the elements are designated using the uppercase form of their first letter. When two components begin with the same letter, another letter of the word is used. Thus, the six categories are *S* (system), *P* (perspective), *A* (approach), *R* (prototype), *E* (mode), and *M* (model). The letters form a little word that has no meaning itself but makes the order of the letters easy to keep in mind: *SPAREM*.

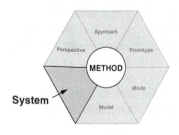

FIGURE 4.4   System for Collaborative School Consultation

Systems

A system is a unit composed of many diverse parts for a common purpose. (See Figure 4.4.) *Systems* (*S*) in which educators function to serve special needs of students include school, home and family, community, medical and dental professions, mental health, social work, counseling, extracurricular functions, and advocacy and support groups. Other systems with which consultants and collaborators might be involved from time to time in addressing very specialized needs are therapy, industry, technology, mass communications, the arts, and special interest areas for talent development.

The most natural system within which to conduct school consultation and collaboration is, obviously, the school context. Educators are involved beyond the academic or cognitive aspects of student development, to address sensorimotor, emotional, social, and life-orientation aspects. School educators include not just teachers both general and special, but administrators, and related services and support personnel. Home educators include parents or other family members who are the caregivers, and the community in general.

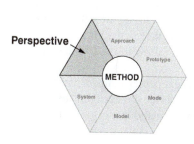

FIGURE 4.5   Perspective for Collaborative School Consultation

Perspectives for Consulting and Collaborating

A *perspective* (*P*) is an aspect or object of thought from a particular viewpoint or outlook. (See Figure 4.5.) Consultation perspectives that have evolved in education and related fields are distinguished by three categories—purchase, doctor-patient, and process.

A *purchase* perspective is one in which a consumer shops for a needed or wanted item. The consumer, in this case the consultee, "shops for" services that will help the consultee serve the client's need. For example, the teacher of a developmentally delayed student might ask personnel at the instructional media center for a list of low-vocabulary, high-interest reading material with which to help the student have immediate success in reading. The "purchase request" makes several assumptions (Neel, 1981) that (1) the consultee describes the need precisely; (2) the consultant has the right "store" and "goods" in the store for that need; (3) the consultant also has enough "inventory" (strategies and resources) to fill the request; and (4) the consultee can assume the costs of time, energy, or modification of classroom procedures.

As a consumer, the consultee is free to accept or reject the strategy or resource, use it enthusiastically, put off trying it, or ignore it as a "bad buy." Even if the strategy is effective for that case, the consultee may need to go again to the consultant for similar needs of other clients. Little change in consultee skills for future situations is likely as a result of a consumer-type interaction. Thus, the overall costs are rather high and benefits are limited to specific situations. However, if the need is immediate and severe, the purchase approach has advantages.

The *doctor–patient* perspective casts the collaborating consultant in the role of diagnostician and prescriptor. The consultee knows there is a problem, but is not in a position to correct it. Consultees are responsible for revealing helpful information to the consultant. With this perspective there are several different assumptions that: (1) the consultee describes the problem to the consultant accurately and completely; (2) after making a diagnosis the consultant explains it clearly and convinces the consultee of its worth; (3) the diagnosis is not premature; and (4) the prescribed remedy is not *iatrogenic* (a term from the medical profession where a treatment is more debilitating than the illness it was designed to treat). An iatrogenic effect from educational services would create more problems for students, educators, or the school context than the initial condition did. For example, taking high-ability students from their general classrooms to meet with gifted program facilitators could result in resentment and antagonism from their peers and perhaps even from their classroom teachers, so that if pressed to choose, many students would reject academic enrichment and perhaps even overcompensate with underachievement in order to regain a desired status with their friends. Or, having a restless, misbehaving primary-level student stay inside during playtime as a corrective measure would make the child even more restless during the next study period.

A classroom teacher might use a doctor–patient perspective by calling on a special education teacher and describing the student's learning or behavior problem. The collaborative consultant's role would be to observe, review existing data, perhaps talk to other specialists, and then make diagnostic and prescriptive recommendations. As in the medical field, there is generally little follow-up activity on the consultant's part with the doctor-patient perspective (just as few doctors call their patients the morning after a procedure to see how they are doing), and the consultee does not always follow through with conscientious attention to the consultant's recommendations.

In a *process* perspective, the consultant helps the client perceive, understand, and act on the problem (Neel, 1981; Schein, 1969). Consultative service does not replace the consultee's direct service to the client. In contrast to the purchase and doctor-patient perspectives, the consultant neither diagnoses nor prescribes. As Neel (1981) puts it, the consultee becomes the consultant's client for that particular problem.

Schein (1978) sorted process consultation into two types—a catalyst type in which the consultant does not know a solution but is skilled toward helping the consultee figure one out, and the facilitator type in which the consultant contributes ideas toward the solution. In both catalyst and facilitator types of process consultation the consultant helps the consultee clarify the problem, develop solutions, and implement the plan.

All of these perspectives—purchase, doctor-patient, and the two types of process— have strengths; therefore, each is likely to be employed at one time or another in schools. One factor influencing the adoption of a particular perspective is the nature of the problem. For example, in a noncrisis situation the consultee may value the process approach. In crisis situations the consultee may need a quick solution, even if temporary, for the problem. In such cases the purchase or doctor-patient perspectives would be preferred because situations that immediately affect the physical and psychological well-being of students and school personnel require immediate attention and cannot wait for process consultation. However, when it is not a crisis situation, and process consultation is employed regularly, many skills and resources that are developed for solving a particular problem can be used again and again in situations presenting similar problems. This makes process consultation both time-efficient and cost-effective for schools.

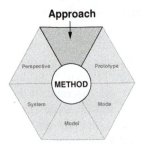

FIGURE 4.6   Approach for Collaborative School Consultation

Approaches for Consulting and Collaborating

An *approach* (A) is a *formal* or *informal* preliminary step toward a purpose. (See Figure 4.6.) Formal collaborative consultations occur in preplanned meetings such as staffing meetings, conferences for developing IEPs, arranged interactions between school personnel and support personnel, and organized staff development activities. They also take place in scheduled conferences with families, related services personnel, and community resource personnel.

In contrast, informal consultations often occur "on the run." These interactions have been referred to as "vertical consultations" because people tend to engage in them while standing on playgrounds, in parking lots, at ball games, even in grocery stores. They are dubbed "one-legged consultations" when they happen in hallways with a leg propped against the wall (Hall & Hord, 1987; McDonald, 1989). Conversations also take place frequently in the teachers' workroom. This aspect is addressed more fully in Chapter 14 as a place and type of informal staff development. It is very important to note and record informal interactions like these as consultations because they *do* require expenditures of time and energy on the part of both consultant(s) and consultee(s) and may have ramifications later in regard to the concern. Highlighting them as consultations helps establish the concept of school consultation, document the time expended and the general topic for purposes of accountability, and promote efforts to construct a suitable framework for allocation of quality interaction time. Informal consultations should be encouraged because they can open the door for more structured collaborative consultation later. Sometimes they become catalysts for meaningful professional development activities as well. In other cases they may activate team effort that would have been bypassed in the daily hustle and bustle of school life.

Prototypes for Consulting and Collaborating

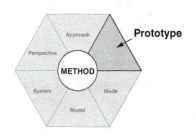

FIGURE 4.7   Prototype for Collaborative School Consultation

A *prototype* (R) is a pattern. (See Figure 4.7.) Consultation prototypes include mental health consultation, behavioral consultation, process consultation, and advocacy consultation. Only the first two will be addressed here.

The *mental health* prototype has a long history (Conoley & Conoley, 1988). The concept originated in the 1960s with the work of psychiatrist Gerald Caplan, who conceived of consultation as a relationship between two professional people in which responsibility for the client rests on the consultee (Hansen, Himes, & Meier, 1990). Caplan (1970) proposed that consultee difficulties in dealing with a client's problems (think "teacher" dealing with "student need") usually are caused by any one, or all, of four interfering themes:

1. Lack of *knowledge* about the problem and its conditions
2. Lack of *skill* to address the problem in appropriate ways
3. Lack of *self-confidence* in dealing with the problem
4. Lack of *professional objectivity* when approaching the problem

The consultant not only helps resolve the problem at hand, but enhances the consultee's ability to handle similar situations in the future. When the mental health prototype is used for consultation and the issue of theme interference is introduced, consultee change may very well precede client change. Therefore, assessment of success should focus on consultee attitudes and behaviors more than on client changes (Conoley & Conoley, 1988). School-based mental health consultation is characterized by consultant attention to the teacher's feelings and meaning that the teacher attaches to the student's behavior (Slesser, Fine, & Tracy, 1990).

The *behavioral consultation* prototype also purports to improve the performance of both consultee and client. It focuses on clear, explicit problem-solving procedures (Slesser, Fine, & Tracy, 1990). It is based on social learning theory, with skills and knowledge contributing more to consultee success than less definitive themes like objectivity or self-confidence (Bergan, 1977). Behavioral consultation probably is more familiar to educators, and therefore more easily introduced into the school context than mental health consultation. Indeed, it is the prototype on which the majority of collaborative consultation models are based. The consultant is required to define the problem, isolate environmental variables that support that problem, and plan interventions to reduce the problem. Bergan (1995) states that his four-stage model of a consultative problem-solving process was grounded on successful identification of the problem as the first stage. This is a very important point that will be emphasized more explicitly in Chapter 5. Problem analysis, implementation, and evaluation followed this stage.

Conoley and Conoley (1988) regard behavioral consultation as the easiest prototype to evaluate because problem delineation and specific goal setting occur within the process itself. Evaluation results can be used to modify plans and promote consultation services among other potential consultees. But behavioral consultation can fail to bring results when it focuses on problematic social behavior such as aggression or being off-task, if that behavior really emanates from poor or inadequate academic skills (Cipani, 1985).

Modes for Consulting and Collaborating

A *mode* (*E*) is a particular style or manner of doing something. (See Figure 4.8.) Modes for school consultation are either direct consultation for the delivery of service to clients, or indirect consultation for delivery of service to consultees.

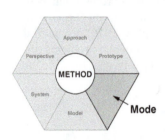

FIGURE 4.8   Mode for Collaborative School Consultation

In a *direct* mode the consultant works directly with a special-needs student. For example, a learning disabilities consulting teacher or a speech pathologist specialist might use a particular technique with the student while a parent or classroom teacher consultee observes and assists with the technique. Direct service typically is provided to students subsequent to a referral (Bergan, 1977). The consultant may conduct observations and discuss the learning or behavior with the student (Bergan, 1977; Heron & Harris, 1987). The consultant becomes an advocate and the student has an opportunity to participate in decisions made pertinent to that need. Another example of direct service is teaching coping skills or study techniques to students for use at home or at school (Graubard, Rosenberg, & Miller, 1971; Heron & Harris, 1987).

The *indirect* service delivery mode calls for "backstage" involvement among consultants and consultees to serve client needs. The consultant and consultee interact and problem-solve together. Then the consultee provides related direct service to the client. So school consultation is indirect service to students resulting from the direct service to teachers or parents.

Models for Consulting and Collaborating

Models are many things—patterns, examples for imitation, representations in miniature, descriptions, analogies, or displays. But a model is not the real thing, just an approximation of it. (See Figure 4.9.) A *model* functions as an example through which to study, replicate, approximate, or manipulate intricate things.

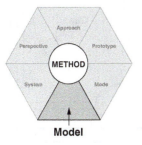

A few of the many well-known models adopted or adapted for collaboration and consultation in schools over the past twenty-five years are:

- Triadic model
- Resource/Consulting Teacher Program model
- Instructional Consultation model
- Conjoint Behavioral Consultation model
- Consultee-centered consultation model
- Teacher Assistance Teams model
- Responsive Systems Consultation model
- Collaborative consultation and its variant models

FIGURE 4.9   Model for Collaborative School Consultation

A very few of those few will be described briefly here. The Additional Resources section has references that can be consulted for more information about models and their applications.

The *triadic* model, developed by Tharp and Wetzel (1969) and Tharp (1975), is the classic model from which many school consultation and collaboration models have evolved. It includes three roles—consultant, consultee (or mediator), and client (or target). In this most basic of the existing models, services are not offered directly, but through an intermediary (Tharp, 1975). The service flows from the consultant through the mediator to the client. The consultant role is typically, although not always, performed by an educational specialist such as a learning disabilities teacher or a school psychologist. The consultee is usually, but not always, the classroom teacher. The client (or target as Tharp termed it in the early years) is most often but not always the student with special needs. An educational need may be a disability or an advanced ability requiring special services for the student. The triadic model requires that both consultant and consultee take ownership of the problem and share accountability for the success or failure of the program (Idol, Paolucci-Whitcomb, & Nevin, 1995). (See Figure 4.10.)

When studying the models, it is important to recall the discussion in Chapter 1 about roles. Roles are interchangeable among individuals, depending on the school context and the educational need. For example, on occasion a learning disabilities consulting teacher might be a consultee who seeks information and expertise from a general classroom teacher consultant. At another time a student might be the consultant for a resource room teacher as consultee, and for parents as the clients who are targets for interventions intended to help their child. Tharp (1975) gives the following example:

> Ms. Jones the second-grade teacher may serve as mediator between Brown, the psychologist, and John, the problem child. At the same time, she may be the target of her principal's training program and the consultant to her aide-mediator in the service of Susie's reading problem. The triadic model, then, describes relative position in the chain of social influence. (p. 128)

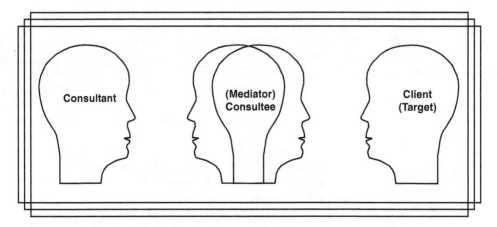

FIGURE 4.10   Example of a Basic Triadic Consultation

Tharp identifies several strengths of the triadic model, including the clarity it provides in delineating social roles and responsibilities, and the availability of evaluation data from two sources—mediator (consultee) behavior and target (client) behavior. However, it may not be the most effective model for every school context and content area, given the process skills and resources that are available. Here is a brief summary highlighting the triadic model's strong points and potential drawbacks:

- *Strengths*—Appropriate in crisis situations; a good way to get started with the consultee; quick and direct; informal and simple; keeps problem in perspective; has objectivity on consultant's part; provides student anonymity if needed; is time efficient; can lead into more intensive collaborative consultation; and may be all that is needed.
- *Potential drawbacks*—Has little or no carryover to other situations; probably will be needed again for same or similar situations; only one other point of view available; consultant needs to have expert skills; essential data may be unavailable; consultant may be held accountable for lack of progress; there is little or no follow-up.

The *Resource/Consulting Teacher Program* (R/CT) model was implemented at the University of Illinois and replicated in both rural and large urban areas (Idol, Paolucci-Whitcomb, & Nevin, 1986). It is based on the triadic model, with numerous opportunities for interaction among teachers, students, and parents. The resource/consulting teacher offers direct service to students through tutorials or small-group instruction and indirect service to students through consultation with classroom teachers for a portion of the school day. Students who are not staffed into special education programs can be served along with exceptional students in inclusive general classrooms. Parents sometimes are involved in the consultation. Teacher education in preparation for the model (Idol-Maestas, 1981), and close coordination between the R/CT and the classroom teacher are required. This accentuates the importance of sharing perspectives and preferences as discussed in Chapters 2 and 3.

The *Instructional Consultation* (IC) model merges skill in collaborative consultation with expertise in specific areas of content. The model responds to several premises that have been offered by educational experts. First, teacher behavior does make a crucial difference to children's achievement (Rosenfield, 1995). Second, many tasks assigned to students are not well matched to their instructional levels. Children should be regarded as having learning disabilities only if they fail to learn *after* having *appropriate* instruction (Rosenfield, 1995). Furthermore, when students are referred for special services, their classroom teachers should have ongoing assistance in developing and managing their learning programs. The IC process begins with entry-level discussion between consultant and teacher about roles, expectations, and commitment. Consultants are case managers who have relinquished the expert role and configured their professional relationships to be collaborative and egalitarian. Steps proceed through problem identification and analysis, classroom observation, procedures such as curriculum-based assessment, implementation of interventions, ongoing evaluation, and termination of the consultation relationship. At termination, a written record of agreed-on findings is submitted to involved parties.

Other Variations of the Triadic and Collaborative School Consultation Models   Most *collaborative consultation* models are derived from Tharp and Wetzel (1969) and Tharp (1975) and include three components: (C) consultant, M (mediator), and (T) target (Idol et al., 1995). Collaborative consultation is a problem-centered approach requiring all parties in the consultation to participate in development of exemplary programs (Idol et al., 1995). The consultant and consultee are equal partners with diverse expertise in identifying problems, planning intervention strategies, and implementing recommendations that carry mutual responsibility (Idol et al., 1986; Raymond, McIntosh, & Moore, 1986). The communication is not hierarchical or one-way. Rather, there is a sense of parity that blends the skills and knowledge of both consultant and consultee, with disagreements viewed as opportunities for constructive extraction of the most useful information (Idol et al., 1995). In addition, both consultant and consultee work directly with the student.

In research to investigate teacher responses to consultative services, Schulte, Osborne, and Kauffman (1993) found that most teachers who were surveyed viewed collaborative consultation as an acceptable alternative to resource rooms. However, scheduling and congruence of teacher time slots can impose limits on success. Idol, Paolucci-Whitcomb, P., & Nevin (1995) recommend that for such a model to be successful, participants will need appropriate interview skills, active listening skills, effective oral and written communication, positive nonverbal language, and well-developed structures for conflict resolution. To reiterate, the collaborative school consultation process must be voluntary and nonsupervisory, and carried out with a demeanor of onedownsmanship.

Many experts assert that the most appropriate model for a specific school context is a combination of the best features from several models to create one that is tailor-made for that context. Additional variations of collaborative consultation that lend themselves to further adaptation for local contexts are discussed next.

Schoolwide Enrichment Model (SEM)   The well-researched SEM (Renzulli & Reis, 1985) provides three types of challenging learning experiences for gifted and talented students in the regular classroom. It involves close collaboration between general education

teachers and gifted program facilitators and includes intensive staff development to prepare all participants for their roles. Discussion of SEM continues in Chapter 10.

Resource Consultation Model   The concept of the Resource Consultation Model was
originally developed by Curtis, Curtis, and Graden (1988) and adapted for education of
gifted students. The consultation is a problem-solving process shared by all school personnel where the primary goal is to use limited and expensive resources more effectively
and efficiently to better serve students (Kirschenbaum, Armstrong, & Landrum, 1999).
It can occur at one of three levels: collaboration on a less formal and less structured
basis; assistance from gifted education personnel (an option that turns out to be chosen
85 percent of the time); or team intervention, if several school personnel will be affected,
such as in a consultation matter involving radical acceleration. It also will appear again
in Chapter 10.

Summary of Strengths of Collaborative Models   In general, collaborative models fit
current school reform goals; inspire professional growth for all through shared expertise;
provide many points of view; focus on situations encompassing the whole school context;
involve general *and* special education staff and often resource and support personnel as
well; generate many ideas; maximize opportunities for constructive use of adult differences; allow administrators to assume a facilitative role; facilitate liaisons with community agents; and are pleasing to families because many school personnel are working with
their child.

Summary of Potential Drawbacks of Collaborative Models   The following are some
of the potential drawbacks of collaborative models: little or no training of educators in collaborative consultation and co-teaching; shortage of time and compatibility of schedules
for interacting; working with adults not the preference of some educators; require solid, not
token, administrator support; confidentiality harder to ensure with many people involved;
could diffuse responsibility so much that no one feels ultimately responsible; and can take
time to see results.

DEVELOPMENT OF PLANS FOR COLLABORATIVE SCHOOL CONSULTATION

When planning for collaborative school consultation, it is helpful to use an informal,
journalistic-style template that directs the study and discussion, such as:

- Why is this type of service best?
- What do we expect to occur?
- Who will be involved?
- When will it take place and for how long?
- Where will it be happening?
- How will we put the plan into operation?
- How will we evaluate the results?

Then, returning to the six components in Figure 4.3 for constructing a method, it is helpful to decide which components and to what extent they will be structured to help frame the plan:

1. *S*ystem (school systems, other social systems)
2. *P*erspective (purchase, doctor-patient, process)
3. *A*pproach (formal, informal)
4. *P*rototype (mental health, behavioral)
5. Mod*e* (direct, indirect)
6. *M*odel (triadic, Resource/Consulting Teacher Program, Instructional Consultation, Schoolwide Enrichment, Resource Consultation, and other collaborative consultation variations).

Referring again to Figure 4.3, the Method area in the center draws from each of the six facets to synthesize all into a method with goodness of fit for the particular school situation. Several practice situations that follow provide opportunities to plan and implement school consultation, collaboration, and/or teamwork. To work through one or two of the situations, it will be helpful to consider the why, who, what, when, where, and how, and choose among options for system, perspective, approach, prototype, mode, and model. It is not necessary to dwell on interaction and coordination processes at this time; the goal is an appropriate structure for a school context.

When thinking about a situation, it is stimulating to address complex circumstances in the way that the eminent thinker Albert Einstein did—that is, as a thought problem to be explored in the mind and not in a laboratory or a classroom. The idea is to manipulate variables and concepts mentally, "seeing" them from all angles as facets of the gem structure described earlier, and withholding judgment until all conceivable avenues have been explored in one's mind. Thought problems are opportunities for intently reflecting on real problems and possibilities before presenting them for discussion and critique by others. This abstract way of pondering problems rather than manipulating components is a practice Einstein employed quite successfully. Indeed, this kind of thinking often occurs informally when co-educators are contemplating multifaceted processes, such as collaborative consultation and co-teaching. The Reflections sections included in this book are thought problems. Reflection 4.1 serves as a warm-up for the case-study situations that follow.

REFLECTION 4.1

Picturing a Collaborative Consultation Model

How do you think an artist might depict educators working together to help a child learn at school? Would it be an abstract design with geometric shapes, and lines to show the interactions? Or would it be a sketch with stick figures to show the teachers problem—solving for the child, who might be in the middle of the sketch? Or would it be a sculpture made of clay or sand?

If you like to draw or sculpt, you could turn Reflection into Action and try your hand at making an illustration of your idea. If you don't care to do that but you have a graphically talented friend, explain the concept and ask if it suggests a picture to that person. The most fun of all might be to ask a school child to make a drawing. It would be interesting to see how the young student perceives adults working together to help every child do well in school.

As a further challenge, think of an illustration for a co-teaching partnership. If you like your idea very much, find a way to make it into a chart or mural for your school to draw attention to the process of co-teaching and what it offers students who experience it.

Case Situations for Formulating Methods

Several scenarios provide examples of situations that can occur in a typical educational context. Decyk (1994) depicts *examples* as instructional workhorses, helping us dig into ideas and plow the land of the abstract, transporting information and ideas from one person to another and from one context to another:

- One person or group may decide that the best way to address a situation is with the *triadic* model and a *purchase* perspective, using *indirect* service from the consultant to the client, in an *informal, mental health* prototype of interaction within the *school system.*
- Another individual or group may approach a particular problem through a variation of a *collaborative consultation* model, with a *process* perspective, using *direct* service to the client from both consultant and consultee, in a *formal* way that approximates a *behavioral* prototype, in a *community work setting* as the system.

Select a situation from the examples that follow or from others generated by your group and apply case-study techniques introduced in earlier chapters to making decisions that have a goodness of fit for <u>S</u>ystem (context), <u>P</u>erspective (viewpoint), <u>A</u>pproach (formal or informal), p<u>R</u>ototype (pattern), mod<u>E</u> (form), and <u>M</u>odel. Also, when thinking about possibilities, it is good to consider what drawbacks might exist in carrying out the proposed method and what could emerge as strengths that provide positive ripple effects.

Situation 1: Ten-year-old Clarisse is new to the school and is placed in a program for students with intellectual disabilities. Her teacher quickly learns that Clarisse prefers to observe rather than participate, and she will not join in with group activities. In her previous school, according to her parents, Clarisse had been allowed to lie on the floor most of the day so she would not have tantrums about participation. Her new teacher and paraprofessional want Clarisse to demonstrate her capabilities but do not want her to get off to a bad start in the new school and do not want the parents to feel negative toward her new teachers. The teacher knows this is a crucial time for Clarisse and wonders what to do.

Situation 2: The speech pathologist has been asked by the gifted program facilitator to consult with her regarding a highly gifted child who has minor speech problems but is being pressured by his parents and his kindergarten teacher to "stop the baby talk." The child is becoming very nervous and at times withdraws from conversation and play. How can the speech pathologist use collaborative consultation to help?

Situation 3: A preschool child with behavior disorders hits other children for no apparent cause in the inclusive day care center. The teacher has tried behavior management strategies and time-out periods. But the child impulsively strikes out whenever another child enters her physical "space." How should the early childhood special education (ECSE) teacher approach her primary caregiver, a grandmother, and who else could be involved to help?

Situation 4: A school psychologist is conferring with a teacher about a high school student she has just evaluated. The student is often a behavior problem, and the psychologist is discussing methods for setting up behavior limits with appropriate contingencies and rewards. The teacher makes numerous references to the principal as a person who likes for teachers to be self-sufficient and not "make waves." How should the school psychologist handle this?

Situation 5: Parents of a student with learning disabilities have asked the special education consulting teacher to approach the student's classroom teacher about what they think is excessive and too-difficult homework. The parents say it is disrupting their home life and frustrating the student. How can this situation be addressed?

Situation 6: A high school learning disabilities consulting teacher is visiting with a principal at the principal's request. The principal expresses concern about the quality of teaching demonstrated by two faculty members and asks the consultant to observe them and then provide feedback. How should the consultant handle this situation?

Situation 7: A pediatrician contacts the director of special education and asks her to meet with a group of local doctors to discuss characteristics and needs of children with disabilities. How should this opportunity be structured for maximum benefit to all?

Situation 8: A middle school student has been failing in several subjects during the semester and has become more and more sullen and withdrawn over the past several weeks. Two of her teachers have arrived independently at the strong possibility that she is being abused by a male relative who is living with her family in the home. What actions need to be taken here?

TECHNOLOGY'S TOOLS FOR STRENGTHENING COLLABORATIVE SERVICES

Tools of modern technology augment the services co-educators can provide for their students in a wide range of venues. A tool is not *the* service any more than a dish is not the meal and a car is not the trip. Tools activate and improve services so that desired things get done; the better the tool, the more helpful and efficient the service. One might say that the technology tool is the tail of the dog; it does not wag the dog; rather, the dog uses its tail to do something—show trust, display affection, express happiness, and so forth. The technology "tail" does something—it facilitates social networking, word processing, information gathering, data entry, and gaming, as just a few of its contributions.

FIGURE 4.11   "Remember, You Work for Me."

It is important to keep "dogs and tails" in proper perspective when selecting technology-based tools for teaching and learning. Teachers are no different from others who work in today's digital, information-laden workplace. They can easily become enslaved to what Hurst (2007) calls *bit literacy overload*. The best approach is to welcome the benefits of communication technology *after* studying potential problems and setting specific guidelines for use, such as:

- Limiting the times one checks e-mail and text messages each day
- Taking care that text messages and other electronic mail convey tone and substance so they are not likely to be misinterpreted
- Forgoing use of electronic connections when person-to-person interactions are almost as convenient and could be much more effective
- Selectively using technological assists that provide more efficiency for routine tasks and make more time available for collaborative activities and direct services to students (See Figure 4.11.)

AN ETHICAL CLIMATE FOR DEVELOPING COLLABORATIVE SCHOOL CONSULTATION

Methods for collaborative consultation in schools are as varied as the school personnel who will use them and the school environments in which they will be used. Models may be drawn on for building the framework(s), but ultimately the development process will be a collaborative endeavor that is itself an example of the methods to be developed for students.

If collaborative efforts markedly reduce the time and instruction truly needed for direct services to students, it will be a situation of diminishing returns (Friend & Cook, 1992). Some parents focus on this as a reason for opposing inclusive classrooms co-teaching practices. The issue must be examined with objectivity and discussed candidly with families.

Some parents might prefer to have school personnel cooperate with *them* rather agree to engage in collaborative efforts. The concept of cooperation is problematic; it is a facilitative endeavor, but not in the same way as collaboration. Cooperation often involves giving up something—changing perspective or preferences to a certain extent. Sometimes cooperation is a necessary approach. Negotiation and arbitration are even more complex social behaviors that impose similar demands of meeting somewhere in or near the middle and giving up something. But collaboration among educators trumps all three and potentially gives up less. Recall the social domain taxonomy in Chapter 2.

Collaboration is not easy; it requires effort and energy and for relatively autonomous individuals to arrive at shared goals along different pathways with very little sacrifice by anyone. An issue is explored, options are analyzed, and often the best solution is not anyone's particular choice, but *everyone's* choice—a new and collaboratively formulated plan.

TIPS FOR STRUCTURING COLLABORATIVE SCHOOL CONSULTATION

1. Be knowledgeable about the theoretical aspects of collaboration, consultation, and co-teaching.
2. Keep up to date on professional issues and concerns because education and the area of special education in particular undergo frequent changes in policies and practices.
3. Read current materials on school consultation and collaboration and highlight references to these processes in other professional material you read.
4. Be realistic and understanding about the demands that are placed on classroom teachers, support personnel, administrators, and family members of students in fulfilling *their* roles.
5. Be on the alert for new methods or revisions of existing methods through which consultation and collaboration can occur in your school context.
6. Visit programs where models different from those in your school(s) are being used.
7. Find sessions at professional conferences that feature different models and methods and attend them to broaden your knowledge about educational systems.
8. Create specific ways that teachers can get your help and make those ways known.
9. Clarify expectations by having dialogue with people in all roles in the school context because expectations will vary from person to person; so the first question must be, "How important are these differences?"
10. Be flexible and adaptable; change takes time, and it must be preceded by awareness of the need to change.

ADDITIONAL RESOURCES

Denton, C. A., Hasbrouck, J. E., & Sekaquaptewa, S. (2003). The consulting teacher: A descriptive case study in Responsive Systems Consultation. *Journal of Educational and Psychological Consultation, 14*(1), 41–73. A case-study analysis illustrating the consulting teacher's role in implementing the Responsive Systems Consultation (RSC), a behavioral approach that features relationships within contexts. The consultation case involves two consulting teachers and a novice second-grade teacher addressing behavioral and academic problems of a student.

Newell, M. (2010). Exploring the use of computer simulation to evaluate the implementation of problem-solving consultation. *Journal of Educational and Psychological Consultation, 20*:228–255.

Renzulli, J. S., & Reis, S. M. (1985). *The schoolwide enrichment model: A comprehensive plan for educational excellence.* Mansfield Center, CT: Creative Learning Press.

Rimehaug, T., & Helmersberg, I. (2010). Situational consultation. *Journal for Educational and Psychological Consultation, 20*:185–208.

Rosenfield, S. (1995). Instructional consultation: A model for service delivery in the schools. *Journal of Educational and Psychological Consultation, 6*(4), 297–316.

Sheridan, S. M., Kratochwill, T. R., & Bergan, J. R. (1996). *Conjoint Behavioral Consultation: A procedural manual.* New York: Plenum.

Tharp, R. (1975). The triadic model of consultation. In C. Parker (Ed.), *Psychological consultation in the schools: Helping teachers meet special needs.* Reston, VA: Council for Exceptional Children.

Wilkinson, L. A. (2005). Bridging the research-to-practice gap in school-based consultation: An example using case studies. *Journal of Education and Psychological Consultation, 16*(3), 175–200.

Wilkinson, L. A. (2005). Supporting the inclusion of a student with Asperger's syndrome: A case study using conjoint behavioral consultation and self-management. *Educational Psychology in Practice, 21,* 307–326.

5

Problem-Solving Strategies for Collaborative School Consultation and Teamwork

USING A STRUCTURED PROCESS FOR COLLABORATIVE SCHOOL CONSULTATION is like preparing food according to a recipe. After the fundamentals of cooking have been mastered, one can adapt those procedures to just about any setting, preference, or creative impulse. Similarly, a basic "recipe" for consultation and collaboration can be adapted to any school context, grade level, subject areas, or special learning need. Just as a recipe should be adaptable to suit individual tastes and nutritional needs, so should collaborative consultation structure be flexible and adaptable to fit the needs and interests of individual students in their school contexts.

A collaborative style is based on respecting and trusting one another. When educators exercise ingenuity in constructing teaching and learning strategies collaboratively, schools are better contexts in which all can perform at their best. Collaborative school consultation is an ideal scenario for incorporating the content of problem-solving techniques into educational contexts to cultivate flexible, divergent thinking. (See Figure 5.1). Teamwork builds *esprit de corps*.

FOCUSING QUESTIONS

1. What are the fundamental components in a problem-solving process?

2. Why is problem identification so important in collaborative school consultation?

3. What basic steps should be included in the collaborative consultation process?

4. What kinds of things should consultants and consultees say and do during their interactions for problem solving?

5. What strategies can be useful to expedite collaborative problem solving?

6. What are interferences and hurdles to overcome when problem solving with co-educators, and how can technological aids in a caring, ethical climate be helpful?

KEY TERMS

brainstorming	Janusian thinking	problem identification
concept mapping (webbing)	metaphorical thinking	problem-solving process
follow through	multiple intelligences	synectics
follow up	PMI (Plus–Minus–Interesting)	TalkWalk

VIGNETTE 5

The setting is the office area of an elementary school, where a special education consulting teacher has just checked into the building and meets a fourth-grade classroom teacher.

Classroom Teacher: Hello (introducing self). I understand you're going to be a consulting teacher in our building to work with learning and behavior disorders.

Consulting Teacher: Hi (introducing self). Yes, that's right. I hope to meet with all of the staff very soon to find out what you need and how we can work together to help with those needs.

Classroom Teacher: Well I, for one, am glad you're here. I have a student who is driving me and my other twenty-two students up the wall.

Consulting Teacher: How so?

Classroom Teacher: Well, since she moved here a few weeks ago, she's really upset the classroom system I've been using for years—successfully, I might add.

Consulting Teacher: Is she having trouble with the material?

Classroom Teacher: No, she's a bright child who finishes everything in good time, and it's usually correct. But she's extremely active—I'd say almost frenetic—as she busy-bodies around the room.

Consulting Teacher: What specific behaviors concern you most?

Classroom Teacher: Well, for one thing, she tries to help everyone else when they should be doing their own work. I've worked a lot on developing independent learning skills in my students, and they've made good progress. They don't need to have her tell them what to do.

Consulting Teacher: So her behavior keeps her classmates from being the self-directed learners that they can be?

Classroom Teacher: Right. I have to monitor her activities constantly, which means diverting my attention from all the other students. She bosses her classmates in the learning centers, and the media center, and even in the lunchroom and on the playground.

Consulting Teacher: How has she done with making friends so far?

Classroom Teacher: It's hard to say. So far I've been proud of the kids because they seem to be giving her some time and the benefit of their doubts while she settles in. But I think their tolerance is wearing thin, and at this rate she will soon be having serious difficulties with casual peer relationships, let alone developing close friendships. This is probably the thing that will concern her socially prominent mom the most. I've only had one interaction with her and it wasn't very promising. She seemed to not want to be bothered with problems.

Consulting Teacher: Okay. For now, shall we concentrate on the daughter? Which of this student's behaviors would you like to see changed first?

Classroom Teacher: Well, I need to get her settled into some activities by herself so she's not bothering other students. Then she would learn more, too.

Consulting Teacher: What have you tried until now to keep her involved with her own work?

Classroom Teacher: I explain to her what I expect, and then I try to reinforce appropriate behavior with things she likes to do. I've also tried some time-out, but she doesn't seem to understand what that is and why it's being imposed.

Consulting Teacher: We could make a list of specific changes in behavior you'd like to see and work out a program to accomplish them. In fact, the technique of webbing might help us explore the possibilities. It could help us identify her interests that we could channel into some directed activities. How about doing one together on this chart paper? Then we'll have a record of our ideas. (Consultant and teacher work together to make the web of the student's behaviors and how one behavioral event seems to lead to another. They start talking about a plan the teacher can begin in the classroom.) There's the bell, and I know you have to go. Want to meet tomorrow to add any afterthoughts to our webbing chart and finalize the plan?

Classroom Teacher: Sounds good. I'd like to get this student on track so the class is more settled. We're getting into some new material that will require everybody's attention. If she can stay on track, I think the other children will like her better, and she'll enjoy learning new things, too. Besides that, standardized tests are coming up soon, and then it will really be a challenge to keep her settled, not only for her sake but also for the good of the others. I could meet with you here tomorrow, if that's okay. It might seem like a small problem to some, but to me it's a big problem that clouds my whole day. I must say, it helps a lot to have someone to talk with about it in a problem-solving way.

THE PROBLEM-SOLVING PROCESS

Co-educators exercise their perception and judgment in order to determine students' needs and set learning and behavioral goals for them. This requires well-honed problem-solving skills. There is not any one cookbook formula or "recipe" of problem-solving strategies, but most of them feature similar steps for working through the process. The skills can be developed with practice and critique. Teachers who have others to observe, collaborate with, and practice instruction and behavioral management techniques in simulated situations will be developing skills for practical use in a wide range of professional situations.

Pugach and Johnson (1995) suggest that co-educators configure two general categories for problem solving in the context of teacher collaboration: school-wide problems and specific student problems. Full inclusion is an example of school-wide problem solving undertaken in a collaborative way by all school personnel. Other examples are programs to eliminate bullying and to build good sportsmanship. The second type, specific student needs, is the more frequently occurring type of situations that teachers must deal with in a problem-solving mode. For instance, should a developmentally delayed student be retained for another year in kindergarten or move on with his inclusionary-classroom schoolmates? What problem-solving strategy will help a teenage girl with a serious obsessive-compulsive disorder who does not take the medications regularly that will help her function appropriately in school? Both school-based and student-based categories are areas in which problem-solving skills can yield positive results in planning educational options for students with special needs.

It is helpful to begin with a study of the fundamental problem-solving process. Key steps given here for solving problems effectively are similar to components of the case study approach; the components are compatible with other well-known problem-solving models:

- Gathering data, guided by the expressed or observed need
- Identifying and defining the problem (*very* important)
- Generating possible actions toward solution
- Critiquing proposed actions
- Making decisions in order to select the best option(s)
- Developing a plan
- Implementing the elements of the determined plan
- Following through and following up to evaluate the outcome(s)

A problem-solving process that encourages high levels of communication and collaboration will allow educators to share their expertise related to the problem. Learning and behavior problems do not always result from student disabilities. Some students are simply "curriculum-disabled" (Conoley, 1985), requiring a modified or expanded approach to the existing curriculum in order to function successfully in school (Pugach & Johnson, 1990). To make modifications and accommodations for special needs, educators must identify aspects of the educational environment, both curricular and extracurricular, and at school and in the home that affect student development.

ACTION 5.1
Adjusting to Address Disability

Reread the previous paragraph, focusing on the term *curriculum-disabled*, and discuss it with colleagues whom you trust to be candid, nonjudgmental, and innovative with their viewpoints. How do you think and feel about the term? Should *schools* adjust in order for students to fit in and be successful, or should *students* adjust and strive to achieve within existing school structures? If you have generated some stimulating ideas from the discussion, what could you do with those ideas?

Delineating the Problem

The first, most critical step in a problem solving process is to delineate, or *identify,* the problem (Bolton, 1986). Sophisticated teaching methods and expensive instructional materials will be worthless if student needs are misidentified or overlooked. It can even

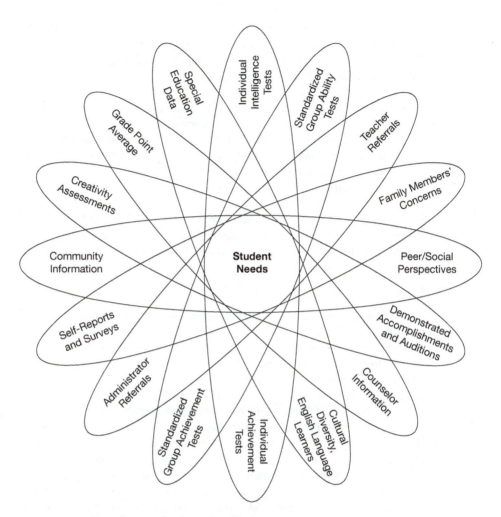

FIGURE 5.2   Data Sources for Assessing Needs

be argued that they will be iatrogenically less than worthless, perhaps causing more harm than good. Delineating problems in collaborative consultations calls for concentrated time and keen focus if the consultation process is to produce results. If the problem is identified appropriately, the rest of the problem-solving process is likely to be successful.

Data from multiple sources about the client (student) will contribute multiple kinds of information on exceptional needs, along with information about the settings in which the needs are evidenced. These information points can be aggregated into a description of specific needs and suggestions of options for help. (See Figure 5.2, which identifies sixteen possible data sources.) Problem-solving tools such as brainstorming, concept mapping (webbing), and lateral thinking will activate thinking to select or design appropriate options that address the learning and behavioral needs.

Co-educators must examine their own abilities to identify personal deficiencies in problem-solving abilities. The four major interfering themes introduced earlier (Caplan, 1970) should be reviewed here as potential impediments to the ability to listen and problem solve on the student's behalf. They are:

- Lack of knowledge and understanding about the student's needs and the goodness of fit with processes of instruction and learning
- Lack of skills in posing options for courses of action that could be taken
- Lack of professional objectivity, so that former experiences or beliefs get in the way and have undue influence
- Lack of self-confidence when addressing the situation and dealing with it

It is important for collaborating teachers to focus on a problem and not on who "owns" the problem. When the problem area is identified, then it will be productive to focus on planning that will lead to short-term progress and, in a positive mode, to long-term solutions.

Generating Possibilities

After a problem has been determined, problem solving calls for generating ideas to come up with potential solutions. Divergent thinking is important for this in order not to get stuck in routine answers. Some consultants find it helpful for the person who "owns" the problem to have first opportunity for making suggestions. This is important for several reasons. When people participate actively in decision making, they feel more ownership toward the results than when they feel coerced into a particular plan. People are more apt to support decisions they helped create than those imposed on them.

An important second reason for prompting the owner of the problem to give initial suggestions is that consultants should avoid giving advice and being perceived as *the* expert. Several researchers have shown that a nonexpert approach to educational consulting is especially effective in special education (Idol-Maestes, Lloyd, & Lilly, 1981; Margolis & McGettigan, 1988). The suggestions and opinions of all others need to be listened to with respect before additional suggestions are offered. Communication skills needed for these kinds of interaction are such an important aspect of successful problem solving that they will be the focus of Chapter 7.

A problem will never be solved if all parties think they are working on different issues. Problems are like artichokes: They have layers. Only after the outside layers are stripped away can problem solvers get to the heart of the matter. Expressing thoughts and feelings with clarity in order to generate best ideas requires effective listening and appropriate assertiveness. Good listening skills facilitate movement to the heart of the problem.

Problems that come up in school consultation often reveal the need for changes in classroom practices. There may be resistance and negativity from classroom teachers. Advice giving and even a hint of hierarchy in roles may be communicated unintentionally if special education consulting teachers appear to present their ideas as being solely theirs and the best at that. Furthermore, if a consulting teacher is regarded as *the* expert, there is pressure on that person and false expectations may be formed. It is hard to win in this kind of situation. The best practice for a collaborating consultant is to communicate parity, flexibility, and a caring, sharing attitude. Three questions assess the existence of a professionally collaborative relationship conducted in an ethical, caring environment:

- Does the consulting teacher give recognition to the consultee's expertise and opinions?
- Does the consulting teacher encourage the consultee to generate ideas and make the decisions?
- Do consultees feel free to *not* do as the consulting teacher might recommend?

Eager consulting teachers who are intent on solving problems and producing quick results and dramatic improvements too often jump in and try to solve problems alone. Consultees may react with resistance or perhaps even hostility by hiding their feelings and withdrawing, and then blaming others if things do not work out.

It is difficult for consultants to avoid the "quick fix" but a quick fix is not an appropriate solution (DeBoer, 1986). It is demeaning to the one who has been struggling with the problem, perhaps for some time. Others need to feel that the collaborating consultant fully understands their unique situation and the source of their frustrations. If they don't, they may resist participating in the problem solving and listening to the suggestions of colleagues. Special education consulting teachers must listen before they can expect to be listened to and treated with parity or be approached voluntarily for help by consultees.

All learning situations and all students are unique. In response to a question about a hypothetical classroom-management scenario, an understanding high school teacher replied, "I don't know all the answers because I haven't seen all the kids." Although students and situations may appear similar in some ways, the combinations of student, teacher, parents, and contexts of school and home are unique for each problem. Furthermore, in many cases, people with problems already have arrived at their answers. They just need help to clarify issues or provide reassurance. When consulting teachers keep talking with consultees, they can begin to work through and solve their own problems. Joint problem identification and idea generation should assure that professional relationships are preserved. Then professional communication is enhanced and all who are involved have stronger feelings of self-esteem and situational control.

Good collaborative consultants do not "solve" problems—they see that problems get solved. So they do "nix the quick fix" and engage in a dedicated way to facilitate problem solving. In his longstanding and very popular leadership training program, Thomas Gordon (1977) focused on questions such as "Whose problem is it?" and "Who *really* owns the problem?" Busy consulting teachers do not need to take on the problems of others. Everyone who owns a part of a problem should participate in solving it. That may involve collaboration among a number of roles—teachers, administrators, vocational and technical arts counselors, social workers, justice system personnel, students, parents, and others. Again, consultants and consultees must focus on a problem rather than on establishing ownership for the problem.

Implementing Plans Agreed On

A problem-solving group needs to select a workable solution that all are willing to adopt, at least on a trial or experimental basis. The consulting teacher should seek mutual participation in making the decision. Group members will accept new ideas and new work methods more readily when they have opportunity to participate in decision making. Many times a complex problem can be solved as each person in the group discovers what the others really want, or perhaps dread, that they will get. Then proposed solutions can be formulated to meet the goals and protect the concerns of all involved.

Better decisions are made with a cool head and a warm heart (Johnson, 1992). Johnson suggests asking oneself if the decision helps meet the *real* need. Real needs are based on situational reality, not illusion or wishful thinking. Co-educators should ask, "Did we have enough information to create options we may not have realized before this? Have we thought through the consequences of each option? Have we *really* thought through all the options?" Taking time to ask all the necessary questions is a key to the decision-making process. Asking many questions and expecting clear answers will help to make options and choices obvious.

Effective collaborators participate in the problem solving process in such a way that all participants feel their needs are being satisfied and an equitable social, emotional, and professional relationship is maintained. The members of the problem-solving team critique all the suggestions made, with each presenting disadvantages and merits of the suggestions from their own perspectives. Agreement is not necessary at this point, because both disadvantages and potential merits of options have been taken into account. Honest and open communication, using good listening skills and an appropriate level of assertiveness, are vital at this step.

Following Through and Following Up

After sorting through data, scheduling and arranging meetings, planning the agenda, and facilitating and participating in the meeting, it is tempting to breathe a sigh of relief when the agreed-on plan is ready, and move on to other things. But collaborators, busy as they are, must follow *through* on progress of the plan, first to be sure it *is* implemented as planned, and later at a designated time to follow *up* with consultees and clients on how the plan succeeded. If the follow-up process indicates that no progress was made or other, unexpected problems surfaced, then the problem-solving activity should be repeated.

PROBLEM-SOLVING ROLES

In collaborative problem solving, the role of the initiator or convener for special needs is to facilitate interaction and teamwork with understanding, skill, objectivity, and self-confidence. Collaborative school consultation encourages collective thinking for creative and imaginative alternatives and allows all who are involved to have their feelings and ideas heard and their goals addressed in practical ways. The ultimate goal is to provide the best learning opportunities possible for students with special needs. At this point it may be helpful to review the descriptions of consultation, collaboration, and teamwork as demonstrated through some examples that differentiate among the three interactive processes.

Problem Solving with Consultation

A preschool teacher is concerned about a child in the group who is not fluent in speech. So the teacher asks the speech pathologist to help determine what to do about it. The speech pathologist consults with the teacher and the child's family to get more information about the observed behavior, and makes additional observations. The consultant then uses her expertise in speech pathology to address the questions and concerns of the teacher and the family.

In another instance, a physical therapist provides individualized therapy for a preschool child who has cerebral palsy. The therapist wants to know about the child's social development as well as performance in pre-academic skills such as letter recognition and sound discrimination. The therapist asks the teacher to serve as a consultant regarding this issue, and the preschool teacher provides the information requested.

Problem Solving with Collaboration

A kindergarten teacher and a music teacher are both concerned about a child's tendency to masturbate during group time, while sitting on the classroom rug. The two teachers meet to discuss their mutual concern. Both parties discuss their observations and engage in problem-solving activities to identify the problem clearly and select possible actions. Both parties agree to make some changes in their respective settings to address the problem. If these collectively determined revisions do not work, they commit to trying other possibilities, including consultation with the child's parents, the school psychologist, and the health nurse.

In another situation, a teacher of students with behavioral disorders, along with the school counselor, three classroom teachers, and a student's parents, meet to discuss inappropriate behavior of that student. The individuals involved in the meeting engage in collaborative problem solving to formulate a plan for addressing the problem. Each individual has a role to play in defining the problem, generating possible actions, and implementing the plan.

Problem Solving with Teamwork

A special education teacher and a general classroom teacher wish to try co-teaching. The teachers meet weekly to co-plan. During the co-planning they decide when, where, and how to share responsibilities for the instructional needs of all students in the classroom during a specified class period each day. Each contributes information about personal areas of expertise and strength whenever feasible. The co-teachers come to consensus on evaluation systems and assign grades for all students by mutual agreement. They no longer speak of "my students" or "your students." Instead, they speak of, plan for, and teach *our students*.

In another situation, a team of professionals provides services for severely and profoundly disabled infants and toddlers. Each professional has an area of expertise and responsibility. The social worker has the leadership role because she is responsible for most family contacts and often goes into homes to provide additional assistance for families. The nurse takes responsibility for monitoring the physical well-being of each child and keeps in close contact with other medical personnel and families. The speech pathologist works with the children to develop speech and language skills. The occupational therapist is responsible for teaching the children self-help skills. The physical therapist follows through with the medical doctor's prescribed physical therapy. Special education teachers provide language stimulation and modeling, coordinate schedules, and facilitate communication among the team that meets twice weekly to discuss individual cases.

A TEN-STEP PROCESS FOR COLLABORATIVE PROBLEM SOLVING

The fundamental principles of a typical problem-solving process have been discussed, and distinctions have been made among problem solving with major focus on direct consultation, problem solving that emphasizes collaboration, and problem solving as a team. It is now appropriate to proceed with a ten-step process for collaborative school consultation.

This process, outlined in Figure 5.3, will help consultants and consultees communicate effectively and coordinate their efforts efficiently to identify educational problems

FIGURE 5.3   The Ten-Step Problem-Solving Process

1. *Prepare for the consultation.*
   1.1 Focus on major topic or area of concern.
   1.2 Prepare and organize materials.
   1.3 Prepare several possible actions or strategies.
   1.4 Arrange for a comfortable, convenient meeting place.

2. *Initiate the consultation.*
   2.1 Establish rapport.
   2.2 Identify the agenda.
   2.3 Focus on the tentatively defined concern.
   2.4 Express interest in the needs of all.

3. *Collect and organize relevant information.*
   3.1 Make notes of data, soliciting from all.
   3.2 Combine and summarize the data.
   3.3 Assess data to focus on areas needing more information.
   3.4 Summarize the information.

4. *Isolate the problem.*
   4.1 Focus on need.
   4.2 State what the problem is.
   4.3 State what it is not.
   4.4 Propose desirable circumstances.

5. *Identify concerns and realities about the problem.*
   5.1 Encourage all to listen to each concern.
   5.2 Identify issues, avoiding jargon.
   5.3 Encourage ventilation of frustration and concerns.
   5.4 Keep focusing on the pertinent issues and needs.
   5.5 Check for agreement.

6. *Generate solutions.*
   6.1 Engage in collaborative problem-solving.
   6.2 Generate several possible options and alternatives.
   6.3 Suggest examples of appropriate classroom modifications.
   6.4 Review options, discussing consequences of each.
   6.5 Select the most reasonable alternatives.

7. *Formulate a plan.*
   7.1 Designate those who will be involved, and how.
   7.2 Set goals.
   7.3 Establish responsibilities.
   7.4 Generate evaluation criteria and methods.
   7.5 Agree on a date for reviewing progress.
   7.6 Follow through on all commitments.

8. *Evaluate progress and process.*
   8.1 Conduct a review session at a specified time.
   8.2 Review data and analyze the results.
   8.3 Keep products as evidence of progress.
   8.4 Make positive, supportive comments.
   8.5 Assess contribution of the collaboration.

9. *Follow through and follow up on the consultation about the situation.*
   9.1 Reassess periodically to assure maintenance.
   9.2 Provide positive reinforcement.
   9.3 Plan further action or continue the plan.
   9.4 Adjust the plan if there are problems.
   9.5 Initiate further consultation if needed.
   9.6 Bring closure if goals have been met.
   9.7 Support effort and reinforce results.
   9.8 Share information where it is wanted.
   9.9 Enjoy the pleasure of having the communication.

10. *Repeat or continue consultation as appropriate.*

and design programs for students' needs. Consulting and collaborating teachers may find it helpful to have a copy of the ten-step outline available for handy reference when they are in problem-solving consultations. If entered into one's electronic file or plan book, it is a good organizational tool and a reassuring resource for every co-educator, particularly for those who are engaging in their first consultations.

Step 1: Preparing for the Collaborative Consultation

Co-educators focus on the major areas of concern and reflect on the circumstances surrounding this concern. They prepare helpful materials and organize them in order to use the collaborative time efficiently. It is helpful to distribute information beforehand so that valuable interaction time is not consumed reading new material. But they must take great care to present that material as tentative and still open to discussion. It is not always constructive to plan in detail prior to consultations. Furthermore, confidentiality is to be maintained by everyone at every juncture.

Occasionally consulting activities happen informally and without notice—between classes, during lunch periods, or on playgrounds. Educators usually will want to accommodate colleagues on these occasions when time and place permit. However, they should look beyond these events for opportunities to engage in more in-depth sessions.

Consultants need to give each collaborator enough advance notice and time to prepare. They will want to provide convenient and comfortable settings for the interaction, arranging seating so there is a collegial atmosphere, with no phone or drop-by interruptions, and assuring privacy. Serving coffee and tea can help set a congenial tone for meetings. (Refer to Figure 5.3.)

Step 2: Initiating the Collaborative Interaction

Educators need to exert much effort in this phase. When resistance to collaborating is high, or the teaching staff has been particularly reluctant to participate, it is difficult to establish first contacts. This is the time to begin with the most receptive staff members in order to build in success. Rapport is established by addressing every consultee as special and expressing interest in what each one is doing and feeling. Teachers should be encouraged to talk about their successes but some are modest and reluctant to do so. The consultant needs to display sensitivity to teachers' needs and make each one feel important. The key is to *listen and observe.*

The convener will want to identify the agenda and keep focusing on the concern. It is helpful to have participants write down their concerns before the meeting and bring them along. These can be checked quickly for congruence and major disagreements. (Again, and with the remaining eight steps, refer to Figure 5.3 for each step.)

Step 3: Collecting and Organizing Information

The data should be relevant to the issue of focus. However, data that might seem irrelevant to one person may be the very information useful to another and essential for identifying the real problem. So participants must be astute in selecting appropriate data that include many possibilities but do not waste time or resources. This becomes easier with experi-ence, but for new teachers, having too much information is probably better than having too little, while bearing in mind that time is limited and must be used judiciously.

A case study method of determining data sources and soliciting information is par-ticularly effective in planning for students who have special learning and behavior needs. Because problem identification is the key factor in planning for special needs, it is critical that sufficient data be obtained from multiple sources. Refer again to Figure 5.2 for identi-fying up to sixteen data sources of information for problem solving to address a student's needs. The more sources that are tapped, the more easily and clearly the need is understood. Think of shading pertinent sections of the figure with colored pencils, paint, or tissue-paper overlays. The darker the center becomes the more assured co-educators can be that needs are being assessed comprehensively.

Step 4: Isolating the Problem

It cannot be stressed too strongly that the most critical aspect of problem solving involves identifying and defining the problem at hand by focusing on needs, not handy solutions. Without problem identification, problem solving cannot occur (Bergan, 1995). The most common problem-solving error is to short circuit the problem definition step and hasten to traditional solutions rather than developing individually tailored solutions (Conoley, 1989). Henning-Stout (1994) notes that less experienced consultants in particular tend to spend insufficient time with the consultee on the nature of the problem and proceed too quickly to developing "the plan." (See Figure 5.4.)

Step 5: Identifying Concerns and Stating Realities Relevant to the Problem

All concerns and viewpoints related to the problem should be aired and shared by each par-ticipant. A different viewpoint is not better or worse, just different. An effective consultant keeps participants focusing on the need by listening, observing, and encouraging everyone to respond. A certain amount of venting and frustration is to be expected and accepted. Teachers and parents will be less resistant when they know they are free to express their feelings without retaliation or judgment. Consulting teachers should remain nonjudgmental and assure supportive confidentiality, always talking and listening in consultees' language.

As information is shared and discussed, the consulting teacher will want to make notes. It is good to have everyone look over the recorded information from time to time dur-ing the session as a demonstration of trust and parity, and a check on accuracy. A log format for recording information and documenting the consultation will be provided in Chapter 6.

Step 6: Generating Options

Now is the time for creative problem solving. If ideas do not come freely, or if partici-pants are blocking productive thinking, the consultant might lead the group in trying one or more of the techniques described later in the chapter. A problem-solving technique not only unleashes ideas, it sends a message about the kinds of behavior and attitude needed to solve problems. "Straw votes" can be taken periodically if that helps the group keep moving toward solutions. "Thinking outside the box" and combining ideas are desirable

FIGURE 5.4   First, Identify the Problem

processes at this stage. It is productive to separate the discussion into two topics, one focusing on benefits and the other on concerns. These two sharing periods would be initiated with the word stems "I like . . . " (where the benefits are shared), and "I wish . . . " or "How could . . . ?" (in which concerns are aired). At this stage the group should modify, dismiss, or solve problems for each concern.

Step 7: Formulating the Plan

After options have been generated, wishes and concerns have been aired, and modifications have been recommended, it is time to make the plan. Participants must remain on task. They need to be reinforced positively for their contributions. Consulting teachers will want to be ready to make suggestions, but they should defer presenting them so long as others are suggesting and volunteering. They must avoid offering ideas prematurely or addressing too many issues at one time. Other unhelpful behaviors are assuming a supervisor/expert role, introducing one's own biases, and making suggestions that conflict with existing values in the school context.

As the plan develops, the group should be clear on just who will do what and when, and where. Evaluation criteria and methods that are congruent with the goals and plan should be developed at this time, and arrangements made for assessment and collection of data on student progress. A vital element to success in collaborative problem solving will be the commitment by *all* participants to follow through with the plan, a step appearing later, as Step 9.

Step 8: Evaluating Progress and Process

This step and the final two steps are frequently neglected. Consultation and collaboration decision making should be followed by assessment of student progress that results from the collaborative plan, and also by evaluation of the collaborative consultation process itself. Figures in Chapter 12 will be useful for this purpose.

The convener will want to make positive, supportive comments while drawing closure, and at that time should evaluate the consultation informally with consultee help and taking care to record the information for later analysis, or evaluate formally by asking participants to complete brief written responses. This can be a good time to plan for future collaboration.

Step 9: Following Through and Following Up

Of all ten steps, Step 9 may be the most neglected. Unsuccessful consultation outcomes often result from lack of follow through on commitments, and then follow up to see if progress has been made or new issues have surfaced. For follow *through* it is in the best interest of the client, consultee, consultant, and future opportunities for consultation to revisit the situation periodically. Participants will want to adjust the student's program if necessary and initiate further consultation if the situation seems to require it. Informal conversations with consultees at this point are very reinforcing.

During the follow *up*, consultants have opportunities to make consultees feel good about their participation. They can make a point of noting improved student behaviors and performance, as well as positive effects that have resulted so far from the collaboration. Also, they may volunteer to help if things are not going as smoothly as anticipated, or if consultees have further needs.

The sweetest words a consultee can hear are "What can I do to help you?" However, this question *must* be framed in the spirit of "What can I do to help you *that you do not have the time and resources to do*?" and *not* with an implication of "What can I do for you that you do not have the skill and expertise to accomplish?" Consultants should respond immediately with materials, information, action, or further consultation that have been promised, and take special care to reinforce things that are going well. Figure 5.5 is an example of a form that could be used.

Step 10: Repeating Collaborative Consultation, if Needed

Further consultation and collaboration may be needed if the plan is not working, or if one or more parties believe the problem was not identified appropriately. On the other hand, consultation also may be repeated and extended when things are going well. The obvious rationale in this case would be that if one modification helped, more will help further. This is very reinforcing for those who are consulting, collaborating, and working together as a team. It also encourages others to participate in the consultation and collaboration processes, too.

FIGURE 5.5   Memo to Follow Through

From: _____ to _____
            (consultant)   (consultee/s)

Date: _____ Re: _____

I am eager to follow through on the plan which we developed on the date above, and also to assist in other ways that may have occurred to you since then.

How do you feel things have progressed since that time? Please be forthright.

_____

_____

What else may I do to help?

_____

_____

                                           (List here any times, descriptions, etc., that would
                                           help me respond specifically to your needs.)

_____   Information   _____

_____   Resources   _____

_____   Meet again   _____

_____   Classroom visit   _____

_____   Conference with: _____

Thank you so much! I enjoy working with you to serve our students and schools.

CASE STUDY IN USING THE TEN-STEP PROBLEM SOLVING PROCESS

When implemented, a ten-step scenario for problem solving might go something like this: A first-year special education consulting teacher asks to meet with the veteran classroom teacher about their student with hearing impairment. Implementation of instructional strategies and curricular adaptations to address the student's IEP goals have been going well. However, the special education teacher believes more could be done in the school environment to help this student fit in socially, emotionally, and physically. In a brief exchange during shared hall supervision with the classroom teacher, she senses that he has some concerns as well, and she suggests a meeting before contacting the parents to see if adjustments to the IEP are warranted.

She prepares for their meeting with an agenda and a summary of ideas and examples for adaptations. She asks to meet in the classroom on the teacher's "turf." As a novice teacher, she wants to use her most polished collaborative consultation skills with this veteran teacher. She knows that as an intuitive thinker her preferred problem-solving style includes a tendency to gloss over facts and move too hastily (eagerly) to looking at ideas for solutions. This is something she has been working on and it will serve her well today because she has observed that this classroom teacher has an opposite style of stating problem, issues, and factual data in succinct detail. She believes that these differences in style can work to their advantage, and benefit the student.

During the interaction, she listens and waits appropriately. She uses verbal forms such as "we" and "How can I assist you in planning for this student's needs?" She asks the teacher about his concerns and listens reflectively until the teacher concludes his comments. She describes a few of what she considers the most powerful items on her idea-suggestion list. They review the student's IEP and then brainstorm, based on their concerns and suggestions as a launch pad. This is where the novice teacher feels she can shine. Next, they generate a description of modifications that focuses on the areas of student need and outlines what would be each teacher's responsibilities. Both contribute their personal expertise on how these modifications can be integrated into general curriculum and other parts of the student's school day. This includes more thoughtful placement in the music room, in assemblies, at lunch, and in playground games.

The two teachers work out the details of the plan, which surprisingly does not take all that much time to accomplish, and they include an early conference with parents for going over the plan. They want to be sure all facets are in compliance with their student's IEP and that they have family support. They make a note to solicit additional ideas from input by the parents. They also plan the means by which they will engage support from other personnel including the music teacher, physical education teacher, bus driver, cafeteria personnel, and school nurse. As they wrap up, the novice teacher confesses to the classroom teacher that this has been one of her first consultations, and she is grateful to him for his part in making it a success. She will be even more comfortable now in the role and enthused about working with other teachers. Her collaborating teacher thanks her for her innovative ideas and says he is sure that more good consultation and collaboration experiences are in her future.

This meeting carries the joint consultation through Steps 1–8 of the problem-solving process. Steps 9 and 10 for following up/following through and repeating the consultation process are yet to come. But both co-educators leave the meeting on this day feeling very good about their collaborative effort. As evidenced by the final exchange between the two, the event was a special boost to the first-year teacher's confidence.

Review as a case study the scenario described above. Then using the ten-step problem solving process, ask:

1. What are the facts in this situation?
2. Who initiated the collaborative effort?
3. What additional information would be helpful?
4. What was the problem and how was it identified?
5. What other realities and concerns became evident?

6. What were options for possible actions?
7. What plan was formulated?
8. What went well in this scenario and did anything not go well, and why?
9. What should happen in follow through and follow up processes?
10. Are further interactions or actions called for?

This is a good time to consider sample phrases of communication that can be helpful in implementing each phase of the ten-step problem-solving process. Copies of these might also go into the consultant's plan book for quick reference during consultations. More communication phrases for a variety of interactional situations will appear in Chapter 7.

What to Say During a Collaborative Consultation

A consulting teacher does not want to parrot points from an outline as though reading instructions for assembling a bicycle. But practicing verbal responses for problem-solving steps will enable the teacher to become more natural and automatic when the need arises. Each number for the phrase sets below corresponds to a numbered step of the ten-step consultation process outlined above. Of course, it is unlikely that all of the comments suggested here would be needed or would fit for any one conference.

1. *When planning the consultation* (Comments in this step are made to oneself.)

   (What styles of communication and interaction can I expect with these consultees?)
   (Have I had previous consultations with them and if so, how did they go?)
   (Do I have any perceptions at this point about client needs? If so, can I keep them under wraps while soliciting responses from others?)
   (What kinds of information might help with this situation?)

2. *When initiating the consultation* (In this step and the rest of the steps, say to the consultee—)

   You're saying that . . .
   The need seems to be . . .
   May we work together along these lines . . . ?
   So the situation is . . .
   I am wondering if that . . .
   What can we do in regard to your request/situation . . . ?

3. *When collecting information*

   Tell me about that . . .
   Uh-huh . . .
   What do you see as the effects of . . . ?
   I'd like to rephrase my question.
   Let's see now, your views/perceptions about this are . . .
   Tell me more about the background of . . .
   Would you give an example of that?
   Sounds tough . . .
   To summarize our basic information then, . . .

4. *When isolating the problem*

> The major factors we have brought out seem to be . . .
> Are we asking the right questions?
> Could you be more specific?
> What do you perceive is the greatest need for . . . ?
> What circumstances have you noted that may apply?
> Are there other parts to the need that we have not considered?
> So to summarize our perceptions at this point . . .
> Are we in agreement that the major part of this issue is . . . ?

5. *When identifying the concerns and stating the realities*

> You say the major concern is . . .
> How do you feel about this?
> Let me see if I understood that.
> But I also hear your concern about . . .
> You'd like this situation changed so that . . .
> How does this affect your day/load/responsibility . . . ?
> You are concerned about other students in your room . . .
> What are some ways to get at . . . ?
> You're feeling . . . because of . . .
> This problem seems formidable. Perhaps we can isolate part of it . . .
> Would you say that . . . ?
> Perhaps we can't be sure about that . . .
> The major factors we have brought out seem to be . . .
> If you could change one thing, what would you change first?

6. *When generating possibilities*

> How does this affect the students/the schedule/the family . . . ?
> Do we have a good handle on the nature of this situation?
> We need to define what we want to happen . . .
> How would you like things to be?
> What has been tried so far?
> What happened then?
> Is this the best way to get it done? The only way?
> How could we do this more easily?
> Could we try something new such as . . . ?
> Could you add to what has been said?
> What limitations fall upon things we might suggest?
> Let's try to develop some ideas to meet the need . . .
> Your idea of . . . also makes me think of . . .

7. *When formulating a plan*

> Let's list the goals and ideas we have come up with . . .
> So, in trying . . . you'll be changing your approach of . . .
> To implement these ideas, we would have to . . .
> What I heard you say was . . . and is that what you meant?

We have considered every possibility brought forth, so which shall it be?
The actions in this situation would be different, because . . .
We've discussed all of the alternatives carefully, so now should we choose?
We need to break down the plan into steps. What should come first? Next?
When is the best time to start with the first step?

8. *When evaluating progress*

Have we got a solid plan?
One way to measure progress toward the goals would be . . .
Some positive things have been happening . . .
How can we build upon these gains?
Now we can decide where to go from here . . .
In what ways did our getting together help?
I can see [the student] progress every day . . .
You're accomplishing so much with . . .
How could I help you and your students in more and better ways?

9. *When following through and following up*

How do you feel about the way things are going?
We had set a time to get back together. Is that time still okay, or should we make it sooner?
I'm interested in the progress you have observed.
I'm following up on that material/action I promised.
I just stopped by to . . .
I wondered how things have been going for you . . .
How are things in your corner of the world these days?
I'm glad you've hung in there with this situation.
You've accomplished a lot that may not be apparent when you're with it every day.
You know, progress like this makes teachers look very good!

10. *If repeating the consultation*

Should we have another go at discussing . . . ?
Perhaps we overlooked some information that would help . . .
We got so much accomplished last time. How about getting together again to . . . ?
That's a great progress report. Would another plan session produce even more of
these very positive results?

ACTION 5.2
Using the 10-Step Consulting Process

Select one or more of the following situations and, with a volunteering collaborator, simulate
a school consultation experience, using the ten-step process and "What to Say" phrases that
seem appropriate:

Situation A: A middle-school student is vision impaired. Her IEP includes having the
teacher modify her paper/pencil tests. What are the ramifications of this for the classroom
teacher's preparations, grading issues, and district-wide testing?

Situation B: It is the first week of school. A high school student new to the area has Tourette's syndrome, and even though he has medication that keeps the syndrome under control, he has asked if he may speak briefly to his classmates during class to explain his condition "just in case." He believes that few in the public know very much about Tourette's syndrome, and one of his chosen causes is to spread awareness. Who should meet about this, and what should their agenda be?

Situation C: A ninth-grade student is considered lazy by former teachers, has failed several courses, and cannot grasp math concepts. He has difficulty locating information but can read and understand most material at his grade level. He is never prepared for class, seldom has pencil and paper, and loses his assignments. Yet he is pleasant and seemingly eager to please, and he will try things in a one-to-one situation. His classroom teachers say he will not pass, and you all have decided it is imperative to meet about this. How will you, the learning disabilities consulting teacher, address the situation?

Situation D: You are attending an IEP meeting on behalf of a third-grade student who is emotionally disturbed and classified as developmentally delayed. You believe she should be placed in a general classroom with supportive counseling service and reevaluated in a year. The other staff participants feel she should have been in special education placement with inclusion only into music, art, and physical education. The mother is confused about the lack of agreement among school personnel. How will you address the concerns of all in this situation, particularly the mother?

Situation E: A sixth-grade student's mother is known as a perfectionist. Her son did not receive all A's on the last report card, and she has requested a conference with you as the classroom teacher, the principal, and the school psychologist. How will you approach this?

Situation F: A first-year kindergarten teacher has learned that one of her students will be a child with cerebral palsy. Although the child's history to date has included continuous evaluation, home teaching, group socialization experiences, special examinations, and therapy sessions as well as family counseling for three years, the teacher is nervous about her responsibilities with this child. As the speech pathologist, how will you build her confidence in caring for the kindergartner's language needs, and her skill in helping the child to develop her potential?

Situation G: The special education director and middle school building administrator have been asked by a group of general education teachers and special education teachers to meet with them. The director and the principal sense that this group was chosen informally by the entire teaching staff to be their spokespersons. They know that these teachers and their colleagues are caring and conscientious educators. The representative group wants to discuss the grave concerns they have about including all students with special needs in the high-stakes standardized tests to be given in a few weeks. When they voice their concerns, request information on how best to prepare the students for these tests, and ask what is to be done with the results of the tests, how might the special education director and building administrator react and respond?

What to Consider if Group Problem Solving Is Not Successful

There is no universal agreement on what makes group problem solving effective, and there is little research to guide consultants as to what should be said and done in collaborative consultation. However, the ten steps outlined above have worked well for many consultants and consulting teachers. If this method of ten steps does not work, consultants should put forth questions such as these:

- Was the problem defined accurately?
- Did all participants practice good listening skills?
- Were feelings addressed empathically?
- Were the nitty-gritty details worked out?
- Were pertinent hidden agendas brought to light and handled?
- Were all participants appropriately assertive?
- Was the consultation process evaluated and then discussed?
- Could any other problem-solving tools have facilitated the process?
- Was there follow-through and follow-up activity after the conference?
- Should participants convene in groups to practice problem-solving techniques?

ACTION 5.3
A Further Problem-Solving Challenge Using Impromptu Scenarios

As a team effort in a group with several colleagues who share your grade level and subject area, construct a scenario to demonstrate the ten-step collaborative school consultation process at your teaching level and in your content area(s). Role play it for other groups, stopping at key points—for example, after problem identification, and again after formulating the plan, and perhaps then just before following through, to ask the observing group what they might do at that point. If promising alternatives are suggested, try each one and follow it to its conclusion, in the manner of the choose-an-adventure books that children like to read and complete.

What techniques worked best? How did individual differences influence the consultation? Were these individual differences used constructively, and if not, what could have been done instead? Did participants become better collaborators as they tried more scenarios?

TOOLS FOR COLLABORATIVE PROBLEM SOLVING

The collaborative format of working together and drawing upon collective expertise to solve problems is widely practiced in business and professional worlds. In the effort to use the best ideas of bright, innovative minds, astute leaders employ a number of group problem-solving techniques.

One of the most frequently occurring examples of problem finding and problem solving in schools is development of a student's Individual Education Plan. The shared thinking in which the interactive IEP team engages is a collaborative method of finding solutions to problems (Clark, 2000). Student needs are the first and foremost consideration, but with all participants aware of the problem-solving process and using some of the suggested lead phrases, the conference should go well. Collaborators will want to reflect later as a group on their success.

Too many general educators have expressed dissatisfaction with the IEP development process, citing blizzards of terms, forms, and paperwork as factors, and even expressing concern that student input was not valued. As noted by Menlove, Hudson, and Suter (2001), dissatisfaction was higher for secondary teachers than for elementary teachers. Reasons given were team disconnect, time and preparation involved, training needed for pertinent knowledge and skills, and IEP relevance to their school context. General educators had the view that the IEP meeting is a special education teacher's meeting, not a team meeting, and when parents were present they did not like to push issues.

On the positive side, general education teachers have been signaling some improvements in time available, information received, communication skills in collaborative settings, and preparation for problem delineation. This is a promising area in which both IEP participatory skills and collaborative skills can be improved simultaneously through well-targeted training programs.

Another instructive activity as a group can be rubric development for a specific purpose, such as learning and behavior expectations on a class trip, or procedures and assessment for a cooperative learning activity. Development of rubrics might even lead to setting up a portfolio system in the classroom.

Yet another exercise could be solving problems collaboratively to use technology for developing differentiated curriculum to fit exceptional learning needs. After generating lists of technological tools, the group could evaluate the lists using the Plus–Minus–Interesting technique described later in this chapter.

A large number of easy-to-use techniques for group participation in problem solving are available. These include, but certainly are not limited to, brainstorming; lateral thinking, Six Thinking Hats, and Plus–Minus–Interesting techniques of de Bono (1973, 1985, 1986); concept mapping; idea checklists; metaphorical thinking; role play; and TalkWalk (Caro & Robbins, 1991). Many more are available on line and in books featuring creative production. Teachers often incorporate these kinds of group problem-solving activity into their curriculum planning for students, but then overlook their potential for problem solving with adults. Here are a few brief descriptions and application activities.

Brainstorming

Brainstorming is a mainstay of creative problem-solving methodology. It facilitates generating many unique ideas. When a group is brainstorming, participants should be relaxed and having fun. There are no right or wrong responses during the process because problems seldom have only one right approach. No one may critique an idea during the brainstorming process. All ideas are accepted as plausible and regarded as potentially valuable. Each idea that is expressed is recorded. In large group sessions, it is most efficient to have a leader for managing the oral responses and a recorder for getting them recorded on a board or screen visible to all.

The classic rules developed by Osborn (1963) and others for brainstorming and used in countless business, education, industrial, and community settings since then are:

1. Do not criticize any ideas at the time they are offered.
2. Remember that the more wild and zany the ideas are, the better.

3. Think up as many different ideas as possible.

4. Try to combine two or more ideas into new ones.

5. Hitch-hike (piggyback) on another's idea. A person with a hitch-hike idea is to be called on before those who have unrelated ideas, so indicate a signal for doing that.

Note that when coaching others (children in particular) in brainstorming techniques, it is good to introduce them to a "humanitarian principle" before the very first session. This means that an idea will not be accepted if it is obviously a harmful or hurtful one. A response to "What are new ways to use old bricks?" that comes out as "To drown kittens" (typically followed with a pause and a quick glance at the teacher by its contributor to wait for classmates' chuckles or teacher's shocked expression) would be handled with a brief but firm "Sorry, but as you know, we abide by the humanitarian principle here." Then the teacher would move quickly on without accepting the idea or scolding the contributor. This response would remain true to the spirit of brainstorming.

Brainstorming is useful when the group wishes to explore as many alternatives as possible and defer evaluation of the ideas until the options have been exhausted. People who cannot resist the urge to comment prematurely on ideas during brainstorming must be reminded on the spot that evaluation comes later. Leaders should call on volunteers quickly and politely ignore those who seem to want to bend the rules.

When the flow of ideas slows, it is good to persevere a while longer. Often the second wave of thoughts will contain the most innovative suggestions. Each participant should be encouraged to contribute, but be allowed to pass if desired.

Individual brainstorming activity can be a very productive precursor to group brainstorming. Recall that personal preferences often have effects on instruction in unexpected ways, and this is one example. Some people like to brainstorm privately, rather like an incubation process, before joining in the group effort. Others enjoy getting right to it.If an agenda that states topics to be discussed is provided ahead of meeting time, with the "heads-up" suggestion that brainstorming might be used as a tool for gathering ideas, those who wish to reflect on the matter beforehand will be better prepared to contribute enthusiastically.

Reverse brainstorming is an unusual technique that can be useful on rare occasions if the group is stuck and needs to find another approach. With this technique, participants propose what would be considered the opposites of good ideas, such as, "If someone wanted to *increase* bullying and extortion on the school grounds, how could that be done?" Or, "If we *didn't* want students to read widely from many sections in the library, how would we discourage them from doing so?" On a cautionary note, participants need to know exactly what the purpose of this technique is and should bring closure to the activity in a positive way by restating, "These are things we want *not* to do, so things we don't want to happen will not." It would be unfortunate if there were accidental eavesdroppers to a reverse brainstorm session who did not know the technique and were not informed as to the intent of the exercise!

Using the Brainstorm Technique   A brainstorming session would be appropriate for this situation. A first-grade student has read just about every book in the small, rural school. The first-grade teacher and gifted program facilitator brainstorm possibilities for enhancing this student's reading options and augmenting the school's resources as well.

Another way to use brainstorming would be to think of ways to welcome and include new students into classroom and extracurricular activities. A third would be to brainstorm ways of getting socially neglected children chosen on teams early in the selection process.

Concept Mapping

Concept mapping (referred to by some as mind-mapping, semantic mapping, webbing, or trees of knowledge or information) is a tool for identifying concepts, showing multiple relationships among them, and reflecting upon the degree of generality and inclusiveness that envelopes them (Wesley & Wesley, 1990). The technique allows users to display ideas, link them together, elaborate upon them, add new information as it surfaces, and review the formulation of the ideas. The process begins with one word, or issue, written on paper, screen, or chalkboard and enclosed in a circle. Then other circles of subtopics, ideas, words, and concepts are linked to that central theme by lines or spokes, connecting and interconnecting where the concepts relate and interrelate. More and more possibilities and new areas open up as the webbing grows. Relationships and interrelationships that can help verbalize problems and interventions are recorded for all participants to see. If the concept map is displayed as a large mural about a topic of general interest, the process can go on and on as more ideas are generated and added.

Concept mapping is taught to students for purposes such as reading comprehension at all grade levels. Buzan (1983) offers strategies for mind-mapping in which learning techniques such as note-taking can be structured to show interrelationships easily. Many students in gifted programs have been introduced to the concept of webbing to focus on a problem of interest and plan an independent study. Sometimes college students are encouraged to try mind-mapping by combining lecture notes and text reading to study for exams. Concept-mapping is a powerful tool for enhancing individual learning. It also can lead to more meaningful and productive professional development activities (Bocchino, 1991).

Using Concept Mapping   A classroom teacher has agreed to work with a student new to the district who has been diagnosed with Asperger syndrome. The student has acceptable social skills in some instances, and is friendly and cooperative. But he also requires individual instruction, is functioning about two years below grade level, and makes threatening comments impulsively to other students. During previous visits the teacher had indicated to the special education teacher that things were going well. Now, in the middle of November, she asks for consultation immediately. She is upset, saying things such as "It just isn't working" and "I've tried so hard," but she has not really described the problem. How might concept mapping or webbing help in this situation? What word or phrase could go into the center to begin the webbing?

Synectics, Metaphors, and Janusian Thinking

Innovators in many walks of life have been trying for decades to introduce more creative thinking into the work field. Workers are trained to "see old things in new ways," so as to invent better ways of performing their work well. The technique, known as synectics (Gordon & Poze, 1975), calls on participants to "make the familiar strange" and "make the strange familiar." Mental connections are made with facts and feelings and broken up so that new connections can be made with new facts and feelings.

When co-educators interact to discuss their differing perspectives and preferences in the spirit of nonjudgmental curiosity and inquiry, they are helping what is strange to become more familiar, and anticipating perhaps that a gem of an idea will begin to form. This can be refreshing and enervating. Ideally, some Actions and Reflections sections in this book will encourage synectical thinking.

Using Synectics, Metaphors, and Janusian Thinking   As an example of synectics, one secondary teacher of students with developmental delays thought ("What if I take something that seems appropriate for very bright students, and design it for my students, who would be quite challenged by it?"). After much thought, planning, trial and error, revision, and preparation of a procedural plan, he set up the catering system described in an earlier chapter in which his students provided snacks at first, then full-fledged meals after the plan was going well, for special events in the schools. The results for students' academic skills, social skills, practical skills in running the business, and feelings of self-confidence and self-esteem were immeasurable. The program became the talk of not only the school but also the entire community. After presentation at a special education meeting, it received statewide attention and accolades. Creative problem-solving tools and activities *can* have real and positive outcomes.

Metaphors are a kind of synectics—mental maps that permit the connection of different meanings through some shared similarity. They appear often in spoken and written communication. For example, poetic sentences such as "Life is a loom," and "The fog swallowed the ship," are metaphorical. But ordinary phrases used every day also are beautifully metaphorical, as "Her flower garden is a paint box of intense colors." "It was a *zoo* at school today." Metaphors connect in order to explain. Many creative people in various fields have broken with conventional thinking by engaging in metaphorical thinking.

The metaphor uses one subject to strengthen and deepen the understanding of another. Metaphors can guide groups for activating change processes. They are useful to generate new ideas, and teach new concepts (Garmston, 1994). Pollio (1987) suggests that some of the most important scientific, philosophical, and technical insights were conceived from an imaginative image. Educators can use metaphors to connect two different viewpoints so one idea can be understood by means of the other.

■ ■ ■ ■ ■

ACTION 5.4

Engaging the Power of Metaphorical Thinking

With a group of your colleagues, generate free-association responses to open-ended phrases such as:

- "Life is a ＿＿＿＿＿." (zoo/pressure cooker/bank/car lot/battle/party)
- "School is a ＿＿＿＿＿." (prison/smorgasbord/twelve-act play/family/game)

A second part of the activity is to continue from the image chosen, as in the following—for examples:

- "If school is a *zoo*, then teachers are _____ and students are _____."
- "If school is a twelve-act play, students are _____, teachers are _____, and principals are _____."

Open-ended phrases then could move to topics such as:

- "Team teaching is _____, and teachers are the _____."
- "Inservice days are a _____ (battery charger?) and teachers are the (dead batteries now all charged up?)."

(Metaphors can be served as tart lessons sweetened with humor and a twist of wry!)

Janusian thinking was recognized by Rothenberg and Hausman (1976) as they studied the Eugene O'Neill play, *The Iceman Cometh*. The term was coined from the Roman god Janus, who looks backward into the old year and forward into the new (January). The process involves using two or more contradictory or opposite ideas *simultaneously*—for example, sweet and salty. This simultaneous consideration of opposites creates tension that can spark original thought. As an example, Mozart told aspiring musicians that the rests in between the notes are as important, if not more so, than the notes themselves. Frank Lloyd Wright valued the concept of Janusian thinking because architects need to conceptualize the inside and outside of a building simultaneously. The key element in the process is simultaneity; thus, convex outer shapes must be reconciled with concave inner shapes in order for the architect to conceptualize the structure.

ACTION 5.5
Exploring the Power of Janusian Thinking

With colleagues, use the technique of group brainstorming, permitting no judging of the ideas, and having a disposition where the strange become familiar, such as in with Sweet Tarts®, dry ice, jumbo shrimp, snow blanket, to generate more examples of Janusian thought. Then shift to a socially focused mode and try for ideas such as "win–win," and "friendly fire." After thinking of several clever product-type examples, the power of the process becomes evident.

But that was the easy task. Now strive for new, Janusian-based concepts that can help students, such as creative homework, innovative drill, elementary/secondary student mentorships, and more. Not so many years ago some considered collaborative consultation to be a Janusian phrase, but no more. (Teachers might be surprised at some profound combinations generated by students if they put them to the task of generating Janusian-structured school terms.)

More Techniques for Collaborative Problem Solving

A number of other collaborative activities for nurturing creative thinking are useful for exchanging information and generating ideas among co-educators to the ultimate benefit of their students. Many of them can be retrieved at websites under their descriptive names or under key words such as creative problem solving, creative thinking, and even creative collaboration. A brief summary of just a few will follow.

Plus–Minus–Interesting   The simple Plus-Minus-Interesting (PMI) process (deBono, 1986) can be completed in a half-hour or so, often stimulating rearrangement of perspectives and sometimes recasting values placed on those perspectives. As an example, in a school considering use of active senior citizens as reading aides, the collaborative team would generate a three-part list to show aspects that rate as pluses, then as minuses, and as things that are interesting but the team would like to investigate further before making a decision. In making a decision, it is not necessary that the pluses exceed the minuses, and sometimes the "interesting features" may even win out as the most contributive to decision making. The discussion and potential resolution that the PMI technique offers is a productive tool in problem solving.

Role Play   A fundamental purpose of role play as a problem-solving practice is to produce new perspectives. For example, for new perspectives in a teacher-parent conflict, the teacher could take the role of the parent, and the parent that of the teacher. Other participants also have specific parts to play. At a critical part in the interaction the leader stops the players and has the whole group explore options that would be possible from that point. Then new solutions may emerge (Torrance & Safter, 1999). In role playing, the convener must be skilled and facilitative, so that the role players understand the purpose and participate intently without self-consciousness.

Talking Stick   A very simple device for encouraging participation in discussions is the use of the talking stick, a practice ascribed to some American Indian tribes. Each person in turn takes the talking stick, restating the previous point made, even if contrary to his or hers, before adding a personal viewpoint to the discussion and then passing the stick on.

TalkWalk   In this unique form of small-group interaction, participants engage in collegial dialogue focused on instructional and curricular issues while they walk together in an open environment (Caro & Robbins, 1991). The fresh air, physical and mental exercise, and exploration of ideas frees up thinking and expression. These domains of activity are reflective of the taxonomy domains discussed in Chapter 2—cognitive, affective, sensorimotor, and social. The technique itself was the collaborative idea of Caro, a physician, and Robbins, an educational consultant. It calls for an element of trust among collaborators who sometimes are reluctant to seek advice from colleagues for fear of seeming incompetent. It can be used as part of a workshop or simply as an informal arrangement among colleagues.

Caro and Robbins suggest that groups of two or three work best. They propose that TalkWalk provides educators with four Es for problem solving: *expertise* from collective experience, *enrichment* to improve sense of self-worth and problem-solving capacity, *expediency* to obtain rapid solutions through assistance, and *exercise* to bring a fresh attitude and perspective to the problem. One walk, for example, might focus on the group's vision for students who are in transition from school to work and independent living. Another might be to join preschool teachers and primary teachers in a TalkWalk to discuss that transition period for very young children. An outcome of such talks could be a plan that will help make the vision become real.

Use of Multiple Intelligences   A unique way to generate many perspectives and perhaps arrive at some clever solutions for problems is to frame the questions in terms of Gardner's (1993) multiple intelligence categories. For example, to build interest, rapport, and skills for team teaching among staff with no experience in team teaching, these questions could help with planning efforts:

- *Linguistic*—How can we use words and stories to describe team-teaching?
- *Logical-mathematical*—How might we measure the benefits and drawbacks of a team-teaching approach in our school?
- *Musical*—Should we create a team song or cheer?
- *Spatial*—Should we make a physical map of where everything will be and what more, or less, we should include in the spaces we will share?
- *Interpersonal*—What kinds of differences in interests, preferences, values, and personal habits would be important to discuss before embarking on a team teaching mission?
- *Intrapersonal*—How would I describe my feelings about giving up some of my professional autonomy, and sharing many of my ideas and techniques?
- *Bodily-kinesthetic*—How can we move throughout the room, arrange materials, and get students' attention when we are teaching together in the same spaces?
- *Naturalistic*—Will our school environment accommodate the aspects of team teaching so that students are comfortable, parents are satisfied, and teachers are positive about the experience?

INTERFERENCES AND HURDLES TO OVERCOME

Co-educators must examine their own perspectives and preferences to identify any potential aspects that will impede *their* abilities to consult and collaborate on behalf of the student. Recall the four interfering themes (Caplan, 1970) that can impede teachers' effectiveness. One area in which the interference is subtle but strong is being divergent thinkers and problem solvers.

Some teachers might demonstrate *inadequate understanding* by over- or under-identifying students. Others may show *lack of skill* by failing to modify curriculum for those with disabilities. *Failure to be objective* is evident when teachers equate student situations to situations in their own lives or to former students. *Lack of self-confidence* is shown in resistance to new plans and inflexibility toward new ideas.

Educators must be knowledgeable, skilled, objective, and self-confident, with a bit of risk-taking mixed in, to engage in divergent-thinking strategies with colleagues. When collaborating, they should use every opportunity to reinforce the efforts and successes of their colleagues, to take risks with curriculum and instruction for the right purposes so long as the risks are not harmful or hurtful, and to convey a desire for learning from them and their experiences. Too often classroom teachers, as ones occupying nonspecialist roles among specialists, and parents, who know their child best but must give them up to schools for hours each day, are somewhat removed from the discussion and overlooked when ideas for addressing special learning and behavior needs are explored.

When communicating and cooperating with consultees to identify the learning or behavior need, it is important that collaborating consultants avoid sending messages intimating that classroom teachers and parents are deficient in skills that only special education teachers can provide (Friend & Cook, 1990; Huefner, 1988; Idol, Paolucci-Whitcomb, & Nevin, 1986). Good communication skills and cooperative attitudes will encourage feelings of parity and voluntariness among all school personnel and parents in the problem-solving process.

Students assigned to go back and forth among resource settings in other schools for part of the week or school day may have teachers who never communicate about them and their work. This is a serious drawback of some cluster group arrangements where students travel from one school to another with no planned interaction among school personnel taking place. Coordination of collaborative effort is vital. This is easier said than done; even the bus drivers sometimes find it hard to coordinate students' comings and goings among buildings.

Special education teachers who cannot identify basal reading curriculum used in various levels, and classroom teachers who cannot identify the nature of instruction taking place in the resource room, make problem identification more difficult (Idol, West, & Lloyd, 1988). Their lack of shared knowledge may even intensify the problems. All parties must think about their own roles in a problem situation and endeavor to learn from each other by interacting, deferring judgment, and coordinating services. A team approach is a productive way to assess the context, conditions, interfering themes, and circumstances surrounding the student's needs and the school programs designed to meet those needs.

Positive and Not-So-Positive Interactions

Some collaborative consultations are more successful than others. In a few instances, they turn out rather discouragingly. The following are examples of collaborators feeling positive:

- Primary-level teachers and I sat down and discussed what materials they thought would be good to order and place in the resource room, for their use as well as mine. Everyone had a chance to share needs, express opinions, and make recommendations.
- An undergraduate asked me about my student teaching and substituting days. She was feeling very down and unsure of her teaching abilities. I reassured her by

telling of some things that had happened to me (and why). I encouraged her to find a dependable support system, and gave her some ideas and things to think about.

- A teacher I have spent several weeks with stopped me in the hall yesterday to ask for an idea to use in her class that next hour. Before she finished putting her question into words, she had thought of an idea herself, but she still thanked me!
- I participated in a parent conference in which the parent wanted to kick the daughter out of the house and into a boarding school. It ended with the daughter agreeing to do more work at home, and the mother agreeing to spend one special hour of together-ness a week with just her daughter.

The following are examples of some not-so-positive situations:

- A kindergarten child was staffed into my program, but the teacher wouldn't let me take her out of "her" class time. So I arranged to keep the child after school. The first night I was late coming to fetch the child, and the teacher blew up about it.
- Our music teacher asks students who cannot read to stand up in class and read, and then pokes fun at them. I approached the teacher about the situation, but the teacher wanted nothing to do with me, and after that made things even worse for the students.
- In visiting with the principal about alternatives in altering classroom assignments, it ended with his speaking harshly and suggesting that I was finding fault with the school staff, which I had not done.
- I give a sticker every day to a student who has learning disabilities if he attends and does his work in the resource room. His classroom teacher complained to the principal about it because "other students work hard and don't get stickers."

REFLECTION 5.1

Establishing Rapport Among Co-Educators for Collaborative Problem Solving

When consulting teachers are getting ready to take part in problem-solving sessions with class-room teachers that they have not worked with very much, or perhaps have never even met yet, what are several things they can think about beforehand, and prepare, and then when on the scene, say and do, to develop rapport and establish strong, friendly collaborative relationships?

TECHNOLOGY FOR COLLABORATIVE PROBLEM SOLVING

The most compelling feature of an excellent technological tool for collaborative school consultants and co-teachers is its ability to save co-educators time. Tools that are asynchro-nous and efficiency promoting will be the ones that busy educators with heavy caseloads and coordinative responsibilities want to reach for first and use.

In schools where teachers apply instructional methods that incorporate technology into their classrooms, students become engaged and motivated in interactive learning

(Martinez, 2010). Martinez describes a project in which ninth graders in a low-performing school read silently for 30 minutes twice a week and then log on to a website to join a group the teacher has arranged. They discuss a topic posted on the Facebook and discussion board and write about what they read. Then they are ready to work in teams for writing and designing a children's book. Elsewhere, in a Northeastern urban public school, teachers use a video-game strategy as a tool for designing a "traveling around the world" game, requiring all the necessary "preparations" to be made and dealing with situations along the way.

In order for beginning teachers to use the technological tools they have grown up with and love in purposeful, innovative ways with their students, teacher preparation programs must provide them with opportunities to practice applications of those tools in ways that will transfer constructively into their future classrooms. This means that their instructors will need to be skilled in coursework for teacher education *and* the technology that can complement and enrich that coursework.

Students in high-technology classrooms with interactive whiteboards, iPads, and handheld video cameras and many more innovative devices, if not staffed by well-coached instructors, are no better off than those without these modern tools (Ferriter, 2011a). News reports have told of iPads going to kindergarten classes so that they can learn the basics of ABCs, 1–2–3s, drawing, and music with iPad2 touchpad tablets. A goal is to hold the attention of the young students as they learn through imagery and sound. Such investments of money and time should be preceded by collaborative consultation among school personnel to determine most important goals for kindergartners and best instructional objectives and assessments to put to use in working toward those goals.

Once again, Ferriter (2011b) asserts that good teaching (and here we could insert "good collaborative school consultation") trumps good tools every time. Educators point to the computers sitting idle against the wall in many schools because instructional goals and teacher skills for their use have not been established and developed. With this caution in mind, co-educators can choose tools wisely that will best help them and their students perform at the highest level possible, and then prepare themselves to be facilitators for smart, sensible use of those tools.

ETHICS FOR COLLABORATIVE AND CONSULTATIVE PROBLEM SOLVING

An ethical climate and impeccably ethical behavior are keenly important in special education. Howe and Miramontes (1992) remind us that actions of special educators have life-long ramifications and must be taken very seriously. Many of the proposed actions require keen judgment to deal with potential consequences. As an example, consider the dilemma of a junior high teacher, alone in her classroom preparing for class, when a student enters the room and grabs her from behind in an inappropriate and forceful way. After talking him into a chair and calming him down, what then? She was virtually certain that the parents' harsh and peculiar child-rearing practices were the root of his alarming behavior. What should happen next? Teachers have little preparation for thorny issues such as this. But, as co-educators in inclusive settings with joint responsibility for students, they must share their concerns, pool their expertise, and collaboratively make decisions for the welfare of a student such as this and for others who could be affected, including the parents. Collegial problem solving must be valued and promoted as a tool to help students in need to succeed (Phillips & McCullough, 1990).

When groups of co-educators gather (and to reiterate a previous point, in some IEP conferences the number of adults in attendance may be as many as a dozen), handling confidential material is compounded. Co-educators need to be watchful for negative outcomes resulting from "groupthink," where negativity, bias, failure to examine risks of proposed choices, and failure to work out plans carefully can result in quite negative outcomes (Murray, 1994). A collaborative ethic guides such groups in discussing sensitive matters calmly, objectively, and respectfully. This ethic empowers professionals to support and motivate each other toward exemplary instructional and management practices.

TIPS FOR PROBLEM SOLVING THROUGH COLLABORATIVE CONSULTATION

1. Have materials and thoughts organized before consultations and develop a list of questions that will help ferret out the real problem.
2. Be prepared for the meeting with a checklist of information typically needed. Do not be reluctant to say that you do not have *the* answer. If it is something you should know, find out as soon as possible and get back to the person who asked.
3. Have strategies and materials in mind that may be helpful to the situation, but do not try to have *all* of the answers or offer solutions too readily because this discourages involvement by others who may have been struggling with the situation for some time.
4. Avoid jargon, and shun suggestions that conflict with school policies or favored practices of individual teachers; whenever possible use the terms *we* and *us*, not *I* and *you*.
5. Make it a habit to look for something positive about the teacher, the class, and the student, and comment on those things, using feedback as a vehicle that can provide *positive* information, not just negative perspectives.
6. Don't try to "fix it" if it is not "broken," or wait for the consultee to make the first move, or expect that teachers will be enthused and flattered to have questions asked about their classrooms and teaching methods.
7. When a teacher seeks advice about a student, first ask what the teacher has already observed. This gets the teacher involved in the problem and encourages ownership in serving the student's special need.
8. Know how to interpret test results and how to discuss those results with educators, parents, and students in a conference setting; if insecure about it, have a practice session with a willing colleague.
9. When possible, provide parents with samples of the child's schoolwork to discuss during the conference, remembering to *refrain from talking* while they peruse the materials. Have a list of resources ready to share with the family for helping with homework, suggesting incentives and reinforcements, and providing study tips.

10. Maintain contact with teachers during the year; the collaborating teacher or family may have detected an improvement that is directly related to your work, and it will be uplifting and energizing for you to know that!

ADDITIONAL RESOURCES

Clark, S. G. (2000). The IEP process as a tool for collaboration. *Teaching Exceptional Children, 33*(2), 56–66.

Gardner, H. (1993). *Multiple intelligences: The theory in practice.* New York: HarperCollins.

Giangreco, M. F. (1993). Using creative problem-solving methods to include students with severe disabilities in general classroom activities. *Journal of Educational and Psychological Consultation, 4*(2), 113–135. Provides specific examples of using the Osborn-Parnes Creative Problem-Solving process for instructional inclusion relevant to students with intensive educational needs.

Gullatt, D. E., & Tollett, J. R. (1997). Educational law: A requisite course for preservice and inservice teacher education programs. *Journal of Teacher Education, 48*(2),129–135.

Osborn, A. F. (1963). *Applied imagination: Principles and procedures of creative problem-solving.* New York: Charles Scribner. The classic problem-solving handbook, with a wealth of ideas, including early instruction on the technique of brainstorming.

Starko, A. (2001). *Creativity in the classroom: Schools of curious delight* (2nd ed.). Mahwah, NJ: Lawrence Erlbaum.

6

Organization and Management of Collaborative School Consultation

SCHOOLS ARE BUSTLING ARENAS OF ACTIVITIES, WITH MUCH MORE ACTIVITY for students than simply books and studies and much more responsibility for teachers and support staff than just instructing and disciplining. Not only do school personnel teach students in academic settings, they also feed them, transport them, keep records, coach, counsel and advise, dispense materials and resources, address social and health problems, and much, much more. If the services of various school-related roles such as library and media specialist, speech pathologist, school psychologist, social worker, counselor, and nurse, were included, the list of responsibilities for educators would be even more daunting. The content of organization and management (see Figure 6.1) for collaboration and consultation includes implementation of strategies to assist co-educators with issues such as stress and burnout, meetings, schedules, recordkeeping, and confidentiality.

When consulting teachers are asked to name the biggest obstacle for performing these responsibilities to the very best of their abilities, the overwhelming response is, "Time!" A study released by the Council for Exceptional Children in October, 2000 (*CEC Today*, Nov. 2000), cited overwhelming paperwork, pressure of high caseloads, lack of needed support by administrators, and shortage of qualified special education teachers as major concerns. Teachers stressed that they needed more time for collaborative planning, and 15 percent of the respondents reported having *no* time for individualized instruction. Only 26 percent reported having more than three hours a day with their intact classes of students. An unfortunate outcome was a lack of time for the planning and collaborating that are vital components of instructional accommodations and modifications for special needs.

Teacher retention is a burning issue in education, particularly in areas of science, math, the arts, and *special education*. Levine (2006) points out that due to population increases, immigration of students, and the inevitability of teachers reaching retirement age, numbers of school-age population are rising while numbers of teachers are decreasing. "Recruiting and preparing strong, effective teachers must be a top priority for those concerned about public education" (p. 220). But several factors erode preparation of teachers and support for teachers after they enter the profession, including ever-expanding costs of maintaining schools, public criticism as reflected in polls and the media, low morale among educators, and an avalanche of regulations and paperwork. Nearly one-fourth of new teachers leave after only two years, and one-third leave within five years (Ingersoll, 2002; Millinger, 2004).

FOCUSING QUESTIONS

1. What aspects of education make school personnel vulnerable to stress and burnout and what improvements in conditions could increase retention of teachers in the profession?

2. What organizational and management tools and techniques help minimize stress and reduce attrition from the teaching profession?

3. What procedures for conducting meetings, interviews, and observations contribute to success in collaborations and partnerships?

4. How can collaborating school consultants manage time, records, and resources more efficiently?

5. What technological tools and processes enable educators to teach, collaborate, and consult effectively?

6. What are important ethical issues in organization and management of collaborative consultation in schools?

KEY TERMS

attrition	eustress	stress management
burnout	interview	time management
caseload	observation	
consultation log or journal	self-efficacy	

VIGNETTE 6

The setting is a coffee shop in a university's student union. Three faculty members from the College of Education—one who teaches educational psychology for elementary education majors, another who teaches educational psychology for secondary education majors, and a third who teaches a class on exceptional children in the inclusive classroom, are sharing views about their new students for the semester.

Instructor for Elementary Educational Psychology Class: I am impressed with the new group of students we have this semester in our teacher education program.

Instructor for Exceptional Child Class: I haven't been here as long as you have, but from what I have observed during my first two class sessions, I agree that they seem to be strong and very capable and dedicated as a whole.

Instructor for Secondary Educational Psychology Class: They're so idealistic. They are sure that they will be able to inspire kids and excite them toward learning. They say they want to make a positive difference in their students' lives. I hope that in two years or so they'll be well prepared and strong enough to deal with all the challenges out there, especially if they accept positions in tough schools with many difficult students.

Instructor for Exceptional Child Class: Yes, or all too soon they'll be joining the ranks of teachers who burn out after just three or four years in the profession. I'm alarmed at the attrition rate for new teachers in this country.

Instructor for Secondary Educational Psychology Class: We should all be alarmed about those figures. The statistics are an urgent message to us in teacher education programs to prepare them as best we can. Of course we all think our own classes are vital toward that effort! But besides knowing their subject matter well, new teachers will need to be competent in many kinds of things. I believe a key area of competence that novice teachers need to develop is collaboration and consultation.

Instructor for Elementary Educational Psychology Class: You raise a good point. Even though we offer that in a graduate-level course, the knowledge and practices it provides are needed by all teachers from day one, not just after they are out in the schools for several years and working toward a master's degree.

Instructor for Exceptional Child Class: And it shouldn't be only for special education majors. It's just as important for the general education teachers to develop those skills, for they are the other side of the equation.

Both Educational Psychology Instructors, in Unison: Well said!

TEACHER ATTRITION, SATISFACTION, AND EFFICACY

The dedication and enthusiasm of educators wishing to mold younger generations and make the world into a better place must be retained and maintained. However, in the complex hubbub of school life, demands on the professional educator can be overwhelming. Stress and fatigue take a toll, with burnout and attrition from the teaching profession an all-too-frequent occurrence. The challenge of professional accountability for student achievement is a heavy burden. High-stakes testing to the neglect of the subject matter they love takes a heavy toll on teachers as well as on students. When teachers are not satisfied in their roles, they become candidates for burnout and attrition. But role-related stress can be minimized. The heavy responsibilities fueling that stress can be controlled by organizing and managing time and resources wisely.

Steep attrition in the first few years of teaching is an escalating situation, with an alarming one-third of new teachers leaving the profession within five years (Darling-Hammond, 2003). Shortages of special education teachers, science teachers, and math teachers, in particular, plague school districts. Nearly one-fourth of new teachers leave after only two years, and one-third leave after two years (Ingersoll, 2002; Millinger, 2004). Sadly, teacher turnover is 50 percent higher in schools with high poverty levels than in other schools (Ingersoll, 2001). Special education teachers as advocates for children with special learning and behavior needs may be setting unreasonably high expectations for themselves and others. Lack of appreciation and reinforcement for their work, along with heavy caseloads, confusion over role responsibilities and not much decision-making authority, are additional stressors, particularly for special education personnel.

An unfortunate reality of the teacher shortage is a distressing exodus of experienced teachers in special education. Many leave within their first few years of teaching and a number of those quit the profession altogether, but more than half transfer to general education positions (Plash & Piotrowski, 2007). As needs for special education teachers mushroom, the numbers of educators who prepare for special education and subsequently enter the field have been dwindling. Demands imposed on classroom teachers by the NCLB mandate weighed heavily on teachers, making it hard for them to feel good about what they do. One fourth-grade teacher spoke for many of her colleagues when she put it this way: "I wanted to be a teacher, and I'm glad to be a teacher, but it's just not fun anymore."

Professional satisfaction is a key variable in the effort to increase retention and enhance the work settings of special education personnel. Some educators remain in the profession and juggle their daily routines within a burgeoning agenda of reform and mandates. Others burn out and leave the profession. Still others simply "fizzle out," "rust out," or "coast out." This last group tends to go through the motions of their profession in lackluster fashion, just getting by until retirement age arrives or opportunity for a better opportunity comes along. These educators create situations that are particularly penalizing for students who have special needs and are most vulnerable to the effects of uninspired teaching.

One factor that can influence professional satisfaction is teacher self-efficacy. This is the belief that people have the ability to mold their own actions in ways that affect the learning and behavior of their students. Teacher efficacy correlates positively with higher student achievement, effective teacher practices, increased family involvement, decreased referral rates to special education, and higher job commitment by teachers (Gibson & Dembo, 1984; Hoy & Woolfolk, 1993). Importantly, teacher self-efficacy has an inverse correlation with burnout among general educators (Friedman, 2003.)

Collective efficacy, or beliefs and efforts of the group, have not been studied to a great extent as yet (Viel-Ruma, Houchins, Jolivette, & Benson, 2010). However, Goddard, Hoy, and Woolfolk-Hoy (2000) found a significant relationship between student achievement in schools and collective efficacy levels. More recently Viel-Ruma, Houchins, Jolivette, and Benson (2010) determined that while collective efficacy did not have a direct effect on job satisfaction among special educators, it directly affects teacher self-efficacy. These researchers recommended professional development programs and strong induction programs to promote self-efficacy. They also spoke out for school improvements in curriculum, discipline, and school status within the community as ways of enhancing collective efficacy.

REDUCING TEACHER STRESS AND TEACHER BURNOUT

Teacher burnout can come about from physical and emotional exhaustion. Prolonged stress or the buildup of stressors causes fatigue and frustration. According to Maslach (1982), a researcher of burnout among service professionals for many years, there are three basic components of burnout:

1. Emotional exhaustion ("I'm tired and irritated all the time. I am impatient with my students and colleagues.")
2. Depersonalization ("I am becoming emotionally hardened; I start to blame the students or their families for all the problems.")
3. Reduced accomplishment ("I feel like I'm not making a difference for my students.")

The results of burnout can be attrition, alienation, cynicism, and physical problems such as heart disease, hypertension, ulcers, headaches, and psychosomatic illnesses. Stressors that cause stress reactions are many and varied. For the collaborative consultant in special education, a stressor could be a new special education regulation, a change in job description, too much paperwork, too many meetings that seem to go nowhere, an angry parent, a student who is behaving in a violent manner, or some or all of the above.

Most educators have a vast repertoire of coping skills, and we all know that stress in general is a normal life process. In fact, there is *eustress* (Schultz, 1980), a little-discussed phenomenon of proactive, positive response to a stimulus, such as that experienced by artists, entertainers, athletes, speakers, and yes, teachers, before going "on stage" that helps people perform at their best. It can even help us learn and grow. Those who have experienced some conditions such as eustress probably are more likely to have good coping skills and to be empathetic with others under stress than people who have not.

On the other hand, *dis*tress (anxiety, sorrow, pain, trouble) wears us down physically and emotionally. Busy, conscientious educators will never be able to reduce or eliminate all the stressors in their lives, but they can develop some positive coping skills that lessen the burden and strengthen resolve to overcome the difficulties.

Teacher education programs must be strong learning centers for preparing preservice teachers to succeed as novice teachers so that they will want to remain in the profession. Management techniques for time and other resources, organizing structures for some of the more burdensome tasks, evaluation procedures that provide careful analysis of the outcomes, and the assistance of technology, are four areas that can minimize stress and reduce attrition from the profession.

Undergraduate students, when queried about their greatest concerns for their first years in the profession, have named areas that fit remarkably into Caplan's (1970) four "lack-of" themes noted in Chapters 4 and 5: knowledge, skill, objectivity, and self-confidence. Their questions, as major concerns driven by these themes, are: Will I know my subjects well enough? Will I be able to prepare good, motivating lessons? Can I manage the classroom and discipline the students appropriately? How will I be when it comes to working with parents? Will I know how to serve all students' special needs? Do I have the skills to provide appropriate feedback and grade students fairly? Can I be confident that I can handle everything and not be a big failure? Teacher efficacy is needed here.

Novice teachers have many pressures that dampen their enthusiasm in the first years of teaching. This is the time when temptation to leave the profession is high. New teachers may be very stressed emotionally, physically, and socially. Their two most frequently cited problems were dealing with special needs of children such as behavioral problems, learning disabilities, and attention deficits, and working with other adults including parents, administrators, mentors, teaching assistants, and co-teachers (Babinski & Rogers, 1998). Understandably, new teachers fear being judged as incapable and failing if they ask for suggestions or outright assistance. Given the importance of perceived self-efficacy, it is important to build it up as a way of retaining new special education teachers.

Strategies for Reducing Stress

Developing adaptive strategies to reduce stress is crucial to maintaining emotional and physical health for all teachers, whether novice or veteran. The techniques individuals use depend on their preferences and life styles. Collaborators must learn to "work smarter, not harder" to accomplish goals for students who are at risk of failure in school. They must take care of themselves so they do not lose their energy and enthusiasm, and students with special needs do not lose their good, caring teachers. Recall the words of the flight attendant who instructs, "In case of emergency, first put on *your* oxygen mask and *then* put on your child's mask." We cannot take care of others if we are in no condition to help.

One group of special education teachers makes a commitment to meet each Friday at a centralized place for lunch and lively conversation. Ground rules stipulate there will be no talking about students, schools, or staff in that public place. The camaraderie and conviviality of the weekly event, looked on favorably by district administrators, is an effective support system for teachers whose roles invite stress.

Building mutually supportive networks of co-educators will minimize, if not totally eliminate, feelings of isolation and helplessness for those in demanding roles. It helps to talk things out with others and develop new outlooks when in the throes of the complex responsibilities inherent in working with special needs students.

The husband of a pregnant teacher in a self-contained classroom for behavioral disorders finally insisted one day that she resign from her position. For months her work had been laced with disappointments and danger, but on that particular day she came home bruised and crying after a chair was thrown at her by a female student. "You *and* our unborn baby are at risk," said the concerned spouse. An overlooked aspect of collaboration and co-teaching roles is the support system it provides. The teacher has an outlet for expressing frustration and a backup in times of crisis or when the going is just getting too rough.

What if burnout has occurred or is at least in the glowing embers stage and ready to flare up at most any time? What if an educator is experiencing low self-esteem, emotional distress, and physical exhaustion now? Strategies such as these can help:

1. Talk to someone, give a positive comment, let it be known you could use one in return, share ideas.
2. Find a former teacher who was very important in your life and tell that person how much you learned with his or her guidance.
3. Schedule some time to be alone and reflect on your profession. Then stick to that promised schedule.
4. Laugh out loud. Each person should have his or her "laugh ration" every day for mental and physical health. So listen to a comedy tape, read a joke book, watch children play.
5. Move, stretch, jog. Mild exercise gets the blood flowing and transports more oxygen throughout the body, helping you feel alert and alive. Sunlight and fresh air help body and mind function well.
6. Play energetic, happy music. Classical music is best. Listening to sixty-cycle music such as that by Bach, Handel, and Mozart has been shown to increase alpha brain wave, the relaxation wavelength (Douglass & Douglass, 1993). On the other hand, rock music is tiring and tends to drain energy away.
7. Break the routine. Take a different route when driving to work. Let everyone cut in front of your car and feel smug about it. Rearrange your schedule or your furniture. Take a vacation if you can and when you do, leave worries and cares behind. Give yourself over to relaxation and rejuvenation.

8. Keep a jar of little treats on your desk, such as encouraging statements, or an envelope with a five-dollar bill for something frivolous inside, to be good to yourself now and again. Positive reinforcement is not just for kids.
9. Use reminders to help remember these and other prevention and intervention strategies. They could be colored ribbons, stick-on happy faces, ads from magazines, letters written to yourself. Put the reminders on your tote bag or briefcase, on your calendar, or dangling from your rear view mirror as in younger, more carefree days.
10. Remind yourself often that prevention and remediation of stress and burnout are the concern of the individual adult, not family or friends or colleagues. Every person needs to make deposits into a personal bank of techniques for keeping the flames of motivation and enthusiasm alive.

MANAGING TIME AND TURF

School improvement issues and legislative mandates may have convinced educators that the concept of collaborative school consultation is a promising method for helping students with special needs. However, for some teachers, the conversion to co-educator concepts and collaborative practices is not so simple and can be unsettling. As for novice teachers who did not have collaborative experiences in their teacher preparation program, collaborative principles can put them off balance just when they are starting out in their first teaching role. They may be thinking:

- Will participation in collaboration and consultation make me appear to be less competent?
- How much of my classroom time with students will be needed to provide this method of service to kids and how do I go about allocating that time?
- Don't I need to work out a plan for my classroom and get experience with that before I collaborate with others and certainly before I co-teach?
- When in the world will I find time and space to interact like this with other teachers anyway?

Studies have shown that collaborating teachers chafe under time pressures of attending meetings, preparing and planning, teaching, conferencing with parents and students, administering tests, communicating with related services and support personnel, observing, evaluating, and problem solving. (See Figure 6.2.) Time, the precious, nonrenewable commodity everyone receives equally, requires decision making about allocation and management. We should devote more time to time—organizing and managing it, and seeking out tools that will help us put it to good use in the most powerful ways possible. Educator ingenuity can produce innovative ways of carving out time in an already-packed day if it becomes a top priority to do so.

A key factor in managing time and arranging schedules is the teacher's caseload. Those having both direct and indirect service roles should have their ratios classified for each category, and students receiving consultative services as well as direct services should be counted twice on the consulting teacher's caseload. Solutions to the time element lie in how educators choose use the time available to them. Time may not be adaptable, but people are. An ancient Chinese proverb says, "You cannot change the wind, but you can adjust the sail." Time management skills can be learned and improved. Because

FIGURE 6.2   "I Need a System Here!"

time management is about choices, it is very personal. The best management plan for one is not the best one for another. A basic five-step plan is useful for making one's own time management plan:

1. Analyze your current use of time.
2. Establish your goals and priorities.
3. Allocate your time and work.
4. Use positive time management techniques.
5. Review the results, rethink any problem areas, and reinforce successes.

Accountability for Collaborative Consultation Time

Many consultants, when asked specifically how they use their time, rely on memory or perceptions. However, to make significant improvements in time management, busy consultants must accurately observe and *record* their use of time. Time logs are a valuable way to observe personal use of time and they ultimately save time rather than waste it. Consultants may choose to use a diary time log, recording everything they do, when they do it, and how long it takes. Another option is to record time in 15-minute segments, or use a matrix that lists times of the day in segments and highlights elements of the consulting role. The matrix can be used to check off quickly those responsibilities that were handled in each segment. Then time spent on each activity can be totaled at the end of the day. When recording use of time, remember to begin early in the day, not waiting until the end of the day and then trying to remember it all, for the log record will come up short almost every time.

It is helpful to review long-term goals daily. They should be posted on the desk, the wall, or in a planner. This simple activity, according to Douglass and Douglass (1993), helps one stay focused. Long-term goals should be subdivided into short-term goals, weekly goals, and daily goals. To minimize the gap between long-term and short-term goals, Douglass and Douglass suggest keeping a master "to do" list with priority codes matching items to your goals, assigning a due date to each project because due dates keep tasks from being put off and foster a sense of completion when accomplished, and estimating time required to complete the task or the project.

Putnam (1993) offers a number of practical tips for making every minute count, including establishing goals and staying focused during work time; delegating routine tasks when possible to students, aides, and parent volunteers; minimizing procrastination; and learning to say "no" by practicing until it feels firm and guilt-free, and then really doing it.

Time management procedures encourage efficient use of abilities and strengths. The purpose of time management is not to get *everything* done, but to meet high-priority goals successfully. Being busy is not the same as being productive. Time management is a skill that can be learned and improved. See Figure 6.3 for one consulting teacher's weekly organizer form.

WEEKLY ORGANIZER

Dates: _____ to _____

Week at a Glance				
Monday /	Tuesday /	Wednesday /	Thursday /	Friday /

To Do (Priority)	To See	
	Person/Place	Time

To Do (Eventually)	To Phone/E-mail	
	Person	Phone number/E-mail address

☺ Notes & Reminders ☺

—by Jane Jacquart

FIGURE 6.3   A Weekly Organizer Form

ACTION 6.1
Using Time Wisely

Physicists define time as nature's way to keep everything from happening at once. By planning time and managing time-wasters, educators can be more productive and less stressed. Try one or more of these strategies and then reflect on how they helped:

1. *Make "to do" lists—monthly, weekly, and/or daily lists.* Make each list at the same time of day on the same kind of paper. Write down all that needs to be done and plan all activities, even those such as talking with friends or playing with the family. Then prioritize the list. Lakein (1973) suggests "ABC-ing" the list, with A as top priority for only those items that *must* be done. Designate B priorities as "nice if done" and C jobs as "maybe later." You might even end up with a D—or "So what?"—list. Handle the C tasks sensibly. If they can't be delegated or ignored, try putting them on the extra-minutes list. If that is not an option, consider bartering, pooling resources, and consolidating activities.

2. *Say "no" when you need to.* Avoid saying "Well . . . ," or "I'll think about it." Certainly avoid, "I will if you can't find anyone else" because they won't. Responding with "This is so important that it needs more attention than I can give it now" is often very effective.

3. *Delegate.* This is the perfect solution for C priorities, if a helper is available. Teachers are habituated into functioning autonomously, but others may be just waiting for a chance to contribute and develop their own skills or to receive recognition for being a good team player.

4. *Set deadlines and time limits.* Plan a personal treat for accomplishing a task by deadline. Limiting time helps get things done efficiently and prevents simple tasks from becoming major projects. It prevents letting the intentions to clean out one drawer become major cleaning of the whole desk, file cabinet, and book shelves, for example.

5. *Organize desk and office area.* A work area can be so cluttered that it is difficult if not impossible to find things, concentrate, or work efficiently.

6. *Get a "do not disturb" sign and use it without guilt.* Some teachers have had great success making and using work-status cubes for their desk *and* even encouraging their students to do the same. Faces on one's cube can convey messages such as "Please do not disturb right now," "I need help," "This is not a good day for me, so be patient, please," or "I'm available if assistance is needed."

7. *Plan time for yourself.* Busy educators often devote so much time and energy to taking care of others that it comes at the expense of neglecting themselves. Take time to relax, visit with others in the building, talk to a child, read a book, go for a walk, or sketch a picture. If you absolutely cannot get away, take a few minutes to imagine where you would like to be and "go there" in your mind for a while.

Finding Time for Collaboration and Teaming

Managing time and schedules in order to collaborate effectively is indeed one of the biggest challenges for co-educators. In Cawelti (1997), teachers report that their instruction improves when they work in teams. But they need to have the time available in order to do that. Many educators believe outcomes-based education and performance-based assessment are promising innovations for schools, but acknowledge that each plan requires additional teacher plan time. How to accomplish that is as yet unresolved.

Time emerged as the key issue inherent in every school-change analysis for many years. Raywid (1993) found that strategies for gaining time included freeing up existing time used for some lesson priority, restructuring or rescheduling time, using available time more efficiently, or buying time from other facets of the school context. Examples from this research include:

- Teachers sharing the same lunch period with their planning period after lunch, which results in 90 minutes of shared time per day
- Teachers interacting while students leave the building a few hours weekly to perform community service
- Substitutes hired with money saved by increasing class sizes by one or two students
- Daylong staff development for three to five days per year in some districts
- Compensatory time for teachers participating in two- to three-day planning sessions during breaks between terms
- Staff development days, with as many as five or more instructional days waived by state legislatures
- Lengthened instructional days
- Special talents and skills programs provided by specialists or hobby days for students while teachers meet to collaborate and plan
- University personnel working in partnership to provide activities that free up teachers to interact

Note that most of the ideas above would require administrator approval and assistance. Building administrators must be the driving force to make such things happen. In some areas, teachers meet to develop rubrics, tests, teaching ideas, and the like. They are not required to make reports or write summaries as justification for time spent. They are just asked to show the products that resulted from the shared time. Other faculties brainstorm in an initial collaborative effort to come up with unique ideas for carving out more extensive collaborative time. Still others have grade-level or departmental plan time on a regular basis during some music, art, and physical education periods.

In one district, teachers were convinced that their high school students didn't get enough sleep. These teachers also were looking for ways and means of collaborating. So a policy was put into place to have late-start days every other Wednesday, moving school starting time from 8:00 a.m. to 8:30, to allow teachers an extra 45 minutes to meet and students an extra 30 minutes to sleep in, visit, or study. Administrators and paraeducators supervised the students who showed up early. The Professional Learning Communities (PLC) model that was first implemented in Adlai Stevenson High School in Lincolnshire, Illinois, guided the time allocated for meeting together. Even experienced teachers reported learning many useful things during their time together. Guidelines for the teachers required that there be no cell phones used and no complaining. Instead, teachers shared ideas and discussed ways to improve student achievement (Silva, Thessin, & Starr, 2011).

In another district, three building administrators made it possible for teachers to form interdisciplinary teams that meet on their own time—Saturdays for breakfast or before or after school—to work on instruction that would use authentic achievement criteria (Stewart & Brendefur, 2005). The trade-off was that they were excused from regular professional development days. As they participated in the learning team, they adjusted to the reality that their work was available for scrutiny by others. A master teacher marveled at how much she learned, saying she could only imagine how much a *new* teacher might have learned. Her administrator became convinced that learning teams could improve instruction.

Other educational leaders have found new ways of creating time to collaborate. Some work with the parent–teacher organization to implement volunteer substitute-teacher programs that free up teachers. Others revise schedules to provide shared planning time, and still others release teachers from school duties such as lunch and bus supervision, and student activities and assemblies. Peer-tutoring programs across classes can free up time for team meetings, although start time and monitoring time must be factored in. Many innovative ideas are available, but generating and implementing the ideas requires time to plan and coordinate them.

In an *Education Update* (ASCD, 2000) from the Association for Supervision and Curriculum Development, finding time for collaborating is described as "not a question of know-how, but of want-to." Teachers want collaborative time to be part of staff development that occurs during the school day, not after school or on Saturdays. They value sharing materials and ideas, developing rubrics, asking big questions, doing joint planning, and making presentations to one another on tried-and-true techniques. When teachers have premium time arranged for working collaboratively on creating helpful strategies for curriculum and instruction, they refrain from using the shared time for routine activities such as grading papers.

A number of strategies for increasing collaboration time have been used successfully at elementary, middle, junior high, and senior high levels, including ideas such as these (ASCD 2000; West, 1990):

- Bringing large groups of students together for speakers, films, or plays
- Using volunteers such as grandparents, parents, community leaders, and retired teachers
- Hiring a permanent "floating substitute"
- Having the principal set aside one day per grading period as "collaboration day" with no other activities on this day
- Having the principal or another staff supervisor teach a period a day regularly
- Having students working on independent or study activities while clustered in large groups under supervision
- Having faculty vote to extend the instructional day twenty minutes for two days a week

TECHNIQUES FOR MEETINGS, INTERVIEWS, AND OBSERVATIONS

Who has not winced at the thought of having another meeting to attend? Meetings, interviews, and classroom observations command precious time as well as physical and mental energy. Collective time and energy are wasted when people are trapped in unproductive meetings. Educators who want to work smarter, not harder, should set goals for having group interactions that are efficient and productive for all.

Conducting Efficient Meetings

Special educators are busy, but classroom teachers are among the most overextended of all. Many express their frustration that the total time is appallingly short for having all of their students together for a class period without someone or another coming and going. Consultation and collaboration will be accepted more readily when consultees know that consultants respect their time and their students' time. So meetings should be planned only if they can contribute significantly to serving students' needs.

The first rule in planning an efficient meeting is to ask, "Do we really need to have this meeting?" If the answer is not a resounding "Yes," then the business probably can be handled in a more efficient way, perhaps by memo, e-mail, phone, or brief face-to-face conversations with individuals. Good reasons for having a meeting are:

- Fulfilling legal obligations (such as an IEP conference)
- Brainstorming for a need in order to generate many ideas
- Problem-solving with several people in diverse roles to explore options
- Reconciling conflicting views among school, students, and home
- Providing a forum for all to be heard
- Building a team to make and implement educational decisions

Unnecessary meetings do waste much school time and teacher time. They also erode participants' confidence in the value of future meetings that may be called. Meetings should be called only when there is verifiable need and an overall purpose with definite objectives. Only people who can make a contribution need to be there. An agenda should be prepared and distributed in advance, and the meeting room and any needed equipment should be made ready ahead of time. Most important, the meeting must begin on time with no waiting for latecomers, and end on time, or early if possible.

Preparing for the Meeting   Leaders or chairpersons of meetings will be more prepared and organized if they follow a planning checklist. (See Figure 6.4 for an example.) The planning sheet should include general planning points such as date, start and anticipated end time, participants, and goals. Checklists designed to set forth preparations for the room and to note participant needs also will be useful.

Participants   After determining a need for a meeting, as noted earlier, leaders and chairs will want to request attendance from only those who can contribute to the topic at hand. The group should be as small as possible, adhering to the principle concerning meetings that the more who are involved, the shorter it should be. Experts on group interaction recommend that the maximum for problem solving is five, for problem identification about ten, for hearing a review or presentation as many as thirty, and for motivation and inspiration as many as possible. If a problem-solving group includes more than six people, it is likely that not everyone will have an opportunity to contribute.

FIGURE 6.4   Checklist to Prepare for Meetings

Date: _____   Place: _____

Time: _____   Topic: _____

Participants: _____

Goals for Meeting: _____

_____

_____

Preparation of Room: Preparation for Participants:

_____ Technology for visuals   _____ Nametags

_____ Screen, bulbs, cord   _____ Pads and pens

_____ Display board and markers   _____ Handouts

_____ Charts, pens, tape   _____ Agenda

_____ Audio capture technology   _____ Ice-breaker activity

_____ Podium, lectern   _____ Map of location

_____ Tables, chairs   _____ Refreshments

_____ Breakout arrangements   _____ Follow-up activity

_____ Other?   _____ Other?

Room Arrangement: _____

_____

_____   (Sketch of Room)

_____

_____

Agenda   Chairpersons for meetings should develop an agenda that addresses the needs of all participants. Sometimes e-mail or memos can be used to solicit agenda items from those who will participate. If an e-mail agenda is sent in advance, a request can be attached soliciting suggestions for additional items. The agenda topics could be given in question format as a variation now and then. For example, rather than "Scheduling for the Resource Room," the issue might be "How can we construct a fair, workable schedule for use of the resource room on M–W–F?" The latter form takes a bit longer to write and read, but it could save several minutes, multiplied by the number of participants present, when the meeting does take place.

With an agenda distributed beforehand and a stop-time given, participants will be more productive and less apprehensive. Sometimes leaders of large group meetings draw upon a teaching technique of placing a short, high-interest activity, relating to the topic but

FIGURE 6.5 Checklist to Prepare Participants

Date: _____ Place: _____

Time Start: _____ Time End: _____ Topic: _____

Roles: Facilitator: _____

Recorder: _____

Timekeeper: _____

Other Participants: _____

Agenda for Meeting: _____

_____

_____

_____

_____ Minutes of Prior Meeting Attached _____

_____ Advance Preparation Needed _____

_____ Next Planned Meeting _____

At the Meeting

Action	Person(s) Responsible	Target Date	Done

needing little explanation, on the chalkboard or overhead screen. Participants focus on the activity as they arrive, becoming centered on the meeting topic(s) as they do so. Meetings are more effective when participants can anticipate the task. (See Figure 6.5 for an example of a pre-meeting communication to prepare participants.)

It is important to allocate time for each item on the agenda. Estimating the time needed for each item will allow the chair to monitor progress during the meeting. It is counterproductive to focus too long on early items and fail to get to the last ones. If more important items are placed far down the agenda and time becomes short, it might even appear that they have been put there by the convener to avoid action or decision making on those topics. Collaborators seeking to build positive relationships among their colleagues will not want that to happen.

Seating Arrangements   Comfortable chairs and seating arrangements that facilitate inter-action are important factors in the success of a meeting. Full-size chairs (not kindergarten furniture) with a little padding, but not too much, should be provided. For best interaction, there should be an arrangement where all can face each other. A circle for six to ten people, a U-shape with peripheral seating if there is to be a visual presentation, or a semi-circle of one or more rows for large groups, works well (Lawren, 1989).

Participant Responsibilities   Along with the responsibility of each participant to inter-act and help brainstorm, problem solve, or decide, three other role responsibilities are important—chair, recorder, and timekeeper. In many cases the consultant will take care of all three roles, particularly if the meeting includes only two or three people. However, if the meeting is long, or the issues are complex and there is much discussion and brainstorming, it is efficient for the chair to ask another participant to record the key points and any decisions made.

One potentially useful strategy for getting the most out of a meeting is to take notes, whether or not they are required. This focuses attention and keeps the writer actively engaged and still. Even adults sometimes find it hard to sit still and listen when there are so many other things vying for one's energy and attention.

During the Meeting   The first order of business is to make sure that all participants are introduced by name and role. Whether the meeting involves two persons or twenty persons, all participants should be made to feel that they have important contributions to make. All should listen attentively to each other, think creatively and flexibly, and avoid disruptive communication such as jokes, puns, sarcasm, or side comments (Gordon, 1974). Talking and whispering in subgroups can be particularly distracting. Ironically, some teachers who will not tolerate such behavior by their students in the classroom are the biggest offenders. Astute group leaders have various ways of handling this disagreeable occurrence. They might go over to the offenders and stand alongside or between them, direct a question to one of them, or request a response from them. Each participant in a meeting should be thinking at all times about what will move the group ahead.

Compromise for consensus is not always the best solution. It may reflect a weak decision, a watered-down plan, or failure by some participants to express their concerns as firmly as they should. During the meeting leaders should encourage opposing views so that they do not surface later when the matter has been closed and opinions no longer would be useful. If any participant wishes to dissent, the time to do so is in the meeting, not in hall-ways after the matter has been decided and open dissent would dampen enthusiasm for the decision. Of course, many consultations and collaborations involve only two individuals—consultant and consultee. But procedures recommended for groups of several or more usually are pertinent to interactions between only two individuals as well.

Winding Up the Meeting   The time should be checked frequently but discreetly without calling attention to timekeeper or clocks so that the meeting can end on time. If a meeting's agenda and group progress become sidetracked, leaders should redirect attention by making a point to refocus the discussion (Raschke, Dedrick, & DeVries, 1988). When time is up, the leader should review any key decisions made and, if needed, set the time and place for the next meeting, perhaps offering a preliminary overview of that agenda.

FIGURE 6.6   Checklist to Evaluate Meetings

	Yes	No	Don't Know or Does Not Apply
1. All participants were prepared in advance with an agenda.	____	____	____
2. The meeting began on time.	____	____	____
3. Facilities were comfortable and pleasant.	____	____	____
4. Privacy was ensured.	____	____	____
5. Participation was evenly distributed with everyone contributing.	____	____	____
6. Time was used well and the agenda was completed.	____	____	____
7. A summary of decisions was made, listing those responsible.	____	____	____
8. Follow-up activities and any needed repeats were planned.	____	____	____
9. The meeting ended on time.	____	____	____
10. Participants evaluated the meeting's structure and outcome(s).	____	____	____

Additional Comments: _____

_____

_____

Minutes of the Meeting   Minutes are a record for designating those who will have a responsibility, for describing plans and decisions, and for listing projected dates to complete tasks. This is an important aspect of the consultation that must not be slighted. Sometimes committees are faulted for keeping minutes to waste hours! But they are necessary to reflect the group's decisions about what is to be done, by whom, and by what date. They should be brief and concise, but they do not need to include each point of the discussion.

Assessment of the Meeting   Some time should be reserved at the end of the meeting to discuss progress made and to evaluate the effectiveness of the meeting. This does not need to be a lengthy process. A brief checklist like the one in Figure 6.6 could be distributed or sent by e-mail to be completed on line and returned in short order. Participants should be thanked for coming, for being prepared, and for participating actively. Finally, there should be early follow up on any tasks assigned.

Brief Agenda Meetings   When educators have a single topic that can be handled in a quick meeting before or after school, they can structure the meeting with a brief agenda meeting process. (See Figure 6.7.) After becoming familiar with this process, team members will be able to have short agenda meetings without much ado. However, they should not try to squeeze a large agenda or issue into this format, for that would be self-defeating to brief agenda purpose.

FIGURE 6.7   Brief-Agenda Conference

Date, Time, and Participants

Data reporting: _____

_____

_____

_____ 3 minutes

1. Problem finding   5 minutes

2. Idea generating   5 minutes

3. Solution finding   12 minutes

4. Follow-through planning   5 minutes

Conducting Effective Interviews

School consultants often need to interview school personnel, community resource personnel, and family members to plan programs for helping students with special needs. Interviewees can contribute useful information for case studies and formulation of learning goals. They can help ferret out options and alternatives from a myriad of possibilities to find curricular fits for special needs, and when they have participated actively, they can be called on to provide data for program evaluation.

Successful interviews require effective communication skills and demeanors of one-downsmanship, parity, and cooperativeness. Queries such as "Tell me more," and "Could you expand on that?" and "Let me see if I understand what you are saying . . . " are examples of the responsive listening and paraphrasing that help to elicit the most useful information. This will be addressed in more detail in Chapter 7; refer also to the "What to Say During a Collaborative Consultation" section in Chapter 5.

The interviewer should take notes, allowing interviewees to look them over at the conclusion of the interview. If a tape-recording is desired, the interviewer must ask permission beforehand to make one. Some feel it is best to avoid taping, because respondents are often less candid, therefore less helpful, if their comments are being recorded.

Interviews must be conducted ethically, collegially, and for a purpose not attainable by less intrusive and less time-consuming methods. Keys to a successful interview include asking the right questions and showing respect and appreciation for the expertise of the interviewee. A follow-up interaction soon after the interview session has occurred will be affirming and reassuring to the interviewee, thus encouraging further collaborations.

Making Prudent Observations

Consulting teachers often need to observe a student, groups of students, or an entire program in operation, and it is becoming more common for general education teachers to observe in other educational settings as well. This is not an easy professional activity to conduct. Consultants who go into classrooms to observe can expect some discomfort and

FIGURE 6.8   "Here's That Teacher Video Recording Again."

anxiety on the part of the observed. There may be latent resentment because the consulting teacher is more or less free to visit in other classrooms, something many teachers would like to do but rarely get the opportunity.

Consulting teachers can facilitate the process of observation, and ease the minds of those being observed, in several ways. First, they should provide a positive comment upon entering the room, and then sit unobtrusively where the teacher has designated. They should avoid getting involved in classroom activities or helping students, even those who raise their hands hoping to be attended to. The most effective observers blend into the classroom setting so they are hardly noticed. Regular visits minimize the likelihood of having students know who is being observed and for what reason. It is concerning to hear a student say, "Oh, here's that learning disabilities teacher to check up on Jimmy again." (See Figure 6.8.)

Records of behaviors must be done in code so that the physical signs of the observer's writing, watching, and body language do not reveal the subject or purpose of the observation. Each consultant should develop a personal coding system for recording information. Observers can watch the targeted student for one minute, and then divert their attention to another student for one minute, continuing the process with other peers. In this way the observed student does not feel "targeted" and the behavior can be compared with that of classmates. The consulting teacher might even teach a lesson while the classroom teacher observes. This can be helpful for both consultant and consultee. See Figure 6.9 for a sample classroom observation form.

Finally, it is important for an observer to exit the room with a smile and a supporting glance at the teacher. Then very soon after the observation, the observer will want to get back to the classroom teacher with positive, specific comments about the classroom first, then feedback on the observation, suggestions for collaborating, and concluding with another positive comment. Although consultants do not observe in classrooms for the

FIGURE 6.9   Classroom Observation Form

Classroom Observation Form
for Social and/or Academic Assessment

Student's Name _____ Teacher's Name _____

School _____ Grade _____

Date _____ Time _____   To _____

Consulting Teacher/Observer _____

_____

Location of Student in Room _____

Percent of Time Student Is: In Seat _____ In Group Activity _____ On-Task _____

Attends to Instruction of Teacher or Aide_____

Responds/Follows Directions _____

Complies with Teacher/Aide Requests _____

Complies with Class Rules _____

Works Independently _____

Completes Work _____

Seeks Help Appropriately _____

Is Distracted _____

Seems Confused/Unfocused _____

Distracts Others _____

Participates in Discussions _____

Participates in Group Activities _____

Shows Respect for Teacher(s) _____

Shows Respect for Other Students _____

Helps Others Appropriately _____

Other Observations _____

_____

Summary/Comments _____

purpose of assessing teacher behaviors and teaching styles, it would be myopic to assume that they do not notice teaching practices that inhibit or enhance students' ability to succeed in the classroom. When the practices appear to be interfering with student achievement, the consultant might ask the consultee in a nonthreatening, onedownsmanship way whether the student achieved the goals of the lesson. If not, is there something the teacher would like to change so this could occur? Then what might the consultant do to help? If the practices are showing positive results, the teacher should be reinforced with recognition of the student's achievement.

To avoid gathering inaccurate information, consultants will want to make repeat observations. In doing so they can use the opportunity to obtain additional information on antecedents to the problem (Cipani, 1985). They also can record benchmarks that indicate progress or backsliding.

Achieving rapport with a consultee while targeting a teaching strategy for possible modification, requires utmost finesse by consulting teachers. To reiterate, the observer should make an appointment as soon as possible after the classroom observation or interview to provide feedback and continue with steps of the problem-solving process.

REFLECTION 6.1

Important Happenings

Once a week, take ten minutes or so at the end of the day to reflect on all the important things that happened in the classroom and in your collaborative consultations that day. Notice how observant one becomes after engaging in this practice for a while.

MANAGING CONSULTATION RECORDS AND RESOURCES

A prominent space scientist commented that physicists can lick anything, even gravity, but the paperwork is overwhelming! Special education teachers can relate to that. They cite the avalanche of computer workflow, paperwork, and record-keeping that just keeps piling up, and the lack of time in which to deal with it adequately, as major causes of stress and burnout. Writing and monitoring IEPs, data recording and analysis, and completing records and forms, rank high as major usurpers of their professional and, too often, personal time.

When asked to estimate the amount of time they spend performing their responsibilities, resource teachers unknowingly will often overestimate the time spent on direct pupil instruction and staffings, and underestimate their preparation for instruction and clerical duties such as data gathering and record-keeping. If teaching is to be perceived as an important service profession, careful records are essential. Records and data, both formal and informal, must be written into the consultant's role description as major responsibilities, with time in the workday allowed for accurate management. Who would want to be treated by a doctor who did not write down vital information after each visit, or served by lawyer who failed to record and file important documents? The key for educators is to manage their student and teacher information data and paperwork so that it does not manage them. Developing efficient systems and standardized forms for record-keeping will help educators, and especially those who collaborate often with colleagues, to work smarter and not harder.

Using a Consultation Journal or Log

One of the most important formats for consultants to develop is a consultation log or journal or electronic file. Consultants should record the date, participants, and topic of each consultation on separate pages, along with a brief account of the interaction, plans made, and consensus reached. Space could be provided for follow-up reports and assessment of the consultation. (See Figure 6.10 for a sample format.) If collaboration and consultation are to gain credibility as essential educational activities, records must be kept to account for the time spent and the outcomes. While teachers typically cannot control the type of records required, they can streamline some of the processes and procedures for collecting and using the information.

It may be productive also to check with one's administrator to find out what specific information would be best. Busy co-educators should not spend time collecting information that is not wanted or needed.

One caution that all educators are aware of but needs to be stressed often is confidentiality in regard to consultation records. Important points of the discussion about student needs and progress might be entered; however, diagnostic classifications and specific planning information—the type that needs family-member permission, should not be recorded there because of privacy issues. A misplaced log or a glance by a curious onlooker could allow access to very personal, privileged information about students and their families. All co-educators will want to have a coding system and secure storage facility for managing confidential data.

Developing Memos and Professional Cards

A consultation memo is a communication tool and also a record of that communication. It must be clear and precise in order to convey, not confound, the message. Information expressed in a simple, organized manner will receive more attention from the recipient. Jargon, acronyms, excess verbiage, and cryptic sentences are to be avoided. Even idioms, as noted earlier, can be problematic, especially to family members who do not speak English as the first language.

Contrary to some beliefs and practices, memos should be rough-drafted and then rewritten in best form, rather than dashed off hastily and flung into a mailbox or an e-mail inbox. This is particularly relevant to the electronic memo where the words must convey the message with no vocal or facial expressions to help and no retrieval possible after the send key is pushed. Furthermore, it is always "out there," as some public figures have learned to their dismay. The memo writer should put the message simply, telling just enough and no more, with accurate information (times, dates, meeting rooms, descriptions, names) in sharp focus that sticks to the point, and as grammatically correct and aesthetically pleasing as possible without spending hours doing it. Recall Mark Twain's note concluding his letter to a friend: "Sorry about the length of this letter; if I'd had more time, it would have been shorter." That is a good maxim to remember for communication with students, families, and colleagues.

Consultants will find it helpful to include a personalized logo on the memo forms they use to communicate with consultees. This logo identifies the consultant at a glance. Thus, a busy recipient immediately recognizes its source and can make a quick note to self

FIGURE 6.10   Consultation Journal Format

Client (coded): _____Consultee (initials): _____

Initiator of Consultation: _____

General Topic of Concern: _____

_____

Purpose of Consultation: _____

_____

_____

Brief Summary of Consultation: _____

_____

_____

_____

Steps Agreed On—by Whom, by When: _____

_____

_____

_____

Follow-Up: _____

_____

Most Successful Parts of Consultation: _____

_____

Consultation Areas Needing Improvement: _____

_____

Satisfaction with consultation process (1 = least, 5 = most)

1. Communication between consultant and consultee   _____

2. Use of collaborative problem solving   _____

3. Consultee responsiveness to consultation   _____

4. Effectiveness of consultation for problem   _____

5. Impact of consultation on client   _____

6. Positive ripple effects for system   _____

about the information needed to respond now or later. It personalizes professional interaction by providing a bit of information about the co-educator, a humorous touch, or the creative element that educators enjoy and appreciate. A carefully designed logo can promote consultation, collaboration, and team effort in a positive light. For example, a lover of dogs might sketch his dog in the corner along with his initial. One who likes to quilt might have quilt designs as a logo. A restorer of old cars could feature a small sketch of a favorite model. A profile-type logo showing several people working together would convey the desire to collaborate.

Another item that improves consultant efficiency is the professional card. Business cards have been a mainstay for communicating basic information in many professions and can be useful in education as well. Administrators could increase recognition of their staff and enhance morale by providing them with attractive, well-designed professional cards. Educators find these cards helpful when they interact with colleagues at other sites, or when they attend conferences and conventions. The cards are convenient also for quickly jotting down requests for information or promises of material to be provided. They help build communication networks among colleagues with similar interests. They also are effective in promoting one's own programs and school district, a good "selling point" to present to administrators when requesting the cards.

Organizing a Consultation Notebook

Some consulting teachers use a loose-leaf notebook divided into sections with index tabs; others accomplish this with electronic files. They categorize the sections by buildings served, students served, teachers served, or a combination of those. One very organized consulting teacher had a section of "Best Times to Meet with Teachers," listing the days and times available for every teacher with whom she collaborated. Each consultant will want to develop the style that works best in his or her school context and role. Figure 6.11 is a list of suggestions for a special education consultant's organization of sections. Figure 6.12 shows a different format used by a consulting teacher for learning and behavioral disabilities. Collaborative consulting teachers may not want or need all of these sections, and may come up with others of their own that they would like to include. Here again, personalizing the role and school context adds to the usefulness.

It bears repeating that a primary responsibility of the collaborator is to ensure confidentiality of information for both student and staff. This can be accomplished in at least two ways—coding the names with numbers or symbols while keeping the code list in a separate place, and marking person-specific files as confidential. A "Confidential" stamp prepared for this purpose can be used to alert readers that the information is not for public viewing. These practices, along with the usual protection of information and data, and the practice of seeing that the recorded information is as positive *and* as verifiable as possible, are common-sense rules that should be sufficient for handling all but the most unusual cases.

An itinerant special education teacher who serves several schools may want to prepare a simple form stating the date, teacher's name and child's code, along with the topic to be considered, for each school. The list can be perused quickly before entering the building, so that no time is lost in providing the consultative or direct teaching service. Some teachers block off and color-code regular meeting times and responsibilities. An electronic

FIGURE 6.11   Consultation Notebook Format

Appointments:	One for week, one for year.
"To-do" lists:	By day, week, month, or year as fits needs. List commitments.
Lesson plans:	If delivering direct service, outline of activities for week.
Consultation logs:	Chart to record consultation input and outcomes (Figure 6.10).
Phone call log:	Consultation time by phone.
Observation sheets:	Coded for confidentiality.
Contact list:	Phone numbers, school address, times available, e-mail addresses.
Faculty notes:	Interests, social and family events and dates, teaching preferences of staff.
Schedules:	For faculty, paras, support staff, regular school events.
Student list:	Coded for confidentiality, birth dates, IEP dates, other helpful data.
Student information:	Anecdotal records, sample products, events, awards, interests, birthdays, talents.
Medication records:	If part of responsibilities.
Materials available:	Title, brief description with grade levels, location.
Services available:	School and community services for resources.
State policies:	Guidelines, procedures, names and phone numbers of agencies/ personnel.
School policies:	Brief description of school policies regulations, handbook.
Procedural materials:	Forms, procedures, for standard activities.
Evaluation data:	Space and forms to record data for formative and summative evaluation (discussed in Chapter 12), and coded if confidential.
Idea file:	To note ideas for self and for sharing with staff and parents.
Joke and humor file:	To perk up the day, and for sharing with others.
Three-year calendar:	For continuity in preparing, checking, and updating IEPs.
Pockets:	For carrying personalized memos, letterhead, stamps, hall passes, paper, professional cards.

calendar makes easy work of this by allowing the consultant to easily set up a color-coding system for different buildings, teachers, and types of tasks. The electronic calendar has added advantages when entering a series of meetings, searching for information about a meeting or student or teacher, storing contact information, adding pertinent information such as an emergency contact or IEP annual review date, listing phone numbers, and inserting detailed information such as class schedule and names of teachers.

An online calendar allows consulting teachers to have access to their calendars from anywhere, any time. It provides a clearer picture of available consultation times. Sensitive information within contact files can be locked and password protected, making it much more secure than a paper-based calendar or notebook. Another helpful strategy is development of a

FIGURE 6.12   Consulting Teacher's Notebook

Table of Contents

comprehensive manual or electronic file of pdf documents that organizes standard procedures and forms used for the school district and required by the state.

Managing Consultation Schedules

The collaborative school consultation schedule is a vital management tool. It not only allows the co-educator to organize that precious commodity of time productively but also demonstrates to administrators and other school personnel by its very existence and the records it contains that the collaborative consultant is goal-directed, productive, and facilitative. Schedules should be posted on line and left in hard copy with office staff or administrative assistants and in teacher workrooms so that colleagues have easy access to the information. School secretaries and teachers should be asked to refer to these schedules. Saying, "Gee, I don't know where the special education teacher is; I can't keep up with those people" does *not* present collaborative consultation in a positive way.

Consultations and collaborative experiences can be keyed on the consultant's schedule with code letters for efficiency. Two collaborating teachers use this code in their notebooks:

- *ID*—informal discussion, spontaneous meeting
- *PM*—planned, formal meeting
- *PC*—phone conversation

- *EM*—e-mail message
- *MM*—major meeting of more than two people
- *FT*—follow-through activity
- *SO*—scheduled observation

The general classroom teacher may use the coded memos in his lesson plans on a daily or weekly basis. The special education teacher may use hers by buildings, teachers, or students in her management book.

Commercial resources are available that provide sample letters and forms adaptable to a variety of educational purposes, from writing a letter of congratulations to thanking a resource speaker for a presentation. Although educators probably will not want to use these patterns verbatim, they can get a "jump start" in preparing some of the more difficult types of communications. Coordination and organization of student files, consultation logs, school procedures, and schedules will necessitate spending a little more time at the outset, but once the procedures are set up, they will be time-efficient and cost-effective in the long run.

Organizing and Distributing Materials

Many school districts now have extensive instructional resource centers where school personnel can check out a variety of materials for classroom use. Even with the busiest resource center in full operation, consulting teachers usually have their own field-related materials and information about special areas that teachers want and need. With little or no clerical help, and oftentimes little storage space available beyond the seats, floor, and trunk of their own vehicles, traveling school consultants need to develop simple and orderly check-out/check-in systems for loaned materials, or soon they will have little left to use and share. One traveling teacher described her unfortunate experience of opening the door to her van and having a strong prairie wind whisk away forever the materials she had brought to share.

Those who travel from school to school, or even travel from room to room in one school, have helpful tips to offer that they have learned about organization and management:

- Color-code electronic files and folders for schools and use a file box with a card for each day that has reminders.
- Keep an idea file of filler activities.
- Use tubs for storage of bulky materials. Plan ahead and put materials in varied colors of tubs for one week, one month, a season, or a thematic unit. Colored tubs help with organization; clear tubs facilitate identification of the contents.
- Have a retrieval box in a certain place for receiving borrowed items that are returned. Keep a check-out catalog so you will know where your materials are. When materials are due, remove due cards for the buildings where you will be that week and collect the materials while there.
- Mark materials belonging to a school with the school's stamp and mark personal materials with a personal label.
- Keep an up-to-date inventory of available materials in both personal and school libraries that are available for borrowing and are organized somewhat by specific student

needs. In some school situations, library pockets and check-out cards will facilitate check-out and return. But the inventory can be most efficiently managed, updated, and made available if it is an interactive electronic file arranged by subject of the material, grade levels for which appropriate, alphabetized name of the item, recommended loan period, and space for a requester to enter name, date, and item borrowed for what length of time, along with the all-important space for the entry of *date returned.*

- Before traveling to a school, scan the check-out file for due dates, and send a friendly e-mail reminder that you will be at their school later that day or the next and could pick up any borrowed materials they no longer need. An alternative would be to drop by classrooms or put memos into message boxes asking for their return, and leave request cards for them to tell you of any additional needs.

- Periodically assess the usefulness of the materials by querying teachers and students who used them. These kinds of interactions build positive attitudes toward collaboration and teamwork, promote the effectiveness of school consultation, and extend the ripple effect of special services.

TEACHER PORTFOLIOS FOR DATA KEEPING AND ACCOUNTABILITY

A teacher portfolio focuses on a *teacher's* learning and accountability to self, co-educators, and administrators. It is useful vehicle for recording progress in collaborative experiences and team interactions, as well as in co-teaching and partnerships with co-educators. It is authentic in purpose and task, multi-dimensional, contributive to an ongoing learning process, and invaluable at teacher evaluation time. The teacher can reflect on the material regularly, streamline it periodically, and add to it from year to year for visible evidence of growth and improvement. The portfolio can be presented as an example of productivity when it is time for them to be formally observed and evaluated by supervisor or administrator. After retirement, when purged of any confidential material, it becomes a fond-memories folio.

Importantly, portfolios are useful tools for sharing ideas during team meetings and professional development activities. They spark discussions about reforms needed in education and excellent practices that deserve replication. They can be shared with students and parents as models for student-developed portfolios. Portfolios can be fun to design and maintain.

The value of teacher portfolios as a record and repository of professional activities and experiences has not been fully explored, but possibilities abound. A few products that bear consideration are:

- Lesson plans that worked well
- Videotapes of classroom activity highlights (with signed parent permission, if students are recognizable)
- Sample tests
- Worksheets or packets that worked well
- An innovative teaching or grading technique
- A sketch or photo of an unusual bulletin board so it won't be forgotten
- A list of professional books read and a mini-review

- Any articles published in newsletters, newspapers, or other professional outlets
- Photos of special class sessions (with signed parent permission)
- Original computer software that worked well
- A highly effective management technique
- Notes from parents or students that were reinforcing

Inclusions in the portfolio that are especially relevant to collaborative consultation and teamwork include:

- Documentation of consultation episodes (coded for confidentiality)
- Descriptions of team-teaching activities
- Stimulating discussions or collaborative activities with co-educators
- Special achievements by students for the participating team of teachers
- Interesting contributions made to teaching and learning by related services and support personnel (For example, a teacher of students with learning and behavioral disorders learned that the school custodian was an expert on bees. Several of her students became keenly interested in a science project on apiaries and apiarists. The teacher consulted with the custodian and together they made plans for a classroom presentation by the custodian. Multiple positive outcomes resulted from this collaboration and she entered a summary into her portfolio.)

ACTION 6.2
Developing a Teacher Portfolio

Develop a plan for your own teacher portfolio. Include a table of contents and design a rubric for showing growth and progress toward your professional goals. Be sure to include a number of collaborative experiences in your collection. Decorate the portfolio in your personal style. It could be fun as well as rewarding to do this project in collaboration with co-educators, discussing elements to put in portfolios, and in particular developing rubrics for the portfolio assessment and perhaps some specific parts of it such as co-teaching skills.

Brief entries that result from actions and reflections activities in this book may be helpful "down the road." Some advanced degree programs in universities require a portfolio presentation as a final examination. Sharing these in a small-group session for professional development could be idea generating and enjoyable for all participants. (Recall the attention to professional perspectives and personal preferences in Chapters 2 and 3; positive examples of these most likely would surface in a portfolio presentation.)

Administrators are interested in more than how effectively collaborating teachers communicate or engage in problem solving. They want to know about practical issues such as how collaborators use the time, types of issues addressed, and whether or not collaborative consultation has been helpful to the participants.

All collaborators, regardless of their general or special education role, should keep records of their consulting and collaborating activities in order to justify the time involved and to validate their roles. The consulting log in Figure 6.10 is a useful form for documenting these data.

Case Study for Accountability in Co-Taught, Blended Classes

Two high school teachers had conceived of a co-teaching project that would combine their one-hour history and one-hour literature classes' students in a two-hour block of time. Their curriculum plans for the two subjects would be integrated and presented at a high level of expectation for student learning. The plan took considerable effort to win the approval of administration and even more to "sell" other teachers on what they would be doing. But after the school year got under way, things went well for several weeks with the students accomplishing the collaboratively developed goals at that expected high level.

Then one day the building principal dropped in and happened to see a cluster of students in the corner in an animated discussion that obviously was not related to the rest of the work going on in class. Later, this group of students learned that the teachers had been questioned by the administrator about students who seemed out of tune with class activity and wasting class time that was monitored by *two* teachers.

The students were chagrined. They immediately put their heads together and prepared and delivered a fervent letter of explanation to the principal about that incident. In it they stated that just minutes before he arrived they had put the finishing touches on their very complex, labor- and time-intensive project for the class that was due that day. They then had a few minutes to collaborate hurriedly on a calculus assignment due next hour that they had set aside to finish the project.

They told in the letter about the success of their blended class as directed by co-teachers and how much they had learned, not only about the interwoven subject matter, but about how to work together successfully in accomplishing high-level goals. This brief episode was a rich learning and teaching experience for all.

A number of co-educators in that building had not been in favor of the blended-class plan, citing waste of personnel and possibly larger classes for others as main points of objection. Was this just a case of bad timing? Could the need for explanation by the students have been avoided? Did they do the right thing? Were there possibly some underlying currents of unresolved issues here? Was the administrator looking for validation of the plan's worth? Building administrators can get caught in the middle of such issues. How could recordkeeping and journals of the collaboration plan and implementation help ease friction in situations such as this? What actions, preparations, (for example, a discussion among faculty of several departments about innovative class configurations), and assessment procedures could be taken to ensure camaraderie among co-educators and, in the longer run, to evaluate this class structure meaningfully?

TECHNOLOGY FOR WORKING SMARTER, NOT HARDER, AS CO-EDUCATORS

A number of technological tools were featured at the 2002 Futures Conference for school psychologists that could fuel change in schools (Meyers, Meyers, & Grogg, 2004). Some of the devices seemed complicated and out of reach at the time, but would likely become available to allow for connected consultations in the near future. The video streaming of the conference and the resultant website underscored possibilities for Internet participation, video conferencing, electronic consultation with staff development, e-Forums for posting questions and answers, exchanges of information through shared network drives, and sophisticated arrangements of time and schedules via e-mail. Such advancements hold exciting promises of instruments and methods for reducing stress levels and workloads of collaborative educators on the verge of fizzle-out, if not burnout.

Currently, interactive teams that reach across organizational boundaries can use technologies such as e-mail, broadcast fax, teleconferencing, and video conferencing to communicate with one another frequently and quickly. Information can be gathered rapidly and exchanged through databases and electronic networks or list servers. Digital pagers and cellular phones make team members accessible, regardless of their location. Think of those traveling teachers not so many years ago, as described in an earlier chapter, needing assistance to get their vehicles out of those snowy ditches! Modern technology can help in many ways. For example:

- *Instant messaging (IM)*—Can be sent at the convenience of one party and then others read and respond to them at their convenience.
- *Databases and information on student progress*—Stored in a file server and accessed by any team member at a convenient time.
- *Notes*—Added on by team members to keep everyone on the team apprised of information or items of concern.
- *Scheduling/appointment calendar*—Appointments and other commitments are entered into the computer calendar. One special advantage is the way the program can handle recurring appointments. For example, if a team-planning meeting is scheduled for 2:00 on Friday afternoons, the consultant can enter that information; the program will automatically write in meeting reminders on the appropriate dates. Another advantage is the ability to view and print out daily, weekly, or monthly calendars, to be shared through the network if desired. Sharing privileges can be customized to allow one or several individuals the right to view or schedule appointments for all or part of a colleague's calendar. Smartphones have made the work of busy educators more efficient and less stressful. Thanks to online scheduling software such as MeetingWizard, finding available dates and times and scheduling meetings between several parties becomes automatic and less labor intensive for busy consultants and teachers.
- *Managing student records*—Databases for organizing large amounts of information in electronic "filing cabinets" allow great flexibility in sorting and retrieving data. For example, a consultant might set up a database file on a caseload of students with each individual record containing a separate entry for categories selected, such as name, address, phone, age, grade, type of disability, parents' name(s), address, and phone number. Once the format is established, the consultant or an assistant enters the information for each record. Then it can be searched and sorted for different types of reports. This search-and-sort capability gives databases flexibility, a considerable improvement over traditional paper filing systems. Confidentiality of the data is, of course, essential.
- *Recording consultations and collaborations*—Information is kept in electronic files rather than paper-pencil format. It can be searched and sorted in various ways to provide

valuable information for making decisions about students and collaboration processes. For example, if one wanted to know how many times a certain consultant or service provider worked with the student during the year, the data could be sorted to have all the entries for the service provider appearing together. Later, one who needed to know what services were provided by whom on a particular date could sort the information by data field. Having a record of these activities helps validate the need for time and places to consult and collaborate. Communication between teachers and paraeducators can be easily facilitated and captured through these electronic formats as well.

■ *Preparing reports and other written products*—Word processors and desktop publishing programs are a *must* for busy consultants and other team members. Once text has been entered in a word processor, it can be changed easily, edited, added to, modified, or reformatted. This capability is particularly useful for routine writing such as consultation logs, letters to parents, memos to other team members, assessment reports, newsletters, and classroom materials that are modified or adapted for specific needs of students with disabilities.

Educators have many decisions to make about what, when, and how to invest in emerging technology. Thoughtful planning and investment decisions are needed to ensure that team members have the right technologies in their schools for management and instructional purposes.

ETHICS IN ORGANIZING AND MANAGING COLLABORATIVE SCHOOL CONSULTATION

Ethical climates for collaboration will nurture teachers who are experiencing stress and perhaps verging on burnout from the profession. It is often the accumulation of mountains of little things, not big crises that push professional educators into disillusionment—in other words, the "nibbled to death by ducks" phenomenon. Caring, supportive colleagues can make all the difference. Many of the tips in this chapter, when carried out with camaraderie and team spirit, will convey caring and respect for the overwhelmed novice teacher, the burdened administrator, or the discouraged veteran teacher.

Co-educators must respect the views and the rights of their colleagues who do not want to collaborate and prefer not to co-teach. They must tolerate kindly the "fly in the ointment"—perhaps the teacher in the building who does not want to be involved in a student portfolio plan or who will have no part of a teacher-developed block schedule that allows for co-teaching. The saying "Honey catches more flies than vinegar" comes to mind and a hesitant teacher might be won over eventually with patience and understanding.

When collaborative consultants visit a teacher's classroom, they should conduct their discussions and observations discreetly and without judgment. Many teachers find it hard to carry on comfortably when they and their teaching methods and classroom environment are being discussed or are under observation by other professional educators. Keeping exceptional needs of students ever in mind, co-educator respect for individuality of teachers is an essential characteristic of the collaborative environment and the ethical climate within that environment.

TIPS FOR MANAGING AND ORGANIZING COLLABORATIVE SCHOOL CONSULTATION

1. Don't schedule yourself so tightly that you have no time for informal interactions and impromptu consultations, because these can open the door for more intensive and productive collaboration; be even more protective of colleagues' time than you are of your own and make good use of it.

2. Furnish treats to colleagues often. (At very nutrition-conscious schools, make the treats vegetables or fruit.)

3. Make concise checklists for procedural activities, such as general items to tell parents at conferences, or items to tell new students and their parents.

4. Go to classroom teachers and ask *them* for help in their area of expertise. Discuss a strategy that you have seen them use and like very much, asking if they would like to share it with others or keep it as a special part of their teaching repertoire, and then respect their views about it.

5. Promote instances of high quality consultation and collaboration, not just the frequency and time spent in the activities.

6. Become more visible, communicating informally with teachers of each classroom and making positive comments about their classroom.

7. Always have an ear open to opportunities to help out, and spin off helping situations to become more established as a consulting teacher.

8. Be realistic and understanding about the demands that are placed upon classroom teachers, administrators, and parents in fulfilling *their* roles; be realistic about what collaborative consultants can do in their roles, and celebrate even small successes.

9. Keep school personnel wanting more consultation service, making it so valuable that if it were taken away from the schools, it would be missed and petitioned to return.

10. Do not expect a uniformly high level of acceptance and involvement from all, but keep aiming for it.

ADDITIONAL RESOURCES

French, N. K. (2000). Taking time to save time: Delegating to paraeducators. *Teaching Exceptional Children, 32*(3) 79–83.

Haynes, M. E. (1998). *Effective meeting skills: A practical guide for more productive meetings.* Los Altos, CA: Crisp.

Sapolsky, R. (1994). *Why zebras don't get ulcers: A guide to stress, stress-related diseases, and coping.* New York: W.H. Freeman.

Stewart, R. A., & Brendefur, J. L. (2005). Fusing lesson study and authentic achievement: A model for teacher collaboration. *Phi Delta Kappan, 86*(9), 681–687.

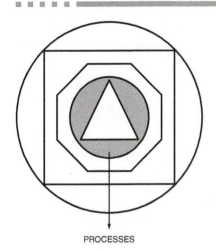

PROCESSES

Processes for Working Together as Co-Educators

PART III, THE SHADED-CIRCLE SECTION FOR PROCESSES, includes three chapters. Chapter 7 focuses on instruction and practice to develop communication skills. Chapter 8 features home and school partnerships for students who have special needs; and Chapter 9 addresses the need for meaningful, productive interactions and partnerships with culturally and linguistically diverse students and co-educators.

7

Communicating as Collaborators, Consultants, and Team Members

COMMUNICATION IS ONE OF THE GREATEST ACHIEVEMENTS OF HUMANKIND. A vital component of human relationships in general, it is the foundation of cooperation and collaboration among educators. Communication is not simply delivering a message. It involves talking, listening, managing interpersonal conflict, and addressing concerns together. Key components of successful communication are understanding, trust, autonomy, and flexibility. Effective communicators withhold judgment and minimize efforts to control the path of communication.

Collaborating educators in the twenty-first century have technology tools that educators in years past could not envision. Tech-savvy consultants must think about how technology-related tools can enhance their roles but also recognize the pitfalls these tools may pose and use them in ways that will communicate their intentions clearly.

Problems and conflicts are unavoidable elements of life, but good communication skills will facilitate problem solving and resolution of conflicts. Ineffective communication creates a void that breeds misunderstanding and distrust. Elements of trust, commitment, and effective interaction are critical for conflict-free relationships. Effective communication (included in the shaded circle for processes in Figure 7.1) becomes a foundation for cooperation and collaboration among school personnel, students, families, and others involved in education.

FOCUSING QUESTIONS

1. What is a primary reason people fail in collaborative efforts?
2. What are key components in sending and receiving messages?
3. How does one establish rapport in order to facilitate effective communication?
4. What are major verbal and nonverbal skills for communicating effectively?
5. What are the primary roadblocks to communication, and how can a collaborative school consultant be appropriately assertive in coping with resistance, negativity, and anger to manage conflict?
6. What are some important things to keep in mind when using electronic communication, social networking, and other Web 2.0 tools in an ethical, collaborative climate?

KEY TERMS

assertiveness

blog

body language

conflict management

empathy

miscommunication

negativity

nonverbal communication

partnership building

rapport building

resistance

responsive listening

roadblocks to

   communication

semantics

Web 2.0 tools for

   collaboration

VIGNETTE 7

The setting is the hallway of a junior high school in mid-afternoon, where the general math instructor, a first-year teacher, is venting to a colleague.

Math Teacher: What a day! On top of the fire drill this morning and those forms that we got in our boxes to be filled out by Friday, I had a disastrous encounter with a parent. Guess I flunked Parent Communication 101.

Colleague: Oh, one of those, huh?

Math Teacher: Jay's mother walked into my room right before fourth hour and accused me of not doing my job. It was awful!

Colleague: (nods head, showing empathy)

Math Teacher: Thank goodness there weren't any kids around. But the music teacher was there telling me about next week's program. This parent really let me have it. I was stunned, not only by the accusation, but by the way she delivered it. My whole body went on "red alert." My heart was pounding, and that chili dog I had for lunch got caught in my digestive system. Then my palms got sweaty. I could hardly squeak out a sound because my mouth was so dry. I wanted to yell back at her, but I couldn't!

Colleague: Probably just as well. Quick emotional reactions don't seem to work very well when communication breaks down. I found out the hard way that it doesn't help to respond at all during that first barrage of words. Sounds like you did the right thing.

Math Teacher: Well, it really was hard. So you've had things like this happen to you?

Colleague: Uh-huh. I see we don't have time for me to tell you about it because here come the thundering herds. But I'll tell you all about it later if you want. Come to my room after school and we'll compare notes—maybe put our heads together to plan some strategies for the future, just in case. And, by the way, welcome to the club!

COMMUNICATION FOR EFFECTIVE SCHOOL RELATIONSHIPS

Teachers manage many kinds of relationships in their work with students who have special needs. Some relationships grow throughout the year or over several years, others are established and stable, and still others are new, tentative, and tenuous. No matter what the type of relationship, and no matter whether it is with families, co-educators, paraeducators, or related-service providers, communication is the key to successful relationships. Furthermore, communication in the twenty-first century has become, paradoxically, simpler and more complex due to the effects of modern technology.

In the chapter "Enter Technology, Exit Talking" of her book *How to talk so people listen: Connecting in today's workplace*, Sonya Hamlin (2006 p. 3) says that "even hello has changed" as a result of modern technology. Her discussion includes examples of how technology has changed the ways we communicate:

- We e-mail the person in the office next door.
- We have a list of 15 phone numbers to reach our family.
- We pull up in our driveway and use our cell phone to see if anyone is home to help carry in the groceries.
- We get up in the morning and go online before getting our coffee.

Computers, cell phones, the Internet, and even television have changed communication in the last decade. However, while all these media may be part of our repertoire when it comes to collaborating with school, home, and community partners, face-to-face interactions are still the standard and the most effective type of communication for most collaboration. People typically communicate in one form or another for about 70 percent of their waking moments. Unfortunately, lack of effective communication skills is a major reason for work-related failure.

A supportive, communicative relationship among special education teachers, general classroom teachers, students, and their families is critical to the success of children with exceptional learning needs in inclusive classrooms. Special educators must model exemplary communication and interaction skills.

Preceding chapters described the contexts of collaborative school consultation and identified potential areas of differences and disagreements among educators who are poised to work together in a number of ways. A framework for working together in purposeful ways was laid out, and techniques for problem-solving, and organizing and managing procedures and resources were presented. Now it is time to move ahead to the challenge of honing communication processes that are the nuts and bolts of collaboration and teamwork.

CHALLENGES IN COMMUNICATING EFFECTIVELY

Consulting is not a one-person exercise. A consultant will pay a high price for using a ramrod approach to push ideas onto others. But communication that minimizes conflict and enables teachers to maintain self-esteem may be the most important process in consulting (Gersten, Darch, Davis, & George, 1991). Unfortunately, development of communication skills is not typically included in teacher education programs. Because the development and use of "people skills" is the most difficult aspect of collaboration for many educators, more and more educators are stressing the need for specific training in collaboration and communication skills if they expect to help students with special needs be successful.

Verbal Aspects of Communication

Semantics play a fundamental role in both sending and receiving messages. As stressed earlier, a person who says, "Oh, it's no big deal—just an issue of semantics" is missing a major point. The semantics frequently *are* the issue and should never be taken for granted. The vital role of semantics in consultation, collaboration, and teamwork cannot be ignored.

Body language also plays a key role in communication. Studies of kinesics, or communication through body language, show that the impact of a message is about 7 percent verbal, 38 percent vocal, and 55 percent facial. We communicate *non*verbally much of the time and in many more ways than we tend to acknowledge. Nonverbal communication includes use of space, movements, posture, eye contact, attention to other things such as the clock, positions of feet and legs when sitting, toying with furniture and doodads, voice volume and rate of speech, and level of energy (Gazda et al., 1999).

Miscommunication breeds misunderstanding. As the noted theologian John Powell put it, "I can't tell you what you *said,* but only what I *heard.*" A person may send the message, "You look nice today," and have it understood by the receiver as, "Gee, then I usually don't look very good." A classroom teacher wanting to reinforce efforts of the special education teacher might say "Gerry seems to get much better grades on tests in the resource room," but the resource teacher may hear, "You're helping too much and Gerry can't cope outside your protection." Figure 7.2 graphically illustrates a potential range of distorted communication.

Differing values, ambiguous language, stereotypes, assumptions, and personal experiences all can serve as filters of language. Preconceived ideas constantly filter the messages we receive, thus preventing us from hearing what others are saying and providing only what people want to hear (Buscaglia, 1986). This can be demonstrated with the well-known game "Telephone." Players stand in a long line or a circle, while one of them silently reads a note or quietly receives a whispered message. Then that person whispers the message to the next one, and the message is delivered to each one in turn. After passing

FIGURE 7.2   Miscommunication

through the filters of many people and being stated aloud by the very last person, the message in most cases is drastically different from the original message. The game results are usually humorous. Real-life results are not always so funny.

Nonverbal Aspects of Communication

Successful collaborative models will facilitate nonverbal communication during interactions and promote careful attention to the body language of others. Nonverbal communication can be organized into six categories: eye contact, gestures, paralanguage (volume, rate, pitch, and pronunciation of the verbal communication), posture, overall facial expression, and even clothing and physical setting chosen for the interaction (White, 2000).

Our facial expressions convey our thoughts and feelings. When gestures and facial expressions do not match verbal content, mixed signals can be the unfortunate result. For example, teachers send mixed signals if they smile as they outline class rules and procedures, but display stern faces when introducing a learning activity. A consulting teacher might err similarly when interacting with parents or co-teachers. Voice tone, pitch, volume, and speed can affect the receiver of a message in positive or negative ways. Sometimes the speaker is unaware of the way a message is being interpreted due to these more subtle nonverbal communication messages. Stress or nervousness might be misinterpreted and interfere with the words or perceived interest in the topic being discussed. A slouching posture or turning away will imply lack of interest or rejection. Members of some cultures—teachers or parents—may feel demeaned when consulting teachers dress too casually and communicate in an overly friendly way.

Ethnic and Gender Differences in Communication

Language is the window through which the realities of experiences are revealed. A number of factors may cloud that window and lead to misjudgments in interpreting communication. Misunderstanding may not be due simply to miscommunication. Gender, ethnicity, or cultural background of the sender or the receiver may affect both sender and receiver. Examples of gender differences in conversational style are discussed by sociolinguist Deborah Tannen and others (Banks & Banks, 2007; Tannen, 1991, 1994). Educational consultants should be aware that such types of communication style differences might lead them to be misunderstood or cause them to misunderstand their consultees. Tannen's research describes differences in communication styles between females (both girls and women) and males (both boys and men) that include:

- Amount of time listening versus talking
- Interrupting
- Physical alignment during conversation
- Use of indirectness and silence
- Topical cohesion

The caveat for gender also applies to cross-cultural interactions. Most consultants are aware that different languages or different dialects may have different words for the same object. Some languages have no words for terms the way educators use them in education. Verbal and nonverbal communication must be attuned to ethnic, racial, linguistic, and cultural differences. Because language and culture are so inextricably bound together, communicating with potential collaborative partners who are from different cultural and linguistic backgrounds is a very complex process (Lynch & Hanson, 1998). For example, eye contact in a classroom may signal disrespect and inattention in one culture but may mean respect in another culture. Cultural differences can extend to use of space, touch, appearance, voice tone, and body language. Educators will continue to be challenged by the cultural diversity of collaborators. Increases in diversity among colleagues, families, and community members require that educational consultants recognize and respect the impact of culture on communication in their work and the respect they will be accorded when they do.

ACTION 7.1
Sending, Receiving, and Sharing Messages

In groups of three, with one person designated as interviewer, another as interviewee, and the third as responder, conduct three-minute interviews to learn more about each other. After each of these segments, the three change roles so that each person has a turn to serve in all three capacities. Each responder may make brief notes to use during a follow up, one-minute share time for introducing his or her interviewee to the whole group. Use questions of this nature, or others given by the convener: What are your special talents? Interests? Apprehensions? Pet peeves? Successes you have had? Long-range goals? Things you want to learn more about?

BUILDING SKILLS FOR COMMUNICATING

With well-developed communication skills, consultants and consultees will be able to engage more effectively in collaborative problem solving. In order to be effective communicators, senders and receivers of messages need competence in five major sets of skills:

1. Rapport building
2. Responsive listening
3. Assertion
4. Conflict management
5. Collaborative problem solving

Rapport building is essential in establishing a collaborative relationship. Responsive listening skills enable a person to understand what another is saying and to convey that the problems and feelings have been understood. When the consultant uses listening methods appropriately, the consultee can have an active role in problem solving without becoming dependent on the consultant. Assertion skills include verbal and nonverbal behaviors that enable collaborators to maintain respect, satisfy their professional needs, and defend their rights without dominating, manipulating, or controlling others. Conflict management skills help individuals deal with the emotional turbulence that typically accompanies conflict and they have a multiplier effect of fostering closer relationships when a conflict is resolved. Collaborative problem-solving skills help resolve the conflicting needs so that all parties are satisfied. Problems then "stay solved," and relationships are developed and preserved. Problem solving was the focus of Chapter 5.

Rapport-Building Skills

Collaboration with other professionals for best interests of students with special needs often means simply sitting down and making some joint decisions. At other times, however, it must be preceded by considerable rapport-building efforts. Both the consultant and the consultee should work to identify the problem(s) and to provide ideas toward solving the problem. Respect must be a two-way street for generating and accepting ideas and building an appropriate consultation climate.

When we take time to build positive relationships that are based on mutual respect and trust, others are more likely to:

- Want to work with us
- Care about our reactions to them
- Try to meet our expectations
- Accept our feedback and coaching
- Imitate our behavior

We are more likely to:

- Listen to and try to understand their unique situations
- Accept them as they are and not judge them for what they are not
- Respond appropriately to their concerns and criticisms
- Advocate for, support, and encourage them in their efforts to serve student needs

What behaviors are central to the process of building a trusting, supportive relationship? When asked this question, many teachers mention trust, respect, feeling that it is okay not to have all the answers, feeling free to ask questions, and feeling all right about disagreeing with the other person. Most of all, people want to feel that the other person is *really* listening. Trust is developed when one addresses the concerns of others and looks for opportunities to demonstrate responsiveness to others' needs. Parents want to be treated with dignity and know that professionals respect their concerns and value their contributions and suggestions about their child's education (Pruitt, Wandry, & Hollums, 1998).

Respecting differences in others is an important aspect of building and maintaining rapport (a partnership). Although teachers and other school personnel are generally adept at recognizing and respecting individual differences in children, they often find this more difficult to accomplish with adults or they simply do not think about it, much less treat it as an important consideration. Accepting differences in adults may be particularly difficult when the adults have different values, skills, and attitudes. Effective consultants accept people as they really are rather than wishing they were different. Rapport building is not such a formidable process when the consultant respects individual differences and conveys high esteem for others.

Responsive-Listening Skills

Plutarch said, "Know how to listen, and you will profit even from those who talk badly." Shakespeare referred to the "disease" of *not* listening. Listening is the foundation of communication. A person listens to establish rapport with another person. People listen when others are upset or angry, or when they do not know what to say or fear that speaking out will result in trouble. People listen so others will listen to them. Listening is a process of perpetual motion that focuses on the other person's ideas as speaker rather than concentrating on one's own thoughts and feelings as listener. Thus, effective listening is *responsive listening* because it is responding, both verbally and nonverbally, to the words and actions of the speaker.

Successful consultants listen responsively and empathically in order to build trust and promote understanding. Responsive listening improves relationships, and minimizes resistance and negativity. Although most people are convinced of the importance of listening in building collegial relationships and preventing and solving problems, few are as adept at this skill as they would like to be. There are several reasons for this. First, most people have not been taught to listen effectively. They have been taught to talk—especially if they are teachers, school administrators, or psychologists. One study (Martin et al., 2006) found in observations of more than 100 IEP meetings that special education teachers talked 51 percent of the time, whereas family members talked only 15 percent of the time. This lopsided ratio may be attributed to teachers feeling pressure to report student progress to parents, but it doesn't leave much opportunity for parents to express their goals and interests during the meeting. This may result in parents' feeling that their concerns are not valued, thus marginalizing the opportunities for successful collaboration. Educators are good at talking and regard it as an essential part of their roles. But effective talkers must be careful not to let the lines of communication get tangled up in a tendency to talk too much or too often.

According to Thomas Gordon, one of the early promoters of effective communication, listening helps keep the "locus of responsibility" with the one who owns the problem (Gordon, 2000). Therefore, if one's role as a consultant is to promote problem solving without cultivating dependence on the part of the consultee, listening will keep the focus of the problem solving where it belongs. According to Gordon, listening also is important in showing empathy and acceptance, two vital ingredients in a relationship that fosters growth and psychological health.

Responsive, effective listening makes it possible to gather information essential to one's role in the education of children with special needs. It helps others feel better, often by reducing tension and anxiety, increasing feelings of personal well-being, and encouraging greater hope and optimism. This kind of listening encourages others to express themselves freely and fully. It promotes self-understanding and problem-solving abilities.

If responsive listening is so important, why is it so hard? First of all, listening is difficult because it is hard to keep an open mind about the speaker. Furthermore, people may be hesitant to listen because they think listening implies agreeing. However, listening is much more than just hearing. Openness is important for effective communication. Co-educators must demonstrate tolerance toward differences and appreciation of richly diverse ideas and values while they are engaged in consulting relationships. A consultant's own values about child rearing, education, or the treatment of children with special needs become personal filters that make it difficult to really listen to those whose values are very different.

Listening is indeed hard work. If the listener is tired or anxious or, conversely, bursting with excitement and energy, it is particularly hard to listen carefully. Feelings of the listener also act as filters to impede listening. Other roadblocks to responsive listening are making assumptions about the message (mind-reading), thinking about our own response (rehearsing), and reacting defensively.

Improving one's own listening skills can help establish collaborative relationships with colleagues, even those with whom it is a challenge to communicate. When both consultants and consultees improve their listening skills, they have a head start on solving problems, sidestepping resistance, and preventing conflicts. The three major components of responsive listening are:

1. *Nonverbal listening*—Discerning others' needs and observing their nonverbal gestures
2. *Encouraging the sending of messages*—Encouraging others to express themselves fully
3. *Showing understanding of the message*—Reviewing what they conveyed, or paraphrasing

Nonverbal Listening Skills   Responsive listeners use appropriate body language to send out the message that they are listening effectively. Nonverbal listening may not be so effective for people who do several things at once, such as peruse their e-mail or text messages while attending a meeting, or talk to a colleague and grade papers, or prepare dinner while listening to a child's synopsis of the day. This is because nonverbal components of listening should demonstrate to the speaker that the receiver is respecting the speaker enough to concentrate on the message and is following the speaker's thoughts to find the *real* message. A person who is attentive leans forward slightly, engages in a comfortable level of eye contact, nods, and gives low-key responses such as "oh," and "uh-huh," and "umm-humm." The responsive listener's facial expression matches the message. If that message is serious, the expression reflects seriousness. If the message is delivered with a smile, the listener shows empathy by smiling.

The hardest part of nonverbal listening is keeping it nonverbal. It helps the listener to think about a tennis game and remember that during the listening part of the "game," the ball is in the speaker's court. The speaker has the privilege of saying anything, no matter how seemingly inconsequential or irrelevant. The listener just keeps sending the ball back by nodding, or saying "I see" or other basically nonverbal behaviors, until he or she "hears" the sender's message. This entails using appropriate nonverbal behaviors and "listening" to the nonverbal as well as the verbal messages of the sender. The listener recognizes and minimizes personal filters, perceives and interprets the filters of the sender, and encourages continued communication until able to understand the message from the sender's perspective. Responsive listeners avoid anticipating what the speaker will say and *never* complete a speaker's sentence.

After listeners have listened until they really hear the message, understand the speaker's position, and recognize the feelings behind the message, it is their turn to speak. But they must be judicious about what they do say. Several well-known humorous "recipes" apply to this requirement:

- Recipe for speaking: stand up, speak up, and then shut up.
- Recipe for giving a good speech: add shortening.
- It takes six letters of the alphabet to spell the word *listen.* Rearrange the letters to spell another word that is a necessary part of responsive listening. (What is the word?)
- In the middle of listening, the *t* doesn't make a sound.

Verbal Listening Skills   Although the first rule for a good listener is to keep one's mouth shut, there are several types of verbal responses that show the listener is following the thoughts and feelings expressed by the speaker. Verbal encouragers are added to nonverbal listening responses to communicate that the listener understands what the other is saying from the speaker's specific point of view. Certain verbal aspects of listening are intended to keep the speaker talking. There are several reasons for this that are specific to the consulting process:

- The consultant will be less inclined to assume ownership of the problem inappropriately.
- Speakers will clarify their own thoughts as they keep talking.
- More information will become available to help understand the speaker's point of view.
- Speakers begin to solve their own problems as they talk through them.
- The consultant continues to refine responsive listening skills.

Three verbal listening skills that promote talking by the speaker are inviting, encouraging, and questioning cautiously. Inviting means providing an opportunity for others to talk, by signaling to them that you are interested in listening if they are interested in speaking. Examples are "You seem to have something on your mind," and "I'd like to hear about your problem," and "What's going on for you now?"

Verbal encouragers are words added to nodding and mirroring of facial responses. "I see," "uh-huh," and "oh" are examples of verbal behaviors that encourage continued talking. These responses by the listener suggest, "Continue. I understand. I'm listening" (Gordon, 1977).

Cautious questioning completes the promoting of continued talking. Most educators are competent questioners, so the caution here is to use minimal questioning. During the listening part of communication, the speaker controls the message. It is always the speaker's "serve." Too intensive and too frequent questioning gives control of the communication to the listener. This is antithetical to the consulting process, which should be about collaboration rather than power and control. Questions should be used to clarify what the speaker has said, so that the listener can understand the message—for example, "Is this what you mean?" or "Please explain what you mean by 'attitude problem.'"

Paraphrasing Skills   Responsive listening means demonstrating that the listener understands the essence of the message. After listening and using nonverbal and minimal verbal responses, a collaborator who is really listening probably will begin to understand the message of the speaker. To show that the message was heard, or to assess whether what was "heard" was the same message the sender intended and was not altered by distortion, the listener should paraphrase the message. This requires the listener to think carefully about the message and reflect it back to the speaker without changing the content or intent of the message.

There is no simple formula for reflecting or paraphrasing, but two good strategies are to be as accurate as possible and as brief as possible. A paraphrase may begin in one of several ways: "It sounds as if . . ." or "Is what you mean . . .?" or "So, it seems to me you want [think] [feel] . . ." or "Let me see if I understand. You're saying. . . ." Paraphrasing allows listeners to check their understanding of the message. It is easy to mishear or misinterpret the message, especially if the words are ambiguous. Correct interpretation of the message will result in a nod from the speaker, who may feel that at last someone has really listened. Or the speaker may correct the message by saying, "No, that's not what I meant. It's this way . . ." The listener may paraphrase the emotional part of the message back to the speaker by saying, "You appear to be very frustrated about . . ." By paraphrasing appropriately, a listener demonstrates comprehension of the message or receipt of new information. This aspect of hearing and listening is essential in communication and in assertion, problem solving, and conflict management as well.

Just by recognizing a consultee's anger, stress, or frustration, a consultant can begin to build a trusting relationship with a consultee. The listener doesn't necessarily have to agree with the content or emotion that is heard. It may appear illogical or even absurd. Nevertheless, the consultant's responsibility is not to change another's momentary tendency; rather, it is to develop a supportive working relationship via effective communication, paving the way to successful cooperation and problem solving while avoiding conflict and resistance.

Parents often comment that they have approached a teacher with a problem, realizing that they didn't want a specific answer, but just a sympathetic ear—a sounding board, or a friendly shoulder. This is a very important consideration. Teachers can communicate clearly to parents their interest in the parents' perceptions and ideas by following three simple steps: listen, empathize, and communicate respect (McNaughton & Vostal, 2010). After listening to the parent's concern, teachers can make a statement of empathy (for example, "I can understand why you are concerned."). Consultants communicate respect by thanking the parent for contacting them and arranging their schedule to attend the meeting and by using all of the nonverbal listening skills described in the previous discussion. Responsive listening is important in establishing collaborative relationships and maintaining them. It is also a necessary precursor to problem solving in which both parties strive to listen and get a mutual understanding of the problem before a problem is addressed.

So when is responsive listening to be used? The answer is *all* the time. Use it when establishing a relationship, when starting to problem-solve, when emotions are high, when one's conversation doesn't seem to be getting anywhere, and when the speaker seems confused, uncertain, or doesn't know what else to do.

This complex process may not be necessary if two people have already developed a good working relationship and only a word or two is needed for mutual understanding. It also may not be appropriate if one of the two is not willing to talk. Sometimes "communication postponement" is best when one is too tired or too emotionally upset to be a responsive listener. When a consultant cannot listen because of any of these reasons, it is not wise to pretend to be listening while actually thinking about something else or nothing at all. Instead, a reluctant listener should explain that he or she does not have the energy to talk about the problem now but wishes to at a later time (for example, "I need a chance to think about this. May I talk to you later?" or "Look, I'm too upset to work on this very productively right now. Let's talk about it first thing tomorrow"). Responsive listening skills that help avoid blocked communication are summarized in Figure 7.3. The checklist might be useful to review as a reminder of one's goal to be a responsive listener before entering a conversation or problem-solving meeting with a parent or colleague, and then again after the interaction to reflect on the listening skills for future refinement.

FIGURE 7.3   Responsive Listening Checklist

	Yes	No
A. *Appropriate Nonverbals*		
1. Good eye contact	_____	_____
2. Facial expression mirrored	_____	_____
3. Body orientation toward other person	_____	_____
B. *Appropriate Verbals*		
1. Door openers	_____	_____
2. Good level of encouraging phrases	_____	_____
3. Cautious questions	_____	_____
C. *Appropriate Responding Behaviors*		
1. Reflected content (paraphrasing)	_____	_____
2. Reflected feelings	_____	_____
3. Brief clarifying questions	_____	_____
4. Summarizations	_____	_____
D. *Avoidance of Roadblocks*		
1. No advice giving	_____	_____
2. No inappropriate questions	_____	_____
3. Minimal volunteered solutions	_____	_____
4. No judging	_____	_____

■ ■ ■ ■ ■

ACTION 7.2

Putting Responsive Listening into Practice

Using the responsive listening checklist in Figure 7.3, find a willing partner such as a classmate, colleague, family member, or friend and have them share a problem situation or something that is bothersome to them. Practice your responsive listening skills. After the interaction, review the checklist together to reflect on what you did well, and what areas need improvement. What did you find most difficult to do in responsive listening?

Assertiveness

By the time a consultant has listened effectively and the collaborative relationship has been developed or enhanced, the consultant may be more than ready to start talking. Once the sender's message is understood and emotional levels are reduced, it is the listener's turn to be the sender. Now the consultant gets to talk. However, it is not always easy to communicate one's thoughts, feelings, and opinions without infringing on the rights, feelings, or opinions of others. This is the time for assertiveness.

Assertiveness skills allow consultants to achieve their goals without damaging the relationship or another's self-esteem. The basic aspects of assertive communication are:

- Use an "I" message instead of a "you" message.
- Say "and" instead of "but."
- State the behavior objectively.
- Name your own feelings.
- Say what you want to happen.
- Express concern for others (empathy).
- Use assertive body language.

Open and honest consultants say what they want to happen and what their feelings are. That does not mean they always get what they want. Saying what you want and how you feel will clarify the picture and ensure that the other(s) won't have to guess what you want or think. Even if others disagree with the ideas and opinions, they can never disagree with the feelings and wishes. Those are very personal and are expressed in a personal manner by starting the interaction with "I," rather than presenting feelings and opinions as truth or expert answers.

In stating an idea or position assertively, consultants should describe the problem in terms of its impact on them, rather than in terms of what was done or said by the other person. "I feel let down" works better than "You broke your part of the agreement." If a consultant makes a "you" statement about the consultee which the consultee thinks is wrong, the consultant will only get an angry reaction and the concerns will be ignored.

Concern for Others During the Interaction   Expressing concern for others can take many forms. This skill demonstrates that although people have thoughts and feelings that differ from those of others, they can still respect the feelings and ideas of others. "I realize it is a tremendous challenge to manage thirty-five children in the same classroom." This statement shows the consulting teacher understands the management problems of the classroom teacher. As the consultant goes on to state preferences in working with the teacher, the teacher is more likely to listen and work cooperatively. The consultee will see that the consultant is aware of the problems that must be dealt with daily. "It seems to me that . . . ," "I understand . . . ," "I realize . . . ," and "It looks like . . . " are phrases consultants can use to express concern for the other person in the collaborative relationship. If the consultant cannot complete these sentences with the appropriate information, the next step is to go back to the listening part of the communication.

How to Be Concerned and Assertive   Assertive people own their personal feelings and opinions. Being aware of this helps them state their wants and feelings. "You" sentences sound accusing, even when that is not intended, which can lead to defensiveness in others. For example, saying to a parent, "You should provide a place and quiet time for Hannah to do her homework," is more accusatory than saying, "I am frustrated when Hannah isn't getting her homework done, and I would like to work with you to think of some ways to help her get it done." Using "and" rather than "but" is particularly important in expressing thoughts without diminishing a relationship. This is a particularly challenging assertion skill. To the listener the word *but* erases the preceding phrase and prevents the intended message from coming through.

It is important to state behaviors specifically. By describing behaviors objectively, a consultant or consultee sounds less judgmental. It is easy to let blaming and judgmental words creep into language. Without meaning to, the speaker erects a barrier that blocks communication and the relationship. Conveying concern and assertiveness at the same time might not come naturally at first. If you are confronting a difficult situation, you might find it helpful to write down how you will phrase what you want to say and practice saying it aloud until it feels natural and you are comfortable with the words and phrasing.

REFLECTION 7.1

Communicating Positively

Compare the following two statements:

1. "I would like to have a schedule of rehearsals for the holiday music program. It is frustrating when I make a special trip to the school to work with Maxine and Juanita, only to find they are practicing for the musical program and can't come to the resource room."

2. "When you don't let me know ahead of time that the girls won't be allowed to come and work with me, I have to waste my time driving here and can't get anything accomplished anywhere."

Which of these two statements is less judgmental and accusatory? Can these two contrasting statements create differing listener attitudes toward the speakers? For many listeners the judgmental words and phrases in the second sentence ("you don't let me know," "won't be allowed," "waste my time") sound blaming. They introduce an array of red flags.

FIGURE 7.4   **Assertiveness Checklist**

	Usually	**Sometimes**	**Never**
1. Conveys "I" instead of "you" message	_____	_____	_____
2. Says "and" rather than "but"	_____	_____	_____
3. States behavior objectively	_____	_____	_____
4. Says what he or she wants to have happen	_____	_____	_____
5. States feelings	_____	_____	_____
6. Expresses concern	_____	_____	_____
7. Speaks firmly, clearly	_____	_____	_____
8. Has assertive posture	_____	_____	_____
9. Avoids aggressive language	_____	_____	_____

Assertive communication includes showing supportive body language. A firm voice, straight posture, eye contact, and body orientation toward the receiver of the message will have a desirable effect. Assertive body language affirms that the sender owns his or her own feelings and opinions but also respects the other person's feelings and opinions. This is a difficult and delicate balance to achieve. Body language and verbal language must match or the messages will be confusing. Skills for being assertive are given in Figure 7.4.

What we say and how we say it have a tremendous impact on the reactions and acceptance of others. When consultants and consultees communicate in ways that accurately reflect their feelings and focus on objective descriptions of behavior and situations, and then think in a concrete manner about what they want to happen, assertive communication will succeed in building strong, respectful relationships. Assertive communication is the basis for solving problems and resolving conflicts.

The Art of Apologizing

Sometimes, despite good communication skills and careful relationship building and problem solving, consultants make errors and mistakes. Good consultants never blame someone else for communication breakdowns; they accept responsibility for their own communication. This is demonstrated when a consultant says, "Let me explain in a different way" instead of conveying, "Can't you understand?" Good collaborative consultants cultivate the art of apologizing.

One of the biggest misconceptions in the area of consultation and collaboration is that apologizing puts consulting teachers and classroom teachers at a disadvantage when working with colleagues and parents. It is simply not true that strong, knowledgeable people never say they're sorry. In fact, apologizing is a powerful strategy because it demonstrates understanding, honesty, confidence, and trust. Apologizing offers a chance to mend fences in professional relationships so that all can continue to trust in one another and in the relationship. Some suggestions from psychologist Barry Lubetkin (1997) about how to apologize include allowing the person you've wronged to vent her or his feelings first, apologize as soon as possible, don't insert "but" after "I'm sorry." Say it once and let that be enough. Most importantly, apologies are empty if you keep repeating the behavior or the mistake.

ROADBLOCKS TO COMMUNICATION

Roadblocks are barriers to successful interaction, halting the development of effective collaborative relationships. They may be verbal behaviors or nonverbal behaviors that send out messages such as, "I'm not listening," or "It doesn't matter what you think," or "Your ideas and feelings are silly and unimportant." Responsible collaborating consultants most assuredly do not intend to send blocking messages. But by being busy, not concentrating, using poor listening skills, or allowing themselves to be directed by filters such as emotions and judgment, well-meaning collaborating consultants inadvertently send blocking messages.

Nonverbal Roadblocks

Nonverbal roadblocks include facing away when the speaker talks or looking at another person in the room when the speaker says something, displaying inappropriate facial expressions such as smiling when the sender is saying something serious, distracting actions such as repetitively tapping a pencil, rattling pocket change, or checking messages on the cell phone while "listening." Interrupting a speaker to attend to something or someone else—an alert message on a cell phone, a sound outside the window, or a knock at the door—also halts communication and contributes in a subtle way toward undermining the spirit of collaboration.

Verbal Roadblocks

Gordon (1977) proposes twelve verbal barriers to communication. These have been called the "dirty dozen," and they can be grouped into three types of verbal roadblocks that prevent meaningful interaction (Bolton, 1986):

1. Judging
2. Sending solutions
3. Avoiding others' concerns

The first category, judging, includes criticizing, name calling, and diagnosing or analyzing why a person is behaving a particular way. False or nonspecific praise and evaluative words or phrases send a message of judgment toward the speaker. "You're not thinking clearly," "You'll do a wonderful job implementing the RTI (Response to

Intervention) curriculum-based assessment model in your classroom," or "You don't really believe that—you're just tired today" are examples of judging. (Notice that each of these statements begins with the word *you.*) Avoiding judgment about parents or others helps teachers avoid deficit-based thinking which hurts everyone it touches (Lovett, 1996). Non-judgmental communication conveys equity in the relationship, which is a critical factor in teamwork.

Educators are particularly adept with the second category of verbal roadblocks—sending solutions. These include directing or ordering, warning, moralizing or preaching, advising, and using logical arguments or lecturing. A few of these can become a careless consultant's entire verbal repertoire. "Not knowing the question," Bolton (1986) says, "it was easy for him to give the answer" (p. 37). "Stop complaining," and "Don't talk like that," and "If you don't start monitoring Jim's oral reading fluency on a more consistent basis . . ." are examples of directing or warning. Moralizing sends a message of "I'm a better educator than you are." Such communication usually starts with "You should . . . " or "You ought to . . . ." When consultees have problems, the last thing they need is to be told what they *should* do. Using "should" makes a consultant sound rigid and pedantic. Avoid giving the impression that you are more concerned with rules or shoulds than with your relationship with the consultee.

Advising, lecturing, and logical argument are all too often part of the educator's tools of the trade. Teachers tend to use roadblock types of communication techniques frequently with students. The habits they develop cause them to overlook the reality that use of such tactics with adults can drive a wedge into an already precarious relationship. Consultants must avoid such tactics as assuming the posture of the "sage-on-the-stage," imparting wisdom in the manner of a learned professor to undergraduate students, lecturing, moralizing, and advising. Unfortunately, these methods imply superiority, which is detrimental to the collaborative process.

Avoiding others' concerns is a third category of verbal roadblocks. This category implies "no big deal" to the message-receiver. Avoidance messages include reassuring or sympathizing, such as "You'll feel better tomorrow" or "Everyone goes through this stage," or interrogating to get more than the necessary information, thereby delaying the problem solving. Other avoidance messages include intensive questioning in the manner of "The Grand Inquisition," and humoring or distracting, "Let's get off this and talk about something else." Avoiding the concerns that others express sends the message that their concerns are not important.

Other powerful roadblocks to communication are too much sending, not enough receiving; excessive kindness; reluctance to express negative information; and inadequate feedback where the sender does not find out if the message has been received, acknowledged, or understood (Fisher, 1993; Rinke, 1997). When consultants use roadblocks, they are making themselves, their feelings, and their opinions the focus of the interaction, rather than allowing the focus to be the issues, concerns, or problems of the consultee. Because it is so easy to use a communication block inadvertently through speaking, it is wise to remember the adage, "We are blessed with two ears and one mouth, a constant reminder that we should listen twice as much as we talk." Indeed, the more one talks, the more likely a person is to make errors, and the less opportunity that person will have to learn something.

REFLECTION 7.2

Roadblocks You Use or May Have Used Unknowingly

After reading about roadblocks to communication, did you find yourself thinking, "I've done that but I didn't think about it being perceived that way. My intentions were good."? Which of the roadblocks have you used that you will now be more aware of and try to avoid in the future? Reflect on different ways you could handle those situations differently.

Terms, Labels, and Phrases as Roadblocks

Inappropriate use of terms and labels can erect roadblocks to communication. Educators should adhere to the following points when speaking or writing about people with disabilities:

- Do not focus on the disability label, but instead on educational needs or accommodations or issues affecting quality of life for them, such as housing, assistive technology needs, and employment opportunities.
- Do not portray successful people with disabilities as superhuman, for all persons with disabilities cannot achieve this level of success.
- Use people-first language, such as *a student with autism* rather than "an autistic student."
- Emphasize abilities and not limitations, such as *uses a wheelchair* rather than "wheelchair-bound."
- Terms such as "physically challenged" are considered condescending, and saying "victim of" is regarded as sensationalizing.
- Do not imply disease by saying "patient" or "case" when discussing disabilities.

Acceptable, up-to-date terminology facilitates active listening and verbal communication.

MANAGING RESISTANCE, NEGATIVITY, ANGER, AND CONFLICT

Communication is the key to collaboration and problem solving. Without back and forth discussions, there can be no agreement. Problem solving often breaks down because communications break down first, either because people aren't paying attention, or they misunderstand the other side, or emotions were not dealt with as a separate and primary issue.

In problem solving, it is critical to separate the person from the problem. Many wrongly believe the myth that conflicts could be avoided if people would just act rationally. Most of us view ourselves as someone who responds intellectually and objectively on the job to issues, people, and situations. In other words, we are the rational party. Others who engage in conflict are often seen as hostile, difficult, and not rational (Anderson, Foster-Kuehn & McKinney, 1996). Collaborative consultants will find themselves often needing to deal with emotions, along with any errors in perceptions or communication, as separate issues that must be resolved on their own. Masking emotions and avoiding difficult issues may seem like the most professional and appropriate way to handle emotional encounters but studies suggest this often leads to deterioration in the relationship (Kramer & Tan, 2006). Expressing the emotions and addressing the issues can lead to positive outcomes if done in the proper time and place. Ignoring emotions during conflict is unrealistic. Conflict is rarely a dispassionate exercise between relative strangers weighing the pros and cons of an issue objectively. Rather than ignore emotions as being counterproductive, we should accept them as an integral factor in the conflict process. Emotions may take the form of resistance, anger, negativity, or outright conflict. If emotions are not recognized and dealt with skillfully, they may become barriers to effective communication when the consultant or consultee experiences them. Sometimes, regardless of how diplomatic people are in dealing with the emotions of others, they run into barriers of resistance in their attempts to communicate.

It is estimated that as much as 80 percent of problem solving with others is getting through the resistance. Resistance is a trait of human nature that surfaces when people are asked to change. Researchers have found that people resist change for a number of reasons. They may:

- Have a vested interest in the status quo
- Have low tolerance for change
- Feel strongly that the change would be undesirable
- Be unclear about what the change would entail or bring about
- Fear the unknown

Resistance often has nothing to do with an individual personally, or even with the new idea. The resistance is simply a reaction to change of any kind. Change implies imperfection with the way things are being done, and this makes people defensive. However, it is good to remember the adage from a wise person, "Change is the only thing that is permanent."

Many people get defensive or resistant or just stop listening when others disagree with them. This often happens because they feel they are being attacked personally. Parents who are asked what time a sleepy student goes to bed at night may become defensive because they feel you are attacking or questioning their parenting, even though you may just want to rule out lack of sleep for some of the behaviors the child is exhibiting in the classroom.

Why Collaborative Partners Resist

It is human nature to be uncomfortable when another person disagrees. It is also human nature to get upset when someone resists efforts to make changes, implement plans, or modify programs for children with special needs. The need for change can generate powerful emotions. Most people are uncomfortable when experiencing the strong emotions of others. When someone shouts or argues, the first impulse is to become defensive, argue the other point of view, and defend one's own ideas. Although a school consultant may intend to remain cool, calm and collected in the interactions that involve students with special needs, occasionally another individual says something that pushes a "hot button" and the consultant becomes upset, or angry, or defensive.

Special education consulting teachers who have been asked to describe examples of resistance they have experienced toward their roles provide these examples:

- Classroom teachers won't share how they really feel about working with exceptional students.
- They act excited about an idea when it is proposed but never get around to doing it.
- They won't discuss it with you, but they do so with others behind your back.
- They may try initially but then give up too soon.
- They take out their frustrations on the students.
- They say that a proposed strategy won't work in their situation.
- They dredge up a past example where something similar didn't work.
- They keep asking for more and more details or information before trying an idea.
- They change the subject, or suddenly have to be somewhere else.
- They state that there is not enough time to implement the strategy.
- They intellectualize with a myriad of reasons it won't work.
- They are simply silent.
- They make it clear that they just prefer the status quo.

When resistance spawns counter-resistance and anger, an upward spiral of emotion is created that can make consulting unpleasant and painful. Bolton (1986) describes resistance as a push/push back phenomenon. When a person meets resistance with more resistance, defensiveness, logical argument, or any other potential roadblock, resistance increases and dialogue can develop into open warfare. Then the dialogue may become personal or hurtful. Nobody listens at that point, and a potentially healthy relationship is damaged and very difficult to salvage.

How to Deal with Resistance and Negativity

An important strategy for dealing with resistance and defensiveness is to handle one's own defensiveness, stop pushing so that the other person will not be able to push-back, delay reactions, keep quiet, and *listen*. This takes practice, patience, tolerance, and commitment. It is important to deal with emotions such as resistance, defensiveness, or anger before proceeding to problem solving. People are not inclined to listen until they have been listened to. They will not be convinced of another's sincerity and openness, or become capable of thinking logically, when the filter of emotions is clouding their thinking.

Negative people and negative emotions sap the energy of educational consultants. Reactions to negativity, conflict, and resistance can block communication and ruin potentially productive relationships. It is important to remember that negative people are not going to change. The person who has to change is the consultant. Negative people tend to harp on the bad things and ignore the positive. They also have a tendency to exaggerate issues, making the situation seem worse than it actually is.

The first point is not to engage in the negativity. When you converse with the negative person for the first time, provide a listening ear and empathy. If the person keeps harping on the same issues after the first few conversations, then it is time to disengage. Try changing topics, and if the person insists on continuing the negative banter, let it continue but don't engage in the negativity. Give a simple reply such as "I see" or "Okay." If you hear anything positive from the person, be sure to give affirmation and reply with enthusiasm.

Refrain from taking negativity personally. Negative people can be quite critical at times. If the negative comments are directed at you, it is natural to be bothered by the words and start questioning if there is something wrong with you. If you observe their interactions with others, you may see similar negativity being directed at them as well, and realize the person's comments are not so much personal attacks but just the way the person deals with everyone. It is more about personality style than about you or something you did or didn't do. Such individuals just may be having a bad time at that point in their lives. A positive approach would be to deal with negativity as a challenge from which much can learned about working with people. When there is a breakthrough in the communication and problem solving, such folks can become one's staunchest allies and supporters.

Accommodating negative or resistant school colleagues or family members of students at their best times and on their turf can be a first step toward this alliance. Communicate in writing in order to diffuse emotional reactions and convey the message one wishes to send. Following up later and remaining patient will model a spirit of acceptance that is spiced with invincibility and yet grounded in purpose.

For application of practical techniques, William Ury of the Program on Negotiation at Harvard Law School, has stressed that one of the keys to working with difficult people is controlling one's own behavior (Ury, 1991). The natural reaction to resistance, challenges, and negativity is to strike back, give in, or break off the communication. But a negative reaction to resistance leads to a vicious cycle of action and reaction and eventual breakdowns of communication and relationships. Instead of reacting, seek to regain a mental balance and stay focused. So, don't react.

Ury (1991) suggests that to curb one's own natural reactions to resistance and negativity, one should "go to the balcony." This means distancing oneself from the action/reaction cycle. Step back and take a deep breath and try to see the situation objectively. Imagine yourself climbing to the balcony overlooking the stage where the action/reaction drama has been taking place. Here, you can calmly look at the situation, with a detached or third party perspective. Going to the balcony means removing yourself from your natural impulses and emotions. So when your "hot buttons" get pushed or when you find yourself getting emotional and reacting instead of acting, go to the balcony!

Ury (1991) also suggests to "keep your eyes on the prize." Dealing with emotional and difficult situations in collaborative efforts usually diverts us from our goals and causes distress, so always keep your mind on the larger picture. In the collaborative consultant's case, the prize is optimal developmental and educational outcomes for students with special needs. If we remember that the communication process is crucial to the relationships among those involved in the student's education, we will remember that diversions are worth dealing with and the eventual outcome is well worth the process.

ACTION 7.3
Managing Resistance

Construct a problem situation involving another person that could happen, or has happened, in your school context and interact with a colleague to try these communication techniques:

Dismiss the negativity with "You may be right" and keep moving forward. Be assertive, as in, "I am bothered by discussing the negative side of things." Ask for complaints in writing (because some people don't realize how negative they sound). Ask for clarification, also, by suggesting that the person describe the problem and clarify the desired outcome. This leads people to thinking about positive actions. Don't defend attacks, and invite criticism and advice instead. Ask what's wrong. Look for interests behind resistance, negativity, and anger by asking questions. Tentatively agree by saying "that's one opinion."

Switch roles and try another episode. Then have a debriefing session to critique the interactions.

Consultants must "hear their way to success" in managing resistance. This may take five minutes, or it may take months and months of careful relationship building. Colleagues cannot always avoid disagreements that are serious enough to create anger and resistance. A comment or question delivered in the wrong manner at the wrong time may be the "hot button" that triggers the antagonism. Consider remarks such as these:

"If you want students to use good note-taking skills, shouldn't you teach them that?"
"Not allowing students with a learning disability to use calculators is cruel."
"Why don't you teach in a way to accommodate different learning styles?"
"You penalize students who are gifted when you keep the class in lockstep with basal readers."
"Shouldn't students be learning their own material rather than tutoring their peers (or younger students)?"

Such remarks can make harried, overworked classroom teachers defensive and resentful. If an occasion arises in which a teacher or parent becomes angry or resistant, responding in the right way will prevent major breakdowns in the communication that is needed.

Why People Get Angry

Anger is felt when a situation is perceived as unfair or threatening, and the person angered feels helpless to rectify that situation (Margolis, 1986). Differences of opinions, values, and behaviors exacerbate these feelings. Coyle (2000) explains anger as a secondary feeling that follows frustration, unmet expectations, loss of self-respect, or fear. The anger is accompanied by anxiety and powerlessness, changing into feelings or actions of power and fight. Anger is directly proportional to a person's feeling of powerlessness. If you ask angry people to tell you what they want, you give them power, thereby reducing their feeling of powerlessness. A growing body of evidence indicates that even minor shifts in a person's mood can exert strong influences on ability to act and think clearly (Axelrod & Johnson, 2005). A person who is in a positive mood tends to see the world in a more positive way, stating that the glass is half full. In contrast, when people are in a negative mindset, they are more receptive to negative interpretations of events and a cynical outlook on life and those around them. For them the glass is half empty. Strong emotions create what has been identified as a cognitive deficit, a reduced ability to formulate rational plans of action, or to rationally evaluate potential outcomes of behaviors. This heightened emotional state can cause people to act in ways that are self-defeating and interfere with the rational pursuit of their actual interests. And sometimes "people vent their anger at those giving them the most help because they feel comfortable directing it there. In most instances, angered people feel unjustly victimized and blame others for their pain and anguish" (Coyle, 2000, p. 43).

How to Deal with the Anger   Unresolved conflict leads to anger, which undermines morale and thwarts productivity. Just as the concept of emotional intelligence has been identified with successful people who have the ability to regulate and learn from their emotional experiences, Axelrod & Johnson (2005) have proposed that people would be well served by developing a form of conflict intelligence. It is important for the collaborative consultant to respond appropriately to angry people. A first rule is to address the problem rather than the person, and then seek to find a shared goal with the angry person. Defer judgment and together explore options. When an angry person is loud and belligerent, speak more softly and calmly. Listen intently with responsiveness, not reaction.

Margolis (1986) recommends that educators learn about those who are angry and get to know them as people, not problems. When they meet with the angry person, they should succinctly state a general and slightly ambiguous purpose for the meeting and ask if that purpose is satisfactory. The tone must be empathic, with careful phrasing of questions and brief summaries at key points during the problem-solving phase. The final summary with agreements and commitments should be written down to provide a record for later referral if necessary. Margolis reminds educators to congratulate all for what they have accomplished during the interaction. Griffin (1998) recommends letting the angry person vent to drain off some of the energy, and move toward transforming an "I versus you" conversation into a "We versus the problem" dialogue.

Why Conflict Occurs in School Contexts

Conflict is an inevitable part of life. It occurs when there are unreconciled differences among people in terms of needs, values, goals, and personalities. If conflicting parties cannot give and take by integrating their views and using their differences constructively, interpersonal conflicts will escalate. School consultants and collaborators are not exempt from the dysfunction that often accompanies conflict. So it is important to develop tools for transforming vague and ambiguous sources of conflict into identified problems that can be solved collaboratively. Lippitt (1983) suggests that conflict, as a predictable social phenomenon, should not be repressed, because there are many positive aspects to be valued. Conflict can help clarify issues, increase involvement, and promote growth, as well as strengthen relationships and organizational systems when the issues are resolved. Gordon (1977) contends that it is undesirable to avoid conflict when there is genuine disagreement, because resentments build up, feelings get displaced, and unpleasant conditions such as backbiting, gossiping, and general discontent may result.

Teachers, administrators, and parents face many possible occasions for conflict when they are involved with educating children who have special needs. Some conflicts occur because there is too little information or because misunderstandings have been created from incorrect information. These instances are not difficult to resolve because they require only the communication of facts. Other areas of conflict arise from disagreement over teaching methods, learning and behavioral goals, assessment methods, and values.

Parent goals and teacher goals for the exceptional student may differ significantly, and support personnel may add even more dimensions to the conflict. At times a parent may criticize a general education teacher or lash out at administrators or school/district policies they feel are standing in the way of their child's success. When this occurs, consulting teachers who do not have a well-practiced communication strategy might fall into the trap of criticizing those who are not present. This might be done because they too feel some of the same frustrations as the parent or maybe they want to position themselves on the side of the parent in contrast to their absent colleague. Showing empathy is one thing, but if the consultant criticizes others, it may further erode the parents' confidence in their child's teacher or the school or district.

In addition to cautioning teachers not to criticize others to parents, McNaughton and Vostal (2010) also remind us not to react hastily and promise something we can't deliver. A wise building contractor once said, "It is better to under-promise and over-deliver than to over-promise and under-deliver." Consultants might find that helpful in their roles as well. Some conflict can even be beneficial if it clears the air of lingering disagreement and doubt so conflicting parties can move ahead. But if differences cannot be resolved through formal or informal conflict-resolution processes, then relationships will surely disintegrate.

Perhaps the most difficult area of conflict relates to values. When people have differing values about children, education, or educator roles within the learning context, effective communication is a challenging goal. As discussed earlier in this chapter, rapport building, listening, and paraphrasing are significant in building relationships among those whose values are in conflict. The most important step is to listen courteously until a clear message about the value comes through, demonstrating respect for the value even if it clashes with yours. Then it is time to assert one's own values, and along with the other person try to reach a common goal or seek a practical issue on which to begin problem solving (Knackendoffel, Robinson, Deshler, & Schumkaer, 1992).

How to Resolve School-Related Conflicts

Some conflicts, particularly those involving values, are difficult to prevent and may seem at the time to be irresolvable. However, if all can agree to common goals or common ground for discussion, conflicts can be resolved.

When emotions or conflict inhibit the communication process, first listen responsively and acknowledge what is being said. The other side appreciates the sense of being heard and understood, and the consultant will gain a vivid picture of their interests and concerns. A useful strategy is to focus on interests rather than positions as a way to circumvent potential conflicts during the communication process.

Resolving conflicts within an "everybody wins" philosophy requires listening skills described earlier in the chapter to find common ground. In dealing with emotions of the speaker, the listener must concentrate with an open mind and attend to the speaker's feelings as well as facts or ideas that are part of the message. The listener must strive to hear the whole story without interrupting, even if there are strong feelings of disagreement. Conflict usually means that intense emotions are involved. Only by concentrating on the message with an open mind can all parties begin to deal with the conflict. Emotional filters often function as blinders. If the emotions cannot be overcome, the best tactic is to postpone the communication, using assertive responses to do so.

Consultants and consulting teachers must put aside preconceived notions about their own expertise and learn from those who often know the student best—family members and classroom teachers. Such consultees respond positively to open-ended questions that let them know they are respected and needed. When consultants open their own minds, they unlock the potential of others.

■ ■ ■ ■ ■

ACTION 7.4
Practice Makes Perfect, or Easier at Least!

With a partner, practice the following ten uncomfortable or embarrassing situations. Use the figures in this chapter to monitor verbal and nonverbal communication, for both sending and receiving.

1. Ask a person who drops by to come back later.
2. Say "no" to someone who is urging you to help with a project.
3. Answer the phone when you have at least three things going on. (Voice tone and rate are particularly pertinent here.)
4. Receive a compliment graciously.
5. Deliver a compliment so that it is not a distorted message or patronizing in tone.
6. Ask a colleague to please (for once!) be on time.
7. Ask an IEP team member to please refrain from checking text messages during a meeting.
8. Respond when someone has interrupted you.
9. Break into the conversation when someone has monopolized the discussion to everyone's frustration.
10. Apologize for an oversight or an ill-chosen remark you made.

As you feel more confident in these real-life "peak" and "pit" situations, think of similar difficult situations you have faced and practice your responses until they become second nature. Then use them!

After listening constructively, consultants need to help establish ground rules for resolving the conflict. The ground rules should express support, mutual respect, and a commitment to the process. Again, this requires talking and listening, dialoguing, and keeping an open mind. It is important not to dominate the dialogue at this time, and by the same token not to let the other person dominate the conversation. This part of the communication might be called "agreeing to disagree," with the intent of "agreeing to find a point of agreement." It is important to share the allotted interaction time equitably and in a way that facilitates understanding. Consultants must use precise language without exaggerating points, or, as discussed earlier, flaunting educationese or taking inappropriate shortcuts with jargon and alphabet soup acronyms.

Although there may be resistance after each assertion, it will gradually dissipate so that *real* communication and collaboration can begin to take place. Figure 7.5 summarizes useful steps for managing resistance and conflict.

FIGURE 7.5   Checklist for Managing Resistance and Conflict

A. *Responsive Listening*

    1. Had assertive posture   _____

    2. Used appropriate nonverbal listening   _____

    3. Did not become defensive   _____

    4. Used minimal verbals in listening   _____

    5. Reflected content   _____

    6. Reflected feelings   _____

    7. Let others do most of the talking   _____

    8. Used only brief, clarifying questions   _____

B. *Assertiveness*

    9. Did not use roadblocks such as giving advice   _____

   10. Used "I" messages   _____

   11. Stated wants and feelings   _____

C. *Recycled the interaction*

   12. Used positive postponement   _____

   13. Did not problem-solve before emotions were controlled   _____

   14. Summarized   _____

   15. Set time to meet again, if applicable   _____

MINI-CASE STUDY: ASSUMPTIONS ABOUT COMMUNICATION

Assume that the first sentence of this chapter is true: *Communication is one of the greatest achievements of humankind.* Then discuss with others the following assumptions about communication during collaborations. Do not hesitate to be frank and candid. Some may wish to play a "devil's advocate" role to tease out connecting assumptions and encourage deeper reflection on communication skills.

> *Assumption 1*: Reactions of others depend on your verbal and nonverbal skills.
> *Assumption 2*: People generally want to do a good job when working together.
> *Assumption 3*: People have a powerful need to "save face" in their roles.
> *Assumption 4*: No one can force another person to relate and communicate.
> *Assumption 5*: The core element of communication is listening.

Now come up with more assumptions that focus on rapport building for good communication.

Fisher and Sharp (1999) suggest that many collaboration setbacks can be traced to four problems: telling others what to think or do; not separating the person from the problem; blaming others; and having flawed assumptions about other teachers, families, community agencies, and even students.

When engineers stress collaboration, they often use the bumblebee analogy. According to the laws of aerodynamics, people have flawed assumptions that bumblebees cannot fly. But as everyone knows, they do. By the same token some might say that groups cannot function productively because of the conflicts, personal agendas, and individual preferences that exist among the members. But they do. Groups of people play symphonies, set up businesses, write laws, and develop IEPs for student needs.

An understanding of adult individual differences, styles, and preferences, as discussed in Chapters 2 and 3, will encourage participants in consultation and collaboration to listen more respectfully and value differences among colleagues. Educational consultants maximize their effects on the lives and education of children with special needs by using good communication skills. They should always keep in mind the ancient rule we instill in children for crossing the street: "Stop, look, and listen." For the collaborative school consultant it means:

- *Stop* talking, judging, and giving advice.
- *Look* at the long-term outcome of good communication (keep your eyes on the prize).
- *Listen* to parents, colleagues, and others who work in collaboration for children with special needs.

The stop, look, and listen rule sets up consultants for success—in establishing collaborative relationships, in developing rapport, in dealing with conflict and emotions, and in solving problems.

TECHNOLOGY TO FACILITATE COMMUNICATION AMONG COLLABORATORS

The Pew Internet and American Life Project Survey, Generations 2010 (Zickuhr, 2010) estimates that more than 79 percent of the U.S. population is online and 94 percent of that group uses the Internet to send or read e-mail. If the growing number of instant messages and text messages, not to mention tweets, are added, the volume of electronic messages sent daily for work and pleasure is staggering. Many do not stop to consider how these hurried messages are being received or interpreted. Even in school settings, educators are sending electronic messages instead of writing letters, phoning, or meeting face-to-face—amazingly, sometimes to colleagues just down the hall.

E-mail for school-based collaboration with colleagues, community organizations, and families, can facilitate *or* can hinder ongoing collaborative efforts. Because electronic communication lacks "tone of voice," body-language signals, and other nonverbal elements, it will be more difficult for educators to get a message across clearly; the unfortunate result could be serious miscommunication. An unread e-mail, a misinterpreted message, or unclear communication related to e-mail, tweet, blog or website requires extra time and work to repair the damage caused. The adage "You can't un-ring a bell" comes to mind.

Over the past forty years, we have seen unprecedented advances in electronic communication. Today, low-cost Internet access devices and the Web facilitate access to information, allow for asynchronous communication, and increase opportunities for collaboration. New and different ways of communicating and collaborating with each other are appearing almost daily. Web 2.0 tools, such as Facebook, Twitter, YouTube, Google Docs, Skype, Glogster, and Moodle, to name just a few, have grown from relative obscurity a few short years ago into the emerging top ten tools for learning in 2011 (Center for Learning and Performing Technologies, 2011).

Online technology tools mentioned here and many others that are available can be used effectively as tools for collaboration. They offer a range of opportunities for interaction, information, and community participation among people of all ages, cultures, and socioeconomic classes. With appropriate technology, collaboration among those in a virtual community is not hindered by language, culture, or disability.

Just as with social etiquette rules that are designed to help people "think before they act," a network etiquette ("netiquette") is designed to make communication easier and safer. Netiquette-conscious users of technology are less likely to create problems for themselves and their recipients through stray or misguided comments or actions via the Internet. Strawbridge (2006) and other experts in Internet etiquette have offered more than 150 netiquette rules for e-mail, mail lists, blogs, online services, and websites. Several of these suggestions are especially relevant to educators and others who engage in team-building and collaborative work. Electronic communication can be a great resource when used well. Many organizations, businesses, and more and more schools are adopting and implementing etiquette rules for Internet activity by their employees so that they will be more efficient and have better protection from liability issues. Rules of politeness, consideration, and respect afforded by netiquette are important to follow for e-mails or other types of electronic communication.

COMMUNICATING ETHICALLY IN COLLABORATIVE WAYS

Effective communication skills form the basis of respectful, egalitarian relationships within an ethical climate to best serve students with special needs. Verbal and nonverbal skills pave the way to effective problem solving and mutual collaboration.

It is often helpful to write down what one plans to say to a teacher or a parent before an interaction and reflect on what the effects might be (Laud, 1998). Novice teachers and more experienced teachers who are still honing their communication skills could keep a log for recording selected interactions, analyzing them, and reflecting on alternative ways to communicate if those interactions were not productive.

Along similar lines, when sending written communication, and especially the irretrievable e-mail, select words and expressions carefully. When in doubt, it is a good idea to have a colleague read the communication before sending it on its way. It is essential to put aside anger or frustration, begin the note on a positive tone, state the problem or concern carefully and objectively in the middle of the communication, and conclude with additional words that are positive and encouraging.

Listening instead of arguing, establishing ground rules that are considerate of the values and opinions of others, and working toward common goals and expectations for student success will help bring teams to the problem-finding and problem-solving stages with parity and respect. Consultants who remain calm and listen—always listen—will be "hearing their way to success" and helping to create an ethical and collaborative climate.

TIPS FOR COMMUNICATING EFFECTIVELY

1. Avoid communication roadblocks. Research shows that positively worded statements are one-third easier to understand than negative ones (Rinke, 1997).
2. Listen. Doing so helps dissipate negative emotional responses and often helps the other person articulate the problem, perhaps finding a solution then and there.
3. Use assertion. Say what you feel and what your goals are.
4. Be aware of your hot buttons. Knowing your own responses to certain "trigger" behaviors and words will help you control natural tendencies to argue, get defensive, or simply turn red and sputter.
5. Attend to nonverbal language (kinesics, or body language) as well as to verbal language when communicating.
6. Don't "dump your bucket" of frustrations onto the other person. Jog, shout, practice karate, sing, to avoid pouring out anger and frustration on others. Fill the buckets of others with "warm fuzzies" of empathy and caring.
7. Develop a protocol within the school context for dealing with difficult issues and for settling grievances.
8. Deal with the present. Keep to the issue of the current problem rather than past problems, failures, or personality conflicts.
9. Use understanding of individual differences among adults to bridge communication gaps and manage conflicts in educational settings.
10. Advocate for training that focuses on communication, problem solving, and conflict management.

ADDITIONAL RESOURCES

Bolton, R. (1986). *People skills: How to assert yourself, listen to others, and resolve conflicts.* New York: Simon & Schuster.

Byington, T. A. (2011). Communities of practice: Using blogs to increase collaboration. *Intervention in School and Clinic, 46*(5), 280–291.

Fisher, R., & Sharp, A. (1999). *Getting it DONE: How to lead when you're not in charge.* New York: HarperCollins.

Fisher, R., Ury, B., & Patton, B. (1991). *Getting to YES: Negotiating agreement without giving in.* Boston: Houghton Mifflin.

McNaughton, D., & Vostal, B. R. (2010). Using active listening to improve collaboration with parents: The LAFF don't CRY strategy. *Intervention in School and Clinic, 45*(4), 251–256.

Stone, D., Patton, B., & Heen, S. (1999). *Difficult conversations: How to discuss what matters most.* New York: Random House.

Strawbridge, M. (2006). *Netiquette: Internet etiquette in the age of the blog.* London: Software Reference Ltd.

Yang, S. H. (2009). Using blogs to enhance critical reflection and community of practice. *Educational Technology and Society, 12*(2), 11–21.

8

Cultivating Home-School Collaborations and Partnerships

EDUCATION OF STUDENTS WITH SPECIAL NEEDS IS A SHARED RESPONSIBILITY. Education of the whole child requires solid, well-functioning partnerships among school, family, and community. In a 2003 Phi Delta Kappa/Gallup Poll of attitudes toward public schools, 94 percent of respondents declared that home life, parent involvement in education, student interest in education, and the community environment are crucial to improving student achievement (Blank, 2004). Current research backs up this viewpoint.

Family members are a child's first and most influential teachers. The nature of education puts families and schools into shared roles for educating children and especially those with special needs. Too often the conventional pattern of relationships between schools and parents is limited to having parents as donors, as "room mothers" and classroom volunteers, or as passive recipients of information via informal newsletters and website posts. The roles of family members and community members should blend into a shared role of collaborative partnerships. Cultivating home-school collaboration (not to be confused with the practice of homeschooling, to be discussed in Chapter 9) allows school educators and home educators to fulfill their commitments toward developing each child's potential. This benefits all who are involved in the process and committed to the educational goals. The process of nurturing home-school interrelationships (see shaded circle in Figure 8.1) allows school educators and parents and other educators in the home to fulfill their commitments toward developing each child's potential.

FOCUSING QUESTIONS

1. How do home-school partnerships benefit students, their families, teachers, schools, and communities?
2. What legislation has mandated parent involvement and supported family empowerment in schools?
3. In what ways has family involvement matured into family partnership and collaboration?
4. What are potential barriers to home-school collaborative partnerships?
5. How can school personnel initiate and individualize partnerships with families and involve students in planning for their own learning, using carefully chosen technological tools as resources?
6. How can educators examine their values and attitudes toward families in order to build collaborative relationships in an ethical environment?

KEY TERMS

cultural and linguistic diversity/culturally and linguistically diverse (CLD)

empowerment
Equal Partnerships Model
family-focused collaboration
home-school collaboration

Individualized Family Service Plan (IFSP)
parent involvement
parent partnerships

VIGNETTE 8

The setting is morning at a junior high school. The consulting teacher for learning disabilities has just arrived at the building, hoping to make some very-much needed contacts with two teachers before they start their classes, when the principal walks out of her office briskly, with a harried look.

Principal: Oh, I'm glad you're here. I believe Ronnie is part of your caseload this year, right? His mother is in my office. She's crying, and says that everybody's picking on her son.

LD Teacher: What happened?

Principal: Yesterday he broke a beaker in the science lab and then he got into a shouting argument with the teacher about whose fault it was. She needed to remove him from the classroom, so she sent him to me. After he cooled down and we had a talk, it was time for classes to change, so I sent him on to his next class. But he skipped out. The secretary called his home and left word on their machine to inform the mother about his absence. He must have really unloaded on her last night, because she's here now, quite upset, and saying that the teachers do not care about her son and his problems. Could you join us for a talk?

LD Teacher: Okay, sure. (Enters the principal's office and greets Ronnie's mother.)

Mother: I am just about at my wit's end. It's not been a good week at home, but we *have* made an effort to keep track of Ronnie's work. Now this problem with his science teacher has him refusing to come to school. Sometimes I feel that we're at cross purposes—us at home and you at school.

LD Teacher: We certainly don't want *that*. I'd like to hear more about your concerns, and the problems your son and his teachers are having. Is this a good time, or may we arrange for one that is more convenient for you?

Mother: The sooner, the better. I don't want him missing school, but with the attitude he has right now, it won't do him any good to be here. My partner and I both work and we don't want him leaving the school to go heaven-knows-where during school hours. I can't just lock him up, although I've heard stories about people who do that.

LD Teacher: Sounds like we both agree that we must get to work on this without delay. Let's move into the conference room now where we can talk about Ronnie's problems here at school. We may want to involve others in our discussions later. Would that be okay with you? We're all concerned about your son, and we want him, and your partner and you, to understand that.

(Parts of this vignette may have triggered some points you would like to discuss. The scene will be the basis of a case study in Chapter 9.)

RATIONALE FOR COLLABORATIVE FAMILY-SCHOOL PARTNERSHIPS

When school personnel and family members work together in a collaborative, respectful, and trustful manner, the results are dramatic. Such partnerships enhance the educational attainment of students. Benefits, including increased satisfaction for home-based educators as well as school-based educators, are evident in a number of research studies. Family-school partnerships are mandated by legislation pertaining to the education of students with special needs.

Broadened Concept of Family

Changing times and changing families require new ideas, new languages, and new models. The first step in these changes is to think in terms of family rather than parent. The U.S. Census defines a family as a group of two people or more (one of whom is the householder) related by birth, marriage, or adoption and residing together; all such people (including related subfamily members) are considered as members of one family. This reflects the reality that many children do not live with both parents, or with either biological parent. In addition, Part H and Section 619 of the Individuals with Disabilities Education Act (IDEA) refer to families rather than parents. Consultants who are collaborating with adults for the development and well-being of children with special needs should use a broad, inclusive definition of *family*.

In another venue, the Second Family Leadership Conference (Family Integration Resources, 1991) recommended that family be defined as a group of people who are important to each other and offer each other love and support, especially in time of crisis.

Consultants need to help school personnel accommodate differences in families—families of children with disabilities, poverty-level families, CLD families—and recognize that they are not homogeneous groups. Educators should respond in individually relevant ways rather than make assumptions about families based on their language, ethnicity, or background. Educators need to learn more about full-service educational models and collaborate actively with related service providers and community networks. If they become knowledgeable about resources and advocate for broader services and access, collaborative efforts with parents will be more successful, to the benefit of students, families, and school personnel.

Legal Mandates for Family Involvement

Families of children and youth with special needs are among the strongest advocates for programs that function in our country. Legislators have been known to tell persons who lobby for special interests that they should model their zeal and intensity of preparation on what the parents of children with disabilities bring to legislative offices and meeting chambers. So a brief overview here of legislative action concerning families and schools will be enlightening. School personnel need to be aware of several mandates intended to ensure and strengthen educational partnerships between home and school. The Education for All Handicapped Children Act of 1975 (P.L. 94-142) prescribes several rights for families of children with disabilities. Succeeding amendments have extended those rights and responsibilities.

Legislation mandating family involvement is part of EACHA, the Handicapped Children's Protection Act, Early Intervention for Infants and Toddlers (Part H of P.L. 99-457), and the Individuals with Disabilities Education Act (IDEA, P.L. 101-476). Passage of P.L. 94-142 in 1975 guaranteed families the right to due process, prior notice and consent, access to records, and participation in decision-making. To these basic rights the 1986 Handicapped Children's Protection Act added collections of attorney's fees for parents who prevail in due process hearings or court suits. The Early Intervention Amendment was part of the reauthorized and amended P.L. 94-142. Passed in 1986, it provides important provisions for children from birth through five years and their families. Part H addresses infants and toddlers with disabilities or who are at-risk for developmental delays. Procedural safeguards for families were continued and participation in the Individualized Family Service Plan (IFSP) was added.

The IFSP is developed by a multidisciplinary team with family members as active participants. Part B, Section 691, mandates service to all children with disabilities from ages three to five, and permits noncategorical services. Children may be served according to the needs of their families, allowing a wide range of services with parent training. This amendment fosters collaboration based on family-focused methods. The legislation speaks of families in a broad sense, not just a mother-father pair as the family unit, and families' choices are considered in all decisions.

The 1990 amendments under P.L. 101-476 increased participation by children and adults with disabilities and their families. An example is the formation of community transition councils with active participation of parents in the groups. Subsequent court decisions and statutory amendments have clarified and strengthened parent rights (Martin, 1991). The spirit of the law is met when educators develop positive, collaborative relationships with families.

The IDEA Amendments of 1997 were signed into law in June 1997, after two years of analysis, hearings, and discussion. This reauthorization of IDEA, as Public Law 105-17, brought many changes to P.L. 94-142. Parent participation in eligibility and placement decisions, and mediation as a means of resolving parent-school controversies are two critically important areas of change. P.L. 105-17 strengthened the involvement of parents in all decision making involving their children (National Information Center for Children and Youth with Disabilities, 1997). The 1997 amendments were reauthorized in 2004 as P.L. 108-446, the No Child Left Behind (NCLB) legislation. NCLB mandated that schools give parents the tools they need to support their children's learning in the home and also that they communicate regularly with families about children's academic progress, provide opportunities for family workshops, and offer parents chances to engage in parent leadership activities at the school site.

Benefits of Family and School Partnership

School, family, and community provide overlapping spheres of influence on children's behavior and achievement. All spheres should be included for involvement by the collaborative team in partnerships with students at the center. Student development and learning at all levels of education are supported by strong home-school relationship.

Extensive research shows that family involvement can enhance a student's chances for success in school and significantly improve achievement. Students have higher attendance rates, more pro-social behavior, better test scores, and higher homework completion rates when their families are engaged in home partnerships with schools. Level of family involvement predicts children's academic and social development as they progress from early childhood education programs through K–12 schools and into higher education (Caspe, Lopez, & Wolos, 2007).

For preschool children, family involvement means improved cognitive and social development. In an experimental research study on parent involvement at the early childhood level, the Harvard Family Research Project found that participation in school activities is associated with child language, self-help, social, motor, adaptive, and basic school skills (Weiss, Caspe, & Lopez, 2006). Frequency of parent-teacher contact and involvement at early-childhood sites is associated with preschool performance (Weiss et al., 2006).

Home-school relationships have positive short-term and long-term benefits for elementary school students as well (Caspe et al., 2007). Barnard (2004) showed that when low-income African American families maintained continuously high rates of parent participation in elementary school, children were more likely to complete high school. Dearing, Krieder, Simpkins, and Weiss (2006) conducted a longitudinal study that showed consistent family involvement was predictive of gains in children's literacy performance. In a meta-analysis of studies examining the relationship of parent involvement with student academic achievement in urban elementary schools, Jeynes (2007) discovered that continuous and consistent parent involvement shields and protects children from the negative influences of poverty; it may be one approach to reducing achievement gaps between white student groups and students of color groups.

At the middle and high school levels, family involvement is a powerful predictor of various positive academic and social outcomes. Because of the adolescent's increasing desire for autonomy and changes in school structure, family involvement in education tends to decrease in middle and high school (Kreider, Caspe, Kennedy, & Weiss, 2007). Nevertheless, family involvement in learning remains important in the adolescent years. Parents can monitor their adolescents' academic and social progress and acquire information they need to make decisions about their children's future, and engage in positive relationships with school staff (Hill & Taylor, 2004). They also have the opportunity to learn skills that help with their child's needs, such as behavior management techniques and communication strategies.

As parents work with teachers, they can provide input about their children's histories and experiences and include their own wisdom about their children's interests and needs. Teachers learn more about students' backgrounds and receive support from family members who can provide encouragement to their children as they study and learn.

School systems benefit from home-school collaboration through improved attitudes toward schools and advocacy for school programs. A positive home-school relationship helps others in the schools and the community. Family involvement increases positive communication among all who are involved on the education team.

All in all, substantial research supports family involvement, and a growing body of intervention evaluations demonstrates that family involvement can be strengthened with positive results for children and youth (Caspe & Lopez, 2006). Therefore, it is crucial as a major factor in encouraging optimal outcomes of students. So how can educators initiate and nurture this very important family involvement?

MOVING FROM PARENT INVOLVEMENT
TO PARTNERSHIPS WITH FAMILIES

A significant goal of family and community involvement with education is empowerment of families. The old way of working with families of children with disabilities often meant "helping them into helplessness." Well-intentioned educators and other professional helpers provided services and solved problems, and families were deprived of the experience of learning to solve their own problems. But families are the constant in children's lives and family members need knowledge, skills, and motivation to become advocates for themselves and their children. Empowerment means that family members take action to reach goals for their children, satisfying their children's wants and needs and building on their strengths. Empowered people have the means and knowledge to act; they know what they want and take action to get it (Turnbull, Turnbull, Erwin, & Soodak, 2006). True educational partnerships support empowerment of families.

Educators should provide families with some of the means they need to become empowered. Turnbull et al. (2006) describe an empowerment model of collaboration. In their empowerment framework, family resources, professional resources, and education context resources are all involved in collaborating for empowerment. Family resources include expectations, motivation, energy, and persistence. Families often need additional skills and knowledge to become empowered as strong advocates for their children and partners with their children's teachers. This knowledge includes information, communication skills, problem-solving skills, and life management strategies. Teachers can use their resources to empower parents and support development of these skills. Providing this support for parents, families, and siblings of children with exceptionalities also means fostering community support and advocacy (Fiedler, Simpson, & Clark, 2007). For example, resources for studying the interests and needs of siblings of people with special health and developmental needs are available online at websites such as www.siblingsupport.org.

■ ■ ■ ■ ■ ▬▬▬▬▬

ACTION 8.1
Communicating about Home-School Collaboration

Write a letter to the editor of your local paper, describing the importance of home-school relationships. Or, prepare a short talk about that topic for the local school board or parent group. Show your letter to a community leader who is concerned about student success in the schools, or practice your talk to others in your group. What are the strongest points of your ideas? How could your presentation of ideas be improved? Consider actually sending your letter or giving your talk in a public forum.

Successful educational consultants realize that involvement is not synonymous with collaboration. Developing a workshop on discipline or a volunteer program without assessing strengths, needs, and goals of the groups involved is a failure to respect the partnership between school and home. True partnership features mutual collaboration and respect for the expertise of all parties.

Educational consultants and their colleagues must be aware of the realities and new legislation facing today's families. Increases are evident in poverty levels, births to unwed adolescent parents, and the rise of nonbiological parents as primary caretakers (foster care, grandmothers, extended family, adoptive parents, and so on). In addition, there are increasing numbers of families with cultural minority backgrounds, single-parent families, parents with disabilities, gay and lesbian parents, and blended and extended families.

Many families are overwhelmed by family crises and normal life events. Others face multiple stressors such as long work hours, illness and disability, and overwhelming responsibilities. Many are discouraged and burned out. Such situations make family collaboration a challenge for collaborative consultants and many families. Despite these potential challenges, an Equal Partnership Model is the goal for home-school collaboration.

The Equal Partnership Model

It is possible for families to be involved in the school life of their children but not be collaborative. Collaboration goes beyond involvement. Educators may provide families with information, parenting classes, and advocacy groups. However, this kind of involvement does not ensure that family needs and interests are being heard and understood. It is more like traveling on a one-way street where, if you miss your mark, you just have to keep going on and doing what you were doing. It is not a two-way street where families meet to show the way, and destination goals are set forth based on family members' concerns and input.

The Equal Partnership Model includes specific skills, attitudes, and behaviors on the part of educational consultants. It is important to distinguish between the narrower concept of parent involvement and the broader aspect of family collaboration in two ways:

1. Parent involvement is parent participation in activities that are part of their children's education—for example, conferences, meetings, newsletters, tutoring, and volunteer services.
2. Family collaboration is the development and maintenance of positive, respectful, egalitarian relationships between home-school. It includes mutual problem solving with shared decision making and goal setting for students' needs.

REFLECTION 8.1

Thinking about the Equal Partnership Model

Think of family-based activities in your school or those you have experienced as a parent, teacher, or student. How would you rate these activities along a continuum from simply providing information to engaging in true partnerships? How might teachers and other school personnel move from involvement (number 1 above) to true collaboration (number 2 above)? What kinds of activities and programs could they initiate for this goal? What could be the challenges, and importantly, the potential rewards of the Equal Partnership Model compared with the traditional pattern of involvement?

Along with the general consulting skills of communication, problem solving, and other skill sets discussed in this book, consultants who strive for the Equal Partnership Model of family-school collaboration should focus on:

- Understanding their own perceptions of parent-teacher parity
- Recognizing family strengths
- Including the expertise of family members

Identifying Family Strengths   The Equal Partnership Model stresses not only respect for the curriculum of the child's home and community, but also the importance of providing opportunities for family members to use their strengths and skills to contribute to the formal education of their children. This relationship is not based on a deficit model of blame and inequality. Families appreciate having their special efforts recognized, just as teachers do. Multi-year research by St. John, Griffith, and Allen-Hayes (1997) showed mixed outcomes when parents were not treated as full partners in the education of their children.

Tools for assessing parent strengths include interviews and checklists that are useful in determining what types of contributions families can bring to the partnership. One example of a strength assessment is provided in Figure 8.2. Family assets can be conceptualized along four levels of involvement (Kroth, 1985), from strengths that all family members have, to skills that only a few family members are willing and able to contribute. For example, all parents have information about their children that schools need. At more intensive levels of collaboration, some family members are willing and able to tutor their children at home, come to meetings, help make bulletin boards, and volunteer to help at school. At the highest level of collaboration, only a few parents can be expected to lobby for special education, serve on advisory boards, or conduct parent-to-parent programs.

Including the Expertise of Family Members   Family members fulfill a range of roles from purveyor of knowledge about the child to advocates for political action. Indeed, they are experts about their children, their families and often about their communities. This expertise should be honored by remembering that families are:

- Individuals with initiative, strengths, and important experiences
- The best advocates and case managers for the child with special needs
- The best information resource about the child, the family, and their culture
- Partners in setting goals and finding solutions

Not all parents are ready or able to provide this expertise. The consultant must respect and support the courage and commitment of family members who struggle with the challenges of daily living faced by all families and those with exceptional needs in particular. Recognizing, supporting, and reinforcing interventions on behalf of the child with special needs will promote an increased sense of competency and help create a safe, nurturing environment for children, while maintaining the unique cultural and ethnic characteristics

FIGURE 8.2   Family Member Participation Checklist

Families! We need your help. Many of you have asked how you can help provide a high-quality educational program for your children. You have many talents, interests, and skills you can contribute to help children learn better and enjoy school more. Please let us know what you are interested in doing.

____   1. I would like to volunteer in school.

____   2. I would like to help with special events or projects.

____   3. I have a hobby or talent I could share with the class.

____   4. I would be glad to talk about travel or jobs, or interesting experiences that I have had.

____   5. I could teach the class how to _____.

____   6. I could help with bulletin boards and art projects.

____   7. I could read to children.

____   8. I would like to help my child at home.

____   9. I would like to tutor a child.

____   10. I would like to work on a buddy or parent-to-parent system with other parents whose children have problems.

____   11. I would like to teach a workshop.

____   12. I can do typing, word processing, phoning, making materials, or preparing resources at home.

____   13. I would like to assist with student clubs.

____   14. I would like to help organize a parent group.

____   15. I want to help organize and plan parent partnership programs.

____   16. I would like to help with these kinds of activities:

At school   _____

At home   _____

In the community   _____

Your comments, concerns, and questions are welcome. THANKS!

Name: _____

Child's Name: _____

How to Reach You: _____

of their family unit (Barbour, Barbour, & Scully, 2008; Caspe & Lopez, 2006; Turnbull et al., 2006).

School personnel must guard against valuing teacher knowledge and experience over family knowledge and experience. As stated earlier, it is vital to recognize that parents are the experts when it comes to knowing about their children, no matter how many tests educators have administered to students, or how many hours they have observed them in the classroom. If professional educators are perceived as *the* experts, and the *only* experts, false expectations may create unrealistic pressure on them. Some family members find it difficult to relate to experts. So a beautiful "boulevard of progress" becomes that one-way street where there are only narrow, one-sided elements of judging, advising, and sending solutions.

Communicating messages of equality, flexibility, and a sharing attitude will facilitate effective home-school collaboration. The message that should be given to parents of students with special needs is, "I know a lot about this, and *you* know a lot about that. Let's put our information and ideas together to help the child."

Just as school personnel have much expertise to share with families about the education of students with special needs, parents have much to communicate to school personnel about their children. This parental expertise can be regarded as "curriculum of the home" and "curriculum of the community" (Barbour et al., 2008). Such information includes parent-child conversation topics, how leisure reading is encouraged, deferral of immediate gratifications, long-term goals, how homework is assisted and assessed, what TV is watched and how it is monitored, who the child plays with, how affections and interests in the child's accomplishments are demonstrated, and what community activities are important in the family's life.

If school personnel do not understand (or attempt to understand) the curriculum of the home and the community, equal partnerships are difficult to establish. Educators can use checklists, conversations, home visits, and community involvements to learn about the strengths, interests, and needs of parents and the communities in which the families live. If school personnel offer workshops and materials that are not based on family interests and needs, a message is communicated that educators know more about their needs than they do; then the family involvement is not a true partnership. Figure 8.3 provides an example of a needs assessment/interest inventory.

Too often parent involvement is perceived as teachers and school personnel *giving* parents "things to do, things to read, things to change." True equal partnership calls for consultants to promote mutual trust, respect, and parity. Not only should families be involved with schools, but educators also must be involved with families. Family-focused collaboration between home-school is based on these principles:

- Families are a constant in children's lives and must be equal partners in all decisions affecting the child's educational program.
- Family involvement includes a wide range of family structures.
- All families have strengths and coping skills that can be identified and enhanced.
- Families are sources of wisdom and knowledge about their children.
- Diversity and individual differences among people are to be valued and respected.

Central to family-centeredness are respect for family concerns and priorities, issues of family competence and assets, and use of family and community resources and supports. Family-centered programs are flexible and individualized; they focus on communication and developing and maintaining relationships. Building family-staff collaboration takes time and expertise. This is a tall order for educational consultants, but empowering relationships and better outcomes for students depend on this shared sense of respect and care.

FIGURE 8.3   Ascertaining Family Interests

Families! We want to learn more about you so that we can work together helping your child learn. Please take a few minutes to respond to these questions so your voice can be heard. It will help the Home-school Advisory Team develop programs for families, teachers, and children.

Check those items you are most interested in.

_____   1. Family resource libraries or information centers
_____   2. Helping my child learn language and social skills
_____   3. Support programs for my child's siblings
_____   4. Talking with my child about sex
_____   5. Helping with language and social skills
_____   6. Mental health services
_____   7. Talking with another parent about common problems
_____   8. Respite care or babysitters
_____   9. My role as a parent
_____ 10. Classes about managing behavior problems
_____ 11. Making my child happy
_____ 12. Managing my time and resources
_____ 13. Making toys and educational materials
_____ 14. Reducing time spent watching television
_____ 15. What happens when my child grows up
_____ 16. Recreation and camps for my child
_____ 17. State-wide meetings for families
_____ 18. Vocational opportunities for my child
_____ 19. Talking to my child's teacher
_____ 20. Talking with other families
_____ 21. Learning about child development
_____ 22. Things families can do to support teachers
_____ 23. Home activities that support school learning
_____ 24. Information about the school and my child's classes
_____ 25. Helping my child become more independent
_____ 26. Others?

_____

_____

_____

Thanks for your help!

Name of family member responding to this form, and relationship to child:

_____

Child's name: _____

POTENTIAL BARRIERS TO COLLABORATION WITH FAMILIES

Most educational consultants recognize the importance of family involvement, but moving beyond the "What can parents do for the school?" question poses a challenge for some educators. Christie (2005) believes it is easier to talk about what parents can do for the school than it is to listen to parents about what they know their children need. Sometimes when parents appear not to care, Christie says, it is because they know that what they have to say probably will not be heard.

The success of family collaboration activities is based on partnerships developed and maintained by using interaction and communication skills such as those described in Chapter 7. However, other barriers may overshadow the need for effective communication. These surface as formidable challenges to educators even before lines of communication are established. Examples of such barriers are time limitations, anticipation of negative and stressful or punishing interactions, denial of problems, blaming, or a personal sense of failure in parenting and teaching. Collaborative consultants who recognize potential barriers to home-school partnerships will be better prepared to use successful and appropriate strategies in bridging the gap between home-school.

Family Structures and Characteristics

Changing family structures make traditional methods of facilitating home-school collaboration somewhat problematic. Historical, attitudinal, or perceptual factors in regard to work and to education can influence family participation. Major changes in immigration patterns and in the diversity of the U.S. population add to the complexity of collaboration with families (see Berger, 2008; Lynch & Hanson, 1998; and Chapter 9 in this book).

Parents of children with learning and behavior problems can be effective change agents for their children; however, they may be inhibited by their own attitudes or circumstances. Many parents, while very concerned about their child's education, are fearful and suspicious of schools, teachers, and education in general because of their own educational history or past negative interactions with school personnel.

Parents of children with special needs face many economic and personal hardships such as work schedules and health concerns. Low-income families may have difficulty with transportation and child care, making it hard to attend meetings or volunteer in school even when they would like to do so (Thurston & Navarette, 1996). Also, families stressed by poverty or substance abuse will be less available to consult and collaborate with school personnel.

A single parent, already burdened with great responsibilities, may be particularly stressed in parenting a child with special needs. This role can be overwhelming at times. For collaborative efforts to produce results, the interaction must fit the single parent's time and energy level. (See Figure 8.4.) School personnel may need to tailor their requests for conferences and home interventions to the availability of the single parent. Sometimes a single parent may need additional emotional support or just someone to chat with about concerns. Compare the tone of Figure 8.4 to that of similar Figure 8.9 later in the chapter.

FIGURE 8.4   "Keep parents informed"

A two-parent, two-home student may face struggles in dealing with repercussions from family strife leading to the divorce, breakup of the family, and passage back and forth between parents, oftentimes with stepparents and new brothers and sisters, and possibly a change of schools, in the mix. Educators at school and at home must organize a cooperative and collaborative team for managing the academic and emotional needs of the students. As just one example, homework assignments can be problematic for a child who will be with one parent for only a short time and then will move on for a turn with the other parent, and return to the first parent to repeat the procedure time after time.

Many types of disability are very expensive for families, and the impact on the family budget created by the special needs of a child may produce formidable hardships. Sometimes families arrive at the point where they feel their other children are being neglected by all the attention to the child with exceptional learning needs. This adds to their frustration and stress. In addition, children with special needs and their families are vulnerable to stereotypes of society about disabilities. The ways in which families cope with the frustrations and stress influence their interactions with school personnel. Providing support networks can help them cope with the situation (Dunst, 2002; Turnbull et al., 2006).

Attitudes and Understandings of Home-School Collaborators

Family members may avoid school interactions because they fear being blamed as the cause of their children's problems. Sometimes teachers do blame parents for exacerbating learning and behavior problems ("I can't do anything here at school because it gets undone when they go home!"). But blaming hampers development of mutually supportive relationships. Family members are very sensitive to blaming words and attitudes from school personnel. A teacher who is part of a therapeutic foster family reported that he felt "blame and shame" after a school conference about the child with emotional and behavior problems who had been his foster child for two months. It is fair to assume that this was not a productive conference.

Judging attitudes, stereotypes, false expectations, and basic differences in values also act as barriers and diminish the collaborative efforts among teachers and families. It is challenging to feel comfortable with people who have very different attitudes and values. Families and teachers should make every effort not to reproach each other, but to work together as partners on the child's team. Educators, including teachers and parents, must abandon postures of blaming or criticism, and move on to collaboration and problem solving. It is important to remember that it does not matter where a "fault" lies. What matters is who steps up to address the problems and needs.

Cultural and Linguistic Diversity among Families

Too often programs for family collaboration are based on middle-class, majority-culture values; however, active parent and community involvement in educational programs for culturally and linguistically diverse (CLD) students is essential. Yet the differences among cultural and linguistic backgrounds of school personnel and their students make home-school collaboration a challenge. The unfortunate portrayal of CLD families as deficient in skills necessary for school readiness is a huge barrier to active parent participation. Misconceptions about parental concern for their children's schooling are all too prevalent among school personnel (de Valenzuela, Torres, & Chavez, 1998).

Effective collaborative consultants recognize that sometimes there are differing views between home-school educators about the involvement of families in education of their children and varying levels of visibility for that involvement. When August and Hakuta (1997) researched patterns of parental involvement (parent behaviors that support education) among Puerto Rican families, Chinese American families, and Mexican American families, they found that parent behaviors nurturing child learning may not always be visible to school personnel or recognized as such.

Educators should take careful note that the concept of *disability* is culturally and socially constructed. Each society's culture defines the parameters of what is considered normal, with some cultures having a broader or different definition of disability from that in U.S. schools (Linan-Thompson & Jean, 1997). This may be one reason ethnically diverse parents tend to be less involved and less informed about their child's school life than mainstream parents. It is important to learn from family members how their beliefs and practices will affect programs for children with special needs. Educational consultants who work with families must be aware of the family's perceptions of disability. Linan-Thompson and Jean suggest taking time to learn about family perceptions of special needs, carefully and thoroughly explaining the whole special education process. They should use informal assessments in addition to formal assessment tools to help explain the disability on less formal terms), and use parents' preferred forms of communication (written note, informal meetings, or video- or audiotapes).

Traditional parent roles as teacher, information source, decision maker, and advocate for transition planning may not be appropriate for all families or sensitive to their situations. It may be more relevant to regard their roles as guide, information specialist, decision maker, and ally. Family members, friends, and community members can be invited to take part in education-related decisions as a way to honor diverse values and traditions of multicultural groups. Educators who develop cross-cultural competencies and collaborate with families who are culturally or linguistically different from themselves must keep in mind that one approach does not fit all ranges of diversity (Parette & Petch-Hogan, 2000).

The following eleven strategies are helpful when collaborating with families from diverse cultural groups:

1. Acknowledge cultural differences and become aware of how they affect parent-teacher interactions.
2. Examine your personal culture, such as how you define family, and your desired life goals and perceived problems.
3. Recognize the dynamics of group interactions such as etiquette and patterns of communication.
4. Go out into the community and meet the families on their own turf.
5. Adjust collaboration to legitimize and include culture-specific activities.
6. Learn about the families. Where are they from and when did they arrive? What cultural beliefs and practices influence their child-rearing practices, health and healing processes, and disability-causation attitudes?
7. Recognize that some families may be surprised by the extent of home-school collaboration expected in the United States.
8. Learn and use words and forms of greetings in the families' languages.
9. Work with cultural mediators or guides from the families' cultures to learn more about the culture in ways that will facilitate communication between school and home. Examples are relatives, church members, neighbors, or older siblings.
10. Ask for help in structuring the child's school program to match home life, such as learning key words and phrases used at home.
11. Most of all, understand your own values, educational and cultural history, and root out and discard any lingering stereotypes or misconceptions.

Having well-publicized policies at the district level encouraging home-school collaboration are vital in providing opportunities for minority family members to become full partners with teachers. Traditional methods of parent involvement such as PTA meetings, open house, or newsletters seldom permit true collaboration, constructing instead a "territory" of education that many parents are hesitant to invade.

Concern, awareness, and commitment on the part of individuals in the educational system are beginning steps in challenging limitations that inhibit collaboration between teachers and families who have language, cultural, or other basic differences. Supporting and reinforcing families in their life roles is not always easy. Members of families with multiple problems often are viewed as having defective or faulty notions of parenting, minimal problem-solving skills, and mental health problems. For families with different values and expectations who must deal with high-risk factors such as poverty, mental illness or drug and alcohol involvement, focusing on strengths and providing positive supports are best approaches for collaborators.

DEVELOPING HOME-SCHOOL PARTNERSHIPS: A FIVE-STEP PROCESS

Home-school collaboration practices have many variations. Effective collaboration efforts depend on attitude of teachers, their beliefs about family roles and the efficacy of family involvement, and their experience, comfort, and communication skills. When school personnel collaborate with family members, they nurture and maintain partnerships that facilitate shared efforts to promote student achievement. As families and teachers plan together and implement plans of action, they find that working as a team is more effective than working alone. Each can be assured that the other is doing the best for the child and each can support the other, thus producing positive educational outcomes for children with special needs. Families that are stressed by poverty or substance abuse will be less readily available to consult and collaborate with school personnel, so educators must be resourceful in developing strategies for encouraging their participation.

Family involvement is usually conceptualized from family member perspectives (Wanat, 1997). In her study that involved fifty-seven parents, Wanat found that parents did not distinguish between involvement at school and at home and they had specific ideas about what constituted meaningful involvement. One parent summarized legitimate parent involvement as "everything you do with the child, because education involves a lot more than just sitting at school." It would be good for education consultants to remember this statement when they work collaboratively with parents.

Five basic steps will assist school personnel in developing successful home-school partnerships:

Step 1: Examining personal values
Step 2: Building collaborative relationships
Step 3: Initiating home-school interactions
Step 4: Individualizing for families
Step 5: Evaluating home-school collaboration

Step 1: Examining Personal Values

Value systems are individualistic and complex. Our values influence our viewpoints toward cultural backgrounds, gender, age, education, family structures, sexual orientation, and many other issues that are part of working collaboratively with families. Therefore, an initial step in collaborating with families is to examine one's own values and beliefs about parents and their interactions with their children and with teachers. Figure 8.5 is a checklist for examining one's own values and attitudes toward parents and other family members. Inventorying and adjusting one's attitudes about families are the hardest parts of consulting with them. Attitudes and perceptions about families and their roles in partnerships greatly influence implementation of the collaborative consulting process.

In addition to examining values and beliefs related to specific parent and teacher roles, consultants should think about their personal values and skills that relate to home-school

FIGURE 8.5   Examining Own Values

Instructions: Rate belief or comfort level, from 1 (very comfortable or very strong) to 5 (very uncomfortable or not strong at all).

How comfortable do you feel with each?

____ Parents and others whom you think are overly protective

____ Homeless families

____ Families who send their children to school without breakfast

____ Parents who have lost control of their children

____ Volunteers in the classroom

____ Being invited to students' homes

____ Teachers who do not follow through

____ Families that include gay or lesbian parents

____ Students attending conferences

____ Parents who do not allow their children to be tested

____ Families from a different racial or ethnic group than yours

____ Family members who do not speak English

____ Others who think special needs children should be kept in self-contained classrooms

____ Teachers who think modifying curriculum materials or tests is watering down the lessons

____ Family members who drink excessively or use drugs

How strongly do you believe the following?

____ Family members should be able to call you or e-mail you at home.

____ Newsletters and listservs are important communication tools.

____ Family members should volunteer in the classroom.

____ General classroom teachers can teach students with special needs.

____ All children can learn.

____ Family members should come to conferences.

____ Resistance is normal and to be expected in educational settings.

____ Children in divorced families have special problems.

____ Family influence is more important than school influence.

____ Sometimes consultants should just tell others the best thing to do.

____ Consultants are advocates for children.

____ Teachers should modify their classrooms for children with special needs.

____ It is a teacher's fault when children fail.

____ Consultants are experts in educating special needs children.

____ Some people do not want children with special needs to succeed.

Do you think all teachers, administrators, counselors, psychologists, parents, grandparents, social workers, and students would have responded as you did? What happens when members of the same educator team have different views?

collaboration. Figure 8.6 provides a self-assessment rating scale for reflecting on personal attitudes and perceptions concerning the collaboration of parents and educators.

School personnel also must keep in mind that family members are not a homogeneous group; therefore, experiences with one family member cannot be generalized to all other parents and families. Resources for examining values and for increasing cultural sensitivity are found in the "Additional Resources" sections in this chapter and in Chapter 9.

FIGURE 8.6   Self-Assessment of Attitudes and Perceptions

Rate yourself on the following, from 1 (very little) to 5 (always).

1. I understand the importance of home-school collaboration.	1 2 3 4 5
2. I recognize the concerns parents may have about working with me.	1 2 3 4 5
3. I recognize that parents of students with special needs may have emotional and social needs I may not understand.	1 2 3 4 5
4. I recognize and respect the expertise of families.	1 2 3 4 5
5. I feel comfortable working with families whose values and attitudes differ from mine.	1 2 3 4 5
6. I am persistent and patient as I develop relationships with families.	1 2 3 4 5
7. I am comfortable with my skills for communicating with families.	1 2 3 4 5
8. I am realistic about the barriers for me in working with families.	1 2 3 4 5
9. I find it difficult to understand why some families have the attitudes they have.	1 2 3 4 5
10. I recognize that some family members will have problems interacting with me because of their experience with other teachers.	1 2 3 4 5

ACTION 8.2
Examining Your Personal Values

Work in small groups, choosing as a group to use either Figure 8.4 or 8.5 to examine and discuss your personal values about parents and families or about family-school partnerships. Individually complete the chosen assessment. Then compare your responses. Discuss the similarities and differences. Why are some of the responses different within the group? Why are others similar? What experiences have you had as students, parents, educators, and community members that are reflected in your responses? Show respect for these differences as you have a group discussion about what has been learned.

Step 2: Building Collaborative Relationships

The second step in collaborating with families is building collaborative relationships. This critical step involves:

1. Appropriate communication
2. Focusing on family strengths
3. Honoring parental expertise
4. Providing social support

Appropriate Communication   Friendly, positive relationships and honest, respectful communication can help bridge barriers that prevent effective home-school collaboration. As emphasized in Chapter 7, basic communication and rapport-building skills are essential for establishing healthy, successful relationships with family members. Astute teachers avoid any words and phrases that may be perceived as thinking that having a student with one or more disabilities is undesirable. They listen for the messages given by parents and respond to their verbal and nonverbal cues. In addition, when communicating with families, school personnel must avoid jargon that can be misunderstood or misinterpreted. Parents often feel alienated by professional educators and one common cause is words (pedagogy, dual-immersion classrooms) and acronyms (IFSP, ITBS) that pepper the conversation without explanation of their meaning (Soodak & Erwin, 1995). Choices of words can ease, or inhibit, communication with parents, and professional educators must respect language variations created by differences in culture, education, occupation, age, and place of origin (Morsink, Thomas, & Correa, 1991).

Teachers and administrators often find that one of the most important, but difficult, aspects of developing relationships with parents is listening to them. The challenge lies in listening to parents' messages even though they might disagree strongly with family members, and their attitudes and values might differ significantly. Although the quality of the interaction should be a primary focus in parent relationships, the numbers and variety of initiated communications are important as well. To initiate partnerships, educators have used effectively such communication tools as phone calls, introductory and welcoming letters, newsletters, teacher-to-parent calendars, and notepads with identifying logos. Each note, phone call, e-mail, conversation, or conference, whether taking place in a formal setting or on the spur of the moment at the grocery store, should reflect the willingness and commitment of school personnel to work with parents as they face immense responsibilities in providing for the special needs of their child.

It is important for teachers to arrange and encourage more regular, informal contacts with parents. Family members often report being put off by the formality inherent in some scheduled conferences, particularly when they are limited to ten minutes, as they often are, with another child's family waiting just outside (Lindle, 1989). Teachers should ask parents to tell their preferred modes of communication. Phone calls and e-mails or text messages are appropriate for positive reports, but should not be used to discuss weighty concerns. Some consultants have found that e-mail and school websites are an effective way to communicate with families. However, keep in mind that many families do not have access to this technology.

Focusing on Family Strengths   Family-focused services and collaboration emphasize an empowerment approach. Rather than focusing on what is going wrong, collaborators focus on family members and the strength of their experiences. The effective collaborative partner provides support and reinforcement for family members in their family roles. In addition to listening to family members and acknowledging their expertise, it is crucial to empower families by giving them positive feedback about their efforts to support their child's education. Families often get very little reinforcement for parenting, particularly for the extra efforts they expend in caring for children with special needs. They should be encouraged and commended for providing time and space for homework and discussing school with their children.

Too few families hear positive comments about their children. They may feel guilty or confused because of their children's problems. Examples of support and reinforcement that teachers can use include thank-you notes for helping with field trips; VIP (very important parent) buttons for classroom volunteers; supporting phone calls when homework has been turned in; and happygrams when a class project is completed. By considering family member strengths as well as needs and interests, educators will be focusing on the collaborative nature of parent involvement. An example of a strengths-assessment form is provided in Figure 8.2, earlier in this chapter.

School educators who use strengths and interests of family and community members to engage them in education of infants and toddlers, preschool and kindergarten students, as well as primary, middle, and secondary students can approach this in many creative ways. Teachers Involve Parents in Schoolwork (TIPS), developed by the National Network of Partnership Schools (Van Voorhis, 2003) is an interactive process for encouraging homework that counts on middle-school families to help sixth- through eighth-graders complete their homework proficiently and earn better grades. At the early childhood level, Mayer, Ferede, and Hou (2006) use storybooks to successfully promote family involvement.

The online Family Involvement Storybook Corner promotes awareness and practice of family involvement through storybooks, at www.hfrp.org/storybook-corner.

Another example is the Raising a Reader Program, at www.raisingareader.org, that is based on the work of Judith K. Bernhard. She and her colleagues built their Early Programs on parent strengths that benefit children by giving parents a prominent role as their children's literacy teachers. Raising a Reader is a nonprofit organization in California whose purpose is engaging parents in a routine of daily "book cuddling" with their children birth through age five.

Providing Social Support   For many families with exceptional children, support networks are a vital part of their lives. Families rely on informal and formal social support networks for information and guidance they need to carry out responsibilities for child rearing, children's learning, and child development. Schools can provide a rich array of child, parent, and family support in the form of information and environmental experiences to strengthen family and child competence and influence student outcomes. Parenting supports include information and advice that can strengthen existing parenting knowledge and skills and facilitate acquisition of new competencies (Dunst, 2000).

For families of children with disabilities, supports are a crucial aspect of family-focused collaboration. Workshops, newsletters, informational meetings, provision of emotional support, and multigenerational gatherings are examples of formal supports needed by families. Schools are instrumental in promoting informal support systems for families. According to extensive research by Dunst (2000) and his colleagues, informal support has a stronger relationship to many child, parent, and family outcomes than formal support. Fiedler et al. (2007) suggest that providing support for all family members and siblings also benefits children with special needs, as does fostering community advocacy and support. Consultants should encourage activities that help families develop informal support networks such as parent-to-parent groups and informal multiple-family gatherings. Families may have the capacity to garner support; however, many families, especially those with young children who have just been referred to special services or diagnosed with a learning or behavior problem, need help from schools in developing social support networks.

Step 3: Initiating Home-School Interactions

Parents want their children to be successful in school. Even parents who are considered "hard to reach" such as nontraditional and low-income families, usually want to be more involved (Davies, 1988). Most, however, wait to be invited before becoming involved as a partner in their child's education. Unfortunately, many have to wait for years before someone opens the door and provides them the *opportunity* to become a team member with others who care about the educational and social successes of their children. Parent satisfaction with their involvement is directly related to perceived opportunities for involvement (Salisbury & Evans, 1988). They are more motivated to carry on when they are aware that the results of their time and energy are helping their child learn. School personnel who are in a position to observe these results can provide the kind of reinforcement that parents need so much.

Research has shown that when family members are welcome in schools and classrooms, and their child's work and experiences are meaningful to them, parents often experience new aspirations for themselves and for their children (St. John et al., 1997). This provides another important reason to work collaboratively and respectfully with parents.

Step 4: Individualizing for Families

Special education professionals are trained to be competent at individualizing educational programs for students' needs. Nevertheless, they may assume that all family members have the same strengths and needs, thereby overlooking the need to individualize family involvement programs (Turnbull et al., 2006). Individualizing for families means knowing the strengths and needs of family members. Using checklists and forms like those provided in this chapter will help teachers learn about the needs parents have for information, translation, social support, advocacy, or referral. By using the assessments discussed earlier, and taking care to avoid stereotypes and judgments, they will be more successful in involving parents as partners in their child's learning program. Individualizing for families based on their strengths and needs promotes family empowerment, or the attitudes and skills to determine their own futures. When educators partner with parents and other family members on behalf of children with special needs, parents become more confident that they have the information and problem-solving skills they need in order to deal with current and future situations regarding their children and families.

Several program attributes can help assure consultants that school-home-community programming will result in family empowerment. Dunst (2002) lists and describes the principles of Family Support America that promote family empowerment. Examples of those principles are:

- Relationships should be based on equality and respect.
- Educators should enhance families' abilities to support growth and development in all family members.
- Schools should affirm and strengthen families' cultural, racial, and linguistic identities and enhance the abilities of families to function in a multicultural society.
- Services and systems for families should be fair, responsible, and accountable to the families served.

Successful work with parents calls for establishing respectful and trusting relationships, as well as responding to the needs of all partners. The degree to which parents are placed in an egalitarian role, with a sense of choice, empowerment, and ownership in the education process, is a crucial variable in successful collaboration.

Considering Culture   Traditional approaches to reaching out to families are not always appropriate for families from cultural and other minority groups. Educators must develop cultural competence that demonstrates acceptance and respect for cultural diversity and differences (Cross, 1996; Lynch & Hanson, 1998). This allows individualization of educational programs for students and individualization of parent interactions to be done in a manner that respects the family's culture. Cross (1996) recommends that educators learn about cultures they serve by observing influential members of different groups. Other recommendations include spending time with people of that culture, identifying a cultural guide, reading the literature (professional as well as fiction) by and for persons of the culture, attending relevant cultural events, and asking questions in respectful ways. Schools can investigate programs that have been proven successful with parents and families from different cultural and socio-economic backgrounds. One program that has been replicated in many communities across the country is the Parent Institute for Quality Education (PIQE). It was started in California to connect families, schools, and community members as partners in advancing the education of every child through parent engagement (www .piqe.org). This organization, to be discussed further in Chapter 13, includes parent engagement education classes, workshops for parents and educators, and activities to promote school success.

Step 5: Evaluating Home-School Collaboration

Evaluation of efforts to provide opportunities for collaboration in schools can indicate whether families' needs are being met and their strengths are being utilized. Evaluation also shows whether needs and strengths of educational personnel are being met. Assessment tools used after a workshop, conference, or at the conclusion of the school year allow school personnel to ask parents, "How did we do in facilitating your learning of the new information or accessing the new services?" Some teachers use a quick questionnaire, to be completed anonymously, to see if the activity or program fulfilled the goals of the home-school collaboration. If data show that the activity gave families the information they needed, provided them with the resources they wanted, and offered them the opportunities they requested, educators know whether or not to continue with the program or modify it.

Educators also should evaluate their own involvement with families. This means assessing their inclusion of family strengths and skills to facilitate educational programs with children who have special needs. Did teachers get the information they needed from families? How many volunteer hours did parents contribute? What were the results of home tutoring on the achievement of the resource room students? What changes in family attitudes about the school district were measured? Chapter 12 contains information about procedures for evaluating collaboration efforts. Note again that the purpose of family collaboration is to utilize the unique and vital partnership on behalf of their children.

CASE STUDY: CARLOTTA'S FEUDING FAMILY

Carlotta, a fifth-grade student in your class who has a diagnosed learning disability, is having difficulty with her homework, especially in math and spelling. Family members try hard to help, but they disagree on the best way to help Carlotta. Her grandmother thinks Carlotta will improve on her own if everybody will "just leave her alone." Her older sister tries to help her with the homework but is not very patient and they end up fighting. Carlotta's father believes she should have a set homework time every evening and should quit piano lessons and soccer. Carlotta makes little progress and tension within the family is palpable. You, her teacher, see the negative effect on Carlotta in the classroom. The mother feels her daughter needs more instructional attention at school because of her learning disability. The mother would also like her to have *no* homework to relieve strain on the family at home. She has requested a conference with the girl's teachers and related services personnel. Think about this situation and then answer the following questions:

1. Who should be involved in the subsequent meeting? Where should it take place?
2. Make a list of things you would *not* want to have happen during the meeting.
3. Make another list of things that you *would* want to have happen.
4. Then combine and arrange all lists into overall "Do and Don't" help sheets for home-school involvement in students' learning programs and study strategies. Embellish with illustrations if appropriate.
5. Develop a group, assigning a person to represent each of the people at the meeting. Have another person be the observer. Role play the meeting. Stop after ten or fifteen minutes and ask the observer to comment on the interactions. Then discuss the meeting as a group. How did you feel in your role? What did the consultant do to make you feel part of the meeting? What could the consultant have done to make the experience better for those in the roles of Carlotta, her father, mother, grandmother, or one of the school personnel?

COLLABORATING IN PLANNING AND CONFERENCING

Working collaboratively and respectfully with parents in formalized planning such as IEP meetings and regular classroom-progress conferences is a vital yet sometimes challenging aspect of home-school collaboration. If parents only hear from teachers when formal meetings are scheduled, they are less likely to see themselves as equal partners. As one parent said to a teacher, "I take care of her at home; you are in charge of the school part. . . ." Planning and progress meetings and conferences should be only one of the many points of contact between school personnel and family members.

Family Partners in IEP, ITP, and IFSP Planning

The Individualized Education Plan (IEP), Individualized Family Service Plan (IFSP), and Individualized Transition Plan (ITP) conferences can be a productive time or a frustrating experience. Parents may be emotional about their child's problems, and teachers can be apprehensive about meeting with the parents in emotion-laden situations with sensitive issues to discuss. A number of researchers have found that too little parent involvement in team decision making, particularly relating to IEP, IFSP, and ITP development, is a major problem in special education programs (Boone, 1989).

School consultants will improve school-home collaboration in these areas if they provide family members with information before the meeting. Consultants can communicate with family members by phone, letter, or informal interview to inform them about names and roles of staff members who will attend; typical procedure for meetings; ways they can prepare for the meeting; contributions they will be encouraged to make; and ways in which follow-up to the meeting will be provided.

Turnbull and Turnbull (2006) discuss characteristics and components of a successful IFSP/IEP conference. Those components include: preparation before the conference; getting started with the conference; sharing expectations and visions for the student; reviewing evaluations and assessments; sharing priorities, resources, and concerns (both the family and the educators); working collaboratively to develop plans, addressing expected outcomes, or addressing issues; determining placement and services; and summarizing.

Then the educator should wrap up the conference and ask for questions or feedback. Educators should keep in mind that family members may be anxious or nervous about the conference and may not have questions at the time of the conference. In addition, their emotions may prevent them from "hearing" everything said during the conference. Finally, they may be on very strict time schedules for returning to work, picking up small children, or keeping a medical appointment. Their time must be valued and their schedules honored.

Specific ways parents can be involved in IEP, ITP, or IFSP development and implementation before, during, and after the IEP conference are provided in Figure 8.7. These lists could be printed in the school handbook.

When parents and teachers work together as equals, they have more opportunities to express their own knowledge and can come to respect each other's wisdom and expertise. Siblings need information about disabilities, opportunities to talk about their feelings, and time to hear about the experiences of other siblings of children with disabilities. Families need others with whom to share their feelings of pride and joy, and to discuss ways of planning for the future (Cramer et al., 1997; Fiedler et al., 2007).

Student-Led Conferences

A student has the greatest investment and most important involvement in constructing an individual education plan for learning. Indeed, it is counterproductive to formulate goals and objectives without involving students in their conferences as a member of the planning team. Having students help plan a student-led conference with family members will give them a sense of ownership in their own learning process. Students and their teachers should talk beforehand about the purpose of their conference and then set some goals for the meeting.

A student will want to decide which samples of work to show and what learning activities to describe. Developing a sample rubric beforehand to evaluate the conference after it takes place will add to the learning process. The classroom teacher or special education teacher, or both, may want to have a brief practice session so the process feels familiar

FIGURE 8.7   Checklist for Families in Developing IEPs

Throughout the year:

  Read about educational issues and concerns.

  Learn about the structure of the local school system.

  Observe your child, noting work habits, play patterns, and social interactions.

  Record information regarding special interests, talents, and accomplishments, as well as areas of concern.

Before the conference:

  Visit the child's school.

  Discuss school life with the child.

  Talk with other families who have participated in conferences to find out what goes on during the conference.

  Write down questions and points you would like to address.

  Review notes from any previous conferences with school staff.

  Prepare a summary file of information, observations, and products that would further explain the child's needs.

  Arrange to take along any other persons that you feel would be helpful in planning the child's educational program.

During the conference:

  Be an active participant.

  Ask questions about anything that is unclear.

  Insist that educational jargon and "alphabet soup" acronyms be avoided.

  Contribute information, ideas, and recommendations.

  Let the school personnel know about the positive things school has provided.

  Ask for a copy of the IEP if it is not offered.

  Ask to have a follow-up contact time to compare notes about progress.

After the conference:

  Discuss the conference proceedings with the child.

  Continue to monitor the child's progress and follow up as agreed on.

  Reinforce school staff for positive effects of the planned program.

  Keep adding to the notebook of information.

  Be active in efforts to improve schools.

  Say supportive things about the schools whenever possible.

and the student is comfortable when the conference takes place. Teachers should prepare family members ahead of time for the student-led conference with a phone call or a brief letter, focusing on the contributions it can make to their child's confidence and pride in achievement.

Parent partnerships can be particularly difficult to cultivate at the secondary level. Much of the difficulty stems from attitudes of teenage students who would just "die" of humiliation if their parents were seen at school by their peers (McGrew-Zoubi, 1998). Other teens might head off a teacher's efforts to involve family members with "Go ahead, but they won't care/come/participate," or "They have to work," or "They don't think it's necessary," or even a harsh appraisal of parent interest such as "They don't have anything to contribute to any meeting about me." Parents probably are not immune from these perceptions and attitudes and some acquiesce to them out of frustration or years-long weariness, while teachers are hard-pressed to find ways of countermanding them.

In some middle school settings where traditional parent-teacher interactions and conferences have been perceived as more problematic helpful, an innovative student-centered model for conferencing has been developed and field tested. In this model, a structure is created in which students are helped to prepare for their own conferences. The new format is communicated to parents and colleagues and procedural operations are developed (Countryman & Schroeder, 1996). In the planning, development, and evaluation phases of this new approach, teachers found that students should have more participation in preparing conference scripts. They need a log to help them organize their products, and they must not overlook bringing to the discussion their classes such as art, music, driver education, family and consumer science, and modern languages or those subjects will not get discussed. Students reasonably express the need to see how teachers have evaluated them before it is revealed at the conference.

Teachers will want to plan carefully for a student-led conference in collaboration with parents or other family members. After planning, they should review the steps and prepare by rehearsing them, focusing especially on the opening few minutes and the closing of the conference. These steps will help guide student and collaborator through the process in advance of the event:

1. Decide what the goal(s) of the conference should be, and why having a student-led meeting is a good idea.
2. Together make a simple, uncluttered agenda, with time limits built in and a definite ending time imposed (preceded by a three-minute wrap-up). If you plan to use the rubric provided in Figure 8.8, go over those with the student now to convey what is expected and how the event will be assessed.
3. Determine how families will be informed and invited, making sure to convey that the student will be in charge. This would be a good time to use an on-line format for the invitation if that is something the student can do well or would like to learn.
4. Have the student sketch a preferred location and a seating arrangement.
5. Together, choose work samples and other information showing progress made, goals accomplished, and goals yet to be met. Think about what other information family members would like to have and what questions they might want to ask or answer.
6. Rehearse! Fix any problem areas. If needed, rehearse again.
7. After the conference, have a debriefing and talk about what went especially well, what needed improvement, and what would be good to do next time. Expect the student-led conference to be a very good learning experience for student, family, and teacher.

A student-guided conference must not be hurried. A thirty-minute segment of time might be reasonable. Busy teachers, particularly those at the secondary level with

FIGURE 8.8   Rating Form, Student-Led Conference

Name: _____

Criterion	Needs Improvement		Fair	Good	Outstanding
1. Was prepared for the conference	0	1	2	3	4
2. Participated enthusiastically	0	1	2	3	4
3. Presented material in organized way	0	1	2	3	4
4. Explained learning process effectively	0	1	2	3	4
5. Assessed achievement realistically	0	1	2	3	4
6. Submitted ideas for next work/studies	0	1	2	3	4
7. Credited resources accurately	0	1	2	3	4
8. Involved all participants in discussion	0	1	2	3	4

Total: _____ of 32

Areas of strengths:

Areas that need more work:

dozens of students, will need strong administrator support and innovative scheduling ideas to make student-guided conferences successful. But for a courageous, energetic school staff, student-guided parent conferences can promote meaningful ownership by students in their own learning. Students and other participants also can benefit from an assessment of conference outcomes by using a rubric designed for the purpose. (See Figure 8.8.)

Benefits from having students participate in conferences for their individualized programs include:

- Receiving information about their progress
- Feeling involved in their own educational planning
- Being more strongly motivated to improve
- Being aware that home-school are working collaboratively on their behalf

MAINTAINING HOME-SCHOOL COLLABORATION AND PARTNERSHIPS

Home-school collaboration is mandated, it is challenging, and it is rewarding. Educators have two choices in collaborating with families: to see school as a battleground with an emphasis on conflict between families and school personnel or to see school as a "homeland"

FIGURE 8.9   "Teacher Says Thanks"

environment that invites power sharing and mutual respect, with collaboration on activities that foster student learning and development (Epstein, 1995). The goal for educators and their partners is to integrate family involvement as part of the school instructional strategy, that is, as part of the curriculum rather than added on to school activities. Successful models for home-school-community partnerships (see Figure 8.9) are those that:

- Respect the family as the child's first teacher
- Empower families and communities to support and advocate for all students
- Understand learning as a lifelong endeavor involving families and communities
- Recognize that all families want the best for their children and can have a positive, significant impact on their children's education

Students, schools, and families are strengthened by appropriate outreach efforts and partnership activities based on values and practices of a family-focused approach. Educators who empower and support families of their students recognize that they are part of powerful partnerships and the work they do with parents is part of the educational legacy they leave with students and their families. Compare the tone of Figure 8.9 with similar Figure 8.4, p. 227.

TECHNOLOGY AND OTHER RESOURCES FOR SCHOOL EDUCATORS AND HOME EDUCATORS

The Internet and local libraries and media centers are excellent sources of information about successful home-school-community collaborative efforts. Many state and national organizations are dedicated to providing helpful information about disabilities, special education, legal issues, and successful parent-as-partner strategies. For example, every state has at least one parent center that is funded by the U.S. Department of Education; see www.parentcenternetwork.org.

Most states have a Parent Training and Information Center and a Community Parent Resource Center that provides training and information to families of children and young adults from birth to age twenty-two who have physical, cognitive, emotional, or social needs, for addressing learning or behavioral disabilities. They help families obtain appropriate education and services for children with disabilities and improve educational programs for all children. They train and inform parents and professionals on a variety of topics, help to resolve problems between families and schools or other agencies, and connect children with disabilities to community resources that address their needs. Other resources include, but are by no means limited to, sites such as:

- National Association for the Education of Young Children, www.naeyc.org
- Harvard Family Research project, www.hfrp.org
- Educate America—Family Empowerment, www.maec.org/
- Family Empowerment Council, Inc, www.familyempowerment.org
- National Network of Partnership Schools and the Center on School, Family, and Community Partnerships, www.csos.jhu.edu/P2000/center.htm
- National Dissemination Center for Children with Disabilities, NICHCY, http:// .nichcy.org
- Children, Youth, and Families Education and Research Network (CYFERNet), www.cyfernet.org

Most of these sites have both Spanish and English versions and are excellent resources for both parents and educators.

ETHICS FOR WORKING TOGETHER WITH FAMILIES AND COMMUNITIES

In an ethical climate for home-school collaboration, educators will demonstrate keen awareness of the realities, sometimes bright but oftentimes grim, in which today's families live and function. Challenges in working with families today are very different from those of past decades due to significant changes in society. Many families are overwhelmed by family crises as well as everyday life events. Some face multiple and prolonged stressors such as poverty, long work hours or multiple jobs, health issues without insurance, bilingual or multilingual communication difficulties between home-school, and more. Families might include a single parent, a blended family, gay or lesbian parents, unwed adolescent parents, nonbiological parents serving as primary caregivers, foster caregivers, grandparents, extended families, and adoptive parents.

Collaborative consultants must avoid judging attitudes, overtones of blaming, stereotyping, holding false expectations, and dwelling on basic differences in values. They must be tolerant if parents wish to obtain second or even third opinions. It is important to have empathy with families, with the awareness that parents may be having considerable difficulty in coming to terms with their child's disability or disabilities. Confidentiality of information and privacy pertaining to family matters must be honored and preserved.

Families and school personnel within an ethical climate will make every effort not to reproach each other, but to work together as partners on the child's team. They will be honest with each other and willing to listen and empathize, acknowledging any anger or disappointment with patience and calmness. In potentially explosive situations the teacher will want to include the principal. All should remain calm and open-minded, and employ responsive listening to learn exactly what the family members' views and concerns are. Teachers who find out that they are wrong should acknowledge that before stating their views. They will want to stress that all parties have the welfare of the child in mind.

Teachers and administrators, and any other school personnel included, will want to keep in mind that most families are doing the best they can; parents of students do not start out the morning saying, "I think today I will be a poor parent." Collaboration will not require total agreement in values or educational philosophy, but school personnel and families must focus on needs and interests of children and their families.

TIPS FOR HOME-SCHOOL COLLABORATION

1. Establish rapport with families early in the year. Call right away, before problems develop, so that the first family contact is a positive one.
2. Invite families in to talk about their traditions, experiences, hobbies, and occupations.
3. Send home "up slips," putting them in a different format from the "down slips" that families too often receive, and have conferences with families because the student is performing *well* in the classroom.
4. When sharing information with families, sandwich any necessary comments about problems or deficits into the conversation between two very positive ones.
5. During interaction with families, notice how your actions are received, and adapt to that; never assume anything.
6. When several staff members will be meeting with family members, make sure each one's role and purpose for being included in the meeting will be understood by the parents. Send follow-up notes to the family after the meeting.
7. Introduce families to all support personnel working with the child.
8. Build interpersonal "bank accounts" with frequent deposits of good will to families. The "interest earned" will be better outcomes for students.
9. Encourage family members to volunteer in the classroom to read stories, help with art lessons, listen to book reports, or give a lesson on an area of expertise such as a job or hobby. If the family has just arrived, they may enjoy telling about their former home-school.
10. Ask families about their educational expectations for their children. Develop a climate of high expectations in the home, school, and community.

ADDITIONAL RESOURCES

Berger, E. H. (2008). *Parents as partners in education: Families and schools working together* (7th ed.). Upper Saddle River, NJ: Prentice Hall.

Caspe, M., & Lopez, M. E. (2006). *Lessons from family-strengthening interventions: Learning from evidence-based practice.* Cambridge, MA: Harvard Family Research Project. Available at www.hfrp. html.

Caspe, M., Lopez, M. E., & Wolos, C. (2007). *Family involvement in elementary school children's education.* Cambridge, MA: Harvard Family Research Project. Available at www.hfrp.org.

Fiedler, C. R., Simpson, R. L., & Clark, D. M. (2007). *Parents and families of children with disabilities: Effective school-based support services.* Upper Saddle River, NJ: Prentice Hall.

Kreider, H., Caspe, M., Kennedy, S., & Weiss, H. (2007). *Family involvement in middle and high school students' education.* Cambridge, MA: Harvard Family Research Project. Available at www.hfrp.html.

Lynch, E. W., & Hanson, M. J. (1998). *Developing cross-cultural competence: A guide for working with children and their families* (2nd ed.). Baltimore: Paul H. Brooks

Murray, M. M. & Curran, E. M. (2008). Learning together with parents of children with disabilities: Bringing parent-professional partnership education to a new level. *Teacher Education and Special Education, 31*(1), 59–63.

Trainor, A. A. (2010). Diverse approaches to parent advocacy during special education home-school interactions: Identification and use of cultural and social capital. *Remedial and Special Education, 31* (1), 35–47.

Weiss, H., Caspe, M., & Lopez, M. E. (2006). *Family involvement in early childhood education.* Cambridge, MA: Harvard Family Research Project. Available at www.hfrp.html.

9

Working Together for Students in Diverse Populations

THE UNITED STATES IS A COMPLEX SOCIETY OF MANY CULTURES, RACES, ethnicities, languages, and group differences for which the melting-pot and salad-bowl metaphors no longer apply. This ever-expanding richness of perspectives, attributes, talents, skills, and styles is better characterized now by images such as mosaic, quilt, or tapestry that can more fully illustrate our broad spectrum of cultures and differences. Each characteristic of socioeconomic, racial, ethnic, religious, age, gender, and ability contributes a unique part to the whole, with our shared values and social institutions providing the frame and the adhesive.

If we choose a tapestry as our metaphor, we can think of the tapestry as made up of threads having many textures, hues, and sizes that are woven into a colorful, vibrant image. Of course there would be the occasional knots, ravelings, and frays, but every thread would be valuable in contributing purpose and texture to the whole design. Appreciation of such differences and respect for diversity are key elements in collaboration to serve the special needs of this diverse population. The process of cultivating this appreciation is represented in the shaded circle of Figure 9.1.

FOCUSING QUESTIONS

1. How does the ever-changing demography of contemporary classrooms relate to school consultation and collaboration?

2. What is meant by *cultural diversity*, and what terms are used for various school programs that serve culturally diverse learners?

3. What is the collaborative consultant's role in working with diverse populations and how can supportive attitudes, sensitivities, and skills for the role be developed and assessed?

4. Why should consulting teachers strive to know their own culture first, before they set out to consult, collaborate, and work as educational teams in multicultural settings?

5. What are differences in culturally diverse communication styles and belief systems that teachers observe among students and colleagues, and how can modern technology help bridge these differences?

6. How can collaborative consultants ethically and constructively team with educational partners to serve needs in culturally and linguistically diverse school settings? Rural and isolated areas? Areas of high mobility? Military-dependent contexts? Settings where students are home-schooled? Gay or lesbian families? Children with disabilities who are abused? Educators who themselves have disabilities?

KEY TERMS

culture

cultural and linguistic
    diversity/culturally and
    linguistically diverse
    (CLD)

cultural competence

cultural and linguistic
    diversity with an

exceptionality or
    exceptionalities/culturally
    and linguistically diverse
    with an exceptionality or
    exceptionalities (CLDE)

diversity

English language learner
    (ELL)

ethnic group

gay, lesbian, bisexual,
    transgendered/transsexual,
    queer (GLBTQ)

multicultural education

underrepresented minority
    (URM)

VIGNETTE 9

The instructor of a course in a program for teacher preparation wants to include awareness and appreciation of cultural diversity as a class activity. Early in the course, she greets the students, hands them a half-sheet of paper with several items to complete, and says, "Please move about the room to obtain a different autograph on each blank line of your paper. You may use your own name once, and only once, if you qualify for an item. When your autograph form is complete, or the signal is given to stop, please sit down and interact with others near you by telling some things about your own cultural background, describing as you do so any memorable multicultural experiences you have had and would like to share, and discussing places and peoples you would like to know more about."

The paper distributed by the instructor was an autograph-signature form that looked like this:

Autograph Form

The challenge for you is to obtain autographs from your colleagues in the allotted time:

1. Someone who speaks Spanish _____
2. Someone who has been in more countries than you have _____
3. A person who owns a world atlas or a globe _____
4. Someone who has eaten blubber or sushi, or ants, or grasshoppers, or another food you do not consider a delicacy _____
5. A person who has driven (legally) on roads to the left of center _____
6. A person who has seen an entire movie in a foreign language _____
7. Someone who knows the time in Sweden right now _____
8. A person who has studied the French or German language _____
9. One who has or did have an international pen pal _____
10. Someone with a friend or a relative from another culture _____

As participants seek out the autographs, and especially as they begin discussing their own experiences with other cultures and languages, the instructor becomes more familiar with the wide range of multicultural experiences within the group. Sharing these backgrounds and learning more about their experiences will be helpful in expanding multicultural understanding throughout the rest of the course.

DIVERSITY AND EDUCATIONAL COLLABORATION AND CONSULTATION

Understanding other cultures is not an easy undertaking, but it is a cornerstone for successful collaboration. Respecting cultural differences and cultural similarities fosters collegial interactions and relationships. Consultants must acknowledge and understand the implications of cultural diversity within society as it affects the educational system. According to 2010 Census Bureau projections (United States Census Bureau, 2010), in the United States within about three decades the group characterized as nonhispanic whites will be a minority. During the year 2010, more babies were born to the minority populations than to the white population. In addition:

- The population of those with Hispanic ethnicity will increase by 188 percent, to 102.6 million, or about one-quarter of the total population.
- Hispanics accounted for more than half the nation's growth between 2000 and 2010, jumping to more than 50 million because of high birth rates and immigration. One in six Americans is Hispanic.
- Asian populations have increased to double digits, with Asians making up 5% of the total population in the United States.
- African Americans make up 12% of the total of the U.S. population of 309 million, with the black population only slightly outpacing the nation's 9.7% growth rate.

These trends are expected to continue, with shifts in the demographics by region. For example, during the year 2010 more babies were born to the minority populations than to the white population. African Americans are moving from cities to suburban areas and from the North to the South. A growing number of individuals identify themselves as multiracial. William H. Frey (2010), demographer from the Brookings Institution in Washington, DC, calls 2010–2020 a pivotal decade because the population is pivoting from a white-black-dominated American population to one that is multiracial and multicultural.

These changes in U.S. demographics and predicted trends for continuing rapid change will have significance for the collaborative work done by educational consultants. Educators and others who work with students with special needs may move to a city or region where cultural differences seem to be overwhelming. Or the school district where a teacher works may change significantly. Although demographics change, co-educators' mission is the same: promoting the education of students with special needs. Therefore, educational consultants must respect and value diversity as they demonstrate knowledge and competence in working with multicultural populations in their schools and communities.

What Is Diversity?

Educational consultants believe that all students, regardless of gender, disability, social class or ethnicity, race, or other cultural characteristics, should have an equal opportunity to learn in school. Therefore, for educational consultants, it is appropriate to define diversity broadly. Many demographic variables (age, gender, residence), status variables (social, educational, economic), and affiliations (formal, informal) contribute to identity as well as to issues related to collaborative relationships. Current uses of the word *diversity* in educational settings relate to ethnicity, language, religion, disability, sexual orientation, and demographic factors of economic level, geographic location, age, gender, and other indicators of group uniqueness. Diversity includes historical and contextual basis and includes not just racial or ethnic groups, but other groups or subgroups such as female, deaf, rural, and military or ex-military. Educational systems will be called upon more and more during the next several decades to serve new pluralities with sensitivity to issues on understanding and appreciation of diversity.

The term *diversity* is used here in a very broad sense. Because the concept of multicultural education grew out of the Civil Rights movement, too often the term *multicultural* is thought of as including only race or ethnicity. Individuals with whom educators will collaborate are members of cultural, racial, or other groups, but within groups there are subgroups, called "micro-cultures." Therefore, within diverse groups there are those who share other factors, such as country of origin, religion, marital status, and education. Banks and Banks (2010) remind us that while membership in cultural or micro-cultural groups can provide important clues about an individual's attitude or behavior, membership in a particular group does not determine behavior. Therefore, educators should avoid thinking about individuals in terms of their group or subgroup identity, such as deaf, African American, lesbian, or single parent. Individuals may or may not identify specifically with the group. These caveats should be called to mind frequently throughout this chapter. Strong group identification might provide vital cues for collaborative efforts; however, consultants should take care to avoid assumptions about individuals based on general characteristics of groups.

What Is Culture?

Banks and Banks (2010) describe culture as knowledge, concepts, and values shared by group members. Although different cultures tend to have different tools, dress, language, food, housing, and other artifacts, it is the values, symbols, interpretations, and perspectives that most distinguish one culture from another. Culture is a dynamic framework that provides guidelines and bounds for life practices. T. L. Cross, of the National Indian Child Welfare Association, describes culture as an organized response to human needs. Food, safety and security, love and belonging, esteem and identity, and self-actualization are shaped by culture (Cross, 2003).

All members of a cultural group are not the same and individuals are not fixed in their attitudes, beliefs, or behaviors. Therefore, educators should think about cultural differences as a continuum. This helps avoid stereotyping and aids in developing accurate perceptions of the diversity of our collaborators. Lynch and Hanson (1998) focus on the cultural continuum in several areas to consider:

- Family constellation
- Interdependence/individuality
- Nurturance/independence
- Time
- Tradition/technology
- Ownership
- Rights and responsibilities
- Harmony/control

The work of Lynch and Hanson (1998) and others in the Additional Resources section of this chapter can assist consultants who want to learn more about these areas, along with development of cultural identity, immigrant culture shock, culture-specific information, and important caveats for gathering this type of information. It is extremely important for educators who collaborate with adults from different cultural backgrounds to study and reflect on the reality of diversity.

What Is Multicultural Education?

Banks and Banks (2010), in their seventh edition of *Multicultural Education: Issues and Perspectives*, use the term *multicultural education* to refer to a wide variety of programs and practices related to educational equity for women, ethnic groups, language minorities, low income groups, and people with disabilities. The historical premise of multicultural education is the assumption that some students, because of their particular racial, ethnic, gender, or other group characteristics, have a better chance of succeeding in educational settings than students who belong to other groups or have different characteristics. Consultants who focus on the education of students with disabilities usually feel right at home in the company of multicultural education advocates.

Is There Diversity in the Teacher Population?

The teaching force does not reflect cultural diversity and it never has. Profiles of prospective teachers continue to be primarily white females from small towns or suburban communities who attended colleges or universities not far from home and plan to return to places similar to home for their teaching career. These teachers reflect middle-class backgrounds and values and have limited travel experience in which to become acquainted with diverse cultures. Eighty percent of teachers surveyed by Futrell, Gomez, and Bedden (2003) felt unprepared to teach a diverse student population. Discrepancy between teacher and student backgrounds argues forcibly for family and community collaborative efforts.

It is essential for educators to become familiar with the cultures of the students and families with whom they work and to have preparation in interpersonal communication and problem solving with culturally diverse populations. Deans and department chairs of teacher education programs are well aware that a critical element in gaining national accreditation for their programs is demonstration of diversity in student enrollment, instructional faculty, and sites for student teaching and field experiences. Once preservice teachers are placed in schools for that first year of teaching, experienced consulting teachers have an important role in mentoring and coaching them to work effectively with culturally and linguistically diverse students.

Diversity-Related Terminology for Educational Collaborators

Changes in the language used in various professional areas to describe programs, students, and instructional strategies related to diversity may be confusing to consultants and consultees. School educators and home educators (family members) may need to ask questions or research the meaning of terms related to diversity that are used in various local school programs. Such terms include English language learner (ELL), English language development (ELD), multicultural education, English for speakers of other languages (ESOL), cultural and linguistic diversity (CLD), and culturally and linguistically diverse students with exceptionalities (CLDE).

The term *English language learner* (ELL) refers to students who are not proficient in English. *English language development* (ELD) refers to all types of instruction that promote the development of oral or written English language skills and abilities. This term replaces those such as *English as a second language* (ESL) and *English for speakers of other languages* (ESOL; Gersten & Baker, 2000).

The phrase *minority group* is now used less frequently than in past decades unless it is in a numerical sense. The more acceptable term *ethnic group* refers to a microcultural group that shares a common history and culture, values, behaviors, and other characteristics that cause members of the group to have a shared identity (Banks & Banks, 2010).

The National Science Foundation (NSF) and many other agencies of the federal government use the term *underrepresented minority* (URM) to refer to individuals from diverse groups who are underrepresented in specific areas such as postsecondary and graduate education in science, technology, engineering, and mathematics (STEM). For example, the NSF funds programs to promote and support STEM education for URMs. In the science field, that generally means women and girls, individuals with disabilities, and individuals from some racial and ethnic groups such as Native Alaskans, American Indians, Native Hawaiians, African Americans, Hispanics, and Pacific Islanders.

The term *tolerance* is used frequently by excellent resources found in the *Teaching Tolerance* magazine, a project of the Southern Poverty Law Center in Montgomery, Alabama. When those at the center were asked why they used the word *tolerance* rather than "acceptance," they responded that the term is the counter-position of intolerance. The center uses the definition established by the United Nations Educational, Scientific and Cultural Organization (UNESCO), which adopted a Declaration of Principles on Tolerance in 1995. UNESCO defined tolerance as ". . . respect, acceptance, and appreciation of the rich diversity of our world's cultures, our forms of expression, and ways of being human." The organization understands that tolerance is fostered by knowledge, openness, communication, and freedom of thought, conscience and belief; and that tolerance is harmony in difference. More information about this perspective can be found at www.unesco.org.

CULTURAL AWARENESS BY COLLABORATIVE CONSULTANTS

Some students, because of their particular racial, ethnic, gender, and cultural characteristics, have a better chance of succeeding in educational institutions as currently structured than do students who belong to other groups with different cultural and gender characteristics (Banks & Banks, 2010). Consultants who work daily with students with disabilities are usually very aware of the harm to students when diversities of educational and cognitive abilities are ignored. Efforts to become more inclusive in education must include expanded knowledge about cultural diversity. Educators must foster positive attitudes toward cultural pluralism and cultivate skills for arranging multiple learning environments that enable individuals from every culture to realize their potential. In addition to their roles of working directly with students from diverse backgrounds, collaborative consultants work daily with other adults who are integral to providing the best education possible for all students. Being sensitive toward cultural differences and knowledgeable about cultural practices will enhance relationships and the process of collaboration.

School districts often employ paraeducators from the local community for many good reasons. One of those reasons is that they are likely to be from the dominant culture of that community and can relate well to students and their families. An obvious example is the ability to speak Spanish and appreciate Hispanic customs such as special holidays.

Lynch and Hanson (1998) compare culture to looking through a one-way mirror; everything we see is from our own perspective and limited view. It is only when we join the observed on the other side of the mirror that it is possible to see others and ourselves clearly. However, getting to the other side of the glass is difficult.

Cultural competence is the ability to function comfortably in cross-cultural settings and to interact harmoniously with people from cultures that differ from our own. Cultural competence brings a set of skills and attitudes that allow collaborators to move to the other side of the one-way mirror. There are many different perspectives on specific skills, attitudes, behaviors, and policies for cultural competence, but whatever definition is used, the bottom line is acknowledging, respecting, and building on the strengths of ethnicity and cultural and linguistic diversity.

Developing Cultural Competencies

How educators interact with diverse groups of people, demonstrate respectful behavior that responds to cultural diversity, and integrate cultural diversity into their curriculum and instruction, has a strong impact on the process and outcomes of collaborative consultation. Cultural competence is a reflective stance of learning, unlearning, and re-learning. There is no clear recipe for achieving cultural competence; however, the journey involves continual, reflective work to:

- Increase self-awareness of cultural and linguistic diversity
- Cultivate appreciation for diversity
- Increase knowledge and understanding of specific cultures
- Promote multicultural education for all students
- Develop skills to work effectively with a variety of students and parents

Increasing Awareness of Diversity

Only after we have assessed our own attitudes and values toward cultural and linguistic diversity will we be able to develop and strengthen our skills for working with diverse populations. When we hone our cross-cultural competencies, we are better consultants for consultees and students from diverse backgrounds. In addition, we are better equipped to promote understanding and appreciation of diverse cultural groups in the school setting. Therefore, we must examine our attitudes and practices about cultures different from our own, and work at broadening the limitations of our thinking.

Sample items for assessing one's multicultural attitudes and practices are provided in Figure 9.2. The items can be used for personal reflection and self-study. Discussion and expansion of the list can form the framework for staff development or be administered

FIGURE 9.2 Examples of Multicultural Assessment Items

A = Always; U = Usually; S = Sometimes; R = Rarely; N = Never

---

Personal Sensitivity

_____   1. I realize that any individual in a group may not have the same values as others in the group.

_____   2. I learn about and avoid words, statements, expressions and actions that members of other culture groups and orientations could find offensive.

_____   3. I read books and articles to increase my understanding and sensitivity about the hopes, strengths and concerns of people from other cultures, experiences and backgrounds.

_____   4. I counteract prejudicial, stereotypical thinking and talking whenever and wherever I can.

School Context Efforts

_____   5. I include contributions of people from diverse populations as an integral part of the school curriculum.

_____   6. I strive to nurture skills and develop values in students and colleagues that will help members of minority groups thrive in the dominant culture.

_____   7. I know where to obtain bias-free, multicultural materials for use in my school.

_____   8. I have evaluated the school resource materials to determine whether or not they contain a fair and appropriate presentation of people in diverse populations.

Parent/Community Relations

_____   9. I invite parents and community members from various cultural backgrounds to be classroom resources, speakers, visiting experts, or assistants.

_____   10. I value having a school staff composed of people from different cultural backgrounds.

_____   11. I exhibit displays showing culturally diverse people working and socializing together.

_____   12. I advocate for schools in which all classes, including special education classes, reflect and respect diversity.

---

as part of a study module for a teacher preparation course on consultation and collaboration. Additional items might be added after discussions about multiculturalism and cultural diversity in schools and communities.

■ ■ ■ ■ ■

ACTION 9.1
Personal Appreciation of Diversity

Complete the checklist in Figure 9.2. Then select two or three of the items for which you gave yourself a "usually" or "always" rating. Think of at least one example, such as number 3, "Name several books you have read" (e.g., *Saltypie: A Choctaw Journey from Darkness into Light*, a children's book by Tim Tingle; or *Beyond Central, Toward Acceptance: A Collection of Oral Histories from Students of Little Rock Central High School*, edited by Mackie O'Hara and Alex Richardson). Select one or two items you would like to incorporate into a plan of personal-awareness development for the school year. Share your thoughts with others in a small group. Work with a colleague to set target dates for your awareness development plan and commit to getting back together in person or via electronic communication on those dates to evaluate the outcomes. As reinforcement for making significant progress, treat yourself to something special!

Cultivate Appreciation for Diversity

Recognition and acceptance of diversity allows individuals and groups to interact effectively (Berger, 2008). Clare (2002) suggests that a person's worldview and perspectives of diversity expand as a result of multicultural experiences and proximity to other diverse groups. Recall the taxonomy for the social domain in Chapter 2 that shows increasingly complex levels of social interactions. These experiences create avenues for personal reflection and shift the way consulting teachers frame collaborative efforts and educational practices.

A primary part of developing cultural awareness is to understand one's *own* culture, beliefs, and values. Recognizing characteristics of one's own culture is especially important for European Americans because of their tendency to view culture through an ethnocentric lens, often believing somewhat naively that theirs is the primary or prevailing culture (Banks & Banks, 2007; Lynch & Hanson, 1998).

ACTION 9.2
Reflecting On One's Own Culture and Family History

Think about your own cultural background. What language did your great-grandparents, or more distant ancestors, speak? When did they come to this country? Why did they come? What family customs, such as holidays, food, and traditions reflect the culture of your ancestors? Food is always a good topic for exchanges about cultural history. What food did your great-grandmother fix for holidays? Where did the recipe come from and how did she learn to make it? Did she pass the tradition on to subsequent generations? Why, or why not?

After you have thought about your own history, practice effective communication skills by listening to descriptions from others about their cultural heritage. Ask questions to learn more about the cultural history of your colleagues. Share your cultural background information with others so that they may practice their active listening skills and get to know *you* better. How does this conversation contribute to your thinking about the phrase *a nation of immigrants*?

After consultants reflect on their own culture, they should work to enhance their abilities for acknowledging cultural differences in responding and relating to others. When considering methods for improving cross-cultural awareness and sensitivity, the best way for consultants to learn about other cultures is by learning from the people themselves, rather than learning about them secondhand as belonging to a particular cultural group. Communication skills and interpersonal skills are important for collaboration with educational partners. Awareness of differences and respect for customs within diverse cultures are major factors for interacting within school settings and engaging in collaborative efforts with school personnel.

Increasing Knowledge and Understanding of Diverse Cultures

One of the biggest challenges for consultants in diverse settings is understanding the consultee's frame of reference, or "entering the consultee's world" and viewing things as the consultee (or client) sees them (Soo-Hoo, 1998). Home communication patterns of students or consultees may be quite different from those they hear and see in school. Expectations between family members and teachers may be at variance.

Collaborators require a deep understanding of the co-collaborator's frame of reference. Sometimes general characteristics of cultural groups provide preliminary insights for consultants as they strive to develop and maintain collaborative relationships. These characteristics include cultural norms for the style of communication behavior and beliefs about families, and their spirituality and nature. A consulting teacher hoping to engage the family in collaborative problem solving may be met with silence or short phrases as a sign of respect, and may erroneously interpret this response as being negative or disengaged.

One cautionary note is that generic cultural characteristics are not the be-all and end-all of cultural diversity. *Any person or family may differ markedly from these generalities.* Although many researchers provide lists of generic cultural characteristics of specific diverse groups, consultants must guard against the myopic perspective that culturally diverse families are a homogeneous group. Educators should respond in individually relevant ways to those with whom they collaborate rather than make assumptions based on group characteristics of microcultures.

Descriptions of characteristics provide only broad-brush strokes for initiating multicultural interrelationships. Furthermore, brief descriptions for cultural characteristics of specific cultures may imply that cultural differences are simple and easy to understand. Cross (2003) gives us an example from his own Seneca teachings. For this Native American group from the U.S. Northwest, the theoretical model for their culture is a relational worldview; and this worldview, Cross says, is different from that found in most educational institutions. For the Senecas, human existence is understood in the form of a four-quadrant circle encompassing mind, body, spirit, and context. Health and well-being depend on the balance among the quadrants. Balance is a constant human process, and the Senecas rely on their culture to provide the resources within each quadrant for staying in balance. Cross points to this relational worldview as being different from a culture that relies heavily on linear thought and the scientific process to understand and solve problems in terms of causal relationships. Developing a cultural perspective is far from simple.

Communication and Culture

Effective intercultural communication for consultants means coping with the stress of dealing with the unfamiliar, establishing rapport with others, sensing other people's feelings, and communicating effectively with people from varying backgrounds. Collaborative consultants benefit from understanding interrelationships between language and cultural meaning.

Bogdan and Biklen (2006) remind us that not all cultures share middle class values and American definitions of terms. Examples of ethnic-based values and behaviors that can affect group interaction are preferences regarding (Adler, 1993; Sue & Sue, 1990):

- Personal space, such as physical distance between communicants and the arrangement of furniture for seating
- Body movement, including body orientation, gestures, and facial expressions
- Time orientation
- Eye movement and position
- Touch

Cultures have differing rules about human communications and relationships. For example, it is not acceptable in some cultures to share beliefs and opinions with people outside the group. Another example is the inclination in some cultures for being quiet in the presence of authority figures. This can be disconcerting to school personnel when trying to solicit input from parents who regard the teacher as the authority.

In some cultures, the way to respond to a question with finesse is to skirt the subject and arrive at it indirectly, while in another culture being direct and forthright is admirable. Public congratulation in certain cultures is offensive because group accomplishment is valued more than individual achievement, whereas in other cultures public congratulation would be an incentive to continue excelling. When Billy Mills, an Oglala Sioux from South Dakota became a track star at the University of Kansas, he won an important race, but not by much. In the movie about his life, *Running Brave*, after the race his coach questioned Billy about his less than stellar performance, to which Billy replied that he had won the race as Coach wanted, but he would not shame a fellow athlete in doing so.

Knowledge of cultural differences in nonverbal communication is important for educational collaborators. For example, knowing that avoiding eye contact is a sign of respect in some cultures will help consultant and consultee avoid interpreting this as disrespect and rudeness. Although it is the opposite of the cultural norms in most educational settings, looking away from the speaker in some cultures indicates paying attention. Variations of actions involving handshakes, head nods, eyebrow raising, and finger-pointing have widely different meanings in different cultural settings.

Monitoring Language and Colloquialisms

Consultants will want to avoid negative words and use language instead that indicates a desire to help students expand their abilities, in contrast to "helping them get better." They need to exercise caution in discussing poor work, bad behavior, or poor attitudes because what is perceived as mild criticism or simply a suggestion in one culture may lead to severe punishment of the child or disillusionment about the student's ability from a family of another culture. Idioms should not be used that might be misunderstood in another language—for example, "Let's put this on the back burner for now," or "We need to get her to up to speed in that," or "Students need to toe the line in his classroom," or "That's a Catch-22." Consultants should listen carefully to family members to learn more about the student and capitalize on strengths, which, for that matter, is good strategy for any situation involving any student. They need to be sensitive to the type of colloquialisms having negative connotations that they use in day-to-day conversations. Some common colloquialisms are based on cultural stereotypes and may be offensive to others. Examples are "circle the wagons," "that cotton-pickin' regulation," "low man on the totem pole," or "Even Ray Charles could see that."

Gendered language also affects interactions, particularly when they intersect with characteristics of some cultural groups. Collaborators must monitor their own behavior for use of fair and balanced gender-specific languages. For example:

- Use *persons* or *women and men*, not *men* or *mankind*.
- Use the term *homemaker*, not *housewife*.
- Avoid saying *female doctor and male nurse*, saying simply *doctor* or *nurse*.
- Instead of saying *He adds the balances*, when the sex of the accountant is unknown, say *The accountant adds the balances*.
- Do not avoid recognizing same-sex partnerships. Same-sex partners are typically referred to as *partner* rather than *significant other*.
- Avoid *man and wife* and instead say *the couple* or *husband and wife*.
- Refrain from terms like *the fair sex*, *woman's work*, and *man-size job*.
- Say *Susan is a successful executive*, not *Susan is a successful lady*.
- Identify someone as a *supervisor* rather than a *foreman*.
- Say *students* or *class* instead of *boys and girls*.

Promoting Multicultural Education

Multicultural appreciation and understanding evolve from direct interpersonal contact and from knowledge of the history and culture of diverse groups, including their stories, values, myths, inventions, music, and art. Many consultants report that making the effort to become involved with families, communities, and cultures not only improves their work with students and families, it also enriches their own lives. When consultants learn about the cultural heritages of their students and the adults with whom they collaborate and honor those heritages, they make every effort to mitigate the negative impact of prejudice and racism and utilize cultural traditions as strengths. Cross (2003) challenges us to "help our children find the strengths, positive emotions, and mental wellness that are a part of every culture" (p. 359). Keep in mind the broader definition of culture and diversity from the first part of this chapter.

Banks and Banks (2010), Glasgow and Hicks (2003), Chisholm (1994), and others offer suggestions for promoting multicultural education for all students. When consultants integrate these suggestions into their work with CLD children, families, and other school personnel on the education team, they are more able to:

- Think beyond content. English language learners come with a variety of challenges and needs, as well as strengths.
- Use technology in ways that are sensitive to cultural and individual differences. Technology is not culture free; it reflects the cultural perspective of software developers.
- Develop a critical understanding of the social-cultural context of interactions and instruction in the setting, and allow this understanding to guide the work.

- Promote a positive ethnic identity, because all cultures add value to schools and to society and are a powerful resource for group members.
- Develop multicultural connections in the school area.
- Prepare for an increasingly likely cultural and linguistic mismatch in this country among school personnel, students, and their families.

COLLABORATION AND CONSULTATION IN DIVERSE CULTURAL SETTINGS WITH DIVERSE TEAM MEMBERS

Consultants have an instrumental role in bringing together diverse groups of educators, including teachers, administrators, related services personnel, families, and community members. They use communication and collaboration skills to help the educational team address and resolve problems and to work for creative solutions.

Collaborative consultation within a true collaborative environment, rather than within an expert model of consultation, is the preferred mode of education for CLDE students (Baca & Cervantes, 2004). In this approach, the expertise of one partner in the team is not valued over that of another; all are recognized as vital to the collaborative process and the education of students.

Collaboration with Partners for CLDE Students

Students who are culturally and linguistically diverse with exceptionality (CLDE) are served by a variety of educational professionals and specialists in the school and the community. There are several models of bilingual special education. In the coordinated services model, students are helped by services of a team composed of a special educator and a bilingual educator. But whichever model is practiced in a particular school, collaboration and consultation will be essential to provide quality services for CLDE students.

Teacher assistance teams are a common strategy for serving exceptional CLD students. The team should include individuals with expertise in appropriate assessment and instructional options related to the cultural and linguistic background of the students, as well as the exceptionality. Bahamonde and Friend (1999) suggest that co-teaching is a promising alternative to current practices of bilingual education. By applying best practices and knowledge from special education to bilingual education, improvements can be documented in student-student, student-teacher, and teacher-teacher relationships. Collaborative consultation is a key feature of co-teaching.

McCardle, Mele-McCarthy, and Leos (2005) suggest that not only should teachers and practitioners become familiar with the cultural norms of the children and families with whom they work, they should also be familiar with the structural parameters of the student's first language. These parameters may affect the learning of English. English language learners' linguistic performance cannot be fully or appropriately evaluated separated from their culture because culture influences how people use language to express themselves and how language is used in a social context.

Consultants need to learn about language and literacy because there is a close link between language and literacy abilities and disabilities (McCardle et al., 2005). Bilingual students are often lost between these two levels of proficiency in their first language (L1) and their second language (L2), usually English. For example, the ways that children develop study habits, reading practices, and writing skills are influenced by home and culture (Maldonado, 1994). The native literacy approach advocated by many in the field means that the children's native language and culture are acknowledged and are the main focus of instruction. This is a vital area for collaboration and consultation among special educators, bilingual educators, and others.

Students in the throes of acculturation may find the learning environment in public schools to be stressful and confusing (Baca & Cervantes, 2004). The interaction of culture and language within the acculturation context and the possible effects of a disability on this interaction are important (Baca & Cervantes, 2004). Success for CLDE students can be maximized with practices that have proven effective. The Additional Resources section provides several suggestions for further reading about using appropriate assessment and instructional strategies.

Collaboration and Consultation in Rural and Isolated Schools

About 9 percent of the nation's students attend rural schools. Students of color are about 25 percent of rural students. Poverty is the biggest threat to educational achievement in rural schools; in the 800 poorest rural districts, the poverty rate is similar to that in urban districts in Los Angeles, New York, and Chicago (Kreiss, 2010). Schools in rural and remote areas are characterized by geographic isolation, cultural isolation, and distance that necessitates significant amounts of teacher time spent in travel from school to school. Often there are too few students for some kinds of grouping, too few staff members covering too many curricular and special program areas, reluctance of students to be singled out, and limited resources.

In rural settings, teachers tend to be highly visible and therefore especially vulnerable to community pressure and criticism. Rural educators are left much to themselves to solve problems and acquire skills for their roles. These qualities of rural school life create advantages for consulting teacher approaches, yet there are certain disadvantages to indirect service delivery. Few rural schools are prepared and able to meet the needs of special needs students without consultation and other indirect services, so it is necessary for consulting teachers to become intensively involved in providing learning options and alternatives for students. Consulting teachers use their roles to coordinate efforts among teachers, administrators, parents, and other community members so that only a few resources will seem like more.

In a comparative study of consultant roles and responsibilities in rural and urban areas, Thurston and Kimsey (1989) found several major obstacles to consultation and collaboration activities. Rural teachers had less formal recognition of their consulting roles. They seemed less confident in their consulting skills than their urban counterparts. Thurston and Kimsey identified several obstacles to rural-area consultation, including: Not enough time; lack of administrative support; too much paperwork; paucity of professional interaction, travel burdens; being different in small communities where differences are very noticeable. Nevertheless, a bright spot on the rural scene has been introduction and installation of high-speed Internet and the resources it makes available immediately to teachers and students. These resources must be absorbed into the rural districts' budgets, already inflated with transportation and low teacher-student ratios. In harsh economic times, when federal funds and grant programs slow to a trickle, it can be difficult to find funds for the technology that rural-area students should have.

Students in rural environments tend to be resourceful, open to a wide range of experiences, somewhat independent, and capable of self-direction, as their ancestors were. These pluses can be used to advantage by consultants in designing collaborative arrangements for special needs. Because they dislike being singled out for special service, it is important to involve them in planning learning programs in which they are comfortable, involved, and interested.

Rural teachers do have advantages in carrying out their consulting roles. They often function as influential change agents. They tend to be creative and innovative problem solvers (perhaps paralleling the farmer/rancher who can fix almost anything with improvisation and what is on hand). In no other setting is the multiplier effect more useful than in rural areas that have limited access and resources. These multiplier benefits can be maximized by playing on the strengths of the rural community, including smaller class sizes, more frequent interaction between students and staff, greater involvement of families in the school and its activities, and students who participate in most phases of school life.

Collaborating with Families Who Move Frequently

With up to 20 percent of the population in the United States on the move each year and many more searching for ways they could relocate to new jobs and new homes, many families find that their school-age children's educational programs are disrupted. Moving and the events leading up to and following it can be traumatic for everyone—even the family pet; for a student with disabilities, they may be particularly troublesome. Records must be forwarded, new teachers and texts and classmates assimilated, and adjustments made to home conditions of sleep, meals, and schedules for routines while the child is getting settled in. In some communities, the predominant language may be different. Customs involving celebrations and holidays may vary dramatically. The older the student, the more difficult the moves, generally speaking, because adolescents are quite peer-oriented and friendship-based. Boys, in particular, are often less capable than girls of making new friends easily, and they may be teased, bullied, or rejected. Children may feel that they cannot measure up to expectations in the new school. One whose disability was accepted by peers in the former school has to begin all over again to win friends and influence adults.

Single-parent families have a particularly difficult time because there is no other adult with whom to share responsibilities and repercussions of the move. The school-age individual may be put into the position of that missing adult without having the coping skills and maturity to manage the stress. Belonging to a minority group (for example, an African American student in a white majority classroom, or a white student in a primarily African American classroom) is another factor in the challenge of feeling welcome and being accepted. Limited ability with English will add yet another dimension to acclimation and academic success.

Neighborhood ties are disrupted by moves, and parents are adjusting to new jobs in many cases. Families who are forced to move due to eviction, ethnic or racial tension, or economic deprivation, will be particularly stressed. Children and teens of agricultural workers whose work takes them to different areas with regular frequency (and some of whom may participate in that work themselves) may arrive late, after school has begun. They often must catch up in academic areas due to constant moves, necessitating that they forgo enrolling in classes such as art, drama, and debate. Gaining English language fluency can take five to seven years; young children can achieve it sooner, but transience remains a big hurdle. Those with disabilities and other special needs beyond these apparent ones are in particular need of consultation and collaboration by those who can provide the array of services they require. Mobility affects not only the students and families who move, but also the institutions they use.

Newly arriving students with special needs should be assisted by the collaborative team in handling any stress and disorientation as soon as they arrive at the new school. Collaborative teams in the new school can help ease their transition through such plans as:

- Synchronizing curriculum for smooth transitions between schools
- Forming peer support groups, particularly helpful when there is seasonal influx that affects employment
- Putting less emphasis on teamwork and cooperation among students, which will help not only new students, but also all others in the process
- Setting up a buddy system that could involve matching the student with an older, confident, and popular student
- Including a variety of learning styles and methods
- Finding mentors (preferably adults) to serve as the new student's advocate and confidant
- Forming parent support groups
- Having periodic orientation programs at various times of the year
- Providing professional development programs for school personnel that focus on the needs of transient students, particularly those with disabilities, in their adjustment to the new school and neighborhood

Students with special needs due to high abilities also can be affected by family moves. This area has not had much research activity, but more could be forthcoming with the growing emphasis on STEM education. One study revealed that gifted students were much more concerned about making new friendships and adjusting to their new school climate than they were about their academic success (Plucker & Yecke, 1999). There seemed to be little difficulty in sustaining their academic performance, but organizational difficulties such as different qualifications for programs and reluctance of school officials to accept test scores were barriers to smooth transitions. The researchers noted that in order to overcome these kinds of administrative hurdles, parents frequently rely on assertiveness in their interactions with school personnel. Collaborative consultants should take this into account without judging and overreacting.

Collaborating with Gay and Lesbian Home and School Co-Educators

The increasing diversity of family structures means that educators interact with those whom students consider to be their family, whether it is a single parent, grandparents, foster parents, multigenerational living groups, or GLBTQ parents. GLBTQ is the abbreviation for individuals who are considered to be in sexuality and gender identity minority groups, such as gay, lesbian, bisexual, transgendered, or queer. "Queer" is a concept and identity that works against problematic forms of normalization of identity and is the preferred term for some members of that heterogeneous group (Mayo, 2010). Families headed by gay and lesbian parents are becoming more common and more visible (Mayo, 2010; Ray & Gregory, 2001). Therefore, educators in areas where school personnel and communities are committed to inclusive schools and active parent-educator collaboration are likely to be interacting with family members who are gay or lesbian.

Homophobia with homophobic harassment and bullying are concerns of GLBTQ families and teachers. GLBTQ parents face barriers to their participation in schools and understandably are concerned when their children are inadequately protected from harassment (Casper & Schultz, 1999). GLBTQ educators, too, face harassment and safety concerns (Wright, 2010). Many educators have come from homogeneous community and family backgrounds and they may bring biases from the past or limited knowledge about issues related to families with GLBTQ consultees. To establish crucial home-school ties and to understand more about a child's out-of-school context, educators must do two things:

1. Examine their personal beliefs and feelings about families and family diversity in all its many facets (Koemer & Hulsebosch, 1996)
2. Become educated about the context of GLBTQ families and their children

Examining one's own beliefs and feelings is not always a comfortable activity. No matter what our personal beliefs, values, and experiences are, as educators we understand that it is not possible to be *for* children and *against* their families. Inclusiveness is a moral imperative in schools, as well as in family and community relationships.

Educators seek and develop relationships with families so they can understand the lives of their students. They need to have effective skills for promoting and maintaining an inclusive learning environment for all children in all types of families. It will be necessary to work out their own feelings and clarify their own values on the issues. Casper and Shultz (1999) have suggested that individuals or groups reflect on such questions as: What types of family differences fit into my borders of tolerance? Do gay and lesbian families fit into this circle? Is discomfort associated with fear or other deep-seated feelings? In what ways can conscious awareness of my feelings enable me to consult with adults in my students' lives and be more inclusive in my interactions with them?

Educators need to recognize that lesbian and gay parents represent a range of diverse social, ethnic, and economic class backgrounds, as do any other group of parents. Along with questioning stereotypes, school personnel who strive for inclusive and respectful home-school relationships should strive to learn more about the families with whom they work.

Golombok and colleagues (2003) offer important findings that help educators understand the reality of families with gay or lesbian parents. Three of these are:

1. The only clear difference between heterosexual and homosexual parents' child-rearing patterns is that co-mothers in lesbian-mother families are more involved in parenting than are fathers in two-parent heterosexual homes.

2. A longitudinal study of adults who had been raised as children in lesbian-mother families found that as young men and women they continued to function well in adult life and maintained positive relationships both with their mothers and their mothers' partners.
3. Research has consistently failed to find differences between children of gay and lesbian families and children in heterosexual families with respect to gender development or psychological well-being. Sexual orientation of parent is not a predictor of successful child development.

Research by Ray and Gregory (2001) shows that children in gay and lesbian families have psychological adjustments similar to those of children growing up in more traditional family structures. They identified common concerns of gay and lesbian parents. First, their type of family structure was not included in the curriculum about homes and families, and this made the children feel isolated. Also, their children were apt to be teased or bullied, and were asked difficult questions by other children, or even teachers, such as, "Why do you have two mommies?" Educators should take note of these very real concerns as they work with gay and lesbian parents.

Although debates take place at both national and local levels about the definition of family and the parameters of a "legitimate" family, educators have an ethical responsibility to collaborate with *all* significant adults in the lives of their students. Co-educators must help school personnel set a comfortable tone within which all parents can feel welcome in classrooms and comfortable with taking an active role in home-school interactions.

Educators play a powerful role in demonstrating dignity and respect toward all. Lamme and Lamme (2001–2002) offer several concrete suggestions for making schools more inclusive and friendly to gay and lesbian parents. Four of the most important to include here are:

1. Refer to families or parents rather than mothers and fathers.
2. Refuse to tolerate harassment and homophobic teasing, just as racist remarks and behavior are not tolerated. None of the children of gay and lesbian parents whom Lamme and Lamme (2001–2002) interviewed had heard an adult intervene when a homophobic remark was made in school.
3. Model and teach respect for all. Do not let homophobic harassment continue unchallenged. Educators should not tolerate popular youth sayings such as "That's so gay," just as they should not tolerate the use of the pejorative word "re-tard."
4. Reconsider special-event, parent-focused activities. Emphasizing a stereotypical father's day or mother-daughter breakfast may stigmatize children in homes with gay or lesbian parents.
5. Learn about community resources for LGBTQ individuals, including faculty and staff in your own school who might provide support to parents, students and other educators.

In addition, educational collaborators can provide leadership in improving a school climate of accepting diversity. Part of diversity training or professional development regarding community-home-school relationships and programs should include the concerns expressed by families with gay or lesbian parents.

Another aspect of sexual orientation affecting school personnel is the increasing number of young gay and lesbian students who are coming out about their sexual orientation, especially those in their early teens who live in urban areas. Some educators might deny that this could be a problem, but others recognize the need that students with sexual-orientation differences have for sensitivity by school personnel. A few states are mandating sensitivity training in their teacher certification programs and developing guidelines and materials for making schools more inclusive places of learning (Anderson, 1997). When caring teachers and administrators provide support to gay and lesbian parents and gay and lesbian students, the instances of abusive language, harassment, and homophobia are reduced (Edwards, 1997). In years past, little information on this subject was available, but now educators, parents, and students talk more openly and share information that can help students feel safe in their school environments and neighborhoods.

Collaborating in Educating Military-Dependent Students

Children and youth who are military dependents and live with families that tend to move frequently live with considerable stress and anxiety. They are overlooked too often as a population with special needs who can benefit significantly from consultation services. Most are quite resilient and make friends easily; they also know how to say good-bye and move on. However, their mobile lives do put demands on their flexibility and typically personable nature, not to mention demands on their schoolwork. (See Figure 9.3.) When they arrive at a new school, they may be behind their age peers in achievement. Others might be ahead of their class and in need of academic challenge. The less frequent the moves, the better the achievement level as a rule. The earlier in the school year the move occurs, the higher the academic success rate (Keller & Decoteau, 2000). One concern that is often overlooked is that their moves frequently take them farther away from their extended families and lifelong friends who could provide some of the support they need (Tovar, 1998).

When families move from site to site, they frequently become frustrated with the tangled web of records (or having *no* records for long periods until they do arrive), referrals, screenings, and conferences. When school records and student information are slow to catch up with the student or are misplaced, then students are at risk of being misplaced in school programs. Parents need quick forwarding of accurate, clear student records to ease their child's transition from school to school. Coordinators for the Army's Exceptional Family Member Program in Hawaii advise parents of exceptional children to deliver copies of program records personally, especially those related to their child's IEP (Keller & Decoteau, 2000). They also recommend that parents get a personal letter from former teachers directed to new teachers on how they worked with that child.

Consultants, aided by up-to-date electronic technology, can become a lifeline for students and their families by assisting busy classroom teachers with organization of student records and coordination of orientation activities and conferences. Consultants also can help smooth the integration of students into activities with their new peers. Much can be done toward making military dependent and transitory students feel welcome in new school environments. Local partnerships among home, community, and military establishment are a first step that benefits all groups. Institutional partnerships among schools, military installations, and colleges and universities have initiated research and programs that

FIGURE 9.3 "This Isn't Like What I Had in My Other Three Schools."

help students succeed academically and socially (Keller & Decoteau, 2000). In all of these efforts, consulting teachers are the foremost facilitators of transitional adjustments for students having special needs.

In their schools, students can be assigned to buddies who help with orientation to the school and integration into peer groups. Selected classmates might interview the "new kid on the block," focusing on things their new peers like to do. Teachers can plan activities in which all students participate in making a class album or collage mural, highlighting unique qualities of everyone in the class. Ethnicity is addressed by reminding students that everyone has a cultural heritage (German, Finnish, Korean, Samoan, Irish, Nigerian, and so on). Each could research his or her own heritage, with a variety of project extensions possible.

Curricular units and learning centers that highlight a student's travels and former experiences will be instructive for other students even as they make the military family's child feel more welcome. New students' strengths should be drawn on to help remediate gaps that may have resulted from their dissimilar educational programs and frequent adjustments to new situations. In addition, students who have traveled widely can be valuable resources for their classmates and teachers, and they should be encouraged to do so.

When families are separated by deployment of fathers, mothers, or sometimes *both* parents to trouble spots and active war zones around the world, consulting teachers become sources of assurance for anxious families who have students with special needs. These caring professionals can provide continuity in learning programs and support for the social and emotional needs of students who may feel afraid, lonely, and confused. Working in a team with families, school administrators, teachers, health and social service personnel, and military staff who oversee family and school concerns will help ensure a stable learning environment for military-dependent students.

Consultants in schools must recognize that returning veterans face many challenges in reintegrating with their families and communities. Values and behaviors that are inherent for success in the military are not those that automatically can lead to success in the nonmilitary environment (obeying orders, depending on a team and protecting its members at great personal cost). Trauma experienced by military personnel in the line of duty may have affected the way in which new information is processed, how relationships are managed, and response modes to situations and surroundings.

Army Captain Joshua A. Mantz, who was shot by a sniper in Iraq, was pronounced dead for 15 minutes but recovered, thanks to heroic efforts of Army medical personnel. Five months after he recovered, he returned to duty in Iraq. Speaking at a conference in Manhattan, Kansas, Captain Mantz described characteristics of military personnel returning from battle situations: "I'd like you to throw out the word 'wounded' as meaning a guy who got shot or burned. Rather, start thinking about it as nobody who deploys to combat comes back not-wounded. Everybody who experiences combat comes back wounded in one way or another" (Mantz, 2010). Partnerships by consulting teachers and classroom teachers with individuals such as Captain Mantz and other combat-wounded veterans are essential in serving the needs of their children.

Collaborating on Behalf of Students Schooled at Home

Reports on numbers of students home-schooled in the U.S. vary widely and not all children who are home-schooled are reported. However, the National Center for Education Statistics in the U.S Department of Education lists the count as 1,096,000 students for the year 2003, which was an increase of 29 percent from 1999.

Families' reasons for home-schooling have been categorized as academic, value-driven, or religious; parents are concerned about moral issues, lack of differentiated instruction, negative peer pressure and bullying, more help for special needs including disabilities and giftedness, and problems that include student suspension or pregnancy. As home-schooling is becoming more accepted and prevalent, educators are seeing the need to develop collaborative partnerships with families who home-school. These partnerships facilitate responding to family requests for the use of school services, including but not limited to speech therapy, foreign language classes, extracurricular activities/sports, enrichment programs, and libraries and other materials. As taxpayers they are entitled to these resources and by law they are entitled to special education services for their children with exceptional needs.

Evidence that home-schooling is successful for most of the students has been documented through such means as success rates in university classes and scores on standardized tests. However, there are not many safety nets for the student if home-schooling does not work. Good home-school experiences require tremendous commitments of time, effort, focus of both student and home-school teachers, and often a loss of a second-income source by families. This is a huge sacrifice, especially if there are disabilities in the family that require special attention.

The home-school process has benefited greatly from distance learning curricula and from resources available on the Internet. Many home-schooling families also take advantage of nearby community colleges and universities. Some parents do not want to commit to home-schooling as a full-time activity, preferring instead to send their children to school while supplementing their education with downloaded curricula or community-based experiences to give them additional opportunities for learning.

Many home-schooling families *do* want to remain a part of the public school community with the understanding that all private-schooled and home-schooled students are eligible to receive services (Council for Exceptional Children, 2000). A growing trend is one in which personnel from public schools and homes work together to educate children. By collaborating with school personnel for a child's special needs, families can be assured that they have taken advantage of everything both home and school have to offer in order to maximize their child's opportunity for success. Collaborative partnerships will allow home and school educators to provide the utmost benefits available for students in whom they have a shared interest.

Collaborating on Behalf of Students with Disabilities Who Are Abused

Newspapers and television newscasts occasionally report extremely disturbing accounts of abuse toward children with disabilities. Research indicates that these children are abused more often than other children (Cosmos, 2001). Furthermore, many cases are not reported; if all were, the incidence rate would be much greater. In a thought-provoking report, Cosmos points out that some children with disabilities are not capable of telling others about their plight. Alarmingly, some who do tell are not believed.

Most abusers are family members, but nonfamily abusers include, shockingly, some teachers, health care and residential care workers, transportation personnel, volunteers, babysitters, and peers (Cosmos, 2001). Types of abuse are many and complex, defying brief descriptions, but they include major trauma, such as injury to the brain from shaking or beating, and neglect, which could be denial of basic needs or being held in isolation, or both. Neglect is the most common form of abuse toward children with disabilities. Special education teachers are in an ideal role to detect child abuse, so they would be in a position to help. But even more importantly they often have an opportunity to notice conditions that *lead* to abuse, so they might help to prevent its occurrence in the first place.

The National Clearinghouse on Child Abuse and Neglect Information (NCCANCH) and other researchers cite symptoms that teachers should be aware of, such as when students are stealing, hoarding things (including food), missing school, appearing to be unsupervised, and displaying emotional trauma in their art and writing, along with being dirty, hungry, and in need of proper clothing and medical care. In the NCCANCH research summaries, recommendations for addressing these situations include working with the school psychologist, requesting help from an outside consultant, and seeking services from related services personnel who can be helpful in their roles such as physical and occupational therapists. Families in which there is abuse are stressed families and a major aspect of intervention is reducing the stress. Collaboration by a number of agencies will be needed. At school, special education teachers and paraeducators should use positive behavioral supports and nonaversive forms of behavior modification. Experts also recommend avoidance of physical restraint with abused students.

One of the most troubling aspects of detecting abuse is when and to whom it should be reported. According to NCCANCH personnel, all fifty states have a mandatory reporting law and most states include teachers as persons who *must* report abuse. So they advise teachers to know their school policy and abide by that. If the policy is not available or not clear, then they should follow reporting procedures for that state. The teacher is not responsible for affirming the abuse, but only to report suspicions of abuse or neglect. Teachers will want to know the policies and then think things through in order to do the right thing in the right way. Once rung, a bell cannot be un-rung, but there are urgent situations in which the bell must be heard.

ACTION 9.3
Promoting Disability Awareness Month

October is disability awareness month. In celebration of diversity and disability, perhaps you and some of your collaborative colleagues could plan to use October as the focus of increasing the cultural competence of your school and community about disability. There are many resources for planning on the Internet. For example, the Indiana Governor's Council for People with Disabilities offers an action kit for download (www.in.gov/gpcpd/). Activities in Indiana have included art contests, plays, parades, and other events. Take some time now to brainstorm with others about possible collaborative community activities in your area to promote disability awareness. Who could be partners in this activity? What are resources you could use? What are some activities you could organize?

Working with Educators Who Have Disabilities

One diverse group that seldom is discussed in educational literature is educators who have disabilities. The teaching ranks undoubtedly include individuals with disabilities—physical, learning, perhaps behavioral—but this is not a widely investigated or talked-about topic. Some adults with physical disabilities such as a missing limb, hearing or visual impairment, disfigurement, or impaired mobility do enter the teaching profession. Young children, and sometimes even socially awkward adolescents, can be quite blunt and curious about disabilities. A group of seventh graders asked their teacher, a combat veteran with a prosthesis instead of a right arm, "Where'd you get that thing?" It made for a good history lesson by that teacher on the aspects of war and its outcomes. In spite of their initial fascination, the group was almost nonchalant from then on, when their papers were handed back by prosthesis, or when they shook "hands" with their right-handed teacher in greeting.

Teachers who have learning problems of their own with memory, spelling, or comprehension have opportunities to model tenacity toward reaching their goals and to share the learning strategies that have helped them be successful. They can inspire children with anecdotes about how hard it was for them to succeed in college, but by having solid goals and good habits to nudge them forward, and by taking advantage of resources offered in schools and communities, they succeeded in completing an education for the profession of their choice.

In the late 1990s it was estimated that 6 to 9 million adults have ADHD, or attention-deficit/hyperactivity disorder ("Adults and Attention Deficit Disorder," 1997). It is quite likely that some of these adults are in the education profession. However, many adults with ADHD tend to excel in crises and have learned adaptive strategies for dealing with paperwork and details. One former salesman found that he could not keep an accurate count of his merchandise, so he left that job and found fulfillment working in a restaurant and teaching reading to those with disabilities.

The incidence of disability among school personnel, the objective analyses of their abilities to handle the conditions, and discussions of the impact this has on schools and students are topics for which more information is needed. School collaboration is an arena in which these topics can be discussed openly rather than left to linger below the surface and adversely affect communication and problem solving, not to mention attitudes of acceptance and professional respect.

Adults who have overcome anxiety disorders, eating disorders, obsessive-compulsive disorders, or alcohol and other drug dependency also have much to offer children and youth by modeling attitudes of coping, resilience, a regimen of good habits, and a conquering spirit. Some cultures throughout the world have very different perceptions of disability from those of Anglo-Americans ("Adults and Attention Deficit Disorder," 1997). Those with "disabilities" are accepted in some areas as having a place in the community with no stigma or problem because they are viewed as having talent or uniqueness to contribute. This is an intriguing concept that poses a challenging topic for educators to address among themselves and with students.

ACTION 9.4
"Develop Your Character"

This activity is designed for pre-service or in-service teachers to be conducted in groups of six or so to explore and discuss beliefs and stereotypes. Prepare four sets of index cards, with each set a different color to represent one of four different categories: Role, Adjective, Group, and Where. Then make a set of characteristics cards for each category. An example of the four sets could be:

Role (blue cards)	Adjective (red)	Group (yellow)	Where (green)
Mom	tall	Mexican	in a wheelchair
Teacher	white-haired	white	in a burka
PTA president	blind	migrant worker	in a Land Rover
Grandfather	Spanish-speaking	African American	in a doctor's coat
School counselor	single	Jewish	in a large family
Foster parent	lesbian/gay	Muslim	in a beat-up truck

Each person in every group gets a card from each category. For example, one person's cards may depict: An African American lesbian foster parent who is in a wheelchair at your school's New Student Orientation.

1. What were your first thoughts when you learned the description of your character? What emotions did you have? What questions did you have?
2. Think about your character. What is your history? Who is your family? How do you deal with intolerance you may face? What do you do for fun? What is your motivation for working with others for the best interests of your child with special needs?
3. Introduce yourself to others in the group.
4. Hold a group discussion, taking the part of your character, on collaboration and consultation for students with special needs in your school and community.
5. Debrief as yourself with the group. What did you learn?

As an extension of this activity, decide on four different sets of categories and make different characteristics cards for each set; then play the game again.

Case Study: Analyzing Stereotypes

With information gained from Action 9.4 and the post-game discussion, use a case study approach to target concerns that surfaced from the activity, and suggest collaborative activities that could address them. Then design a plan for doing the activities. Decide how to put the plan into motion, how to follow through and follow up on results, and how to evaluate effects of the process on altering negative stereotypes.

TECHNOLOGY FOR COLLABORATION WITH DIVERSE INDIVIDUALS

Technology-based communication can be a great equalizer when working with diverse collaborative partners. Communication and working together via technology such as Skype, chat rooms, blogs, and conference calls can overcome the reticence that parents and community members may have if they look or sound different from others in the group. Fox, Morris, and Rumsey (2007) demonstrated that participants in a focus group adjusted quickly to an online chat room environment, and the text-based venues transcended both age and gender.

Other research has shown that individuals self-disclose their thoughts or emotions more freely in an on-line environment than in a face-to-face group. In addition, using these and other electronic tools to collaborate with others reduces problems of travel and transportation and trying to a comfortable space to meet. According to Darlene Koenig (2011), technology tools such as Twitter, Google Docs, and their "cousins" shrink the spaces between cultures even as they expand the reach of a typical classroom. Again, as noted in Chapter 8, it is important to keep in mind that technology is not always the best choice for sensitive situations. Some tools could have an iatrogenic effect if collaborating and consulting educators do not have access to the *right* tools and the skills for using electronic techniques appropriately. Recall that the tool is just that; the purpose and substance of the interaction transcend the tool in importance. This will be apparent in Reflection 9.1.

REFLECTION 9.1

The Wrong Tool, Technique, and Timing

Have you had an experience where you sensed that technology, even simple e-mail or text messaging, was not helping in a special-needs situation and perhaps even had a detrimental effect? For example, think again about idioms in language and imagine that a grandfather is newly arrived in the United States to be the primary caregiver for his grandson while his daughter, a widowed single mom, works. This young boy has cerebral palsy with good cognitive function but serious physical disabilities.

The grandfather opens e-mail from the school at midday, finding a message from his grandson's young paraeducator that is laced with (1) technical terms for equipment his grandson uses at school and (2) teachers' language that is colloquial and vague ("Let's talk turkey. I won't beat around the bush about this," and then, "The completed homework was a feather in his cap," and "He is on cloud nine today," ending with "His feeling of low self esteem bit the dust with that activity"). Grandfather, without the physical presence of a teacher or a friendly voice on the telephone, and shy about his lack of English-language skills, is confused. What is the para conveying with these strange phrases? He cannot be sure he is deciphering them correctly and he doesn't wish to worry his weary daughter unnecessarily. What is problematic here—the para's poor choice of a tool, the fact that a para and not the boy's teacher was sending school-to-home messages, the reluctance of the grandfather to burden his daughter, or none of these factors? It's a simple incident with potential for complex effects.

CULTURALLY RESPONSIVE, ETHICAL COLLABORATIVE CONSULTATION

If a consultant is not familiar with cultural similarities and differences, the collaborative process is likely to lack mutual goals and successful outcomes. Then both consultant and collaborative partner(s) will experience frustration, disappointment, and, in some cases, disenfranchisement. On the other hand, culturally sensitive consultants can initiate meaningful cross-cultural collaborations, and instigate activities that draw out contributions from culturally diverse groups.

Multicultural education is *not* an activity for the last thirty minutes of school on Friday. Appreciation for cultural and linguistic diversity must be infused throughout the entire school program every day. Collaborative consultants can be facilitative and supportive in this endeavor. They are in a position to encourage use of diversity-focused resources within the entire community. They can bring in eminent citizens representing culturally diverse groups to tell about their heritage, interests, and roles in society. They might pair them with students having special needs, particularly if they share the same cultural background.

Awareness and appreciation of individual differences and cultural diversity are vital attributes for consultants as they work with a wide range of resource and support personnel, teachers, families, and the students themselves. An educational consultant's respect for diversity demonstrates and models acceptance of individuals and their cultural heritage. Culturally competent and sensitive collaborative consultants can do much to illuminate the brilliant textures and hues in the tapestry of diversity.

TIPS FOR WORKING WITH DIVERSE POPULATIONS

1. Learn about the values, beliefs, and traditions of other cultures in your school by attending community activities sponsored by those cultural groups.
2. Read fiction and nonfiction about people, families, and communities who are very different from your own.
3. Get to know the families of culturally and linguistically diverse students by making special efforts to reach out to them. Let them know you want to learn more about them because you care about their children.
4. Sit in on classes in bilingual education programs.
5. Develop collaborative relationships with teachers of English language learners or culturally and linguistically diverse students with exceptionalities, even if you are not working with any of the students at the present time.
6. Make the most of opportunities to travel to new places, interact with people from other cultures, and learn at least a rudimentary part of a new language.
7. Attend professional conferences that feature speakers and presentations focusing on diverse populations.
8. Have families from other countries or cultures talk to students about customs in their culture.
9. Ask families from diverse groups what their family goals are and discuss with them a variety of ways those goals could be addressed in the school curriculum.
10. Be realistic about what collaborative consultation can do, and celebrate even the smallest successes.

ADDITIONAL RESOURCES

Baca, L. M., & Cervantes, H. T. (2004). *The bilingual special education interface* (4th ed.). Upper Saddle River, NJ: Merrill.

Banks, J. A., & Banks, C. A. M. (Eds.). (2010). *Multicultural education: Issues and perspectives* (7th ed.). Hoboken, NJ: Wiley.

Chisholm, I. M. (1994). Preparing teachers for multicultural classrooms. *Journal of Educational Issues of Language Minority Students, 14,* 43–68.

Lynch, E. W., & Hanson, M. J. (1998). *Developing cross-cultural competence: A guide for working with children and their families* (2nd ed.). Baltimore, MD: Paul H. Brookes.

National Association for Bilingual Education: www.nabe.org

National Association for Multicultural Education: www.nameorg.org

Northwest Regional Educational Laboratory: http://educationnorthwest.org/rel-northwest (A guidebook called *Culturally Responsive Practices for Student Success* is available on the NWREL website.)

Teaching Tolerance: www.teachingtolerance.org (*Teaching Tolerance* is an excellent periodical that is available free for teachers. Sign up on their website.)

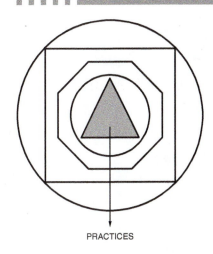

PRACTICES

Practices for Working Together as Co-Educators

PART IV, THE SHADED-TRIANGLE SECTION FOR PRACTICES, includes three chapters. Chapter 10 features techniques for delivery of collaborative instruction to students with exceptional learning needs in a consultative, or collaborative mode that may include co-teaching. Chapter 11 defines the roles of paraeducators and their teacher supervisors. Chapter 12 focuses on essential evaluation practices for assessing the outcomes of collaborative school consultation.

10

Collaborating and Co-Teaching for Students with Special Needs

STUDENT ABILITIES AND NEEDS LIE ALONG A CONTINUUM OF LEARNER DIFFERENCES; they do not fall into discrete, separate categories. It follows that there is no uniform instructional strategy for every student's needs. Alternatives must be available to provide accessible curriculum and appropriate instruction for individual learners. In the past, many educators aimed at teaching to the middle of the class, all the while knowing that did not meet the needs of all students but doing the best they could under the circumstances.

A one-size-fits-all approach to instruction can be particularly detrimental to students with disabilities and is stunting to students with high abilities. Teachers are challenged to develop and deliver lessons that provide multiple pathways to accessing information, learning content, and demonstrating their learning in a variety of ways. Educators differentiate learning goals for students' special needs and make adaptations for students to those goals when necessary. Adaptations can be in the form of accommodations (aids and supports) or modifications (altered goals and expectations).

Co-planning and co-teaching are useful practices for providing differentiated curriculum in inclusive classrooms. (See shaded triangle in Figure 10.1.) Such curriculum may be remedial, review, student-interest based, accelerated, enriched, or a combination of differentiations. Regardless of the intervention or interventions to be used, it is important for special educators and general educators to work together so appropriate differentiated curriculum and alternatives for learning are developed and made available to fit *all* students' needs.

FOCUSING QUESTIONS

1. What effect can Universal Design for Learning (UDL) have on collaborative consultation and co-teaching for students with disabilities?
2. How does planning for co-teaching differ from planning for typical lessons?
3. What are some typical approaches to co-teaching?
4. What are appropriate accommodations and modifications for students with disabilities?
5. What other instructional strategies, supports, and technologies can benefit students with disabilities and students with advanced abilities in general classrooms?
6. What ethical concerns make it important to inform all who are involved in the students' learning programs about differentiations that are included in their IEPs?

KEY TERMS

acceleration
adapted outcomes
adapting tests, texts
brain networks—recognition, strategic, and affective
Common Core Standards
co-planning
co-teaching
curriculum accommodations
curriculum adaptations
curriculum compacting
curriculum modifications

differentiated instruction
digital text
enhanced outcomes
enrichment
flexible pacing
functional outcomes
multiple means of representation, engagement and expression
National Instructional Materials Accessibility Standard (NIMAS)

Parallel Teaching approach
preassessment
Response to Intervention (RTI)
scaffolding
Station Teaching approach
Teach and Monitor approach
Team Teaching approach
Universal Design for Learning (UDL)

VIGNETTE 10.A

At lunchtime two secondary-level teachers take their lunchroom trays from the salad bar to a relatively quiet, cleared area where they can talk. Lori asks Mark about an activity that she was not able to attend the previous week.

Lori (Secondary Classroom Teacher): Mark, you were going to fill me in on last week's professional development session about Universal Design for Learning that I missed. Is this a good time?

Mark (Secondary Classroom Teacher): Sure. And it will be good for me to wrap my thoughts around it again, because I think you and I might want to work together to give some of it a try with our classes. They presented it as a collection of best practices that are to be strategically placed at each phase of the teaching and learning process. These maximize learning and give all students access to the curriculum. In thinking about all of the needs in our inclusive classes, that has appeal, don't you think?

Lori: So we wouldn't make adaptations for certain students after the fact, but plan lessons at the front end so that they're accessible to the broad spectrum of students we have?

Mark: That's the main idea I took away from the session. The overall concept is an outgrowth of the universal design movement in architecture. As you know, architecture is my true love, so I really related to that. As a result of the Americans with Disabilities Act, the universal design movement shelved the "one size fits all" mentality about architecture and the environment to accept one that's precisely the opposite—multiple ways of getting in, out of, and around buildings and functioning successfully in the environment. Regardless of whether someone can see, hear, walk, read, or speak, appropriate alternatives are provided so that anyone who can't do what others might be able to do can experience the environment in a fair and equitable way.

Lori: So this brick-and-mortar plan for using physical space became a concept that works for curriculum. That's interesting.

Mark: Yes, UDL provides supports for students in the classroom and reduces the barriers curriculum often throws up that shut them off from learning. It maintains high achievement standards for all learners, too. Here, I have an extra copy of the handout from the session that explains what the presenters called multiple pathways for using UDL.

UNIVERSAL DESIGN FOR LEARNING

The Universal Design for Learning (UDL) paradigm features flexible curriculum development, teaching, learning, and assessment to accommodate individual differences. Rather than providing remediation for students so that they can learn from a set curriculum, UDL recognizes that there is no one optimal solution for everyone. It has alternatives that make curriculum accessible and appropriate for individuals with different backgrounds, learning styles, abilities, and disabilities in widely varied learning contexts. See the Center for Applied Special Technology (CAST), at www.cast.org. For UDL, special educators and general educators must work together to ensure they select appropriate alternatives that address the unique needs of students. When curriculum alternatives are insufficient for individual students, or when non-UDL curriculum is used, the special educator has an additional challenge of finding or creating adaptations to accommodate, and in some cases modify, the learning goals for students in accordance with their IEPs.

Co-planning and co-teaching are important roles for collaborating consultants, whether or not the classroom teacher is using UDL curriculum. Five aspects of working together for students with special needs who learn differently will be discussed here:

1. Planning and delivering differentiated instruction
2. Planning individualized alternatives for certain students
3. Planning and making adaptations
4. Planning remedial instruction
5. Planning for other instructional strategies and supports

Aspects of Universal Learning Design

The paradigm for teaching, learning, assessment, and curriculum development that emerged in the 1990s when CAST coined the term *Universal Design for Learning* (UDL) is a refinement of differentiated instruction (Pisha & Coyne, 2001). "Universal" doesn't imply one optimal solution for everyone. Instead, it calls for multiple approaches to meet the needs of diverse learners. This involves:

■ *Multiple means of representation*, meaning that whatever content or information is to be learned can be represented in different ways. For example, a teacher can have many books or websites at different reading levels to deliver the same information. Or a teacher can use lecture to deliver information, but also provide visuals of main points, guided notes, and/or an audio file for students to access at a later time.
■ *Multiple means of engagement*, tapping into learners' interests and offering practice opportunities that provide appropriate challenges for each student. Just like when a child is learning to ride a bike for the first time and the supervising adult needs to determine the right amount of support—when to remove the training wheels and how long to hold on while running alongside—teachers need to implement a scaffold that

provides the right amount of support students need while they acquire new skills. This involves creating many pathways for students to actually learn the material presented. Some students may benefit from small-group learning opportunities, others may require more focused practice with precise feedback, and still others may benefit from working independently. Some students will need to write, some will need to talk through ideas before they understand, and others may need to represent their learning physically.

■ *Multiple means of expression*, providing learners with alternatives for demonstrating what they have learned. Again, the creation of many paths is key. Some students are good test-takers, whereas others are not. Some students write well and other students express themselves better orally. Most learning objectives can be manifested in multiple ways. Giving choices within a framework of options will likely provide increased motivation for students to participate meaningfully and demonstrate what they have learned.

Every brain processes information differently, and the way a person learns is as unique as an individual's DNA profile or fingerprints. In its research, CAST identified three primary brain networks and the roles they play in learning:

■ *Recognition networks*—Gathering information and facts and how we identify and categorize what we take in through our senses (for example, how you recognize a person's voice even without seeing the person, or how you can automatically put together a string of letters to form a word). These are recognition tasks—the "what" of learning.

■ *Strategic networks*—How we plan and perform tasks, including organizing and expressing our ideas—the "how" of learning.

■ *Affective networks*—How students are motivated and engaged, what piques their interest or excites them. These are affective dimensions or the "why" of learning.

Teachers can customize their teaching for individual differences in each of the three brain networks and thus reach and engage all students rather than just a few. The flexible UDL curriculum provides alternatives to address the broad range of learner differences. With this type of curriculum, it is imperative that special educators and general educators work together to ensure that appropriate alternatives are selected to address unique student needs. General education teachers are typically considered the content and grade-level experts, whereas special education teachers possess advanced training in matching specialized teaching methods and learning strategies to specific student learning needs. In other words, general educators are in the best position to determine the big ideas that all students need to learn in their content area or grade level, and special educators can help determine if those goals are appropriate for individual students and suggest alternatives when necessary. As noted earlier, if curriculum alternatives are insufficient for individual students, or if non-UDL curriculum is used, then the special education teacher has the additional challenge and responsibility of finding or creating accommodations, and in some cases modifying the learning goals for students with disabilities.

COMMON CORE STANDARDS[1]

As general education teachers and special educators join together in jointly planning and delivering instruction, they will be influenced, no doubt, by the movement toward adopting a set of common standards across the country. The Common Core State Standards Initiative is a state-led coordinated effort to provide a clear and consistent framework for what all students should learn. Issues about each state having their own standards included concerns that different states covered different topics at different grade levels. But part of the rationale was that with the Common Core Standards, students across the country, for example, will progress through a coherent sequence of mathematics standards, alleviating the inevitable problems that arise when students move from one state to another or when students from different parts of the country complete different grade levels with vastly different skills.

The movement toward the Common Core Standards has not been without controversy and renewed debates about who decides what students should learn. Some teachers fear losing control of their instructional autonomy. Proponents of the Common Core Standards argue that the standards will establish *what* students need to learn but they will not dictate *how* teachers teach. Much of the discussion seems to center around the meaning of terms such as *curriculum, frameworks*, and *curriculum guidelines*. These are terms not always easy to define and often have multiple meanings. To some, the term *curriculum* can mean a scripted, day-to-day lesson plan, while to others it signifies a set of big ideas that can be approached in many different ways.

It is difficult to say how this will all sort out in the months and years ahead but as these issues and philosophical differences are debated and ultimately implemented in schools and classrooms across the country, students will be best served if educators, both general and special, work together rather than parallel to each other. The general educator may take the lead in interpreting the standards but together, the collaborative teachers will develop lessons to meet the standards by incorporating UDL principles.

PLANNING AND DELIVERING DIFFERENTIATED INSTRUCTION

As a result of recent federal legislation and policy changes related to the education of students with disabilities, these students are being held to high expectations and must be assured access to the same general education curriculum as students without disabilities to the maximum extent possible. Accountability for all students to make not just social gains, but academic gains as well (Dukes & Lamar-Dukes, 2009) has become increasingly important in the years since PL 94-142 was first passed in 1975. Clearly, for this mandate to be realized, general and special educators must work together in planning and delivering instruction to shared students. Co-teaching is an instructional delivery model used to teach students with disabilities in the least restrictive integrated classroom settings where general and special educators collaboratively plan and deliver instruction for all students.

[1]Common Core Standards, © Copyright 2010. National Governors Association, Center for Best Practices and Council of Chief State School Officers. All rights reserved.

Co-teaching has rapidly evolved and has been recognized as one way to ensure students with disabilities have access to the general education curriculum, taught by highly qualified teachers, while still receiving the individualized, special education and other supports to which they are entitled (Friend, Cook, Hurley-Chamberlain, & Shamberger, 2010).

Co-teaching allows teachers the opportunity to share expertise with general educators having knowledge of the curriculum content and special educators knowing the instructional strategies most appropriate for students who learn differently. These potential benefits also create new challenges for planning lessons in general classrooms. Without co-planning, co-teaching often involves a special educator helping the classroom teacher, or the classroom teacher helping the special educator, or "turn-taking" at best. This arrangement brings little satisfaction to either teacher, nor is it likely to result in the high-quality student outcomes that educators and parents desire. Some describe co-teaching as a professional marriage (Scruggs, Mastropieri, & McDuffie, 2007), but one could argue that it is often an "arranged marriage" rather than one of choice. Regrettably, co-teachers too often are placed together as a matter of convenience and miss out on the development stages we all know are critical in a lasting relationship. This can lead to communication problems and misunderstandings, and in some cases, an end to the relationship while declaring that co-teaching was a tried-and-failed attempt at inclusion (Sileo, 2011).

Others assert that co-teaching involves both art and talent (Reinhiller, 1996). No doubt this is true, but it is not very reassuring to new teaching partners who are trying to figure out exactly how to implement this co-teaching arrangement. They need to maximize their co-teaching time, especially in light of increased pressure for accountability in the education of students with disabilities in general education classrooms. The good news is that much has been written about co-teaching and it is now widely accepted as an appropriate model for collaboration (Friend et al., 2010; Scruggs et al., 2007).

Typical Lesson Planning

Most agree that before engaging in co-teaching a lesson, potential co-teachers must begin by co-planning. Special educators and general educators must blend differing approaches to planning lessons. General classroom teachers usually plan for groups of students whereas special education teachers tend to plan for individuals. Research conducted by the Joint Committee on Teacher Planning for Students with Disabilities (1995) indicated that general education teachers do not individualize instruction as a rule, although they might differentiate by planning for *all*, *most*, and *a few* students. They do not typically engage in a linear planning process of going from objectives to activities followed by determining evaluation methods. Even though general educators may know how to use that type of planning, they tend to start by selecting a theme or topic for a lesson and then planning content and activities for the entire class or large group.

Special educators, on the other hand, are trained, even required by federal law, to base lesson plans on individualized learner goals or what is specified in the learner's IEP. The planning steps are based on traditional, linear lesson-planning models—goals, objectives, activities, and evaluation. This linear process may not be the best way for co-teachers to plan lessons, nor does it reflect the way teachers typically plan lessons. General classroom teachers obviously are concerned about student learning, but they must keep their groups of students engaged in activities throughout the school day for the sake of class-room order and whole-group learning. Advocates of students with disabilities often voice concerns that exceptional students' needs are not always met in inclusive settings. These concerns have largely focused on meeting students' needs through adaptations or modifications of the general education curriculum and instructional practices. Some have suggested one possible reason for the struggle of students with disabilities in the general education curriculum and setting has to do with lesson plan development. For example, Schumm and Vaughn (1995) found that although teachers felt accommodations were helpful for students, they reported being unable to modify their instruction due to factors such as time limitations, classroom management issues, and the complexity of vastly different achievement levels of students in their classrooms. In short, many teachers feel ill equipped to plan for and teach students with disabilities.

Co-Planning Lessons

The challenge for co-teachers is to reconcile the individualized and group planning processes and develop UDL lessons for the benefit of *all* students. This process must address the concerns of general educators mentioned earlier such as being sensitive to time constraints, management and engagement issues, and result in addressing the needs of all learners. According to McTighe and Brown (2005), differentiated instruction has four guiding principles: It (a) focuses on essential ideas and skills in each content area; (b) is responsive to individual student differences; (c) integrates assessment and instruction; and (d) adjusts content, process, and products to meet individual student needs. Spooner, Baker, Harris, Ahlgrim-Delzell, and Browder (2007) found that even a simple introduction to UDL can help teachers design lesson plans that are accessible for all students.

These results were achieved by providing an introduction of UDL, including a description of the three principles of UDL and how to incorporate these principles into daily lesson planning (Spooner et al., 2007). In describing the individual components, visual cues were used, such as re**present**ation, **express**ion, and **engage**ment (that is, underlining and putting key words in bold print) to provide participants with a strategy to help remember the critical elements of UDL when planning their own lessons. It is important for teachers to remember the keyword *present* when thinking about the UDL concept of re**present**ation that includes creating innovative ways of presenting content material to students. Additionally, CAST provides some general recommendations on how teachers can use appropriate teaching methods to support the three primary brain networks:

To support diverse recognition networks:

- Provide multiple examples of critical content (including nonexamples)
- Highlight critical features or essential components
- Provide content using varied media formats and tools
- Support background knowledge through assessment and scaffolding when needed

To support diverse strategic networks:

- Provide flexible models of skilled performance by demonstrating multiple times and at varying levels
- Provide opportunities for supported and productive practice

FIGURE 10.2   UDL Lesson Analysis Form (Elements)

UDL Elements	Examples in Current Lesson	Ideas for Enhancing the Lesson
RePRESENTation (Content) Giving students various ways to acquire information and knowledge		
ENGAGEment (Process) Engaging students in activities that help them make sense of the content. Tapping into students' interests, offering appropriate levels of challenge and motivation.		
EXPRESSion (Products) Providing students alternatives for demonstrating what they know		

- Provide ongoing, relevant feedback, skillfully coaching and adjusting for students with a range of remediation needs (Ginsburg, 2010)
- Offer flexible opportunities for demonstrating the skill by varying the requirements and expectations for learning and expressing knowledge

To support diverse affective networks:

- Offer choices of content and tools
- Offer varying levels of challenge in materials and tasks, providing scaffolding as needed
- Offer reward choices
- Offer choices of learning context such as working independently or with a partner, resources to use such as book or web-based information, responding to questions through written (handwritten or word processed), scribed or recorded formats.

Using a simple planning format that incorporates the three primary UDL elements (see Figure 10.2), along with the related brain networks and the role they play in how students learn (see Figure 10.3), general and special educators are able to jointly analyze lessons already created and in use in the general education setting as their initial step in co-planning using existing lessons.

Teaching partners would first look for examples of the UDL elements already in place within the lesson. Next, they would brainstorm ideas for enhancing the lesson in each of the three primary UDL elements and the related brain networks with each teacher bringing unique knowledge and expertise to the table. Additionally, the special education teacher might provide information regarding individual student characteristics and

FIGURE 10.3   UDL Lesson Analysis Form (Brain Networks)

Brain Networks	Examples in Current Lesson	Ideas for Enhancing the Lesson
Recognition • Provide multiple examples • Highlight critical features • Represent information in multiple media and formats • Provide supports for limited background knowledge and establish a context for learning		
Strategic • Provide flexible models of skilled performance • Provide opportunities to practice with supports • Provide ongoing, relevant feedback • Provide flexible opportunities for demonstrating skills • Provide novel problems to solve		
Affective • Offer choices of content and tools • Provide adjustable levels of challenge • Offer a choice or rewards • Offer a choice of learning content		

needs. The special educator could note for example, one student's difficulty reading grade level material independently, or might share that another student benefits from using a word processing program with word prediction capabilities and a talking spell checker when doing written assignments. This type of information could easily be shared using a form similar to the one shown in Figure 10.4. By using such a form, the general education teacher is better informed about the special learning needs of some students in the class and the potential barriers that printed textbooks or note-taking requirements might pose for some students. Having this basic background knowledge, the teacher is in a better position to plan effective UDL lessons on the front-end rather than having to retrofit lessons, much like adding a ramp to the outside of a building that is inaccessible to some because of stairs. These types of "add-ons" are never quite as elegant or work as smoothly as when these considerations are part of the initial plan. By engaging in this initial "fix-up" of existing lessons, teachers begin to routinely incorporate these UDL principles into their initial planning stages.

FIGURE 10.4   **Analyzing Student Needs with Potential Lesson Barriers**

Students with Special Needs	Characteristics or Specific Needs	Potential Barriers to Learning
Student #1		
Student #2		
Student #3		
Student #4		
Student #5		

Co-planning works best when teaching partners share a common planning period (Friend et al., 2010; Scruggs et al., 2007) and, at least initially, can meet once a week for planning, with an aim to narrow this eventually to twice a month (Murray, 2004) as the teaching partners gain skills and knowledge about content, teaching styles, UDL principles, and teaching options from one another.

Lack of sufficient and joint planning time is frequently high on the list of barriers to co-teaching, so teaching partners should think flexibly and creatively in terms of where and how co-planning can occur. While face-to-face joint planning may be the ideal, especially during the initial stages, teachers may find that sometimes they can utilize technology for collaborative planning. Using free web-sharing tools such as Google Docs, teachers can pass lesson plans back and forth electronically, making recommendations and adjustments in their own time, with a final copy for each teacher clarifying the responsibilities of each partner during delivery of instruction.

Stewart and Brendefur (2005), in their study of collaboration among teacher teams, were told by participants that they found power in collaborative planning and found value in observing colleagues teach. Collaboration helped to organize teachers' thoughts about teaching a lesson and to bring instruction to a higher level with more student-centered lesson planning.

Delivering Differentiated Instruction

A key element of co-teaching is the shared responsibility of the teachers in both planning and delivering instruction. Co-teaching usually occurs for a set period of time, such as one class period each day, certain days of the week, or for one lesson topic. Some teachers have been misled to believe that co-teaching is necessary for every inclusionary situation and that students should never be taken out of the general classroom for special help. However, co-teaching should only be used when it is the best option for meeting the needs of a significant number of students. Pairing two teachers to deliver instruction to one group of students is a relatively expensive option and should only be utilized when the number of students with disabilities in the inclusion class justifies the presence of two teachers (Friend & Bursuck, 1996).

That being said, a number of studies report teachers benefiting professionally from co-teaching experiences. This includes general educators learning how to adapt lessons for all students and special educators gaining a better understanding of the critical content and teaching realities of the general education classroom (Scruggs et al., 2007). In their meta-synthesis of qualitative research on co-teaching in inclusive classrooms, Scruggs et al. (2007) reported increased cooperation among students in co-taught classrooms and academic benefits as a result of extra teacher attention.

Preparation for Co-Teaching

Teachers need to prepare the classroom before implementing co-teaching. As Keefe, Moore, and Duff (2004) note, "As a successful co-teacher, you need to (a) know yourself, (b) know your partner, (c) know your students, and (d) know your "stuff" (p. 37).

Co-teaching partners need to discuss their views on teaching and learning and resolve any major differences. (Refer to Chapters 2 and 3 for the discussions on teachers' differences in perspectives and preferences.) They also need to discuss nitty-gritty details regarding shared classroom space, instructional noise levels, and classroom rules and routines during co-teaching. In addition, they should agree on how grades will be assigned to students (a topic examined in detail in Chapter 2). Other matters to resolve are whether substitute teachers will be needed, roles of paraeducators, how to inform parents of the new approach, and most importantly, a schedule for planning time together at least once weekly.

ACTION 10.1
Variations in Teacher Perspectives

With colleagues or classmates, brainstorm and compile a list of teaching style differences that might be problematic if two teachers were to pair together for co-teaching. For starters, put on the list preference for direct versus indirect teaching approaches, hands-on learning compared to reading about a topic, assessing student learning through student-directed projects or by using paper-pencil, objective-style tests. What kinds of student classroom behavior might be tolerated or even encouraged by one teacher, yet be upsetting to another? You might start this list with behaviors such as: Getting out of seat during the lesson; talking; making noises; being habitually late; and so forth. Discuss the importance of those on your lists through the lenses of teachers' perspectives. What differences surface about importance and possible responses or actions to take? Then discuss how these variations in teacher perspective might affect co-teaching relationships.

Selecting the Best Co-Teaching Approach

Co-teachers can use one of several approaches to present their lessons to heterogeneous groups, and they should vary the approaches often. Some examples of approaches are Teach and Monitor, Parallel Teaching, Station Teaching, and Team Teaching. Vaughn,

Schumm, and Arguelles (1997), Bauwens and Hourcade (1997), and Reinhiller (1996) provide descriptions of additional co-teaching arrangements.

Teach and Monitor   One of the most common approaches is for both teachers to be in the classroom during instruction, but one takes primary responsibility for lecturing or presenting the lesson. The other teacher helps monitor performance of students and provides additional assistance to the students who need it. This approach does not require as much advanced planning as other approaches and is simple to implement. However, the teacher who circulates around the room could easily begin to feel like a "teacher's aide." One parent recently reported that her child came home from school saying they had a new "student teacher" in her room. In reality, the "student teacher" was the special education teacher who was co-teaching in the classroom. This observation is not provided to minimize the role of student teachers, but to illustrate the point that both teachers might not be recognized as co-equals by the students and as such may not be equally effective in providing direct instruction. So in order to minimize potential limitations of the Teach and Monitor approach to co-teaching, the teachers should alternate roles regularly.

Variations of this approach are Speak and Chart and Speak and Add. With Speak and Chart, one teacher lectures while the other writes the outline or notes on the chalkboard. With Speak and Add, one teacher lectures and the other occasionally jumps in to add or clarify points from time to time. Duet is a planned variation of Speak and Add in which each teacher takes turns presenting portions of the material in a coordinated fashion. These co-teaching structures often become blended, as the example of Lori and Mark's co-teaching experience later in this chapter's case study will illustrate.

Parallel Teaching   A second form of co-teaching is Parallel Teaching. Both teachers plan a lesson, but they split the class and each delivers the lesson to a smaller group at the same time. Parallel Teaching might also utilize a parallel curriculum, that is, both teachers teach a similar topic but one teacher teaches it at a more advanced level than the other. For example, after having read a story to the entire class, one teacher takes the highest achievers to create a new ending for the story, while the other teacher works with the other students on vocabulary meaning and retelling the story sequence.

Station Teaching   A third method of co-teaching is Station Teaching. This approach occurs when teachers co-plan instructional activities that are presented in "stations" or learning centers. Each station presents a different aspect of the lesson and allows teachers to work with small groups of students. This way each teacher works with all students in the class as they rotate through the stations.

Team Teaching   Team Teaching is sometimes used as a synonym for co-teaching. However, this approach can be a variant approach whereby the special education teacher joins with one or more other special education teachers to form a team. The team is responsible for all of the children in the classroom or ones at a particular level.

A variation of team teaching was observed in one school that involved ignoring categorical labels for service of students. Instead, all students identified for special education services were assigned to special educators according to their age or grade-level placement.

The special educators, regardless of categorical specialization, were assigned to grade-level teams and assumed primary responsibility for all students with special needs at the assigned grade level. In addition, the special educators met weekly to discuss matters of concern. Each special educator was a member of a grade-level team and met regularly with that team to discuss common issues. The special educators moved in and out of the classrooms at that grade level to co-teach as needed, to adapt materials, or sometimes to present a special lesson.

A high school math teacher described a pre-algebra class that she and the special education teacher co-teach. They have a shared planning time every other day because the school uses block scheduling. Within that time, they usually are able to set out a general plan for the week and then attend to specific problems or coordinate activities as needed. They share actual teaching responsibility more than they use a Teach and Monitor approach. This is purposeful, so students perceive them *both* as math teachers, and not one as math teacher with the other as special education teacher for certain students. What one of the co-teachers likes best about the approach is the camaraderie she shares with another adult. It lessens her feelings of isolation. However, she is quick to point out that co-teaching in situations when partners do not share a similar philosophy of classroom management, or do not appreciate and value temperament differences, would be challenging.

Co-teaching occasionally transpires almost spontaneously. Two third-grade teachers had adjoining classrooms and early in the school year they could see that some students' math skills had slipped during summer vacation. So one teacher worked on basic skills with a blended group of students from both rooms while her colleague provided enrichment activities for students who were ready to move on. Then one day they had a "lightbulb moment." The curriculum and students were mismatched! So the co-teachers exchanged the curriculum plans. The enrichment group did modified bundling to grasp the concept of huge numbers after they complained about hearing adults on TV stammer over keeping words like *billion* and *trillion* straight because the amounts were almost beyond comprehension. The other group was more enthusiastic about math after constructing geo boards and building birdhouses and figuring out recipes, and they began to understand tens and ones through these construction activities. The teachers continued to monitor, co-plan, and move students back and forth among groups from time to time.

At the university level, team teaching is generally voluntary and instructors select their partners, unlike K–12 team teaching which typically is set up to facilitate inclusion of students with special needs (Sileo, 2011). Even so, preservice teachers can learn about co-teaching in a university environment. Winn and Messenheimer-Young (1995) recommend allowing students significant time for reflection on the experience.

CASE STUDY PLAN: CO-TEACHING WITH UDL

You might recall the conversation between Lori and Mark at the beginning of the chapter regarding the staff development session on UDL. As a result, they decide to co-teach an American history lesson about the Battle of Gettysburg during the Civil War:

- First, Mark provides his lecture materials from past lessons. They review the lecture outlines, textbook materials, and assignments and discuss what could be eliminated or added to the original lecture and textbook material. They decide that all students can benefit from the lecture, including Randy, who is developmentally delayed. Most students can read the textbook assignment, which is ten pages, except Colin who needs it read aloud and Randy who cannot read it at all.

- They decide that most students, with the exception of Randy, will benefit from two of the assignments in the textbook.
- Mark is concerned about the ability of some students with learning difficulties to benefit from some of the content. Lori wonders if students with high ability will be challenged. They decide to use cooperative learning methods to deal with some of those concerns. Lori will prepare "challenge tasks" that will be required for the students with high ability although anyone who wishes can try to do them. Mark has group-study worksheets they could use, but Lori recommends several changes. Mark thinks of some other items that could be eliminated or added to help the students in the class who have learning difficulties.
- Mark volunteers to make the revisions since he has the original worksheets on his computer.
- Although Lori is the teacher assigned for the course, they decide Mark should present the lecture because he has done it many times previously. However, Lori will be in the classroom to add information whenever it seems appropriate to help clarify a point.
- Lori will direct the cooperative learning activities. She has already established teams in the class and this content fits that structure well. Mark will have his para come into the classroom during that time, freeing him up to consult with another teacher.
- Lori thinks the students need a summative experience requiring them to demonstrate individual accountability. Mark and Lori discuss what the activity could be and Lori agrees to prepare it (a test this time). They will divide the tests, each grading half. When the tests are graded, Lori will record the scores in her grade book and Mark will give team rewards. Mark will give the test orally to the students with learning disabilities and prepare a modified test for the para to administer to Randy in the resource room.

■ ■ ■ ■ ■

ACTION 10.2
Case Study Plan in Action

Now, based on the co-teaching case study so far, partner with a colleague or classmate and fill in a blank copy of the interactive lesson planning forms presented earlier in the chapter (see Figures 10.2 and 10.3). Did the format and prompts built into the planning form spark ideas for other things that Mark and Lori might do or help you elaborate on some of their ideas?

No matter how well the teachers plan, some co-teaching actions must be spontaneous. This became obvious as Lori and Mark put their plan into action. Mark presented the lecture, while Lori monitored, as planned. But Lori spontaneously "jumped in" from time to time to clarify information. At one point, she went to the chalkboard and drew a diagram to more clearly illustrate a point that seemed confusing to students. The next day, as planned, Lori took over when the class began team study in the cooperative learning format. She instructed students to get into their teams, gave instructions for team activities, and told how they could earn bonus points. Now the para was monitoring and noticed that Randy needed more explanation, so he wrote out the steps for Randy. Once students were engaged in teamwork, Lori and the para "cruised" the classroom, stopping to help individuals or teams as needed and providing positive reinforcement for team effort. Later they met to reflect on results of the plan.

On Friday, both teachers were present while students took individual tests. The para took Randy to the resource room to help him take a modified test while Mark read the test to the students with learning disabilities. He read questions orally for them when needed. He noticed two students having difficulty writing their answers and pulled them aside one-by-one to let them dictate answers to him. Then he asked them to do an additional task while the rest of the class finished their tests. Lori involved the very able students in other activities after they finished their tests and Mark continued to monitor the test-takers. Lori and Mark divided the tests to grade as planned. Later they met to reflect on results of the UDL plan.

DESIGNING CURRICULAR ADAPTATIONS COLLABORATIVELY

Federal law requires that accommodations be made for individuals who qualify for certain types of carefully defined disabilities. Section 504 of the Rehabilitation Act of 1973 calls for public agencies to provide reasonable accommodations for individuals with disabilities, even those who do not qualify for IDEA, such as some students with attention deficit disorders or health impairments. The intent of both laws is to provide access to participation in school programs. Although Section 504 provisions and IEPs may specify accommodations needed by individual students, consultants should help all parties who are involved in teaching these students to plan and prepare accommodations. Many authors use the terms *adaptations*, *accommodations*, and *modifications* interchangeably. For purposes here, curriculum *adaptations* are delineated as accommodations and/or modifications.

Curriculum *accommodations* are assistive aids and supports that help a student achieve the same outcomes as most other students in the class by adjusting the requirements. Therefore, an accommodation changes the path the student takes and the way he or she demonstrates learning, but it doesn't modify the initial learning goal or the final learning outcome. Examples of accommodations include reading a test to the student, writing answers dictated by the student, putting text in a digital format so a screen reader can be utilized, putting text into Braille, or providing sound amplification.

Curriculum *modifications* involve changing the goals or the content and performance expectations for what the student should learn. This might be, for example, reducing the number of spelling words for a student to master or allowing a student to create an outline of the major points rather than writing an essay. In the UDL case study, Randy took part in the American history class and then completed a modified test.

The key to effective accommodations and modifications is the word *appropriate*. Today, with the special education population included in high-stakes testing, accommodations must be appropriate without reducing the minimal objectives expected of all students. Accommodation strategies—for example, "Read tests aloud and provide extended time"—should be individualized to meet the learner's needs and not generically applied to all special education students.

Consulting teachers might want to draw on the concept of scaffolding rather than accommodations. Scaffolding, as presented by Vygotsky (1978) is a structure for learning with which adults or more accomplished peers can help develop a student's independent problem-solving skills with collaboration and guidance that will facilitate cognitive development. The scaffolding is used temporarily for enabling a student to benefit from classroom learning and then it is faded once the student no longer needs it. While that is the goal of general educators and is reasonable for some students with disabilities, many individuals with disabilities will need scaffolding or accommodations for a lifetime. Consider the special needs of students who are deaf or hard of hearing.

Making Text Accessible

In the upper elementary and secondary grades, the textbook has an increasingly prominent role; it is often the primary source of information about a subject. Unfortunately, the printed textbook and instructional materials used in the general education curriculum are not useful to many students with disabilities. The very materials that are there to support learning actually create barriers to learning for students who are not able to glean information from these materials. No reasonable person would question converting printed text for someone who is blind to another format such as Braille or audio format, yet some would expect students who are challenged by printed text because of a learning disability to read unaltered grade-level printed text.

Another way must be found for students with special needs to learn from materials that seem inaccessible to them. Hehir (2007) argues that school time devoted to activities focusing on changing the disability may take away from valuable time needed to learn academic material. Academic deficits may actually be exacerbated by ingrained prejudice against performing activities in more efficient, nontraditional ways, such as reading with Braille or text-to-speech software. For example, many older students with dyslexia and other specific learning disabilities who are in inclusionary classrooms have been expected for years to handle grade-level or higher text rather than having the book made available in an audio file format. Disabilities such as dyslexia that affect ability to handle print can pose grave consequences for student success if accommodations aren't made.

National Instructional Materials Accessibility Standard (NIMAS)

Until recently, few students with disabilities had access to books they needed. Sometimes the problem was technical: Schools did not have the technology they needed to provide accessible versions to students even if they were made available. In other cases, the problem was lack of awareness: Many teachers and schools did not understand the issue of access or potential solutions. But for too many students the problem was the result of a frustrating distribution system; students couldn't get the materials in a timely fashion. The dissemination of accessible materials was inefficient, and raised barriers rather than opportunities.

One of the most frustrating barriers to accessibility is created by multiple formats. The U.S. Department of Education has endorsed a common National Instructional Materials Accessibility Standard (NIMAS). NIMAS is a technical standard used by publishers to produce source files using Extensible Markup Language (XML) that may then be used to develop multiple specialized formats for students with print disabilities. Source files are prepared using XML tags to mark up the structure of the original content and thus provide a way to present content in any number of formats such as Braille, large print, talking books using human voice, and text-to-speech.

New to IDEA with the 2004 amendments, NIMAS is designed to maximize access to the general education curriculum for blind or other print-disabled students through timely provision of accessible instructional materials created from NIMAS source files. As a result of this standard, the printed instructional materials, including textbooks, are to be made available free of charge by publishers in the NIMAS-specified format to blind and other persons with print-related disabilities in elementary and secondary schools. Prior to NIMAS, converting print textbooks into specialized formats was complex and time consuming, often taking months to complete. The adoption of the NIMAS not only improves the speed of the process, but also the quality and consistency of books converted into specialized formats.

Zabala and Carl (2010–2011) outline four steps that IEP teams should follow in order to ensure that students who need accessible instructional materials (AIM) have them available to them and receive them in a timely manner: (1) determine the need, (2) select the format(s) needed, (3) acquire formats, and (4) select supports needed for use. How does a specialized format of a print-based material differ from an alternative material? The specialized format includes exactly the same information as the print version of the material. It doesn't change the content, it merely changes the way in which the content is presented (Braille, audio, large print). An alternative material, on the other hand, may address the same general goals or content but the material is changed in some way, usually made less complex, so that it can be understood by the student. Examples would include reducing the complexity of the vocabulary, reducing the length of text or sentence complexity, or a host of other options.

When general education teachers and special educators collaborate on decision making such as seeking out and arranging for appropriate materials, the match between the integrity of the content and the individual needs of the student with a disability can be realized.

Adapting Tests

Many students with learning and behavior problems have difficulty taking tests about subject matter they have learned. As a student progresses to higher grade levels, the ability to demonstrate knowledge through tests becomes more and more important. Consultants at upper grade levels will need to give careful attention to the test-taking skills of students with learning and behavior difficulties.

When students have difficulty taking teacher-made tests in content subjects, consulting teachers should give attention to a number of elements about the nature of the tests and ways to either help students take the tests as written, or collaborate with the teacher to make test adaptations. Students can benefit from being taught effective study skills and test-taking strategies. Other suggestions to consider when consulting with classroom teachers about how to prepare students for tests, alternative test construction, and test administration include:

- Prepare study guides to lead students through reading material, emphasizing important information
- Give practice tests
- Have students test one another and discuss answers
- Give more frequent mini-tests rather than one test on large blocks of content
- Back up the written tests with audio-formatted tests
- Provide extra spacing for essay questions and short-answer items
- Underline key words in test directions as well as test items
- Provide additional time for students who have processing difficulties or write slowly
- Administer tests orally or convert to a digital format that will convert text to speech

Teachers are likely to be more resistant to test adaptations than to adaptations of classroom materials. Likewise, even when they believe it is a good thing to do, they are not very likely to make the adaptations themselves, either because they lack knowledge in this area, or they feel they don't have sufficient time. Consultants can teach classroom teachers elements of accessible test construction. For example:

- Keep sentence structure as simple as possible. Text should include only words essential for responding to the item.
- Vocabulary and item stem should be grade appropriate when a readability analysis is applied.
- Test questions should be directly related to the objectives of the class.
- Item stem should be as direct as possible and use active voice.
- Item stem, answer stem, and any related visuals should be on the same page.
- Item stem should be worded positively (in other words, avoiding *not* questions).
- Use bold font on essential words or vocabulary terms.
- Answer choices should be about equal length.
- Have all text printed in standard typeface, using a minimum of twelve-point text.
- Allow for sufficient space between lines.
- Include ample white space to prevent the item from appearing cluttered.
- Keep the right margin unjustified (staggered).

An existing teacher-made or publisher-produced test can be adapted using some of these guidelines:

- Changing the format so the items are easy to read, more space is allowed for discussion, or the order of items is rearranged to make them more predictable
- Rewriting directions or providing cues such as highlighting, underlining, and enlarging
- Providing prompts such as "Start here" or "Look at the sign on this row"

- Adjusting the readability level of the questions
- Providing outlines or advance organizers
- Providing spelling of difficult words
- Allowing students to use outlines, webs, or other visual organizers

Making Modifications

Students whose cognitive disabilities prevent them from benefiting from the general class-room curriculum, even with accommodations, need curriculum modifications. Students with mild or moderate cognitive disabilities may need adapted outcomes while students with severe cognitive disabilities will need different goals or outcomes. Whenever possible, a theme or topic being studied by the rest of the students in the classroom should also be studied by these students.

Adapted Outcomes   Students with moderate learning and behavior problems can succeed very well in most classrooms but may need modified outcomes such as reduced number of practice problems or highlighted text. Other examples include the following: In math, the student works on the same concept but the number of required practice problems may be reduced; in social studies, the teacher might mark certain parts of the text material that must be read and the remainder skimmed; and in science, the teacher might limit the number of concepts within a domain to be mastered. In short, these students are expected to master most but not all of the content. Most of the items listed in Figure 10.5 are adapted outcomes.

Functional Outcomes   For students with severe cognitive challenges, curriculum goals may focus on areas such as social/behavioral development, language development, concept development, basic skills, or self-help skills. For example, if the class is studying plants, but a certain student's goals have to do with counting and language development, that student may count, sort, and talk about seeds. These students may also need accommodations to help them attain their goals. The primary reason for inclusion in the class is to participate in the social context and culture of the group.

Enhanced Outcomes   Students with high ability also need modified curriculum. Cooperative learning is an effective instructional strategy for many students for a variety of reasons. However, it should not be justified for gifted students through inference that they require remediation in social skills. Nor should it be used to make gifted students available as handy tutors (Robinson, 1990). While occasional peer tutoring can be challenging and rewarding for the gifted student, collaborative activities are not intended to set very able students up as surrogate teachers for other students.

When gifted students are included in general classrooms, as the majority are for most of their school day, their learning needs also must be considered. Providing appropriate learning environments for them necessitates intensive collaboration and consultation among gifted program facilitators, classroom teachers, and resource personnel so that classroom modifications and resource adaptations will help gifted students develop their learning potential. This is discussed in more detail later in the chapter.

FIGURE 10.5   Suggestions for Adaptations

Instructional Level
Let student work at success rate level of about 80%.
Break down task into sequential steps.
Sequence the work with easiest problems first.
Base instruction on cognitive need (concrete, abstract).

Curricular Content
Select content that addresses student's interest.
Adapt content to student's future goals (job, college. . .).

Instructional Materials
Fold or line paper to help student with a spatial problem.
Use graph paper or lined paper turned vertically.
Draw arrows on text or worksheet to show related ideas.
Highlight or color-code on worksheets, texts, tests.
Mark the material that must be mastered.
Reduce the amount of material on a page.
Use a word processor for writing and editing.
Provide a calculator or computer to check work.
Tape reference materials to student's work area.
Have student follow print text, listening to audio format.

Format of Directions and Assignments
Make instructions as brief as possible.
Introduce multiple long-term assignments in small steps.
Read written directions or assignments aloud.
Leave directions on chalkboard during study time.
Write cues at top of work page (for example, noun = . . .).
Ask student to restate/paraphrase directions.
Have student complete first example with teacher prompt.
Provide folders for unfinished work and finished work.

Instructional Strategies
Use concrete objects to demonstrate concepts
Provide outlines, semantic organizers, or webbings.
Use voice changes to stress points.
Point out relationships between ideas or concepts.
Repeat important information often.
Use color-coded strips for key parts.

Teacher Input Mode
Use multisensory approach for presenting materials.
Provide a written copy of material on chalkboard.
Demonstrate skills before student does seat work.

Student Response Mode
Accept alternate forms of information sharing.
Allow audio-recorded or written report instead of oral.
Allow students to dictate information to another.
Allow oral report instead of written report.
Have student practice speaking to small group first.

Test Administration
Allow students to have sample tests to practice.
Teach test-taking skills.
Test orally.
Supply recognition items and not just total recall.
Allow take-home test.
Ask questions requiring short answers.

Grading Policies
Grade on pass/fail basis.
Grade on individual progress or effort.
Change the percentage required to pass.
Do not penalize for handwriting or spelling on tests.
Use scoring templates and rubrics.

Modifications of Classroom Environment
Seat students according to attention or sensory need.
Remove student from distractions.
Keep extra supplies on hand.

Classroom teachers may believe they do not know how to adapt instruction, but the most plausible explanation is that they do not have time to do it. Consultants and collaborators must consider whether their suggestions for classroom modifications are reasonable and feasible for the situation. (See Chapter 7 for ways of dealing with consultee resistance.)

Many of the resources available for helping teachers make classroom modifications represent the views of special educators rather than the collaborative views of classroom teachers and special education teachers. However, the list given in Figure 10.5 was prepared jointly by elementary classroom teachers and special education collaborating teachers, and as such it can be a helpful resource for sharing with classroom teachers during collaborative consultations.

Using IEP Information Collaboratively

When teachers and other instructional support personnel such as paras collaborate about shared students, it is important to use sensitive information from IEPs in a way that is useful but also maintains the confidentiality of the information. General education teachers with a classroom full of other students should not be burdened with sifting through massive IEP documents to keep track of goals and objectives of shared students relative to their class or content areas. Likewise, paras need the big picture of what goals the student is working toward and clear directions and guidance in terms of what they are to do while working with the student.

Consultants should devise a way to provide IEP highlights to teachers and paras in a format that will be useful to them without violating a student's rights. This might be a document called "IEP at a Glance" or "IEP Snapshot." To protect this information, it could be shared in a password-protected computer file or a paper copy placed in a locked file cabinet. Only individuals who know the password or who have been given access to the locked file could access the information. However, one limitation of putting information in locked files is that it is too easily forgotten—out of sight, out of mind. Perhaps a periodic e-mail message with the relevant information and a personal note about the student's progress or lack of it would be a way to keep everyone informed about progress toward meeting IEP goals and objectives. Of course, the e-mail material must be kept as secure as any printed, and perhaps even more so because of its potential for being sent far and wide erroneously.

RESPONSE TO INTERVENTION

Response to Intervention (RTI) has been gaining momentum and expanding across grade levels and content areas since it first came on the scene as a result of two major efforts by the federal government. The Reading First program that was ushered in with No Child Left Behind in 2002 encouraged schools to use the RTI framework for their literacy programs. Two years later, the 2004 reauthorization of IDEA also changed federal law concerning identification of children with specific learning disabilities. Schools are no longer required to consider whether a child has a severe discrepancy between achievement and ability and can now use RTI as one tool for determining if a child has a specific learning disability (SLD).

The long-standing discrepancy model of SLD identification has been criticized on many fronts, and often described as a wait-to-fail model where students had to wait to be so far behind before they became eligible for special education services. RTI was promoted as an alternative prevention model not only for students with potential learning disabilities, but also as a built-in support and monitoring system for all students. This three-tiered prevention model works to support students with varying instructional and behavioral needs (Brown-Chidsey, 2007):

1. In Tier 1, research-based core group instruction is provided to all students. Universal screening of all students is done, typically three times a year. Students identified at risk based on benchmarks established for the universal screen are then monitored on a more frequent basis while they continue in the core group interventions.
2. In Tier 2, students identified as at risk in Tier 1, who did not respond adequately to the core group instruction, are now targeted for additional small group interventions provided in the general classroom and they continue to be assessed or progress monitored more frequently. Those making too little progress are considered for Tier 3 interventions.
3. In Tier 3, students receive individualized, intensive interventions targeting their specific skill deficits. Those not responding at this level typically are considered for eligibility under IDEA.

RTI has many beneficial features. It helps ensure that all students have equal opportunity to learn (Brown-Chidsey, 2007). It is a data-based, systematic method that lets co-educators know what is working and what is not working. The process has been growing exponentially and expanding far beyond its initial application to early literacy. A summary feature is that it reduces the number of children and youth who are referred for special education, and the number of students identified for SLD has been steadily declining since 2005. Not surprisingly, it does require much collaboration between general education and special education teachers.

RTI comes with cautions. It must be implemented by educators having considerable training in the model. Identification of students for special education must focus on assessments that directly relate to instruction and services must focus on intervention, not eligibility. Experts in the field of learning disabilities have spoken out against its sweeping application as a replacement model for SLD identification. However, as a preservice teacher noted while participating in a team, RTI was very helpful in improving a teacher's lessons and being able to learn from watching others teach. A number of websites, such as those of the National Center on Response to Intervention (www.rti4success.org) and Intervention Central (www.interventioncentral.org), feature explanatory material, articles, and materials teachers can use when implementing RTI. Initially, RTI was used almost exclusively for beginning reading skills but now is being implemented in early childhood settings through high school and has been moved into math, written language, spelling and even behavior benchmarking and monitoring.

Monitoring Student Progress

Frequent monitoring of progress is a key component of the RTI model but it has always been at the heart of what special education is all about. Special educators focus on daily and weekly student progress. Since it is rare in schools today for a special education teacher to provide all of the direct instruction to students with special needs, it is more important than ever to track progress and determine if the interventions being implemented in the general education classroom are working. In fact, it might be the most important function performed by the special educator in inclusive schools. Consider the example of a consulting teacher for learning disabilities named Sara:

Sara was now in her second year at an inclusive school. She had sixteen students in her caseload—mostly third- and fourth-graders. Sara spent at least one hour a day in each classroom where her students were placed. In addition, she taught math to several small groups in which her students were included. Although she believed her students were making satisfactory progress in basic skills, she wasn't sure. She began using curriculum-based measurement (CBM) procedures, taking reading and math probes once each week. After a few weeks of charting data she realized that four of her students were not making progress in reading. She had not been working directly with these students in reading and did not realize the problems they were having. She immediately took steps to make changes in their reading instruction.

Monitoring Classroom Grades   Secondary-level teachers can monitor student progress by the number of completed assignments and grades in general classroom courses. This information must be interpreted cautiously, however, because teachers' grading standards vary greatly. Special educators in inclusive schools should discuss grading philosophies and processes with each teacher and plan a system for grading students with adapted curriculum. (Refer to Chapter 2 for teacher perspectives on grading policies.)

COLLABORATING AND CO-TEACHING FOR STUDENTS WITH HIGH ABILITIES AND TALENTS

Students differ, and the magnitude of these differences can be great. They cannot be eliminated. As noted in Chapter 2, effective teaching (and who does not desire that?) tends to increase the range of individual differences among students. When instruction is effective, *all* students learn. Those who have difficulty in learning will achieve much, and those who learn very easily, or who already knew the material being taught, will achieve even more.

VIGNETTE 10.B

Anna, a second-grade student reading at the sixth-grade level or beyond, returned home from school and laid a second-grade basal reader on the kitchen table. She announced to her mother that the class's homework assignment was to read aloud to parents the word list in the back of the book, practicing any words they did not know.

Anna's mother sighed inwardly and strengthened her resolve to request a parent conference next week to talk about the snail's pace and unnecessary drill in reading, her daughter's favorite and best activity. For now, to Anna she said, "Just put the book in your backpack and return it to school tomorrow."

"For your homework this evening, let's get your new dictionary and read as many pages in it as that word list takes up in the reader. We'll see how many new, interesting words we find on those pages and think of ways we could use them in the stories you like to write. Then we'll practice ones that you don't know. Okay?"

REVISITING THE REALITY OF INDIVIDUAL DIFFERENCES

Students in inclusive classrooms do not develop skills neatly and tidily at the same pace and within the same time frame. The conventional way of structuring schools has been to sort and place children in classroom groups by age and grade level. But in most of these age-/grade-level groups, we can find rather predictable percentages of the students functioning, or capable of functioning if given the opportunity, at two or four or six—or even eight—grade levels above expected achievement levels. Some would call such students overachievers. That is a misnomer because one cannot achieve over and above what one does. The "overachiever" has simply been mislabeled by persons who are *under-expecting.*

How do educators decide which students have special needs and should be served with special-needs programming? The simplest methods are often the most effective. Parents know their children best, so they should participate in the process. But that is a complex, multifaceted undertaking and may not be the most efficient place to start. A more practical way to begin is with classroom teachers who see students in a variety of "kid roles" for cognitive functioning, social interactions, emotional situations, and physical performances. However, there *is* a major problem even with that. Observations of student potential, if they are to be of value, must be predicated on making available the means by which students *can*, and are *willing to, reveal* their potential. Clark (2013) aptly explains the need to create a responsive, nurturant school environment so that children's abilities will "bubble up" to be recognized. It does not take too much imagination to realize that providing such environments for learning also would give educators a head start on providing them the differentiated curriculum they need.

Checklist Tools for Recognizing Exceptional Ability and Talent

Assuming that rich, responsive environments are in place so children and adolescents can show what they are capable of learning and doing, the logical place to begin identifying advanced abilities and talents is with the classroom teacher. Building administrators and parents can be brought into the process next as collaborators, coordinated by the person(s) designated in the school or school district as the gifted education facilitator.

An example of a teacher checklist that works well is provided in Figure 10.6. (It also is a useful tool for designing a staff development activity about characteristics and needs of high-ability learners.) The checklist may be completed by the classroom teacher for one student or a few designated students, but better yet, for the entire classroom. High scores on items 1 through 7, due to the cognitive nature of those tasks, approximate the level of two standard deviations on standardized individual intelligence tests—the score that serves as a guideline for many gifted education program entries. Items 8–12 focus on styles and manners of learning, and items 13–19 on performance and motivation. Items 20–25 indicate creative thinking and doing. Items 26–30 pinpoint social preferences that relate to learning and doing with others. The seven lettered items at the end of the numbered list are factors that, if present, may provide further evidence of exceptional ability.

One third-grade teacher decided to put her entire class roster through the checklist. She told the gifted program facilitator, "In regard to Joey, I won't be referring him to the gifted program at this time, but I am starting to *think differently about him now* [emphasis

FIGURE 10.6   Teacher Referral Checklist

The following criteria are useful in assessing high potential of students. Please use one form per student to assign a value of *3* (to a considerable degree), *2* (to some degree), or *1* (to little if any degree) for each characteristic.

1. Learns rapidly and easily _____
2. Uses much common sense and practical knowledge _____
3. Retains easily what has been presented _____
4. Knows about many things of which other students are unaware _____
5. Uses a large number of words easily and accurately and appreciates word power _____
6. Recognizes relationships, comprehends meanings, and seems to "get more out of things" _____
7. Is alert with keen powers of observation and responds quickly _____
8. Likes difficult subjects and challenging tasks for the fun of learning _____
9. Asks penetrating questions and seeks out causes and reasons _____
10. Is a good guesser with an intuitive sense _____
11. Reads voraciously well beyond age level, and sets aside time for reading _____
12. Questions the accepted ways of doing things _____
13. Prefers to work independently with minimal direction _____
14. Has a longer attention span than age peers _____
15. Has little patience for routine drill and practice _____
16. Tends to be critical of self and others, with high standards and seeking perfection _____
17. Seldom needs more than one demonstration or instruction in order to carry out an activity _____
18. Perseveres on projects and ideas _____
19. Is withdrawn yet very capable when pressed _____
20. Demonstrates remarkable talent in one or more areas _____
21. Uses materials in innovative and unusual ways _____
22. Creates unusual stories, pictures, examples, models, or products _____
23. Has many interests and follows them with zeal _____
24. Makes extensive collections, with sustained focus _____
25. Invents contrivances, gadgets, and new ways of doing things _____
26. Prefers to be around older students or adults, communicating effectively with them _____
27. Has an advanced sense of humor and "gets it" when others may not _____
28. Influences other students to do things _____
29. Is serious-minded and intolerant of prolonged foolishness _____
30. Shows much sensitivity toward people, social issues, and right and wrong _____

Please check any of the following factors which apply. If present along with a number of the attributes above, they may provide additional validation of high ability.

A. A disability that affects learning and/or behavior _____
B. Living in a home where English is the second (or third) language _____
C. Transience (three or more moves) during the elementary school years _____
D. Social or educational isolation from resources and stimulation _____
E. Home responsibilities or employment that interferes with school _____
F. Irregular school attendance _____
G. Little or no interaction between school personnel and family _____

Additional comments:

FIGURE 10.7   Building Administrator Referral Checklist

The following criteria are useful in assessing high potential of students. Please use one form per student to assign a value of *3* (to a considerable degree), *2* (to some degree), or *1* (to little if any degree) for each characteristic.

1. Is quite advanced in academic areas _____

2. Shows superior leadership qualities _____

3. Demonstrates a high degree of critical thinking and prefers intellectual challenge _____

4. Is motivated by curiosity and seems to be self-directed _____

5. Has many interests and is involved in many activities and projects _____

6. Is full of ideas and demonstrates flexibility, originality, and resourcefulness _____

7. Is keenly observant and questioning _____

8. Is usually serious-minded and intolerant of foolishness _____

9. Has a high energy level with unusual perseverance _____

10. Has family members who are intensely concerned with enrichment and acceleration _____
    in the curriculum and with the learning environment of the school

Please check any of the following factors which apply. If present along with a number of the attributes above, they may provide additional validation of high ability.

A. Irregular school attendance _____

B. Limited contact between school personnel and family _____

Additional Comments:

---

added] and plan what I can do to differentiate some of the lessons for him here in the classroom." Things are off to a great start here, and not only Joey, but others in the class just may be the beneficiaries of this classroom teacher's insight.

Figure 10.7 is a checklist for building administrators. Principals know all students, but perhaps are not as familiar with particular facets of their abilities. They do see the bigger picture and often gain illuminating information from families about student capabilities or from students as they watch them come and go in curricular and extracurricular activities. School administrators respond best to succinct fact sheets, information bulletins, and in this case short checklists. A written note of explanation and request from the gifted program facilitator should be attached to the form. Teacher checklists and administrator checklists should provide space for making additional comments. Confidentiality of the information during distribution and collection processes must be assured.

Secondary teachers often respond helpfully to checklists that are in question format, or in face-to-face interviews with gifted program facilitators, to describe specific (sometimes annoying or overbearing) behaviors, such as:

Do you have a student (or more than one) who:

- Finishes what should have been a twenty-minute assignment in five minutes?
- Volunteers off-the-wall comments or suggestions during discussions?
- Is highly intolerant of stupidity, especially if perceived in an authority figure?
- Is impatient with sloppy or disorganized thinking to the point of rudeness?
- Recognizes sophisticated punch lines and gets more out of humor?
- Plans activities efficiently but can procrastinate to the point of desperation?
- Would rather argue than eat?
- Has probably read every book available on subjects of personal interest?

At the other end of the age spectrum, educators who work with preschool children and kindergartners respond helpfully (and seem to enjoy doing so because they may have been flummoxed by some of the children's capabilities and behaviors) to lists of characteristics such as:

- Asks many questions, often on topics typically interesting to older children
- Demonstrates early use of a large vocabulary and multiple meanings of words
- Understands abstract concepts such as time, coins, larger numbers, calendars
- Relates experiences with great detail and makes up vivid, dramatic stories
- Has a long attention span and deep concentration level for such an early age
- Learned to read at a very young age with little or no formal teaching
- Expressed self in complete sentences at an early age
- Shows precocious interest in values, purposes, and reasons

Not all children and certainly not all teenagers allow their abilities and talents to shine. Students with high potential can be chronic underachievers after languishing in mundane, "boring" curriculum for years. (The *b* word—*boring*—should not be used as a verbal "weapon" by students against teachers or children against their parents, for *everyone* should be bored at some points in their lifetime in order to reflect and ponder, stir up the imagination, and steep themselves in wonder that leads to creativity.) However, students who coast through easy material at the early grades can find themselves embarrassingly lost with basic concepts when subjects get harder in the upper grades.

Children with high abilities may have physical disabilities or behavior disorders. Attention-deficit/hyperactivity disorder (ADHD) is not uncommon among children singled out as gifted. Learning disabilities can overshadow high abilities, and conversely, high ability can mask disabilities, so the student loses both ways. Outstanding ability is not cultivated and disability is not remediated. Collaborating classroom teachers and special education teachers, along with counselors and school psychologists, need to be vigilant in watching for signs of dual (or more) exceptionalities.

Illness or a dysfunctional home may eclipse evidence of high ability and talent. Very capable children and youth raising the most concerns among school personnel in regard to their progress will be those in subgroups such as students with disabilities, English language learners, and children of families who are poor (Christie, 2004). A consulting teacher may find evidence of one or more of these influences on the summary of checklist information.

NEEDS OF LEARNERS WITH HIGH ABILITY AND TALENTS IN SCHOOL-BASED LEARNING PROGRAMS

A simple equation can aim educators toward the kinds of special services that students with high ability require: *Characteristics + Needs = Curriculum Implications*. Going a step further with the equation, curriculum can be tailored to those characteristics and needs with four types of modification:

1. *Release from repetition* of material already learned
2. *Removal of ceilings* on prescribed curriculum
3. *Flexible pacing* for progress through curriculum that allows time and space for accelerative, enriching learning experiences, and provides opportunities for learning activities some of the time with mental peers
4. *Self-directed learning and production* of professional-quality products for authentic (beyond-school) outlets

That said, the modifications beg the question of how these four areas are to be accomplished in schools where compulsory attendance is the law and educators and policymakers have the unequivocal responsibility to provide the framework that will structure it. Collaborative consultation and working in teams are the keys that can make that framework relevant for all students.

Differentiating the School-Based Curriculum

Tomlinson (2000) frames and activates that business of schools with a clear mission statement:

> What we call *differentiation* is not a recipe for teaching. It is not an instructional strategy. It is not what a teacher does when he or she has time. It is a way of thinking about teaching and learning. It is a philosophy. As such, it is based on a set of beliefs. (6)

But as teachers struggle with organization and management issues required for differentiation, students "mark time in place" day after day while waiting for something interesting and challenging to happen. As mentioned earlier, some "sleep through" their classroom situations only to "wake up" later and find that they have missed important elements needed for understanding key concepts. Other students "tune out" and create their own personal diversions during the school day, sometimes by "acting out." But most simply bide the time by reading, daydreaming, playing little games such as writing class notes backward or with the other hand, writing or texting messages to friends if they can get away with it, analyzing and charting their teachers' idiosyncrasies, or surreptitiously interacting with other disengaged students.

Should Differentiated Curriculum Be Accelerated or Enriched?

There is no need to debate the choice between accelerated curriculum and enriched curriculum. Curriculum that enriches student learning *is* accelerating, and curriculum that accelerates *will*, by definition, be enriching.

Implementing enriching, accelerated instructional strategies requires careful organization and coordination among general education teachers, special education personnel, resource personnel, school administrators, and families, with intensive involvement and collaboration by students in their own learning programs. Classroom teachers should introduce fundamentals at the levels and paces (note the plurals) that can be accomplished by each student. No one should have to repeat, repeat, and repeat again the content that has been learned. The key is *flexible pacing*, with movement through the curriculum at speeds, breadths, and depths that stimulate and challenge exceptionally able minds. This may sound simple, but it is not. Most prominently, it does not fit the "teach to the middle" paradigm that gets the class to the same place by summer so they can all begin *together* again in the fall. Flexible pacing of the curriculum puts a tremendous burden on classroom teachers in addition to their responsibilities of teaching, reteaching, and providing correctives for students who have not yet made adequate progress on district- and state-stipulated goals. It places the teacher at risk of incurring the displeasure of next year's teachers for whom they just made *their* jobs more difficult. Therefore, all teachers from year to year must have assistance from curriculum specialists—gifted program facilitators, who can seek out learning options and alternatives, coordinate them, gather resources needed, and design challenging curriculum and other learning activities. With concerted collaborative efforts between classroom teacher and facilitator, students do not languish in unchallenging curriculum and nonstimulating classroom environments. Consulting teachers collaborate and work in partnerships with:

- Teachers in the classroom to develop learning options and alternatives, to organize the individual or small-group plans, and occasionally to co-teach with them
- Resource personnel, support personnel, and mentors outside the school environment to engage in extension of learning opportunities for students
- School administrators to approve and activate the extended learning programs
- School counselors and school psychologists to interpret assessment tools and assist with finding opportunities for students beyond the school setting
- Families and the students themselves to use the differentiated curriculum options and alternatives efficiently

CO-EDUCATING FOR VERY ABLE AND TALENTED STUDENTS' NEEDS

Gifted program personnel have known for some time now that they need to work in new and different ways. Collaborative school consultation is a golden window of opportunity for making changes and improvements as gifted program facilitators collaborate and co-educate with others for exceptionally able children and youth (Dettmer, 1993). The field called *education of gifted* ("gifted education," in the vernacular) has made important contributions in the past to learning programs for students and for teachers as well, who often learn more than the students in preparing for them. But much more can be done. See Figure 10.8 for opportunities of collaborating, consulting, co-teaching, and partnering in teams to provide the changes and developments for very able students.

FIGURE 10.8   Window of Opportunity for Gifted Program Collaborators

1. Promote excellent education for _all_ students to take place in every school and community program.

2. Set high learning standards and expectations for all students, elevating the floor of expected outcomes, and raising the ceiling of anticipated outcomes.

3. Use multiple assessments for determining abilities of young learners so curriculum can be provided that meshes with those abilities and will increase them. So much time has been "spent" for many years and too often continues to be used for "identifying" students formally and then labeling them as qualified for placement in gifted programs. Meanwhile, in retrospect, too many of those programs have been not all that substantive or in synchrony with their schools and communities.

4. Develop the kinds of programs all students need to create, experiment, explore, produce, express themselves, and build meaningful relationships with friends, including opportunities to engage in learning some of the time with mental peers.

5. Structure gifted program personnel roles for working in different ways. Prepare preservice teachers to recognize and appreciate giftedness and value it rather than be put off or intimidated by it. Have gifted program teachers-to-be prepare in their teacher preparation programs to roll up their sleeves in classrooms for engaging in co-teaching, or teaching while the classroom teacher has opportunities to do other activities to enhance her resource base, or demonstrating teaching techniques, or developing resource materials. Many gifted education personnel have become experts at this.

6. Integrate education of gifted with general education in as many meaningful ways as possible. Make the differentiation seamless, so everyone, teacher or student, is working at a personal level and interest level that challenges and satisfies, with no one singled out for undue attention.

7. Plan for professional development that will add to school and district capabilities for motivating and challenging all learners, just as is expected for their athletes.

8. Monitor the progress of all students where gifted programs are offered. The "rising tide" of enhanced curriculum and expectations should "raise all ships."

9. Be on the watch at all times for student ability, motivation, and creativity that "bubble up" as validation of the health and vitality of the curriculum and the instruction; then suggest to policymakers ways in which schools and educators could continue to improve and showcase the community's focus on excellent education.

10. Advocate to the general public, to policymakers and school boards, to families in the community, and to co-educators at all times for excellent education that will tap the abilities of all students and gratify all educators at home and in school (Dettmer, 1993).

ASSESSING WHAT HIGHLY ABLE STUDENTS KNOW AND CAN DO

A key part of tailoring curriculum and integrating learning alternatives to fit very able students' learning programs is using preassessment techniques to find out what they already know. Teachers should test students' achievement levels with *out-of-level* (power) tests because to miss only one or two on a grade-level test (and everyone is prone to this occasionally) can prevent the test from showing what the examinee really can do with more challenging tasks. Collaborators should evaluate students' aptitudes by gathering as much other multi-sourced evidence as possible. (See Figure 5.2 in Chapter 5.)

Simple preassessment techniques that can be indicants of the need for differentiated curriculum and guides for providing enriched and advanced curriculum have been used successfully as classroom teachers, gifted program facilitators, and students' family members collaborate. Examples are:

1. Pretest, and if material is known, advance to the next unit or chapter. (Retain the pretest scores to make comparisons with advanced test scores later.)
2. Allow the student to "stop off" during a particular unit of special interest and do more in depth study, catching up with the class later through compacted curriculum and test-out opportunity.
3. Replace assigned seatwork or homework with opportunities for more in-depth study of that subject through the use of library, Internet, or people resources.
4. Allow the student to use alternative test forms such as essay, construct-an-exam options, in depth reaction papers, or compare-and-contrast papers.
5. Allow coursework to be undertaken in two subjects simultaneously, attending each class half time and completing half of the assignments as determined by pretest and curriculum compacting in which content that has been mastered is set aside and not required.

Many more preassessment techniques could be generated by classroom teachers and collaborating gifted program facilitators. See Figures 10.10 and 10.11 later in the chapter for more general possibilities in and out of school.

Textbook Analysis

Love of reading, and interest in science and mathematics have been dulled in many bright students by uninspired teaching and uninspiring materials. Basal readers, in particular, with their readability formulas and syllable schemes have "dumbed down" stories so that children sometimes cannot even follow the meager plots and mundane story lines.

One way to judge the suitability of basal materials for very able students is to do a textbook analysis. Consulting teachers and classroom teachers working in teams can examine grade-level texts for enrichment material and may find that together they can devise instructional strategies even better for their purposes than those in the basal series.

■ ■ ■ ■ ■

ACTION 10.3
Collaborative Textbook Analysis

Two groups of teachers have taken it upon themselves to critique content-area textbooks as a prelude to serving on curriculum committees for selecting new textbooks that will give teachers real assistance in differentiating for a wide range of student needs. Here is an abbreviated version of their several-page reports:

Group 1: We evaluated the XXX social studies text at the fifth grade level. It is superb, having been critiqued by several consultants, university instructors, and fifth grade teachers as well as teachers from other grade levels. Bloom's taxonomy is used as a format for unit questions, with categories that include focus, critical thinking, connect, and activity. Factual information is presented in different ways, with occasional side notes relating the historical topic to the present time. Special pages appear every so often for a unit to continue the lesson with exploration ideas or activities. One section on making decisions poses a problem from the past and asks "What would you do?" In the back is a small version of encyclopedia called Minipedia. Also there are an atlas and a time and space databank, which are wonderful reference tools for students and teachers. With this textbook, the teacher has an opportunity to enrich and accelerate social studies content for students.

Group 2: Our group critiqued a math text at the kindergarten level. It contains a lot of material on copying abstract symbols, on counting in isolated situations, and on analyzing pictures of objects. But kids need to work with things and learn about numbers in real life situations. Use of concrete materials was not emphasized here. The enrichment masters seem to be for assigning more of the same when students finish their workbook pages too early, and the answers are to be written rather than circled. (To take up more time?) They represent no more cognitive effort than the regular lesson. One "gifted student" activity is provided for each unit that perhaps offers some possibilities, but these are obscurely placed and total only nine in all. We feel that if teachers construct their lessons around material provided by this rather typical text, it is no wonder so many students get turned off by math!

Try analyzing a text series that your school uses, or one from your teacher education media center for classroom materials. Think about enrichment and acceleration for advanced needs and correctives and remediations for those needing more practice. What do you find? What were your more specific criteria as you examined the materials? Who determines the selection and purchase of teaching materials?

EXAMPLES OF CURRICULAR STRATEGIES FOR VERY ABLE LEARNERS

A graphic that is popular with educators of gifted students shows the taxonomy of the cognitive domain as a pyramid for dividing categories of thinking by complexity. The wide slabs at the bottom depicting knowledge and comprehension too often capture 80 to 90 percent of learning time and resources. But students who learn rapidly and easily should have an inverted pyramid of taxonomic emphasis, not because they don't need knowledge and understanding, but because for the most part they have acquired it already for the subjects being taught, or can do so very rapidly. Freeing rapid learners from a rehash of what they already have learned or can learn in minimum time would allow them the time they need for engaging in higher orders of thinking and doing. If not by such means, then how would it be possible for them to extend their learning?

Curriculum should draw out high-order application, synthesis, evaluation, and creative thinking in everyday classroom discussions and assignments. Questions provided in Reflection 10.1 are a start.

REFLECTION 10.1

Good Thinking!

Look at the following questions and reflect on the frequency with which you use such questions as discussion enhancers in your teaching. Versions of this list, when custom tailored by instructors for their subjects, can be taped into plan books and used as prompts during instruction to enhance discussion, writing, and group-oriented activities. Reflect on the practice of beginning a discussion with a challenge to the class: "Let's do some deep, wide, and complex thinking today." and then use some of these questions to guide the discussion.

- Who has some ideas about this?
- Why do you think that occurred?
- What may happen next?
- If you could, what would you change about . . . ?
- Do we have any new information to consider?
- What you said was good. Now let's think about it this way . . .
- We can't seem to solve this. How else could we approach it?
- Is there anything important we left out?
- Will you give an example, please?
- Yes, that is a reasonable answer. Where do we go from here?
- I see that you have an idea/answer. How did you arrive at it?
- Could you say that another way?
- What would be an exciting or innovative way to do that?
- What caused . . . to . . . the way it did?
- Do you agree with . . .'s suggestion?

For challenging students to think even higher, wider, and deeper, select from the following questions.

- If you could interview a famous person, who would it be?
- If you could have picked an important event in history to have attended, which would it have been, and why?
- If you could have two notable persons meet for a discussion, who would you choose, and what would you have the topic(s) be?
- If you were to redo something you have written, drawn, composed, or invented, how would you change it?
- How would you put your feelings about something you like very much into a work of art or science?
- How could you combine poetry, music, video, and art to convey what life is like or was like in a particular time and place of interest to you?
- What writer, artist, or scientist would you select as a very influential person, and why?
- Of the things you have written, composed, drawn, performed, invented, or discovered, which did you like best and why?
- What might creative expression be like in other civilizations—past, present, and future?

During departmental team-planning time, collaborating teachers could discuss student growth in complex thinking skills, creative problem-solving skills, and demonstrations of tolerance for differing opinions and values. If educators expect students to think and perform at more complex and individually expressive levels than recall, recitation, explanation, and translation, they must convey that intent to students as well and recognize them for that. Very able students will accept readily the challenge to analyze, synthesize, and evaluate. With encouragement, they can become partners in curriculum development rather than passive recipients. Figure 10.9 can be introduced to students as early as the primary grades and on into secondary school as a tool for illustrating the progression of high-order thinking by way of the basic and important knowing and understanding categories. Growth toward higher order processes depicted on the taxonomic

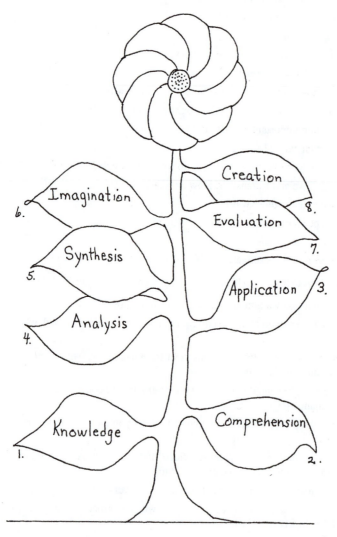

FIGURE 10.9   Blooms for Thinking and Doing

"plant" illustration is the right and responsibility of *every* learner at all ability levels. Nurturing the roots and cultivating the lower "leaves" from which all other "leaves" grow, will enable all learners, not just those in gifted programs, to "bloom" into the most knowledgeable, productive, and creative persons they can be.

Charts can be displayed showing the Blooms concept and reminding students to think "big." Older students can be informed that periodically their teachers will be evaluating the complexity of both answers they give *and questions* they ask, and recording an evaluation of that alongside grades for test scores or project assessment. The weight for test scores versus discussion "scores" would not be equal due to subjectivity of the latter, but would be taken into account when assessing learning. In co-educator meetings, general education and special education teachers will want to discuss their findings.

SAMPLE OF INSTRUCTIONAL MODELS FOR DIFFERENTIATING INSTRUCTION

Many teaching models and instructional approaches are well suited to curriculum differentiation, including multiple talents, autonomous learner, multiple intelligences, and others. Two that put significant emphasis on collaboration among general education, special needs education, and resource personnel will be described briefly here. Others are available among the numerous sources of materials for education of gifted students that can be found on line, with publishers of educational materials for students with high potential, and with facilitators for gifted education programs in the schools.

The Enrichment Triad Model

Renzulli's Enrichment Triad Model (1977) is one of the most widely used models for serving very able and talented students in inclusive schools. *All* students in the general classroom participate in exploratory activities (referred to as Type 1 in the model) on interesting topics through learning centers, field trips, resource speakers, learning packets, and more. *All* students in the classroom also participate in process-building activities (Type 2) to develop skills in problem-solving, creative thinking, inquiry, study skills—the possibilities are unending. Classroom teachers and gifted program consulting teachers collaborate in the general classroom for these activities.

For enrichment and production (Type 3), students who are very able, very motivated to learn and do, and show early signs of creative thinking and doing, are invited to participate in activities such as independent studies, research, and project development as they would be done by professionals. These tend to take place in a resource room or beyond the school setting, but not necessarily. Interest inventories and learning styles surveys guide the planning of these intense activities in which students study and produce or perform as professionals. Curriculum compacting (Renzulli & Reis, 1985)—that is, removing requirements of some regular classroom learning activities—"buys" time for engaging in the more challenging curriculum of Type 3 experiences. Just as teachers condense daily lessons and assignments for children returning to school after an illness, so do they compact curriculum for students who learn more quickly and easily than the majority of students. Students can pursue individual interests and independent study rather than repeat material they already have mastered. Curriculum compacting, and the preassessment process described earlier, will provide must-have information to guide development of differentiated curriculum. Students sometimes request to be placed in the talent pool for Type 3 activities. They and their teachers and parents will soon know if it is a good fit; the model is appropriate for moving into and out of such enriching opportunities.

The Enrichment Triad Model is a long-standing, well-researched, and highly respected model. It is built on a solid foundation of practices and ongoing programs of school-wide staff development with intensive collaboration and consultation among classroom teachers, special education personnel, and outside resource people.

Resource Consultation Model

In many schools, there is little collaboration between general classroom teachers and gifted education teachers, with classroom teachers making very few efforts to modify the curriculum for their most able students (Kirschenbaum, Armstrong, & Landrum, 1999). The Resource Consultation Model calls for teachers of gifted students to work in ways that may be different from ways they have worked in the past (Ward & Landrum, 1994).

The consultation occurs at different levels. In level one, teachers collaborate on an unstructured, informal basis for serving student needs. At level two, teachers seek assistance from specialized personnel for education of gifted students. Level three provides team intervention with several staff members involved in the decision-making process. Aims of the model are to enhance student academic performance for highly able learners *and* their age peers, to improve teacher competencies in providing differentiated instruction, to demonstrate effectiveness of the consultation approach, and to redefine the role of the gifted education specialist. Research studies (Landrum, 2001) show that positive spillover effects of the resource consultation model result in diverse and more frequent services to gifted students, and make the specialized services available to other students in the general classroom. Enhanced staff development creates positive ripple effects of gifted education teachers learning more about the general education program, and classroom teachers and other specialists becoming more familiar with the gifted education program.

Differentiated Learning Options in the School Environment

An inclusive school increases responsibilities of classroom teachers to provide for learning needs of highly able students. But few teachers have been prepared for differentiating curriculum to serve gifted and advanced learners (Rakow 2012). Differentiation is more than just being "different." The ideal situation, according to Rakow, is for classroom teachers to collaborate with gifted program facilitators in designing advanced activities and materials.

VanTassel-Baska (1989) notes several mistaken beliefs that need to be altered regarding differentiation for highly able students. First, consultants and consultees should not assume that curriculum must *always* be different from what all learners have. Nor do all learning experiences need to be product oriented. Then, too, one curriculum package or a single learning strategy will *not* provide all that is needed. Figure 10.10 provides suggestions for learning options within the school environment.

FIGURE 10.10   Learning Opportunities in the School Setting

- Differentiated curriculum in the classroom
- Curriculum compacting
- Use of books from the library as basal readers for both comprehension and skill building
- Telescoped curriculum where a course of study is collapsed into a shorter time frame
- Continuous progress courses, moving ahead as content and skills are acquired
- Grade skipping
- Early entrance to school (however, not permitted in some states)
- Test out
- Cross-age tutoring, with very able students teaching younger students of high ability
- Programmed instruction packages for rapid progress in areas of keen interest
- Seminars within schools or in collaboration with other schools or universities
- Advanced Placement courses
- Mini-replications of existing research studies
- Conversations with/observations of book authors, artists-in-residence, scientists
- Enrichment activity calendars for classroom teachers with a daily enriching activity
- Resource room time for independent study, research, or project development
- Honors classes
- Dual enrollment
- Discussion groups for moral dilemmas, great books, or current issues
- Special units of study that have a concentrated international perspective
- Biographies and autobiographies, to study great leaders of past and present
- Collection and analysis of the world's wisdom (proverbs, fables, maxims, credos, etc.)
- Summer school enrichment courses
- International Baccalaureate program
- Extra classes for extra credit
- Cluster grouping to work with mental peers on advanced topics
- Extended library, lab, practice, or computer time, or more time to work on projects
- Small-group discussions and investigations with mental peers (and more)

Some teachers are openly negative toward accelerating or compacting content for very able students. Some of their concerns must be heeded, such as the possibility that vital content and needed practice will be skipped; however, most concerns are not justified. The research is clear that acceleration is *not* harmful as a general rule to the academic, emotional, or social well-being of students who already may be tuned out, bored, or discouraged. That said, very able students need not always accelerate at a fast pace through the curriculum. On occasion they may welcome the opportunity to slow down and study a subject in depth and detail, catching up with the class later by completing regular assignments on a compacted basis. At other times, in their social environment the price of being different and doing different things at school can be quite high. In these situations, their wishes to be "one of the group" should be heeded.

Differentiated Learning Opportunities Beyond the School Setting

Some arrangements that would benefit very able learner the most are accessible only outside the school setting. When students leave their school campus for enrichment activities or accelerated course work, special educators and classroom teachers must assume responsibility for collaborating and communicating often to ensure that the students accomplish school district and state requirements, and that they continue to be involved in the life of the school. They also must deal with student supervision and liability issues. Figure 10.11 provides suggestions for some of the more commonly used off-campus learning opportunities.

FIGURE 10.11 Learning Opportunities Beyond the School Setting

- Early graduation from high school
- Early entrance to the university, with or without a high school diploma
- Career shadowing
- Academic competitions—regional, state, national, international
- Community service (sometimes for high school credit)
- Student exchange programs—urban to rural, west to east, north to south, U.S. to other countries
- Mentorships
- Tutorials with experts in a field of keen interest or exceptional talent
- Travel study programs
- Concurrent enrollment in high school courses and college courses
- Part time enrollment in vocational-technical schools to learn a trade
- University credit by examination
- College correspondence courses
- Field trips
- College-level independent studies
- Internships and apprenticeships
- Periodic contributions of writing and reporting for newspaper and media
- Presentations and performances of advanced work, to audiences outside the school (and more . . .)

ACTION 10.4
Scavenger Hunt

Get several educator colleagues involved in a hunt to find interesting, unusual, promising resources for enriching and accelerating student learning. Allow a certain length of time to search in instructional media centers, libraries, museums, historical societies, university campuses, neighborhoods, or towns and bring back innovative ideas for teaching and learning. Share and discuss these potential resources among the group and try some of them with students, if possible.

MINI-CASE STUDY

It is imperative that classroom teachers, gifted program teachers, building administrators, and family members, at the least, collaborate to provide highly able and very talented students the learning experiences they need to grow and develop their skills. This must be accomplished, however, while respecting highly intelligent children's needs for challenging content and adolescents' needs to build social and emotional relationships to complement their cognitive-based interests.

A brief exchange between gifted-program facilitator and a student on her caseload at a large high school is illuminating. The gifted program facilitator, who arranges for mentorships, independent studies, Advanced Placement classes, field trips (some of them international), academic contests, the honors program, and gifted program professional development sessions for the school, was walking to her office when she saw one of the gifted program's students approaching. Just before they met, the student seemed to be intent on something happening to the other side of her, and they passed without speaking. The next day, when the student arrived in the facilitator's office for a scheduled appointment, she commented about the rather transparent avoidance somewhat apologetically, "Sorry about yesterday, Mrs. Casey. But everyone knows who you are and what you do. So sometimes I may see you in the hallway when it just isn't in my best interests for me to act as if I know you very well. I hope you understand and don't mind."

What do you think was the student's motivation for (1) ignoring Mrs. Casey and then (2) volunteering an explanation? What do you think Mrs. Casey said to her in return? What, if anything, should Mrs. Casey do about this?

Educational programs for highly able students come in many sizes, settings, formats, locales, and levels of intensity. Figure 10.12 provides a visual summary of issues and topics to consider in planning wisely for the needs of such students in building their futures.

FIGURE 10.12   Collaboration and Teamwork for the Future with Exceptional Abilities and Talents

TECHNOLOGY FOR CO-TEACHING STUDENTS WITH SPECIAL NEEDS

Technology, when integrated into personalized learning activities, can help students learn what they need to learn by studying topics they choose that interest them (Richardson, 2012). Web 2.1 technologies can provide tools such as blogs and social bookmarks so that, as Richardson proposes, students connect to authors, videographers, and other resource persons online. Other technologies may be less social but also effective for inpersonalized learning, such as Google Docs for students to update their progress and receive teacher feedback. Richardson promotes technology as facilitating both learning and assessment.

As was discussed earlier in this chapter, often students with print-related disabilities need learning materials in specialized formats called accessible instructional materials (AIM). When co-teachers acquire specialized instructional materials, accommodations and/or modifications may be needed to effectively use AIM in general education settings.

For example, the student may need additional time to complete tasks due to the time required to use a specialized format. A free web-based tool, the AIM Navigator, is available at http://aim.cast.org/experience/decision-making_tools/aim_navigator and can be used to facilitate the decision-making process about accessible instructional materials for an individual student. The AIM Explorer can be found at this same site and is a free downloadable simulation tool that combines grade-leveled digital text with access features common to most text readers and supported reading software. It allows the user to manipulate features such as magnification settings, colors of text and background, text-to-speech (synthetic and human), text highlighting, and layout options to help educators and struggling readers decide the best way to configure these supports to help with access to, and understanding of, the text. Both are useful tools for teachers collaborating on making text-based materials accessible to students with a variety of needs and will facilitate those students being able to benefit from the general education curriculum.

In addition to converting printed text to specialized formats such as digital text, Edyburn (2006) suggests that teachers compensate for a student's difficulty with printed text in a number of different ways, including altering the size of the text, translating the text to a different language when English is a second language, providing vocabulary and concept development to scaffold for student understanding, providing similar text at different reading levels, decreasing the amount of reading, or teaching students learning strategies in order for them to become more strategic in their interaction with the text. For example, free web-based applications such as Babel Fish (http://babelfish.yahoo.com) are quick and easy tools for translating text or web pages from one of several languages into another. These can provide helpful scaffolds for students who are English language learners struggling to comprehend text used in classroom instruction.

Other strategies such as concept-teaching routines or analogical anchoring developed at the Center for Research in Learning at the University of Kansas also can help support struggling readers with vocabulary and concepts encountered in grade-level materials (Deshler et al., 2001). Using tools like the concept diagram for helping students grasp critical concepts will go beyond simple text adaptations to deepen their understanding (Bulgren, Schumaker, & Deshler, 1993). Unit and lesson organizers can enhance learning for students by providing a graphic organizer to help them transform content into a learner-friendly format (Boudah, Lenz, Bulgren, Schumaker, & Deshler, 2000). Teaching routines and organizers such as these enhance content learning rather than watering it down. These tools and others like them can assist collaborating teachers in having meaningful conversations about how to select and best teach important concepts in content-area classes.

As another strategy, Rotter (2006) suggests applying basic rules of graphic arts and design to all written materials. These simple guidelines can be applied to almost any type of written materials including everything from graphic organizers, commercially prepared materials, tests, digital slide presentations, and guided notes. Elements of design have a direct relationship on how well the message of the material will be transferred to the reader and how clear visual signals can help the reader grasp concepts more readily. Rules of graphic design help teachers prepare their instructional materials to make them easier for students to read, organize information more clearly, and improve comprehension.

ETHICS FOR CO-TEACHING STUDENTS WITH EXCEPTIONAL LEARNING NEEDS

Many positive benefits result from consulting, collaborating, and co-teaching to tailor the curriculum and manage classroom procedures for students who learn differently, whether it is because of disabilities, behavioral disorders, or high abilities.

Classroom teachers and special education teachers may want to co-teach a lesson or perhaps even a unit. They might exchange roles for a time, to gain new perspectives on the students and the material. They can work together with a particular student as a partnership of three or more to plan, implement, and evaluate differentiated learning experiences. As they collaborate to design personalized programs and free up time for learning alternatives, they can more readily provide seamless attention to special needs.

Not all teachers wish to co-teach, and those wishes should be respected. Some classroom teachers are uncomfortable with having other teachers in the classroom as they teach. Co-teaching must be entered into willingly and implemented with positive attitudes among all who will be involved. Building trust among collaborating teachers, families, and students as partners is a major determinant of success in co-teaching, and effective communication is a major tool in building that trust.

In a collaborative, ethical climate, schools are more lively places for learning, staff members are more enthusiastic, and families become more supportive. When allowed to have a "voice" in their learning, students are for the most part delighted with the opportunity. In an ethical and caring environment, teachers can model interpersonal skills for their students and find outlets for expression of their best and most creative ideas, affirming and reinforcing their decision to have a career in education.

TIPS FOR COLLABORATIVE PLANNING AND TEACHING

1. Co-teaching requires careful planning. Planning time must be built into the restructured school day.
2. Co-teachers will want to discuss their philosophies about teaching with their collaborator, especially in areas such as grading and reporting procedures, and interactions with families of students.
3. When co-teaching, clarify classroom rules and procedures, both big and small ones, such as routines for leaving the room, discipline matters, and division of chores such as grading or making bulletin boards.
4. Devise a way to keep track of individuals who are providing services for students so that monitoring does not become a problem.
5. Rather than just telling classroom teachers about materials modification, *show* them. Give some examples or do one for them.
6. Request demonstration lessons from classroom teachers who are "game" for this, featuring *their* most outstanding teaching techniques, but do not expect enthusiastic participation by all teachers.
7. Offer to re-format a test for a teacher (to double-space, type in large print, or organize it differently) for use with any student who has a learning problem.

8. Before ordering computer software or apps, have students try it out first. This gives them an opportunity to be consultants for teachers and cultivates student ownership in educational planning and evaluation.

9. When preparing and distributing materials for classroom use, don't just drop them off and run. Help the teacher or student get started, and stay awhile to see how it goes.

10. Keep a supply of materials to send to classrooms for students who need reinforcement—even those with whom you don't work who could benefit.

11. Have a favorite dozen or so successful strategies available for demonstration teaching or sharing.

12. Be understanding of classroom teachers' daily trials with some special needs students. Celebrate with classroom teachers even the smallest student progress.

13. Talk with school librarians and public librarians, asking them to order books and periodicals about needs of students that would appeal to families and community members. Give them the name, author, publisher, and, if possible, the ISBN.

14. Drop off samples of periodicals such as *Educational Leadership*, *Phi Delta Kappan*, *Early Childhood Today*, *Journal of Emotional and Behavioral Disorders*, *Journal of Learning Disabilities*, and *Gifted Child Today* at offices of pediatricians, obstetricians, and dentists for their waiting rooms. If possible, briefly visit with the medical staff about potential value of these materials to families and community members.

15. Talk with very able students to learn what has worked for them and what has not been helpful.

16. Observe other facilitators and collaborative consultants in schools that have outstanding programs for highly able students. If visiting several, select ones that use different approaches, to broaden your perspective.

17. Build networks of interaction among school personnel, parents, and community members who could serve as tutors, monitors, mentors, and independent study facilitators for special needs.

ADDITIONAL RESOURCES

Center for Applied Technology (CAST). *Resources to help implement UDL and make curriculum adaptations.* Available at www.cast.org.

Dettmer, P. (1991). Gifted program advocacy: Overhauling bandwagons to build support. *Gifted Child Quarterly, 35*(4), 165–171. Suggests ways in which twenty role groups can support differentiated learning programs for students with high ability and offers a fifteen-point plan of advocacy.

Dettmer, P. (1993). Gifted education: Window of opportunity. *Gifted Child Quarterly, 37*(2), 92–94. Stresses the importance of collaboration among classroom teachers and gifted program facilitators for addressing special needs of very able students.

Fennick, E. (2001). Co-teaching: An inclusive curriculum for transition. *Teaching Exceptional Children, 33*(6), 60–66. Describes how co-teaching in high school life skills classes can provide instruction for transition, job skills, and daily living skills in inclusive environments.

Friend, M. (2007). The coteaching partnership. *Educational Leadership, 64*(5), 48–52.

Hughes, C. E., & Murawski, W. A. (2001). Lessons from another field: Applying co-teaching strategies to gifted education. *Gifted Child Quarterly, 45*(3), 195–204. Offers a new definition of collaboration within the context of gifted education and expands on co-teaching as a collaborative strategy.

Descriptions and examples of adaptations of five models for co-teaching originally developed for students with disabilities are provided.

Kirschenbaum, R. J., Armstrong, D. C., & Landrum, M. S. (1999). Resource Consultation Model in gifted education to support talent development in today's inclusive schools. *Gifted Child Quarterly, 43*(1), 39–47.

Mastropieri, M. A., Scruggs, T. E., & Berkeley, S. L. (2007). Peers helping peers. *Educational Leadership, 64*(5), 54–58.

Morocco, C. C., & Aguilar, C. M. (2002). Co-teaching for content understanding: A schoolwide model. *Journal for Educational and Psychological Consultation, 13*(4), 315–347. A model for co-teaching involving collaboration between a content-area teacher and a special education teacher. Success is dependent on collaborative school structures, equal status rules for teachers, commitment to all students' learning, and strong content knowledge.

Pisha, B., & Coyne, P. (2001). Smart from the start: The promise of universal design for learning. *Remedial and Special Education, 22*(4), 197–203.

Reinhiller, N. (1996). Co-teaching: New variations on a not-so-new practice. *Teacher Education and Special Education, 19*(1), 34–48. Co-teaching approaches as a collaborative model, a special education instructional strategy, and an activity are discussed. Challenges, barriers, and benefits to these innovations are delineated.

Renzulli, J. S., & Reis, S. M. (1985). *The schoolwide enrichment model: A comprehensive plan for educational excellence.* Mansfield Center, CT: Creative Learning Press.

Stewart, R. A., & Brendefur, J. L. (2005). Fusing lesson study and authentic achievement: A model for teacher collaboration. *Phi Delta Kappan, 86*(9), 681–687.

VanTassel-Baska, J. (1991). Gifted education in the balance: Building relationships with general education. *Gifted Child Quarterly, 35*(1), 20–25. This article focuses on the relationships among gifted education, special education, and general education and discusses the importance of establishing links with general education and educational reform movements.

11

Supervising and Collaborating with Paraeducators

MUCH OF THE DISCUSSION ABOUT SCHOOL CONSULTATION AND COLLABORATION to this point has been in reference to classroom teachers and special educators. Now the focus will shift to an increasingly visible and important partner in special education—paraeducators (sometimes referred to as *paraprofessionals* or shortened to *paras*). Without these often underpaid and overworked partners, including students with disabilities in general education settings would be difficult, if not impossible. The use of paraprofessionals in public schools has become one of the primary mechanisms by which students with disabilities are being supported in general education classes. These practices are included in the shaded triangle of Figure 11.1.

The role of paras has changed rather dramatically over the years as they have moved from working primarily under the direct supervision of the special educator in a special education classroom setting to now more likely being seen in a general education classroom working directly with students while often being supervised from a distance by the special educator who is assigned to the supervisory role. This service delivery option has had a tremendous impact on the special educators who supervise paras. It is not uncommon for special educators to be responsible for directing a half dozen or more paras. Special education teachers who entered the profession to work with children with special needs often feel more like an air traffic controller than a teacher. Scheduling and communication logistics dominate a large part of their role. These teachers frequently report that it is a role they felt unprepared for as a novice special education teacher.

Paraeducators and teachers have an important interactive relationship. They are partners in accomplishing the tasks inherent in the teacher's role; however, the teacher has responsibility for supervising the para's work and assessing outcomes of the para's performance. In short, teachers supervise and direct the work of paraeducators.

FOCUSING QUESTIONS

1. Why is it important for the paraeducator role to be defined clearly?
2. How should teachers plan for and communicate about the para's responsibilities?
3. How are paraeducators selected and prepared for their roles?
4. In what ways do teachers supervise and direct para activities?
5. What assistance and supports can technology provide to the broad roles in which many paraeducators are placed for serving students with exceptional needs?
6. What elements are needed to provide an ethical climate in which paraeducators can work best?

KEY TERMS

paraeducator   preservice teacher   supervising teacher
   (para, paraprofessional)

VIGNETTE 11

Jackie recently completed her teacher training program and was hired as a special education teacher in a community not far from where she attended school. She was excited when offered a job in a highly sought-after district with little turnover in the teaching staff. She couldn't have dreamed of a more perfect job, or so she thought. After being in the job for four short months, things weren't going as she had envisioned.

Jackie's biggest problem was with her paraeducators. This blindsided her because during her student internship semester and subsequent practica in special education classrooms, she found she really enjoyed working with the paraeducators in those programs and had considered them both friends and colleagues. After all, they were close in age to herself, and her cooperating teachers seemed to have a good working relationship with them. She even commented in her portfolio that they all functioned together as an effective team.

When Jackie walked into her new job, she looked forward to having the same type of working relationship with her paras. She felt fortunate when interviewing for the position that there would be four paras working with her to help support students in the various classrooms. All the paras had been there five or more years, and two had been there more than ten years, so she was encouraged by their dedication to their jobs. She felt fortunate that she would not have to do para orientation and training that was talked about in one of her university courses on collaboration in special education. She had enough on her plate just getting oriented herself.

Jackie welcomed the paras' knowledge of students on her caseload and how returning students had been served during the previous year. She felt like she was able to hit the ground running, without missing a step, due to the collective experience of her para team. It took about six weeks for things to settle in and as new students were placed on her caseload and she had a chance to visit classrooms and observe, Jackie felt she was ready to try some new things. Later in the chapter, the attention will focus on a case study in Jackie's context to see how her plan for trying new things has worked.

PARAEDUCATORS AS PARTNERS

Paraeducators are essential partners in providing special education services; therefore, teachers and consultants to whom these partners are assigned must give special consideration to their needs. Many of the concepts and skills presented in other parts of this book apply to working with paraeducators.

This section emphasizes special skills that relate specifically to supervising and communicating with paras.

Since the early 1990s, significant changes in special education have fueled an increase in the reliance on paraprofessionals to support students with disabilities. In recent years, schools have turned increasingly to paras because of large caseloads for special education teachers, the need for more individualized attention to students at risk due to economic disadvantage or other circumstances, and the cultural and linguistic fit with students by many paras who live right in the school's neighborhood (French & Pickett, 1997). Paras are particularly important members of the teaching team in rural communities. They may be the most constant element in the school life of students with special needs if they stay there when teachers move on (Ashbaker & Morgan, 1996; Demchak & Morgan, 1998).

Increasingly, paras are being used in general education settings, particularly for students with low-incidence disabilities such as autism, intellectual and multiple disabilities, and emotional disturbance (Suter & Giangreco, 2009). In their review of a decade of literature on paraprofessional support of students with disabilities, Giangreco, Edelman, Broer, and Doyle (2001) noted that when the Education of All Handicapped Children Act (P.L. 94-142) was first passed in 1975, there were discussions concerning training a whole new cadre of personnel, essentially paraprofessionals (now *paraeducators* in much of the literature), to meet the needs of the new population of students with more severe disabilities who would be entering the public schools. At the time, some believed these students did not need highly trained teachers with teacher education degrees. Others felt differently and assumed that given proper support and instruction, students with more severe disabilities were in fact educable, and needed specialized and individualized instruction from highly trained special educators. In the end, federal officials agreed with the latter group and advocated for professional teachers to serve students with severe disabilities. In looking at the landscape of services for students with moderate to severe disabilities in today's schools, we should note the increasing reliance on paraprofessionals to support students with more severe disabilities in the general education classroom. Some might ask whether we have come full circle.

Paraeducator Requirements

As one outcome of the No Child Left Behind Act (NCLB), by end of the 2005–2006 school year, all paraprofessionals were to hold an associate degree, have completed two or more years of college, or passed a district- or state-approved paraprofessional assessment. Additionally, NCLB more clearly set the boundaries of the roles that instructional paras could fulfill by requiring that they act under the direct supervision of highly qualified teachers.

The use of paraeducators is now a well-established and growing trend. In 2008, slightly more than 391,000 full-time-equivalent (FTE) paraprofessionals were employed in special education in the United States, for students ages six to twenty-one (U.S. Department of Education, 2008b). That was up almost 9 percent from just two years before. Twenty-six states reported employing more special education paras than special education teachers (U.S. Department of Education, 2008a). It has become common for special educators to be responsible for directing the work of more than four paras on average—and in some cases as many as fourteen (Giangreco & Broer, 2005).

Over the years, the manner in which paraprofessionals are used has also changed. Paras increasingly are being called on to support students with disabilities in general education classrooms. This was not always the case. Initially, paras employed in special education typically worked under the close supervision and direction of a special educator who was present with them in a resource or self-contained classroom all or most of the time. Today, paras are more likely to be assisting students with disabilities within general education classrooms; and sometimes they have very limited contact with the professional special education teacher listed on the student's IEP as the one who supervises them (Giangreco, Suter, & Doyle, 2010). This raises many questions. Are the roles and duties that paras are asked to perform clearly delineated and appropriate? Do they have adequate training to carry out their duties? Are they being adequately supervised? The extensive literature review by Giangreco and colleagues (2010) indicates that often, through no fault of their own, too many paras remain inadequately trained and supervised to do the jobs they are asked to undertake. Overreliance on paras or inappropriate use of their services can result in a host of unintended negative consequences.

Under the NCLB legislation, teachers have been held more accountable for supervising their paraeducators, and administrators have been expected to give paras more support, avoid misassignments of their responsibilities, and provide professional development to help them perform their roles effectively. *Neither paras nor teachers typically have had formal preparation for collaborating with one another in productive ways.* Frequently, the relationship is hampered by inadequate communication, lack of time for planning together, and lack of clear job descriptions.

A fine line often exists between paras' assistance to teachers in implementing their plans and functioning as instructor and decision maker. With more and more pressures evolving from inclusionary practices, paras are sometimes being asked to extend their roles inappropriately to include assessment, curricular adaptations, instruction, and communicating with families.

With these issues, along with heavy caseloads and lack of time, paraeducators have many pressures. They may feel a lack of respect. Their salaries tend to be appallingly low. Some resent the absence of opportunity for advancement. Many articulate a need for more intensive clarification and preparation for the para role. Research by Giangreco, Edelman, and Broer (2001) identified several themes suggesting how school personnel can respect, appreciate, and acknowledge paraprofessionals. They can receive:

- Non-monetary signs and symbols of appreciation
- Adequate compensation
- Trust for carrying out important responsibilities
- Non-instructional responsibilities
- The respect of being listened to
- Orientation experiences and support for their roles

Special education supervising teachers have little control over how much their paras are paid, but they could have substantial influence over most of the other identified areas. Successful matches of role delineation, skill development, expectations, and support can help instill respect and appreciation for the role. Paraeducators often serve as "connectors" between parties such as students, parents, teacher and community service providers. Being a respected and valued member of the team is paramount for them to work effectively.

Delineating the Paraeducator Role

Paraeducators may be found in virtually any educational setting, ranging from a preschool class for children with special needs, to a first-grade classroom having students with disabilities, to a grocery store for coaching adolescent students with developmental disabilities in learning a new job, to a resource room for gifted adolescents with needs for advanced and expanded curriculum. Paraeducator responsibilities vary widely, from teaching a lesson, to grading homework and tests, to participating in classroom activities, to sometimes just "being there" for the students and teacher.

An extensive literature review by Giangreco, Edelman, Broer, and Doyle (2001) had noted the greatly expanding roles and duties for paraprofessionals during the 1990s, especially those where students with disabilities are served in general education settings. They found that paras continue to work with students who have the most challenging behavioral and learning characteristics, engaging in a broad range of roles without preparation for many of them. The researchers listed eight major role categories of such duties:

1. Providing instruction in academic subjects
2. Teaching functional life skills
3. Teaching vocational skills at community-based work sites
4. Collecting and managing data
5. Supporting students with challenging behaviors
6. Facilitating interactions with peers who don't have disabilities
7. Providing personal care
8. Engaging in clerical activities

In their updated review of previous findings, Giangreco and colleagues (2010) found that current literature supports the earlier findings that para roles have become increasing instructional. With the understanding that highly qualified educators, both general and special education teachers, are responsible for making the plans that the para then implements, evidence continues to appear that paraprofessionals work autonomously with very little direction. Paraeducators report making instructional decisions, providing the majority of instruction to some students, and doing so without adequate professional direction from the teachers who are their direct supervisors. This certainly begs the ethical question as to whether our least qualified personnel are being assigned to provide the bulk of instruction and support to our students with the most challenging behaviors and learning needs. With the current emphasis on Response to Intervention (RTI) and teacher and student accountability regarding instruction, it is more imperative than ever before that paras, as key players in academic programs for students with disabilities, be closely supervised in their performance of those duties. This is particularly important in situations where most students on a special education teacher's caseload are served in a full inclusion model. A special education teacher functions more as a case manager, overseeing and directing the activities of many paraprofessionals who work with students on IEPs in the general education classroom. These paras must not only be supervised in the performance of their duties, but they must also be guided and coached on the nuances of instruction for students with disabilities. Just as importantly, teachers who are planning the instruction for students must receive ongoing feedback from the paraeducator in both formal progress of monitoring data as well as more informal feedback about a host of other variables that have impact on student performance and motivation.

The relationship between the special education teacher and paraeducator differs somewhat from the other collaborative roles. Unlike the consulting teacher and the consultee teacher, classroom teachers and paraeducators do not have parity in the school program because they are not equally responsible for decisions about student needs and instructional interventions. The teacher is expected to supervise and direct the paraeducator, who is employed to assist the teacher and, therefore, to follow the teacher's direction. Even so, the paraeducator is necessary as a partner to the teacher's success and to the success of the teacher's students. Indeed, the prefix *para-* means "to come alongside," or "to help another." Paraeducators are employed in schools to come alongside teachers and help them with the demands of their jobs.

Some people use the term *instructional paraprofessional* to designate a person who helps with instruction of students. Nevertheless, paraeducators do not plan instruction nor are they responsible for evaluating student performance. But they can do a great deal to help students learn and gain confidence with their schoolwork and assist teachers and special educators in implementing the students' IEPs.

Prior to supervising or working with a paraeducator, it is helpful to identify key tasks as part of a teacher's role, specify what the teacher does when carrying out that role, and then stipulate what role the paraeducator might have in comparison to what the teacher does. This is a useful exercise for the teacher to clarify, distinguish between the two, and then articulate it to the para so both are clear about how their roles are intertwined but different. Figure 11.2 provides an example of what this might look like on a few key teacher and para tasks.

Paraeducator Responsibilities

Every paraeducator position has its unique characteristics and responsibilities, but some are more commonly utilized than others. Paras report delivering instruction planned by professionals as the most common use of time along with behavior support (Giangreco & Broer, 2005). Less frequent, but still reported by paras and teachers as being part of a para's role, are supervision of students, clerical tasks and assisting students with personal care. These tasks might be in the form of one of the following:

1. *Supporting and monitoring students*—Reading to students and listening to them read, providing guided practice for students needing scaffolding on a math lesson that was presented by the teacher, administering routine curriculum-based measurement (CBM) probes as part of ongoing student progress monitoring, helping students with health care or other personal needs, assisting with small-group activities, observing and recording student behavior, supervising playground activities

2. *Preparing instructional materials*—Making materials for specific lessons, duplicating materials, taking notes in a secondary content class to help students fill in their own notes and prepare for tests, making instructional games and learning centers or self-correcting materials to provide additional practice on a skill or topic area,

FIGURE 11.2   Interrelated Roles of Teacher and Para on Key Tasks

EXAMPLE TASKS	Teacher Role	Para Role
INSTRUCTION	Delivers whole class, small group, and one-on-one individualized instruction.	Reinforces lessons and skills introduced by the teacher or carries out individual and small group instruction directed by the teacher and when para has been explicitly trained to deliver a specific instructional format.
PLANNING	Plans the lessons and determines which instructional procedures will be used.	Carries out the teacher's plans and reports to teacher about student progress.
BEHAVIOR MANAGEMENT	Observes and analyzes student behavior (Functional Behavioral Assessment) and then, often in consultation with others, develops a behavioral intervention plan.	Observes and records student behavior and carries out any behavior plan that is in place for a student or other classroom management system.
WORKING WITH FAMILIES	Initiates written and verbal contact, conferences, and shares student progress.	Participates in conferences or other meetings with parents as appropriate and when invited by the teacher or supervisor.
ASSESSMENT	Administers, scores, and interprets both formal and informal tests and reports results to necessary persons.	Administers informal tests and routine progress monitoring probes and CBMs with prior training and records results for the teacher to review and share.

making arrangements for community-based instruction and field trips, collecting and compiling upcoming assignments from general education teachers to share with special education supervisor for planning purposes

3. *Communication support*—Participating in team meetings and parent conferences as appropriate, preparing student performance charts, providing feedback about student progress

4. *Support of routine business*—Recording attendance, checking papers, filing materials, entering data for progress monitoring

As noted earlier, more and more students with disabilities are receiving their education in the general education classroom where paraeducators often are assigned to work with individual students or small groups of students to support them in the inclusion setting. This can present a challenge for a special educator who is responsible for supervising the work of the paras and monitoring student progress, but who may not be present to oversee day-to-day instructional activities and behavior support strategies being implemented. The special education para supervisor must have a system to ensure ongoing two-way communication between them. Often paras have the most direct avenue for contact and support of students with disabilities whose primary placement is in the general education classroom. In order for the special education teacher to develop appropriate interventions and ensure that instruction and behavior plans are being implemented appropriately, the special education teacher should build weekly meeting time with the para into their schedules. This meeting should have a consistent format and structure to promote most efficient use of time. This weekly meeting can fulfill the dual purpose of monitoring and planning for students as well as establishing and building a positive working relationship between the supervisor and paraprofessional. Depending on the situation, possible topics for discussion at such a meeting are outlined in Figure 11.3. In addition to the weekly meeting, it is helpful to have a daily communication procedure that provides a definite, reliable way to touch base with one another. This could be in the form of a student folder where the para records brief notes on a log sheet to keep the teacher informed about student day-to-day performance. It might be a list of words the student missed in the oral reading time, math concepts covered in the lesson on which the student needs additional guided practice, a sentence or two about behavior incidents, or notes about student successes. This can also be a place for the para

FIGURE 11.3   Topics for Para/Supervisor Weekly Conferences

Possible Discussion Topics for Weekly Conference Between Para and Special Education Supervisor include:

1. Schedule para's time and delegate tasks for the upcoming week.
2. Discuss general role of para in the classroom.
   - This is a good time to discuss how the para interacts with the student(s) and classroom teacher.
   - Share any feedback you have been given by the classroom teacher regarding the para or the students being served.
   - Ask the para for feedback about the effectiveness of interventions being implemented, student behavior, academic performance, progress toward goals and overall motivation and attitude.
   - Solicit input from the para in terms of how the students being supported in the classroom are fitting in and interacting with other students and the teacher. (Do they seem to be an integrated member of the class or more of a "visitor" on the side?)
3. Review any data being collected by the para regarding student performance and discuss what the next step should be. This might include progress-monitoring graphs or charts of basic academic skills, student work samples, behavior observation logs, anecdotal daily log notes, and the like.
4. Talk through your analysis of the information and seek input from the para.
5. Finalize plans for the upcoming week, including any changes that will be made, and ensure that the para has the necessary training and information to carry out the plan. Sometimes the special education teacher might need to provide a brief demonstration or model the teaching behavior on how to provide feedback to the student.
6. Finally, ask the para if there are any additional topics to cover or issues that need to be brought to your attention. Make sure to convey that you value their contributions and input.

to jot down questions or topics to be discussed at the next weekly conference. Some find that rather than physically dropping off a student folder or clipboard with these notes to the special education classroom or teacher's office, a more efficient tool is using e-mail or some type of electronic log sheet. As always, keeping such communications private from other students and even from adults who do not have permission for access, is mandatory. Electronic tablets and other such devices are becoming more common in the classroom for recording data and communication purposes and this simply extends the application of that technology and puts it in the hands of paraprofessionals. This reality begs the question of preparing the para for such responsibility with proper training and guidelines.

As has been mentioned earlier, paraeducators may assume a range of job responsibilities while supporting students in the classroom. Depending on the skills and training of the paraeducator, this could include carrying out academic and social skill interventions designed by the teacher, making on-the-spot curricular modifications, and managing student behavior, all while developing working relationships with others on the team. Paraprofessionals and their supervisors and teachers should discuss what tasks are appropriate for the para to carry out, which should be done only by a highly qualified teacher, and which might be done by either the para or the teacher. Figure 11.4 provides an example of how this might look. It is designed so both the para and teacher fill it out separately and then compare their selections and discuss any items where there was not agreement. The items on this form can be easily adapted to more closely fit a particular situation.

There is often a fine line between what is an appropriate responsibility for the para and is being clearly directed by a qualified teacher and what crosses the line and borders on educational malpractice by essentially leaving paras on their own to teach students with special needs. In fact, many paraeducators appear to assume primary responsibility for the included students in the general education classroom. Breton (2010) indicated that almost 40 percent of paras he surveyed interacted directly with the special education teacher on less than a weekly basis. Another 16 percent said they never received consultation on providing direct instruction to students from their supervising special education teacher.

Paras are often aware that it is the classroom teacher's responsibility to provide the primary instruction in academic and social skills, to make modifications, and respond to student misbehavior. Nevertheless, some paras often take on these responsibilities that go beyond their role and job description (Marks, Schrader, & Levine, 1999). Explanations for this behavior include:

- Paras don't want students to be a "bother" to the teacher.
- Paraeducators feel an urgency to meet a student's immediate academic needs.
- Paras may believe their own performance will be based on positive relations with the teacher.
- Paras are often faced with the need to make on-the-spot modifications when teachers are not readily available.

In many situations, paraeducators have become the primary vehicle for accommodation for students with severe or multiple disabilities in inclusive schools. Lohrmann and Bambara (2006) contend that providing in-class supports such as paraeducators is a critical factor in the acceptance by general education teachers of the inclusion of students with

FIGURE 11.4 **Teacher and Para Role Clarification**

Both the para and teacher should complete this separately and then compare and discuss any answers that vary.

ACTIVITY	PARA	TEACHER	EITHER
Listen to student read orally and record words read correctly and errors			
Monitor student progress by administering daily math probes			
Assist students with assignment			
Deliver rewards and consequences as indicated on the student's behavior plan			
Provide corrective feedback			
Help with arrangements for field trips or community based instruction			
Prepare materials for lessons following teacher directions			
Observe and record student behavior			
Share academic or behavior information with a parent			
Supervise students (lunch, playground, loading bus)			
Complete routine paperwork			
Attend to student's physical needs in bathroom or lunchroom			
Program communication phrases into a student's augmentative communication device			
Gather instructional resources for a lesson on teaching fractions			
Read a test to a student			
Score an objective style test			

developmental disabilities and challenging behaviors in their classrooms. In most instances, paraeducators stay in close proximity to the student with a disability in these classrooms, attending to their students' physical needs such as toileting, and to instructional needs such as reading aloud to students or recording their answers. Paraeducators may even adopt an advocacy role, making it their responsibility to work toward acceptance of the included student, or to "represent" the student in ways that would support acceptance (Broer, Doyle, & Giangreco, 2005; Giangreco & Boer, 2005). While on the face of it, this may seem a laudable character trait of paraprofessionals to become so invested in the students they serve that they do whatever it takes for the student to be successful in the inclusive classroom. But, when paras take on roles that have been described in the literature as mother, friend, protector and primary teacher (Broer et al., 2005) that can be cause for concern.

Often, especially when paraprofessionals are assigned to individual students, a primacy and sometimes-exclusive relationship develops between the students with a disability and the person who is literally at their side for a significant part of the school day. Giangreco and Broer

(2005) found that paras assigned to individual students in their study reported spending 86 percent of their time in atypical proximity—within three feet of their assigned student. To an outside party looking in at the situation, this might send up some warning flags as to whether this is a healthy situation if our goal is to help these students gain independence and develop friendships with their peers in natural settings. Possibly the bigger issue is that fewer than 15 percent of the paras in the study indicated a concern that this unusual proximity to students for so much of their time at school might be unnecessary and interfere with teacher and peer interactions.

Since the paras seem to be unaware of the harm they may be causing, it is important for teachers and supervisors of paraprofessionals to sensitize their own paras and teachers in those classrooms to reactions reported by some former students who had paras. It is not likely that many students would want to attend school all day with their mother always at their side, yet this is how many students have reported feeling with a para who is almost constantly within three feet of them. Mothering supports, no matter how well intentioned, perpetuate the thinking that what students with intellectual disabilities need in school is mothering rather than appropriate supports and effective instruction delivered by a highly qualified teacher (Broer et al., 2005).

It has also been suggested that in addition to making paras and teachers more sensitive to this issue, changes in program structure might be needed. This could include such remedies as rotating paraeducators, carefully analyzing the need for and assignment of one-to-one paras, exploring alternatives to the current use of paras, and developing more socially valid ways of providing needed supports in general education classrooms by means of peer tutors and similar peer-based models. When an exclusive para is deemed necessary, the goal should be to gradually but deliberately begin to fade out such intensive para support. Students with disabilities should also be given age-appropriate input about the types of support they will receive and instructed in self-advocacy skills (to be discussed in Chapter 15) so they can share in the decision-making process.

Supervision of paraeducators can be complex and challenging. Unfortunately, many teacher education programs give little or no attention to the topic in their programs. When it is addressed in preservice programs, it is most likely discussed with future special education teachers and rarely included in courses for general education teachers. This neglect is similar to that of neglecting collaboration and consultation skill development in preparation programs for general education teachers, thereby excluding one-half of the interaction process by this oversight. One could argue that a special education teacher is the person most likely to be responsible for supervising paraprofessionals (or collaborating with a co-teacher) and, therefore, the one in most in need of the training. Yet it seems reasonable for the general education teacher to also have some knowledge about the para role and skill in interacting with special education colleagues. In reference to the paraeducator, awareness should include:

- What a paraprofessional can and cannot do
- How to best utilize para support in an inclusive classroom
- Ways to provide feedback and communicate effectively
- How to handle issues with paras
- Who to contact if the problem is not resolved expeditiously

Although most special educators today expect to direct the work of paraprofessionals, the majority report receiving little or no training in how to carry out this important function and most say they rely primarily on their on-the-job experiences. This might explain why many special educators responsible for overseeing paraeducators fail to use effective supervision practices. French (2001) reported that in her research, the majority of teachers she studied did not plan for paraprofessionals, and most of those who did delivered plans orally rather than providing written directions the para could refer to when carrying out an instructional or behavioral plan. So, while new special educators realize that paraprofessionals are very much a part of their role in the delivery of special education, few feel they have been adequately prepared in exactly *how* to supervise paras and even fewer have had practice in doing so prior to their on-the-job experience. When novice special education teachers engage in para supervision without adequate training, they may make mistakes that could have long-term ramifications and need to be repaired. The situation could be compared to starting a building project without a blueprint. But people and relationships are harder to rebuild than bricks-and-mortar building, not to mention the lost opportunities for students that cannot be regained.

One area of particular importance in regard to para and teacher relationships and success of the supervisory relationship is that of personality variables. (See Chapters 2 and 3 for discussions of individual differences among adults in the work setting.) Individual differences also can be problematic when there are large discrepancies in age, culture, educational level, or ethnic background. Young novice teachers may feel inadequate or awkward when having to supervise a para enough older to be the teacher's parent. In another supervisory relationship, a new teacher may be faced with supervising a para who has been in the position for several years and seems to be a lot more knowledgeable about the students, teachers, parents and school culture than the supervising teacher, thus making it seem like the tables are turned.

In spite of challenges in addressing the roles and responsibilities of paras, there are positive effects. As suggested earlier, many paras can be supportive links to the community. Their positions cost the schools relatively little. Laudably, most paras are pleased to work patiently and caringly with students who can be difficult at times. They often tend to view these students in different and positive ways. They are able to contribute information that helps classroom teachers and consulting teachers provide appropriate learning experiences. Much more effort should be made to prepare educators to collaborate with and supervise paraeducators, and schools should put strong emphasis on recruiting exemplary candidates for paraeducator roles and preparing them well.

Persons who are attracted to paraprofessional positions report some of the same reasons for choosing to become a para. Many like the schedule compatibility with family circumstances, and being involved in work within their communities that fulfills their love of working with children (Giangreco et al., 2010). These factors may attract a person to the job, but given the relatively low pay that most paraprofessionals earn, it is unlikely a skilled and motivated person will stay in the position very long if there aren't other factors that make the job enjoyable. A great deal of time and training is invested in a para during the first year or two of employment, so it only makes sense that retention of qualified and effective paras should be a priority of both the district and the supervisor. There are many intangible ways to foster retention of good paras.

One special education teacher who has successfully retained many in her core group of paras for several years describes her team as being like a family. She meets with her paras as a group a few days before school starts to go over important information about the upcoming school year and students they will be supporting. When there are new hires, she uses the skills and experiences of her returning paras to help with the orientation and training of the new paras, thus communicating her confidence in their abilities and leadership skills. They all work together to prepare for the start of the school year, each contributing their own particular skills and interests. They organize and arrange the room, put together student folders and materials, discuss how they will communicate on a daily basis about each student, determine topics of interest for professional development and, since the supervising teacher loves to cook, she prepares a special lunch to serve when they meet on the first day. The group also shares a pizza lunch twice a month to bring everyone together. This not only helps them bond as a team socially but it is an avenue for group brainstorming and problem solving.

The paraeducator and teacher relationship can be likened to a couple on the ballroom dance floor. The two gracefully perform together to the rhythm of the music, one partner leading and the other following. Both partners use the same basic dance steps, but the unique timing of special moves, as guided by the leading partner, keeps them from impeding others or digressing from their areas.

The para–supervisor relationship becomes less obvious when a para is employed to work with a team. In that case, it can be likened to having an orchestra: The para plays an important role in a group performance directed by a conductor. Co-teachers, in contrast, can be thought of as engaging in a musical duet. Each follows the same score, but with different, preplanned parts. All must maintain the rhythm and harmony to produce a pleasant experience.

The co-teaching team will need to determine who is to assume supervisory responsibilities for paraeducators. The best selection will likely be a person who:

- Holds ultimate responsibility for the outcomes
- Is in the best position to direct the para
- Can provide training for the assigned duties
- Can observe and document para performance

Supervision requires specific, sophisticated skills and behaviors. A supervisor must plan, schedule, coordinate, and evaluate another person's actions. As noted earlier, it is not unusual in these current times of fiscal austerity for special education teachers to be assigned as many as five or six paras whom they direct and supervise. The supervisor is responsible for the para's actions and the para is accountable to the supervisor. Regardless of how much or how little education or preparation a person has before taking a para position, a supervisor should provide on-the-job training. For example, co-teachers may develop a teaching plan that includes the para for part of the implementation. For the plan to be successful, the supervisor or co-teacher must get the para ready for implementing the pertinent parts of the plan.

A number of functions associated with para supervision have been introduced thus far (French, 2000; Wallace, Shin, Bartholomay, & Stahl, 2001). They include:

1. Communicating and planning with the paraprofessional
2. Managing schedules (prioritizing tasks, preparing schedules)
3. Delegating responsibilities (assigning tasks, directing instructional supports, monitoring performance)
4. Orienting (introducing people, policies, procedures, job descriptions)

5. Providing on-the-job training (modeling teaching, coaching new skills, giving feedback)
6. Evaluating (tracking performance, summative evaluation of job performance)
7. Strengthening public relations in the communities and managing the work environment (maintaining lines of communication, managing conflicts, solving problems)

The more individuals with whom the para works, the more complex the supervision processes. When paras are in the general classroom most of the school day, it is essential for the classroom teacher to be involved in the supervision. In some instances the classroom teacher may take major responsibility for the supervision. If communication processes among all parties are open, this arrangement can work well. This is best discussed at a meeting with all three parties involved—para, classroom teacher, and special education supervising teacher. The general education teacher may not fully understand the para's role in the classroom and not be well versed in what the para is permitted by law to do or not do as a paraprofessional. Having a meeting with all parties prior to placement avoids problems and misunderstandings down the road. The teacher and para are made aware of the proper channels of communication if a conflict develops between the two. The first section of the para orientation plan checklist (refer to Figure 11.5) breaks out some of the points that could be discussed at such a meeting.

Selection and Preparation of Paraeducators

Most paraeducators bring many useful skills to the job. Some have teaching experience. A few may even have teacher certification but may have been unable to find a teaching job available in the area where they must live. When selecting a paraeducator, administrators should look for a person with:

- A high school diploma, at least, so as to meet national entry standards for paraprofessionals such as those set forth by NCLB
- Evidence of good attendance at work
- Adherence to ethics and confidentiality in their work
- Ability to follow teachers' directions and written plans
- Ability to communicate effectively with students and adults
- Good relationships with young people
- Willingness to learn new skills
- Flexibility
- A sense of humor (It always helps!)

Many of the common difficulties between paraeducators and their supervising teachers can be minimized or avoided completely if the relationship begins with a well thought-out orientation session. An example checklist of items to include during a para's orientation is included in Figure 11.5. As you will notice, orientation and training are not one-shot events. There are things a paraprofessional needs to know immediately and other things that are important but can wait until after a week or two on the job. Other information and training needs will be ongoing and almost indefinite as the paraeducator grows professionally.

FIGURE 11.5   Para Orientation Plan Checklist

Get to Know the People and the School
- Provide a tour of the school
- Introduce key people para needs to know
- Provide a school and student handbook and a school calendar
  - Highlight emergency procedures and other important information

- If the para is working with you in a special education classroom, go over classroom routines including:
  - general student behavior expectations
  - a schedule of when students arrive and leave
  - where materials and supplies are located
  - how to contact the office,
  - any clerical or record keeping duties the para might need to do

- If the para will be working in an inclusive classrooms supporting students, arrange a formal meeting with the teacher, yourself and the para. Be sure to cover the basics including:
  - the role of the para in the class,
  - how the para will be introduced to the class and parents
  - having teacher share expectations for the para (such as where the para will be located in the classroom, classroom management policies, work style and interaction preferences)
  - clarifying whether the para is to assist only a particular student, a group of students, or any student in the classroom even if they do not have an IEP, 504, or behavior plan.
  - what records or log the para will keep to report on student progress (reporting to both the general and special education teachers)
  - discussing proper communication channels if there is an issue or concern (Will the teacher have a role in the para's evaluation?)
  - discussing how feedback will be given to the para and the special education supervisor

- Discuss confidentiality–VERY IMPORTANT

After a Week on the Job
- Introduce para to other teachers and staff
- Discover para's interests, skills and relevant background related to students or education (and consider using both an inventory or a checklist as well as an interview/discussion format)
- Discuss additional details about job related tasks (answer para questions)
- Provide additional background on specific student characteristics and needs
- Provide ongoing mini "need to know" training sessions (how to provide positive corrective feedback, how to administer a word identification probe, and so forth)

After a Month on the Job (and continuing on an ongoing basis)
- Develop a plan for acquisition of new skills needed in carrying out the para's role (para, teacher, and supervisor all having input)
- Ask for input from para about program improvement and convey that you work as a team for the benefit of students you serve

---

The foundation for the relationship is often built during the initial orientation. With development of a job description, trust can emerge along with high expectations and mutual support.

Supervisors are ultimately responsible for the actions of paraeducators in the classroom; however, a certain amount of leeway should be granted if the paraeducator has experience or insight into the behavioral or academic interventions that might be most beneficial. The para sometimes has the advantage of more frequent one-on-one contact with the student and may also see the student across different settings and with different teachers. With this additional insight, their ideas might improve effectiveness of the intervention. Ongoing communication, in which the teacher invites the paraeducator to provide input, will validate the para's ideas and knowledge gained from working with particular students in different classroom environments. Paraeducators should have differing assignments and responsibilities based on their experience, training, and confidence level.

The National Resource Center for Paraeducators (NRCP; www.nrcpara.org) has established three levels of responsibilities for paraeducators:

- *Level I* responsibilities include supervising and monitoring students; preparing learning materials; providing personal assistance to students; reinforcing learning experiences that are planned and introduced by teachers; and conducting themselves in a professional and ethical manner.
- *Level II* responsibilities include all Level I responsibilities as well as having more autonomy in delivering lessons developed by the teacher; assisting students in completing projects assigned by the teacher; collecting ongoing assessment data as directed by the teacher; implementing teacher-developed behavior management plans; and participating in regularly scheduled teacher and paraeducator meetings that may include other team members to plan for students in the general education setting.
- *Level III*, the highest level, responsibilities include additional tasks of collaboration and information sharing with teachers for planning purposes; modifying curriculum and instructional activities for individual students under the direction of teachers; and assisting teachers in maintaining student records.

When training paraeducators, Pickett and Gerlach (2003) recommend that a teacher provide a rationale for a given skill or strategy, explain why it is important, and give a clear, step-by-step description. Next, the teacher should demonstrate or model the skill in the setting where the para is to implement it. Then, the teacher should observe the para implementing the procedure, and provide feedback. Finally, the teacher should provide ongoing coaching unobtrusively while the para is working with students.

Matching Paras with Teachers   When initially pairing paras with teachers, it is helpful to openly discuss work style preferences, both of the para and teacher. A number of such informal inventories exist but a supervising teacher can easily develop one like the example in Figure 11.6. This example has questions appropriate for the paraeducator, but the statements could be easily changed to develop a complementary version for the teacher or supervisor to complete. For example, item 2 could be changed from "I like to receive regular corrective feedback" to "I prefer to *give* regular corrective feedback rather than waiting until end-of-semester formal evaluations." Some items, such as 6, "I am a 'detail' person," could appear on both para and supervising teacher's form. Having both the para and teacher complete complementary forms such as this serves as a good discussion starter about work style preferences.

It is unlikely that two people will be a perfect match, and that isn't necessarily the purpose, nor may it even be desirable, but it starts the conversation about how the two can

FIGURE 11.6   Work Style Inventory

	1 – Strongly Disagree to 5 – Strongly Agree				
1. I like to be supervised closely.	1	2	3	4	5
2. I like to receive regular corrective feedback.	1	2	3	4	5
3. I like to have clear guidelines and expectations.	1	2	3	4	5
4. I like to have written instructions when implementing instruction or a behavior plan.	1	2	3	4	5
5. I like to know exactly what I will be doing in advance.	1	2	3	4	5
6. I am a detail person.	1	2	3	4	5
7. I like to provide input regarding students.	1	2	3	4	5
8. I consider myself a very punctual person.	1	2	3	4	5
9. I need a quiet place to work without distractions.	1	2	3	4	5
10. I thrive on having a routine that is followed daily.	1	2	3	4	5
11. I like working with other adults.	1	2	3	4	5
12. I like to have choices in how I work or how I complete a task.	1	2	3	4	5
13. I prefer to be told exactly how to do each task.	1	2	3	4	5
14. I like tasks that require me to be creative.	1	2	3	4	5
15. I think of myself as being spontaneous.	1	2	3	4	5

best work together. When responses on items are in conflict with one another, differences in styles and preferences can be discussed and followed up by discussion of ways to accommodate or work around them. Sometimes opposites work well together when strengths and preferences for different types of tasks can be identified. Recall the discussion in Chapter 3 about the value of differing styles in team situations. A teacher may enjoy the creative aspect of planning and teaching new and interesting lessons but detest the record keeping part of the job. If the para who works with them enjoys tasks of recording student progress on charts and graphs and analyzing the data, then it may seem like a perfect marriage of opposite work styles. On the other hand, if one person is of a type who is neat and tidy and the other is much less so, then sharing a desk could present problems. Knowing these differences from the start can allow each to be a bit more sensitive to the other's style. If sharing a desk is the only option, maybe a compromise of each having a separate drawer and agreeing that shared space will be maintained at a certain level of organization will resolve the difference at a workable level.

With the rapidly increasing cultural and linguistic diversity of students in special education, having diversity among paraeducators who support them is important. Efforts should be made to create a staff of paraeducators who reflect the cultural and linguistic backgrounds of the students. This is especially important in communities where teachers may not be familiar with the culture and versed in the first language of students. Paras often have fulfilled a role very effectively as a community partner and liaison in home–school relationships. They can serve as translators of the culture and language for both educators and families. Hispanic and Native American families especially rely on the interconnectedness of the extended family and informal community-based networks for emotional and social support (Geenen, Powers, & Lopez-Vasquez, 2001). Thus, paras from the community may be able to facilitate meaningful collaboration with culturally and linguistically diverse (CLD) families. Paras who are not familiar with cultural and linguistic diversity should participate in the same relevant staff development and self-assessment as other educators.

District-Level Staff Development for Paras   Although states are required to provide appropriate training, preparation, and supervision for paraeducators, the type and amount of training provided vary from state to state. Lasater, Johnson, and Fitzgerald (2000), using more than twenty-five years of experience as staff developers and data from a nationwide survey validating guidelines on standards and skills required by paraeducators and teachers, recommend conducting needs assessments targeted specifically to para roles and issues. This should be followed by professional development sessions in settings similar to those for training other professionals, with professional credits and stipends provided for attendance. This communicates that paraeducators are valued and important to the instructional process. During these professional development sessions, time should be allocated for questions and discussion of issues.

The ultimate goal of paraeducator staff development is to build a solid knowledge base that reflects students' needs and goals. Finally, remember that paras, like teachers, value information they can take back to the classroom and implement immediately. So the training should be practical and provide alternatives for responding to implementation challenges.

On some occasions, it may be beneficial to have some joint professional development sessions with teacher and para partners. Topics for joint sessions could include exploration of roles and responsibilities, team-building activities, and communication skills. This dual training model not only provides needed information and skills to both teacher and the paraprofessional, but it also has the added benefit of enabling the partners to discuss the information and its application to their unique situation. Finally, remember that no matter how much advance preparation the paraeducator has received, teachers to whom a para is assigned must provide orientation and on-the-job training. The job of the supervising teacher is to provide training that will help the paraeducator function in the specific situation of the assignment.

Yet another option for providing training is to supply written as well as online materials that paras can study independently at a time convenient to them or access on a need-to-know basis. The supervising teacher can create or obtain a guide that can be given to the paraeducator for self-study. One example of such a guide is *Essential Skills for Paras* (Kaff & Dyck, 1999). Topics addressed in this guide include responsibilities of most paraeducators; labels used to categorize students with disabilities; terms and phrases frequently used in schools; a discussion of ethics for paras; basic principles of direct instruction methods; and guidelines for reporting student behavior. Online training modules can serve a similar purpose. For example, paraprofessionals in Nebraska can access the Project PARA: Paraeducator Self-Study Program (http://para.unl.edu/ec) and receive feedback about their performance as they complete each module.

Supervisors should discuss roles, skills, and needed training on an ongoing basis. New federal and state preparation and training requirements for paraeducators have created a need for documenting training and skill-development activities. At the very least, every paraeducator should maintain a file folder documenting the training by means of certificates, transcripts, meeting/training agendas, products, or other evidence of completed activities. If some type of skill inventory has been completed, and training modules are selected and completed based on that inventory, this should be included in the documentation as well. Project PARA: Paraeducator Self-Study Program (http://para.unl.edu/ec) is set up to include eight units of instructional resources for paras, including pretests for self-assessment of skills prior to beginning each unit. After completion of the unit, a post-test is taken. The ParaEducator Learning Network (www.paraeducator.net) is a commercial program used by many districts across the country to provide online training and documentation for paraeducators in a variety of skill areas.

Training Paras to Deliver Instruction   One of the primary instructional roles of paraeducators is carrying out plans developed by the supervising teacher. This instructional role often takes place away from the supervising teacher where direct observation and monitoring is not possible. In light of this, supervising teachers have an obligation to train and prepare their paraeducators adequately for delivering instruction and then provide the necessary supervision to assure it is being delivered as directed. A detailed lesson plan is the first step in clarifying what the teacher wants the para to do during the instructional session. The plan should include the objective(s) of the lesson, materials needed, a step-by-step outline of the activities, description of instructional procedures, reinforcements needed, and data collection, record keeping, and evaluation that will be required. The teacher's lesson plans should be explicit and provide a means for the paraeducator to communicate ongoing student progress and other daily and weekly anecdotal information from which lesson adjustments can be made. In the end, the supervising teacher needs to be informed and connected to each student who is working with a para in order to make knowledgeable and informed decisions about lesson and behavioral intervention plans.

During initial training with paras regarding teaching a lesson written by the teacher, the supervisor should use a sample lesson to explain clearly and demonstrate carefully each step by means of explicit modeling. In addition to the teaching procedures, the supervisor should also point out ways to keep students engaged and how to provide corrective feedback and effectively reinforce positive behavior and student learning. Record-keeping procedures and how to monitor and document student progress should also be discussed.

After describing and modeling the lesson, the teacher should have the para role-play the lesson while the supervisor takes notes and provides feedback. Some teachers who are responsible for supervising several paraprofessionals and/or who routinely have their paras implement specialized-teaching routines, might find it helpful to create some short instructional videos of herself or himself modeling how to teach a lesson (or find a similar, suitable example on the Internet that could be viewed by the para). An advantage of the video option is that a para can watch a video anytime, and the teacher and para don't have to wait until they have mutually shared planning time, another example of the asynchronous benefit of modern technology. Keep in mind that if the video training option is used for the demonstration and model phase, it is still important for the supervising teacher to directly observe the paraeducator practice-teach the lesson and provide feedback before assigning the para to teach a lesson independently.

Strategies for Ongoing Communication with Paraeducators

A variety of ways are available for paras and supervising teachers to communicate; the method chosen will depend on the preferences of those involved. Logistics, access, level of comfort with technology, number of parties involved, caseload, and supervision load are factors and preferences to be considered. As mentioned earlier, some choose to use an ongoing paper-and-pencil log in a student folder in which the paraeducator and teacher can share information such as data on student progress, anecdotal notes, questions about adaptations or adjustments to lessons, and so on. In other situations, a supervisor may have opportunity to touch base with paraeducators and debrief at the beginning or end of the day. Still others may find technology applications helpful for sharing lesson notes, changes in schedules, and other necessary communication. Portable technologies such as tablets can be used to capture on-the-spot notes, which can be downloaded later by the supervising teacher or printed out and placed in a file for the teacher's review. If e-mail is used for communication between the para and teacher, it is important that paraeducators are informed about issues of confidentiality and how e-mail should and should not be used. Some teachers and paras have found that text messaging with cell phones is an unobtrusive way to send a quick message about an unexpected change in the schedule, or to alert the teacher to a problem that needs immediate attention, or to ask a quick question of the para or teacher. The use of cell phones in schools, whether for sending a text message, making or receiving phone calls, or reading e-mails, can be convenient for a variety of purposes that would otherwise be much more difficult or time-consuming. But, when cell phones are used, there is a risk that they will be used inappropriately. If overused, cell phones could become a distraction and be counterproductive. Teachers should talk to paras upfront about whether cell phones are an appropriate way to communicate with each other and, if so, set clear guidelines for their use.

Need for Confidentiality by the Paraeducator

The Council for Exceptional Children (CEC) has published standards for paraprofessionals working in special education, and the National Resource Center for Paraprofessionals (NRCP) also provides standards for knowledge that paraeducators are expected to possess if they work in special education programs. One of the CEC standards for paraprofessionals specifically addresses professional and ethical practice. It includes knowledge about ethical practices for confidential communication and kinds of biases and differences that affect one's ability to work with others. Because there is no single professional association for paraeducators, standards such as those proposed by CEC or NRCP are voluntary. No outside agency monitors unprofessional behavior, although school administrators can bring disciplinary action if a paraprofessional acts in a way considered inappropriate by school district standards.

Ashbaker and Morgan (2006) target criteria of professionalism for paraeducators such as dress and appearance, regard for health and safety of students and staff, communication and conflict resolution skills, collaboration with teachers and parents, and confidentiality in the use of information. It is of utmost importance that paraeducators understand the necessity for confidentiality when working with students. Teachers need to impress on paraeducators the importance of keeping confidential and secure any information such as academic achievement, test scores, descriptions of student behavior, attendance, family problems, and other information of a personal nature. Additionally, job descriptions for paraprofessionals should include ethical guidelines in dealing with students, families, and others (Trautman, 2004). A statement such as "Keep information that pertains to school, school personnel, student, and parents or guardians confidential" could be printed and placed on the cover of notebooks with student information, at the top or bottom of a memo pad used to communicate with staff, or as part of one's signature line on outgoing e-mails. This serves as a polite yet constant reminder about the confidentiality and ethical behavior related to their role and sensitive information. Paras should be directed to take any concerns they have directly to the supervising teacher rather than sharing those concerns with others. Figure 11.7 offers a dozen tips for carrying out paraprofessional duties in an ethical manner. This list should be shared on the first day with a new para, provided on a handout for the para's notebook, and revisited often at conference time or when needed.

When a teacher is absent and a substitute teacher is called in, confidentiality can be a concern if teachers have failed to plan ahead for ensuring para confidentiality (Fleury, 2000). Teachers will want to discuss with paras at the beginning of the year the possibility

FIGURE 11.7   A Dozen Tips for Carrying Out Paraprofessional Duties in an Ethical Manner

As a member of the educational team, you are expected to carry out your paraprofessional role with high ethical standards. You will be handling confidential information and need to act in an ethical manner in difficult situations. Use this information to guide your actions.

1. Read the district's paraprofessional handbook and school policy manual and follow the guidelines.
2. Only perform instructional and noninstructional activities for which you are qualified or have been trained. (If you do not feel you have the skills to perform a duty that has been assigned to you, you should tell your supervising teacher and seek needed training.)
3. Do not share confidential student information.
4. Do not engage in inappropriate conversations about students or staff.
5. Always follow the directions of your supervisor who bears the ultimate responsibility for managing instruction and behavior of students.
6. Any information about a student should only be shared with a parent when the supervising teacher is present. It is not the role of the paraprofessional to share student progress information, test results, behavior concerns, or any other similar type of information.
7. Respect the dignity and privacy of all students, families, and staff members.
8. Do not engage in discriminatory practices based on the student's race, disability, gender, cultural background, sexual orientation, or religion.
9. School matters and problems should only be discussed while on duty during the school day and with the appropriate personnel. Coffee shops, gyms, restaurants, sporting events, the family dinner table, and other social functions are not appropriate venues to share information that must be kept confidential.
10. Always present yourself as a positive adult role model to students and represent the school, its staff and programs in a positive light.
11. Respect the teacher as your supervisor. Follow the lessons and programs designed by the teacher. Discuss concerns involving teaching methods or other classroom issues directly with the teacher. If the issue is not resolved, then discuss your concerns only with your supervisor. Don't talk about it to other paras, parents, or teachers.
12. If issues arise regarding students, family members, or staff such as other paraeducators, only discuss them with your supervisor. If the issue is not resolved, follow the proper grievance procedures outlined by your district.

of teacher absence and of having a substitute teacher for a period of time. A teacher should provide guidelines on maintaining confidentiality in the presence of the substitute teacher and knowing the parameters for sharing information with the substitute only when it is absolutely needed. The para's role in the presence of a substitute teacher should be discussed. Many teachers have substitute-teacher notes or a special folder with basic information for the substitute that includes the schedules of the paras and the duties and assignments they perform throughout the day. Finally, teachers should convey in their notes to the substitute teacher, how the paras can assist in maintaining the daily routine of the classroom, a concern that is so important for the students *and* their teacher.

Sometimes it is the paraeducator who will be absent and, again, advance planning for an unexpected or even a planned absence can go a long way in making for a smooth transition when a substitute assistant is called in (Fleury, 2000). Ideally, it is less complicated when the substitute is familiar with the program and students, and has filled in before for an absent teacher or para. These subs may be at the top of the "substitute call list." But it is not wise to assume that the person substituting understands issues of confidentiality. Those should be discussed at the beginning of the day. Much like a plan prepared for a substitute teacher, it is helpful to have a similar plan on file should the para be absent. This would include the para's schedule, a brief overview of specific methods or reinforcers used with students, and classroom management routines. It is important to be class specific, not child specific, at this time. If the absent para was assigned to a student with unpredictable behavior, consider reassigning that student temporarily to someone who knows the student. Encourage the substitute to ask questions about your teaching methods or behavior management tools, but be aware that sometimes you will not be able to fully answer the question because of the need to preserve confidentiality.

FRAMEWORK FOR WORKING WITH PARAEDUCATORS

Para supervision requires skills beyond consulting, collaborating, or teaching. The supervisor is responsible for the para's actions and the para is accountable to the supervisor. Whereas collaborating teachers mutually develop a teaching plan, the supervisor will tell the para what parts of the developed plan to implement. Most paraeducators are assigned to one supervising teacher who is responsible for planning what paraeducators should do from day to day, and for scheduling where and when the paras will do it, as well as communicating this information to others.

French (2000) suggests a number of practical ways a supervising teacher can select classroom tasks for delegating to a paraeducator. She describes delegation as getting things done through another who has been trained to handle them, by giving that person authority to do it but not giving up teacher responsibility. Selection of the task is determined by considering it in the light of time sensitivity and the consequences of *not* doing it. A task that needs to be done soon and that has major consequences should *not* be delegated. Such tasks include student behavior crises, meetings regarding the crises, student health crises, and monitoring of students in nonclassroom settings. Tasks that are not time sensitive but have major consequences also should not be delegated. This might include such things as designing individual behavior plans, assessing student progress, developing curriculum, and planning instruction.

The following steps can be helpful in deciding what can be delegated to paras and how to set up the delegated tasks for successful completion:

1. Analyze the task, and if it can be delegated, identify the steps it contains.
2. Decide what to delegate, keeping in mind the skills and preferences of those involved.
3. Create a plan that specifies the purpose of the task, how to do it, and criteria for successful completion.
4. If more than one para is available, match para skill sets to the task at hand and choose the best person for the job.
5. Make yourself available to answer questions and provide clarification.
6. Monitor performance without hovering over the para. When the task is complete, acknowledge the para's efforts and reinforce the good work. Be tolerant of the reality that the para may not do some things exactly as you would have done them.

Special educators responsible for supervising paras need to define clearly and monitor carefully the paras' responsibilities. Breton (2010) points out that the least professionally qualified individuals, the paraprofessionals, often have primary responsibilities for teaching students who present the greatest academic and behavioral challenges. "Too often students with disabilities are placed in general education classrooms without clear expectations established among the team members regarding which professional staff will plan, implement, monitor, evaluate, and adjust instruction" (Giangreco, Edelman, Luiselli, & MacFarland, 1997, p. 15). These researchers suggest assigning paras as classroom assistants rather than as assistants for single students. They note that if co-teachers fail to plan instruction, the responsibility often falls on the para, which is clearly beyond reasonable expectation for them. Others recommend ongoing collaborative meetings for sharing expertise areas and for discussing and clarifying areas of responsibility, including strategies and a plan for "fading" the level of support provided by the paraeducator (Marks et al., 1999).

Sometimes paras inappropriately take the students in their charge away from the general classroom group (Giangreco et al., 1997). Paras must be instructed that students are to be physically, programmatically, and interactionally included in classroom activities planned by qualified teachers. To help instill this awareness, teachers need to make sure they consider the para's role when co-planning lessons, and whenever possible include the para in the planning process.

REFLECTION 11.1

Clarifying the Para Assistant Role

Jane is one of three paras assigned to Martin, a teacher of students with behavior disorders. Jane is an experienced para and has clear notions of what she should do in the inclusive classroom where Martin has assigned her. Martin told Jane simply to be in the classroom to intervene whenever a particular student, Bart, gets off task or refuses to do work. She is not to help him with his work, but only to take steps to keep him "under control." Jane doesn't think that is a good use of her time. She wants to help this student and others who might be having difficulty with the assignment. She thinks she should help clarify confusing information and outline class lectures on the chalkboard as she did in the previous school where she was assigned. Is it appropriate for Martin to have these somewhat limited expectations for Jane even when she isn't pleased about it? Does the classroom teacher have a voice in this? How could this conflict be addressed?

Managing Schedules and Time   Challenges of arranging consultant and co-teaching schedules are magnified when several paraeducators are part of the scheduling demands. Because schedules are likely to change from week to week, it is helpful for everyone to have a schedule each week that indicates who does what, when, and where. The schedule should be available to all special service staff and the building office personnel.

The challenge of finding time to plan and discuss student needs with a para mirrors the issues of time discussed elsewhere for collaborating teachers. Teachers and paras in self-contained special classes may have break periods at the same time, but that is not likely when the para is working in a different classroom, as is often the case in inclusive schools. In an ideal situation at least twenty minutes a day is set aside for para–supervisor planning.

The more individuals with whom a para works, the more complex the supervision process is. When paras are in the general classroom most of the school day, classroom teachers must also be in a supervisory role for them. If communication processes among all parties are open and ongoing, this arrangement can work well. Sometimes, however, much confusion can occur.

It is one thing to plan for oneself and quite another to organize and plan for another person such as a paraeducator. French (1997) provides several examples of forms teachers can use to plan for paras. Another type of plan would be a daily schedule that would list all time periods through the day, where the para is to be during each time period (e.g., "room 25" or "the work room"), and what activity or responsibility the para will have (such as co-teach the group with Martin or adapt the textbook for student Willy). Plans of this nature can be printed on paper or shared in a web-based format using free and accessible web-sharing tools such as Google Docs, where the paraeducator and professional can easily add comments and provide feedback to one another.

Another challenging part of supervising paras will be to determine *when* the supervisory responsibilities will be performed. Teachers who oversee paras must carve time out of their day to plan, schedule, and develop teaching activities for the paraeducator to implement with students. Additional time will be needed to train the para in how to deliver the plans effectively. This can be best described as on-the-job training, coaching, and feedback. According to French (1997), "Teachers who fail to spend outside time for planning, training, coaching, and feedback with paraeducators report that they are dissatisfied with the performance of the paraeducators with whom they work" (p. 73).

Examples of other information to provide the paraeducator are:

- A copy of school handbook(s) providing school policies and regulations
- Information about the students included in one's caseload
- Teachers' guides for instructional materials that will be used
- First aid information
- Emergency information, such as locations of storm shelters
- Classroom rules and other expectations for classroom management

- Behavior management guidelines for specific students
- Procedures for accessing media and checking out materials

Although supervising teachers are responsible for planning carefully and communicating responsibilities to paraeducators, it will not always happen. As part of the orientation and training of paras, it is good to remind them that not every situation they will encounter can be anticipated or clearly spelled out as to what they should do. There will not always be time to read the handbook (such as when a major storm is imminent). There will be times when they are uncertain about their responsibilities and the best advice you can give is to use common sense (Kaff & Dyck, 1999). Of course, they should be reminded to always request details about their designated tasks and to practice good communication skills, but when uncertainties arise, they may have to rely on their best judgment of what their cooperating teacher or supervisor would want them to do under the circumstances.

Evaluating the Paraeducator–Teacher Relationship

Extensive use of paraeducators has changed the role of teachers. Supervising and directing the work of paraeducators is now added to the teacher's role. According to French (1999), "Even though teachers are no longer solely responsible for providing instruction, they remain wholly accountable for the outcomes of the instructional process" (p. 70).

Teachers may find evaluating paras neither easy nor particularly pleasant, especially when performance is substandard. However, the task may be made less discomforting by following three suggestions:

1. *Be clear and concise in telling paras exactly what you expect.* Preparing job descriptions will get you off to a good start. Say "When you help co-teach in science, please refrain from responding to questions, and show the student instead how to find answers in the textbook or other resource materials" rather than "Would you please help students in the science class during study time?"
2. *Tell paras what you like about the way they do their jobs.* Everyone likes to have good performance acknowledged.
3. *Tell paras if there are things that they are not doing well.* Talking about what you don't like as well as what you do like is not only a teacher's responsibility, it also shows you care about the personal relationship. Many teachers do not feel comfortable talking about problems, so they dodge around troublesome issues far too long. But constructive feedback gives you and the para a chance to work out differences and misunderstandings. (Recall that Chapter 7 provided material to help with communication in sensitive areas.) If your paras see you engage in self-evaluation of your own teaching through video recording and analysis or even informal debriefing immediately after teaching a lesson, then they will view the self-analysis as an expected part of teaching and not punitive when they are asked to do it as they teach a lesson. You can also model this behavior by sitting down with paras and looking over student progress data, analyzing how, for example, you could change the level of corrective feedback during your lesson to see if it will have a positive impact on student performance.

Feedback should relate to the task or action, not the person. The tone should be objective and not blaming. Keep the focus on what you can do to improve student outcomes. Also, give feedback sooner than later. If too much time passes, it won't be as meaningful and or as likely to be incorporated because the opportunity will have passed. If the feedback is at all personal or could be perceived as negative, be sure to choose an appropriate place and time and make sure it is done privately. Some examples of how the feedback might be given include:

- Start by describing the context: "I'd like to talk with you about what happened when you were in Ms. Winkler's room helping Davis and other students during the math lesson earlier today."
- Describe your reactions and reasons: "I noticed that some of the students who sit near Davis seemed distracted by your conversation with him and sometimes seem to struggle to see the teacher working the problems on the board because of where you were standing next to Davis when helping him."
- Ask for the change you'd like to see: "It might work better for you to let Ms. Winkler finish the lesson before you start assisting Davis with the assigned problems. Maybe you could discuss moving Davis's seat to a place where it would be less distracting to other students when you are helping him."
- Allow time for the other person to respond.

It is never easy to discuss problems. If a problem is of a more personal or difficult nature than the example here, consider planning out what you will say and rehearse it before you meet with the para. Remember, you can only control what *you* say and what *you* do. You cannot control the other person.

A supervising teacher should listen to the para's input and suggestions that result from his or her observations and knowledge of the students. It is important to learn what is happening to and for the students assigned to the para's responsibility. Sometimes the paraeducator is the only adult who observes what a student does during a particular activity. The para's observations and the way these are communicated to the supervising teacher are important factors in the decisions that will be made about that student. The supervising teacher should direct the para to report outcomes related to specific goals and objectives on students' IEPs, such as learning outcomes, specific behaviors, and relationships with others. Ask the para to provide information to answer the following questions:

- What was the event?
- Who was there?
- When did it take place?
- Where did it take place?
- What was going on before the event?
- How did the event take place? (What was said or done by all those mentioned in "Who" above?)
- What was the outcome (the natural consequence) of your intervention?

Caution the paraeducator to avoid interpreting, judging, labeling, speculating about the student's motives, dwelling on covert behaviors, or making judgments about feelings.

Ask for only the facts and get them written out if at all possible. Once again, it is important to remember that paraprofessionals don't walk into the job having been trained in how to describe behavior objectively. Share some examples of poor interpretations of behavior (for example, "He was daydreaming.") as compared to more objective behavioral descriptions that would be more suitable for documenting student behaviors (such as, "He stared at the bulletin board with a blank look on his face for three minutes."). Figure 11.8 provides a checklist that may be useful in guiding evaluation before or after instructional activities.

Paraeducators, according to Ernsperger (1998), can play key roles in helping students avoid going to or have a smoother return from more restrictive settings. However, to maximize the effectiveness of paraeducators specifically and special education in general, consultants and teacher teams should be keenly aware of the need for well-designed preparation programs, role clarification, appropriate supervision, and adequate compensation for their work.

FIGURE 11.8   Paraeducator Teaching Checklist

Ask yourself the following questions before and after teaching students. Identify those areas in need of improvement. Reward yourself for areas well done.

Getting Ready to Teach

Do I know the special instructional needs of all the students I will be teaching?
Is the teaching environment comfortable with no distractions?
Do I have all the necessary materials for this lesson?
Have I asked the teacher to clarify any parts of the lesson I do not understand?
Have I adapted material if needed?
Do I know the content I am preparing to teach?
Am I prepared to use at least three different activities related to the lesson goal?

While You Are Teaching

Do I take a few moments to establish rapport with students each time?
Have I verbally cued students to attend before starting the lesson (for example, "Eyes up here")?
Are my instructions concise and clear?
Have I reviewed relevant past learning?
Is the lesson goal clear to me and my students?
Have I modeled a skill when appropriate?
Do I keep the student(s) engaged in the task at least 70% of the time?
Do I ask questions of selected students by name instead of calling on volunteers?
Do I provide praise for effort?
Do I give brief, immediate, corrective feedback to the student who errs?
Does every student have an opportunity to respond many times during the lesson?
Do I provide questions and cues to help students use what they already know to discover new
   information?
Do students respond correctly 80–90% of the time?
Do I check for skill mastery before closing the lesson?
Do I change activities when it is clear a student is experiencing frustration?
Do I keep the lesson interesting by changing activities?
Am I using rewards for individual students correctly as instructed by my supervising teacher?

Giangreco, Edelman, Broer, and Doyle (2001) suggest that education teams or schools strengthen paraprofessional support by examining their own status and priority needs and take constructive action to improve. This assessment could begin, the researchers suggest, with an examination of issues they noted in their extensive review of the literature, including acknowledging paraprofessional work, orientation and training; hiring and assigning, interactions with students and staff, roles and responsibilities, and supervision and evaluation. Carrying out the assessment of progress with issues such as these may be part of the special education administrator's role or it may be a responsibility of the school administrator.

CASE STUDY: SUPERVISING PARAEDUCATORS

Recall that in Vignette 11, Jackie wanted to try some new ways of doing things with her paraeducators. She had been exposed to some teaching methods and routines in her special education intervention courses that she thought would work well with some of the students. She was also noticing that the paras seemed to be in close proximity at all times to students they were supporting in the classroom. She knew from discussions in her university program that this could have a detrimental effect on students making friends and learning to advocate for themselves with regard to their needed educational accommodations. Of even greater concern to Jackie was that the paraeducators appeared to be taking over the instructional responsibilities for these students and the teachers appeared to be hosting rather than teaching these students.

In light of these observations, Jackie decided to assign some of the paras to different classrooms, partly to discourage students (and teachers) from developing too much dependency on one particular para. She thought that many of the teachers were getting a little too comfortable in letting the paras take responsibility for the students they were there to support. Things did not go well. The paras were visibly angry with her and she learned from another teacher that they were talking about her behind her back and even calling her teaching abilities into question. She suspected that a few teachers did not like the changes she had made.

In addition to reassigning the paras, Jackie tried to implement a communication system that would provide her with daily reports from the paras, including what happened in the classrooms each day and data that monitored student progress. She did this by asking each para to keep a daily log as they worked with students and return it to her at the end of the day. She also wanted to begin weekly debriefings and training meetings with all her paras to start training them in the skills they would need to implement the new teaching routines.

Much to Jackie's disappointment, the logs were often incomplete and poorly written. When Jackie asked one of the paras to improve the quality of her logs, the para said it seemed pointless to have to write everything out that she already knew in her head. It didn't stop there. The paras found excuses to miss the weekly meetings or seemed disinterested in what Jackie was sharing. One even went as far as texting on her cell phone while attending one of the meetings. Jackie felt intimidated by a couple of the paras who were old enough to be her mother and felt they knew better than she what the students needed. She knew the district para evaluations would be due at the end of the semester and she was not looking forward to that task.

- Where did Jackie go wrong?
- What would you have done differently at different points along the way to avoid where she ended up?

- Does Jackie share all of the blame?
- What behaviors did the paras engage in that might be considered unethical?
- Are the classroom teachers responsible in any way?
- Can the situation be fixed? If you were in Jackie's shoes, what would you do now? What tools or strategies have you learned about in the chapter that will help you avoid a similar situation?

TECHNOLOGY FOR SUPERVISING AND COMMUNICATING WITH PARAEDUCATORS

Just as teachers have needed to become tech savvy in multiple areas, so, too, must paraeducators. This includes utilizing technologies to aid in the delivery of instruction, being able to capture behavior for later review and analysis, making record-keeping tasks easier, becoming knowledgeable about assistive technology devices and how to match them with students, and finally, using technology to work smarter, not harder, to connect with others in new and innovative ways. As special education teachers become responsible for overseeing more and more paraprofessionals, two of the greatest challenges will be management of multiple paraeducators and efficient and effective communication between paras and their supervising teachers.

A cell phone and text messaging can be helpful tools when used by a teacher or para to alert the other about a change in the schedule or an emergency situation where help is needed. Using electronic note-taking devices as a way to reflect on a lesson quickly or record student data efficiently can make sharing of information much faster and easier. This can be done either using a basic tablet primarily as a word processing or data-capturing device or some schools might have access to a more sophisticated electronic tablet such as an iPad that can serve multiple functions with specialized apps for instruction, productivity, assistive technology, augmentative communication, and many functions that have yet to be developed but are limited only by our imagination.

When a student comes into a general education classroom with specialized equipment and assistive technology, the teacher might feel overwhelmed and wonder how to carve out time to learn how to use the specialized equipment. This is an area where a para can be helpful. A paraprofessional can learn about a device or an application and help with integrating it into a useful place in the classroom. The para can show the teacher some of the basic functions and capabilities and they can work together to maximize its capabilities in that setting. The para might also use technology to adapt materials for the teacher to use web-based file sharing applications for sending lesson plans or tests back-and-forth to make necessary adaptations and modifications.

Technology can be a valuable tool when a para is asked to collect student behavior data or to video record some examples of baseline behavior and then use periodic video captures to document progress and the effectiveness of an intervention or behavior plan. A supervising teacher may video mini training lessons and archive them on a webpage for paras to access when they need to learn a new skill or learn how to implement something directed by the teacher. This makes the problem of finding time for the para and supervising teacher to meet for training a nonissue. Paraeducators often receive an extensive amount of their training and required staff development through sophisticated and comprehensive paraprofessional online training modules. Supervising teachers should have a basic understanding of what type of training paras are receiving in such online training modules and may even help guide the paraeducator in selecting modules that will be most beneficial to the para's role.

ETHICAL CONSIDERATIONS WHEN UTILIZING PARAEDUCATORS

Five areas in which it is important for paraeducators and their supervising teachers to create an ethical climate for students and school personnel are the para role, responsibilities in that role, relationships with students and parents, relationships with teachers, and relationships within the school. Confidentiality of information and rights of privacy for students and families are especially important. Paraeducators should be encouraged to carry out their paraprofessional duties in an ethical way by reviewing ones such as those in Figure 11.7. Regular review of a list like this will allow them to continue monitoring their performance and to develop in these vital areas.

With the increasing utilization of paraeducators, we must ask ourselves what we want from special educators in inclusion-oriented schools. Do we want our special education teachers to be managers of paraeducators who provide the bulk of specialized instruction to students with disabilities? Or do we want special education teachers spending more time directly teaching students with IEPs and co-teaching with general education teachers? Giangreco and Broer (2005) reported that special education teachers spend a significantly smaller percentage of time on instruction than do the paras they supervise. It raises a question about the quality of instruction these students are receiving, especially in the age of mandates for having highly qualified teachers work directly with students. If the tables were turned and we were doing this in general education, would it be accepted as good practice? What is a reasonable number of paraprofessionals for a single special educator to direct and supervise without tipping the scale of reasonableness? The Bright Futures Report (Kozleski, Mainzer, & Deshler, 2000) listed the relatively small percentage of time special educators spent in instruction as being one of the key contributing factors to explain why many special education teachers say they are leaving the field. Like other teachers, they went into special education to teach and work with students with special needs directly, not to be paper pushers and supervisors for other adults who teach for them.

Another ethical concern that warrants further scrutiny is the alarming number, over half, of all special education paraprofessionals, who are assigned to students on a one-to-one basis (Suter & Giangreco, 2009). Broer et al. (2005) reported the potential detrimental effects (for example, stigmatization, isolation, lack of friendships, over-dependency on the para, disenfranchisement) of having individual paras assigned one-to-one with students. Often, these one-on-one paras are described by their former students as being unnecessarily motherly or parental. At the very least we need to consider-alternatives to our current utilization of paraprofessionals and explore other options for providing students with the supports they need to be successful in inclusion-oriented schools.

TIPS FOR COLLABORATION WITH PARAPROFESSIONALS

1. Discuss the school district's mission statement, your building(s) philosophy, and your own teaching philosophy and values with the paraeducators assigned to you before they begin working with you and the students.

2. Visit other schools where there are clear procedures for scheduling, directing, super-
    vising, and evaluating the work of paraeducators. Implement practices that are prom-
    ising for your school setting.
3. Encourage paras to share their ideas on student behavior and learning, and incorpo-
    rate those ideas into the instructional plan when appropriate. (See Figure 11.9.)
4. Give frequent constructive feedback. Simple statements like "You did a great job
    modeling how you find the main idea" and "Maybe he would perform better if you
    changed the order and put his favorite task after a less favored task" are important
    communication examples to express to the paraprofessional.
5. Be aware of how you communicate. Different approaches work better with different
    people. Avoid personal attacks or put-downs, and make every attempt to ensure that
    you are conveying information in your para's preferred communication style.
6. Introduce family members to the paraeducators who will work with their child.

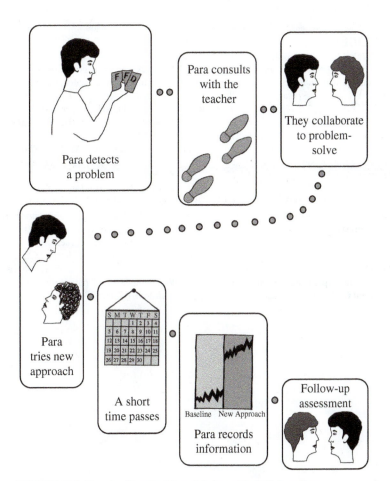

FIGURE 11.9 Step-by-Step Problem-Solving with Collaboration

7. When a para asks for advice, first ask what the para has observed. This gets the para involved and encourages active participation in observing students, deciding on a plan, and implementing that plan.

8. Advocate for well-designed, well-conducted, and carefully evaluated staff development activities prepared specifically for paraeducators, and help them take place, if possible.

9. Discuss ethical standards with your paras on a frequent basis by first providing staff development on confidentiality and ethical behavior for paraprofessionals. Provide examples of applications that are as close as possible to what the para might experience on the job.

10. Practice the adage we all learned as children: "If you can't say something nice (respectful, appreciative, supportive) about a colleague or student or family, then say nothing at all."

ADDITIONAL RESOURCES

Broer, S. M., Doyle, M. B., & Giangreco, M. F. (2005). Perspectives of students with intellectual disabilities about their experiences with paraprofessional support. *Exceptional Children, 71,* 415–430.

Devlin, P. (2008). Create effective teacher–paraprofessional teams. *Intervention in School and Clinic, 44*(1), 41–44.

French, N. K. (2000). Taking time to save time: Delegating to paraeducators. *Teaching Exceptional Children, 32*(3), 79–83.

Giangreco, M. F., & Broer, S. M. (2005). Questionable utilization of paraprofessionals in inclusive schools: Are we addressing symptoms or causes? *Focus on Autism and Other Developmental Disabilities, 20*(1), 10–26.

Mueller, P. H., & Murphy, F. V. (2001). Determining when a student requires paraeducator support. *Teaching Exceptional Children, 33*(6), 22–27.

Outlines a process that helps IEP teams determine when to assign paraeducators to support students with disabilities.

Riggs, C. G. (2001). Ask the paraprofessionals: What are your training needs? *Teaching Exceptional Children, 33*(3), 78–83.

Suter, J. C., & Giangreco, M. F. (2009). Numbers that count: Exploring special education and paraprofessional service delivery in inclusion-oriented schools. *The Journal of Special Education, 43*(2), 81–93.

Thurston, L. P. (2000). *The positive para: Helping students develop positive social skills.* Lawrence, KS: Curriculum Solutions, Inc.

Wallace, T., Shin, J., Bartholomay, T., & Stahl, B. J. (2001). Knowledge and skills for teachers supervising the work of paraprofessionals. *Exceptional Children, 67*(4), 520–533.

12

Evaluation of Collaborative School Consultation

WHY DO COLLABORATIVE SCHOOL CONSULTANTS NEED TO KNOW ABOUT EVALUATION? Why should collaborative school consultation (CSC) programs and activities be evaluated? What are the benefits of evaluating collaborative activities? In this age of heightened accountability and data-based decisions making, evaluation of educational activities has become increasingly important. Here are some examples of how the practice of evaluation (see shaded triangle in Figure 12.1) is used in school settings:

■ The school district received a year of funding from the state library to develop a parent-teacher center for families of children with disabilities. Future funding for the center depends on evidence that the center is having a positive impact on children, parents, siblings, and neighborhoods. An evaluation of the program can provide evidence needed to receive further funding.

■ The local school board wants useful information in order to make a decision to continue, eliminate, or expand the school's after-school bilingual special education program.

■ Every year the theater department of the local community college works with all fifth-graders and their parents to write and produce a play based on current events. Special education teachers and general education teachers work collaboratively with the theater department for this activity. There is a new chairperson of the theater department, and she wants to know if the project is worth all the time and effort her students and faculty put into this joint effort.

■ Co-teaching in the school district's inclusive classrooms takes time and energy. With all the mandated testing and programs, the middle school principal wants to know if co-teaching is worthwhile. Program evaluation will help the principal and others make decisions about staffing integrated classrooms.

Evaluation is particularly important for programs in which there is a strong focus on process skills and outcomes that can affect students in profound ways. Consultants cannot know if consultation activities are effective unless they conduct evaluation; administrators and policymakers are not eager to support programs for which there are no meaningful data. Engaging in an ongoing systematic evaluation is the best way to be more confident that appropriate decisions are made.

FOCUSING QUESTIONS

1. Why is evaluation important for collaborative school consultation in educational and community settings?

2. What are some important considerations for consultants when they work with colleagues to evaluate collaborative activities for students with special needs?

3. What are key steps in designing and implementing evaluation of collaborative school consultation programs and activities?

4. How can consultants use self-assessment to improve their skills?

5. What is the role of the consultant in large-scale program evaluation in school and community settings?

6. What are useful technological tools and important ethical issues inherent in the evaluation of collaborative consultation in schools?

KEY TERMS

evaluation	impact	stakeholder
formative evaluation	self-assessment	summative evaluation

VIGNETTE 12

The setting is the conference room of a special education program office where the superintendent, Ms. Tolavar, the director of special education, Mr. Ramirez, and a parent, Mrs. James, who represents the Special Education Advisory Group, are seated. The Advisory Group is a group of parents, community members and advocates who have an interest in the special education programs in the school district.

Superintendent: Mrs. James, I have asked Mr. Ramirez, our director of special education to meet with us today to help address your questions. I've explained to him that you are here representing the Advisory Group and that the group is concerned about the alterations we have made in our special education programs in the district.

Parent: That's an adequate summary. The focus on the consulting model of providing special education services is confusing to many of us who remember the progress our children made when they were in small classrooms with one or two teachers and a low student-teacher ratio. Others in the group are wondering how this consulting program affects the other children. Questions about the special education program have come up at several of our meetings and I told the group I would try to get more information about the results of the program from you. We would like evidence that this indirect way of educating students with special needs, using teachers who collaborate and students who tutor other students, is the right way to educate children who have learning problems.

Superintendent: Mr. Rameriz, do you have data that we can show Mrs. James about the impact of the special program?

Director of Special Education: Yes, I could get some test scores and observational summaries from teachers' consulting logs and their portfolios. These data do not fully address your request, however. Our collaborative consultation program is rather new. Most of us believe it is already producing some positive outcomes, but we realize we must provide better documentation of the results. We are starting to plan for a structured program evaluation to get the appropriate data for assessing our results and communicating them to parents and other stakeholders.

Superintendent: I regret we do not have a full range of data about the impacts of our program at this time, Mrs. James. The Advisory Group is important to us in the evaluation process. After we do some further work on this topic, may we call on *you* to collaborate with *us* on developing a more specific plan? We really would like for you and others in the group to be involved. You are stakeholders in the program and the results we hope it provides. Your input will help us improve the program for your daughter and other students as well.

THE ROLE OF EVALUATION IN COLLABORATIVE SCHOOL CONSULTATION

Evaluation is a complex endeavor. The American Evaluation Association (www.eval.org) includes thousands of members who focus on the evaluation of widely varying activities such as school and community programs, federal policies, health related programs, environmental issues, and international development. It seems that everybody is interested in evaluation because everybody wants to know "What works?" or "Am I getting my money's worth or taxpayers' money's worth from this public program?" or "How do we strengthen this program so it really makes a difference for the academic success of students with disabilities?" All these are questions that can be answered by evaluators, using rigorous and appropriate methods. Collaborative consultants in school settings typically are not professional evaluators and are not expected to have the skills of a professional evaluator. However, consultants for educational programs should have a basic knowledge of evaluation; they may be called upon to conduct simple evaluations of collaborative efforts, to work collaboratively with evaluators, or to be one of the many partners in large evaluations that involve services to students with special needs and their families. In considering the evaluation of CSC processes, activities, and programs, several questions must be answered:

1. What is evaluation?
2. Who cares about evaluation?
3. What are the purposes of evaluation?
4. What types of evaluations are used for CSC activities and programs?

What Is Evaluation?

Evaluation is a hot topic these days. Everybody wants to know the value of programs, products, and portfolios. In general, evaluation involves fixing a value or determining the worth of something. In most education settings, evaluation relates to determining the worth of an educational program such as an IEP, a peer-tutoring program, an after-school program, a co-teaching arrangement, or a family involvement program.

Program evaluation is defined here as an activity directed at collecting, analyzing, interpreting, and communicating information about the workings and effectiveness of designated educational programs (Rossi, Lipsey, & Freeman, 2004). Evaluation of collaborative activities and programs is important for three reasons:

1. If the program is to be continued as an item in the school district budget, and if it is to be funded and staffed adequately, school administrators need to know about the impact of the program.
2. School personnel will want to know whether their hard work is paying off. They will want to continue successful practices and discontinue or modify activities that do not have an impact. Thus, evaluation data will help to make continuous improvement in the program.
3. Evaluation results are an excellent source of information for explaining, validating, and providing accountability for collaborative consultation programs and efforts. Evaluation results provide justification for the time used to invest in these kinds of efforts. This is especially important when some are skeptical about indirect services and are pushing for more direct services to students with exceptional learning needs.

A school or district may have an assigned evaluator whose job is to assess programs and activities within the school. Local universities may have faculty or graduate students who can assist in evaluation activities. Whether schools are working with outside professional evaluators or in-district evaluators, the process is a collaborative activity. A good evaluation involves stakeholders in all aspects of program assessment.

Although evaluators and researchers use many of the same methods as researchers, research and evaluation are different in several ways. They have different purposes, different users, a different focus, and different uses for the findings (Preskill & Russ-Eft, 2005). A research question is usually in the form of a hypothesis that is tested; research findings build a knowledge base about specific areas, such as the relationship of socio-economic status to referral for special education services. Research results are published in research journals for other researchers to replicate or for practitioners to use to inform their practice. Evaluators respond to the questions of stakeholders and focus their methodology on answering those questions, such as investigating the impact of a parent reading program on the literacy achievement of their children. Evaluation findings may be presented in a variety of ways, as discussed later in this chapter. The users of evaluation findings are the stakeholders—funders, educators, parents, students, community members, and others. The resources at the end of this chapter contain much more extensive descriptions of the differences and similarities in research and evaluation.

Who Cares About Evaluation?

Individuals who care about specific evaluations are called *stakeholders*. Stakeholders usually focus on the benefits of a program or activity because their children are involved, their time is involved, or their money is involved. Stakeholders have legitimate reasons for wanting to know if programs are producing the outcomes they expect to see. Stakeholders are involved in the program or are invested in the expected outcomes of the program.

Participatory or collaborative evaluation is organized around a team, usually an evaluator and key stakeholders (Patton, 2008). Stakeholders are other educators, parents, community members, students, and school administrators. In educational settings, stakeholders are directly involved in all phases of the evaluation (Rodriguez-Campos, 2005). The consultant may provide leadership for evaluation, or may simply be a stakeholder who is active in the process. Regardless of the role of the consultant in program evaluation, she or he should be familiar with evaluation designs, methods, and models.

When collaborative consultants organize in leadership roles or as participants on evaluation teams, they should always communicate the purpose and importance of soliciting involvement by all stakeholders, working to establish relationships with them and to achieve buy-in from participants. In fact, many evaluators involve stakeholders at the evaluation design phase of a project and ask them to help design the evaluation questions. For example, if school personnel want parents to believe in the home-tutoring program, they should find out what questions parents have about the program. Then they can design the evaluation to elicit responses for the questions. In interviewing parents or asking teachers to fill out a survey, evaluators should always make sure people know why they are being asked to participate in an evaluation, whether the data will be treated as grouped or individual data, and how the data results will be used.

What Are the Purposes of Evaluation?

In a nutshell, the purpose of evaluation is to answer the questions stakeholders have about a specific activity or program. When planning program evaluation, evaluators need to review the questions they intend to have the evaluation address. These are called the evaluation questions, and they are the basis for all evaluations, from small classroom-based evaluations of activities to large multimillion-dollar evaluations of government programs such as the DARE program.

These questions are usually related to the expectations of school districts, families, communities, or other stakeholders. Questions may address how the program is progressing and what improvements are needed to make it better. Questions may also be about what impact the program is having on participants.

Case Study 1: Who Are Stakeholders and What Do They Want to Know?

Three middle schools in a large city collaborated with two engineering companies and the Engineering Department at the local university to host an engineering summer camp. The goal of this project was to create a residential summer camp for middle school students with disabilities who were interested in taking science and math courses in high school and possibly attending college to major in engineering. The expected outcome for the camp was increased interest and excitement about engineering and technology and the ways it can be used to help individuals, organizations, and society. This camp developed activities to increase academic skills and build self-confidence in the areas of math and science and to promote taking four full years of mathematics in high school. Program activities included hands-on experiential workshops and field trips and exposure to role models (high school students, college students, and scientists with disabilities). Follow-up activities during the school year and outreach to parents were part of the intervention program. School math and science teachers were part of the camp's administrative staff, and they were learning about engineering and career opportunities along with the students. The project was funded by the engineering companies, the university's Department of Engineering, the State Department of Education, and the National Science Foundation.

After you have read this case study, work in teams and discuss the following questions:

1. Who are the stakeholders in the engineering summer camp program?
2. What do you think these stakeholders want to know?
3. What evaluation questions might the stakeholders have?

What Types of Evaluations Are Used for Collaborative School Consultation?

Professional evaluators use many different types of program evaluations and methods (Mertens, 2010; Patton, 2011; Rossi et al., 2004). But most educational program evaluation features the accumulation of information for one of two primary purposes: formative evaluation or summative evaluation.

Formative evaluation provides information for making decisions to modify, change, or refine a program during its implementation. If a program is not producing expected outcomes, then program staff and administrators will need to know that so they can make immediate changes. The process of formative evaluation often points to the need for specific program changes, providing important information for ongoing program improvement. Formative evaluation means continually examining the impact of a program to fine tune it until it reaches the outcomes that are expected. Without formative evaluation, practitioners could spend their time and efforts on programs that are not resulting in changes for students that they expect. Or, educators could keep changing a program that does not even need modification because "it works as it is."

Summative evaluation, on the other hand, provides documentation on attainment of program goals. It is used most often by administrators who are seeking to determine whether a program should be started up, maintained, ended, or chosen to be the one from among several alternatives. Summative evaluation usually includes an assessment of the impact of a program or activity. Can student development be attributed to the program or could the outcomes be the result of some other factor or factors? Summative evaluation may be conducted to determine the collective impact of a project on students, teachers, parents, schools, and communities. Summative evaluation is completed at the end of the program, but utilizes data collected before and during the program. This type of evaluation is expected to provide information about the viability of the program, to test the effectiveness of a completed new program, or to indicate whether a product or process is ready for dissemination or replication. Summative evaluation indicates the short-term and long-term outcomes of the project and should relate program activities to these outcomes.

STEPS IN DESIGNING COLLABORATIVE SCHOOL CONSULTATION EVALUATION

Evaluation should be planned carefully before a project or activity begins. A variety of evaluation designs is available from which evaluators can choose. Consultants for school districts who need to evaluate processes such as collaboration, consultation, and co-teaching typically select a practical action research design in which the practitioner is the researcher, or in this case, the evaluator. Action research is an approach to investigation that enables teachers to find effective solutions to problems they confront in their daily professional activities (Mills, 2010). Stringer (2007) conceptualizes action research as a wheel and considers the process an iterative, or cyclical one, with self-repeating steps. A practitioner starts with a problem and tries out various strategies to solve the problem. Collecting data before and after the application of the problem-solving strategies allows the practitioner to test the impact of the interventions. This aspect of the action research cycle can be used to evaluate CSC processes and activities. So the pre-baseline, intervention, post-baseline approach can be used as a simple evaluation design in classroom or school settings.

Whether the consultant uses an action research model for evaluation or collaborates with a professional evaluator or evaluation team, steps in the process are somewhat similar. The steps are:

1. Describing the purpose of the evaluation
2. Articulating the stakeholders' evaluation questions
3. Articulating the activities of the program
4. Measuring outputs and expected outcomes of an activity
5. Collecting and analyzing data
6. Reporting and using findings

Describing the Purpose of Evaluation

The purpose of evaluation typically is established by those who will use it. Evaluation must be built into the program from the outset. Evaluators should design the evaluation as early as possible so planning and implementation are congruent with expected outcomes. All stakeholders should be involved in a discussion about purposes of the evaluation.

The Logic Model for Evaluation   Educational consultants often find it helpful to develop a logic model as they collaborate with stakeholders about programs involving collaborative efforts on behalf of students with special needs. A *logic model* describes inputs, activities, outputs, and outcomes of an activity or program. (See Figure 12.2.) Many evaluators use a logic model to design their evaluation method and communicate results to stakeholders. Various formats are available for displaying the conceptual logic of a program. A quick web search for logic models will produce many designs and a wealth of information. Some websites have templates for use in developing logic models.

FIGURE 12.2   Logic Model Evaluation Template

RESOURCES	ACTIVITIES	OUTPUTS	SHORT- & LONG-TERM OUTCOMES	IMPACT
In order to accomplish our set of activities we will need the following:	*In order to address our problems or assets we will accomplish the following activities:*	*We expect that once accomplished these activities will produce the following evidence of service delivery:*	*We expect that if accomplished these activities will lead to the following changes in 1–3, then 4–6 years:*	*We expect that if accomplished these activities will lead to the following changes in 7–10 years:*

Source: W. K. Kellogg Foundation. 2004. *Logic Model Development Guide*. Battle Creek, MI: Author. Illustration courtesy of The W. K. Kellogg Foundation, Battle Creek, Michigan.

Whatever logic-model format is used, it will be a systematic way to depict relationships visually among resources for operating the program, activities that have been planned, and outcomes the program is geared to achieve. In addition, a logic model provides stakeholders with a road map that shows the sequence of related events that connects the need for the program to desired outcomes. A logic model can show the relationship between planned work (resources and activities) and intended results (outputs, outcomes, and impact). Figure 12.3 is an example of a hypothetical logic model prepared for a collaborative family–school program of information exchange activities based on activities described by Hughes and Greenhough (2006) in their research about a parent-school partnership program.

In considering a logic model, these definitions are helpful:

- *Activities*—The events, strategies, implementations, workshops, and the like that a project carries out to meet its goals and produce expected changes in participants.
- *Outputs*—Quantitative data or products related to project activities, such as the number of teachers attending a workshop about Universal Design for Learning, the number of parents checking out books from a resource center, the number of students with disabilities taking Advanced Placement courses, hits on a school homework website, or student test scores.
- *Outcomes*—Results of participation in project activities, such as changes in knowledge or attitude, increased use of a specific practice, or improvement in grades.
- *Impact*—Lasting outcomes attributable to the project, such as changes in environmental conditions or the increase in the power of evaluation to promote projects.

Figure 12.3   Logic Model Evaluation Plan for Home-school Collaboration Project

RESOURCES	ACTIVITIES	OUTPUTS	SHORT- & LONG-TERM OUTCOMES	IMPACT
In order to accomplish our set of activities we will need the following:	*In order to address our problems or assets we will accomplish the following activities:*	*We expect that once accomplished these activities will produce the following evidence:*	*We expect that if accomplished these activities will lead to the following changes:*	*We expect that if accomplished these activities will lead to the following impact on home-school collaboration:*
■ Government policies (Every Child Matters: Change for Children) ■ Primary and secondary schools in Bristol and Cardiff ■ Teachers and administrators in target schools ■ Students and parents in target schools ■ Funding of the Home-school Knowledge Exchange (HSKE) Project	■ Video Activity—Video based on literacy teaching to inform parents of new literacy methods used at school and to encourage parents to do literacy activities at home (school-to-home communication). ■ Shoebox Activity—Students filled shoeboxes with items from home that were special to them; contents were used as part of the curriculum across all subjects (home-to-school communication).	■ Feedback from parents ■ Feedback from teachers ■ Demonstrated evidence of teachers' knowledge of out-of-school lives of their students ■ Demonstrated increased parent-child school-related interactions ■ Demonstrated increased parent-teacher interactions	■ Better communication between school and home ■ Increased parental appreciation and support of school learning activities ■ Parents learning about how reading and writing were taught ■ Teachers providing curriculum enrichment that is relevant to students' out-of-school lives ■ Improved trust and mutual understanding between teachers and parents	■ Increased trust between parents and teachers ■ Increased willingness to listen to parents and their priorities ■ Increased parental appreciation of educational methods ■ Increased parental support of school activities ■ Students see link of out-of-school lives with classroom and curriculum ■ Ongoing exchange of "funds of knowledge" between school and home

Source: Based on Hughes, M., & Greenbough, P. (2006). Boxes, bags, and videotape: Enhancing home-school communication through knowledge exchange activities. *Educational Review, 58*(4), 471–487. Illustration courtesy of the W. K. Kellogg Foundation, Battle Creek, Michigan.

Articulating Evaluation Questions of the Stakeholders

Most educational programs are expected to produce changes in one or more of three categories of changes. These expected changes then are articulated as evaluation questions. The three categories, with examples of evaluation questions are:

1. *Awareness, attitudes, knowledge and skills*—Did awareness, attitudes, and/or knowledge change as a result of participation in this activity?
2. *Behaviors, practices, and policies*—What was the impact of the intervention on participants' behaviors?
3. *Environmental, social, economic, or educational system*—In what ways did the school change as a result of the intervention?

REFLECTION 12.1

Identifying Components of a Logic Model for Evaluation

Think about one intervention or activity for improving social or academic outcomes of students with special needs that was designed to broaden participation in scientific careers. Or use one of the four brief examples of how evaluation is used in school settings found at the beginning of this chapter. Then reflect on these questions:

1. What outcomes do you expect after a participant completes the activity?
2. What outcomes will you expect six months after the activity concludes?

Articulating the Activities of the Program Being Evaluated

In planning an intervention and describing the logic of the program, an important step is listing the activities of the program. What is the program going to do to produce the outcomes desired? What activities can improve educational outcomes for students with special needs, provide information or services to parents, or enable teachers or faculty to be successful in working with diverse student populations? These activities are often the first phase in program development; however, they should always be based on the desired changes in student behavior, parent perceptions, or teacher instruction. The first question should be: What changes do we want to see? The second question should be: What will we do to make those changes happen? The answers to this second question are the activities you will facilitate to produce the changes you expect.

ACTION 12.1

Developing Evaluation Questions

A local engineering company and a local state university have teamed up to develop research internships for students with disabilities who show interest and capability for working in an engineering research lab or a science lab at the university during eight weeks in the summer.

Students participating in the internships will be paid a generous stipend and travel or living expenses. Three students in the local high school are going to be part of this program: Graciella, who is visually impaired; MaDawn, who has multiple sclerosis and is in a wheelchair; and Wayne, who has a learning disability.

Gather into groups of five or six. Each person in the group should assume one of the following roles: parent, high school student, pre-engineering or physics teacher, special education teacher, professional engineer, and transition counselor. In your role, think of the outcomes you expect for this summer research experience. Write down the evaluation questions you would have if you were a stakeholder in this program. Compare your questions with those of other "stakeholders" in your group. How are the questions different? Why? What collaboration skills are needed for you to reach consensus on several evaluation questions? Role play the process of agreeing on three or four of the evaluation questions. What was difficult? What was easy?

Measuring Outputs and Expected Outcomes for Activities

When matching expected outcomes with goals and activities of your program, you can expect that each collaborative program will have its own particular goals and specific activities to help meet those goals. Step 4 is to assign specific measurable objectives or outcomes to each program activity. An evaluator then will select or design measures that can do this. For example, stakeholders involved in a tutoring program might want to measure achievement gains for tutees, and perhaps look at subject-matter grades. Self-efficacy, along with attitude toward the subject matter, perceptions of the teacher, and attitudes of the parents might also be outcomes to be measured.

To measure these outcomes, an evaluator might interview students and parents for their thoughts about the impact of the program (see Bodgan & Biklen, 2006 for methodology). Another method might be to survey community volunteer tutors (see Dillman, 2007, for methodology). The evaluation measures may use qualitative methodology (Bodgan & Biklen, 2006; Patton, 2008), quantitative methodology (Posavac & Carey, 2006), or mixed methods (Creswell & Plano-Clark, 2006; Mertens, 2010). Examples of quantitative data are surveys, enrollment figures, attendance figures, dropout rates, and test scores. Qualitative methods include interviews, focus groups discussions, checklists, rubric scores, and open-ended survey questions.

The evaluation should include a variety of measures to document achievement of each program objective. Many different sources of information should be used, including but not limited to:

- Direct observations of behavior
- Long-term projects
- Parent input
- Student self-assessment records
- Logs and journals of consultation activities
- Surveys of stakeholder attitudes, perceptions, or knowledge
- Videotaped conferences

- Anecdotal records
- Student grades
- Data from counselor and school psychologist
- Teacher portfolios
- Professional development activity evaluation forms

Collecting and Analyzing Data

When the measures have been determined, methods to gather outputs or outcome data are selected. An evaluation team should decide collaboratively on ways of obtaining the data. Much of the data will exist within classrooms, or student files, or school computer data banks. The challenge is to determine what is needed and then plan a strategy for collecting and summarizing the data in a meaningful, time-efficient way. Important aspects of the program must get measured, and the evaluation instruments must be sensitive enough to pick up all outcomes that result from the project. An evaluation is only as good as the data. Incomplete, flawed, out-of-date, or irrelevant data lead to results that are not valid and in some instances might be harmful. "Garbage in, garbage out" is a phrase frequently used by evaluators.

Instrumentation and process for data collection should be put into place at the beginning of a project. A consultant, working with an evaluation team, should decide how to evaluate the program as early as possible, during the planning of the program, activity, or intervention. Of course, baseline data must be collected before the program activities are put in place or the intervention has begun.

Data collection activities must be congruent with the type of data to be collected. For example, evaluators could use a survey to obtain information about teachers' perceptions of the new parent-teacher center in the district. Or they could use an online survey system such as SurveyMonkey.com to e-mail a survey to teachers. It is essential to let teachers know why they are being asked for feedback, and to inform them that their names will not be used in any reports made from the data. Summative evaluation procedures should be extensive enough to document achievement of each program goal. This language probably sounds familiar, for that is exactly what is required when an IEP is developed for a student. The similarity is not coincidental. Principles guiding IEP development must guide all good program development.

Evaluation instruments and procedures must be as objective and unbiased as possible. Unfortunately, unbiased opinions and objective information are not easily obtained. For example, a consultant might ask consultees to complete checklists such as the ones presented in this book, but respondents may not be willing or able to offer objective opinions.

As noted earlier, lack of objectivity can interfere when working with the special needs of students. Consultees may give high ratings indiscriminately to avoid losing a colleague's friendship or to cloak the reality of not knowing enough about the issue to provide a constructive response. Exaggerated ratings are of little benefit for evaluation purposes and if inaccurate they may be another example of an iatrogenic effect that compounds problems rather than creates solutions. For these reasons, consultants need information from multiple sources, in different circumstances within the school and home context, and at varying times throughout the school year. All who participate in the evaluation process must be thanked genuinely and generously.

The data analysis method must fit the chosen methodology. Some complex programs may require extensive databases and statistical programs. Evaluation personnel should check with the school district to find out what types of database and statistical programs are available. Stakeholders may be interested only in pre-post comparisons, or tables with collected information, or charts that visually represent the results of the evaluation. Most common office productivity software includes a database program that can convert databases to charts or tables. Involving stakeholders in making decisions about the representation of the data will help ensure that they remain interested and involved through the entire process so that the hard work of evaluation pays off with smart decisions.

Reporting and Using Findings

The final element of evaluation involves communicating or reporting the results of the evaluation in a manner that is useful. Evaluation has value only if the results will be used to facilitate improvement of programs or to develop better programs, or lower the costs of the program, or improve methods of operation. Evaluation findings provide information about what works and what doesn't work. The data should promote self-reflection and evidence-based thinking, and point out actions that need to be taken—for example, curriculum revisions and adaptations, testing modifications and accommodations, reassignment of school personnel, reconfiguration of schedules, reallocation of funds, and so forth.

The report of evaluation findings should be constructed to answer the evaluation questions in specific ways. Providing graphs, tables, and a brief summary of the results of the evaluation is often sufficient to make the report useful for those reading it. Again, reports of findings should be based on stakeholder needs. Funders may want detailed reports much like a journal article or a corporate report. Parents may want a summary with examples, graphs that do not take a great amount of their time to interpret, and pictures. A school administrator or collaborating teachers may want an executive summary with the findings and recommendations listed. Matching the type of report to stakeholder needs and interests will help to assure that evaluation findings are used in making decisions about programs and activities, and not left languishing on shelves or in drawers.

CONDUCTING EVALUATION FOR COLLABORATIVE SCHOOL CONSULTATION

A collaborative team designs an evaluation plan to address the six steps discussed above. In summary, they are:

1. Purpose of the evaluation
2. Stakeholders' evaluation questions
3. Activities of the program being evaluated
4. Outputs and expected outcomes of program activities
5. Data collection and analysis
6. Report and use of findings

An evaluation plan is a guide for conducting an evaluation. It contains a time line, and it designates which team members of the team will be responsible for what actions. Planning and conducting an evaluation of collaborative school consultation programs and co-teaching programs are intense endeavors, and educational personnel will be using all their collaborating and consulting skills in carrying out a successful process. Each stakeholder brings an agenda and skill set to the table; all stakeholders must be heard. As with other collaborative activities, participation in the planning and having a voice in the work will help assure continued cooperation and buy-in to the collaborative consultation process. Figure 12.4 is a planning template for developing an evaluation and may be used as a guide when working with a team to make decisions about a program evaluation.

Many times a consultant will be part of a larger team to plan and conduct an evaluation of a large-scale program, such as a state-wide inclusionary robotics competition or a new initiative for providing professional development in Universal Design for Learning for all teachers in the district, or a project to pair math educators and special educators in Response To Intervention collaborations for students with learning disabilities. The consultant may be the only person on the larger team who has knowledge and experience in

FIGURE 12.4   CSC Evaluation Planning Template and Checklist

Name of program or activity: _____

Purpose(s) of the program or activity: _____

Evaluation team members: _____

    1. Agreed purpose of the evaluation: _____

    2. A) Stakeholders: _____

       B) Stakeholder evaluation questions: _____

       _____

3. Activities:	4. Expected outcomes:	5. Outcome measures:
_____	_____	_____
_____	_____	_____
_____	_____	_____

    6. Date collection (using outcome measures):

Instrument	Date	Who
_____	_____	_____
_____	_____	_____

    7. Analysis of data: _____

    _____

    8. Report(s) of findings: _____

    9. Use of findings: _____

exceptionalities, and part of that person's work will be to advocate for inclusion in general educational programs.

Some consultants have found resources that are helpful in providing an overview about legal, social and pedagogical issues regarding students with disabilities. One such resource is *Basics About Disabilities and Science and Engineering Education* (Sevo, 2011). The book, which can be downloaded free at www.lulu.com/sevo, contains information about basic statistics, history, research, and legal issues. It is not just about science and engineering. The annotated bibliography and the recommended resources are especially helpful to consultants for providing information about disabilities to team members.

Case Study 2: Evaluation of a District-Wide Program for Mothers

A city-wide school district has adopted a program, Success Skills for Moms (SSM), as part of its ongoing family literacy program. The program was designed for single poverty-level mothers who have young children with disabilities or children who are at risk for school failure. SSM was developed by educators and researchers and has been adopted in many other cities in the region. The school board has agreed to fund the program for a two-year trial but wants to have evidence of the impact of the program before they commit to a longer funding period. You are part of the group that has made the decision to adopt this program as part of the literacy initiative. The adoption committee hopes the program will help single mothers in their community improve their lives, their parenting skills, and their children's educational prognosis.

SSM is a series of interactive workshops where women who have completed the program are co-facilitators in the workshops. Workshop participants are regarded as the experts in their own lives; thus the curriculum is a series of activities combining educational and community living skills and knowledge with the participants' expertise as parents and community members. The workshops include these topics: early childhood education basics; advocating for your child; finding and using community resources; time management; money management; preventing and solving problems; food for families; continuing education; and crisis management.

1. Draw a logic model for the program. Fill it in as you proceed with the following discussion questions.
2. What is the purpose of the evaluation?
3. Who are the stakeholders?
4. What do the stakeholders want to know?
5. What outcomes are expected to happen as a result of the planned activities and the program?
6. How can those outcomes be measured?
7. Who will collect and analyze the data? When?
8. How should the findings be reported? To whom?
9. How do you recommend the data be used to make decisions about program changes or program efficacy?

(This case study is loosely based on a program described by Thurston [1989].)

The following ten points are other important considerations in planning and implementing effective evaluations for collaboration, consultation, and co-teaching activities:

1. The evaluation process should be ongoing.
2. Multiple sources of information should be used.
3. Valid and reliable methods of gathering information should be used.
4. Data gathering should be limited to that which addresses pertinent questions and documents attainment of specified consultation goals.
5. The evaluation should be realistic, diplomatic, and sensitive to diversity issues.
6. Legal and ethical procedures, including protection of privacy rights, must be followed.
7. Anonymity of respondents should be maintained whenever possible, and respondents should be informed about whether the data are to be reported as grouped data.
8. The evaluation needs to be cost-effective in terms of time and money (for example, whenever possible use existing data).
9. Data that are collected must be put to useful purpose; if not, data should not be collected.
10. Formative evaluation should result in program change; summative evaluation should result in decision making about the program.

SELF-EVALUATION OF COLLABORATIVE CONSULTATION SKILLS

Important reasons for conducting self-evaluation are to examine one's own collaborative work and the processes used, as well as to glean information for professional development. Self-evaluation, self-assessment, reflection, and self-direction are excellent methods of professional development for teachers. Without some type of self-evaluation, a consultant may perpetuate ineffective processes, resulting in a decline of collaborative consultation quality over time. Three areas need to be considered:

- Conceptualizing a framework for self-evaluation
- Examining methods for self-evaluation
- Using self-evaluation for self-improvement

A Framework for Self-Evaluation

Self-evaluation is not synonymous with the accountability required by administrators. Its purpose is to engage in self-improvement and make personal change. Results are only to be shared if the self-evaluating person wishes to do so. Self-evaluation is related to ongoing professional development and involves self-assessment and reflection as well as planning strategies for self-improvement. The basic framework for self-evaluation aligns with the action research or action evaluation model described earlier. The three steps in self-evaluation are:

1. Self-assessment
2. Self-improvement strategies
3. Post-strategy self-assessment or reflection

Methods for gathering self-assessment data for steps 1 and 2 are discussed in the next section. When thinking about designing and implementing strategies to improve collaboration or co-teaching skills, ground the strategies for your performance on baseline data from your first self-assessment. If this is your first self-assessment, you can use any other existing data that are relevant. Critiques or evaluations from past assessments would be a possibility. Then write down goals and objectives. Prioritize the behaviors needing change and write behavioral objectives for them. State desired criteria for evaluation—for example, saying "Okay" no more than two times in a twenty-minute consultation session. Include dates for achievement of each objective. Then select strategies that can help you make the needed changes you have targeted. Formulate the strategies from material presented in other chapters of this book, in other professional books and journals, or in professional development meetings and workshops. After you have worked on the targeted behavior, skill set, or knowledge, collect feedback with the self-assessment method you used for your baseline data collection point. Chart your progress in achieving your goals. Periodically check to determine your progress in the self-selected area for change. It is very easy to assume (often erroneously) that change has taken place if this step is bypassed. If goals focus on verbal skills, audiotapes probably will be sufficient for follow-up data, but if they include nonverbal skills, use of videotapes should continue.

The final step is to celebrate! It's not easy to change. When a criterion is met, a self-reward is due for a job well done. Objective data can be shared with a supervisor. Growth could be charted in the manner that student progress is documented. Self-assessment should be an ongoing process propelled by realistic expectations.

Methods of Self-Assessment for Self-Improvement

Consulting teachers and co-teachers can choose from a variety of methods for conducting self-evaluations. Audio- or videotaped materials, portfolios, checklists, and reflective journals are some of the possibilities.

Audio- or Videotaped Materials   This method uses audio- or videotaping of collaborative activities such as teacher meetings or parent conferences. Although it is time consuming and somewhat cumbersome, there are great payoffs in actually watching and listening to oneself collaborate with others. In choosing this method of self-assessment, here are several important tips:

- Set the consultee at ease by explaining the purpose of the videotape recording.
- Do a few trial runs before involving a consultee in order to become comfortable with the video camera and accustomed to seeing yourself on tape.
- Don't focus on traits that have nothing to do with the quality of consultation. Specific skills must be targeted for observation. Observe or listen to the tape several times, each time focusing on just one or two behaviors for data collection. Checklists and rating forms such as those in Figures 12.4 and 12.5 may be useful. Consultants can make their own checklists that focus on communication skills they would like to improve.
- Tabulate behaviors using a systematic observation method so information can be interpreted meaningfully and progress followed objectively.

- Be sensitive to the rights of privacy for the consultee. Arrange the seating during a videotape recording session so that you face the camera and the consultee's back is to the camera.
- Do not show the tape without signed permission from the consultee.

Teacher Portfolios   The teacher portfolio, as presented in Chapter 6, is an effective vehicle for collecting the authentic assessment information that educators can use to evaluate their own skills and continuing development. A teacher portfolio focuses on the educator's

FIGURE 12.5   Collaborative Consultant Behaviors Checklist

Consultant _____ Observer _____ Date _____

	Yes	Needs Work	Does Not Apply
1. *Welcome*			
Sets comfortable climate	____	____	____
Uses commonly understood terms	____	____	____
Is nonjudgmental	____	____	____
Provides brief informal talk	____	____	____
Is pleasant	____	____	____
2. *Communication Exchange*			
Shares information	____	____	____
Is accepting	____	____	____
Is empathic	____	____	____
Identifies major issues	____	____	____
Keeps on task	____	____	____
Is perceptive, providing insight	____	____	____
Avoids jargon	____	____	____
Is encouraging	____	____	____
Gives positive reinforcement	____	____	____
Sets goals as agreed	____	____	____
Develops working strategy	____	____	____
Develops plan to implement strategy	____	____	____
Is friendly	____	____	____
3. *Interpretation of Communication*			
Seeks feedback	____	____	____
Demonstrates flexibility	____	____	____
Helps define problem	____	____	____
Helps consultee assume responsibility for plans	____	____	____
4. *Summarizing*			
Is concise	____	____	____
Is positive	____	____	____
Is clear	____	____	____
Sets another meeting if needed	____	____	____
Is affirming	____	____	____

learning. It is useful for evaluating progress in collaborative experiences and team interactions, as well as co-teaching and partnerships with co-educators. It is multidimensional and authentic in purpose and task, and it contributes to an ongoing learning process. The material can be evaluated, streamlined, and added to from year to year as visible evidence of growth and improvement. When educators develop professional portfolios to evaluate their own professional growth and development, they demonstrate the value and importance of authentic assessment.

The mainstay of assessment by portfolio is development of sound rubrics. This could be accomplished with several colleagues who want to prepare their own teaching portfolios. As suggested in Chapter 6, designing a rubric for a collaborative activity is a good way to engage in meaningful collaboration. It is also a useful tool for professional development.

Checklists   A variety of tools throughout this book can be used for self-assessment, including the checklist in Figure 12.5 and the rating scale in Figure 12.6. Journal articles about teacher assessment often contain helpful checklists. Consultants may want to design their own checklists based on their specific professional duties and responsibilities. It is always helpful to have others read over self-made checklists to assure that they are clear and comprehensive.

FIGURE 12.6   Consultee Assessment of Consultation and Collaboration

Please evaluate your use of the consulting teacher service provided in the _____
program by providing the following information. Respond with:

1 = Not at all   2 = A little   3 = Somewhat   4 = Considerably   5 = Much

1. The consulting teacher provides useful information. _____

2. The consulting teacher understands my school environment and teaching situation. _____

3. The consulting teacher listens to my ideas. _____

4. The consulting teacher helps me identify useful resources that help my students' special needs. _____

5. The consulting teacher explains ideas clearly. _____

6. The consulting teacher fits easily into the school setting. _____

7. The consulting teacher increases my confidence in the special programs. _____

8. I value consulting and collaborating with the consulting teacher. _____

9. I have requested collaboration time with the consulting teacher. _____

10. I plan to continue seeking opportunities to consult and collaborate with the consulting teacher. _____

Other comments: _____

_____

Video recording, having a colleague observe and report, and often just reflecting on one's habits objectively are all potentially helpful ways of growing professionally. Reflection leads to insights about oneself, prompting changes in self-concept, changes in perception of an event or person, or plans for changing some behavior (Canning, 1991).

TECHNOLOGY FOR EVALUATION OF COLLABORATIVE SCHOOL CONSULTATION

FIGURE 12.7 Data Collection Yields Information for Evaluation

A variety of technological resources can be used to help collaborative consultants implement evaluation processes. Spreadsheets for data collection, online survey sites, and web-based logic models will save time and energy when planning evaluations and collecting and analyzing data. Many free tools are available from Google (www.google.com). For example, Google Refine helps organize messy data sets, and Google Calendar can facilitate coordination of meetings in collaborative groups. Google Tasks is an application embedded within Google Calendar that creates to-do lists, sets due dates, and provides details to help the busy collaborator manage professional and personal tasks. When the data are in, you can let the evaluation begin! (See Figure 12.7.) There are websites that help with designing rubrics for conducting self-assessments and collecting the data electronically.

ETHICAL ISSUES IN EVALUATING COLLABORATIVE SCHOOL CONSULTATION

When co-educators engage in interactive situations, especially those that focus on accountability and evaluation, they will want to keep the needs of their colleagues in mind. Ethical climates for collaboration will nurture and support teachers who are experiencing stress and perhaps on the verge of burnout from the profession. It is often the accumulation of mountains of little things—being "nibbled to death by ducks"—and not the big crises, that push professional educators into disillusionment. Caring, supportive colleagues can make all the difference. The processes described in this chapter, when carried out with camaraderie and team spirit, will convey caring and respect for the overwhelmed novice teacher, the burdened administrator, or the discouraged veteran teacher. Respect for privacy and confidentiality of information are essential characteristics of the collaborative environment. Other ethical considerations for evaluation are found in the guidelines of the American Evaluation Association, the *Guiding Principles for Evaluators*, available at www.eval.org

TIPS FOR EVALUATING COLLABORATIVE SCHOOL CONSULTATION

1. Build into evaluation procedures some ways of improving on less-than-successful collaborations.
2. Advertise and celebrate successes and gains, even seemingly small ones, in collaborative and team-based efforts. They may result in big changes someday!
3. Don't try to fix it if it isn't broken.
4. Identify exemplary consulting and collaborating, especially when it occurs close to home.
5. Consult a technology specialist on a regular basis to remain current in the ever-changing uses of technology, especially for data collection and data analysis. Why do it the laborious "old" way when a newer, more efficient one is available?
6. Keep public remarks about colleagues on a positive, professional level. This is especially relevant when evaluating oneself or others. It is easy to find reasons to blame; it is much harder to find solutions from which all can benefit and then set about to implement them collegially and constructively.
7. Observe programs in other schools and share observations with key people in your school(s).
8. Before sending confidential information through electronic networks, make sure steps have been taken to keep hackers and other would-be technology thieves from gaining access to the information. Information concerning assessment and evaluation is quite sensitive in nature and could be damaging if obtained by those who are not stakeholders.
9. Constantly monitor and update your methods of protecting confidential information.
10. Don't try to do everything yourself, especially when it comes to planning large-scale evaluation programs; involve stakeholders in every phase of the process.

ADDITIONAL RESOURCES

Bogdan, R., & Biklen, S. (2006). *Qualitative research for education: An introduction to theory and methods* (5th ed.). Boston, MA: Allyn & Bacon.

Mertens, D. M. (2010). *Research and evaluation in education and psychology: Integrating diversity with quantitative, qualitative, and mixed methods* (3rd ed.). Thousand Oaks, CA: Sage.

Patton, M. Q. (2008). *Utilization-focused evaluation* (4th ed.). Thousand Oaks, CA: Sage.

Rodriguez-Campos, L. (2005). *Collaborative evaluations: A step-by-step model for the evaluator*. Tamarac, FL: Lumina Press.

Rossi, P. H., Lipsey, M. W., & Freeman, H. E. (2004). *Evaluation: A systematic approach* (7th ed.). Beverly Hills, CA: Sage.

Wholey, J. S., Hatry, H. P., & Newcomer, K. E. (2010). *Handbook of practical program evaluation* (3rd ed.). San Francisco, CA: Jossey-Bass.

Yarbrough, D. B., Shulha, L. M., Hopson, R. K., & Caruthers, F. A. (Eds.) (2011). *The program evaluation standards: A guide for evaluators and evaluation users* (3rd ed.). Thousand Oaks, CA: Sage.

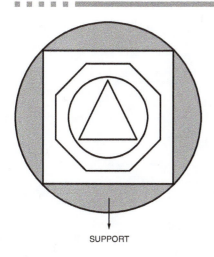

SUPPORT

Support for Working Together as Co-Educators

PART V, THE SHADED OUTER CIRCLE OF SUPPORT, encompasses all five parts and concludes the book. Chapter 13 highlights interagency collaborations, transition periods for students, related services, and support personnel. Chapter 14 addresses leadership and administration, mentorships, and professional development. Chapter 15 promotes the positive ripple effects of collaborative consultation and provides a competency checklist for co-educators who collaborate and co-teach.

Developing and Utilizing Collaborations with Educational Personnel and Community Organizations

AN ANCIENT PROVERB REMINDS US THAT A CHILD'S LIFE IS LIKE A TABLET on which every passerby leaves a mark. It is the responsibility of all members in every society to mark that tablet well.

All children have individual needs, and all are entitled to a free appropriate public education (FAPE) that addresses their special needs. In order to serve students in ways that are right for every child and productive for society, educators should partner with many individuals, organizations, and agencies including:

- Related services and support personnel within the school system and in public organizations
- Public, private, or community organizations and programs
- Government or community agencies that provide funding for services or enrichment programs that can be developed collaboratively for students and families

Collaborations and networks among general and special education teachers, related services and support personnel, families, and the communities they live in can expand the multiple opportunities that students have to succeed in school and in local activities outside of school. Those involved with the formal and informal education of children and youth work in many arenas of school, work, play, and community life. Support for consulting, collaborating, and co-teaching is essential for maximal educational and developmental outcomes for children (See the all-encompassing shaded circle in Figure 13.1). As Helen Keller wisely said, "Alone we can do so little, together we can do so much."

FOCUSING QUESTIONS

1. How can collaborative consultants facilitate communication and coordination among a variety of educational and community agencies for the diverse needs of students with learning and behavioral problems?
2. How can related services and support personnel as a team contribute to the learning programs of students with special needs, and who will coordinate these efforts?

3. How can consultants work with educational and community organizations to assist children and youth as they make transitions at critical educational junctures?

4. How can educational consultants work with school and community partners to develop proposals for funding special projects that benefit children with disabilities?

5. In what ways can school collaborators use technology to build partnerships among educational and community agencies?

6. What are characteristics of an ethical climate in which all work together for the benefit of all students?

KEY TERMS

Americans with Disabilities
    Act (ADA)
community of practice
curriculum of the community
early childhood education
    (ECE)
early childhood special
    education (ECSE)

free appropriate public
    education (FAPE)
Individualized Transition Plan
    (ITP)
interagency collaboration
related services personnel
Request for Proposals
    (RFP)

science, technology,
    engineering, and math
    (STEM)
support personnel
transition services

VIGNETTE 13

An informal conversation takes place at City Hall before the monthly meeting of the city council. Several council members and visiting citizens, including some school personnel, converse about the recent vandalism and several arrests of school-age youth that have taken place in their community.

Mr. Alvarez (Middle School Teacher):   You know, I've been teaching for many years, and I remember when our main discipline problems in schools were running in the halls and talking without permission. Today our problems span everything from drug use, physical and verbal abuse, sexual harassment, assault and destruction of property, to acts of violence such as rape and murder.

Ms. Cohen (Mother of an Elementary School Student):   Yes, I agree with your assessment. My husband and I strongly believe that violence in schools and communities is undermining children's physical and mental health and safety. Furthermore, it erodes their sense of security and interferes with their readiness to learn. A heart-wrenching addition to that is the incidence of suicides among young people across the nation.

Mr. Adamson (Council Member):   The pressure on school officials and community leaders to ensure the existence of safe and orderly schools is strong. I read in the latest national poll on public perceptions of schools that parents and community members name school safety as one of their top concerns.

Ms. Dinkens (High School Assistant Principal):   I can assure you that our teachers are very concerned about the safety of their students and themselves right in their own classrooms.

Ms. Cohen: We need to put in place some community policies that will help school officials lay out strong guidelines in the schools against violence and destruction, and provide the tools and public support to enforce them.

Ms. Dinkens: I agree. There are other things, too, that we can do as a community early in the lives of children to get them on track for succeeding in school and becoming productive citizens of society someday. We have an array of related services personnel and support personnel in our school district, and I have felt for some time that we could be integrating their services more collaboratively to help our children and youth

Mr. Adamson: We all need to work together as a community to figure out some strategies for making this as healthy and productive a school environment as we can. After all, our schools are our country's lifeblood and the showcases for our communities. I want *this* community to shine so others will want to live here, and work, and operate businesses, and raise their families here.

This chapter's vignette presents issues that bind school, family, and local community members together in their concern. Such concern can be addressed with collaborative efforts of schools, community organizations, parents, and local government leaders. Schools are often the brokers and bridges for interagency collaborations aimed at eliminating problems in the school setting. In this collaborative process, all school personnel, parents, students, and community members must work together to adopt prevention and management measures that will help make schools rich learning environments and make communities safe places to live. These groups should work together in designing locally appropriate crisis intervention programs to be implemented in the unfortunate event that disturbing situations do occur.

COLLABORATION WITH EDUCATION, COMMUNITY, AND AGENCY PARTNERS

As a process, collaboration is a means to an end rather than an end in itself. The goal is success in school for students with special needs. But schools are not alone in the responsibility to help students succeed; they cannot do it all. Students are in school for much less time than it would seem. They typically attend six hours a day, 180 days a year for 12.5 years. Some educators describe the school time as "the 13 percent factor"; others calculate sleep, school time, and inevitable absences a bit differently and come up with a "9/91 percent factor". Either way, it is an amazingly low figure. Furthermore, it is only allocated time, not actual time engaged in learning. And this is only the time *allocated* for learning; a measure of actual time students are *engaged* in academic learning would be much less. (This is also one of the shortest school years, if not *the* shortest, in the developed world.) For the remaining 91 or so percent of the time, the child is at home with friends, relatives, caregivers, or others elsewhere in a community, or alone.

Much of what students learn comes from experiences, associations, and interactions they have outside the scheduled school activities. This secondary curriculum may be a dominant part of any student's life (Barbour & Barbour, 2001), especially when traditional and formal school curriculums are not compatible with the special needs of many students. Community settings offer many alternative therapies or learning environments that promote socialization, language, and cognitive and physical development. Non-school facilities in the community provide the added component of parental involvement, and links to the community and other institutions in the community.

This "curriculum of the community" (Barbour & Barbour, 2001) has great potential for enhancing the social networks of students and families, inculcating natural resources into the education of students, and providing services such as entertainment, recreation, and informal education. In addition, the informal curriculum enables the involvement and collaboration of several organizations within a community (Barbour & Barbour, 2001). Schools and communities can address their considerable responsibilities in helping students learn by employing a wide spectrum of resources and collaborating with many agencies to help them stay in school as active, successful learners.

Developing Collaborative Partnerships

Educators endeavor to develop connections and networks that provide opportunities for students with special needs. They reach out beyond traditional teaching roles within the school to find the right people, places, and things that can help students succeed. But it is not easy. It takes time and energy, and it requires communication skills, management ability, and diplomacy. Inevitable barriers make the process more challenging, such as failure to identify the student needs appropriately, turf issues among personnel, potential liability issues, lack of clarity on fiscal responsibilities, and need for shared agreements involving personnel, facilities and equipment.

Engaging Related Services Personnel

Schools are required by the Individuals with Disabilities Education Act (IDEA) and Section 504 of the Rehabilitation Act of 1973 to provide an array of services for students designed to address their special needs. Special educators and related service personnel work together to prepare students for postsecondary education, employment, and independent living. Related services roles are described in IDEA 1997 as facilitators of transportation and the developmental, corrective, and other supportive services needed to help a child who has a disability benefit from special education. Figure 13.2 shows services that are included within this definition. That list is not exhaustive and does not include all services

FIGURE 13.2   Related Services for Students in Special Education Programs

Audiology	Psychological services
Counseling services	Recreation services
Early identification and assessment services	Rehabilitation counseling services
Medical services	School health services
Occupational therapy	Social work services
Orientation and mobility services	Speech-language pathology services
Parent counseling and training	Therapy programs in art, dance, music
Physical therapy	Transportation services

the school district may need to provide (for example, mobility specialists or interpreters). Other services might be artistic and cultural programs, art, music, and dance therapy, if they are needed in order for the child to benefit from special education and receive free appropriate public education. Parents are not charged for these services when they are part of the student's educational program. The services are to be real and substantial. They are defined and determined by how they relate to the student's IEP.

To be eligible for related services, a student is assessed in areas of health, vision, hearing, social and emotional status, general intelligence, academic performance, communicative status, and motor abilities. A variety of assessment tools and strategies must be used to gather the information in order to have a complete picture of the student's needs.

Related services personnel are the professionals who are part of the educational team that works with students with special needs. For example, the services of school psychologists may be part of an IEP, or the psychologists may provide support to teachers, students, and others. School psychologists are integral partners in the education of students with special needs because they provide information about purposes, interpretation, and uses of tests. Counselors trained in individual guidance and group guidance techniques are important participants or presenters in staff development activities and problem-solving sessions. School nurses and social workers contribute valuable data in both informal consultations and IEP conferences. They are often able to target seemingly insignificant data toward meaningful problem identification. Collaborating consultants should always remember that these professional personnel are key partners in educating students. Professional courtesy and respect as well as use of the other collaboration processes that have been discussed here are critical for teamwork that facilitates student success.

Engaging School and Community Support Personnel

Every school has many other support personnel, without whom school life for everyone would be uncomfortable and disorganized. Some of these are listed in Figure 13.3; they includes people who are integral to all school programs and activities such as office staff, food service staff, bus drivers, custodians, and volunteer aides. Although these individuals may not be part of a student's IEP, they interact frequently with students and are integral in the educational environment of all students and teachers.

FIGURE 13.3   Other Support Services for Students in Special Education Programs

Assistive technology personnel	Reading specialists
Custodial and maintenance services	School aides
Food services	Secretarial/Receptionist services
Media/Library/Technology specialists	Security services
Mentors/Apprenticeship and career-shadowing supervisors	Specialists for talent development
	Senior citizens/Grandparents
Paraprofessionals	Special education administrators
Parent volunteers	Student teachers

Just as the roles of consultant, consultee, and client are interrelated and interchangeable according to the focus of the service, so the roles and responsibilities of support personnel are interrelated and interchanging according to the part each plays for teacher instruction and student learning. For example, school bus drivers and cab drivers are involved in the lives of students in special education programs in ways that go beyond just picking them up and delivering them home again. They are a key link between home and school, being the first person to see the student in the morning and often the last of the school staff to see them in the afternoon. Sometimes it is even appropriate for them to help with intervention programs as partners in reward-and-reinforcement systems for students, or in extending learning activities beyond the classroom in practical, real-world ways.

Maintenance workers and school custodians have various titles and responsibilities across school districts and geographic regions. Collaborators should learn what terms are used in their schools and what interests are represented among the staff. An understanding custodian who is tuned in to both teachers' needs and students' needs has always been regarded as teachers' best friend and helpmate in the school setting. This is especially relevant to the special education teacher, who encourages custodians to be involved in planning and monitoring special programs for students with special needs. (Recall the bee expert in a previous chapter.)

Individuals in the community can provide valuable support services for unique needs of students. These include a multitude of roles, including Boy Scout and Girl Scout leaders, 4-H leaders, private music and art instructors, media representatives, interest-area speakers, mentors, tutors, judges of events and products, and community organization members. Community personnel, whether they are in professional positions or volunteers (or both) provide important services that can enrich the lives of students who have special needs and can extend and multiply the education offered to them. These community members are personnel in libraries, park systems, colleges, industries, businesses, and many other professions. Community leaders can assist with career shadowing by students who express interest in specific vocational areas. Others might provide knowledge and experiences from their own lives as members of a specific cultural group. Special activities, managed through clubs, workshops, interests groups, or travel, are an important component of services arranged to accommodate special needs.

Ghosh and Rezazadeh (2011) provide perspectives on useful collaboration among pediatricians and psychologists for children with attention-deficit/hyperactivity disorder.

They propose that it is essential for families and health teams to have information and suggestions they can apply to addressing children's problems. They recommend an interdisciplinary and collaborative model of consultation where teams are built whose members can participate in real-time discussions about a child's special needs. Shaw, Glaser, and Ouimet (2011) cite the relationship between medical and educational systems as a necessary one because most medical issues of children have educational ramifications and many can be addressed helpfully with preventative strategies in educational environment. In their words, "Ideally, every school would have a medical liaison" (p. 113), but such collaboration between systems, while widely proposed, is not yet a common, mature practice.

A frequently overlooked source of help that more and more schools are learning to value and call on is senior citizens, including grandparents of students, to instruct, give demonstrations, provide comfort, relate their own experiences, model behavior, and advocate for children and youth. Schools and universities have a variety of support personnel who could assist with student needs. All these institutions are catalysts for the increasingly popular practice of using community resources to accentuate learning. Every community—large or small, urban or rural, accessible or isolated, wealthy or poor—has agencies and potential resources that can contribute meaningfully to learning programs for special needs of children and adolescents.

UTILIZING RESOURCES FOR ASSISTANCE TO SCHOOLS AND FAMILIES

A consulting teacher will find it helpful to develop a directory of referral agencies, with addresses and phone numbers, to have available for consultations and staffings. As one example, a consulting teacher in a midsize town in the Midwest prepared a referral directory containing more than 100 sources of assistance. Some were national sources that could be called toll free, such as the Missing Children's Network. Others were state-level agencies, such as the Families Together agency. Still others were county agencies, such as the county family planning clinic. But within this average town, many sources were available "just down the street," including a crisis center and a community theater.

Another special education teacher in a large town with a land-grant university found more than 200 agencies, from Alcoholics Anonymous and LDA (Learning Disabilities Association of America) to a living with cancer group and MADD (Mothers Against Drunk Driving), to the World Friendship Organization and a young moms' group. Resourceful consulting teachers will involve personnel regularly from a variety of agencies to collaborate in planning and implementing student programs that provide assistance for students' special needs.

■ ■ ■ ■ ■

ACTION 13.1
Searching for Resources

Have a personal scavenger hunt or go with a small group of your colleagues to discover new resources for student and adult learning. Find people, places, and things that can enhance special abilities and serve special needs. As you do this, if someone asks what you are doing, explain and then engage them in conversation about education. Invite them to be advocates and collaborators in enterprises that will help students succeed in school.

A school-related group such as the parent/teacher organization (PTO) or a committee of teachers, or a student group seeking a service project, could develop a community resources information page for the school and compile the individual pages into a community resources notebook. Persons or agencies targeted for inclusion in the notebook first should be contacted to obtain their permission and to gather information from them for entering on the page. Figure 13.4 shows an example of a resource template for recording information. The notebook must be reviewed and updated periodically to keep it current and useful; this in itself can be a rewarding collaborative activity for a cross section of school personnel.

FIGURE 13.4   Community Resources Information

Name of Individual or Agency _____

Phone Number _____ Fax _____ E-Mail _____

Address _____

Occupation or Emphasis _____

Area(s) of Expertise/Contribution _____

Preference for Grade Level or Subject Area _____

Preference for Group Size with Which to Work _____

Time of Day Preferred _____

Preference for Day(s) of Week and Month(s) of Year _____

Maximum Times Would Care to Assist in a Year _____

Special Arrangements Needed _____

Special Equipment Required _____

Any Further Clarifications _____

Record of Dates Contributed, with Description of Activities of the Contribution:

_____

_____

For More Information Contact (Resource Personnel) _____

(School Personnel) _____

Educators have a variety of national resources available for collaborative discussions and planning related to school improvement and school safety issues. In regard to safety, the National Youth Violence Prevention Resource Center which is part of the Centers for Disease Control and Prevention's Striving To Reduce Youth Violence Everywhere project (STRYVE) (www.safeyouth.gov) and the North Carolina Department of Juvenile Justice and Delinquency Prevention's Center for the Prevention of School Violence (www .ncdjjdp.org) have information and programs. Informative resources for schools, parents, and community members can be found at www.keepschoolssafe.org, and others will appear when key words such as school violence, bullying, vandalism committed by teenagers, teen suicide, drugs in schools, and other similar terms are searched online.

DEVELOPING COLLABORATIVE COMMUNITY RELATIONSHIPS

Consultants should plan carefully how to work with different services agencies, professional cultures, and norms and standards (Shaver, Golan, & Wagner, 1996). None of these entities likes to waste limited time engaging in meaningless meetings any more than busy teachers and consultants do. Many of the strategies addressed in previous chapters will guide educators in developing good working relationships with those who are not professional educators and in resolving major obstacles to understanding.

A group of teachers in a special project to include students with severe disabilities in their general education classrooms reported that the most helpful aspects of the specialist support they received were these: a shared framework and goals, physical presence of the collaborator, validation of the classroom teacher's contribution, and teamwork (Giangreco et al., 1993). If problems did appear, they tended to be caused by separate goals of the related services specialist, disruption of classroom routine, or overuse of special education practices. In this project both teacher and consultant needed to consider more fully the context of the regular classroom and show respect for values and needs of that classroom, its students, and its teacher. In this study conducted to analyze the benefits of inclusion for students with severe disabilities, seventeen of the nineteen teachers reported that they were transformed by their experience. Not only were their attitudes toward the students changed; in some cases the teachers said that they changed their attitudes about themselves as well (Giangreco et al., 1993).

Collaborative teams with support services and school and community personnel are not always easy to coordinate, even when the group has a common goal (for example, assuring the post-secondary success of students with learning disabilities). In describing the co-teaching relationship, Sileo (2011) suggests that newly formed relationships must be nurtured to create a stronger relationship because the teamwork required is hard work and it is important that teams be successful and long lasting. In order to facilitate appropriate support services for students, collaborative co-educators can do several things, such as:

■ Become knowledgeable about the roles, capabilities, and responsibilities of support personnel.

- Have IEPs and the more informal learning plans include all areas of student learning and involve all possible roles that can help the students succeed.
- Within the bounds of necessary confidentiality and ethical school practices, ask support personnel for their viewpoints and opinions about helping students with special needs.
- Inform support personnel about the collaborative consultation role, schedules, and responsibilities.
- Show support for professional staff development activities that focus on inclusion and collaboration and encourage involvement of co-educators.
- Have professional development sessions that provide information about exceptional learning needs and the value of working as teams for these students

Engaging in Interagency Partnerships

Collaborations can be productive in terms of providing successful outcomes for students with special needs and in building exciting new partnerships among communities. Interactions with school personnel are essential for building successful interagency partnerships that focus on the success of students. Here are several examples of interagency partnerships that combine the resources of schools, universities, families, volunteers and community based organizations to serve students beyond the school day:

1. The Parent Institute for Quality Education (PIQE) (www.piqe.org) is a nationally recognized program that started in 1987 by Rev. Vahac Mardirosian and Dr. Alberto Ochoa of San Diego State University as a result of conversations with parents in a predominantly Latino elementary school in the San Diego area. Their first program, Parent Engagement Educational Program, has evolved into a nine-week curriculum delivered to parents in their primary language to help parents become educational advocates for their children K-12. PIQE has operated offices in several states to offer classes in 16 languages. Ongoing evaluation on the impacts of their programs has demonstrated the success of this collaborative effort.
2. Communities in Schools unites community resources such as health care and mental health professionals with teachers, parents, principals, and volunteers on behalf of children (Barbour & Barbour, 2001). Many highly successful outcomes have been realized for students and families. Business-school partnerships have also shown promise for impacting schools, communities, and students. Critical features of these partnerships include strong leadership and support from local power brokers; open communication; respect for differences in skills, ideas, cultures, and values of other partners; decision making based on common ground; long-range goals; careful planning; continuous assessment; and keeping the community informed (Barbour & Barbour, 2001).
3. El Valor (www.elvalor.org) is a nonprofit community based organization founded in 1973 by the late Guadalupe S. Reyes who dreamed of a community in which all members, including her son with special needs, could live, learn and work. The collaboration started in the basement of a church in the Pilsen area of Chicago, where they started the first bilingual, bicultural rehabilitation center in Illinois. El Valor,

meaning "courage," has grown into a multicultural, multipurpose organization that reaches thousands of families in the Chicago area and millions throughout the nation. El Valor has distributed evidence-based practices and curricula such as Mis Padres, Mis Maestros (My Parents, My Teachers), a program for parents with children birth to five years. El Valor has worked with more than 1,000 individuals with disabilities and their families from diverse communities.

The participation of educators in these collaborations has had great benefits for students, families and communities. After studying the development of interagency collaborative educational projects, the Southwest Educational Development Lab in Austin, Texas, offered these steps for organizing and managing collaborative interagency projects (SEDL, 2000):

1. Convene a group. Include all stakeholders.
2. Assess student and community needs.
3. Establish purposes and priorities.
4. Study effective ways of working together.
5. Plan the project.
6. Implement the plan.
7. Evaluate the results.
8. Sustain the achievement.

REFLECTION 13.1

A Ten-Year Dream

Reflect on the three examples of interagency collaborations above. Think of your current or future role with students with special needs—parent, teacher, administrator, volunteer, community agency worker, advocate, or other. Put yourself ten years into the future. What would you like to see in a headline in your local paper related to students with special needs? Write down the headline. Now, think about how this accomplishment involved interagency collaboration. Who are the stakeholders? What are the headlining student outcomes? Finally, think about what you can do today, this month, and this year to get started on this dream to make the headline real. What will be the challenges? What new skills and understandings will you need to be a part of this future happening?

"If you think in-school collaboration and co-teacher consultation are challenging, wait until you try interagency collaboration!" says one experienced educational consultant. Turf issues, lack of clarity on fiscal responsibilities, and requirements for shared personnel, facilities, and equipment agreements are among the barriers to successful interagency collaboration. On the other hand, many educators have had experience with interagency collaboration while working with the Interagency Coordinating Council, established under Part H of P.L. 99-457 (the Handicapped Infant and Toddler Program), and with the Community Transition Council, as established under P.L. 101-476.

Working successfully to implement high-impact programs for students with special needs requires a commitment of time and effort. How can groups work together despite their differences? Suggestions involve efforts to:

- Work to assure that your communication is clear, on-topic, and assertive. Use the skills for communication addressed in Chapter 7.
- Take time to learn from each other. Listen respectfully and remember that all stakeholders have their own ideas and areas of expertise. Build a sense of community.
- Obtain and maintain high levels of support at all organizational levels.
- Keep in mind that the more democratic the process is, the better. However, build toward consensus rather than "majority rules." The idea is to construct a sustainable, successful project together.
- Work to develop high levels of trust. Keep your "eyes on the prize" of successful outcomes for students, families, and communities.
- Think long term; think firm foundations. As with the examples above, a few dedicated individuals from educational and community organizations worked collaboratively to build partnerships that sustained over time and produced positive outcomes for students.
- Most important of all, celebrate small successes and share the credit for successes with all partners.

School–community collaboration requires patience, effort, and new perspectives about what is important in teaching and learning. A quote from Mark Twain helps educators remember that collaboration is sometimes a slow process: "A habit cannot be tossed out the window.... It must be coaxed down the stairs one step at a time." Cross-agency collaboration creates multiple opportunities for learning and enhances the diversity of experiences for students with disabilities. It uses the informal curriculum of the community. The results will be longer-term, consistent, community-developed educational supports for student success. The challenges may be great, but there are resources in educators' own backyards to benefit students in a variety of ways.

SPECIAL NEEDS ADVOCACY AND EDUCATION ACROSS EDUCATIONAL, COMMUNITY, AND GOVERNMENTAL SPECTRUMS

Schools are not alone in their responsibility for removing barriers that keep students from succeeding in the adult world. Personnel in mental health, employment and training, child development, recreation, health, and welfare services, as well as education, have a vital interest in promoting school success for all children. Educational consultants must consider the community an integral part of the preparation of all students for a successful adult life. Building educational and community partnerships requires adaptation of the advocacy role as well as the educational role by individuals and organizations. Figure 13.5 lists some examples of groups with which special education collaborators can partner to advocate for students with special needs.

FIGURE 13.5   Integrating Efforts through Collaboration

Collaborative consultants can integrate and collaborate with other educators in these ways:

With general education teachers:
1. Establish joint ownership of the student and the learning situation.
2. Respect the views of all.
3. Keep problems "in house."
4. Request regular interaction and feedback from them.

With other special education colleagues:
1. Openly deal with the discomfort of having others give critique and feedback.
2. Arrange and coordinate planned interactions.
3. Together develop support systems.

With support and related services personnel:
1. Become more knowledgeable about their roles and responsibilities.
2. Make sure to integrate major ideas they produce.
3. Plan and implement student programs that reflect coordinated involvement and not fragmentation.

With building administrators:
1. Inform them in as brief and practical a manner as possible.
2. Don't carry tales from a school/district to others.
3. Don't be a spy, or judge, even if asked.
4. Request regular feedback as to your own effectiveness.

With attorneys/hearing officers:
1. State your credentials, certifications, training, and experiences relative to the case.
2. State the nature and extent of knowledge about the student.
3. Discuss assessments, curricula, and modifications used, and their reliability, validity, and appropriateness.
4. Explain all terms, using no acronyms or jargon.
5. Remain calm, honest, and cooperative.

With legislators:
1. Be brief, accurate, and substantiating with all material delivered.
2. Thank legislators for their past interest and help.
3. State situations realistically without unreasonable demands.
4. Consider the whole picture, as the legislator must, and not just one's own primary interest.

With the public:
1. Be perceptive about issues of culture, diversity, and conflicting interests.
2. Demonstrate reasonable expectations while upholding standards and delivering challenges.
3. Express your dedication to students and commitment to excellent schools.

Educators understand that advocacy for individuals with special needs is part of their role in educational and community settings. They collaborate with parents, who are experts about their own children and public officials, who are experts in community-based programs or legal issues related to individuals with disabilities. However, special education professionals have extensive background and training in working with individuals with special needs. This experience and expertise may be called upon as communities strive to make their towns and businesses "disability-friendly." For example, in March 2011, the revised regulations implementing the Americans with Disabilities Act (ADA) took effect. These revised rules are the first major revision by the Department of Justice of its guidance on accessibility in 20 years (www .ada.gov). The new rules adopt the 2010 ADA Standards for Accessible Design, which have been retooled to be more user friendly. As communities work to implement these standards that promote independent living for individuals with disabilities, the education consultant with expertise in disabilities can play an important advocacy role in these collaborative endeavors.

It is a challenge for educators to form new paradigms that decompartmentalize services for students with special needs. But stepping outside the in-school educator role is necessary for providing the advocacy needed for student success. Guthrie and Guthrie (1991) stated that service providers must step outside the boundaries of their job descriptions on occasion to do what needs to be done for students. They suggested going to community centers, schools, and homes, devoting more time than usual to families and outside resources. These functions are compatible with the processes and content familiar to educators in school consultation roles. Guthrie and Guthrie warned against "all-talk, no action" posture, excessive jargon, and failure to follow up. These points are readily recognizable to school consultants, who have developed skills in avoiding such pitfalls.

Many families of children with special needs face a multitude of problems and require services beyond the school environment. The reality is that no one agency can provide all necessary services for children with disabilities and their families. Educators partner with others in the community to advocate for these services and educate others about programmatic issues. Collaborative strategies help provide better services to families using several human service systems and keep children and families from falling through the cracks by ensuring that they receive needed services.

All in all, when personnel within various systems collaborate, they avoid service duplication and reduce the total cost of services. Collaborative consultation ensures having fewer gaps in services, minimizes conflict, and clarifies responsibilities. Interagency collaboration includes three elements (Bruner, 1991):

1. Jointly developing and agreeing to a set of common goals and directions
2. Sharing responsibility for obtaining the goals
3. Working together to achieve the goals and using the expertise of each collaborator

The ultimate goal is ensuring the future success of students with special needs by eliminating or reducing difficulties that place them at risk—infant mortality, delinquency, violence such as school shootings and bomb threats, youth unemployment, child abuse and neglect, drug involvement, suicide, mental illness, and poverty. Interagency collaboration is not a quick fix. It is time-consuming and process intensive. It takes commitment and flexibility to discover new roles and relationships. These new roles and responsibilities call for collaborative skills that require wide knowledge and much practice.

ORGANIZING INTERAGENCY COLLABORATION FOR TRANSITION SERVICES

Transition is an umbrella term for activities and opportunities that prepare students for significant changes in their lives. It can be described as the process of moving from one service delivery system to another (Fowler et al., 2000).

Requirements for transition were modified by IDEA 1997. The IDEA amendments called for inclusion of a statement in the student's IEP by age sixteen (unless the team decides otherwise) that focuses on courses of study such as vocational education or preparation for college and also a statement that the student has been informed of legal rights that transfer to the student when reaching the age of majority. Transition services are to be a coordinated set of activities including instruction, related services, community experiences, employment, and adult living objectives; therefore, extensive interagency collaboration is necessary. Schools are responsible for generating Individualized Transition Plans (ITPs) to assess students' career interests and help them focus on career possibilities.

Collaboration across Critical Educational Junctures

Transition points can be called "critical junctures" between systems. These include such points in time as birth to preschool, preschool to kindergarten, elementary to middle school, and high school to work or postsecondary education. Transition calls for intensive collaborative efforts among educational institutions, families, and agencies such as those who provide rehabilitation or school-to-work services.

Collaborations in Early Childhood Education

Concern for preschoolers with special needs has been gaining momentum since the 1960s. In 1975, after passage of P.L. 94-142, interest increased in identifying special needs among preschool children. Public Law 99-457, the Early Intervention Amendments to P.L. 94-142, extended FAPE to children from ages three to five by October 1991 in all states wanting to participate. It also phased in early intervention services for children from birth through two years of age. Part H created a new program for preschoolers from birth to three years of age and stipulated the development of an Individualized Family Service Plan (IFSP) for each child and family served. This amendment called for collaboration based on family-focused methods, and it continued procedural safeguards for families. The legislation expanded beyond academic concerns to include family members, social workers, speech and language pathologists, medical personnel, and other professionals. It authorized funding for state grants and multidisciplinary experimental, demonstration, and outreach programs.

Increased services such as these for preschool children with disabilities require dedicated cooperation among professionals, parents, and other caregivers, with collaboration at the heart of the programs. Making the services available and conducting them effectively is a challenging order for communities. But doing so is extremely important because these services are usually the first experience with schools for parents of young children.

Early Intervention for Special Needs   The earlier the attention to special needs of pre-school children, the more successful the interventions and remediation programs in schools will be. Preschool programs with family involvement and emphasis on socialization, readi-ness for academic learning, language development, and emotional independence will do much to ensure success in school. Keeping very young children in neighborhood programs reduces the need to transport them to other sites and allows them to be in the same area as their siblings. This is an advantage for the child and for the entire family.

To underscore these salient points, education for students with special needs to keep them from falling behind is most effective during the early childhood years. P.L. 99-457 requires family-centered and community-based direct services for all children from infant to five years old with special needs that call for direct services. Early childhood education (ECE) and early childhood special education (ECSE) reduce special education costs and improve teaching envi-ronments. Early childhood education programs can save school systems several thousands of dollars per child over the course of the child's K–12 school experience. However, in order to have programs of high quality, there must be qualified and stable staff, low child–teacher ratios, curriculum that is aligned with local school district curriculum, and *community collaboration* with schools. Teachers need to be trained specifically in early childhood education and certi-fied as such. There should be preparation and accreditation for early childhood teachers and a smooth transition plan in place for preschoolers from early childhood education to K–12 school.

Early intervention is cost-effective and educationally sound. Benefits to the child, the family, and the public are quite significant in reducing later academic failure and social problems such as teenage pregnancy, crime, and school dropout.

Teams for Early Childhood Special Education   ECSE has moved toward full inclu-sion, with consultation services provided by ECSE itinerant consultants who must have expertise across all disabilities including multiple disabilities (Harris & Klein, 2002). Set-tings include a variety of venues such as family daycare, childcare centers, child education centers, Head Start programs, and prekindergarten classes. The nature and responsibilities of educator roles in these settings can be clouded. One thing is clear, however. Successful delivery of inclusion support by ECSE itinerant consultation is dependent on teamwork (Harris & Klein, 2002, p. 239). To meet the challenge, ECSE itinerant consultants must receive intensive training in principles and practices of consultation and teamwork for ECSE contexts (Harris & Klein, 2002).

Teams for ECSE can differ from K–12 teams in that the child may receive services across a variety of settings such as placement in a special education preschool class *and* after-school care in an inclusive setting. Multiple resources may be needed to address med-ical, financial, family counseling, rehabilitation, and other needs. Team leadership often falls on the ECSE itinerant consultant as case manager for orchestrating services as varied as occupational therapist, audiologist, families, and other caregivers. Programs may not be as structured and standardized as they are in K–12 schooling, and expectations of team members can range widely from basic social skills to meeting specific IFSP or IEP goals (Harris & Klein, 2002). So the ECSE team is challenged in many ways.

To accentuate these challenges, time is the enemy. A month or two is a long time in a very young child's life when complex, intensive interaction is needed for planning interventions and remediation. All team members must be knowledgeable about other members' roles and backgrounds, and they must communicate with their perspectives in mind and "on the table" for consideration without unwarranted delay.

Early childhood special education personnel have many responsibilities as collaborative consultants and members of teams where the stakes are high for very young children and their families. They should:

- Help families determine their most needy areas and direct them to appropriate support groups
- Work with families and children on early intervention plans that facilitate transition in the critical time of movement from preschool to kindergarten
- Counsel families to keep files and records of materials accumulated in the care of their child so that resource personnel will have the information needed to provide those interventions thoughtfully and purposefully

Transition from Early Childhood to Kindergarten

Early intervention programs for infants and toddlers with disabilities proliferated following the early childhood legislation. Parents and other caregivers outside the school now play a more integral part in the education and well-being of these children. Disabilities of children in the early intervention programs tend to be severe; therefore, the interventions require integration of multiple services from specialists in several disciplines. Recall the observation in an earlier chapter that an IEP conference might have a dozen participants.

Families are an integral part of the therapy in home-based programs. Therapists go into homes to provide stimulation for the children, and guidance and instruction for the parents. Staff and parents are in consultation and collaboration with all available resources, including health and medical personnel, social services personnel, public school personnel, and community resources such as preschool and day care centers. These programs typically are year-round, not nine-month programs.

Federal legislation (P.L. 102-119) requires that states develop interagency agreements to address roles and responsibilities for transition from early intervention services to preschool services and to provide guidance for local communities through specification of state level responsibilities (Fowler et al., 2000). Preparation of such agreements is a daunting task, requiring skillful collaboration by team members. Issues to be dealt with include ways of (Fowler et al., 2000):

- Transmitting information from one agency to another
- Preparing the child and family for services
- Providing services in least restrictive environments
- Delivering service for children who turn three late in the school year or in summer
- Using IFSPs
- Selecting methods to determine eligibility for services (The interagency agreement and its implementation should be monitored and evaluated on a regular basis.)

Transition from preschool settings to kindergarten school programs also calls for strong, continuous efforts in collaborative school consultation. Although there are many models and programs for early childhood education, P.L. 99-457 reaches far beyond classroom interventions. Preschool teachers should prepare children for the local settings into which they will make the transition. Children need special skills to be ready for kindergarten and sometimes they need preparation for the local setting. Contributions of early childhood educator personnel to elementary school programs are invaluable for getting new kindergarten students off to a successful start. Collaborative efforts between preschools and kindergarten and elementary school educators are essential for the success of students with special needs as they make this critical transition.

Transition from Middle School to High School

The most pressing need for a preteen is to make a comfortable move from elementary school to the very different middle school climate and then to high school. If support systems are not in place for students with disabilities at these important junctures, students may drop out, become alienated, or experience failure in school (Council for Exceptional Children, 1997). Services related to postsecondary education for students should begin much earlier than the high school level. Students in intermediate and middle school grades can begin to set their life goals through career awareness, social skills, money management skills, involvement in extracurricular activities, self-advocacy skills, and development of portfolios, to mention just a few examples.

A collaborative project by the National Association of Secondary School Principals, Phi Delta Kappa International, and the Lumina Foundation for Education, designed to collect opinions of middle school students about their current school activities and their preparation for success in high school and college, showed that the students were optimistic and positive but not necessarily attuned to the reality of American high schools (Bushaw, 2007). The researchers concluded that schools may be operating on a "sort and select" mission that reaches only some students. They urged that this mission be replaced with a goal of preparing *all* students for postsecondary opportunities linked to their interests. The responses of polled students, when asked how much information they had received about how to choose high school courses that prepare them to attend college, showed that 68 percent had "some or none." Only 11 percent had "a great deal." It does not take a giant leap of imagination to conclude where students with disabilities fit into this scene. Several suggestions by researchers can be summarized here as:

- Eliminating the sink-or-swim transition from middle school to high school, with ninth grade in particular being the key link in the school chain where students begin to disengage
- Partnering with parents and caregivers, beginning in middle school, to make available more information about postsecondary options
- Helping students better understand their interests and relate them to a program of study
- Enlarging perceptions of college to include community college, part-time study, work combined with study in the career environment, and study programs offered through distance learning

Each of these suggestions is relevant to success for students with special needs; each is also doable when they are the focus of a strong collaborative effort.

Transition from Secondary School to Postsecondary Opportunities

At the opposite end of the continuum from early childhood needs and continuing beyond those of the middle school child are the needs of students leaving school to enter the world of work and adult living. Heightened awareness of this important transition period for young people with disabilities grew in the 1980s, when program goals for serving students with disabilities were built on education services that could help them lead meaningful and productive lives. One of the realities was that no one parent, teacher, or school counselor could provide all the necessary assistance. All school professionals and agencies with services for the welfare of students need to be involved in partnerships and team efforts to assist the student and the family.

As in transition from middle school to high school, comprehensive assessment of student abilities, interests and needs is vital. Curriculum selection and instructional strategies should include a variety of job-related and postsecondary education explorations. When college education is not a feasible option for young people because of their abilities, job training is essential, along with skills needed to succeed in that work and to experience pleasure and feelings of accomplishment by doing the work. In model programs, students spend part of their day on academic subjects and the rest of the day at work sites. Some programs even allow students to earn academic credits at the work site. Many postsecondary service organizations, such as rehabilitation agencies, are essential partners in the transition from school to work for students with special needs.

Because of increased services offered at the secondary and postsecondary levels, federal legislation related to accessibility and reasonable accommodations, and the increased independence offered by assistive technology, colleges and universities are seeing an increased number of students with disabilities on their campuses (Belch, 2004–2005). Data collected in the fall of 2000 and reported by Henderson (2001) indicated that 6 percent of first-time full-time freshmen who were attending four-year colleges self-reported having disabilities. Successful transition and adjustment require collaboration on the part of all those involved with educational and support services for students with special needs.

Students with disabilities who plan to attend a college or university also need preparation to use the transition services that will be available at that institution. Partnership with college student services offices is an important collaborative relationship to build for educators responsible for high school transition services. Students might visit campuses or take precollege courses. Perhaps most important of all is that they be introduced to sources of assistance on campus to whom they can go for help in choosing appropriate classes and arranging with their instructors for accommodations and modifications with their instructors.

University educators and administrators must acknowledge the needs students have for developing skills to facilitate successful adjustment to college life and then assist them with those needs. Unfortunately, the dropout rate for students with disabilities is extremely high. The rate of attaining a college degree for students with disabilities was reported as 14 percent in 2000 (Harris and Associates, 2004). In her extensive review of research about college retention of students with disabilities, Holley Belch (2004–2005) found that the key elements for success were a sense of belonging and inclusion, involvement in both in- and out-of-class activities, a sense of purpose and intentionality, self-determination, and integration of successful universal design strategies in the curriculum and co-curriculum. These four attributes are not typically developed or nurtured as part of the work of a transition team for students; however, these skills, along with self-advocacy, are essential for postsecondary success of students with disabilities.

Educators have many partners in the transition to postsecondary education endeavor. For example, the National Science Foundation (NSF) funds collaborative programs across high schools and two- and four-year colleges to increase the number of students with disabilities who successfully complete degrees in science, technology, engineering, and mathematics (STEM) fields (www.nsf.gov). These projects, called Alliances for Students with Disabilities in STEM, include students with learning disabilities, autism, physical disabilities, hearing and sight impairments, and others. Supportive personnel are critical to the success of the alliances, and interagency collaboration is a hallmark of the program. Alliance partners provide a range of services, such as mentoring, internships, research experiences, social activities, and stipends for participation. These alliances and their work are described in a website funded by the Research in Disabilities Education (RDE) program of the NSF (www.washington.edu/doit/RDE/). The NSF-funded website includes materials designed to increase awareness of how people with disabilities can be successful in STEM and other educational programs, as well as how to make websites, course materials, and other printed materials more welcoming and accessible to individuals with disabilities. This website is an important resource for sharing with transition collaborators.

COLLABORATING ON GRANT PROPOSALS FOR EXTERNAL FUNDING

As school and community partners work collaboratively to improve the educational and social outcomes of children with disabilities, school consultants are often called upon to be part of a proposal-writing team to secure funding for new projects or programs. Grant money is available from a wide variety of sources, including the federal government, state governments, private donations, foundations, local businesses, local clubs and organizations, donations to fundraising activities, and corporations. These sources have programs and projects in mind that fit their philosophies and goals. They set their own procedures, which must be followed explicitly by proposal writers if they wish to be in the running to receive the grant funding.

Several benefits can result from submitting a collaborative grant proposal. The first is the collaboration experience gained by the team regardless of whether the grant proposal is funded. Few significant proposals are developed in these times that do not include a number of colleagues interacting to conceptualize and develop the plan, and then carry out the project after it is funded. Some people have major roles and others serve in minor ways, but all can participate and ultimately profit in tangible and intangible ways. Another benefit is the collection of resources and support needed to meet the goals of the grant. When multiple resources are targeted and letters of support are generated, more people become involved as supporters of innovative school programs.

When a grant proposal is funded, the benefits soar. Money and resources become available for carrying out projects that were only dreams or wishes before funding. This has an energizing, morale-boosting effect that reverberates throughout a school system. The amounts of money do not need to be sizable for these positive outcomes to be realized. Some of the most invigorating projects have resulted from relatively small grants, such as those from community groups or local businesses.

School consultants and collaborators are in ideal positions to work with others to secure grant funds. When projects impact students with special needs, school consultants provide an important voice in the development of such projects. Some larger districts employ proposal writers, but those individuals need to collaborate with other school and community personnel to develop successful proposals. As a proposal writing team works together, there are some important procedures that are vital to success of the endeavor: (1) identifying a need; (2) targeting a funding source; and (3) preparing the proposal using the helpful ten-step procedure.

Identifying a Need. Successful proposals emanate from an identified need, such as summer internships or work experiences for students with special needs. A good match must be found between that need and the philosophy and goals of an appropriate funding source. The proposed project may be wonderful, and the benefits for students very promising, but if it does not address the interests of the potential donor, it will be rejected.

Targeting Funding Sources. Several general sources of funding are available—public agencies, private foundations, and business entities. Proposals are solicited by public agencies, such as state departments of education, regional rehabilitation organizations, or, at the national level, the U.S. Department of Education or the National Science Foundation. Many large companies give grants as part of their tax structure. Smaller, local businesses, local charitable trusts or service organizations may have funds available for projects that benefit local schools, communities, or individuals. Requirements for proposals are somewhat different between public and private sources, so they must be studied carefully.

Preparing the Proposal. Development of a proposal begins with the idea for the project and continues through two phases: (1) planning; and (2) preparation. The most productive strategy is to spend about 80 percent of time and energy on planning the project, and the remaining 20 percent on writing the proposal. Those who switch these priorities often end up with weak projects that are hard to carry out even if funded.

The proposal must be prepared carefully and correctly according to the guidelines given, and submitted on time. Proposal writing requires both technical writing and creative writing, but, most of all, it requires excellent organization. Proposal preparation is hard work and astute grant writers follow these basic steps to avoid major pitfalls. They:

1. *Identify a need.* What is the problem that stems from that need? Is it potentially fundable? Priorities shift as other issues surface to capture public attention and funding agencies' interests. In the post-2010 era, there continues to be an emphasis on math and science education, preparing high quality teachers, workforce development and educational research that produces evidence-based practices which can be translated into effective classroom pedagogy. These are large topics, but they can be developed into smaller, doable activities and programs that would benefit students with special needs.

2. *Explore the research base* for information about the identified need. Ideally, proposers have conducted a needs assessment in their community or school system. These data will be extremely helpful in proving a need for a proposed project.

3. *Get together a team* of productive people. Having multiple perspectives and a wide range of competencies will vastly improve the proposal. Teams are particularly helpful for collecting the demographic data required for some proposals. Also, the more people who are involved in preparing the proposal, the greater the interest generated in supporting and participating in the project after it is funded. The team should include individuals with expertise and experience in the topic of the proposal. For example, a proposal to improve the success of students with disabilities in the transition to post-secondary education should include personnel from disabilities services offices at local community and 4-year colleges, transition specialists, students, parents, rehabilitation personnel, and educators. Teams should consider an evaluation specialist as a team member, especially if the funder requires extensive evaluation.

4. *Identify possible funding sources.* Federal funding sources are listed at www .grants.gov and in the *Federal Register.* Find out if someone in your district has access to this document. Most private funding sources have information that can be accessed on the Web. For example, the Philanthropic Ventures Foundation (www .venturesfoundation.org) has information about special education resource grants including an on-line guide and an on-line short course on proposal writing. The Foundation Center (www.fdncenter.org) also has a variety of online resources. However, a good place to start is with state or local foundations, trusts, and businesses. They have a vested interest in the well-being of students and families. It may be helpful to make a file containing basic information about each funding source so the team will know when to apply and the types of projects that are funded.

5. *Obtain the guidelines* for the selected funding source(s). A guidelines packet may be called an RFP (request for proposal) or a solicitation. From this point on, each step of the process carries an admonition—*Read the guidelines*! Read to be sure there is a good fit between your idea and the funding source. Look for the ability of that source to meet your budget request, for directions on how to submit the application, for criteria to be used in evaluating the proposal, and most of all, for the *application deadline.*

6. *Design the project.* As stressed earlier, this phase should take up the major time and energy directed toward the project. Again, read the guidelines thoroughly and often and be keenly aware of the deadline date. The Logic Model described in Chapter 12 is helpful in designing a project.

7. *Prepare a budget adequate for the project,* but not "padded." All items should be tied to the activities of the project and the key personnel costs involved. A budget set too low signals poor planning that could undermine the project. Budgets provide for indirect costs (overhead), any cost sharing or subcontracting for services, and, primarily, direct costs of the proposed project—salaries and fringe benefits, equipment, supplies and materials, travel (which is getting quite restrictive with many funding agencies), consultant fees, computer expenses, printing and duplicating, postage and telecommunication, along with other direct costs specific to the focus of the project.

8. *Interagency collaborative support* is a particularly desirable component of most large, externally funded projects, and a requirement of some agencies for submitted proposals. Collaboration and obvious teamwork usually result in a much stronger project in this day and age than do solo projects.

9. *Establish contact with the funding agency* and put to good use any suggestions their grants officers have for proposal development. Most organizations and agencies welcome conversations with those wanting to apply for funding. The primary job of those individuals (called program officers at Federal agencies) is to facilitate smart funding decisions so that their organization meets its mission. Determine if they are allowed to assist you in your proposal development; and always ask for their preferred mode of communication—email, phone, Skype, or another medium. For state and local funders, a scheduled visit is advised.

10. *Meet the deadline.* Most funders, large or small, are serious about their deadlines. If it is not met, the proposal may be eliminated and the time, energy, and costs expended in producing it are wasted. Local trusts, service organizations, businesses or charities have their own deadlines, which may be several times a year.

If a proposal is not funded, the developer(s) should ask to receive the reviews. This may mean a phone call or a visit if the funding organization is local. Reviewing comments is a form of professional development and can help make any next attempt more productive. If the review marks were good, but not quite good enough for the proposal to be selected, the proposal might be revised or modified and resubmitted. Proposals that are not funded should not be cast aside in a spirit of disillusionment, but critiqued thoroughly for possible revision and resubmission.

When proposals are funded, grant recipients often find that they become more and more successful with future applications. It appears to be a phenomenon of "the rich getting richer," but there is logic to this. The applicants have become more adept at preparing the proposals, and even more meaningfully, funding agencies believe that success of well-designed, funded projects will breed success for their contributed funds as well.

In summary, the ingredients for successful pursuit of external funds are an innovative idea, a team of qualified individuals, a close fit with the funding source, and a well-written, persuasive, potentially contributive proposal. The process does take effort, and some co-educators might want to pool their time and skills with each completing a part of the project.

Case Study: Teamwork for a Proposal to Obtain External Funding

The parent advocacy group in the local middle school has approached the school administration about developing a summer STEM (science, technology, engineering, math) camp for students with disabilities. Many students in the school have the potential for post-secondary education at the community college or university level, and parents want to encourage STEM-related interests and capacities of middle school students for STEM education and careers. The principal brought up this idea with the special education consultant as well as the science and math faculty in the school. They agreed to have an initial meeting with the advocacy group and other community stakeholders to discuss the idea and develop a proposal for external funding from state and local organizations. Using the points brought forth in the previous section on proposal development for external funding, and your collaborative problem-solving skills, assume the roles of teachers, administrators, and community members who would initiate and participate in the process. Then discuss how the situation might evolve collaboratively, remembering that the best teams typically are those with diversity of perspectives and preferences. Focus on the collaborative process for developing a project rather than the details of implementing a STEM program. Use the following points as a general guide:

- Description of the situation from the perspective of all stakeholders
- Additional stakeholders who could be involved to assure success of the project
- Intent of the project and potential problems
- Questions to ask, who to ask, and possible answers

TECHNOLOGY THAT FACILITATES CROSS-AGENCY COLLABORATION

Collaborating educators in the twenty-first century have technology tools that educators in years past could not have even envisioned, much less accessed and used. Many new forms of professional communities (sometimes called *communities of practice*) are developing via electronic means such as websites, blogs, and interactive chats. New tools make electronic interfacing with colleagues possible asynchronously rather and reduce the tedium of many clerical tasks. This gains time and energy needed for engaging in collaboration and co-teaching.

Many tools of technology are excellent vehicles for engaging in collegial activities to bolster energy and enthusiasm while in demanding situations for much of the day. However, use of technology must be accompanied by ample funding for high-quality maintenance and upgrades. (See Figure 13.6.)

FIGURE 13.6   "I Need Tech Support!"

One example of a community of practice is the DO-IT (Disabilities, Opportunities, Internetworking, and Technology) program at the University of Washington (www .washington.edu/doit/). This program focuses on promoting the success of individuals with disabilities and the use of computer and networking technologies to increase their independence, productivity, and participation in education and careers. DO-IT provides resources, publications, and videos that include information about evidence-based practices and universal design. Individuals can sign up as a member of the DO-IT community of practice and receive e-mail alerts about new research and other useful information.

Although the Internet and other electronic communication devices provide a wealth of information and resources to improve educational outcomes for students with special needs, several issues need to be reviewed. These involve confidentiality of information, assurance of privacy, vigilance in constructing firewalls to shut out pornography and profanity, adherence to copyrights and intellectual property rights, regard for disability, gender, and socioeconomic situations of collaborating partners who may not have funds for maintenance and support, access to the most recent technology, and development of skills for using it if it were available.

ETHICS FOR COLLABORATING ACROSS SCHOOL PROGRAMS, COMMUNITY ORGANIZATIONS, AND AGENCIES

If co-educators from a broad spectrum of roles are to collaborate successfully as team members in helping students with learning and behavioral disabilities, they must make every effort to respect and value the talents and skills of others who can help. When involved in interagency partnerships, collaborating professionals need to work diligently at understanding the perspectives and preferences of others. Awareness is growing in schools and communities that school systems alone cannot be expected to address learning and behavior problems of millions of children. Many collaborative initiatives are being explored that could expand services to help students learn and grow. Full-service schools, as interagency collaboratives that integrate schools and human services, are one example of these initiatives (McMahon et al., 2000).

For early childhood educators, codes of ethics and practices have been developed by the National Association for the Education of Young Children and the Council for Exceptional Children's Division for Early Childhood to point out the need for knowledge and skills. Collaboration with colleagues is included as an aim, but guidelines for working with adults are not clear-cut. More effort is needed to develop specific recommendations.

All service agencies have the same goal: to make a difference in the world by helping those in the community to grow, be productive, and lead fulfilling lives. Resources—from social worker to music teacher to audiologist to security officer to special education administrator to Big Brother volunteer to school secretary and on and on—can be tapped in many ways for students who have difficulty learning and relating in society. Keen awareness and understanding of roles will nurture an ethical climate for collaboration. Respect and support for all, with thoughtful consolidation of efforts by those in home, school, and community, will make positive differences in students' lives. The most important steps in interagency collaboration are for all entities, including the family, to know and relate to the work of the others.

TIPS FOR INTRA-AGENCY AND INTERAGENCY COLLABORATION

1. Don't try to do everything yourself.
2. Develop rapport with media specialists. Give them advance notice of upcoming topics and try not to make too many spur-of-the-moment requests.
3. Make friends with custodians in your attendance centers and refrain from making excessive demands on their time and energy.
4. Keep public remarks about colleagues on a positive, professional level. If you must vent, try using a journal at home. Reviewing it now and then may show you the way to improve the situation.
5. Remember special things about the faculty in each school, and start a card file or electronic files or notes with comments that will be useful in personalizing the interactions. If you find a news article pertaining in a positive way to a colleague or a student, clip it out and send it along with a congratulatory note.
6. Do not expect the same levels of involvement and commitment from everyone.
7. Have open houses, extending invitations to school board members and community organizations, with follow-up thank-you notes to those who visited.
8. Drop off samples of periodicals such as *Educational Leadership, Phi Delta Kappan, Early Childhood Today, Journal of Emotional and Behavioral Disorders, Journal of Learning Disabilities,* and *Gifted Child Today* at offices of pediatricians, obstetricians, and dentists for their waiting rooms. If possible, have a brief visit with the medical staff about potential value of these materials to families and community members.
9. Build networks of interaction among school personnel, parents, and community members who could serve as tutors, monitors, mentors, and independent study facilitators for special needs.
10. With a colleague, discuss developing a proposal that would provide funds for a project you would like to do with students or co-educators. If possible, write and submit this proposal.

ADDITIONAL RESOURCES

Nelson, G., Amio, J. L., Prilleltensky, I., & Nickels, P. (2000). Partnerships for school and community prevention programs. *Journal of Educational and Psychological Consultation, 11*(1), 121–145.

Pianta, R. C., & Kraft-Sayre, M. (2003). *Successful kindergarten transition: Your guide to connecting children, families, and schools.* Baltimore, MD: Brookes.

14

Leadership, Mentorships, and Professional Development for Collaborative School Consultation

ENVISIONING COLLABORATIVE EDUCATIONAL ENVIRONMENTS is a relatively easy process; developing such environments and implementing them require much more effort. The leadership of experienced school administrators and well-prepared teachers can be catalyzing in a collaborative environment. Leadership in schools is not a position, but a *way of thinking and doing* in the educational setting. As leaders, administrators can forge alliances for *doing* with other social service agencies, business foundations, judicial systems, library and media centers, colleges and universities, families, civic groups, and members of the community (Lugg & Boyd, 1993). As leaders, mentors, and professional developers, teachers can steer their colleagues toward determining what students can do and what more they *could* do with the assistance of special services. Getting everyone involved in leadership builds leadership density in schools, which benefits all (McNulty, 2003). A collaborative esprit de corps is activated when all school personnel learn together, with the support of strong leadership from school administrators, co-teachers, and professional development personnel (see Figure 14.1).

FOCUSING QUESTIONS

1. How do superior leadership skills and mentor–mentee partnerships enhance collaborative school consultation?

2. What leadership can school administrators and school boards provide to nurture collaborative relationships and team partnerships among school personnel?

3. How can professional development personnel promote collaborative consultation among a broad range of school personnel with multiple roles and assignments?

4. What part can the teachers' workroom/lounge have in stimulating collaborative consultation and teamwork?

5. How does modern technology alter leadership and professional development in the twenty-first century?

6. What ethical guidelines are needed for carrying out roles of leadership, mentorship, and professional development activity?

KEY TERMS

leadership in education	presenter–presentee	school administrator
mentor–mentee	professional development	school board

VIGNETTE 14

Several teachers in an elementary school setting are conversing in the teachers' workroom on Friday afternoon.

Fourth-Grade Teacher: What a week! I think my to-do list included everything but my students and the curriculum. Maybe the schedule will ease off a bit next week.

Fifth-Grade Teacher: Guess you didn't look at your office memo yet, hmmm? There's a reminder about the staff development sessions next Tuesday and Thursday mornings before school—something about collaborative consultation with special education.

Fourth-Grade Teacher: Oh, good grief. Consultation? You mean programs by those imported experts breezing in from more than fifty miles away with a bunch of slick, commercial PowerPoint presentations? I think my sister's school district upstate just had something like that.

Third-Grade Teacher: I believe this group involves our own special education staff. We're supposed to find out about what we all can do together now that so many children with learning and behavioral problems are in our classrooms for most of their class time.

Art Teacher: Great. Just how does that involve me? I had my required course in special education. What I really need is a bigger room and more supplies.

Fourth-Grade Teacher: And then if we're expected to collaborate with these people, where will we find the time?

Physical Education Teacher: Uh-huh. It will be hard enough just carving out the time to go to the meeting about it. I'm scheduled to be at a district track meet that day.

Third-Grade Teacher: Ha! Now you all know you'd rather be trying to focus on some new-fangled proposal when you really just want to be getting your classroom good-to-go.

Fourth-Grade Teacher: Well, if they don't wind it up by 8:20 sharp, I'm out of there!

LEADERSHIP IN INCLUSIVE, COLLABORATIVE SCHOOL ENVIRONMENTS

Leadership is an enigmatic quality. For many years, sociologists, psychologists, and educators have tried to define leadership, with only marginal success. It is one of those constructs that we can't describe, but we know it when we see it.

Perhaps this simple definition will serve the purpose here: *Leadership* is the capacity to influence people and represent them, and to carry out responsibilities on their behalf.

"To expand a bit on that, some would add "Good leaders help others to progress in such a way that they think they did it all themselves." Eminent leader and former United States president Harry Truman said it in words something like this: "Great leaders have the ability to get others to do what they really don't want to do—and to like doing it!

Effective leaders nurture responsive followers. They make others feel more empowered. They thrive on the successes of those who follow their lead. They take pleasure in seeing a collaborative team spirit coalesce and they constantly strive to help others improve and grow. Strong educators are not threatened when they note signs of leadership in others. They call on the combined strengths and efforts of others to address the concerns together to achieve success (Miller, Devin, & Shoop, 2007).

In the everyday work world, leaders use phrases and expressions that make others want to succeed. They avoid phrases such as "It'll never work in our district," or "That's been tried before with no success," or "We're too new/old/big/small/inexperienced/set in our ways, to do that in our school." Expressions that leaders avoid because they dampen enthusiasm are, "It could never work here in our area," or "We've done it before," or "With more experience you would not even have suggested it," or "The time is not right for that." How much more effective the communication would be if useful comments were shared, as suggested by Annunzio (2001)—for example, "It seems unworkable to me, so help me understand how it *could* work," or "I'll explain what we tried before, and you can explain how your idea is different," or "That sounds innovative, but there may be some obstacles, and if there are, how could we overcome them?"

Not all leaders are openly active and dynamic in their leadership style. Some very successful leaders have reflective leadership styles, shaping others' values quietly by teaching and modeling. Active leadership skills are developed in situations where there are opportunities to lead by enhancing communication skills (including listening skills), honing creative problem-solving and critical thinking skills, and practicing the "people skills" of conflict resolution, meetings management, and organizational procedure that were introduced earlier. Reflective leadership skills grow through activities such as researching universal problems and learning how social policies are developed and implemented. Problems are solved in a climate of interdisciplinary teamwork. In the collaborative environment, leadership often is diffused and passed around among diverse groups of individuals to use all available talents and skills in addressing the issues and concerns.

COLLABORATIVE SCHOOL CONSULTANTS AS MENTORS

Effective leaders and enthusiastic followers are positioned well for roles as mentors and mentees (those who are mentored). The mentorship concept originated and was recorded many centuries ago in Greek literature to describe the relationship of Odysseus, son of Telemachus, and Mentor, chosen by Telemachus to be Odysseus' model and guide. Mentor was directed to be part "parent" and part peer—model, guide on the side, expert, diagnostician, appraiser, and advocate for Odysseus—all taking place in the full press of daily business and Mentor's own work.

In modern times, the relationship between mentor and mentee is based on shared talent and passion for the field of common interest; it is special and personal. The mentor recognizes budding talent in the mentee but does not push for the mentee's commitment or achievement of greatness. However, the mentor does share a sense of timing—when to bear down, when to ease off, and when to take advantage of a teachable, leadable moment. A mentor coaches toward the bent of the mentee, modeling indirectly through experience rather than just dispensing information to be ingested (or, with some, simply ignored). A mentor–mentee relationship is an ideal situation for novice teachers to gain experiential learning from master practitioners. Such relationships can encourage beginning teachers early in their careers so as to *keep them there,* thus avoiding burnout and attrition.

When studying effects of mentoring on special education teacher retention, Whitaker (2000) noted the alarming statistics that approximately 15 percent of new teachers leave after their first year of teaching, and 10 percent to 15 percent more do so after the second year, compared with an overall annual rate of 6 percent attrition for teachers nationally. Whitaker's research showed that the effectiveness of mentoring correlates significantly with special education teachers' plans to remain in special education. A careful matching of a special education teacher mentor with one who teaches students having the same disabilities is particularly relevant. Unstructured, informal, and frequent contacts are very important in the mentor–mentee relationship.

Marsal (1997) proposed that mentoring relationships established between beginning teachers and their experienced, effective colleagues can reduce the alarming rates of attrition from the teaching profession during the first five years. As a supporter of the Council for Exceptional Children (CEC) Guidelines for Developing a Mentorship for Beginning Special Education Teachers, adopted at the 1997 CEC convention, Marsal challenged each CEC member to find at least one person with potential for being a fine educator and to mentor that person in his or her local context.

Development and practice of consultation, collaboration, and co-teaching skills are superb conduits through which modeling and mentoring can occur. Some interesting mentorship programs have been developed using the services of retired teachers who welcome the opportunity to become involved, just as grandparents welcome grandparenting—loving every minute with their young charges and sharing their years of experience and wisdom, then going home at the end of the day invigorated and satisfied, with few to no carry-over responsibilities.

Some mentorships develop serendipitously and phase out casually. However, for a more planned and structured arrangement, it is helpful to match mentor and mentee by teaching styles, curricular specialties, and extracurricular interests such as sports, music, or debate. Having frequent communication about successful and not-so-successful teaching events, thinking recursively about instructional activities and the whole school day, discussing ideas for instruction and aspirations for students, analyzing texts and tests, can be middle steps in mentoring. (See Figure 14.2.) In a rich collaborative environment, both mentor and mentee will gain, as will their students.

The mentorship roles must be voluntary. An unstructured and informal mentorship is often most effective. One caution pertaining to this professional relationship is that there must be advance preparation for the inevitable termination of the relationship. Mentorships do end eventually and when this is taken into account at the outset, most often in the

FIGURE 14.2   Mentorship Means Caring and Sharing

format of a mutually agreed-on limit of weeks or months, the way is prepared for when and how it will be over. In this way neither participant feels "stood up" or let down. Formal mentorships that are terminated smoothly often develop into long-standing professional friendships.

A different approach to new-teacher education is an induction program (a highly organized and comprehensive form of professional development) in five countries—Switzerland, France, Japan, New Zealand, and (Shanghai) China. The program lasts at least two years; it involves new teachers in practice groups that network to learn effective problem solving, and includes mentoring as a component of the induction process (Wong, Britton, & Ganser, 2005). The approach may differ among countries, but all have three commonalities: a high level of structure, a focus on professional learning, and an emphasis on collaboration. Collaboration is considered the strength of the model, which contrasts with a common complaint of isolation that often is expressed among new teachers in U.S. schools. Wong et al. (2005) report that:

> New teachers want more than a job. They want to experience success. They want to contribute to a group. *They want to make a difference.* Thus collegial interchange, not isolation, must become the norm for teachers. (p. 384; emphasis added)

This is remarkably reflective of teachers' aspirations that were summarized in an earlier chapter.

THE SCHOOL ADMINISTRATOR'S ROLE IN INCLUSIVE, COLLABORATIVE SCHOOLS

A building principal's role and responsibilities are just short of overwhelming. So many school issues compete for a principal's time and energy that consultants must make special efforts to accommodate their principals' heavily committed schedules when seeking their involvement in consultation and collaboration. But regardless of the heavy schedules and myriad responsibilities, building administrators *must* be involved; their roles are key in allowing collaboration to happen and encouraging it to be successful. They are the ones who approve and make allocations for the time, space, and materials so necessary for effective consultation and collaboration. They assign paraeducators and coordinate teamwork that takes place among building personnel. They also approve professional development for educational reform and new programs.

Building principals should work with consulting teachers to clarify collaborative consultation roles and ensure that such roles have parity among the school staff. They can assist teachers greatly by freeing up some of their classroom time and arranging for substitutes or other alternatives so consultation and collaboration among school personnel can take place. It is very important that they encourage school personnel to interact, partner on projects, and work together in teams. When building administrators expedite the arrangements, promote them, and most of all, *attend* the activities with an encouraging attitude as they do so, the positive ripple effects can be profound.

In a review of educational research on the principal's role in creating inclusive schools for diverse learners, Riehl (2000) notes that school leadership has moved well beyond application of knowledge and skills as a science of administration might suggest, and even beyond the finesse of process as an art of administrative performance, to become school administration as a form of *practice*. According to Riehl, school administration as a practice "creates a 'horizon' that envisions what schools create and where they might lead" (p. 69).

A study by Foley and Lewis (1999) indicated that the traditional secondary-level administrator's role as manager and primary decision maker for operation and function of the school, with responsibility for centralized control of school activities and resources, is not congruent with the principles of collegiality, parity, and shared decision making that have become the underpinnings of collaborative-based structures. Foley and Lewis suggest

■ ■ ■ ■ ■

ACTION 14.1
Questions Put to a Building Administrator

The context is an inclusive school working toward a more collaborative environment. Keeping leadership, followership, mentor, and mentee roles in mind, in a classroom–teacher mode, pose these eight questions to your school's administrator in a conversation about consultation, collaboration, and teamwork with school personnel:

1. Must I have a student with disabilities in my classroom? If so, who has the responsibility of developing curriculum and lessons for him or her?

2. If I don't agree with what the special education teachers or support staff asks me to do and I discuss the issues with them but we don't resolve it, what should I do next?

3. Why does the special education teacher have a smaller caseload than I do?

4. Whose responsibility is it to supervise and evaluate the special education staff and support personnel staff?

5. How may I request services for a student that are not available now in our school?

6. Where will I find the time to confer and collaborate with consulting teachers?

7. How can I go about setting up co-teaching with a colleague? And if it doesn't work out after a dedicated fair trial, what do we do?

8. Am I accountable for standardized test scores of all students in my room, including those with disabilities?

a shift in authority that encourages the principal to be a team member and to support others in leadership roles and collaboration as well.

In their handbook *A Principal's Guide,* Bateman and Bateman (2001) target the principal's role in special education and discuss what principals need to know in order to implement best practices in their schools. Topics covered include eligibility, assessments and evaluations; inclusive schools; special education laws; policy issues concerning discipline, due process, accommodations and adaptations of materials, instructional strategies, and assessments; selection and evaluation of special education teachers; and more (Council for Exceptional Children, 2001). It is vital for all school administrators, along with general and special education personnel and related services and support personnel, to study and reflect on such issues.

Getting Off to the Right Start with School Administrators

Four guiding questions for collaborative school consultation were introduced in Chapter 1. It is time to reiterate those questions here in order to focus on a plan for setting goals as co-educators. The questions are:

■ Who am I [to be] in this [collaborative school consultation] role?
■ How do I carry out responsibilities of the role?

FIGURE 14.3   Ten Steps to Follow in Working with School Administrators

1. First, read, study, think, interview others, and complete coursework or professional development sessions, if possible, to gain information and skills about collaborating and consulting as teams of co-educators.

2. Formulate your own personal philosophy of collaboration as a co-educator.

3. Observe the chain-of-command conventions in your assigned school(s), by first meeting with a central administrator, if feasible, to learn administrators' perceptions of the collaborative consultant role or co-teacher role for the district.

4. If an advisory council is part of the administrative structure, engage members in discussion about consultation and collaboration roles. The council should include general and special education teachers, support personnel, administrators, families, and other community leaders, and perhaps a student or two. If there is no advisory council, find out if and how one could be formed and consider taking a leadership role in doing so.

5. Meet with all building administrators to whom assigned, using excellent responsive listening skills to learn their viewpoints before sharing yours. *This is an extremely important step.*

6. After meeting with principals of your assigned attendance centers, reorganize your thoughts and ideas based on information you collected, and gather more information if necessary.

7. Develop a tentative role description and goals based on views expressed by central and building administrators' views and advisory council views as well as your own perspective.

8. Return to central administration and/or building administrators as appropriate in your district(s), conveying the description and goals to them and revising if necessary.

9. After honing the plan to a concise format, put it up for discussion, explaining it to teaching staff and nonteaching staff and refining it even further based on their comments. Try to include something that is suggested by each and can help all.

10. Convey the essence of the plan to co-educators during a professional development or staff meeting, and to parents during a parent-teacher meeting or individually to family members.

- How do I know whether I am succeeding?
- How can I prepare for such a role?

Sometimes just getting started is the hardest part of doing something that has great potential for being a pleasant and fulfilling professional experience. See Figure 14.3 for ten steps that will put co-educators on the right track to success by paving the way with school administrators, especially their building principals.

SCHOOL BOARD MEMBERS AS PARTNERS IN EDUCATION

School districts in the United States are governed by boards of education. The school board is arguably the most influential group in a community because its members oversee education for children and youth of the community; therefore, these elected members are framing the future. Being a school board member in a community may be the most significant responsibility that can be fulfilled by a citizen of that community.

A school board sets policies for operation of the district's schools, including the hiring of staff, approval of curriculum, and care for the attendance centers and other school property. Hiring duties include the all-important task of selecting a superintendent of schools. The superintendent is the agent of the school board, and the board is agent of the community. The aggregate of individuals making up the board are to speak as one body in formulating policy for the community's schools, enforcing the policies, and evaluating the outcomes of policies; they do not speak as individuals. This is important to remember when interacting with a school board member.

Effective school board membership calls for members to focus on policy and not become mired in regulations or procedural matters that focus on "buses, ballgames, buildings, and budgets," as some would label them. These areas are vital to the operation of schools, but it is very important that school boards also discuss and make decisions about matters such as curriculum, goals for student achievement, teacher selection and contracts, special education programs, and the structure and philosophy of inclusionary schools. Teachers who are leaders and aim to introduce concepts such as curriculum revision, changes in basal textbooks, block scheduling, collaboration among co-educators, or co-teaching arrangements, should bring their proposed plans to the school board's attention by way of their school administrator.

Board meetings typically are held monthly and sometimes more often; they tend to be long, often arduous, and sometimes contentious because of the high stakes—the community's children—involved. Nevertheless, teachers should attend meetings now and then, even when their own topics of immediate concern are not on the agenda. Doing so demonstrates to the board that teachers want to be informed and involved. A group of co-educators, representing all grade levels and curricular areas, could collaborate on occasion to present a report to the school board about a current topic such as the efforts they are making to plan and teach together. Sometimes boards have additional meetings—typically a workshop session when there is a new educational trend or innovation they want to learn more about, or a public forum where parents and taxpayers can become more informed about their schools. Faculty and other school personnel should discuss the news reports that come out after board meetings and generally are made available in local newspapers and sometimes in school newsletters.

When school personnel want the news to flow the other way—from school to board—they must remember that board members are typically some of the community's busiest people. So they will react most favorably to comprehensive, concise written reports or fact sheets. Examples of what teachers have done, what students have accomplished, and how the schools can be showcased, will set a positive tone for introducing any proposed policy changes or innovative ideas. Administrators and teachers may want to invite interested students to attend meetings occasionally, and if the topic warrants it, to present an issue, or better yet, to share highlights of good news with the board about school and student accomplishments.

Too few educators and others in the general public know very much about school boards—how they are selected, qualifications for running (which are surprisingly minimal), their term of office, whether they are reimbursed or not, and perhaps most intriguing, reasons a candidate puts herself or himself up to run for a school board position. Teacher education programs should provide preservice teachers with more knowledge about their employer—the school board, and practicing teachers need to become familiar with who is on the board, why they are members, and what transpires at board meetings.

School board members must be active listeners and skilled decision makers. They also must be attuned to the adage that no one can please all of the people all of the time. With that firmly in mind, they can give their best efforts in:

- Collaborating with fellow board members
- Articulating policies to their constituents as a body and not individuals
- Demonstrating creativity in problem identification and problem solving
- Looking at the long-term needs and goals, not just those for the immediate term
- Arriving at consensus as decision makers
- Functioning as change agents for their communities

Collaboration, consultation, and co-education are important tools for school boards as well as for school personnel in fulfilling their responsibilities.

PROFESSIONAL DEVELOPMENT FOR CO-EDUCATORS

Professional development (PD) is a major factor in the success of school consultation, collaboration, and co-teaching. When carefully planned and well delivered, it strengthens interactive processes. School personnel now in the profession and preservice teachers preparing for careers in education need professional development experiences to build the scaffolding that will support their consultation, collaboration, and co-teaching efforts and further develop their professionally relevant people skills. Furthermore, consulting teachers for students with exceptional learning needs often are called on to prepare material for staff development, and some are asked to present sessions for their colleagues or for families of the students with special needs.

That is the good news. The not-so-good news is, unfortunately, that attitudes toward professional development are often anything but positive and stimulating. Opinions about PD experiences range from indifference to resentment to disdain. The harshest criticisms focus on a lack of clear purpose and relevance to anything they are doing or needing, poor use of their time, problematic scheduling, and questions about how the material will affect them and their students.

In order to provide the most constructive professional development experiences possible, planners and presenters must address five points:

1. How do adults respond to and acquire new information and ideas for their work?
2. What should co-educators know and do in order to serve students with special needs effectively?
3. What kinds of materials and assistance will be most helpful for collaborating educators?
4. How might the material be presented effectively and evaluated efficiently?
5. How can follow-up and support be provided after the professional development activities? (This is *very* important.)

The collaborative consultation role is ideal for planning and coordinating inservice and staff development activities about special needs. Special education personnel often inherit these responsibilities either as part of a plan or by default. Disadvantages as well as advantages exist in being a "prophet in one's own land" and conducting professional development activities. But one of the biggest advantages for planners/presenters is knowledge of the school context, along with being aware of what participants probably already know and what they still need or want to know. Advantages for presentees are that their co-teachers are familiar to them and can be accessed easily for more information or answers to questions.

The first step for professional development personnel is to acknowledge that each person's perception of the environment reflects one's own stage of development and is filtered through one's own perspectives and preferences. Presenters must attend to different needs of participants, including those who (Garmston & Wellman, 1992):

- Are looking for facts, data, and references
- Are wishing to relate the topic to themselves
- Are wanting to ponder and explore the topic(s)
- Would like to adapt, modify, or create new ideas and processes

Components of Effective Professional Development

With adult learner characteristics and individual style variations in mind, professional developers will need to arrange for participant comfort, give participants options and choices, manage their valuable time well, deliver practical and focused help, and follow up on the effectiveness of the experience. Busy educators value activities in which they work toward realistic, job-related, useful goals. They need to see results for their efforts as demonstrated by success when they do use the material within their school context. Staff development must illustrate clearly ways in which new practices can improve student performance, and how these practices can be implemented without too much disruption or extra work (Guskey, 1985). This is particularly important when focusing on consultation and collaboration because this kind of professional activity often involves more time and effort at the outset. Too often professional development is designed to focus on "attitude adjustment" before there are validations of successful strategies. So it begins at the wrong place—that is, telling teachers why they should do something and then expecting them to want to do it. In Guskey's well-received model of teacher change, staff development is presented to generate *change in classroom teaching practices.* This causes change in student learning outcomes, resulting in changes in teacher beliefs and attitudes. An idea is presented that teachers can use successfully. They do so and they like it. *Then* they will "buy into it" as valuable to them; thus, the professional development is effective.

Kelleher (2003) describes professional development as a form of adult learning that must be concerned primarily with student learning. A speaker or an activity might be interesting to participants, but the test of success is what teachers *do* with the new information they receive. Kelleher recommends allocating professional development budgets so as to encourage teachers to focus heavily on activities related to peer collaboration.

A peer-collaboration strand that features teachers collaborating in writing curriculum and assessments, examining student work, observing each other's classrooms, and mentoring new teachers can have significant impact on student achievement.

Assessing Needs for Professional Development

What do participants already know about a specified topic at this point? What do they want to learn? How can they be involved in planning, conducting, and evaluating experiences for their individual needs? This information should be solicited through needs assessment instruments. Most school personnel have had prior experience with completing needs assessments. It is a good professional activity to both complete and construct needs assessment instruments. Formats for needs assessments include:

- Checklists
- Questionnaires and surveys
- Open-ended surveys directed at areas of concern
- Interviews
- Brainstorming sessions
- Informal techniques such as interviews, surveys, observations, buzz groups

Needs assessments might ask personnel to check topics of need or to describe their concerns that can then be developed into a staff development activity.

Presenting Professional Development Activities

Garmston (1988), an expert in providing practical, helpful coaching for professional development planners, compares presenting inservice session or staff development with giving presents. He suggests the "present" should be something participants (presentees) want or can utilize, personalized to individual taste as much as possible, attractively wrapped, and a bit fun and perhaps suspenseful.

Presenters of professional development experiences should:

- Know their audience's needs and interests
- Have something on the agenda that appeals to everyone
- Conduct the activity in an interesting, efficient, multimodal format
- Package the material attractively
- Pace the session so all major points are covered within the time span allocated
- Ensure that no one's input is overlooked
- Provide an element of surprise and intrigue
- Deliver follow-up, support, and additional information

Formal and Informal Approaches to Professional Development

Professional development can be formal or informal in nature. Formal activities can be conducted through scheduled sessions, attendance at conferences, presentations, modules, courses, brochures, retreats, and other planned activities. Informal activities occur through

FIGURE 14.4   **Formal and Informal Professional Development**

	Formal	Informal
Plan	Typically structured Example: Workshop	Usually casual Example: Newsletter column
Method	Designed with care Example: Speaker/discussion	Somewhat spontaneous Example: Hall chat
Evaluation	Data collection Example: Checklist	Reflection Example: Journal note

conversations, observations, reports about one topic that then include another aspect of education, memos, references to media productions, Internet forums and chat rooms, mini-presentations by co-educators at faculty meetings, newsletters, and purposeful reading material. (See Figure 14.4.)

One enterprising group of teachers organized a series of sessions called "THT— Teachers Helping Teachers," in which they took turns delivering short sessions on topics in which they had expertise. Soon the idea caught on among other teachers. A teacher who had an exemplary skill to share prepared and presented, with administrator support, a half-day session for teachers in another school within the district. Other teachers followed suit at various times throughout the school year to present on topics reflecting their own particular interests and skills. When co-educators ask what they can do to help each other, they are cultivating professional development in collaborative school environments.

Steps in Providing Professional Development Activities

There is no single inservice and staff development format that will be appropriate for every school context. However, the following steps can be adapted to a variety of schools and staff needs:

1. Discuss attitudes and views about professional development with a variety of colleagues.
2. Conduct a needs assessment.
3. Select the topic to be featured.
4. Determine the audience to be targeted.
5. Choose a catchy, upbeat title for the activity.
6. Determine presenters who will contribute.
7. Decide on incentives, promotion, and publicity.
8. Outline the presentation and prepare opening remarks carefully.
9. List the equipment and room arrangement needed.
10. Plan thoroughly the content to be covered.
11. Prepare handouts and visual materials.

12. Rehearse the presentation and note the time element.

13. Determine an evaluation procedure for the activity.

14. Plan for follow-through and follow-up activities.

Finding Time for Professional Development Activities

Time is the enemy when planning whole-faculty or small-group faculty sessions where teachers can concentrate and reflect. Before-school and after-school hours might seem *workable* because participants are coming to school anyway, or are required to stay after school for a specific length of time. But are they *preferable*? Most teachers dislike these times, finding it hard to focus on their own learning at an early hour when their thoughts are centered on beginning the school day efficiently, and feeling that by day's end their energy and emotions will be lagging and other responsibilities beckoning. Saturday sessions are no more popular because they encroach on the family time and community life so necessary for sustaining teacher vitality and support. (See Figure 14.5.)

The arrangement preferred by teachers is released time. But this means that teachers' responsibilities with students during that time will need to be assumed by others. Numerous suggestions have been offered by professional development experts for carving time out of schedules and responsibilities, such as occasionally hiring substitute teachers, having a permanent substitute cadre that conducts planned enrichment activities, providing roving substitute teachers, or arranging teams whereby one teacher teaches two or more classes to free up team partners for professional development activities.

FIGURE 14.5 **"I Wish Professional Development Days Weren't on Saturdays!"**

The substitute cadre eliminates the necessity for detailed lesson planning by the teacher, because the enrichment activities are planned and provided by the substitute. Roving substitutes allow released teachers to have short periods of time for observing, coaching, gathering research data, or assisting in another classroom. Loucks-Horsley, Harding, Arbuckle, Murray, Dubea, and Williams (1987) counsel that the time issue is a "red herring" because the problem often lies in the constructive *use* of time, not its availability.

Presenter and Participant Responsibilities

Colleagues who deliver inservice and staff development on their own professional turf may face some difficulty in being accepted as "prophets in their own land" (Smith-Westberry & Job, 1986). They will want to scrutinize their own capabilities and deficits first. Practice sessions can help presenters gain confidence and skill. Smith-Westberry and Job recommend video capture practice sessions, uncomfortable though that may be, and critiquing the recorded sessions carefully to correct deficiencies. Presenters must extend the professional courtesy of obtaining permission from participants before the recording session is conducted, and place participants so they are not identifiable.

Participants, as presentees, have the responsibility to participate wholeheartedly in the activity, to help with the evaluation, and to commit themselves to follow-up activities. One of the most important contributions on their part is to overcome negative attitudes (such as those that surfaced in this chapter's opening vignette) and anticipate positive outcomes.

Follow-Up to the Professional Development Experience   Follow-up activity is the breeze that fans the fires of change when sparked by an activity (Dettmer, 1990). Educators sometimes avoid trying new concepts and techniques because they are uncomfortable with them or uncertain about the outcomes. It is easy to revert to business as usual once an activity is over. So follow-up is vital, just as it is with the collaborative consultation process. Possibilities include peer coaching, discussion groups, observations at sites where the innovation is occurring, newsletters, and interviews. Data gathered during follow-up and follow-through activities can be used to plan future professional development projects. An example of one brief follow-up instrument is included in Figure 14.6. Of course, personal contact is best; therefore, the evaluator should consider conducting this follow-up as an interview.

One caution must be extended. When educators are introduced to new concepts and challenged to try new approaches, some discomfort is inevitable. The adage that training may make one worse before it makes one better is an important point to consider. It is easy and convenient to revert to former ways because learning and implementing new ways, and especially giving up old and familiar ways, can be hard. This accents the need for follow-through efforts and perseverance on the part of the professional developer.

Evaluation of Professional Development   Evaluation of a professional development activity is imperative for at least two reasons. First, development is conducted to implement change, so information must be gathered to assess the change (Todnem & Warner, 1994). Second, there is pressure now more than ever before for accountability

FIGURE 14.6   Follow-Up Information for Professional Development

Please take a few minutes to respond to these questions about the recent staff development held
___/ /___ on the topic of _____ . In doing so you will be helping staff developers and presenters
plan effective staff development experiences for you and your colleagues.

1. Have you implemented any idea or strategy that was presented during the staff development?
   If so, please describe it briefly and rate the success level:

   _____

   _____

   _____

   _____ 1 = not effective   _____ 2 = somewhat effective   _____ 3 = very effective

2. Is there something more you would like to learn about this topic? If so, please describe your need.

   _____

   _____

   _____

3. If you did not use the staff development information, please tell why you did not.

   _____

   _____

   _____

4. This item is *very* important. Did the information or enthusiasm you received have positive ripple effects
   that you could identify and describe? If so, please do, and also rate the extent to which this happened.

   _____

   _____

   _____

   _____ 1 = a little   _____ 2 = somewhat   _____ 3 = to a great extent   _____ 4 = profoundly

in education. Evaluators will want to know if participants are using the information that
was presented, and whether the material has made a difference in their classrooms and
the school in general.

The tool used most often for evaluation is a questionnaire that participants complete
immediately following the activity. The evaluation should include both objective responses
and an invitation for open-ended responses. A Likert scale of five to seven values is preferable to a yes/no format. See Figure 14.7 for an example of an inservice/staff development
evaluation tool.

FIGURE 14.7   Evaluation Form for Inservice/Staff Development

Professional Development Evaluation

Date _____

Name (optional) _____   Teaching Area and Level(s) _____

Site of the Professional Development _____ Topic _____

Rate the following with a value from 1 through 5:

1 = None   2 = A little   3 = Somewhat   4 = Considerably   5 = Much

1. The event increased my understanding of the topic. _____
2. The goals and objectives of the event addressed needs I had identified. _____
3. The content was well developed and organized. _____
4. The material was presented effectively. _____
5. The environment was satisfactory. _____
6. I gained ideas to use in my own situation. _____
7. I will use at least one idea from this event. _____
8. Strengths of the event: _____
9. Ways the event could be improved: _____
10. I would like to know more about: _____

Outcomes of Professional Development

Professional development for consultation, collaboration, and special needs of students has the potential to create positive ripple effects that have no bounds. It can encourage:

- Increased respect for individual differences, creative approaches, and educational excellence
- Teacher proficiency in innovative curriculum and teacher strategies
- Staff and parent involvement, encouraging satisfaction with the educational system
- Collegiality and collaboration among all school personnel as well as family and community members

In order to attain these positive outcomes, professional development experiences must be planned, conducted, evaluated, and followed up efficiently.

THE TEACHERS' WORKROOM AS FORUM FOR COLLEGIAL INTERACTION

Very little has been written about the teachers' workroom, sometimes known as "the lounge," even though as a general rule not much lounging goes on there. This lack of attention to the place is surprising because most teachers are there for at least a while at some time or another periodically. Some go frequently, and others hardly ever do. Visits usually fall within one of three purposes—physical, social, or professional. There may be the physical benefit of refreshment, a quick "nap," or a restroom break. A few minutes of socialization with adults, squeezed between intensive hours with children and adolescents, is beneficial for some. Professional reasons include attending to tasks such as grading papers or reading materials, or getting one's thoughts and plans together before the next barrage of youthful energy bursts into the classroom.

Oftentimes teachers drop into the teachers' workroom for an opportunity to interact with colleagues and share reflections about teaching practices and student needs. Good ideas for collaboration and co-teaching can spring from, or slowly unfold from, these brief moments and come back to mind at a later time with more focused attention.

Sometimes "break room moments" are problematic because occasionally the discourse can become quite negative and cynical. When this kind of talk negatively affects one's morale, being there becomes iatrogenic and probably should be avoided. Nevertheless, the teachers' workroom generally is accepted by educators as a useful hub of interaction and this may be appreciated most of all by special education teachers. They have opportunity there to develop rapport with general education colleagues and learn more about their classrooms and students.

It is important that special education teachers spend enough time in the teachers' workroom ("Don't the special ed people want to be a part of our faculty?"), but not *too* much ("Don't those special ed people have anything to do?"). Of course, care must be taken to keep the professional conversation general in nature. Confidentiality and ethical treatment of information are necessary behaviors for all teachers, and special education teachers in particular.

In this room that is provided for relaxation, reflection, and refreshment, a collaborative spirit can be nurtured and carried out the door to classrooms and offices beyond. Some special education teachers have had success with posting a "brag board" of commendations honoring any student or adult in the school.

ACTION 14.2
Designing a Teachers' Workroom

Having suggested some of the benefits that the teachers' workroom can provide to busy educators, it must be said that not all workrooms are ideal physical environments in which to interact, relax, or for that matter, work.

In your thoughts or on sketch paper, have fun creating a "dream workroom" to serve school personnel with their physical, social, and professional needs. What would it look like? What would it sound like? How would it function as a physical place? How might co-educators nurture the collaborative spirit there? What would it take to construct and outfit such a room? Could some of your suggestions be carried out right away, with little cost and disruption to the school? Who would do this, and how? There have been schools where school staff took it upon themselves, with a little money from the office fund, to refurbish their workroom area, and then to relish the benefits that resulted.

More research is needed on the problems and possibilities of an adult gathering area in the school building. Consulting teachers will find many opportunities there for developing rapport with consultees and initiating constructive interactions. Some may think suggestions for using teachers' lounges as professional development and collaboration forums are "off the wall" ideas, but the walls of such places contain knowledge and wisdom and they can be places of rejuvenation for harried teachers. This important school place must be used wisely and judiciously.

CONFERENCES AND CONVENTIONS FOR PROFESSIONAL GROWTH

Conventions, conferences, and workshops provide opportunities for personal and professional growth. The atmosphere at well-structured events typically is charged with energy and enthusiasm. A smorgasbord of choices is available at the best conventions to whet adult learners' appetites for information. Participants learn from interacting with one another, they renew acquaintances, and they often make new connections. Networks of collaboration can be established among educators with common interests. Some gather to plan writing projects for submission to professional journals or for cross-country research projects.

Leadership skills are honed by submitting proposals to present at the event. In-district partnerships can bloom if colleagues or parents are asked to go along. One concept that is effective for some convention themes is a team model of participants in which a classroom teacher or two, a special education teacher, and a building administrator attend the event together as an instructional team.

Professional events are meant to be invigorating and informative. Convention-goers can gain the most from the experience by planning their time carefully, getting to sessions early for the handouts and good seats, making sure to visit exhibit areas for new ideas and materials (and sometimes publisher giveaways toward the end of the conference), taking advantage of sessions to showcase strategies that work and resultant student products, and allowing some time and energy to go beyond the convention site for some rejuvenating fun and relaxation. They should take along a supply of the professional "business" cards that they have asked their school administrator to develop for them.

CASE STUDY FOR BLENDING COLLABORATIVE SCHOOL CONSULTATION WITH RESPONSE TO INTERVENTION

(Before working through this case study, it might be helpful to review the RTI section in Chapter 10 and elements typically addressed in a case study such as those in Chapter 2.)

Margo is the new principal of an elementary school where collaborative school consultation has been a well-received indirect service delivery model for students with special needs. Margo likes this service delivery and its features very much, and is eager to build on its potential in ways that might improve overall school performance and student achievement. She also believes that the RTI programs she has studied in educational literature and observed in practice around her state could serve her school well. So she has set a goal of implementing the RTI approach for identifying and serving exceptional needs. She expects it to build on four strengths of the school:

1. Solid family and community partnerships in education
2. Keen interest among home and school educators for developing students' academic excellence in reading, writing, math, and science instruction
3. Strong, community-based citizenship programs where students are taught to develop responsible behaviors for treating other people and property with respect
4. Teacher responsibility for making important educational decisions based on frequent assessment throughout the year of student progress toward reading, writing, math, and science standards based on Common Core Standards (2010)

Margo plans to implement the Response to Intervention (RTI) program and blend it with aspects of collaborative consultation and team teaching activities that are popular and have been working reasonably well. But some teachers who have been there for many years are resistant toward the plan. They bring to mind the adage that "no one likes change except a wet baby." However, they make some important points, such as the reality that RTI is still evolving. As case in point, it began as an alternative to identification of learning disabilities and early identification of struggling readers but has broadened to other academic areas and to grades beyond primary level. Emotional, behavioral, and social skills also have become areas of focus for RTI. So any description should be broad and flexible.

Nevertheless, Margo is confident that she and the key teachers who are supportive of her goal can work successfully to develop positive attitudes for implementation of the blended approach. She invites teachers to discuss their concerns individually with her. She remains open to all opinions, yet firm in her goals for the school and the students. She follows through efficiently to see that each exploratory activity is conducted carefully and no one's concerns slip through the cracks unheeded.

Margo confers with district administrators, including the director of special education, asking them to give additional support to teachers during the transition time. In order to provide staff development, she solicits help from the school counselor and music teacher to organize school-wide assemblies for Friday afternoons so teachers can have released time for the professional development that will be needed. She begins to design activities that will construct the foundation of a plan for the collaborative school consultation/RTI service. (Recall from Chapter 10 that to be successful the RTI must be implemented by educators having considerable training in the model.)

Margo assembles an advisory group of teachers representing each grade level, along with a number of family members who are keenly interested in school success and student progress, and the school psychologist who was involved with an RTI approach in her former school. Some participants in the newly formed group are enthusiastically supportive of the principal's proposal and others are not so sure, although they have not chosen to transfer to another school. Margo believes this contrast in opinions will promote lively, productive discussion to formulate a plan agreeable to most if not all.

At the first meeting of the combined group, teachers who were familiar with RTI, or had done their homework on the subject, offered pros and cons to Margo's plan. Using Erchul's study (2011) that compares fundamentals of school consultation and RTI, one group of teachers made positive comparisons such as the helpful problem-solving nature of both approaches, their emphasis on problem prevention, compatible use of scientific literature and research findings, and perhaps most relevant of all, a shared focus on the need for treatment integrity (the extent to which the approach is implemented in the way it is supposed to be).

A few of the still-reluctant teachers and parents countered that the approaches have some important differences in terminology, and semantics are important when making comparisons. They contended that an RTI focus could include several roles, such as educational administrators and school psychologists. Some even quoted researchers (Reynolds & Shaywitz, 2009) who profess that RTI is on shaky ground with practices that could be more iatrogenic than helpful. Others said that two important realities are that general education teachers are not free to decline participation in the indirect services RTI requires, and conversely, special education consulting teachers need to accept and facilitate some of the direct service aspects of RTI.

Using a simplified case study approach for this situation, and in consideration of the facts that have been presented here briefly, what is your overall impression of Margo's goal for incorporating collaborative school consultation and the RTI approach to serve students' special needs? What challenges are in store for her and the school personnel in attaining those goals? How do you think Margo should go about planning and implementing professional development activities to introduce RTI to the faculty and participating parents? She wants to promote the potential benefits but not dodge negative aspects.

Do you think Margo's idea for preceding professional development with preplanning by an advisory council is a good one? (If you think it is not a good idea, why not?)

What are key steps Margo will want to follow in implementing her plan that has been modified by input from others? What should come first? What are steps that may be overlooked, for which she must be especially mindful, and how will she assess the results of the plan both formatively and summatively?

Have you been involved in program changes of a major kind? What hurdles blocked progress? How were they removed? How was the program evaluated and what transpired from the evaluation?

TECHNOLOGY FOR PROFESSIONAL DEVELOPMENT ACTIVITY

More and more people are turning to social networking and other Web 2.0 applications as a way of connecting and communicating with others. Some social media sites, such as LinkedIn, clearly have a more professional purpose than other social application sites, such as Facebook, but the lines are becoming blurred. Educators are using sites regarded as *social-only* in innovative and creative ways. For example, a consultant uses a Twitter account to ask a question and get the opinions of other consultants or teachers, or to share links with colleagues and families about interesting things happening at school. With any new medium, and especially social media, consulting teachers are advised to proceed with caution. When posting or tweeting on school issues, educators must be mindful of confidentiality guidelines for conveying information. Direct messages in one-to-one conversations should be used if the content or message is about individual students and not appropriate or of particular value to one's at-large collaborators.

In the end, the information is public, not private. It only takes one disgruntled student, parent, or colleague to share information that was intended only for friends or specific colleagues in negative ways with others for whom it was not intended. Even if the information is not especially controversial, others could misinterpret it. Before posting anything on a public site, think about how it would be if it were read by _____ (you fill in the blank).

If you do decide to use social media tools in professional collaborations, look for good examples that are professional models. Subscribe to practitioner and expert blogs, follow well-respected educators on Twitter or web feeds with an RSS reader, and see how others are connecting with online communities. For example, online *communities of practice*, as noted in Chapter 13, are groups of individuals focused on a common area of interest such as developing strategies for teaching students with disabilities or connecting with other consultants to discuss successful strategies, find solutions to problems, or learn about effective service delivery models that others use.

In an online forum, participation is not limited by geography. This allows sharing of perspectives from different parts of the country and even circling the globe. Many technology tools are available to use within online communities of practice, including e-mail, wikis, topical discussion boards, chat rooms, podcasts, and blogs.

A number of social bookmarking sites, such as Diigo, have group educator accounts that can be used for online group bookmarks, annotations, and group forums. Privacy settings can be put into place for students so only teachers and classmates can communicate with them. Ads that inevitably pop up on these free sites should be limited to education-related sponsors. Twitter is great for on-the-go microblogging, although a message, or "tweet" is limited to 140 or fewer characters and such brevity can be good or not good. All in all, Wenger, White, Smith, and Rowe (2005) have found that using technology tools leads to richer discussions and more meaningful participation.

REFLECTION 14.1

Social Networking and Web 2.0 Applications for Collaboration

If you are not familiar with educational applications of social networking tools such as Twitter or Web 2.0 tools such as Diigo, Delicious, and other similar social and group bookmarking sites, take some time to investigate how other educators are using them. After you see what others are doing, think about how you might use these tools to enhance your role as a collaborative school consultant. Some tips to keep in mind as you reflect on these new tools are:

1. How could you use Twitter to promote others in their endeavors?
2. How would you go about learning to use URL-shortening tools such as TinyURL and all the variants to tidy up and shorten your tweets?
3. What questions would you like to pose? Twitter is a great tool for getting answers and opinions from others. Rather than putting more frivolous social question stems on Twitter, such as "What are you doing?" or "What's happening?" ask questions such as, "What has your attention?"

4. To promote a blog post, what questions could you ask or what context could you give so that your followers will want to go to the blog and read more, rather than just supply the link? The same applies to social bookmarking sites such as Delicious and Diigo; don't just copy and paste links but instead take the extra step to tag them appropriately and provide annotations.

Now do you feel more ready as a collaborating educator to use social media productively in innovative ways? To turn this reflection into an action, get together with others and use the questions to generate even more ideas than you did individually.

AN ETHICAL CLIMATE FOR LEADERSHIP AND PROFESSIONAL DEVELOPMENT

In an ethical climate, collaborating teachers will find ways to inform school administrators about their demanding roles as collaborative school consultants. They in turn will appreciate and respect demanding roles and responsibilities of their building principals, superintendents, and special education directors.

Collaborating teachers will want to locate their schools' mission statements. The school handbook may be the place to begin. If none can be found, it could be said that the school is overdue to have one. A volunteer teacher–parent group or, better yet, the advisory council, if there is one, would be the most logical team to construct a mission statement. Students should be included, of course. Emphasis on creating an ethical, caring climate for students, teachers, administrators, and all other staff members, should be the agenda for the activity.

In an ethical climate, the classic advice from Mom is evident: "If you can't say something good about someone or something, don't say anything at all." Adhering to this advice makes the hallways more pleasant, the teachers' workroom conversation less negative, teacher–student exchanges more respectful, and collaboration and teamwork much easier to implement and practice.

TIPS FOR PROVIDING LEADERSHIP AND PROFESSIONAL DEVELOPMENT

1. Join a dynamic professional organization and become actively involved in it.
2. Consult technology experts regularly to remain current in the ever-changing field of technology and strongly recommend that your district or school employ support personnel to provide maintenance and support for the hardware and software.
3. Find sessions at professional conferences that feature different models and methods of collaborative activities and attend them to broaden your knowledge.
4. Organize a system to know when all co-educators have been reached with specific professional development activities.
5. Make a personal pledge to read at least an article a week from a professional journal.

6. Work with a group of collaborating colleagues to write a guide on the use of consultation and collaboration. Then present it to new faculty members and periodically conduct refresher sessions on the most important issues.

7. Work with the building principal (who will clear it with central administration) to plan and carry out a come-and-go open house in your school for school board members, following it up with thank-you notes to those who stopped by.

8. Remember Ralph Waldo Emerson's words: "It is one of the most beautiful compensations of this life that no man can sincerely try to help another without helping himself."

9. Knowing how to collaborate does not guarantee one the opportunity. Value it as a tool for activating long-range planning and coordination among educators.

10. Continue to read, study, attend educational conferences, and take courses that focus on collaboration, consultation, and co-teaching.

ADDITIONAL RESOURCES

Darling-Hammond, L. (2003). Keeping good teachers: Why it matters, what leaders can do. *Educational Leadership, 60*(8), 6–13.

Martin, K., & Coleman, P. (2011). Licensing teacher leaders: The Kansas Model. *Delta Kappa Gamma Bulletin, 77*(3), 6–9.

McMahon, T. J., Ward, N. L., Pruett, M. K., Davidson, L., & Griffith, E. E. H. (2000). Building full-service schools: Lessons learned in the development of interagency collaboratives. *Journal of Educational and Psychological Consultation, 11*(1), 65–92.

Miller, T. N., Devin, M., & Shoop, R. J. (2007). *Closing the leadership gap: How district and university partnerships shape effective school leaders.* Thousand Oaks, CA: Corwin.

Reason, L. L., & Wellman, B. (2007). How to talk so teachers listen. *Educational Leadership, 65*(1), 30–34. Teacher leaders encourage professional growth through conversation and a collaborative stance of co-developing ideas and co-analyzing situations and data.

Riehl, C. J. (2000). The principal's role in creating inclusive schools for diverse students: A review of normative, empirical, and critical literature on the practice of educational administration. *Review of Educational Research, 70*(1), 55–81.

Whitaker, S. D. (2000). Mentoring beginning special education teachers and the relationship to attrition. *Exceptional Children, 66*(4), 546–566. Teacher leaders encourage professional growth through conversation and a collaborative stance of co-developing ideas and co-analyzing situations and data.

15

Synthesis and Support for Working Together as Co-Educators

NEVER IN RECORDED HISTORY HAS SO MUCH of our world changed so rapidly and dramatically as it is changing today. We do not know for certain how these changes will affect schools and educators, but one thing is clear: Students now at risk with exceptional learning needs will be placed in greater jeopardy than ever by the accelerating demands on them to keep pace and measure up in competitive, high-pressure environments.

Teaching and learning are key elements in preparing students to meet demands brought on by change. Collaborative school consultation and teamwork among all educators in school, home, and community partnerships will provide support (see Figure 15.1) that is vital in preparing and enabling all students to be successful learners, self-assured individuals, and productive members of society.

FOCUSING QUESTIONS

1. How is a visionary perspective relevant to student needs and the roles of collaborative school consultants?
2. In what ways can collaborative consulting teachers advocate for students and ways of serving their special needs?
3. What positive ripple effects are put into motion by successful collaborative school consultation and teamwork efforts such as co-teaching?
4. What benefits result from successful collaborative school consultation?
5. How will technological advances affect teaching and learning in the decades to come?
6. What competencies and ethical guidelines are needed to ensure the success of collaborative school consultation and team efforts?

KEY TERMS

advocacy

competencies for collaborative
    school consultation

ethics

multiplier effect

positive ripple effect

synergy

VIGNETTE 15

Another school week is over. The events of the past week are history. What will happen beyond this moment is the future. As teachers finish their bus duties and other supervisory tasks and head for their rooms to pick up work they will take home for the weekend, one teacher glances through an issue of Scientific American *lying on a table in the teacher's workroom and is intrigued by an article titled "The Limits of Intelligence" by Douglas Fox (2011). In it, she reads*

> So have humans reached the physical limits of how complex our brain can be, given the building blocks that are available to us?... The human mind, however, may have better ways of expanding.... After all, honeybees and other social insects do it: acting in concert with their hive sisters, they form a collective entity that is smarter than the sum of its parts. Through social interaction we, too, have learned to pool our intelligence with others. (p. 43)

The teacher checks out the magazine and puts it into her bag. The collaborative consultation program begins in her school next week. This is good material to ponder over the weekend.

CHALLENGES IN WORKING TOGETHER FOR THE FUTURE

As co-educators work hard in their demanding roles to fulfill professional and personal goals, they are hardy pioneers and sometimes even courageous trailblazers in their search to find better ways of helping children grow and develop into all they can be. Teaching was once a lonely endeavor in public but closed environments. That is no longer the case and most assuredly will not be in the future that is in store for them.

Crafting and perfecting roles that call for interaction and partnerships is demanding and sometimes unsettling, with no simple formulas. But now is the time for educators to have visionary scope—looking inward to analyze their profession in microscopic detail, scanning outward in all directions with periscopic breadth and depth, focusing collectively on kaleidoscopic colors and shapes that reveal the beauty and usefulness of diversity and individual differences, and peering telescopically onward toward the lofty goals they have dreamed of for themselves and their students. Microscope, periscope, kaleidoscope, and telescope are metaphorically useful ways of reflecting on what educators can do together. (See Figure 15.2.)

FIGURE 15.2 Education: A Visionary Scope

Collaboration will become more and more a common process in the future. Those who accepted the challenge in Chapter 1 to watch and listen each day for the word *collaborate* most likely found an amazingly frequent occurrence of examples, in newspaper and news magazines, TV shows, science journals, sportscasts, music reviews, economic reports, diplomacy efforts, and on and on. Working together has become essential to just about every component of life in the twenty-first century. As educators collaborate and consult within the school context, they instill in students the framework of skills that will be needed for their continued collaboration throughout the global world.

Elliot W. Eisner (2003), noted educator and administrator at Stanford University, underscores the collaborative perspective by emphasizing that instruction must teach students to exercise judgment, think critically, acquire meaningful literacy, serve others, and work together with others in all walks of their life. With school consultation and collaboration as a contributing process to teaching and learning, there is hope for creating both the social flexibility and the satisfying individuality that students will need. Collaborating educators can work together to enhance their repertoire of instructional and advisory practices that will enable students to succeed in spite of, perhaps even because of, their special needs. The best educators have always been those who expand, change, modify, and tailor requirements so that the important material is taught, but in a way and to the extent that serves each student's individual interests, needs, abilities, and talents.

The challenge of thinking in new ways about school-based education is not a call to make it easier or to avoid accountability or abandon the values that historically have provided meaning and given educators direction. Rather, it is a challenge to participate in creating a new vision of helping students to achieve their potential in a wide-open, fully connected world. The time to think in new, exciting ways *is* now. As a well-known adage reminds us, "The journey of a thousand miles begins with a single step."

ADVOCACY FOR STUDENTS WITH SPECIAL NEEDS

At a well-attended conference on special needs of students in schools, a member of a state's legislative body, who served on a key education committee in the legislature, directed some strong remarks to her audience. She asked pointedly from her place on the podium, "Can you name the representatives and senators who serve you in our state legislature? Do you know their positions on key issues?" She then charged each one there to let not one more day go by without knowing such important answers to those questions. It gave the educators much to ponder and homework to do!

Getting to know policymakers and elected officials, communicating with them about the needs of students, and building bridges of communication are responsibilities of collaborative school consultants and necessary steps of advocacy. When communicating with public officials, personal letters are more effective than form letters. *Many* letters will get more attention than copies of one letter signed by many. Letters that are short, concise, friendly in tone, and free of stereotyped phrases, derogatory comments, and unreasonable requests will have a positive impact. Thanking legislators for their interest in the past and support they have given, along with descriptions of specific ways that their support already has helped communities, will be particularly powerful. Think of a letter as a vehicle of appreciation, information, and documentation, and then a vehicle to carry ideas for actions that would help, along with suggestions for ways in which they might be carried out. Examples of student work and achievement, and newsletters and clippings that commend students and schools, can provide convincing evidence when included with the letters (with parent and administrator permission, of course).

Student Self-Advocacy

Self-advocacy is knowing what one wants, what one is entitled to, and how to achieve one's goals (Kling, 2000). Educators can help students become effective advocates for themselves by teaching them self-advocacy skills. Students must be aware of their disabilities, be able to state the facts, describe their strengths and limitations, and assess their problems and some possible solutions.

Successful advocates know their rights, their needs, and their best supports. It is important also that they know the best times to approach others with requests that serve their needs. Students who learn to do this can gain a sense of control and influence over their employment conditions and living situations. This self-awareness is especially important for students who are in the transition phase between high school and postsecondary school or a vocation.

SYNERGY OF CONTEXTS, CONTENT, PROCESSES, PRACTICES, AND SUPPORT

Effective school consultation results from the interaction of *process* skills, *content* strategies, *practices*, and *support* venues within the immediate school *context*. Contexts of a school setting for collaborative consultation and teamwork are givens. Some of the content strategies for consulting and collaborating and co-teaching must flow from existing school philosophies and structures. But it is the processes and practices, and some of the support areas, for collaborating and networking that are the most malleable and accessible for creating change.

Collaboration that occurs in conjunction with consultation requires harmonious, efficient teamwork. Collaborative consultation is not an oxymoron as some have suggested. It is *synergy*—"a behavior of whole systems unpredicted by the behavior of their parts taken separately" (Fuller, 1975, p. 3). When interactive teamwork is effective, there is synergy. A synergistic combination of context, content, process, practice, and support is a recipe for success in the school setting.

Positive Ripple Effects of Collaborative School Consultation

Positive ripple effects, or multiplier effects, as they have also been referred to from time to time, provide compelling arguments for consultation, collaboration, and co-teaching. They create benefits beyond the immediate situation involving one student and that student's teachers. When collaborating with co-educators, many skills and talents will "bubble up" to be shared and expanded. All will learn and improve their skills.

As discussed earlier, consulting teachers who might be concerned that general education teachers will be given full responsibility for special learning needs and their own positions will be eliminated should not fret. When teachers become more proficient as collaborative colleagues, they tend to find those services more in demand and indispensable, not less so. Using specialized intervention techniques for many more students than the ones formally identified for special education programs is a positive outcome to expect from collaborative school consultation. Multiple benefits can extend well beyond the immediate classroom because consulting teachers are in a unique position to facilitate interaction among many target groups. The effects that ripple out from mutual planning and problem solving across grade levels, subject areas, and schools are powerful instruments for initiating positive changes in the educational system.

Multiplier effects provide compelling arguments for consultation, collaboration, and teaming. They augment benefits beyond the immediate situation involving one student and that one student's teachers. Co-educators, in collaboration with their colleagues, are modeling this powerful tool for their students who soon will be collaborating and teaming with others in their own workplaces.

Levels of Service

Direct services for consultees delineate one level of positive effects (see Figure 15.3). At this level, the consultation and collaboration are most likely to have been initiated for one client's need. (Recall that a client can be an entity such as a student group, school, family, or community, as well as a single student.) But consultation benefits often extend beyond Level 1 of immediate need. At Level 2, consultees use information and points of view generated during the collaboration to be more effective in other similar but unrelated cases. Both consultant and consultee repertoires of knowledge and skills are enhanced so that they can function more effectively in the future. When collaborative consultation outcomes extend beyond single consultant–consultee situations of Levels 1 and 2, the entire school system

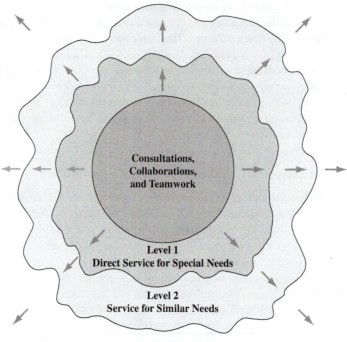

Consultations,
Collaborations,
and Teamwork

Level 1
Direct Service for Special Needs

Level 2
Service for Similar Needs

Level 3
Service Contributing to Institutional Changes
and Professional Development

FIGURE 15.3   Positive Ripple Effects of Collaborative School Consultation

can be positively affected by Level 3 outcomes. Organizational change and increased family involvement are potential results of Level 3 outcomes.

Level 1 Effects   Level 1 effects can result from the following types of school situations:

- The special education teacher for learning disabilities engages in problem solving with a high school teacher to determine ways of helping a student with severe learning disabilities master minimum competencies required for graduation.
- The audiologist helps the classroom teacher arrange the classroom environment to enable a student with hearing impairment to function comfortably in the regular classroom setting.

Level 2 Effects   Level 2 effects include these examples:

- The classroom teacher becomes more familiar with the concept of hyperactivity in children, subsequently regarding fewer children as having attention-deficit/hyperactivity disorder, and adjusting the classroom curriculum to address very active children's needs more appropriately in that classroom setting. This reduces labeling of children as hyperactive and lessens referrals to special education programs.

- The classroom teacher becomes comfortable with enrichment activities provided for very able students through collaboration with the gifted program facilitator, and makes enriching activities available to a larger group of very able children in the classroom who can handle them with no difficulty and thrive in the process.

Level 3 Effects   Level 3 effects enable these kinds of outcomes:

- The efforts toward collaboration and teamwork result in a professional development plan called "Teachers Helping Teachers," during which teachers in a school system provide training for interested colleagues, and sometimes parents as home educators, in their areas of expertise.
- The school district's emphasis on consultation, collaboration, and co-teaching pleases families who find that their children are receiving more integrated, personalized instruction for their learning needs. Families become more active and interested in the school's programs, and more positive and encouraging of their children's efforts at home.

A positive outcome of collaborative consultation is increased skills among teachers for providing interventions and remediation techniques to many more students than those identified for services. All in all, the multiplier effect of these interactive processes is a powerful tool for serving *all* students' needs and abilities in more individualized ways, with the positive effects reaching far beyond school contexts as graduates enter their chosen fields of work and areas of community life. Ripple effects happen in the water and they happen on the land. Most assuredly they happen as well in the hearts and minds of young people and their teachers.

BENEFITS OF COLLABORATIVE SCHOOL CONSULTATION

To review and summarize, school environments that promote collaborative consultation tend to involve all school personnel in the teaching and learning processes. Information is shared and knowledge levels about student characteristics and needs, with strategies for meeting those needs, are broadened. Importantly, many of the strategies are helpful with other students who have similar but less severe needs. A number of specific benefits such as these can be expected from well-conducted collaborative school consultation and teamwork for special needs.

Augmented support and assistance is available for students in the inclusive classroom. Consulting special education teachers help classroom teachers develop repertoires of materials and instructional strategies. Many resource teachers find this more efficient than racing from one student to another in a resource room while they all work on individual assignments. A special education teacher succinctly put it this way: "In my resource room, by the time I get to the last student, I find that the first student is stuck and has made no progress. So I frantically run through the whole cycle again. Tennis shoes are a must for my job!"

Consulting teachers also find ways to help classroom teachers become confident and successful with special needs students. At times, they can assume an instructional role in the classroom, which frees the classroom teacher to study student progress, or set up arrangements for special projects, or work intensively with a small group of students. When general classroom and special education teachers collaborate, each has ownership and involvement in serving special needs. In stressful situations, collaborators strengthen each other's resolve and effort by providing both material and emotional support (Conoley & Conoley, 2010). Such support is invaluable across all domains—mental, emotional, physical, and social.

Collaborative efforts to serve students in heterogeneous settings help minimize stigmatizing effects of labels such as "delayed," "having disabilities," "exceptional," or even "gifted." They also can reduce referrals to remedial programs. Fewer referrals for special education services mean reduced expenditures for costly and time-consuming psychological assessments and special education interventions. Educators can focus more of their limited time and energy on teaching and facilitating, and less on repetitive processes of testing and measuring. In addition, a ripple effect extends services to other students by encouraging use of modifications and alternatives for *their* special needs.

When classroom teachers are efficient in working with a wide range of student needs, administrators benefit from eased pressure of parent and student disgruntlements. Principals find it stimulating to visit and observe in classrooms as part of the team, collaborating to identify ways of helping every student succeed in the school and reinforcing teacher successes with all students. This is for many administrators a welcome change from issues of discipline or classroom visitations they make for purposes of teacher evaluation.

Another important and frequently overlooked benefit is the maintenance of continuity in learning programs as students progress through their K–12 school experiences. This, too, is a savings in time, energy, and resources of the educational staff and often the parents as well.

A collaborative consultation approach is a natural system for nurturing harmonious staff interactions. Teachers who have become isolated or autonomous in their teaching styles and instructional outlook often discover that working with other adults for common goals is quite stimulating. Sharing ideas can add to creativity and flexibility in developing educational programs for students with special needs. In addition, more emphasis and coordination can be given to cross-school and long-range planning, with broader accumulation of resources for student needs.

Families of exceptional students who become extremely frustrated with the labeling, fragmented curriculum, and isolation from peers endured by their children respond enthusiastically when they learn that several educators are functioning as a team for their children. Parental attitudes toward school improve; parents are more likely to become involved in their children's learning programs, more eager to provide input with their ideas, and more helpful in monitoring their children's work. They are particularly supportive when consulting services allow students in special education programs to remain in their neighborhood schools and receive more assistance from interagency sources for their children's special needs.

Collaborative consultants are integral in planning professional development for special education programs. They can identify areas in which teachers need awareness and information sessions, and coordinate workshops that help related services and support personnel become more knowledgeable about exceptional learning needs. Sometimes serendipity lends a hand, as it did in the middle school case study for Chapter 2 when the professional development coordinator benefited from her co-educator's awareness of their colleagues' perspectives on a PD event she had coordinated.

COMPETENCIES OF EFFECTIVE COLLABORATIVE SCHOOL CO-EDUCATORS

Throughout the book, competencies for collaborating, consulting, co-teaching, and working in teams as co-educators have been woven into descriptions of processes and content for various school contexts. The emphasis has been, directly or indirectly, on key points:

- Effective co-educators are knowledgeable about both special education and general education curriculum and methods.
- Effective co-educators are interested in current trends and topics, and they are innovative in generating new ideas.
- Effective co-educators recognize and value personal and professional diversity among colleagues.
- Effective co-educators understand how schools function and have a panoramic view of the educational scene.
- Effective co-educators are practical and realistic along with being innovative. This requires that they be assertive and take risks when needed but remain diplomatic and fair.
- Successful collaborators relate well to teacher colleagues and other school personnel, administrators, parents, and of course students.
- Successful collaborators have good communication skills and a patient and understanding demeanor.
- Successful collaborators have mature, objective viewpoints toward all aspects of education.
- While working to help students learn, successful collaborators retain perspective on the entire school context.
- Successful collaborators link people with resources, refer people to other sources when needed, and teach when that is the most appropriate way to serve students' needs.
- A collaborative consultant is self-confident but if running low on resources or ideas does not hesitate in finding a consultant for herself or himself.
- Perhaps most of all, a collaborative school consultant is an agent for change and progress.

As one highly experienced, long-time consulting teacher put it, "You have to be abrasive enough to create change, but pleasant enough to be asked back so you will do it some more" (Bradley, 1987). The checklist in Figure 15.4 summarizes the main competencies and can be used for self-assessment, evaluation by a supervisor, or assessment by a professional colleague whose views are valued highly.

Preservice teachers in teacher education programs and novice teachers in their first position may look at the competencies checklist and wonder, "Will I be prepared for this kind of professional activity? How do I ensure that I am?" They can have a good start by attending to the top-twelve collection of practical recommendations in Figure 15.5.

FIGURE 15.4   Competencies for Collaborators, Consultants, and Team Members as Co-Educators

Criterion Area and Competencies	Needs Work	Improving	OK	Good	Excellent
Knowledge and Awareness of Collaboration/Consultation					
Understands concepts of collaborative consultation	1	2	3	4	5
Analyzes own perspectives/preferences	1	2	3	4	5
Shows respect for others' perspectives/preferences	1	2	3	4	5
Utilizes collaborative consultation theory and research	1	2	3	4	5
Understands collaborative models and programs	1	2	3	4	5
Application of Collaborative/Co-Educator Relationships					
Values diversity and individuality	1	2	3	4	5
Practices effective listening skills	1	2	3	4	5
Practices effective nonverbal skills	1	2	3	4	5
Practices effective verbal skills	1	2	3	4	5
Establishes co-equal relationships	1	2	3	4	5
Problem-Solving Techniques					
Demonstrates skill in problem finding	1	2	3	4	5
Collects and processes pertinent data	1	2	3	4	5
Uses effective problem-solving strategies	1	2	3	4	5
Selects appropriate methods for special needs	1	2	3	4	5
Follows through with decisions, follows up on plan	1	2	3	4	5
Organization and Management					
Manages time and resources efficiently	1	2	3	4	5
Coordinates collaborative consultation effectively	1	2	3	4	5
Conducts successful observation and interviewing	1	2	3	4	5
Provides resources and personnel for special needs	1	2	3	4	5
Conducts assessment of collaborations/co-teaching	1	2	3	4	5
Partnerships with Co-Educators					
Co-plans effectively with co-educators	1	2	3	4	5
Co-teaches successfully with co-educators	1	2	3	4	5
Directs paraeducators capably	1	2	3	4	5
Works well with related services/support personnel	1	2	3	4	5
Engages in respectful, productive family interactions	1	2	3	4	5
Change Agents for Positive Ripple Effects					
Provides leadership in collaborative settings	1	2	3	4	5
Interacts effectively with school administrators	1	2	3	4	5
Makes appropriate decisions for student well-being	1	2	3	4	5
Uses technology effectively and innovatively	1	2	3	4	5
Demonstrates skills of mentoring/modeling	1	2	3	4	5

FIGURE 15.5   Competencies for Preservice and Novice Teachers to Develop

A top-twelve list of practical recommendations for preservice and first-year teachers complements the general competencies checklist for all collaborative school consultants in general education and special education roles. Some have been sprinkled into various chapters, where relevant, but they are collected here as a helpful dozen.

1. While in the teacher education program, including your field experiences and student teaching experiences, keep an idea journal.
2. If a teaching portfolio is required for graduation, plan the contents so they will be useful idea generators in your brand-new position.
3. Save your class textbooks and course packets for major subjects such as educational psychology, methods and content-areas, introductory special education, and assessment. Also, *taking* an assessment course is highly recommended. If taken as a graduate course, it can be a good launch pad for working toward a graduate degree.
4. When enrolled in courses such as educational psychology, look for ways of applying the material to future teaching situations; for example, when studying negative and positive reinforcement, or developing class rules, create sample plans that could be modified a bit and drawn upon later for a real, specific classroom. Talking through these activities collaboratively with classmates will result in even better products to stow away for use in the near future.
5. Video yourself teaching, lecturing, conferencing, and interacting with students, then study them just as a football team studies game films to improve their playing. Older teachers may dislike doing videos, but the younger generation tends to be more comfortable in front of video cameras. Of course, confidentiality and privacy of participants must be assured, so here again, written permission from all participants is a wise policy.
6. Join a new-teacher support group; if none is available, start one. Novices need high-quality feedback on their teaching performance. If none is forthcoming, ask for it (Grossman & Loeb, 2010); it is likely that your supervising administrator will be impressed with your request.
7. Find key "magnet-type" teachers in your first assigned building(s) and ask for some collegial time to draw upon their expertise. In exchange for the time, offer to take their bus or lunchroom duty for double the length of time the person contributed to you. This generous offer should ensure that you use the interaction time judiciously!
8. Return to your own early school days and visit with your favorite teachers, telling them how much you valued their guidance and asking them to talk with you about their teaching philosophy and practices. Most will be flattered and touched by your desire to do this. Perhaps you will receive such a visit from some of your own former students someday.
9. Take every opportunity to observe collaborative and co-teaching activities in schools during your field experiences or practicum. As noted earlier, it would be good experience to attend an IEP conference, but only with the administrator's written permission, written permission by the student's family, and your assurance of preserving complete confidentiality.
10. Take notes (without recording names—using code if necessary) when observing or working in schools. Sketch classroom layouts, catalog ideas for materials, and observe teaching procedures.
11. Make broad-stroke plans for your first day, month, week, and year. For example, a dedicated first-grade teacher would want to plan out that first day in 10-minute increments, with flexibility to tweak the plan in progress, of course.
12. Do not be concerned about appearing to be inexperienced. Every teacher has a first-year experience. Neither should you regard your veteran colleagues as "old school" and inflexible. All can learn from each other and enjoy doing it. The school environment has become much more collaborative and supportive in the past decade or two.

TECHNOLOGY FOR POSITIVE RIPPLE EFFECTS THAT SERVE THE SPECIAL NEEDS OF ALL STUDENTS

Schools are connected electronically, with multiple opportunities for collaboration, professional development activities, and collegial interactions. By networking with diverse sources, co-educators can assemble information and disseminate what is new or most useful in their learning environments. Networking for professional development produces synergy and creates ripple effects that compound the effects of the process.

Above all, in the educational profession as in the medical profession, the proposed element must first do no harm. Issues to be studied very seriously by school personnel involve:

- Security of information
- Assurance of privacy
- Vigilance in constructing firewalls to shut out objectionable material and contacts
- Adherence to copyrights and intellectual property rights
- Fair and equitable use in regard to disability and gender and socioeconomic level
- Careful attention to feelings of inadequacy and reluctance among some educators in regard to technology.

Young people around the globe have embraced technology as an essential element in their daily lives. Many students with learning and social differences have been helped with various types of technology during their school years. Furthermore, many of them have *contributed* to the development of technological tools, having the stories of their amazing innovation and entrepreneurship told and retold in the media. They are aware of the digital divide that separates their generation with its technological acumen from earlier generations whose teachers must "learn the ropes" as if it were a foreign language. That said, however, school personnel of all ages know that technology is the universal language of the future. It does not come without qualifiers, particularly in the area of education and even more particularly in special education. It must be used wisely with keen attention to good judgment, sensible amount of time for being "on," realization that it should not replace face-to-face human contact, confidentiality, etiquette (in technology parlance known as "netiquette"), and understanding within the ethical climate of its power and its limitations.

The younger generations of educators have strengths in using technology that can be mentoring assets for less able veteran teachers who just might become their technology mentees. Young novice teachers who grew up using technology can be another source of help. When they assist veteran teachers with technology, positive ripple effects can promote even richer collaborations. Professional development sessions involving novice teachers as presenters and mentors, and veteran teachers as presentees and mentees, can become interesting teams for making decisions about best systems and incorporating them into interactive school settings. To add to the positive ripple effects, technologically capable students could become partners in professional development activities. They may even recommend having members of their families participate as experts or as learners.

Obviously, many veteran teachers are technologically savvy, and this reality will include more and more teachers as the younger generations replace those who retire. But there will always be individuals who are less comfortable with electronic tools and prefer libraries, books, telephones, and encyclopedia, working alongside others who are experts with every advanced tool on the technological market. Such is the marvelous diversity among groups of co-educators who respect each other and do not hesitate to lend their talents and skills to one another.

ETHICS OF COLLABORATIVE SCHOOL CONSULTATION

Ethics and the ethical climate have been included in every chapter of the book. Consultation, collaboration, and teamwork in school contexts require particular emphasis on ethical interaction for several reasons:

- Special needs of students exist that cannot be met elsewhere.
- Confidential data must be shared among a number of individuals.
- Collaborative consultants are out and about much more than classroom teachers, interfacing with many people in homes and schools and across the community.
- Parental permission is not always required, but many of the issues to be dealt with approximate the sensitivity of issues that do necessitate parental consent, with common sense dictating confidentiality in most situations involving special learning and behavioral needs.
- Collaborative consultants have complex roles with many demands placed on them, but too often those in the roles have received little or no training for them.
- School consultation implies power and expertise until (and *only* until) the collaborative spirit can be cultivated.
- Collaborative consultants may be asked on occasion to act inappropriately as a middle person, or to form alliances, or carry information, and they must respond ethically.
- There is some risk of diminishing return if collaborative efforts considerably reduce the amount of time available for direct service to the child (Friend & Cook, 1992).
- Adults often have difficulty adapting to individual differences in teaching styles and preferences of colleagues, and some erect barriers to working together.
- Just as with mentorships, it is important to recognize the rare times when it is in the best interests of all concerned, but the student most of all, to withdraw from a consulting situation. Disengagement is recognized in psychological consultation as the termination of a consultative relationship. This is reality, so having a transition plan for moving into other relationships and experiences can ease feelings of loss and sadness, and help to dispel feelings of inadequacy or failure.

The persuasive aspects of consultation require a close, careful look at ethical practices (Ross, 1986). In sum, ethical consultation is implemented by adhering to principles of confidentiality in acquisition and use of information about students, families, and individual school settings. It also includes a high regard for individual differences among colleagues and the constructive use of those differences to serve students' needs. It gives evidence of concern and empathy for all, onedownsmanship (downplaying

FIGURE 15.6   Advocacy: Carrying the Ball for Special Needs

status differences and communicating as partners) in the consultative role, advocacy for those with special needs, and mutual ownership of problems and rewards in the school environment. (See Figure 15.6.)

As expressed by Gullatt and Tollett (1997), we know that society is becoming more legally complex with many legal issues arising in school contexts. Yet few states require an educational law course as part of teacher education coursework for licensure, either at the graduate level or the undergraduate level. Issues that should be addressed in the scope of school law include special education, student discipline, liability insurance, negligence, student/teacher rights, confidentiality and privacy, photographing of students, conducting research in schools, freedom of press, ever-changing laws and regulations, and much more. Occasionally school personnel are even called as expert witnesses to give testimony and depositions involving student or family rights and due process, and are summoned to testify at a hearing.

Gullatt and Tollett recommend that universities and legal authorities collaborate with local educational authorities to design professional development workshops for informing teachers of current educational law and new legislation as enacted by state and national legislative bodies. They propose that each school designate a resource teacher to be responsible for collecting and distributing information about school law. Ethical issues could be included in this assignment and kept on the front burner of co-educators' collective agenda.

The involvement of family members in a collaborative consultation process raises legal, ethical, and confidentiality issues (Kratochwill & Pittman, 2002). Consultants and collaborators should review legal requirements relating to confidentiality, such as the

Family Educational Rights and Privacy Act of 1974 (Buckley Amendment), and truth-in-testing laws within states that legislate them. Requirements such as these stipulate the need for confidentiality of student data and regulate parental access to information about their children.

One concern is that privacy or confidentiality may not be an absolute right, especially when minors are involved and there is risk of serious harm (Taylor & Adelman, 1998). Sometimes professionals cannot maintain confidences legally or ethically. Such conflicted intentions can interfere with trust between consultant and client or consultee, but the concern may be outweighed by a responsibility to prevent serious harm. Taylor and Adelman point out that most ethical guidelines recognize such extenuating circumstances. They suggest that the problem might be reframed and focused on how to go about sharing the information appropriately.

Hansen, Himes, and Meier (1990) offer helpful suggestions to educators for exercising ethical behavior in their roles, such as:

- Promote professional attitudes and behaviors among staff about confidentiality and informed consent.
- Choose carefully the language and specificity of information they enter in written records.
- Take care in discussing problems of children and their families.
- Focus on strengths of clients and share information only with those who need it to serve the student's needs.

Most issues involving special needs of children and adolescents are not so complex and fraught with legal entanglement. In these less complex and dramatic instances, several well-known maxims can be applied to a caring, facilitative, commonsense attitude toward the implementation of collegial and ethical practices for addressing exceptional needs:

- Keep your words sweet, for you may have to eat them.
- Better to bend than to break.
- Only a fool would peel a grape with an ax.
- Eagles do not hunt flies.
- It is very hard to put the toothpaste back into the tube.
- What breaks in a moment may take years to mend.

Case Study: Planning Ahead for Collaborative School Consultation and Teamwork

If you are selected for developing a case study to conduct with co-educators in your school that allows them to reflect on contexts, content, processes, practices, and the support needed for strong collaborative consultation programs, what will be key elements of your case study? What will be your plan for facilitating the case study activity to achieve the greatest benefits for all—teachers, related services personnel, support personnel, students, and their families? How will you assess short-term and long-range outcomes of the activity? What will you do with the data from your evaluation?

IN CONCLUSION

Teachers are guides for today's children and youth as they grow into their future. All students will need skills, developed in their homes, their communities, and most certainly their schools, that ready them for the challenges in their lives, and others that have not even been realized as yet:

- Ethical behavior and social responsibility
- Communication, collaboration, and teamwork
- Critical thinking and problem solving
- Creative thinking and innovation
- Risk taking and entrepreneurship
- Reading comprehension and multiple languages
- Technology
- Citizenship and principles of government
- Global awareness

An apple has been a traditional gift from student to teacher for decades, perhaps centuries, representing the bright, caring relationship between teacher and student. The days of the little red schoolhouse with an apple lovingly placed on the lone teacher's desk in the single classroom by an adoring student are long gone. Different conditions greet teachers today, in their crowded classrooms and huge, bustling school buildings that are teeming with a diversity of students—some outspoken and angry, others withdrawn and seemingly unreachable, many wishing school days would never end, and too many thinking they just might opt out of it all tomorrow.

Now the apple signifies important work still to be done. When individual teachers step out of their classrooms and look and listen, they know they are no longer alone in their school building addressing the challenges. There are opportunities to collaborate in diverse ways with many co-educators. If each one has a symbolic apple and slices it, an outcome is its bounty of seeds. Teachers know that if they slice it horizontally, the image of a star will appear. It is a beautiful image. Then when they take those harvested seeds and plant them far and wide, who can count all of the apples that will grow eventually from those few small seeds?

TIPS FOR PUTTING IT ALL TOGETHER

1. Promote an exchange-of-roles day, on which consultants teach classes and teachers observe, plan modifications, and consult with others.
2. Make a personal pledge to engage in a collaborative activity at least once a week.
3. Formulate a personal philosophy of collaboration, consultation, and teamwork as a co-educator.
4. Join a dynamic professional organization and become actively involved in it.
5. Observe programs in other schools and share observations with key people in your own school context.

6. Engage in research efforts for new knowledge about collaboration, consultation, teamwork, and networking with co-educators.
7. Remember that knowing how to collaborate does not guarantee one the opportunity to do it! *Create* the opportunity.
8. Advocate for students at every opportunity and in every way you can.
9. Reach out to preservice and novice teachers to build their confidence and expand their skills.
10. Be available available, available, available—and never give up!

ADDITIONAL RESOURCES

Wong, H. K., Britton, T., & Ganser, T. (2005). What the world can teach us about new teacher induction. *Phi Delta Kappan, 86*(5), 379–384.

Also, professional periodicals, including but certainly not limited to:

Educational Leadership
Phi Delta Kappan

Teacher Education and Special Education
Journal of Educational and Psychological Consultation

Also look for collaboration and team teaching articles in subject-oriented journals and periodicals, at elementary and secondary levels.

Appendix: Website Resources

Accessible Instructional Materials (AIM) Center, http://aim
.cast.org/experience/decision-making tools/aim
navigator

American Evaluation Association, www.eval.org

Americans with Disabilities Act, www.ada.gov

Babel Fish, http://babelfish.yahoo.com

Books by Ruta Sevo on Lulu, www.lulu.com/sevo

Center for Applied Special Technology (CAST), www.
cast.org

Children, Youth and Families Education and Research
Network (CYFERnet), www.cyfernet.org

Council for Exceptional Children—Professional Standards,
www.cec.sped.org/Content/NavigationMenu/
ProfessionalDevelopment/ProfessionalStandards/

DO-IT (Disabilities, Opportunities, Internetworking, and
Technology) program, www.washington.edu/doit/

Educate America—Family Empowerment, www.maec.org/

El Valor, www.elvalor.org

Family Empowerment Council, Inc., www.familyem-
powerment.org

Foundation Center, www.fdncenter.org

Google, www.google.com

Grants, www.grants.gov

Harvard Family Research Project, www.hfrp.org

Harvard Family Research Project: Family Involvement—
Early Childhood Education, www.hfrp.org/fam-
ily-involvement/early-childhood-education

Intervention Central, www.interventioncentral.org

Joint Committee on Standards for Educational Evaluation, www.jcsee.org

Kansas State University, www.vimeo.com/16928841

Keep Schools Safe, www.keepschoolssafe.org

National Association for Bilingual Education (NABE),
www.nabe.org

National Association for Multicultural Education (NAME),
http://nameorg.org

National Association for the Education of Young Children (NAEYC), www.naeyc.org

National Center for Education Statistics, http://nces.ed.gov

National Center on Response to Intervention, www.
rti4success.org

National Dissemination Center for Children with Disabilities (NICHCY), www.nichcy.org

National Education Association, www.nea.org/assets/
docs/05espparahandbook.pdf

National Network of Partnership Schools—Center on
School, Family, and Community Partnerships,
www.csos.jhu.edu/P2000/center.htm

National Resource Center for Paraeducators (NRCP),
www.nrcpara.org

National Science Foundation, www.nsf.gov

North Carolina Department of Juvenile Justice and Delinquency Prevention, www.ncdjjdp.org

Northwest Regional Educational Laboratory, www.
nwrel.org

ParaEducator Learning Network, www.paraeducator.net

Parent Institute for Quality Education, www.piqe.org

Parent Technical Assistance Center Network, www.
parentcenternetwork.org

Pew Internet & American Life Project (2010),www.
pewinternet.org

Philanthropic Ventures Foundationventuresfoundation.
orgProject PARA: Paraeducator Self-Study Program, http://para.unl.edu/ec

Raising a Reader, www.raisingareader.org

Raising a Reader: Families—Tips for Parents, www.
raisingareader.org/site/PageServer?pagename=
families_tips_for_parents

Research in Disabilities Education program (RDE) of the
NSF, www.washington.edu/doit/RDE

Sibling Support Project, www.siblingsupport.org

Striving to Reduce YouthViolence Everywhere
(STRYVE), www.safeyouth.gov

Teaching Tolerance: A Project of the Southern Poverty
Law Center, www.teachingtolerance.org

References

Adler, S. (1993). *Multicultural communication skills in the classroom.* Boston: Allyn & Bacon.

Adults and Attention Deficit Disorder. (1997, September 2). *New York Times/Manhattan Mercury,* B-10.

Anderson, J. D. (1997). Supporting the invisible minority. *Educational Leadership, 54*(7), 65–68.

Anderson, J. W., Foster-Kuehn, M., McKinney, B. C. (1996). *Communication skills for surviving conflicts at work.* Cresskill, NJ: Hampton Press, Inc.

Annunzio, S. (2001). *eLeadership.* New York: Free Press.

ASCD. (2000). Finding time to collaborate. *Education Update, 42*(2), 1, 3, 8.

Ashbaker, B., & Morgan, J. (1996). Paraeducators: Critical members of the rural education team. In D. Montgomery (Ed.), *The American Council on Rural Special Education Conference-Rural Goals 2000: Building programs that work* (pp. 130–136). Stillwater, OK: Oklahoma State University.

August, D., & Hakuta, K. (1997). *Improving schooling for language-minority children.* Washington, DC: National Academy Press.

Axelrod, L., & Johnson, R. (2005). *Turning conflict into profit: A roadmap for resolving personal and organizational disputes.* Edmonton, Alberta, Canada: The University of Alberta Press.

Babinski, L. M., & Rogers, D. L. (1998). Supporting new teachers through consultee-centered group consultation. *Journal of Educational and Psychological Consultation, 9*(4), 285–308.

Baca, L. M., & Cervantes, H. T. (2004). *The bilingual special education interface* (4th ed.). Upper Saddle River, NJ: Merrill.

Bahamonde, C., & Friend, M. (1999). Teaching English language learners: A proposal for effective service delivery through collaboration and co-teaching. *Journal of Educational and Psychological Consultation, 10*(1), 1–24.

Banks, J. A. (2003). *Teaching Strategies for ethnic studies* (7th ed.). Boston: Allyn & Bacon.

Banks, J. A., & Banks, C. A. M. (Eds.). (2007). *Multicultural education: Issues and perspectives* (6th ed.). Hoboken, NJ: Wiley.

Banks, J. A. & Banks, C. A. M. (Eds.) (2010). *Multicultural education: Issues and perspectives* (7th ed.). Hoboken, NJ: Wiley & Sons.

Barbour, C., & Barbour, N. H. (2001). *Families, schools, and communities: Building partnerships for educating children.* Upper Saddle River, NJ: Merrill Prentice Hall.

Barbour, C., Barbour, N. H., & Scully, P. A. (2008). *Families, schools, and communities* (4th ed.). Upper Saddle River, NJ: Prentice Hall.

Barnard, W. M. (2004). Parent involvement in elementary school and educational attainment. *Children & Youth Services Review, 26*(1), 39–62.

Bateman, D., & Bateman, C. F. (2001). *A principal's guide to special education.* Reston, VA: Council for Exceptional Children.

Bauwens, J., & Hourcade, J. J. (1997). Cooperative teaching: Pictures of possibilities. *Intervention in school and clinic, 33*(2), 81–89.

Belch, H. A. (2004–2005). Retention and students with disabilities. *Journal of College Student Retention, 6*(1) 3–22.

Bergan, J. R. (1977). *Behavioral consultation.* Columbus, OH: Merrill.

Bergan, J. R. (1995). Evolution of a problem-solving model of consultation. *Journal of Educational and Psychological Consultation, 6*(2), 111–123.

Bergan, J. R., & Tombari, M. L. (1976). Consultant skill and efficiency and the implementation and outcome of consultation. *Journal of School Psychology, 14*(1), 3–14.

Berger, E. H. (2008). *Parents as partners in education: Families and schools working together* (7th ed.). Upper Saddle River, NJ: Prentice Hall.

Blank, M. J. (2004). How community schools make a difference. *Educational Leadership, 61*(8), 63–65.

Blaylock, B. K. (1983). Teamwork in a simulated production environment. *Research in Psychological Type, 6,* 58–67.

Bloom, B. S., Engelhart, M. D., Furst, E. J., Hill, W. H., & Krathwohl, D. R. (1956). *Taxonomy of educational objectives; Handbook I: Cognitive domain.* New York: McKay.

Bocchino, R. (March, 1991). Using mind mapping as a note-taking tool. *The Developer, 1,* 4.

Bogdan, R., & Biklen, S. (2006). *Qualitative research for education: An introduction to theory and methods* (5th ed.). Boston: Allyn & Bacon.

Bolton, R. (1986). *People skills: How to assert yourself, listen to others, and resolve conflicts.* New York: Simon & Schuster.

Boone, H. A. (1989). Preparing family specialists in early childhood special education. *Teacher Education and Special Education, 12*(3), 96–102.

Boudah, D. J., Lenz, B. K., Bulgren, J. A., Schumkaer, J. B., & Deshler, D. D. (2000). Don't water down! Enhance content learning through the unit organizer routine. *Teaching Exceptional Children, 32*(3), 48–56.

Bradley, M. O. (1987). Personal communication.

Breton, W. (2010). Special education paraprofessionals: Perceptions of preservice preparation, supervision, and ongoing developmental training. *International Journal of Special Education, 25* (1), 34–45.

Broer, S. M., Doyle, M. B., & Giangreco, M. F. (2005). Perspectives of students with intellectual disabilities about their experiences with paraprofessional support. *Exceptional Children, 71,* 415–430.

Brown-Chidsey, R. (2007). No more "waiting to fail." *Educational Leadership, 65*(2), 40–46.

Brown, D., Wyne, M. D., Blackburn, J. E., & Powell, W. C. (1979). *Consultation: Strategy for improving education.* Boston: Allyn & Bacon.

Brownell, M., Adams, A., Sindelar, P., Waldron, N., & Vanhover, S. (2006). Learning from collaboration: The role of teacher qualities. *Exceptional Children, 72*(2), 169–185.

Bruner, C. (1991). *Thinking collaboratively: Ten questions and answers to help policymakers improve children's services.* Washington, DC: Education and Human Service Consortium.

Bulgren, J. A., Schumaker, J. B., & Deshler, D. D. (1993). *The concept mastery routine.* Lawrence, KS: Edge Enterprises.

Buscaglia, L. (1986). *Loving each other: The challenges of human relationships.* Westminster, MD: Fawcett.

Bushaw, W. J. (2007). From the mouths of middle-schoolers: Important changes for high school and college. *Phi Delta Kappan, 89*(3), 189–193.

Buzan, T. (1983). *Use both sides of your brain.* New York: Dutton.

Canning, C. (1991). What teachers say about reflection. *Educational Leadership, 48*(6), 18–21.

Caplan, G. (1970). *The theory and practice of mental health consultation.* New York: Basic Books.

Caplan, G. (1995). Types of mental health consultation. *Journal of Educational and Psychological Consultation, 6*(1), 7–21.

Caplan, G., Caplan, R. B., & Erchul, W. P. (1995). A contemporary view of mental health consultation: Comments on "Types of Mental Health Consultation." *Journal of Educational and Psychological Consultation, 6*(1), 23–30.

Carlyn, M. (1977). An assessment of the Myers-Briggs Type Indicator. *Journal of Personality Assessment, 41*(5), 461–473.

Caro, D. J., & Robbins, P. (1991, November). Talkwalking—thinking on your feet. *Developer,* 3–4.

Carpenter, T. (2012). Virtual schools a reality. *The Topeka Capital-Journal,* January 23, 2012.

Carver, C. L. (2004, May). A lifeline for new teachers. *Educational Leadership, 58*–61.

Caspe, M., & Lopez, M. E. (2006). *Lessons from family-strengthening interventions: Learning from evidence-based practice.* Cambridge, MA: Harvard Family Research Project. Available at www.hfrp.html

Caspe, M., Lopez, M. E., & Wolos, C. (2007). *Family involvement in elementary school children's education.* Cambridge, MA: Harvard Family Research Project. Available at www.hfrp.html

Casper, V., & Schultz, S. B. (1999). *Gay parents/straight schools: Building communication and trust.* New York: Teachers College Press.

Cawelti, G. (1997). Making the most of every minute. *ASCD Education Update, 39*(6), 1, 6, 8.

CEC Today. (March 29, 2011). *Common Core Standards: What special educators need to know.* Council for Exceptional Children Web Site: Arlington, VA.

CEC Today. (1997, April/May).

CEC Today. (2000, October).

Center for Learning and Performing Technologies (2011). Top 100 tools for learning 2011 [Data file]. Available from Center for Learning and Performing Technologies Data Website: http://www.c4lpt.co.uk/toolbox.html

Chisholm, I. M. (1994). Preparing teachers for multicultural classrooms. *Journal of Educational Issues of Language Minority Students, 14,* 43–68.

Christie, K. (2004). AYP: The new purple pill for the slower learner. *Phi Delta Kappan, 85,* (5), 341–342.

Christie, K. (2005). Changing the nature of parent involvement. *Phi Delta Kappan, 86*(9), 645+.

Cipani, E. (1985). The three phrases of behavioral consultation: Objectives, intervention, and quality assurance. *Teacher Education and Special Education, 8,* 144–152.

Clare, M. M. (2002). Diversity as a dependent variable: Considerations for research and practice in consultation. *Journal of Educational and Psychological Consultation, 13*(30), 251–263.

Clark, B. (2002). *Growing up gifted* (6th ed.). Upper Saddle River, NJ: Merrill.

Clark, S. G. (2013). The IEP process as a tool for collaboration. *Teaching Exceptional Children, 33*(2), 56–66.

Common Core Standards (2010). © Copyright 2010, all rights reserved. National Governors Association.

Conley, D. T. (March, 2011). Building on the common core standards. *Educational Leadership, 66*(6), 17–20.

Conoley, J. C. (1985). Personal correspondence.

Conoley, J. C. (1987). National Symposium on School Consultation. Austin: University of Texas.

Conoley, J. C. (1989). Professional communication and collaboration among educators. In M. C. Reynolds (Ed.), *Knowledge base for the beginning teacher* (pp. 245–254). Oxford, England: Pergamon.

Conoley, J. C. (1994). You say potato, I say . . . : Part I. *Journal of Educational and Psychological Consultation, 5*(1), 45–49.

Conoley, J. C., & Conoley, C. W. (1982). *School consultation: A guide to practice and training.* New York: Pergamon Press.

Conoley, J. C., & Conoley, C. W. (1988). Useful theories in school-based consultation. *Remedial and Special Education, 9*(6), 14–20.

Conoley, J. C., & Conoley, C. W. (2010). Why does collaboration work? Linking positive psychology and collaboration. *Journal of Educational and Psychological Consultation, 20:* 75–82.

Correa, V. I., Jones, H. A., Thomas, C. C., & Morsink, C. V. (2004). *Interactive teaming: Enhancing programs for students with special needs* (4th ed.). Upper Saddle River, NJ: Prentice Hall.

Cosmos, C. (2001). Abuse of children with disabilities. *CEC Today, 8*(2), 1, 5, 8, 12, 14–15.

Council for Exceptional Children. (1997). Working with paraeducators. *CEC Today, 4*(3), 1, 5.

Council for Exceptional Children. (2000). Home schooling—A viable alternative for students with special needs? *CEC Today, 7*(1), 1, 5, 10, 15.

Council for Exceptional Children. (2001). A principal's guide to special education. *CEC Today, 8*(2), 10.

Countryman, L. L., & Schroeder, M. (1996). When students lead parent-teacher conferences. *Educational Leadership, 53*(7), 64–68.

Cox, D. (July, 2011). The limits of intelligence. *Scientific American, 305*(1), 36–43.

Coyle, N. C. (2000). Conflict resolution: It's part of the job. *Delta Kappa Gamma Bulletin, 66(4), 41–46.*

Cramer, S., Erzkus, A., Mayweather, K., Pope, K., Roeder, J., & Tone, T. (1997). Connecting with siblings. *Teaching Exceptional Children, 30*(1), 46–49.

Creswell, J. W., & Plano-Clark, V. L. (2006). *Designing and conducting mixed methods research.* Thousand Oaks, CA: Sage.

Cross, T. (1996). Developing a knowledge base to support cultural competence. *Prevention Report, 1,* 2–5.

Cross, T. L. (2003). Culture as a resource for mental health. *Cultural Diversity and Ethnic Minority Psychology, 9*(4), 354–359.

Curtis, M. J., Curtis, V. A., & Graden, J. L. (1988). Prevention and early intervention assistance programs. *School Psychology International, 9,* 257–264.

Davies, D. (1988). Low-income parents and the schools: A research report and plan for action. *Equity and Choice, 4,* 51–59.

Darling-Hammond, L. (2003). Keeping good teachers: Why it matters, what leaders can do. *Educational Leadership, 60*(8), 6–13.

DeBoer, A. L. (1986). *The art of consulting.* Chicago: Arcturus.

de Bono, E. (1973). *Lateral thinking: Creativity step by step.* Boston: Little, Brown.

de Bono, E. (1985). *Six thinking hats.* New York: Harper & Row.

de Bono, E. (1986). *CORT thinking: Teacher's notes* (Vols. 1–6, 2nd ed.). New York: Pergamon.

de Valenzuela, J. S., Baca, L., & Baca, E. (2004). Family involvement in bilingual special education: Challenging the norm. In L. M. Baca & H. T Cervantes. (Eds.), *The bilingual special education interface* (4th ed., pp. 360–381). Upper Saddle River, NJ: Pearson.

de Valenzuela, J. S., Torres, R. L., & Chavez, R. L. (1998). Family involvement in bilingual special education: Challenging the norm. In L. M. Baca & H. T. Cervantes (Eds.), *The bilingual special education interface* (3rd ed., pp. 350–370). Upper Saddle River, NJ: Merrill.

Dearing, E., Kreider, H., Simpkins, S., & Weiss, H. B. (2006). Family involvement in school and low-income children's literacy performance: Longitudinal associations between and within families. *Journal of Educational Psychology, 98,* 653–664.

Decyk, B. N. (1994). Using examples to teach concepts. In *Changing College Classrooms, by D. F. Halpern & Associates,* 1994, p. 40. San Francisco: Jossey-Bass.

Demchak, M. A. & Morgan, C. R. (1998). Effective collaboration between professionals and paraprofessionals. *Rural Special Education Quarterly, 17*(1), 10–15.

Deshler, D. D., Schumaker, J. B., Lenz, B. K., Bulgren, J. A., Hoch, M. F., Knight, J., & Ehren, B. J. (2001). Ensuring content-area learning by secondary students with learning disabilities. *Learning Disabilities Research and Practice, 16*(2), 96–108.

Dettmer, P. (1981). The effects of teacher personality type on classroom values and perceptions of gifted students. *Research in Psychological Type, 3,* 48–54.

Dettmer, P. (1989). The consulting teacher in programs for gifted and talented students. *Arkansas Gifted Education Magazine, 3*(2), 4–7.

Dettmer, P. (Ed.). (1990). *Staff development for gifted programs: Putting it together and making it work.* Washington, DC: National Association for Gifted Children.

Dettmer, P. (1993). Gifted education: Window of opportunity. *Gifted Child Quarterly, 37*(2), 92–94.

Dettmer, P. (1994). IEPs for gifted secondary students. *The Journal of Secondary Gifted Education, 5*(4), 52–59.

Dettmer, P. (1997, September). *New blooms for established fields.* Presented at the annual conference of the Kansas Association for Gifted, Talented, and Creative, Hutchinson, KS.

Dettmer, P. (2006). New domains in established fields: Four domains of learning and doing. *Roeper Review, 28*(2), 70–78.

Dettmer, P., & Lane, J. (1989). An integrative model for educating very able students in rural school districts. *Educational Considerations, 17*(1), 36–39.

Dillman, D. A. (2007). *Mail and Internet surveys: The tailored design method* (2nd ed.). Hoboken, NJ: Wiley.

Dion, A. (2011). Act it out. *Teaching Tolerance, 39,* 15.

Dougherty, A. M., Tack, F. E., Fullam, C. B., & Hammer, L. A. (1996). Disengagement: A neglected aspect of the consultation process. *Journal of Educational and Psychological Consultation, 7*(3), 259–274.

Douglass, M. E., & Douglass, D. N. (1993). *Manage your time, manage your work, manage yourself.* New York: AMACOM.

DuFour, R. (2004). What is a professional learning community? *Educational Leadership, 61*(8), 6–11.

Dukes, C., & Lamar-Dukes, P. (2009). Inclusion by design: Engineering inclusive practices in secondary schools. *Teaching Exceptional Children, 41*(3), 16–23.

Dunn, R., & Dunn, K. (1978). *Teaching students through their individual learning styles.* Reston, VA: Reston Publishing.

Dunst, C. J. (2002). How can we strengthen family support research and evaluation? *The Evaluation Exchange, 8*(1), 5.

Dyck, N., & Dettmer, P. (1989). Collaborative consultation: A promising tool for serving gifted learning-disabled students. *Journal of Reading, Writing, and Learning Disabilities, 5*(3), 253–264.

Dyck, N., & Dettmer, P., & Thurston, L. P. (1985). *Special education consultation skills project.* Manhattan, KS Kansas State University, College of Education, unpublished manuscript.

Dyck, N., & Kaff, M. (1999). *Essential skills for paras.* San Antonio, TX: PCI Educational Publishing.

Edwards, A. T. (1997). Let's stop ignoring our gay and lesbian youth. *Educational Leadership, 54*(7), 68–70.

Edyburn, D. (2006). Text modifications. *Special Education Technology Practice, 8*(2), 16–27.

Eisner, E. W. (2003). Questionable assumptions about schooling. *Phi Delta Kappan, 84*(9), 348–357.

Epstein, J. L. (1995). School/family/community partnerships: Caring for the children we share. *Phi Delta Kappan, 76*(9), 701–712.

Erchul, W. P., & Martens, B. K. (1997). *School consultation: Conceptual and empirical bases of practice.* New York: Plenum.

Erchul, W. P. (2011). School consultation and Response to Intervention: A tale of two literatures. *Journal of Educational and Psychological Consultation, 21*(3), 191–208.

Ernsperger, L. (1998). Using a paraeducator to facilitate school reentry. *Reaching Today's Youth: The Community Circle Caring Journal, 2*(4), 9–12.

Family Integration Resources. (1991). Second Family Leadership Conference. Washington, DC: U.S. Department of Education.

Federico, M. A., Herrold, Jr., W. G., & Venn, J. (1999). Helpful tips for successful inclusion: A checklist for educators. *Teaching Exceptional Children, 32*(1), 76–82.

Ferriter, W. M. (2011). Becoming digitally resilient. *Educational Leadership,* 68(6), 86–87.

Ferriter, W. M. (2011a and 2011b). Good teaching trumps good tools. *Educational Leadership, 68*(5), 84–85.

Fiedler, C. R., Simpson, R. L., & Clark, D. M. (2007). *Parents and families of children with disabilities: Effective school-based support services.* Upper Saddle River, NJ: Prentice Hall.

Fisher, D. (1993). *Communication in organizations* (2nd ed.). St Paul, MN: West.

Fisher, R., & Sharp, A. (1999). *Getting it DONE: How to lead when you're not in charge.* New York: HarperCollins.

Fisher, R., & Ury, W. (1991). *Getting past no: Negotiating agreement without giving in.* New York: Bantam Books.

Fisher, R., Ury, B., & Patton, B. (1991). *Getting to YES: Negotiating agreement without giving in.* Boston: Houghton Mifflin.

Fleury, M. L. (2000). Confidentiality issues with substitutes and paraeducators. *Teaching Exceptional Children, 33*(1), 44–45.

Foley, R. M., & Lewis, J. A. (1999). Self-perceived competence of secondary school principals to serve as school leaders in collaborative-based educational delivery systems. *Remedial and Special Education, 20*(4), 233–243.

Fowler, S. A., Donegan, M., Lueke, B., Hadden, D. S., & Phillips, B. (2000). Evaluating community collaboration in writing interagency agreements on the age 3 transition. *Exceptional Children, 67*(1), 35–50.

Fox, D. (July, 2011). The limits of intelligence. *Scientific American, 305*(1), 36–43.

Fox, F.D., Morris, M., & Rumsey, N. (2007). Doing synchronous online focus groups with young people: Methodological reflections. *Qualitative Health Research, 17* (4), 539–547.

French, N. K. (1997). Management of paraeducators. In A. L. Pickett & Gerlach (Eds.), *Supervising Paraeducators in School Settings.* Austin, TX: PRO-ED.

French, N. K. (1998). Working together: Resource teachers and paraeducators. *Remedial and Special Education, 19,* 357–368.

French, N. K. (1999). Paraeducators and teachers: Shifting roles. *Teaching Exceptional Children, 2*(2), 69–73.

French, N. K. (2000). Taking time to save time: Delegating to paraeducators. *Teaching Exceptional Children, 32*(3), 79–83.

French, N. K. (2001). Supervising paraprofessionals: A survey of teacher practices. *Journal of Special Education, 35,* 41–53.

French, N. K., & Pickett, A. L. (1997). Paraprofessionals in special education: Issues for teacher educators. *Teacher Education and Special Education, 20*(1), 61–73.

Frey, W. H. (2010). *State of Metropolitan America.* Washington, DC: The Brookings Institution.

Friedman, I. (2003). Self-efficacy and burnout in teaching: The importance of interpersonal-relations efficacy. *Social Psychology of Education, 6,* 191–215.

Friend, M. (1984). Consultation skills for resource teachers. *Learning Disability Quarterly, 7,* 246–250.

Friend, M. (1988). Putting consultation into context: Historical and contemporary perspectives. *Remedial and Special Education, 9*(6), 7–13.

Friend, M. (2007). The coteaching partnership. *Educational Leadership, 64*(5), 48–52.

Friend, M., & Bursuck, W. D. (1996). *Including students with special needs: A practical guide for classroom teachers.* Boston: Allyn & Bacon.

Friend, M., & Cook, L. (1990). Collaboration as a predictor for success in school reform. *Journal of Educational and Psychological Consultation, 1*(1), 69–86.

Friend, M., & Cook, L. (1992). The ethics of collaboration. *Journal of Educational and Psychological Consultation, 3*(2), 181–184.

Friend, M., Cook, L., Hurley-Chamberlain, D., & Shamberger, C. (2010). Co-Teaching: An illustration of the complexity of collaboration in special education. *Journal of Educational and Psychological Consultation, 20,* 9–27.

Fuller, R. B. (1975). *Explorations in the geometry of thinking synergetics.* New York: Macmillan.

Futrell, M., Gomez, J., & Bedden, D. (2003). Teaching the children of a new America. *Phi Delta Kappan, 84*(5), 381–385.

Gallessich, J. (1974). Training the school psychologist for consultation. *Journal of School Psychology, 12,* 138–149.

Gardner, H. (1993). *Multiple intelligences: The theory in practice.* New York: HarperCollins.

Garmston, R. (1988, October). Giving gifts. *The Developer,* 3, 6.

Garmston, R. J. (1994). The persuasive art of presenting: What's a MetaPhor? *Journal of Staff Development, 15*(2), 60–61.

Garmston, R. J. (1995). Techniques to increase collaboration. *Journal of Staff Development, 16*(3), 69–70.

Garmston, R. J., & Wellman, B. M. (1992). *How to make presentations that teach and transform.* Alexandria, VA: Association for Supervision and Curriculum Development.

Gazda, G. M., Asbury, F. R., Balzer, F. J., Childers, W. C., Phelps, R. E., & Walters, R. P. (1999). *Human relations development: A manual for educators* (6th ed.). Boston: Allyn & Bacon.

Geenen, S., Powers, L. E., & Lopez-Vasquez, A. (2001). Multicultural aspects of parent involvement in transition planning. *Exceptional Children, 67*(2), 265–282.

Gersten, R., & Baker, S. (2000). What we know about effective instructional practices for English-language learners. *Exceptional Children, 66*(4), 454–470.

Gersten, R., Darch, C., Davis, G., & George, N. (1991). Apprenticeship and intensive training of consulting teachers: A naturalistic study. *Exceptional Children, 57*(3), 226–236.

Ghosh, S., & Rezazadeh, S. M. (2011). Consultation with pediatricians in the management of attention-deficit disorder. *Journal of Educational and Psychological Consultation, Focus on Autism and Other Developmental Disabilities, 20* (1), 10–26.

Giangreco, M. F. (1993). Using creative problem-solving methods to include students with severe disabilities in general classroom activities. *Journal of Educational and Psychological Consultation, 4*(2), 113–135.

Giangreco, M. F., Dennis, R., Cloninger, C., Edelman, S., & Schattman, R. (1993). "I've counted Jon": Transformational experiences of teachers educating students with disabilities. *Exceptional Children, 59*(4), 359–372.

Giangreco, M. F., & Broer, S. M. (2005). Questionable utilization of paraprofessionals in inclusive schools: Are we addressing symptoms or causes. *Focus on Autism and Other Developmental Disabilities, 20*(1), 10–26.

Giangreco, M. F., Edelman, S. W., & Broer, S. M. (2001). Respect, appreciation, and acknowledgment of paraprofessionals who support students with disabilities. *Exceptional Children, 67*(4), 485–498.

Giangreco, M. F., Edelman, S. W., Broer, S. M., & Doyle, M. B. (2001). Paraprofessional support of students with disabilities: Literature from the past decade. *Exceptional Children, 68*(1), 45–63.

Giangreco, M. F., Edelman, S. W., Luiselli, T. E., & MacFarland, S. Z. C. (1997). Helping or hovering? Effects of instructional assistant proximity on students with disabilities. *Exceptional Children, 64*(1), 7–18.

Giangreco, M. F., Suter, J. C., & Doyle, M. B. (2010). Paraprofessionals in inclusive schools: A review of recent research. *Journal of Educational and Psychological Consultation, 20*, 41–57.

Gibson, S., & Dembo, M. (1984). Teacher efficacy: A construct validation. *Journal of Educational Psychology, 76*(4), 569–582.

Ginsburg, D. (2010, October 5). Differentiated instruction: A practical approach [Web log blog "Coach G's Teaching Tips"]. Retrieved from http://blogs.edweek.org/teachers/coach_gs_teaching_tips/2010/10/differentiated_instruction_a_practical_approach.html

Glasgow, N. A., & Hicks, C. D. (2003). *What SUCCESSFUL teachers do: 91 research-based classroom strategies for new and veteran teachers.* Thousand Oaks, CA: Corwin.

Goddard, R. D., Hoy, A. K., & Woolfolk-Hoy, A. (2000). Collective teacher efficacy: Its meaning, measure, and impact on student achievement. *American Educational Research Journal, 37*, 479–507.

Golombok, S., Perry, B., Burston, A., Murray, C., Mooney-Sommers, J., Stevens, M., & Golding J. (2003). Children with lesbian parents: A community study. *Developmental Psychology, 39*(1), 20–33.

Gordon, T. (1974). *T.E.T.: Teacher effectiveness training.* New York: Wyden.

Gordon, T. (1977). *Leader effectiveness training, L.E.T.: The no-lose way to release the productive potential in people.* Toronto: Bantam.

Gordon, T. (2000). *P.E.T.: Parent effectiveness training: The proven programs for raising responsible children.* New York: Three Rivers Press.

Gordon, W. J. J., & Poze, T. (1975). *Strange and familiar.* Cambridge, MA: SES Associates.

Gordon, W. J. J., & Poze, T. (1979). *The metaphorical way of learning and knowing.* Cambridge, MA: SES Associates.

Graubard, P. S., Rosenberg, H., & Miller, M. B. (1971). Student applications of behavior modification to teachers and environments or ecological approaches to deviancy. In E. A. Ramp & B. L. Hopkins (Eds.), *A new direction for education: Behavior analysis* (pp. 80–101). Lawrence: University of Kansas.

Gregorc, A. F., & Ward, H. B. (1977). A new definition for individual: Implications for learning and teaching. *NASSP Bulletin, 61*, 20–26.

Griffin, J. (1998). *How to say it at work: Putting yourself across with power words, phrases, body language, and communication secrets.* Paramus, NJ: Prentice Hall.

Gronlund, N. E. (2000). *How to write and use instructional objectives* (6th ed.). Upper Saddle River, NJ: Merrill.

Grossman, P., & Loeb, S. (2010). Learning from multiple routes. *Educational Leadership, 67*(8), 22–27.

Gullatt, D. E., & Tollett, John R. (1997). Educational law: A requisite course for preservice and inservice teacher education programs. *Journal of Teacher Education, 48*(2),129–135.

Guskey, T. R. (1985). Staff development and teacher change. *Educational Leadership, 42*(7), 57–60.

Guthrie, G. P., & Guthrie, L. F. (1991). Streamlining interagency collaboration for youth at risk. *Educational Leadership, 49*(1), 17–22.

Hall, G. E., & Hord, S. M. (1987). Change in schools: Facilitating the process. Albany: State University of New York Press.

Hamlin, S. (2006). *How to talk so people listen: Connecting in today's workplace.* New York: HarperCollins.

Hanna, G. S., & Dettmer, P. A. (2004). *Assessment for effective teaching: Using context-adaptive planning.* Boston: Allyn & Bacon.

Hansen, J. C., Himes, B. S., & Meier, S. (1990). *Consultation: Concepts and practices.* Englewood Cliffs, NJ: Prentice Hall.

Harris, K. C. (2004). The relationship between educational consultation an instruction for culturally and linguistically diverse exceptional (CLDE) student: Definitions, structures, and case studies. In L. M. Baca & H. T. Cervantes, *The bilingual special education interface* (4th ed., pp. 337–359). Upper Saddle River, NJ: Pearson.

Harris, K. C., & Klein, M. D. (2002). Itinerant consultation in early childhood special education: Issues and challenges. *Journal of Educational and Psychological Consultation, 13*(3), 247–257.

Harris, L., & Associates, Inc. (2003). *N.O.D./Harris survey of Americans with disabilities.* New York: Author.

Harrow, A. J. (1972). *A taxonomy of the psychomotor domain: A guide for developing behavioral objectives.* New York: McKay.

Hawthorne, E. M. (Fall, 1991). Case study and critical thinking. *Issues and Inquiry in College Learning and Teaching,* 60–87.

Hehir, T. (2007). Confronting ableism. *Educational Leadership, 64*(5), 8–14.

Henderson, C. (2001). *College freshmen with disabilities.* Washington, D.C.: American Council on Education/ HEALTH Resource Center.

Henning-Stout, M. (1994). Consultation and connected knowing: What we know is determined by the questions we ask. *Journal of Educational and Psychological Consultation, 5*(1), 5–21.

Heron, T. E., & Harris, K. C. (1987). *The educational consultant: Helping professionals, parents, and mainstreamed students.* Austin, TX: PRO-ED.

Hill, N. E., & Taylor, L. C. (2004). Parental school involvement and children's academic achievement: Pragmatics and issues. *Current Directions in Psychological Science, 13*(4), 161–164.

Howe, K. R., & Miramontes, O. B. (1992). *The ethics of special education.* New York: Teachers College Press.

Hoy, W., & Woolfolk, A. (1993). Teachers' sense of efficacy and the organizational health of schools. *Elementary School Journal, 93,* 356–372. https://www.ideadata.org/PartBdata.asp

Huefner, D. S. (1988). The consulting teacher model: Risks and opportunities. *Exceptional Children, 54*(5), 403–414.

Hughes, M., & Greenhough, P. (2006). Boxes, bags, and videotape: Enhancing home-school communication through knowledge exchange activities. *Educational Review, 58*(4), 471–487.

Hunter, M. (1985, May). Promising theories die young. *ASCD Update,* 1, 3.

Hurst, M. (2007). *Bit literacy: Productivity in the age of information and e-mail overload.* New York, NY: Good Experience Press.

Hutchings, P. (November, 1993). *Casing cases: Using cases to improve college teaching.* American Association for Higher Education. Washington: D.C.

Idol, L. (1988). A rationale and guidelines for establishing special education consultation programs. *Remedial and Special Education, 9*(6), 48–58.

Idol, L., & West, J. F. (1987). Consultation in special education (Part II): Training and practices. *Journal of Learning Disabilities, 20,* 474–497.

Idol, L., Paolucci-Whitcomb, P., & Nevin, A. (1986). *Collaborative Consultation.* Austin, TX: PRO-ED.

Idol, L., Paolucci-Whitcomb, P., & Nevin, A. (1995). The collaborative consultation model. *Journal of Educational and Psychological Consultation, 6*(4), 329–346.

Idol, L., West, J. F., & Lloyd, S. R. (1988). Organizing and implementing specialized reading programs: A collaborative approach involving classroom, remedial, and special education teachers. *Remedial and Special Education, 9*(2), 54–61.

Idol-Maestas, L. (1981). A teacher training model: The resource/consulting teacher. *Behavioral Disorders, 6*(2), 108–121.

Idol-Maestas, L. (1983). *Special educator's consultation handbook.* Rockville, MD: Aspen.

Idol-Maestas, L., & Celentano, R. (1986). Teacher consultant services for advanced students. *Roper Review, 9*(1), 34–36.

Idol-Maestes, L., Lloyd, S., & Lilly, M. S. (1981). Non-categorical approach to direct service and teachers education. *Exceptional Children, 48,* 213–220.

Ingersoll, R. M. (2001). Teacher turnover and teacher shortages: An organizational analysis. *American Educational Research Journal, 38*(3), 499–534.

Ingersoll, R. M. (2002). The teacher shortage: A case of wrong diagnosis and wrong prescription. *NASSP Bulletin, 86*(631), 16–31.

Jennings, J. (2011). The policy and politics of rewriting the nation's main education law. *Phi Delta Kappan, 92*(4), 44–50.

Jersild, A. T. (1955). *When teachers face themselves.* New York: Teachers College Press.

Jeynes, W. H. (2007). The relationship between parental involvement an urban secondary school student academic achievement. *Urban Education, 42*(1), 82–110.

Johnson, L. J., & Pugach, M. C. (1996). Role of collaborative dialogue in teaching conceptions of appropriate practice for students at risk. *Journal of Educational and Psychological Consultation, 7*(1), 9–24.

Johnson, S. (1992). *"Yes" or "No": A guide to better decisions.* New York: HarperCollins.

John-Steiner, V., Weber, R. J., & Minnis, M. (1998). The challenge of studying collaboration. *American Educational Research Journal, 35*(4), 773–783.

Joint Committee on Teacher Planning for Students with Disabilities. (1995). *Windows on diversity.* Lawrence, KS: University of Kansas.

Jones, S. L., & Morin, V. A. (2000). Training teachers to work as partners: Modeling the way in teacher preparation programs. *The Delta Kappa Bulletin, 67*(1), 51–55.

Jukes, I., McCain, T., & Crockett, L. (2011). Education and the role of the educator in the future. *Phi Delta Kappan, 92*(4), 15–21.

Jung, C. G. (1923). *Psychological types.* New York: Harcourt Brace.

Kaff, M., & Dyck, N. (1999). *Essential skills for paras.* Lawrence, KS: Curriculum Solutions.

Kansas State University, http://vimeo.com/16928841

Kauffman, J. (1993). Foreword. In K. R. Howe & O. B. Miramontes (Eds.), *The ethics of special education.* New York: Teachers College Press.

Kauffman, J. M. (1994). Places of Change: Special education's power and identity in an era of educational reform. *Journal of Learning Disabilities, 27*(10), 610–618.

Keefe, E. G., Moore, V., Duff, F. (2004). The four "knows" of collaborative teaching. *Teaching Exceptional Children, 36*(5), 36–42.

Keirsey, D., & Bates, M. (1978). *Please understand me: Character and temperament types.* Del Mar, CA: Prometheus Nemesis.

Kelleher, J. (2003). A model for assessment-driven professional development. *Phi Delta Kappan, 84*(10), 751–756.

Keller, M. M., & Decoteau, G. T. (2000). *The military child: Mobility and education,* Fastback #63. Bloomington, IN: Phi Delta Kappa Educational Foundation.

Kellogg, W. K. (2004). *Logic model development guide.* Battle Creek, MI: W. K. Kellogg Foundation.

Kerns, G. M. (1992). Helping professionals understand families. *Teacher Education and Special Education, 15*(1), 49–55.

Kirschenbaum, R. J., Armstrong, D. C., & Landrum, M. S. (1999). Resource consultation model in gifted education to support talent development in today's inclusive schools. *Gifted Child Quarterly, 43*(1), 39–47.

Kling, B. (2000). ASSERT yourself: Helping students of all ages develop self-advocacy skills. *Teaching Exceptional Children, 30*(3), 66–71.

Kluth, P., & Straut, D. (2001). Standards for diverse learners. *Educational Leadership, 59*(1), 43–46.

Knackendoffel, E. A., Robinson, S. M., Deshler, D. D., Schumaker, J. B. (1992). *Collaborative Problem Solving.* Lawrence, KS: Edge Enterprises, Inc.

Koemer, M. E., & Hulsebosch, P. (1996). Preparing teachers to work with children of gay and lesbian parents. *Journal of Teacher Education, 47*(5), 347–354.

Koenig, D. (2011). Social media in the schoolhouse. *Teaching Tolerance*, 39, 42–45.

Kozleskie, E., Mainzer, R., & Deshler, D. (2000). Bright futures for exceptional learners: An action agenda to achieve quality conditions for teaching and learning. *Teaching Exceptional Children, 32*(6), 56–69.

Kramer, M. W., & Tan, C. L. (2006). Emotion management in dealing with difficult people. In J. M. H. Fritz & B. L. Omdahl (Eds.). *Problematic relationships in the workplace* (pp. 153–178). New York: Peter Lang.

Krathwohl, D. R., Bloom, B. S., & Masia, B. B. (1964). *Taxonomy of educational objectives; Handbook II: Affective domain.* New York: McKay.

Kratochwill, T. R., & Pittman, P. H. (2002). Expanding problem-solving consultation training: Prospects and frameworks. *Journal of Educational and Psychological Consultation, 13*(1 & 2), 69–95.

Kreider, H., Caspe, M., Kennedy, S., & Weiss, H. (2007). *Family involvement in middle and high school students' education.* Cambridge, MA: Harvard Family Research Project. Available online at www.hfrp.html

Kreiss, C. (2011). What is rural America? *Teaching Tolerance* 39, 28–31.

Kroth, R. L. (1985). *Communication with parents of exceptional children: Improving parent-teacher relationships.* Denver: Love.

Kummerow, J. M., & McAllister, L. W. (1988). Teambuilding with the Myers-Briggs Type Indicator: Case Studies. *Journal of Psychological Type, 15*, 25–32.

Lakein, A. (1973). *How to get control of your time and your life.* New York: McKay.

Lamme, L. L., & Lamme, L. A. (2001–2002). Welcoming children from gay families into our schools. *Educational Leadership, 59*(4), 65–69.

Landrum, M. S. (2001). An evaluation of the Catalyst program: Consultation and collaboration in gifted education. *Gifted Child Quarterly, 45*(2), 139–151.

Lasater, M. W., Johnson, M. M., & Fitzgerald, M. (2000). Completing the education mosaic: Paraeducator professional development options. *Teaching Exceptional Children, 33*(1), 46–51.

Laud, L. E. (1998). Changing the way we communicate. *Educational Leadership, 61*(4), 23–28.

Lawren, B. (1989, September). Seating for success. *Psychology Today,* (16), 18–19.

Lawrence, G. (1993). *People types and tiger stripes: A practical guide to learning styles* (3rd ed.). Gainesville, FL: Center for Applications of Psychological Type.

Lawrence, G., & DeNovellis, R. (1974). *Correlation of teacher personality variables (Myers-Briggs) and classroom observation data.* Paper presented at American Educational Research Association conference.

Lee, J. O. (2011). Reach teachers now to ensure common core success. *Phi Delta Kappan, 92*(6), 42–44.

Lessen, E., & Frankiewicz, L. E. (1992). Personal attributes and characteristics of effective special education teachers: Considerations for teacher educators. *Teacher Education and Special Education, 15*(2), 124–132.

Levine, A. (2006). *Educating school teachers.* The Education School Project. September, 2006, from www.edschools.org

Lilly, M. S., & Givens-Ogle, L. B. (1981). Teacher consultation: Present, past, and future. *Behavioral Disorders, 6*(2), 73–77.

Linan-Thompson, S., & Jean, R. (1997). Completing the parent participation puzzle: Accepting diversity. *Teaching Exceptional Children, 30*(2), 46–50.

Lindle, J. C. (1989). What do parents want from principals and educators? *Educational Leadership, 47*(2), 12–14.

Lippitt, G. L. (1983, March). Can conflict resolution be win-win? *The School Administrator,* 20–22.

Lohrmann, S., & Bambara, L. M. (2006). Elementary education teachers' beliefs about essential supports needed to successfully include students with developmental disabilities who engage in challenging behaviors. *Research and Practice for Persons With Severe Disabilities, 31,* 157–173.

Loucks-Horsley, S., Harding, C. K., Arbuckle, M. A., Murray, L. B., Dubea, C., & Williams, M. K. (1987). *Continuing to learn: A guidebook for teacher development.* Andover, MA: Regional Laboratory for Educational Improvement of the Northeast and Islands.

Lovett, H. (1996). *Learning to listen: Positive approaches and people with difficult behavior.* Baltimore: Paul H. Brookes.

Lubetkin, B. (1997, January). Master the art of apologizing. *The Manager's Intelligence Report.*

Luft, J. (1984). *Group processes: An introduction to group dynamics,* 3rd Ed. Palo Alto CA: Mayfield Publishing.

Lugg, C. A., & Boyd, W. L. (1993). Leadership for collaboration: Reducing risk and fostering resilience. *Phi Delta Kappan, 75*(3), 253–256, 258.

Lynch, E. W., & Hanson, M. J. (1998). *Developing cross-cultural competence: A guide for working with children and their families* (2nd ed.). Baltimore: Paul H. Brookes.

Mager, R. F. (1997). *Preparing instructional objectives* (3rd ed.). Atlanta: The Center for Effective Performance.

Maldonado, J. A. (1994). Bilingual special education: specific learning disabilities in language and reading. *Journal of Educational Issues of Language Minority Students, 4,* 127–148.

Mantz, Josh (October 2010), *Combat Stress: Redefining the Wounded Warrior and Family,* Kansas State University (http://vimeo.com/16928841).

Margolis, H. (1986). Resolving differences with angry people. *Urban Review, 18*(2), 125–136.

Marks, S. U., Schrader, C., & Levine, M. (1999). Paraeducator experiences in inclusive settings: Helping, hovering, or holding their own? *Exceptional Children, 65,* 315–328.

Margolis, H., & McGettigan, J. (1988). Managing resistance to instructional modifications in mainstream settings. *Remedial and Special Education, 9,* 15–21.

Marsal, L. S. (1997). Mentoring & CEC guidelines for developing a mentorship program for beginning special education teachers. *Teaching Exceptional Children, 29*(6), 18–21.

Martin, J. E., Van Dycke, J. L., Greene, B. A., Gardner, J. E., Christensen, W. R., Woods, L. L. (2006). Direct observation of teacher-directed IEP meetings: Establishing the need for student IEP meeting instruction. *Exceptional Children, 72,* 187–200.

Martin, R. (1991). *Extraordinary children—ordinary lives.* Champaign, IL: Research Press.

Martinez, M. (2010). Teacher education can't ignore technology. *Phi Delta Kappan, 92*(2), 74–75.

Maslach, C. (1982). *Burnout: The cost of caring.* Englewood Cliffs, NJ: Prentice Hall.

Mayer, E., Ferede, M. K., & Hou, E. D. (2006). The family involvement storybook: A new way to build connections with families. *Young Children, 61*(6), 94–97.

Mayo, C. (2010). Queer lessons: Sexual and gender minorities in multicultural education. In J. A. Banks & C. A. M. Banks (Eds), *Multicultural education: Issues and perspectives, 7th ed.* (pp 209–227). Hoboken, NJ: Wiley & Sons.

McCaffrey, M. E. (2000). My first year of learning: Advice from a new educator. *Teaching Exceptional Children, 33*(1), 4–8.

McCardle, P., Mele-McCarthy, J., & Leos, K. (2005). English language learners and learning disabilities: Research agenda and implications for practice. *Learning Disability Research and Practice, 20*(1), 68–78.

McCarthy, B. (1990). Using the 4MAT system to bring learning styles to schools. *Educational Leadership, 48*(2), 31–37.

McDonald, J. P. (1989). When outsiders try to change schools from the inside. *Phi Delta Kappan, 71*(3), 206–212.

McDonnell, L. M., McLaughlin, M. J., & Morrison, P. (1997). *Educating one and all: Students with disabilities and standards-based reform.* Washington, DC: National Academy Press.

McGrew-Zoubi, R. R. (1998). I can take care of it myself. *The Delta Kappa Gamma Bulletin, 65*(1), 15–20.

McMahon, T. J., Ward, N. L., Pruett, M. K., Davidson, L., & Griffith, E. E. H. (2000). Building full-service schools: Lessons learned in the development of interagency collaboratives. *Journal of Educational and Psychological Consultation, 11*(1), 65–92.

McNaughton, D., & Vostal, B. R. (2010). Using active listening to improve collaboration with parents: The LAFF don't CRY strategy. *Intervention in School and Clinic, 45*(4), 251–256.

McNulty, R. (2003). Making leadership everyone's responsibility. *Education Update, 45*(7), 2.

McTighe, J., & Brown, J. (2005). Differentiated instruction and educational standards: Is détente possible? *Theory Into Practice, 44,* 234–244.

Menlove, R. R., Hudson, P. J., & Suter, D. (2001). A field of IEP dreams: Increasing general education teacher participation in the IEP development process. *Teaching Exceptional Children, 35*(5), 28–33.

Mertens, D. M. (2010). *Research and evaluation in education and psychology: Integrating diversity with quantitative, qualitative, and mixed methods* (3rd ed.). Thousand Oaks, CA: Sage.

Meyers, J., Meyers, A. B., & Grogg, K. (2004). Prevention through consultation: A model to guide future developments in the field of school psychology. *Journal of Educational and Psychological Consultation, 15*(3 & 4), 257–276.

Michaels, K. (1988). Caution: Second-wave reform taking place. *Educational Leadership, 45*(5), 3.

Miller, T. N., Devin, M., & Shoop, R. J. (2007). *Closing the leadership gap: How district and university partnerships shape effective school leaders.* Thousand Oaks, CA: Corwin.

Millinger, C. S. (2004). Helping new teachers cope. *Educational Leadership, 61*(8), 66–69.

Mills, G. E. (2010). *Action research: A guide for the teacher researcher, 4th ed.* Upper Saddle River, NJ: Pearson.

Morsink, C. V., Thomas, C. C., & Correa, V. I. (1991). *Interactive teaming: Consultation and collaboration in special programs.* Columbus, OH: Merrill.

Murphy, E. (1987). *I am a good teacher.* Gainesville, FL: Center for Applications of Psychological Type.

Murray, C. (2004). Clarifying collaborative roles in urban high schools: General educators' perspectives. *Teaching Exceptional Children, 36*(5), 44–51.

Murray, J. L. (1994). *Training for student leaders.* Dubuque, IA: Kendall/Hunt.

Myers, I. B. (1974). *Type and teamwork.* Gainesville, FL: Center for Applications of Psychological Type.

Myers, I. B. (October 16, 1975). *Making the most of individual gifts.* Keynote address at the First National Conference on Uses of the Myers-Briggs Type Indicator. Gainesville, FL: University of Florida.

Myers, I. B. (1980). *Introduction to type.* Palo Alto, CA: Consulting Psychologists Press.

Neel, R. S. (1981). How to put the consultant to work in consulting teaching. *Behavioral Disorders, 6*(2), 78–81.

Nevin, A., Thousand, J., Paolucci-Whitcomb, P., & Villa, R. (1990). Collaborative consultation: Empowering public school personnel to provide heterogeneous schooling for all—or, who rang that bell? *Journal of Educational and Psychological Consultation, 1*(1), 41–67.

Oja, S. N. (1980). Adult development is implicit in staff development. *Journal of Staff Development, 1*(1), 9–15.

Osborn, A. F. (1963). *Applied imagination: Principles and procedures of creative problem-solving.* New York: Scribner.

Page, S. E. (2007). *The difference: How the power of diversity creates better groups, firms, schools, and societies.* Princeton, NJ: Princeton University Press.

Parette, H. P., & Petch-Hogan, B. (2000). Approaching families: Facilitating culturally, linguistically diverse family involvement. *Teaching Exceptional Children, 33*(2), 4–12.

Patton. M. Q. (2008). *Utilization-focused evaluation (4th ed.).* Thousand Oaks, CA: Sage.

Patton, M. Q. (2011). *Developmental Evaluation: Applying complexity concept to enhance innovation and use.* New York: The Guilford Press.

Phillips, V., & McCullough, L. (1990). Consultation-based programming: Instituting the collaborative ethic in schools. *Exceptional Children, 56,* 291–304.

Phillips, W. L., Allred, K., Brulle, A. R., & Shank, K. S. (1990). The regular education initiative: The will and skill of regular educators. *Teacher Education and Special Education, 13*(3–4), 182–186.

Pickett, A. L., & Gerlach, K. (2003). *Supervising paraeducators in schools settings: A team approach.* Austin, TX: PRO-ED.

Pisha, B., & Coyne, P. (2001). Smart from the start: The promise of universal design for learning. *Remedial and Special Education, 22*(4), 197–203.

Plash, S., & Piotrowski, C. (2007). Retention issues: A study of Alabama special education teachers. *Education, 127,* 125–128.

Plucker, J. A., & Yecke, C. P. (1999). The effect of relocation on gifted students. *Gifted Child Quarterly, 43*(2), 95–106.

Pollio, H. (1987, Fall). Practical poetry: Metaphoric thinking in science, art, literature, and nearly everywhere else. *Teaching-Learning Issues,* 3–17.

Posavac, E. J., & Carey, R. G. (2006). *Program evaluation: Methods and case studies* (7th ed.). Englewood Cliffs, NJ: Prentice Hall.

Preskill, H. & Russ-Eft, D. (2005). *Building evaluation capacity.* Thousand Oaks, CA: Sage.

Pruitt, P., Wandry, D., & Hollums, D. (1998). Listen to us! Parents speak out about their inter actions with special educators. *Preventing School Failure, 42,* 161–166.

Pryzwansky, W. B. (1974). A reconsideration of the consultation model for delivery of school-based psychological services. *American Journal of Orthopsychiatry, 44,* 579–583.

Pryzwansky, W. B. (1986). Indirect service delivery: Considerations for future research in consultation. *School Psychology Review, 15*(4), 479–488.

Pugach, M. C., & Johnson, L. J. (1989). The challenge of implementing collaboration between general and special education. *Exceptional Children, 56*(3), 232–235.

Pugach, M. C., & Johnson, L. J. (1990). Fostering the continued democratization of consultation through action research. *Teacher Education and Special Education, 13*(3–4), 240–245.

Pugach, M. C., & Johnson, L. J. (1995). *Collaborative practitioners, collaborative schools.* Denver, CO: Love.

Pugach, M. C., & Johnson, L. J. (2002). *Collaborative practitioners, collaborative schools* (2nd ed.). Denver, CO: Love.

Putnam, J. (1993). Make every minute count. *Instructor, 103*(1), 39–40.

Putnam, L. L., & Mumby, D. K. (1992). Organizations, emotion, and the myth of rationality. In S. Fineman (Ed.), *Emotion in organizations* (pp. 36–57). Newbury Park, CA: Sage.

Rakow, S. (2012). Helping gifted learners soar. *Educational Leadership, 69*(5), 34–40.

Raschke, D., Dedrick, C., & DeVries, A. (1988). Coping with stress: The special educator's perspective. *Teaching Exceptional Children, 21*(1), 10–14.

Ravitch, D. (2011). Obama's war on schools. *Newsweek,* pp. 20–21, March 28 & April 4, 2011.

Ray, V., & Gregory, R. (2001, Winter). School experiences of the children of lesbian and gay parents. *Family Matters,* 28–32.

Raymond, G. I., McIntosh, D. K., & Moore, Y. R. (1986). *Teacher consultation skills* (Report No. EC 182–912). Washington, DC: U.S. Department of Education. (ERIC Document Reproduction Service No. ED 170–915).

Raywid, M. A. (1993). Finding time for collaboration. *Educational Leadership, 51*(1), 30–34.

Reinhiller, N. (1996). Co-teaching: New variations on a not-so-new practice. *Teacher Education and Special Education, 19*(1), 34–48.

Reis, S. M., Burns, D. E., & Renzulli, J. S. (1992). *Facilitator's guide to help teachers compact curriculum.* Mansfield Center, CT: Creative Learning Press.

Renzulli, J. S. (1977). *The Enrichment Triad Model: A guide for developing defensible programs for the gifted and talented.* Mansfield Center, CT: Creative Learning Press.

Renzulli, J. S., & Reis, S. M. (1985). *The schoolwide enrichment model: A comprehensive plan for educational excellence.* Mansfield Center, CT: Creative Learning Press.

Reynolds, M. C., & Birch, J. W. (1988). *Adaptive mainstreaming: A primer for teachers and principals.* White Plains, NY: Longman.

Richardson, W. (2012). Preparing students to learn without us. *Educational Leadership, 69*(5), 22–26.

Riehl, C. J. (2000). The principal's role in creating inclusive schools for diverse students: A review of normative, empirical, and critical literature on the practice of educational administration. *Review of Educational Research, 70*(1), 55–81.

Rinke, W. J. (1997). *Winning Management: 6 fail-safe strategies for building high-performance organizations.* Clarksville, MD: Achievement.

Robinson, A. (1990). Cooperation of exploitation? The argument against cooperative learning for talented students. *Journal for the Education of the Gifted, 14*(1), 9–27.

Rodriguez-Campos, L. (2005). *Collaborative evaluations: A step-by-step model for the evaluator.* Tamarac, FL: Lumina Press.

Rosenfield, S. (1995). The practice of instructional consultation. *Journal of Educational and Psychological Consultation, 6*(4), 317–327.

Ross, R. G. (1986). *Communication consulting as persuasion: Issues and implications.* (Report No. CS506–027). Washington, DC: U.S. Department of Education. ERIC Document Reproduction Service No. ED 291–115.

Rossi, P. H., Lipsey, M. W., & Freeman, H. E. (2004). *Evaluation: A systematic approach* (7th ed.). Beverly Hills, CA: Sage.

Rothenberg, A., & Hausman, C. R. (1976). *The creativity question.* Durham, NC: Duke University Press.

Rotter, K. (2006). Creating instructional materials for all pupils: Try COLA. *Intervention in School and Clinic, 41*(5), 273–282.

Roy, P. A., & O'Brien, P. (1991). Together we can make it better in collaborative schools. *Journal of Staff Development, 12*(3), 47–51.

Safran, S. P. (1991). The communication process and school-based consultation: What does the research say? *Journal of Educational and Psychological Consultation, 1*(4), 343–370.

Salzberg, C. L., & Morgan, J. (1995). Preparing teachers to work with paraeducators. *Teacher Education and Special Education, 18* (1), 49–55.

Schein, E. H. (1969). *Process consultation: Its role in organization development.* Reading, MA: Addison-Wesley.

Schein, E. H. (1978, February). The role of the consultant: Context expert or process facilitator? *Personnel and Guidance Journal, 56*(6), 339–343.

Schulte, A. C., Osborne, S. S., & Kauffman, J. M. (1993). Teacher responses to two types of consultative special education services. *Journal of Educational and Psychological Consultation, 4*(1), 1–27.

Schultz, E. W. (1980, Fall). Teaching coping skills for stress and anxiety. *Teaching Exceptional Children,* 12–15.

Schumm, J. S., & Vaughn, S. (1995). Meaningful professional development in accommodating students with disabilities: Lessons learned. *Remedial and Special Education, 16,* 344–355.

Scruggs, T. E., Mastropieri, M. A., & McDuffie, K. A. (2007). Co-Teaching in inclusive classrooms: A meta-synthesis of qualitative research. *Exceptional Children, 73,* 392–416.

SEDL. (2000). Collaborative strategies for revitalizing rural schools and communities. *Benefits, 5.*

Sevo, R. (2011). Basics about Disabilities and Science and Engineering Education. www.lulu.com/sevo.

Shaver, D., Golan, S., & Wagner, M. (1996) Connecting schools and communities through interagency collaboration for school-linked services. In J. G. Cibulka & W. J. Kritek (Eds.), *Coordination among schools, families, and communities: Prospects for educational reform* (pp. 349–378). Albany: State University of New York Press.

Shaw, S. R., Glaser, S. E., & Ouimet, T. (2011). Developing the medical liaison role in school settings. *Journal of Educational and Psychological Consultation, 21*(2), 106–117.

Sheridan, S. M. (1992). What do we mean when we say "collaboration"? *Journal of Educational and Psychological Consultation, 3*(1), 89–92.

Shroyer, G., Yahnke, S., Bennett, A., & Dunn, C., (2007). Simultaneous renewal through professional development school partnerships. *Journal of Educational Research, 100*(4), 211–224.

Sileo, J. M. (2011). Co-teaching: Getting to know your partner. *TEACHING Exceptional Chidren, 43*(5), 32–40.

Silva, E. (2010). Thessin, R. A., & Starr, J. P. (2011). Supporting the growth of professional learning communities. *Phi Delta Kappan, 92*(6), 48–54.

Simpson, E. J. (1972). *The psychomotor domain, vol. 3.* Washington, DC: Gryphon House.

Slesser, R. A., Fine, M. J., & Tracy, D. B. (1990). Teacher reactions to two approaches to school-based psychological consultation. *Journal of Educational and Psychological Consultation, 1*(3), 243–258.

Smith, J. D. (1998). *Inclusion: Schools for all students.* Belmont, CA: Wadsworth.

Smith-Westberry, J., & Job, R. L. (1986). How to be a prophet in your own land: Providing gifted program inservice for the local district. *Gifted Child Quarterly, 30*(3), 135–137.

Soo-Hoo, T. (1998). Applying frame of reference and reframing techniques to improve school consultation in multicultural settings. *Journal of Educational and Psychological Consultation, 9*(4), 325–345.

Soodak, L. C., & Erwin, E. J. (1995). Parents, professionals, and inclusive education: A call for collaboration. *Journal of Educational and Psychological Consultation, 6*(3), 257–276.

Spooner, F., Baker, J. N., Harris, A. A., Ahlgrim-Delzell, L., & Browder, D. M. (2007). Effects of training in universal design for learning on lesson plan development, *Remedial and Special Education, 28,* 108–116.

St. John, E. P., Griffith, A. I., & Allen-Hayes, L. (1997). *Families in schools: A chorus of voices in restructuring.* Portsmouth, NH: Heinemann.

Stewart, R. A., & Brendefur, J. L. (2005). Fusing lesson study and authentic achievement: A model for teacher collaboration. *Phi Delta Kappan, 86*(9), 681–687.

Strawbridge, M. (2006). *Netiquette: Internet etiquette in the age of the blog.* London: Software Reference Ltd.

Stringer, G. E. (2007). *Action Research.* Thousand Oaks, CA: Sage.

Sue, D. W., & Sue, D. (1990). *Counseling the culturally different: Theory and practice* (2nd ed.). New York: Wiley.

Talley, R. C., & Schrag, J. A. (1999). Legal and public foundations supporting service integration for students with disabilities. *Journal of Educational and Psychological Consultation, 10*(3), 229–249.

Tannen, D. (1991). *Gender and discourse.* New York: Oxford University Press.

Tannen, D. (1994). *You just don't understand: Women and men in conversation.* New York: William Morrow.

Taylor, N., & Adelman, H. S. (1998). Confidentiality: Competing principles, inevitable dilemmas. *Journal of Educational and Psychological Consultation, 9,* 267–275.

Tharp, R. (1975). The triadic model of consultation. In C. Parker (Ed.), *Psychological consultation in the schools: Helping teachers meet special needs.* Reston, VA: Council for Exceptional Children.

Tharp, R. G., & Wetzel, R. J. (1969). *Behavior modification in the natural environment.* New York: Academic Press.

Thessin, R. A., & Starr, J. P. (2011). Supporting the growth of professional learning communities. *Phi Delta Kappan, 92*(6), 48–54.

Thomas, C. C., Correa, V. I., & Morsink, C. V. (2001). *Interactive teaming: Enhancing programs for students with special needs* (3rd ed.). Upper Saddle River, NJ: Prentice Hall.

Thurston, L. P. (1989). Women surviving: An alternative approach to "helping" low-income urban women. *Women and Therapy, 8* (4), 109–127.

Thurston, L. P., & Kimsey, I. (1989). Rural special education teachers as consultants: Roles and responsibilities. *Educational Considerations, 17*(1), 40–43.

Thurston, L. P. (2000). *The positive para: Helping students develop positive social skills.* Lawrence, KS: Curriculum Solutions, Inc.

Thurston, L. P., & Navarrete, L. (1996). A tough row to hoe: Research on education and rural poor families. In *Proceedings of American Council on Rural Special Education (ACRES),* Baltimore.

Tiegerman-Farber, E., & Radziewicz, C. (1998). *Collaborative decision-making: The pathway to inclusion.* Upper Saddle River, NJ: Prentice Hall.

Todnem, G., & Warner, M. P. (1994, September). Demonstrating the benefits of staff development: An interview with Thomas R. Guskey. *Kansas Direct Connection.* Hays, KS: Kansas Staff Development Council.

Tomlinson, C. (1999). *The differentiated classroom: Responding to the needs of all learners.* Alexandria, VA: Association for Supervision and Curriculum Development.

Tomlinson, C. A. (2000). Reconcilable differences? Standards-based teaching and differentiation. *Educational Leadership, 58*(1), 6–11.

Torrance, E. P., & Safter, H. T. (1999). *Making the creative leap beyond.* Buffalo, NY: Creative Education Foundation Press.

Tovar, N. H. (1998). Addressing the needs of school-age military dependents. *Delta Kappa Gamma Bulletin, 64*(4), 23–28.

Trautman, M. (2004). Preparing and managing paraprofessionals. *Intervention in School and Clinic, 39*(3), 131–138.

Truesdell, C. B. (1983, Spring). The MBTI: A win-win strategy for work teams. *MBTI News, 5*(2), 8–9. 268.

Turnbull, A. P., & Turnbull, H. R., III. (1997). *Families, professionals, and exceptionality: A special partnership* (4th ed.). Upper Saddle River, NJ: Merrill.

Turnbull, A., Turnbull, R., Erwin, E. J., & Soodak, L. C. (2006). *Families, professionals, and exceptionality: Positive outcomes through partnership and trust* (5th ed.). Upper Saddle River, NJ: Pearson.

United States Census Bureau (2010). *2010 National Population Projections.* Washington, D.C.

U.S. Department of Education (2008a). Table 3-2. *Teachers employed (FTE) to provide special education and related services to students age 6 through 21 under IDEA, Part B, by certification status and state:* Fall 2008 [Data file]. Available from Individuals with Disabilities Education Act (IDEA) Data Web site: https://www.ideadata.org/PartBdata.asp

U.S. Department of Education (2008b). Table 3-4. *Paraprofessionals employed (FTE) to provide special education and related services to students age 6 through 21 under IDEA, Part B, by qualification status and state:* Fall 2008 [Data file]. Available from Individuals with Disabilities Education Act (IDEA) Data Web site: https://www.ideadata.org/PartBdata.asp

Ury, W. (1991). *Getting past no: Negotiating with difficult people.* New York: Bantam Books.

Van Voorhis, F. L. (2003). Interactive homework in middle school: Effects on family involvement and science achievement. *Journal of Educational Research, 96,* 323–338.

VanTassel-Baska, J. (1989). Appropriate curriculum for gifted learners. *Educational Leadership, 46*(6), 13–15.

Vaughn, S., Schumm, J. S., & Arguelles, M. E. (1997). The ABCDEs of co-teaching. *Teaching Exceptional Children, 30*(2), 42–45.

Viel-Ruma, K., Houchins, D., Jolivette, K., & Benson, G. (2010). Efficacy beliefs of special educators: The relationships among collective efficacy, teacher self-efficacy, and job satisfaction, *Teacher Education and Special Education, 33*(3), 225–233.

Vygotsky, L. S. (1978). *Mind in society: The development of higher mental processes.* Cambridge, MA: Harvard University Press.

Wallace, T., Shin, J., Bartholomay, T., & Stahl, B. J. (2001). Knowledge and skills for teachers supervising the work of paraprofessionals. *Exceptional Children, 67,* 520–533.

Walsh, J. M. (2001). Getting the "big picture" of IEP goals and state standards. *Teaching Exceptional Children, 33*(5), 18–26.

Wanat, C. L. (1997). Conceptualizing parental involvement from parents' perspectives: A case study. *Journal for a Just and Caring Education, 3*(4), 433–458.

Ward, S. B., & Landrum, M. S. (1994). Resource consultation: An alternative service delivery model for gifted education. *Roeper Review, 16,* 275–279.

Webster's New Collegiate Dictionary (8th ed.). (1996). Springfield, MA: Merriam-Webster.

Webster's Third New International Dictionary, unabridged: The great library of the English language. (1976). Springfield, MA: Merriam-Webster.

Weiss, H., Caspe, M., & Lopez, M. E. (2006). *Family involvement in early childhood education.* Cambridge, MA: Harvard Family Research Project, www.hfrp.html

Welch, M. (1998). The IDEA of collaboration in special education: An introspective examination of paradigms and promise. *Journal of Educational and Psychological Consultation, 9*(2), 119–142.

Welch, M., & Sheridan, S. M. (1995). *Educational partnerships: Serving students at risk.* Fort Worth, TX: Harcourt Brace.

Welch, M., Sheridan, S. M., Fuhriman, A., Hart, A. W., Connell, M. L., & Stoddart, T. (1992). Preparing professionals for educational partnerships: An interdisciplinary approach. *Journal of Educational and Psychological Consultation, 3*(1), 1–23.

Wenger, E., White, N., Smith, J. D., & Rowe, K. (2005). *Technology for communities. In work, learning and networked: Guide to implementation and leadership of intentional communities of practice.* Retrieved from http://technologyforcommunities.com/CEFRIO_Book_Chapter_v_5.2.pdf

Wesley, P. W., & Buysse, V. (2006). Ethics and evidence in consultation. *Topics in Early Childhood Special Education, 26*(3), 131–142.

Wesley, W. G., & Wesley, B. A. (1990). Concept-mapping: A brief introduction. *Teaching Professor, 4*(8), 3–4.

West, J. F. (1990). Educational collaboration in the restructuring of schools. *Journal of Educational and Psychological Consultation, 1,* 23–41.

West, J. F., & Brown, P. A. (1987). State departments of education policies on consultation in special education: The state of the states. *Remedial and Special Education, 8*(3), 45–51.

West, J. F., & Idol, L. (1987). School consultation (Part I): An interdisciplinary perspective on theory, models, and research. *Journal of Learning Disabilities, 20*(7), 385–408.

West, J. F., Idol, L., & Cannon, G. (1988). *Collaboration in the schools: Communicating, interacting, and problem solving.* Austin, TX: PRO-ED.

Whitaker, S. D. (2000). Mentoring beginning special education teachers and the relationship to attrition. *Exceptional Children, 66*(4), 546–566.

White, G. W. (2000). Nonverbal communications: Key to improved teacher effectiveness. *Delta Kappa Gamma Bulletin, 66*(4), 12–16.

Will, M. (1984). Let us pause and reflect—but not too long. *Exceptional Children, 51,* 11–16.

Will, M. (1986). Educating children with learning problems: A shared responsibility. *Exceptional Children, 52*(5), 411–415.

Williams, J. M., & Martin, S. M. (2001). Implementing the Individuals with Disabilities Education Act of 1997: The consultant's role. *Journal of Educational and Psychological Consultation, 12*(1), 59–81.

Winn, J. A., & Messenheimer-Young, T. (1995). Team teaching at the university level: What we have learned. *Teacher Education and Special Education, 18*(4), 223–229.

Woolfolk, A. (2007). *Educational psychology.* Englewood Cliffs, NJ: Prentice Hall.

Wong, H. K., Britton, T., & Ganser, T. (2005). *What the world can teach us about Teacher Induction, Phi Delta Kappan, 86* (5), 379–384.

Working Forum on Inclusive Schools (1994). *Creating schools for all our students: What 12 schools have to say.* Reston, VA: Council for Exceptional Children.

World Book Dictionary: Volumes 1 and 2. (2003). Chicago: World Book, Inc.

Wright, R. E. (2010). LGBT educators' perceptions of school climate. *Kappan, 91*(8), 49–51.

Zabala, J., & Carl, D. (2010, December/2011, January). The AIMing for achievement series: What educators and families need to know about accessible instructional materials. Part Two: Navigating the decision-making process. *Closing the Gap, 29*(5), 12–15.

Zickuhr, K. (2010, December 16). Generations 2010. *Pew Internet & American Life Project.* Retrieved on May 17, 2011, from http://www.pewinternet.org/Reports/2010/Generations-2010.aspx

Name Index

455

Subject Index